THE SEARCHERS AND ME

THE SEARCHERS AND ME

A History of the Legendary Sixties Hitmakers

Frank Allen

to Tony
Happy 60th

Aureus

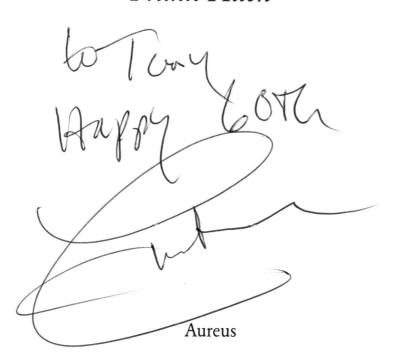

Also by Frank Allen and published by Aureus:
'Travelling Man - On The Road With The Searchers'

First Published 2009

This publication is printed on paper derived from sustainable forests. The cover is made from recycled material.

ISBN 978-1-899750-41-2

Printed and bound in Great Britain by Athenaeum Press Ltd., Gateshead, Tyne & Wear

A catalogue record for this book is available from the British Library.

Aureus Publishing Limited
Castle Court
Castle-upon-Alun
St. Bride's Major
Vale of Glamorgan
CF32 0TN

Tel: (01656) 880033 Fax: (01656) 880033
Int. tel: +44 1656 880033 Int. fax: +44 1656 880033

E-mail: sales@aureus.co.uk
www.aureus.co.uk
www.thesearchersandme.com

Contents

The Searchers And Me is dedicated
to the memories of
Johnny Sandon, Tony Jackson and Chris Curtis

Acknowledgements

I would like to thank Wendy Burton for her invaluable help and support all the way through. She assisted me with considerable archive research and spent endless hours proofing and correcting my efforts, providing encouragement when needed along with praise and criticism when appropriate. It was a long hard slog which she willingly undertook. I am sure that without her involvement it would have been a much lesser work.

For the contents of their memory banks and their valuable time given up to share their reminiscences I would like to thank:

John McNally, Mary McNally, Roy Clough, Serena Cairns, Tony West, Spencer Leigh, Tony Hatch, Margo Newman, Dee Dee Sperling, John Kay, John Carter, Pete Townshend, Martin Wyatt, Cliff Bennett, Alan Mosca, Teresa Cullen, Peter Scotti, Billy Kinsley, Tim Viney, Gary Jackson, David Wigg, the National Newspaper Library, Colindale, the British Library, Marylebone, the BBC Archives, Caversham, all of those people whom I have inadvertently omitted and those who allowed me to use their photographs. I have given them credit where I had the information. If there are those who have not received a credit it is simply because the name of the photographer was lost or not known for which I apologise. You have my gratitude. I hope that is enough.

Lastly I would like to thank all the followers and fans of the Searchers who have kept us going through five decades and who badgered me into taking on this daunting yet exhilarating project and convinced me that there might actually be people out there who would want to read the story.

Foreword by Pete Townshend

Frankie Allen. Who is he? You may well ask. The history of contemporary British Rock and Pop began in 1958, very slightly earlier than most of us care to remember. There are dozens of important characters who should be noted and regarded, Frankie is one of them. By the time the Beatles and the Stones hit the USA in 1963, in the UK there was already a thriving music scene in which pure rock and pop (the music of Buddy Holly, the Everly Brothers and so on) was played alongside music that was rarely heard on the radio. The R&B of James Brown and Bobby Bland was played alongside Hank Williams and Johnny Cash. The best band for all this music in my West London neighbourhood was Cliff Bennett's band, the Rebel Rousers. They had a guitar player or two of course, very good ones, but the brass player(s) and keyboards were still an important part of the sound. When I first saw them Frankie was in the band and the keyboard player was Nicky Hopkins who later played with the Stones and The Who on their first recordings.

Where the Beatles and the Stones (and subsequently the Kinks, the Searchers and the Pirates) led with innovative guitar sounds, with not a sax or a piano or organ in sight, the Rebel Rousers were almost a Big Band of the kind I grew up with; my father had played sax professionally in a post-war dance band called the Squadronaires who almost never featured guitar. At least the Rebel Rousers had a sax player! So they weren't REALLY rebels in my eyes. They were just brilliantly good, and they played music that no one else touched.

Frankie Allen was one of the perennial Faces of a slightly older group of musicians who preceded the Detours (who became The Who) to the West London scene. I first knew him as bass player with the Rebel Rousers. I was schooled in the art of spot-the-handsome-man by my mother and Frankie was good to look at. He was also gregarious, friendly and a terrific musician. Later, he joined the Searchers who - to my mind - pre-empted the jangling guitar sound of the Byrds by several years, and that of the La's by over thirty.

The bands of this period, 1961-1964, did not automatically expect to make it in the USA. Once Freddie & the Dreamers had become a huge hit act, simply because Freddie did a silly dance, anyone serious about their craft just gave up on the USA. Bizarre, because the USA was where most of our beloved music originated. Bands like the Rebel Rousers and the Searchers were big in the UK, and they toured mainly in Germany, Holland and Scandinavia, with rare trips to America. To this very day the Searchers along with the Tremeloes - a huge British pop band of the early sixties - and others still tour Germany with great success.

So Frankie's memoirs of these early years is worth close examination. In a sense it tells us more about why and how the now mammoth British institutions like the Beatles, the Stones and The Who managed to penetrate the pop business in the States, and brought that country's own magnificent musical heritage back into its common domain. We were working on an incredibly solid bedrock. What drove the first wave of West London bands like the Rebel Rousers was sheer love of music, the camaraderie of being in a band, and the lack of prejudice musicians carried (whether racial, sexual or political, none of it mattered).

Sting says the post '60s bands were like gangs, the inference being you had to get out as soon as you were mature enough to do so. To some extent I agree. But in the kind of scene Frankie grew up in that was probably not the case. The bands were musicians, not social scientists or rebels. Despite the name of Cliff Bennett's amazing band, they were not rebels, but enthusiasts of music that they felt had to be shared. Just as Alexis Korner was inculcating pure country blues down at the Ealing Club, just three miles down the High Road in Uxbridge Cliff Bennett was bringing us slimmed-down big band R&B and a little later Motown, Memphis and New Orleans R&B that often, literally speaking, tore to bits the club above Burton's Tailors. The police were called as often to deal with the sheer exuberance brought on by the music as to quell fights between drunken young men.

Cliff Bennett had a hit or two, but has not enjoyed the recognition he deserves. For me - without him, without The Shadows (which means the other Cliff deserves a mention too), without Johnny Kidd & the Pirates or Gene Vincent (sometimes based in the UK for periods), The Who would never have happened. Sometimes when we look back today as musicologists it all seems to be about what grew from the Ealing Club. But what grew from Burton's in Uxbridge was equally crucial to what The Who went on to achieve.

Read Frankie's story and come to understand how Britain, England, London, especially the West of London, formed a crucible for the immense pop and rock explosion that was soon to follow, and in which Frankie himself featured as a member of both Cliff Bennett's band and then the Searchers. Finally, if you have never heard a record by the Searchers, hurry and listen. *Needles And Pins* is a masterpiece really, both as a song and as a recording. Amazing guitar sound for the time and still clangs away today. I really do believe the sound was a precursor to the jangling of the American Byrds. They were, and still are, seminal listening for the uninitiated. Listen too to some Cliff Bennett. It will make you smile, and bring you firmly into the sunny present day. Finally listen here to Frankie. Here is a man who still lives in popular music for love, and only love. And is adored in return by all who know him.

Pete Townshend

Foreword by Bruce Welch

I was standing in a shop doorway watching a band at a street fair. 'It's no good hiding in there' the lady said. 'I know who you are. You're with a famous sixties group aren't you? Oh, what's your name again? It's slipped my mind.'

Just then her friend came over and the lady said, 'You know who this is, don't you?' Her friend looked at me quizzically, not having a clue. I thought I'd give them a break. I said the group's name begins with S.

Still nothing. I said we had a singer who is really famous and it was Cliff and The S. 'Of course,' they both cried. 'The Searchers.'

So there we are. For the past fifty years I've been in the wrong band. I'm off to practise 'Needles And Pinsa' with those rock gods Frank Allen and John McNally. Should be a blast.

Enjoy the book.

Bruce Welch O.B.E.
The Shadows

Introduction

Being asked to write my first book Travelling Man back in 1999 was a scary moment. I had written an article with that title but was not at all sure if I had the necessary knowledge or capability to write an actual full length book. My attention span has always been short and I am easily distracted. And basic GCE English does not necessarily a writer make. I therefore settled on a plan which I figured I could complete without having to unduly tax my limited and rapidly disintegrating memory banks or my reasonable but not exceptional literary skills.

Travelling Man became a book of humour as much as a tome about the Searchers. It dealt with in the main the touring side of my life as a musician. As a substitute for a plethora of biographical detail I decided to build it around my style of humour. I wanted to write a book that people could read on a train and fellow passengers would wonder what on earth you were chuckling about. And, by the feedback I have received through the years, I was reasonably successful in my aims. It is still in print, people still bring it along to our shows to be signed and I still get immense pleasure from the compliments they bestow on me. I am a shallow enough person to revel in flattery.

But I always knew that the story of the Searchers would eventually have to be written by someone. I just didn't know if I possessed enough facts, enough detail to undertake such a mammoth task myself. A publisher once told me that the thing fans love in a biography is detail. If I could not remember the detail could I gather what I needed from research? In the end I concluded that if I was not willing to take on the challenge I was not fit to call myself a writer. And if such a biography was to be written at all then I would rather it came from within our ranks.

Luckily I had kept diaries, not for the whole of our career but certainly for the last couple of decades and the early years had been captured for posterity in such institutions as the National Newspaper Library and the British Library. All it needed was time and effort. And I have a sneaky feeling there is more than enough detail for even the most finickity of 'anoraks' with the inclusion of the various line-up changes in both the

Searchers and the Rebel Rousers, the tour dates as we trudged our tiny talents across the country and the lists of instruments bought, swapped, lost and part-exchanged in those impecunious days when the purchase of an imported American guitar was a major transaction that one never undertook lightly. The importance of such minutiae will be lost on many and perhaps be deemed over indulgent but are mightily significant to anyone who was a teenager and dreamed of being a rock star back in the fifties.

I knew of course that I would have to deal with the arguments and the fallouts and in particular with the departure of one of the best known Searchers of all, Mike Pender. I was especially determined to be objective about this part of our history. Of course I was going to be critical just as I would expect him to be of me or John McNally. But I did not want to be unreasonable or unkind. I might disagree with his actions, his views or his attitude but I also happily accept without rancour that he has a side and a view that differs from mine. For every opinion there is an opposing one. I tried hard not to come across as bitter. We all have our own personal outlook on events and relationships in our lives. Who is to say who is right?

As regards the legal issues between us I had to be factual. Fortunately I had retained the reams of legal correspondence that flowed from our expensive solicitors, piles of papers that gave a slight glimpse into what those enormous sums of money were paying for. All the dates and details relating to events leading up to our court appearances were all quoted from those papers. Thank goodness they were there. I dearly wanted everything to be correct.

As the weeks, months and years went by I found the process of delving into the history of the band a fascinating experience and with no time limit set I could make my own speed and enjoy the journey which was at times a hard slog but never dull. I am sure that the one feeling that will remain with me is that I could have done it better. I have no doubts about that whatsoever. With only two books behind me I am still a novice writer but perhaps I will be spurred on to more projects that will be improvements on those gone by.

The story of the Searchers is not one crammed with sex, drugs and rock and roll. There is precious little scandal. And although these components are the stuff that headlines (and huge sales) are made of it is still a history that needed to be documented. They were exciting and groundbreaking times. The various members, myself included, who came and went played an important part in the rise of Brit Pop throughout the musical world and while other outfits may have taken the use of the twelve string guitar, strong melodies and rich harmonies to another level, the influence of the Searchers on artistes who have since become global superstars (Bruce Springsteen, Tom Petty, Marshall Crenshaw, the Byrds and others) is a fact that we are very proud of indeed.

When I was a kid just getting into my first skiffle group and trying so hard to make my chafed and bleeding fingers form the two or three basic chords I needed to tread in the footsteps of my idol Lonnie Donegan I saw it merely as a compelling and fun way to brighten up a childhood in a dull and grey post war Britain. I had my private dreams but I never had the gall to envisage music as a profession. That was surely never a future that was the entitlement of working class lads like me. And when it did in fact become a serious paying concern I did not imagine the pattern of my life being transformed by an unlikely alliance with a bunch of guys from a city two hundred miles away in the distant North.

But thank goodness the fates conspired to bring about those happy coincidences that shaped my future. I share a debt of gratitude to all of those guys I met in Hamburg. John McNally, who is still today, along with myself, the keeper of a name that in a minor way I like to think is a national treasure. As far as I am concerned it will always be his band and that despite being a Searcher since August 1964, I will eternally be the 'new boy'. Tony Jackson, whose position as bass player I usurped and who missed so badly the exciting life that had abandoned him. Chris Curtis who was charismatic and crazy but always loveable and the owner of a good and generous heart. And, yes, to Mike Pender whose talent helped make the group what it was. We went through some stressful and acrimonious times but it wasn't always like that. We had a lot of laughs along the way and if our priorities and needs were different well, that's what makes each of us different from the other.

I hope you enjoy my efforts. The story can never be a complete one. I do not possess the knowledge or the skills to assemble every single undisputed fact and there will be those who see the events differently or who are privy to information that remained unknown to me but I have done the best I could.

1

Hail Hail Rock & Roll

'Well since my baby left me. Well I've found a new place to dwell.' My God, what was this? I'd never heard anything like that before. *'It's down at the end of Lonely Street at Heartbreak Hotel.'*

The sound coming out of the speaker hit my ears like an explosion. It was the early months of 1956 and I was a mere twelve and a half years old. On reflection and with an additional fifty years of musical experience behind me it is now apparent that this fairly basic and gently rolling blues, although sung with the energy, rawness and unbridled passion of youth and topped off with a somewhat lavish helping of a new audio device known as reverb, was pretty tame and almost understated. But for me, in those innocent and musically barren times, it changed everything.

For most people there is a point in your existence where you just know that for you things will never be the same again. A seminal moment in time which tells you that your life has gone out of control and has chaotically careered down a side road you never even noticed was there. Unplanned, unexpected and sometimes a bit frightening. The voice coming from the speaker was wild and abandoned and the intense slap-back echo seemed to stir such primitive urges somewhere deep inside me that it almost felt wicked to be listening with such undiluted pleasure.

And this was coming not from the radio but the new medium of television. Very few people had television sets in 1956. We certainly did not. I was experiencing this revelation courtesy of the folk next door who had invested in this new and marvellous luxury item. Our house was a television-denied zone and steam radio was all we could, or perhaps would, aspire to at that point. My parsimonious parents did not waste money on unnecessary luxuries.

Our neighbours the Brodies however, who with double the number of hungry kids to raise, not to mention two large aviaries in the garden full of equally hungry budgerigars, were most likely less well off than us, saw life as for living while you were able and figured that money spent on enjoying it while you could was money well spent and that tomorrow would somehow take care of itself. They bought their primitive set as soon as they were able. And anyone in the street was welcome to share in their largesse.

On any evening you would find a dozen or more people, adults and kids, in rows in front of the Brodies' tiny fourteen-inch black and white screen, some on the settee and chairs and the remainder squatting on the lino covered floor, to revel in the comedy of I Love Lucy starring the zany bee-stung-lipped Lucille Ball, the drama of Highway Patrol featuring a corpulent but nonetheless impressively macho Broderick Crawford or the thrill of unexpected riches as naïve and unsophisticated contestants won astonishingly modest prizes in the quiz game Take Your Pick, hosted by 'your quiz inquisitor' Michael Miles. Turn down the money for the wrong box and you could end up with a stick of rock. Choose the right one and your magnificent reward could be (wait for the fanfare) a washing machine. Who Wants To Be A Millionaire? with its truly life changing riches on offer was still five decades away.

There was very little pop music on the screens in those pioneering days and The Jack Jackson Show was what passed for cutting-edge stuff. Jackson was an ex-dance band leader-turned-deejay who had seen the shape of things to come. Big bands were on the wane but radio was here to stay and television was taking off in a big way. His radio show had transferred successfully to the small screen and although there were other presenters of pop platters he was the only one so far who delivered anything that might resemble an image of being in tune with youth.

Indeed the very word deejay was new currency in the mid-fifties. Like most of the current trends it was hijacked from America but in those innocent years it would have been considered unseemly and un-British to adopt the seriously hip attitude of the prototype original, a Jewish radio jock from Cleveland, Ohio, by the name of Alan Freed, the guy who had to all intents and purposes invented the term rock and roll or at least usurped it and foisted it onto a ready and willing great white public.

Freed was a truly cool dude who identified with the new music, championed its cause and promoted its exponents. He was arguably the father of rock & roll who not only gave airtime to the rising young white performers of the day but appreciated even more the art and talent of the maligned and downtrodden American negro musicians who purveyed the hitherto denigrated and so called 'jungle rhythms' of the black ghettos. Playing black records, or 'race music' as it was called then, was a risky business but Freed flouted all conventions and his Moondog Show became required listening for anyone fitting the newly coined label of teenager.

Jack Jackson on the other hand was a cuddly uncle figure of a white man from

Horsley, Derbyshire, in the centre of England. He was already fifty years old by the time Presley arrived on the scene. Jackson's technique consisted of lifting segments from the latest singles and reassembling the pieces like a musical mosaic into comedy vignettes to be acted out by his two cohorts on the family based programme.

Glen Mason, a personable and good-looking young Scottish dance band vocalist, would lip-synch alongside a rubber lipped Libby Morris, an ample-framed matron with a face like a smacked arse. She would gurn her way into the hearts of the viewers with facial contortions that instantly removed any serious lyrical or musical content at a stroke. The public loved it and tuned in religiously every week.

Once in a while you might be treated to a guest performer plugging their latest release or be informed of the latest trends on the other side of the Atlantic. In those days before air travel became affordable and available to the average person, America was an inaccessible fairytale land. The American culture and way of life was a romantic notion that only existed in the movies or on television or in your wildest dreams. And dreams were the only things we could afford.

In fact most of the superior original US recordings never even made it across the pond. There were simply too many for what was then an embryo market which the men in suits did not understand. And anyway most of them got covered by inferior British artistes before the originals could ever get a release. Knowing no better we often accepted dross in our ignorance. In those days we took what we were given and were grateful.

But on this momentous night the purveyor of this unbelievable new sound was not there in the studio. He was not even there on film. We simply heard a portion of the record and gazed on a photograph as Jack Jackson told us of a new musical sensation from the States called Elvis Presley. I stared at the screen, mesmerised by the image in vision and sound that I was experiencing.

If the opening bars of *Heartbreak Hotel* were mind blowing, the sight of the face behind the voice propelled my elation into the stratosphere. Here was a smouldering-eyed young guy with the face of a Greek god and a charisma that was quite apparent even from that one still picture showing on the miniscule monochrome screen. There had never been a singer before who sounded that good. There had never been a matinee idol who looked as handsome as this new and exciting young rock & roll sensation. Presley did not have star potential. He was already a star simply by being.

Rock & roll had introduced itself barely a year or so before in the shape of Bill Haley & his Comets, ostensibly a western swing outfit from the very un-western location of Detroit, Michigan. And it was not a particularly pleasing shape. With his trademark kiss-curl haircut, a big-bodied Gibson guitar strapped around his neck and an outrageous plaid jacket over his well upholstered frame he resembled nothing so much as a singing butcher. He was plump to the point of danger. Two more good meals and he would have been considered fat.

The instrumentation was the usual guitars, stand-up bass and drums and augmented not only by a saxophone and a pedal steel, an item that firmly displayed their country roots and a previous incarnation when they were known as the Saddlemen, but also an accordion of all things, an instrument never known for its cool quotient. Accordions were things to be avoided at all costs. They were played by and listened to by geeks and nerds who were the remnants of a dying breed and, come the rock & roll revolution, they would surely be destroyed. It was not until years later that I discovered the amazing possibilities of an accordion in the right hands. The wonders and delights of Cajun sounds and the sheer joy of zydeco were far off in the musical distance.

The Comets certainly packed a power that had hitherto been missing form pop music but the act comprised more camp comedy than rock & roll menace as they clowned around the stage brandishing their instruments which, in the case of the bass, would mean standing on it while playing and, in the case of the sax, writhing around on the floor whilst attempting to deliver an acceptable solo.

But *Rock Around The Clock* was certainly a great disc and had deservedly become the anthem of untamed youth when it was featured in Blackboard Jungle, a rebellious black and white youth movie of chaos and danger in the classroom featuring Glenn Ford and Vic Morrow. The drums featured a heavy off beat that was insistent and addictive. The guitar solo delivered by Frank Beecher, although in fact played on the recording by session musician Danny Cedrone, was fast and furious. Haley's vocals effectively cut through the backing. And the concise and simple lyrics and tune could be sung by a three year old. How could it fail?

But what gave it the dramatic edge that rock & roll needed was the reaction of the moviegoers as the soundtrack boomed out from the large cinema speakers. The whole theme of the film was seen as an excuse and an enticement to be bad. Young people were weary of being patronised and ignored. They were tired of wearing cut down versions of their parents' fashions. No longer were they prepared to accept an adult's idea of good music. They had money. They had style. And now they wanted power. They desperately wanted that essential requirement, their parents' seal of disapproval.

When the dramatic and raucous soundtrack struck up it was a signal to riot. Rows of cinema seats were pulled from their moorings and hurled across picture houses across the land. Fights started. People got hurt. Some, only a few, died in such skirmishes. Flick knives and knuckle-dusters were the weapons of choice in the mid-fifties. The authorities were outraged and in a great many places rock & roll was banned. Perfect. For rock & roll a ban meant that its success and future were guaranteed.

But for me, after hearing the new messiah on the Jack Jackson Show, Haley was yesterday's man. The next morning after hearing this new sound I rushed to school and asked my pals if any of them had heard it too. No one had. I tried to describe the experience with little success. How could I? I couldn't even remember his name. I mean, what kind of a name is Elvis? Or Presley, come to that? These were not names I had ever encountered before. Maybe they were made up? It sounded that way. In the event I got it wrong. In my confused state I remembered him as Melvin Purves. But pretty soon everyone had heard of him and the whole world knew his name.

There was precious little exposure for pop music back then in Britain. Certainly the BBC limited needle time on the radio to a paltry few hours a week in the fifties, on top of which the powers that be were still locked in their safe little world of the prewar dance band era and clean cut sanitised crooners whose aim was to satisfy the taste of your parents. Youth counted for little in the scheme of things back then. If you were young you had to grab your chances when and where you could. In prim and proper post war Britain it was considered impolite to grab. But society was changing and manners and morals were quickly being cast aside as the times began to adjust to that change.

The development of the transistor meant that radio sets could now be miniaturised and each night kids across the land would tuck themselves under the blankets, an ear clamped to the speaker with the dial tuned to Radio Luxembourg on 208 metres Medium Wave. The station, situated in the tiny European principality, was a commercial enterprise and record labels bought space during which they could shamelessly plug their latest releases. It was the only source from where you could be sure of a decent amount of pop coverage.

The limited transmission power of the Luxembourg set-up and the unstable weather condition that hampered the radio waves meant that listening in was a troublesome experience. The signal would fade in and out and the fading out always seemed to happen in the middle of your own particular favourite sounds.

On Tuesdays and Thursdays at ten o'clock it was time for The Capitol Show. Its brassy big band theme tune had riffs which were interspersed with the names of the artistes whose discs were to be played during the next half hour. And at least the small Hollywood-based Capitol label, whose exotic headquarters was designed to looked like a stack of records, had paid a little more lip service to the new music than some of the other companies. Following the phenomenal success of Elvis they too had made forays into the world of rock & roll.

If the announcer called out the name of Gene Vincent I was overjoyed. He was more primitive and used even more echo than Elvis and his debut hit, *Be Bop A Lula* was fabulous. The effects on the vocals were so intense as to make the lyrics, which were quite bizarre anyway, almost unintelligible. And if you flipped it over to the B-side, *Woman Love,* you would be hard pressed to make out more than a few odd words every now and again. Sheer bliss. And sheer agony when a superbly executed guitar solo by Vincent's unbelievably dextrous sideman Cliff Gallup would be cut off in its prime by some turbulence over the English Channel.

Tommy Sands was another new idol on Capitol although his success was to be very limited. Following on from his debut disc *Teenage Crush* he seemed to stall and from then on his greatest achievement, if you discount his acting role in The Longest Day, was marrying into the Sinatra family by whisking Frank's daughter Nancy down the aisle. Still, I was grateful for anything in those days.

In the event of the omission of any true rockers on the programme I was prepared to accept the inclusion of a country act like Sonny James whose *Young Love,* covered and converted into a bigger hit by film heartthrob and vocally challenged Tab Hunter, was within my defined range of acceptability. After all a lot of country material was pretty close to the teen-oriented style of rockabilly. Sometimes it was hard to see the join. At a pinch I might even hang on to hear Tennessee Ernie Ford, although that was scraping the barrel a bit. But if all I was going to be offered was Frank Sinatra warbling on yet again with songs for swinging lovers it was time to switch off and go to sleep.

Outside of Radio Luxembourg there was a paucity of the new music over the airwaves. Jack Payne, yet another elderly ex-band leader, also hosted a television programme called Off The Record but he was careful in the main to avoid any discs that might in any way pander to or satisfy the emotionally and aurally starved teenager.

Two Way Family Favourites, a radio request show designed to bridge the gap between our armed forces abroad and their loved ones at home, was the main outlet for popular recorded music in Britain. Its midday spot on Sunday, juxtaposed with the hit comedy show Life With The Lyons, provided a comfortable musical backdrop to the family group gathered round the kitchen table to share a roast lunch.

In the main it consisted of light music reflecting adult taste and still firmly entrenched in the comfort zones of the war years. In those days Johnnie Ray, the Cry Guy with the slightly manic and awkward looking gyrations and heartfelt sobbing vocal style, was as wild as it got. And in truth he was pretty wild. And good too. He borrowed heavily from black influences and translated them into a unique style of performance that belonged to no-one else.

Such A Night, which sent his audiences into paroxysms of delight as he mumbled and shuddered through the sexually charged tune, had been previously put out by Clyde McPhatter and the Drifters who, being black, could never get the national exposure necessary to lift them into the best-selling lists. Its explicit lyrics, coupled with a set of gyrations which could just about be construed as simulating copulation, promptly got him banned from the airwaves.

Young women screamed as he sang and lusted after him, naively unaware that Ray himself was more likely to lust after their boyfriends. They were innocent times indeed. His arrest for importuning an off-duty policeman in a gentlemen's urinal was rapidly quashed due to his strong friendship with Dorothy Kilgallen, a powerful journalist with friends in very high places. Johnnie's devoted public to the greater extent remained blissfully unaware of their heartthrob's rather bohemian proclivities.

Not surprisingly one record that found itself on the Family Favourites playlist week after week was *I'll Be Home* by Pat Boone. Its lyrics and sentiment encapsulated the programme's entire raison d'etre. Boone's interpretation of the song, originally recorded by a black doo-wop vocal group called the Flamingos, was emotionally strong and haunting. It was one of his better covers, possibly because it required a tuneful voice, which was his forte. On the other hand his putrid offerings of smoothed out and watered down versions of *Tutti Frutti* and *Long Tall Sally*, both of which started out in life as vastly superior and emotionally charged Little Richard rockers, were hugely successful sales-wise but appalling in their mediocrity. Boone was emotionally divorced from the whole meaning and spirit of the songs. He felt nothing when performing them. And while I loved his voice on *I'll Be Home* I felt nothing listening to this twaddle.

The world was wising up. Britain certainly had its own racist roots but it was far removed from the intense degree of racial bigotry that was endemic in the USA and the South in particular. When records by Fats Domino, The Platters and the aforementioned Little Richard started to receive airplay, the youth of Britain bought the discs by the bucketload and revelled in the sheer abandon with which they were sung. The revolution had arrived and at just the right time for me. After all I was reaching a milestone in my life. I was about to become a teenager and I suddenly knew that there were only two kinds of music. Rock and Roll.

2

School And Skiffle

I was born Francis Renaud McNeice on 14th December 1943 in a ground floor bedroom at 33 Woodrow Avenue, Hayes, Middlesex, an end-of-terrace house in an undistinguished working class neighbourhood fifteen miles out of London proper and only a few miles away from the fast growing but still fairly small airport at Heathrow. The kind of mundane suburban environment where in their wisdom they see fit to tear down the trees and name streets after them. There was precious little wood left in Woodrow Avenue.

I was the first of my immediate family to be born south of the border. My brother Jackie was born a Scot three years previously in the family home town of Greenock, Renfrewshire, a shipbuilding community on the banks of the Clyde, thirty miles south west of Glasgow. The war was at its height and the shipyards were a prime target for the Luftwaffe. Showing early but sensible signs of innate cowardice they moved lock stock and barrel to the relative safety of London. The east end of the capital had received a significant battering but elsewhere the suburbs remained unscathed. I believe I was developing in the womb at the time but was not to plop out into the world until we had reached England. To this day I am not sure whether I am Scottish or English.

We were poor but of course I never knew that. Everyone I knew was in the same boat. There was no money about and rationing meant that we were all scrambling about to get whatever food was available. Life was much simpler then and, in those primitive times before foreign travel, television and electronic luxuries, I never felt deprived. There was nothing around to be deprived of. Recreation for kids in those days, however much money you had, meant heading for the park and creating what fun you could from the depths of your own imagination. I enjoyed my childhood in Harlington. Do adults enjoy adultery as much as infants enjoy infancy I wonder?

If you didn't have a toy gun well, there was always a broken stick that could approximate the shape. There were trees to climb. And streams to swing over and splash about in and any accidents were generally slight and part of our learning curve. We always seemed to eat well although on reflection our diet was greasy and fat filled. Everything, apart from the traditional Sunday roast, was fried. It's a miracle my arteries saw me into adulthood.

Our parents drank and smoked as we were being born and our cots were decorated with bright lead-based paints. We shared a soft drink with half a dozen pals and no one actually died. If our foods were full of sugar and we didn't become overweight it was probably because we spent most of our free time outside playing, expending energy in the open air.

Danger appeared for the greater part to be absent and if we disappeared out of sight all day that was fine as long as we were home when the street lights came on. If our home made go-carts careered out of control down the hill we soon learned to deal with grazed knees and the odd broken limb after crashing into a wall or a bush a few times. There were no Play Stations, Nintendos or X Boxes. Even by the late fifties if we had a television it had two channels on it, not ninety nine. Cable was something that tied a ship to shore. No DVDs with surround sound, mobile phones or personal computers. What we did have were friends and we went out and found them face to face, not in a chat room somewhere out in cyberspace.

Poverty, I have always maintained, is a relative thing. When people proclaim that we must eradicate poverty I insist that it is an impossibility. The pauper is simply the lowest man on the totem pole. Today you are considered poor if you can't afford a car, a Spanish holiday or the latest Game Boy consoles and Nike sneakers for your kids. And if that is your situation the state will probably give it to you anyway. In my youth people in such a situation were called rich and we could only dream, our snotty little red noses pressed hard up against the windows of affluence.

All that happens is that the goalposts are moved. If the majority drive Rolls Royces then the poor man is he who can only run a Ford. In truth the only true poverty is that which threatens your life outside the commonly accepted parameters of expectancy as governed by the conditions in which the rest of your community live. If, in a third world country, you don't have enough food to keep you and your family alive then you are truly poor. Nothing else really counts. You just have to deal with it.

My father's family, the McNeices, originated from the Northern Irish town of Ballymena and emigrated to Scotland in search of work, which was plentiful on Clydeside. Ships constituted the major form of commercial transportation and the yards of Port Glasgow were operating to capacity.

The origins of my mother's family lay in France. My great grandfather, I am assured, was a ship's cook from Marseille who jumped ship in Glasgow and married a local girl. My middle name of Renaud was also my mother's maiden name. It appears to have been a Scottish, or at least Celtic, tradition to incorporate surnames into the names of our offspring, at least in our family.

My grandmother, Annie McGee, became a Renaud on marriage and her daughter who of course was my mother, became Sarah McGee Renaud until her last name changed on marrying Dad to Sarah McNeice. They skipped the custom when my brother came along. He was simply John McNeice. But I was named Francis after my mother's brother and the family name of Renaud was slipped back in between. Rather posh I think for someone with such a lowly start in life.

My father was David McCormack McNeice, although he was always called Davy, and I assume the same method was used on his side of the family. On the whole double-barrelled surnames seem quite pretentious for such a dirt poor working class bunch as us. In the end though names counted for very little. My mum was always Sadie and my father Davy. Brother John was always referred to as Jackie and I never once heard my family call me anything other than Frankie. The name Francis was reserved for formal documents only.

My father was a person who knew his place. All through his life he suffered from a deep sense of insecurity both personal and financial which to a great extent he passed on to me, and although I'm sure we were not exactly at the bottom of the bottom of the pile there did not appear to be too many further down.

Our portion of the family home was rented from the couple who occupied the top half. The Walshes were a volatile couple who argued constantly, something that rarely happened in our home. I would play with their young daughter Madeleine but when the shouting started and fists were raised I would get frightened and run downstairs to the safety of my family. I heard my parents talking to my aunt one day, laughing about how Mr Walsh, in the throes of a particularly heated confrontation, had thrown his wife out into the back garden naked. Even at three years old I knew that adults were not supposed to appear in public without so much as a nice thick vest on. It sounded very exciting. But at the same time I was glad it never happened in our home

When the war finally ended Britain emerged the winner if indeed it's possible to be truly victorious in such matters. There are those who believe you can no more win a war than you can win an earthquake. In 1945 peace was finally declared and the time eventually came when we had to move on. An Englishman's home is his castle and the Walsh's wanted their castle back. There was no right of tenure in those days and we simply had to get out. Jackie and I were handed over to Aunt Nan (Annie) and Uncle Frank Renaud till things were sorted out. Goodness knows where my Mum and Dad stayed.

Eventually we were found temporary accommodation by the council authorities. And what they came up with is still looked on by friends as a Pythonesque invention of my fertile imagination. We were billeted in a Nissen hut. Not, I must affirm, a prefab. Prefabs were luxury compared to our primitive dwelling. Ours was a semi-circular corrugated tin hut set on a disused military camp in Yeading, about a mile from Woodrow Avenue. And I still have my father's identity card with the address on as proof. We lived in Hut 34, The Gunsite, Yeading Lane. The domed shell was split to form bedrooms (I'm still not sure how many there were) and there was a solid fuel stove in the centre of the main living area with a pipe leading straight up through the roof. I can't remember a bathroom. Eating was a priority in those days. Washing was not.

Apart from my parents we also had Gran on my mother's side living with us. Back then families had consciences and still felt the moral obligation to accept responsibility for their parents. In return she provided a necessary baby-sitting service while Mum and Dad went out to work. Mum was a cook in a school canteen while my Dad, now discharged from the army, had gone back to his old trade of painting and decorating.

Still living in the tin shack, I eventually started school at Yeading Primary a short walk away down Carlyon Road where coincidentally I was to buy my first detached house many years later. I doubt if my future purchase, a mock Tudor property behind a high wall at number one, was standing at that time but if it was I never noticed. To get to school we had to cross the fields adjacent to the gun site and cut through an estate of new houses that was still under construction.

My abiding memory of those dwellings was that they featured the very latest cast-iron radiators which I dearly coveted. Forget the deadly sin of coveting thy neighbour's ass (in the traditional farming sense of the word). I coveted his central heating. Central heating was an unashamed luxury in the fifties and the one thing that I was determined to achieve in life above all else. Winters were bitterly cold and small solid fuelled fireplaces that were the norm were hardly sufficient to cope with the freezing conditions when ice would form on the insides of the windows. I hated cold weather and still do. It felt as though I lived in that Nissen hut for years. It was actually about nine months, which I suppose does constitute a lot of child years. I think when you are three or four, a month is a year.

Further on from the fields we had to cross the main road which these days would be unthinkable for kids of our tender years. But cars were scarce and we were rarely in any great danger. School was fun once we got there. I had good pals to play with. It was while there that I had my first encounter with racism.

I had a friend called Dev. He was from India which was plain to see by his colour but which meant absolutely nothing to me. I do remember visiting his house, which was much grander than the conditions we lived in and impeccably clean. And I remember the curious smell pervading the rooms as I entered. It was an odd odour but not unpleasant. A smell which I later understood was curry. It was a loving environment and his mum was always smiling and welcoming to a smelly little runt like me. And believe me I am sure I did smell. And I was most definitely a scruffy little tow rag.

Dev and I were on our way home from school one day when we passed the grocers. Shop displays were different in those pre-supermarket days. Containers were laid out on tables in front of the store and goods in the main were sold loosely. You would by biscuits by weight. We bought broken biscuits at knock-down prices. After all they got broken up once you'd put them in your mouth so what was the difference? Pre-packed goodies were unnecessarily expensive and not for people like me.

There was a tin containing dates, sticky and tempting, and the fact that flies tended to buzz about them, occasionally landing and sampling before being shooed away by the shop lady, was no deterrent whatsoever. Dev decided to buy some and was served with no problem. They looked sweet and tasty. Once he had his I too wanted some but the woman behind the counter refused to sell them to me.

My mother wouldn't want me to eat those, she explained. It was all right for them, she said, obviously referring to Dev and any other filthy unwelcome Asians who knew no better and cared less. From a shelf she lifted a packet of factory wrapped dates protected from the flies and the elements by a layer of professionally applied cellophane. Despite my youth I instinctively recognised the slight to my friend. Not only that, but the hygienically superior offering looked nowhere near as appetising as the others, flies or no flies. I refused and we left. Whether Dev was offended by the insult I never knew. I was too ashamed of what happened to bring the subject up. How in God's name he should be ashamed is unfathomable. He lived in a real house made of bricks and mortar, which it is quite possible they owned, while I lived in a tin shed.

After a lot of harassing the authorities and innumerable visits by my father to the council offices we were finally offered a new home. It wasn't a matter of checking it out and deciding if it was suitable. It was a case of giving an immediate yes or no to a verbal description by someone whose job it was to allocate a paltry number of houses to a seemingly unending line of homeless people. We said yes.

I never set eyes on our new home until the day we moved in. It was a thrilling time. What we had said yes to was not a palace. What it did have over the Nissen hut was solid brick walls, a proper kitchen and living room and three bedrooms. What it did not have was electricity, a hot water system or central heating. The latter would have been the impossible dream anyway. The rooms were lit by fragile gas mantles and the bath water had to be heated first in a free-standing gas boiler in the small kitchen and transported via whatever receptacles were at hand into the ground floor bathroom. But at least we had a bathroom.

Mum and Dad had the main bedroom, Jackie and I shared one of the two singles while Gran had the other. Our new school on the main Bath Road which ran alongside the airport was a fifteen minute walk away. Dad soon gave up the painting and decorating to take on a new occupation at the British Overseas Airways Corporation as a cleaner of aircraft interiors, and Mum began cooking at yet another school which conveniently backed onto our rear garden.

It was 1952 and a fresh start not only for us but also the British nation. We had emerged from the war victorious, we had a new Queen, Elizabeth the Second and Edmund Hillary and Sherpa Tensing were getting ready to conquer one of the great remaining challenges, Mount Everest, just in time for her coronation in the summer of '53. There was a serious danger of Britain actually becoming great again.

In my ignorance as a small child I was completely unaware that my grandmother had some mental problems. Apart from imagining she had cancer she was apparently under the false impression that her presence was a burden on the family and in the middle of the night of July 19th 1952 she let herself out of the house and walked to Hayes Town, a distance of five miles. No mean feat for a frail woman of sixty-eight. In those far off hard times sixty-eight was an advanced age. These days we can almost consider it no age at all.

Once she reached her destination she calmly walked into the Grand Union Canal and drowned. Her death certificate reads 'not being of sound mind did kill herself'. I was too young to understand. Too young to feel any amount of true grief. And selfish enough to realise that this tragedy would benefit me by the acquisition of my own room. My brother Jackie, although three years older and therefore fully matured in my eyes, was equally concerned with little but self interest. He was due to go out with Mum and Dad the next day to buy his first pair of jeans, a most important rite of passage in a young lad's life. The trip, quite naturally, was postponed. He was not pleased.

My primary education was completed at the William Byrd Primary School from where, on passing my 11-plus exams, I transferred to Spring Grove Grammar School in Isleworth. It was my school of choice and a strange choice at that. It was over an hour's journey from my house requiring three bus rides most days. On a lucky day, if I timed things right, I could reduce that to two but it made no difference. I still had to allow the extra in case I missed the bus.

My choice was governed by two facts. A boy who lived six doors away, David Turner, who was three years older than me, had been going there for a while so at least I knew something about the place and I thought the uniform looked cool. The black jacket with crested badge, topped off by a matching white-ringed cap and a rather snazzy striped tie looked smart. Even at that tender age I was beginning to be affected by fashion although these days I base my fashion sense on what doesn't itch.

The building itself was a revelation. A mansion once lived in by one of the immensely wealthy Pears soap family, perfectly suited to the ideas above my station that were beginning to manifest in my increasingly pretentious character. It was built on grounds where once stood the house of Sir Joseph Banks, the botanist on Captain Cook's voyage of discovery to Australia. If the outside was impressive the interior was spectacular. A mahogany staircase rose in the entrance hall to greet an intricate stained glass window. The corridor to the left of the stairs led to the music room, panelled and decorated as delicately as a Wedgwood vase and boasting a minstrels' gallery at one end. This room in turn led into what was our art room, its glazed ceiling providing the perfect lighting conditions for the painting of schoolchild masterpieces. An alcove on one of the long sides was lined in exotic mosaic tiles and resembled a corner of an eastern potentate's palace.

But the *piece de resistance* was the Banksian Room. This was an enormous glass conservatory to rival anything at Kew Gardens. The Pears family would have housed their extensive collection of flora and fauna but for us it was a space for whatever lesson required it. I never fully realised the privileges I was being given by being educated in these glorious surroundings but I did at least have a modest appreciation of it. Even then I was not a total Philistine.

My mother had been told by the headmistress at Yeading Primary that I was an unusually bright child. But any seedlings of knowledge that had been so lovingly planted were about to have their growth stunted by the advent of rock & roll. I had been listening to music all of my short life so far and happily warbled the tunes of my childhood. Doris Day sang *Whip Crack Away* as she steered the Deadwood Stage into town under the guise of sharp shooting Annie Oakley. Jo Stafford caused me to conjure images of romantic shoreline communities to whom she announced that *The Shrimp Boats Are A Coming*. And the booming stentorian tones of Frankie Laine sang the praises of *A Woman In Love* although at that tender age I never knew much about women and less about love, unless it was for music.

In the UK we had home-grown stars like Dickie Valentine, Alma Cogan and David Whitfield. Malcolm Vaughan captured the religious audience with his huge hit recording of *Saint Therese Of The Roses*. I learnt the words and discovered I could be rewarded with one shilling a time for singing the song at our local British Legion. When I got greedy and offered my services more times than was decent in polite society they asked me to give someone else a chance.

All this schmaltzy safe stuff, firmly stamped with the adult seal of approval, was fine to a point but once Elvis Presley arrived most of it became surplus to requirements. I not only wanted to sing the new music I also wanted to play it. Elvis had a guitar. I had to have a guitar. Indeed it seemed like every teenage kid in the land wanted a guitar.

I bugged my parents unmercifully. The fact that they had shelled out for a piano a few years earlier, having been given the solemn promise that I would take lessons and practice religiously, did not help my cause. After passing the first two basic exams in theory and practical I got bored and the shiny black instrument stood in the corner of the room unused. Unless of course my Dad felt like knocking out a tune, which he had a modest talent for, albeit that it was all on the black notes and with the sustain firmly on to give it maximum volume and resonance. He could also deliver a tune on our three-string banjo. Never heard of a three-string banjo? Well actually they don't make them. Ours was a regular four-string model but somewhere along the line it had been dropped causing a section of the headstock, complete with peg and tuner, to detach itself from the neck. He just carried on playing.

Persistence pays off. I finally got my beloved guitar as a Christmas present. It was a cheap steel strung flat top in a dark brown stain with palm trees and the words Palm Beach stencilled on the front. It cost six pounds and nine pence. The canvas carrying bag and the book which gave you some chord diagrams and told you how to tune it were extra.

Many decades later I was given a book called Two Rooms which comprised the songs of Elton John and Bernie Taupin. Just inside the cover there was a picture of Taupin as a young boy in a cowboy suit and holding an identical Palm Beach guitar. I wondered if that could be the very same one that I had owned. I had eventually sold mine to one of the girls at school who lived in Cranford but I suppose that somehow it could possibly have made its way to Lincolnshire where the young Bernie Taupin lived. I'm almost sure I could still recognise it although they must have made hundreds. One of the plastic tuning pegs had broken away and without the money to affect a repair I used to carry a pair of pliers in order to adjust the strings. Sure, the peg head would have been replaced but there was also a distinctive patch of stain that had been removed just below the sound-hole. I wonder? If ever I run into him I will be sure to check. It would be nice to think that it had played a dual role in music history.

Rock & roll was my goal but skiffle had come to popularity via the arrival of Lonnie Donegan's Rock Island Line, Chas McDevitt's *Freight Train* which featured the vocals of the intriguingly named Nancy Whiskey and *Don't You Rock Me Daddy-o*, from the Vipers. Their guitarist Wally Whyton had written the song, or at least adapted it from a standard negro folk ditty, but a sneaky Lonnie Donegan had filched it from under their noses and rocked it up into a massive hit. With skiffle you only needed three chords and the most rudimentary strumming technique to play a song. So, until I could improve my musical skills, skiffle it was. I formed the Ambassadors Skiffle Group with some older guys at the school and we humped our equipment, tea chest bass and all, on and off an endless succession of double-decker buses in order to play wherever anyone would let us.

Our main stomping ground in those earliest of days was the Windmill pub in Bell Road, Hounslow. The manager paid us ten shillings between us and we had to pay for our own drinks. Except me. While the older guys would drink cider or perhaps, in the case of the ones who looked mature enough, a shandy, I only drank lime juice and soda so they gave me that for free. Considering the appalling noise I'm sure we must have made, the customers would have probably preferred us to drink arsenic. But we were performing musicians at last and in heaven.

We even had our own groupies although they were pure as the driven snow as they travelled around with us for support. My girlfriend was Lyn Coleman who came along to cheer and whom we inveigled to write letters of protest to the local press on the occasions when a rival group would beat us in a skiffle contest. Her pocket money, courtesy of generous parents, beat my meagre two shillings and sixpence by a mile and she would buy me the packets of iced caramels and sugar bon bons which I loved but could ill afford. In later years she went on to marry, and eventually divorce, our singer.

The rest of the guys in the group clubbed together to buy an add-on pickup for my guitar so that I could play solos but what I really craved was an electric guitar. My woodwork teacher at school, an incredibly nice and enthusiastic man called Mr Sonji, allowed me to construct one as an end of term project. He immediately became my hero. Everyone around me was telling me to chuck this music lark and get serious about my education and here was wonderful Mr Sonji telling me to go for it.

The solid bodied guitar, vaguely in the style of a Fender Jazzmaster if you closed one eye and squinted a lot with the other, looked quite cool. Sadly, I had no real idea of what I was doing or the precision required to deliver a tuneful sound when finished. On top of which I had no money with which to buy pickups or an amplifier. It was laid to rest out of sight in a cupboard and eventually disposed of. I was no Brian May when it came to the subject of home made guitars.

In the summer of '57 the rest of the group and I undertook the big adventure into the big city of London to see the National Skiffle Concert at the Royal Festival Hall which might not have featured Lonnie, by now a superstar and too big for such things, but boasted such great stars of skiffle as Chas McDevitt, Dickie Bishop and his Side-kicks and Johnny Duncan and the Bluegrass Boys. There was also the Avon Cities Jazz Band featuring the Ray Bush Skiffle Group but I hated jazz and I had never heard of Ray Bush so they didn't count.

Before the concert we made a pilgrimage to Old Compton Street and stared into the window of the Two Is coffee bar where Tommy Steele and most of the Larry Parnes stable of stars had been discovered. Too scared to wander onto such hallowed turf we settled for the Heaven and Hell next door where we were horrified to learn that a frothy espresso coffee cost one shilling. Absolutely outrageous. I talked about it for weeks.

The concert itself was wonderful. I was in awe of the professional performers on the stage of this state-of-the-art auditorium. Dickie Bishop's band even had an electric bass guitar, an instrument as rare as rocking horse shit in England although the Fender bass had been pretty standard in the States for a while. Don Wilson's German made instrument was a Framus Star Bass, the kind we would soon be seeing hung upon the lithe frame of Shadows bassist Jet Harris. Little did I know that evening that for a short while a couple of years on Don Wilson would be plucking away on bass guitar in my own little semi-professional outfit.

We had a great time that day but had to admit that skiffle was just a step on the ladder. The clarion call of rock & roll was getting louder and louder and we just knew we were duty bound to answer the call.

3

From Skiffle To Rock

If you want to run with the big dogs there's no point in pissing like a puppy. We'd learnt our three chords and murdered *Tom Dooley* enough times to get us put away for life. It was time to move on.

A neat looking orange sunburst Framus arch top guitar with a Hofner pickup that had tone and volume controls built into a visually impressive shiny chrome tailpiece for me, combined with a uniform of black slacks, black shirts and bright yellow ties purchased from Levitts Gentlemen's Outfitters in Hounslow transformed us into the Raiders Rhythm Group. At the same time we dumped the tea chest bass and washboard and drafted in a drummer. Impressive stuff albeit that he only possessed a snare drum and nothing else.

In the main our set consisted of American material. *Donna* by Ritchie Valens, *Teenager In Love* by the vocally magnificent Marty Wilde whose home-grown version even managed to eclipse Dion and the Belmonts' original and Diana by Canadian boy wonder Paul Anka were the hits of the day. My speciality was cringingly precocious interpretation of Bill Parsons' *All American Boy*, complete with fake Southern accent. The British scene had opened up. Marty Wilde and Billy Fury had firmly established themselves and Cliff Richard had arrived to prove that we had artistes to rival anything that America could throw at us. *Move It* was possibly the greatest home-grown rock & roll record ever, with Johnny Kidd & the Pirates' *Shakin' All Over* running a close second.

My repertoire of pop songs had increased in inverse proportion to my academic prowess and by the end of my schooldays in 1960, having followed closely the maxim that you should not learn more than you absolutely need to get through life, I ended my formal education clutching a GCE certificate with a lamentable three passes in English Language, French and Woodwork. I was given two weeks of freedom by my parents after which time I was expected to find paid employment.

Penguin Books was a stone's throw away along the Bath Road and appealed to my literary sensibilities which were seemingly lurking in the background even then. I was taken onto their payroll and promptly set about becoming the worst despatch clerk in history, sharing our raised platform with a prematurely middle-aged guy called Laurie and a pleasant but very dizzy blonde called Inge Stark who declared to everyone that this was merely temporary. She was going to be a film star. Oh Inge, where are you now?

It was the time of the Lady Chatterley trial and the warehouse was stacked high with heavily guarded copies of the controversial tome awaiting the outcome of The Crown versus Penguin Books. One day it was found necessary to deliver a copy to one of the jurors and I was deputed to undertake the task. Fortunately they had neglected to seal the envelope and I spent the tube journey salaciously devouring the contents of the relevant pages. I was red faced, my heart was thumping and I had an erection. I was getting a lot of those lately.

I had even tried to do something about it. I had a girlfriend called Josephine with whom there was a lot of fumbling but very little else to outrage the morals of society. My friends decided this had to change and it was planned that during a party one evening at a house in Eastcote that I was to take advantage of a bedroom which they would make sure remained empty and at our disposal.

We climbed the stairs with a great deal of trepidation and I set about trying to figure out how it was done. The main problem was that I knew sod all about women's clothing and I had done no research whatsoever. It was the days of knickers and suspender belts and I was under the false impression that in order to remove the former you first had to unclip the latter. Too embarrassed to look, or worse to ask Josephine for any help with the instructions, I attempted to tackle these ghastly garments that were coming between us. It was impossible. It felt like I should be using a spanner. On reflection I should simply have used was the American method. One yank and they're down.

The excitement was too much and to my undying shame and almost before it began the whole sordid episode was prematurely over. I had wasted precious seconds of my life simply in order to embarrass myself. On reflection this disaster was a godsend. In the foolishness of youth the thought of using protection had not entered my foolish head. The very idea of unwanted progeny as a result of this hasty and unnecessary act of lust and discovery had been completely dismissed by me and as we all know it is at such times when fate will intervene and destroy you. As a wise man once said, condoms should be used on every conceivable occasion. Silently we dusted ourselves off, repositioned our clothing and went down to face the smirks in the party room below. The incident was never referred to again. Not by me anyway. And it was a very long time before I tried it again. The lovely Josephine remained chaste and unsullied by the occasion.

The group was going well. I was making money to boost my modest wages which were six pounds a week and often my gig money outstripped that considerably. I talked my Dad into signing as guarantor for a beautiful Hofner Club 50 electric guitar, pretty near top of the range in those pre-US instrument days, and the group had metamorphosed into The Skyways, put together with an Anglo-Indian pal boasting the exotic name of Brian St George.

We were improving and becoming more professional by the day. We even had a full size stand up bass played by a guy called Alan. Alan also possessed the group transport, a gunge green sit-up-and-beg Ford Anglia fitted with a roof rack to take the bass. This lasted as long as it took for the bass to break free and splinter into a dozen pieces in the road. Exit Alan and bass and enter Johnny Marin who was willing to buy a rather more transportable Framus bass guitar and amplifier in order to join our ranks. It was both a better image and a better size. My Club 50 was discarded in favour of an American made Harmony Meteor as soon as the import bans on instruments were lifted. And when time was up for the Skyways I dropped the axe altogether and formed The Frank Allen Combo. My plan to become Elvis was progressing nicely.

Yes, I had acquired a new name along with everything else. Francis McNeice was hardly the handle of a teen idol and as a lead singer (and I must stress that the title was no indication of quality whatsoever) I decided that I should find something short and snappy.

I was travelling to Harrow on the top deck of a 140 bus and checking out the names on the shop fronts. Just past the White Hart roundabout in Yeading I spotted a knitting wool establishment called Lyn Allen. It was short, stylish and, most importantly, sounded believable. From that point on I was Frank Allen. If I had chosen the shop next door I would have become Frank Ironmonger.

The direction my band was going to follow was mapped out very early on. In late 1959 Brian St George talked me into going with him to the St Giles Hall in the nearby village of Ickenham to see a band from West Drayton called the Rebel Rousers. What I saw and heard that evening just blew me away. It was a five piece group at the time fronted by a young guy called Cliff Bennett who possessed one of the best voices I had ever heard in or out of the charts. The solid rhythms which punched out the backing behind him were far in advance of anything you would have expected from a semi-pro outfit.

Their set consisted of rockers by Gene Vincent and Jerry Lee Lewis interspersed with some of the lesser-known blues based material that was coming out of Atlantic, Vogue Coral or more often than not Sam Phillips' tiny but groundbreaking Sun studios in Memphis. *Lonely Weekends* by the unknown Charlie Rich. She Said Yeah by Larry Williams. And a whole bunch of stuff taken from Conway Twitty's debut album. Vic (Sid) Phillips was a multi instrumentalist who stuck pretty much to the piano back then but doubled on sax and even slung a guitar around his neck for the Johnny Cash song *Big River*. The bass player was Ben Jordan and the drummer was a guy called Alfie James.

Mick Currell's lead guitar was fine for the time if unspectacular and he soon settled happily into the more comfortable and appropriate position of rhythm when within months they were to turn professional and acquire a sensational player in the shape of Mick Borer (a.k.a. Micky King) who could duplicate any solo ever played by Gene Vincent's guitarist Cliff Gallup with consummate ease. The Rebel Rousers also had style in bucketloads and the very best equipment and I knew there and then I wanted to be in that band.

We stayed back to talk to them after the show and pretty soon The Skyways were filling the vacant interval spot. All through the changes in line-up and name over the next couple of years the content of our shows approximated those of my idols, who had now become Cliff Bennett & the Rebel Rousers. And like Cliff I eventually abandoned my guitar to become a writhing, hip-swinging lead vocalist, realising there were better players than I to improve our sound. There were also far better singers but I hoped no one would notice.

Towards the end of 1960 Don Wilson, the electric bass player I had watched from the stalls of the Festival Hall back in 1957, invited me to combine our respective groups. He had been running the East London based Rod Price Combo but egos had clashed and their lead singer was ousted, much to his chagrin. I delivered myself and a guitarist, Mick Barker, and together with their drums, bass and piano we had a perfect combination for the stuff we wanted to play.

On our very first gig, a village hall in Wiltshire, we turned up to note the unexpected presence of the aforementioned Rod Price with his new band who were under the erroneous impression that they would be fulfilling any previously contracted dates. Sadly for them they were sent scuttling on their way by local promoter Brian Orford and we took to the stage for a triumphant debut. Sadly for us Don Wilson's car ceased to proceed after only a few miles of our return journey to London due to a surfeit of sugar in the fuel tank. It appeared that hell hath no fury like a lead singer spurned.

We continued to watch Cliff Bennett's band and jealously coveted both their talent and their equipment, both of which were sadly lacking in our own ranks. When the embargo on US-made guitars ended the superior Fenders and Gibsons arrived in Britain. The Shadows had the first batch of Fenders (Hank Marvin already had his specially-imported Stratocaster, ordered and paid for by boss Cliff Richard) and the Rebel

Rousers had the next. Drummer Ricky Winter had shelled out a small fortune for a set of Trixon drums. They were also using a Binson Echorec reverb unit. This amazing device, which could replicate the sounds that up to then you only heard on record, had been popularised by the Italian easy-listening maestro Marino Marini who scored in the charts with *Volare* and *Ciao Ciao Bambino*.

Whatever it cost the Rousers had to have one and they did. Whatever it cost we could not afford one and our vocals remained dry. Until, that is, one night which remains in my memory as one of the most shameful nights of my life.

We had just finished a gig and Don who was an adult and who had been drinking was feeling merry and pretty wired up. I did not drink but was buzzing anyway as was our new guitarist who had been drafted in to replace a departing Mick Barker. I don't recall whose insane idea it was but we decided there and then to steal one.

A couple of weeks earlier we had played at a ballroom on the south coast in which the owner had installed one of these magic items. We resolved to simply drive there in Don's Renault car, enter the place by whatever means, remove the Echorec and provide it with a better home. When we arrived at the place the door was quite naturally locked. A couple of heaves at the door and it wasn't. We climbed the stairs to where the office with the PA equipment was stored to be confronted by a guard dog. How on earth we never spotted the dog on our previous visit I'll never know.

But luck was on our side. The dog had just given birth to puppies a few days before and she simply looked up at us with a very weary look as her offspring suckled away relentlessly. As a guard dog that night she was as much use as a concrete lifebelt. But the puppies could probably have sucked us to death.

We gathered up the goods and quickly left. Unfortunately the departure was not quite as quick as we had planned. The car refused to start. There we were having just committed a felony, outside the scene of the crime and pushing a dark green car along the narrow street trying to bump start it. Justice should have decreed that a copper would have come round the corner just then, but we were being given a chance. The engine burst into life and we high tailed it out of there. Don must have had more alcohol than he realised. Winding our way back through Earl's Court to join the main A4 to Harlington he managed to sideswipe a couple of vehicles.

Some time later when I thought about the insanity of it all and the possible repercussions I was mortified. I was even more disturbed by the realisation that we had stolen from a perfectly innocent, and probably good, fellow human being. My conscience never quite got over it and even today it still bothers me. So much so that many decades later when I found it necessary to claim for an expensive Rolex watch which I thought had been lost forever but which eventually turned up two years on I sent the timepiece back to the insurance company in the knowledge that I no longer had any entitlement to it. My friends thought I was crazy. I felt all the better for it.

The songs we performed may have been the same as the Bennett outfit but the talent most certainly was not. We had a fairly good band by now complete with a piano that allowed us to do the Jerry Lee material but I was never more than a passable lead singer and my fragile ego was severely dented after an engagement in 1961 at the Kew Boat House, a prestigious first floor ballroom on the banks of the Thames in West London.

In local terms it was a major venue for both non-names and star attractions. Saturday night at the Boat House was the cool place to be. It was operated by the Jones brothers who brought in major acts like Gene Vincent and Johnny Kidd from time to time, boosting the regular bands like the Riversiders and Cliff Bennett & the Rebel Rousers. Don Wilson was older than us and had adopted the role of our manager. When he picked up the loot that night the owner, Paddy Jones, offered the opinion that the group was okay but the singer just shouted, the singer being me. Oh shit. The talent police had finally arrived.

He passed on the information to me merely as a piece of helpful advice rather than as any act of malice, but I was shattered. I began to think that maybe I was in the wrong job. I was never blessed with an abundance of self confidence but this left me feeling like someone who only broke into a song because he couldn't find the key. I voiced my concern to Don who was sorry he had spoken out. He didn't agree with Paddy. I was doing just fine, he assured me and no other promoter had expressed any such reservations. It didn't help much and the self doubts continued to multiply inside my head. I was about to chuck it all in. But then fate intervened, if I believed in fate, which I most certainly do not.

I received a visit from Brian St George, who had by coincidence joined the Rebel Rousers, to tell me he was quitting the band. He'd had enough of the bear baiting and the piss-taking that, in truth, is a part of every group's corporate psyche. Brian was of Anglo-Indian parentage, although not overtly so in any physical sense apart from a most definite swarthy complexion. From time to time the difference was rather ungallantly pointed out to him and he was landed with the nick-name of Gazebo Shiggins. Why, I do not know and what the connections with this odd, and not particularly Asian, name and his ethnic origins were escapes me. But an insult perceived is as good as an insult received and in this case the dragon had finally managed to slay St George.

Seizing my chance I contacted Cliff only to be given the news that they had decided to carry on as a five piece, considering the post of rhythm guitar to be surplus to requirements, not to say financially more advantageous. I accepted the news with resignation and struggled on to figure out the next move in my rather precarious future. A few days later however I got a call to say that they had been booked as a six piece to record their first radio show for the BBC, the prestigious and much listened to Saturday Club. Would I join them for that one date so that they would not be in breach of contract. I accepted straight away and began to construct my devious plan of action.

Cliff arranged to pick me up in his shiny new metallic grey Sunbeam Rapier, a truly beautiful automobile that was not only elegant but also expensive. The rest of the group would make their way to the Playhouse Theatre studios at Charing Cross in the band's transport, a white Ford Thames minibus.

In the fifteen miles or so journey to the banks of the Thames I did the kind of selling job that would have made a double glazing salesman proud. By the time we pulled up outside the foyer I had convinced Cliff that my harmonies, not to mentioned the body of sound supplied by a rhythm instrument, were absolutely invaluable to the success of their unit. Once I had convinced him I knew that the opinions of the others were completely without value. After all, in a democracy your vote counts. In feudalism your Count votes. And Cliff was without a doubt the grand fromage in this little principality. By the end of the day I had taken over the hire purchase payments on a Fender Stratocaster and a Selmer Truvoice Selectortone Amplifier and I was at long last a Rebel Rouser.

4

Sax, Drums And Rock & Roll

In 1961 life was good for me. I was seventeen, the proud owner of top of the range equipment as befitted my new status. The Stratocaster was as good as it got and the Selectortone amp delivered an ear shattering fifteen watts output and an impressive row of push-button tone controls. With all the chutzpah of youth and despite possessing a talent too small to fill a gnat's handbag, I was now a professional musician. How long it would last I had no idea. Maybe two or three years at which point the talent police would arrive, warrant processed and truncheons in hand. But at that point in time I cared little. I had a whole lifetime ahead of me and right now I felt immortal.

Along with the guitar and amp I had also inherited from Brian St George a shiny silver grey mohair suit which, due to the fact that my predecessor was a few impressive sizes larger than me, contained enough spare material to redeploy as an adequate albeit somewhat ostentatious car cover, should I ever need one. The new line-up of the Rebel Rousers gathered at the Gaumont State Ballroom in Kilburn and struck up appropriately dramatic rock & roll poses while a friend and fan called Steve snapped away for what were to be our publicity photos. This was all too exciting for words.

I had also become a recording artiste. The group's managers, Bob and Jean Alexander, had secured a deal with Joe Meek, whose independent setup in a tiny flat at 304 Holloway Road in North London was one of the first to make finished masters which were then leased to the major labels for general distribution. These were pioneering days and such an arrangement was rare. The Big Three companies, Decca, EMI and Philips had the market pretty well sewn up between them.

Meek was an oddball. He had come up to London from Newent in Gwent in the mid fifties, which is situated more or less mid-way between Gloucester and Ross-on-Wye on the edge of the picturesque Forest of Dean, to be a jobbing sound engineer working on current hits like *Bad Penny Blues* by the Humphrey Lyttelton Jazz Band, and *Lay Down Your Arms*, a touch of patriotic pop pap which was a huge success by

Anne Shelton. Young, curious and enthusiastic, he began to experiment with echo, with limiters and compressors managing to get a big sound in a tiny space and at the same time minimizing the problems caused by the overspill from instruments onto open microphones. With a total disregard for convention the young audio hooligan Joe broke all the established rules of recording.

While traditional producers, used to easy listening and sweet sounds, tried to contain and minimise the drums and bass and concentrate simply on the vocal clarity, Meek was intent on providing his discs with a bedrock of power that would not simply satisfy and interest but also excite the pop-obsessed youth of the land who were his target customers. The limiters and compressors would allow the kick drum to punch through whilst at the same time stopping the length of the sound from obliterating the rest of the instruments. It gave his recordings a distinctive staccato sound and his heavy use of echo in a rather more modest way almost, though not quite, approximated the ground breaking 'wall of sound' technique introduced by Phil Spector in the States.

The entire instrumentation was set up in the main lounge of approximately fourteen feet by twelve while an adjoining smaller room contained what was laughingly called his recording equipment. It was a chaotic hotchpotch of second-hand amplifiers and a jumble of leads that seemed to have no formal arrangement and could just as easily have been a dumping ground for unwanted and obsolete electronic tat. But in that tiny space Meek achieved minor miracles in the embryonic world of audio.

In those primitive times there was no multi-tracking and any overdubbing had to be sound-on-sound, losing a generation of quality each time you wanted to add something. The drums and vocals for the most part were put down simultaneously with an arrangement of baffles preventing an undue amount of overspill. Extra vocal backing or orchestral arrangements could be layered on in a separate session but from that point forward you were limited to the amount of ornamentation that could be added before the original signal was too distorted for commercial use. Your ear for sound and sense of balance had to be extremely acute to work in this manner. Meek's was.

In other ways he was a strange and troubled person. Being a gay man when such people were simply 'queer' and with no sign of toleration let alone acceptance on the horizon, he led a twilight life filled with real danger in an age when to be a practising homosexual was still illegal. Indeed Joe, whose real name was Robert George Meek, had been arrested and fined for 'cottaging', using public toilets for the purpose of engaging in sexual acts with other males. We never broached the subject with him and indeed Joe's other world never actually intruded into our dealings with the man.

I recall him as an unremarkable figure in appearance, pretty average in height and build, baby-faced and a trifle plump and while having a slightly camp nature not overtly so. His hair was very rock & roll with a quiff that was a bit dated even then and he wore angora sweaters over the top of very tight black pants which I considered a bit odd. On reflection I suppose that should have given me a clue. But those two minor idiosyncrasies I suppose were not really sufficient to have poor old Joe irrevocably marked down as an out and out rampant woolly-woofter. We were all aware that he 'danced at the other end of the ballroom' but I would never have been bold enough to ask him which dances he preferred or indeed how often he tripped the light fantastic.

I had heard the rumours and kept an eye out around the flat for any signs of his secret life. Some dubious toiletries or lubricants perhaps. Or maybe the odd male porn mag or physique publication. But no. Disappointingly it was all very much above board. The only bathroom items that caught my eye were several tubes of Lenium which I at first thought might be sexually associated ointment but which upon examination turned out to be nothing more outrageous than an anti-dandruff shampoo. No scandal there, unless he got his kicks from erotically shampooing the heads of his amours with an indecent degree of sensitivity.

My main recollections of any feminine side to Meek was his tendency to get extremely frustrated and upset at the bouts of unprofessional anarchy introduced into the recording sessions by a group of untamed animals like the Rebel Rousers. Any overdubs of vocals or hand claps were hindered by unstoppable fits of giggles which could take an age to suppress. During these interruptions the over sensitive Joe would be reduced to real tears of frustration which would require him to leave until he could get his emotions back under control. The consciences of the hard-hearted Rebel Rousers were not troubled in any way by his discomfort.

When I first joined the others in the middle of '61 at the flat above the unimposing leather goods shop they had already put down the A-Side, a Meek-penned rocker called *You've Got What I Like*. We were now there to record a flip side, *I'm In Love With You*, yet another Meek song written under his song writing pseudonym of R. Duke.

Our debut single for the EMI controlled Parlophone label, to which Joe licensed the master tapes, was launched on the general public in July of that year. It came and went without causing too much disturbance in the world of popular music. It was a Jerry Lee Lewis styled belter using a piano whose sound was augmented by the insertion of drawing pins into the hammers giving it extra attack and sustain. The tune was ordinary, and while Cliff's Jerry Lee impersonation was terrific in the end it sank without trace. It was an excellent disc but we were a couple of years behind the times. Old style rock & roll was quickly transmuting into lushly arranged pop and Lewis was fast becoming a dinosaur, albeit an immensely talented one.

The dream of chart success was just that. A dream. I don't remember us getting despondent about our lack of sales. After all we were a working rock band and the road was our livelihood. We were making respectable, if unremarkable, money performing at ballrooms around the country, mainly sticking to the Home Counties.

Our kingdom was the club scene in Middlesex. The Blue Moon in a small hall attached to the Hayes Football Club or the Fender Club at the Memorial Hall in Harrow Weald. At Burtons Ballroom in Uxbridge we were kings. The line up of customers would begin to assemble early evening well before opening time on Saturday nights and snake down the long narrow staircase and out onto the pavement stretching way past the Queen's Head in Windsor Street. If you wanted to get in you had to be early. It was always sold out. Fire regulations in those days were rather lapse. One decent conflagration there would have doubtless seen many deaths. There would have been no way of getting out quickly. Such a large gathering in such an inaccessible environment would today be quite illegal.

One week it would be us and the next week it would be Brian Poole & the Tremeloes. Both bands drew the crowds and the competition to be top dogs was fierce, but as far as we were concerned it was our turf.

We did make the occasional foray into territories further afield. Grantham in Lincolnshire was long distance. Scotland was an adventure of almost unimaginable proportions. In July of 1961 Dave and Bill Fehilly, two enthusiastic if unsophisticated promoters of ballroom concerts way up in the Scottish highlands, had booked us for a run of out-of-the-way country dates. They were rock & roll fans and loved our debut disc.

We were vain enough to be flattered by the attention and naïve enough to undertake a journey which in those pre-motorway times was a two day epic. We set off in a state of expectation that we would no doubt witness hordes of wild haggis-chasing burly ginger-bearded men in richly patterned skirts across the heather covered moors. Berwick on Tweed was our first overnight bed and breakfast stop after a gruelling marathon that took from dawn to dusk. And heading onwards the next day we continued north leaving Edinburgh behind for the wimps heading on past Inverness for distant parts that most Scots would never see or ever desire to.

The audiences were grateful. After all we were a recording group, albeit an unsuccessful one as yet, and very little in the way of English entertainment ventured their way. Elgin Drill Hall was an excellent place and the beat-starved audience loved Bennett's immaculate voice and the rough, tough pounding sound of the Rebel Rousers. Onwards and upwards we travelled for another show in Wick high on the East Coast and deep into woolly-back territory.

As if the air wasn't already getting thin enough we were scheduled for a show even higher up in the Orkney Isles the next day. Alas our judgement in the way of timing was somewhat underdeveloped. The narrow tree lined dirt tracks that passed for roads took much longer for our slow and bulky hired Bedford minibus to negotiate than we had foreseen, and when we finally reached the point where the land stopped and the sea began we lined up along the quay to watch the ferry in the distance as it slowly and majestically sailed to a now entertainment denied land. There was indeed only one ferry on any given day.

The large proportion of the town gathered excitedly on the dockside to greet us finally accepted that the musical Sassenachs were not going to appear after all, and they trundled back to the dance hall to make the best they could of a bad job. On the mainland we checked into a guest house one day early and went for a fish supper.

Back at our digs an impromptu party was evolving. A jut-jawed Scot name Arnold, the owner of a chin that could well have been the prototype for the more celebrated though less spectacular Bruce Forsyth model, unleashed an accordion and proceeded to treat us all to a selection of Celtic melodies which continued long after we, who were burned out and knackered after a stressful day, had retired to bed. It really is quite astonishing just how far the sound of a piano accordion can penetrate at two o'clock in the morning. The only thing needed to complete this surreal Scottish scene was the sight and sound of a man in a skirt trying to strangle an octopus. Mercifully we were spared.

When the dance at Thurso Town Hall the next evening ended we set off on the long journey south. I, being a non driver, tried to get what sleep I could in the cramped and uncomfortable confines of our transport which was straining to accommodate the six of us. I drifted in and out of consciousness as mile piled upon mile dreaming of sci-fi days in the future when perhaps splendid multi-laned thoroughfares would stretch uninterrupted from one end of the country to the other. Somewhere around about Carlisle I lost the will to live.

Despite our lack of success on record we carried on with our futile assault at the charts. The follow up in October, very much in the style of the first and naturally written once more by Joe Meek, was called *That's What I Said* and supposedly inspired by the Ray Charles classic *What'd I Say*. I'm glad no one was so insensitive as to ask Ray what he thought of it. I can't imagine the answer would have pleased us.

It fared no better than the first but Meek seemed not to be deterred. If someone had possessed the foresight to turn the disc over and favour the B-side, yet another Meek song called *When I Get Paid* – no problem. It would still have been a flop. Lots of energy. Wonderful playing. But gimmicky and too formulaic for Bennett's voice which needed, and deserved, the room to accommodate phrasing and personality. Joe's songs were not only too structured and naïve in their assembly but left no room whatsoever for improvisation. He would even direct Cliff when to growl and grunt.

No matter. At least we could genuinely boast that we were a recording group and we continued on our merry circuit of the clubs in and around London. We were earning decent money. I was still without transport or indeed a licence by which I would be allowed to endanger the roads, but Cliff had taken to the internal combustion engine like a man possessed. His first purchase, a shiny brand new Hillman Husky estate car in red and cream. This was soon replaced by a rather more serious piece of road equipment. An MGA sports car, initially in black but refinished by him for whatever insane reason in pea green. Why anyone would want to replicate the colour of the contents of a baby's nappy I'll never know, but Cliff seemed happy enough with it.

Caught by the car bug in a big way he then exchanged the MG for a straight-off-the-assembly-line Sunbeam Rapier in a rather beautiful metallic gun metal grey finish with red faux leather upholstery. It was stunning but such beauty came at a price. Sadly, the price was too much for him to pay and when the financiers came to repossess the car he could only look from his bedroom window in sorrow as he flung the keys down and watched them drive it off. The Morris min-van which replaced it never quite cut the mustard I'm afraid but needs must when the devil, or Cliff Bennett, drives.

As hitless groups went we possessed a reasonably high profile. On top of our regular releases on vinyl we were frequently heard on the radio. The Melody Maker of January 20th 1962 announced our forthcoming appearance on Saturday Club. We were regulars on what was one of the most important pop radio programmes and this time we were sharing the bill with such diverse musical talents as Karl Denver, Dick Charlesworth, Jackie Lynn, The King Brothers, Janice Peters and Don Rennie, a line-up which was on the whole pretty forgettable.

Every week we would scour the music papers hoping for a mention or maybe a review of our latest single. Had we looked more carefully we might have taken note of a record reviewed in the January 27th 1962 edition. The title was *My Bonnie* and featured The Saints on the B-Side, an adaptation of the old chestnut *When The Saints Go Marching In*. The reviewer wrote that the singer had an expressive voice and a dynamic delivery with admirable support from the backing group. He added that it should have wide appeal and confirmed the talents of the band of whom we would, he said, be hearing a lot more. Prophetic words. The singer was Tony Sheridan and the group, who had been credited on the German version as the Beat Brothers and as yet were completely unknown and still months away from securing a record deal in their own right, was the Beatles.

As we approached the spring of '62 our third offering on vinyl was a particularly awful and puerile Meek-penned piece of trite egomaniacally entitled *Poor Joe*. Poor Joe indeed. Poor us was more like it. We had to perform this pointless piece of pop poop. It would have been more suited to John Leyton, the handsome but weak voiced Meek protégé for whom Joe wrought miracles with huge hits like *Johnny Remember Me*, *Wild Wind* and *Son This Is She*.

On second thoughts I think I praise the tune too much. Had he foisted this on Leyton he might have been forced to abandon his pop career for acting a tad earlier than he eventually did. And I might add he did it to some degree of success. Meek had even managed to provide the blond bouffant haired and vocally challenged Heinz, his personal private obsession, with a hit record, *Just Like Eddie* proving that he knew more than a bit about sows' ears and silk purses. But when presented with a silk purse in the shape of Cliff Bennett's talent he had no difficulty whatsoever transforming it into a sow's ear.

For the flip side we used *Hurtin' Inside*, a Brook Benton number that we had been playing on stage. Brook Benton was an idol of Cliff's and indeed for one night only in 1961, at the St Mary's Ballroom in Putney, he was announced as Cliff Benton as a tribute to the American baritone renowned for his richly toned and beautifully executed low notes. But it just didn't sit right and by the next show he was plain old Cliff Bennett again, the name he had been given at birth.

Over in the States Chubby Checker had introduced the latest dance craze, The Twist, and in a somewhat pathetic attempt to attach ourselves to this new sensation we suffixed the title of our latest platter with the word *Twist* in parentheses. The Twist was a life-changing dance. Unbelievably when it first hit the ballrooms of Britain it was banned by some managers as simulating copulation which was an odd concept that this craze kept dancers apart while everything that had previously gone before allowed you to press your bodies against each other.

We had made no changes whatsoever to the tempo which was nothing like those of Chubby's hits and were fooling no one. Simply adding the word 'twist' did not turn it into one and I'm damn sure nobody was fooled. It was a much better piece of product than the A-side but still destined for the remainder bins from the get go. Once more our disc bombed. We were on a losing streak but at least we were consistent. Taking Brook Benton's name was not a success and neither was stealing Benton's song.

We remained carefree and hitless on top of which big changes loomed for the Rebel Rousers. For a while we had risen to being a seven-piece outfit having acquired a second tenor sax player in the form of Maurice 'Moss' Groves. A chubby affable Brummie, who had been playing in a Midland outfit with the distinctly un-modern name of the Modernaires until he encountered the Rousers and saw the light. So thrilled was he at joining us that on his wedding night, instead of going on honeymoon he and his new bride Anita travelled down to London so that he could play with us at the famous Wimbledon Palais.

To a lad from Birmingham a gig at the Palais was unimaginable glory, a veritable shrine in the world of popular music and he was not about to miss out on such a momentous occasion for something as petty as marriage. In fact the Wimbledon Palais was simply a dance hall. Nothing more and nothing less. Its reputation was unwarranted. The Joe Loss Orchestra played on one stage and the latest pop act on the one at the opposite end. And, surprise, surprise, people danced in between. Anita must have been a very forgiving, and very disappointed, lady.

Now girl friends and wives had arrived on the scene and loyalties for the first time were divided. We had three defectors in our ranks and we had to reassess and reassemble the band. It was thankfully a friendly exercise. There was no animosity. We simply got on with the recruitment process.

Moss was staying with us but his fellow sax player, Sid Phillips, was quitting to marry his girlfriend Mavis and to resume his 'proper job' of typewriter mechanic. Bass player Ben Jordan and guitarist Mick Borer, who had long since replaced our original guitarist Mick Currell, had also decided to quit for love and a perceived stability that was never a part of the pop world.

Ben was a really nice guy who like the rest of us loved rock & roll. He looked cool, played his expensive Fender instrument with his thumb and once he grasped his part he was rock solid in the bass department. There was nothing over technical about bass playing in those days so Ben's replacement we figured would not be too much of a problem, but it would be harder to find substitutes for Sid Phillips and Mick Borer.

We had been used to coping with changes in personnel. Drummer Ricky Winter, who had himself replaced the original cow spanker Alfie James, had in turn been replaced some time ago by Mick Burt. Ricky had met Becky, a girl whose family owned a thriving flower business in nearby Kingsbury. In one fell swoop he was offered a wife, a highly remunerative and secure position and a brand new Vauxhall Cresta car. How could he turn it down? He was not a complete idiot. I believe he may also have been fond of Becky too.

This was a very incestuous business. Mick Burt curiously had once been in a line-up of one of my old semi pro bands (are you keeping up with this?). He would play with us while on weekend leave from his National Service duties with the RAF Mick was happy to continue making a din on the Rousers' drum rostrum so there was no problem there. But we were three short and when scouting around for replacements we didn't have to look very far.

Screaming Lord Sutch had been a serious force and a character on the live circuit for a number of years. His brand of shock rock, loosely based on a persona pioneered by the American bluesman Screaming Jay Hawkins and years later on extended and improved beyond recognition by Alice Cooper, packed the crowds into ballrooms across the UK. Young girls screamed and ran for cover as the white-faced ghoul emerged from a coffin, clothed in a black cape and dripping with fake blood, raised his top hat letting his outrageously long hair (for those days) fall into their faces. It sounds tame now but way back then it was the cutting edge of mock horror. Sutch was the ballroom circuit equivalent of Hammer Films.

As inept as he was in the vocal arts, being the owner of a voice that could curdle milk within the space of a few horrendous bars, he had an uncanny knack of recruiting skilled musicians whose careers were in their infancy but who were to achieve enviable reputations in the rock & roll industry.

Guitar hero Ritchie Blackmore served his time with both Dave Sutch and Mike Berry's group the Outlaws before conquering the US, and therefore the world, with Rainbow. Drummer Mitch Mitchell received his call up to the Savage ranks before entering the mainstream as one third of the Jimi Hendrix Experience. A young Paul Nicholas was for a time the pianist with Sutch and while not being any great shakes in the musical department he did eventually go on to have a number of high scoring chart records (*Dancing With The Captain* and *Grandma's Party* etc) not to mention a hugely successful acting career on television in such series as *The Lovebirds* and *Just Good Friends*.

In desperate need of new players we took the drastic decision to more or less steal the whole of Screaming Lord Sutch's band apart from the drummer. Carlo Little, who actually taught Keith Moon how to play, was excellent but we already had a drummer. The rest of his line-up at that time was Ricky Brown (a.k.a Ricky Fenson) on bass, Bernie Watson on guitar and Nicky Hopkins on piano. Brown was a pretty straight forward no nonsense street-wise kid. The other two were great musicians but completely off the wall. In fact I think they had battered the wall down. Or maybe in the face of Nicky and Bernie the wall simply gave up and crumbled of its own accord.

Bernie was a curious elf of a person with a mop of dyed blond hair and a loathing of the audience that resulted in him sitting down to play with his back to the crowd. Nicky's piano artistry was nothing short of mind blowing but his long lean anorexic frame and sunken haunting eyes that were devoid of all expression gave him the look of a particularly ailing and undernourished zombie.

We put in our request for their transfer. Ricky Brown dismissed it out of hand. Nicky said yes straight away but Bernie's answer eventually was no. In general those two absolute weirdos came as a pair but fortunately Nicky stuck to his decision. After all the Rebel Rousers were the number one band among musicians. There were band members all over the land who would have sold their mates down the river in an instant to join Cliff's outfit.

To get round the problem of a bass player, or rather the lack of one, we decided that a rhythm guitar could be dispensed with. This was not news to me. I had known from the start that I had conned my way into this superfluous position and was all too aware of how tenuous my position in the group had been. I reckoned I could switch to bass without any trouble. After all I had been showing Ben some of his parts anyway. It was settled. One day I strummed a six string Fender Stratocaster. The next day I plonked the four thicker strings of a cherry red Gibson EB0 bass guitar, bought from Besson's music shop in London's Shaftesbury Avenue via an Irish salesman called Jack for a hundred and eight pounds. An added bonus was that the reduction in manpower would give us more cash to distribute between us. Lovely.

As a substitute for Watson we asked Dave Wendells, an extremely competent and keen guitarist, who coincidentally had been at Spring Grove Grammar School at the same time as me albeit two years older, to join us. Dave, an incredibly nice guy, was thrilled to pieces and rehearsals began. No sooner had rehearsals started than the news came that Bernie Watson changed his mind.

For Cliff the music was everything and mere sentiment took second place. Wendells was a terrific guy and deserved greater consideration. But personal considerations were far outweighed by more important musical ones. Dave, who had quit his job in another band and therefore burned his bridges, was out before he was even in, left high and dry to sort out whatever future he may or may not now have. The rock & roll world can sometimes be a harsh one. How Cliff managed to break the news I will never know. I could not have done it.

But we finally had our new Rebel Rousers, a new set of cheap striped shirts and we were enjoying the fresh burst of enthusiasm – for a while. We even had a tour to look forward to. *Hey Baby* by Bruce Chanel had stormed up the charts helped by its catchy mouth organ riffs which in a stroke firmly banished any misconceptions one ever had about that most un-cool of instruments, previously only remembered for Larry Adler's rendition of the saccharine-sweet theme from the film *Genevieve.*

Chanel was being brought to the UK by wrestling promoter Paul Lincoln, the proprietor of the famous rock & roll coffee bar the Two Is, who was an associate of our manager. The rest of the bill consisted of Dick Charlesworth's City Gents (trad jazz was going through a revival phase), Beryl Bryden, a big buxom woman whose name meant nothing to anyone except skiffle anoraks who were aware that she was the washboard player on Lonnie Donegan's *Rock Island Line*, Johnny Kidd and the Pirates and Frank Ifield, an affable Australian import whose attempts at the charts in Britain had so far come to nothing.

Bruce Chanel was to be backed by an outfit called Bobby Brown and the Barons. He had brought his own harmonica player with him, a guy called Delbert McClinton whose own less than meteoric career achieved the kind of speed that would make a particularly pensionable tortoise look like a speed freak. His time was eventually to come after many decades had passed with the resurgence of the country music scene in the eighties when he became a serious force in the genre. But for the time being he was just Bruce Chanel's side man We were to have our own spot and were also required to provide the backing for Frank Ifield.

It was fun. For the first time we enjoyed the luxury of performing in theatres which, in our world, only the big boys did. But the timing was all wrong. We might have turned up every night but the audiences did not. At least not in enough numbers to make the enterprise a commercial success. Bruce was a very pleasant chap, reassuringly modest and easy to get along with, but unfortunately he was not the stuff that dreams or screams were made of. His stocky frame and sober-suited appearance made him look like the kind of benevolent bank manager who would give you an overdraft without question but who was hardly likely to unleash erotic thoughts in the minds of teenage girls.

To be fair Bruce did get his share of fan frenzy. After all he was famous, he was American and he had been in the charts although the record had dropped out by the time he arrived on our shores. You've got to be a real dog to be in the entertainment industry and not be able to attract at least a fair proportion of totty. But he was no teenage idol. In fact Delbert fitted the part better. With his sharp, youthful looks and groovy flat top haircut he was the typical all-American boy.

The City Gents were a more than competent group, predictably kitted out in pin striped suits and bowler hats but in the eyes of pop devotees they were way down the pecking order below such current favourites as Kenny Ball and Acker Bilk who were selling discs by the truckload and packing out halls across the land.

Beryl, lovely and cuddly as we found her and a joy to be with, was an irrelevance. The sight of a middle aged woman draped in an unprepossessing frock and with a laundry implement clamped between her knees brought a reaction that was somewhere between sheer disbelief and abject horror.

Johnny Kidd and the Pirates were a strong act around the ballrooms but not strong enough to add any great weight to what was still a weak bill in commercial terms.

Frank Ifield was excellent, blond, tall and handsome with a terrific voice. Unfortunately again the timing was all wrong. He was introducing a new song that he had just recorded but which had not yet been released. It was called *I Remember You* and featured the same hypnotic harmonica style that was clearly influenced by our current top of the bill.

His act, and this song in particular, went down extremely well every night despite the fact that from the beginning to the end of our three-week trek I never once managed to play the correct bass part to the unusual chord sequence in the run-out to the end. To his credit Frank never once commented or complained. Maybe he just never noticed. A couple of months after the tour finished *I Remember You* was at Number One and Frank was at the beginning of a lengthy run of chart successes that made him one of the biggest stars in the land. Sadly, too late to be of any help to our sparsely attended tour.

Our postage stamp of a spot allowed us time for four songs by Cliff plus a couple of instrumentals, *Nut Rocker* (a number one for B. Bumble and the Stingers) which featured Nicky's brilliant piano playing and *Czardas* (previously a Meek produced single for Nero and the Gladiators), a showcase for the nimble fingered Bernie, before his appearance. We even introduced a bit of comedy into our routine with Bernie Watson and myself 'accidentally' bumping into each other during one of the slow sequences in *Czardas*. Gosh, what hilarity we thought at rehearsals. How they would laugh. And how they didn't. The guitar playing in this reworking of Monti's classical piece was fast, spectacular and a guaranteed show stopper despite our appalling attempts at visual humour which, by all rights, should have emptied the theatre nightly. Those that weren't empty already, that is. I can only belatedly thank those audiences for their kindness and tolerance.

But whatever horrors we inflicted on the paying customers it was all forgiven when Cliff sang. Always somewhat inhibited in movements and stage presence, his vocal skills were unparalleled and were in fact getting better by the day. He had crossed from being a Jerry Lee Lewis clone into a fine interpreter of American rhythm and blues.

It was an exciting experience for us but when it all ended we discovered that our fees had suddenly been adjusted to reflect the size of the crowds. Or rather the lack of them. We were paid half of our contracted amount. The rest was never seen. Maybe we could have argued the toss but we were dealing with tough men, the hard-nosed wrestling fraternity of London who handled death, danger and intimidation on a daily basis. We did not frighten them. They certainly frightened us. We cut our losses and put it down to experience.

But hey, that's the price of an education. We were young. We'd get over it. And anyway greater glories were on the horizon.

5

Germany Calling

We were well into 1962. Things were getting better and they were getting worse. Work was flooding in and if it seemed unlikely that we were about to become millionaires in the very near future the date sheet was looking healthy and our fortunes were progressing nicely in a modest kind of way, but meanwhile the changes in personnel had brought about their own problems.

To say that Hopkins and Watson were an odd couple is a bit like saying Michael Jackson is not quite your average guy. Bernie's tendency to sit facing away from our audience and his most disconcerting habit of turning occasionally to scowl and swear at them was at odds with our general philosophy of keeping the paying customers on our side. We were not yet in the days when the Rolling Stones turned contempt into an art form and decades away from punk's passion for outright abuse which often culminated in the artistes endearing habit of expectorating over the front row, the playful little scamps.

Nicky Hopkins had his own peculiarities. Apart from looking like an extra from the Chamber of Horrors he adopted an on stage attitude of intransigence and rebellion. We were the Rebel Rousers but we hardly expected the rebellion to be waged against ourselves. To be hoisted by our own petard was not our aim but hoisted we were. Whilst loving much of the content of our set, if an item was not to Nicky's liking he would simply refuse to start it after I had made the introduction.

I recall the main object of his hate was the instrumental *Last Date*, a country tune originally recorded by Floyd Cramer. Nicky played it superbly. Or at least he did when he deigned to play it at all. He considered it to be sentimental twaddle and would sit there scowling at the keyboard, his hands clamped to his knees

Maybe I should have been a bit more accommodating. I liked the tune and wanted it in the set but on reflection it maybe wasn't the kind of material we should have been weaving our musical future with. And it was never likely to tax Nicky's exceptional skill on the keyboards. It must have been like asking Jimi Hendrix to play *Apache*. I was indulging my own personal tastes and not seeing the bigger picture. To be fair, if I had to put up with Nicky it was also true that Nicky had to put up with me.

Outside their musical idiosyncrasies Messrs Hopkins and Watson had a very unhealthy obsession with people who suffered disabilities. In particular those who would have been referred to in those naïve and politically incorrect days as spastic. The mere glimpse of anyone with a deformity would send them into fits of girlish giggles. They would follow this up by adding entries into what they called their 'Goodies Book'. It was a standard lined school exercise book in which they inserted hand drawn illustrations of their sightings. Occasionally they would clip suitable, or perhaps it should be unsuitable, pictures from magazines and paste them in. Very odd. The irony is that neither of these two very strange people would have looked out of place as entries in their own volumes.

But it was a great band and we had an acceptable if fragmented and tenuous working relationship with these two guys who, in every other respect than music were as like us as little green men from Mars.

One night at the Majestic Ballroom in Reading in the Spring of '62 we were approached by Roy Young whom we all recognised as the Little Richard styled rock & roll pianist from *Drumbeat*, the same show that had featured Adam Faith as a regular. Roy was the 'nearly man' who had to all intents and purposes, or at least to our knowledge, disappeared from the face of the earth when his undoubted but largely unappreciated talents failed to translate into chart success and the series ended.

It turned out that he had acquired a whole new career in Germany as a resident headline attraction at a newly opened venue in the heart of Hamburg's red light district. The Star Club, the brainchild of an ex-pugilist called Horst Fascher and financed by his gangster boss Manfred Weissleder, an entrepreneur whose wealth came from a string of sex clubs on and around the Reeperbahn, had been recently opened to great acclaim.

The converted cinema opened for business in the summer of 1962 at number 39 on the Grosse Freiheit. Its conversion consisted of little more than installing a number of bars, switching the seating into an arrangement of banquettes around tables for drinks and placing beat groups on the existing stage where the screen had once been. But it was a step up from the previous rock aficionados' favourite haunt, a smaller and more basic establishment set up by Peter Eckhorn on the Reeperbahn itself called the Top Ten.

Weissleder and Fascher's policy was altogether more ambitious than anything that had gone before. Instead of a succession of competent but inexpensive and unknown bands recruited mainly from the UK in the manner of Peter Eckhorn's Top Ten they were going to augment the attractions with a list of major stars from the States and the Continent. Serious stuff.

But they were still going to need a seven days a week, fifty two weeks a year supply of good if less than stellar bands to fill the long opening hours of their brainchild venue and ensure its success. Roy had been deputed to sign up the best talent available and it was hardly a surprise to find out that Cliff Bennett was high on his shopping list.

The very thought of grabbing the chance of working in a foreign land was enough for us to agree whatever the terms. The fact that they were paying fees way in excess of anything we were currently achieving on our home territory was a clincher. The equivalent in Deutschmarks of fifty pounds each per week was a king's ransom. We'd have slept with the boss for that kind of money. For much less actually.

When the dates were set we began to grapple with the logistics of this little adventure. There were forms to be filled in for work permits in those pre-European Community days, for which we needed to appear at the German embassy in London. They had to be stamped in passports which we did not yet possess. Indeed none of us, except I believe Moss, had been out of Great Britain or had ever flown before. We decided from the get go that we would fly. After all we all lived right next to Heathrow. The cost of travel was coming out of our own pockets but damn the expense.

It then occurred to us that a great chunk of our money would be swallowed up in transporting our amplifiers and drums. We traipsed down to the airport and used their freight scales to assess the weight and cost. At that point we realised that our seemingly high wages would be very much needed to offset the considerable charges. Maybe the pot of gold at the end of the rainbow was going to have a hollow ring to it after all. If the gold was missing when we finally finished totting up the bill for this little lot then we were certainly going to need the empty pot to piss in.

But we thankfully found that the fates were with us when another group sharing a bill with us one evening passed on the information that there was no need to take anything other than our personal instruments. The club not only had its own PA system, backline and kit but it was also of a quality that made our rag bag assortment of home made cabinets and unreliable domestic amps look like chucking out day at Radio Rentals. A Ludwig drum kit, a concert grand piano, three bright new state of the art Fender amps and, if you had someone to play it, a Hammond organ.

With such an exciting and momentous event on the horizon we tried to stifle our impatience and bided our time by fulfilling our obligations to the regular venues where the faithful followed and happily shelled out their half a crowns for two hours of British beat music.

Friday was the Fender Club in Harrow Weald, actually the Memorial Hall glammed up with the name of the top flight make of American guitar that so many of us used. Saturday night saw us at Burtons in Uxbridge where the Queens Head below in Windsor Street made a killing from the interval crowd. Dance halls were in the main unlicensed in those days. Soft drinks only. And a Coke still meant a sweet fizzy pop. It wouldn't get you drunk and it certainly wouldn't get you high.

Sunday was usually the Blue Moon Club which occupied the small function room attached to the Hayes Football Club in Church Road. This time it was the Royal Oak which counted its financial blessings during the break from the music.

When we weren't at any of those we might play the British Legion in Kenton or the Ritz, Kingsbury or perhaps the sweaty stifling confines of the Railway Hotel in Wealdstone. Southall Community Centre, the Clay Pigeon at Eastcote and the Boat House at Kew were also vying for our services. We loved all of those places but now Germany beckoned. This was another level entirely. The days couldn't pass quickly enough.

It was mid June when we finally set off from Heathrow and I found my first flight terrifying. For anyone to assume that you could lift a great hunk of metal crammed full of people using no other method than a bit of air being swirled around and around by twisted sticks was arrogance of the highest order. It was, as far as I was concerned, flying in the face of God, although by that time I had actually stopped believing in Him, Her or It. I truly wished I was somewhere else. My only belief was atheism which of course is a non-prophet organisation but if it turned out that God really did exist after all he would surely take his revenge on those who were sending things to fly in his face, and when he did I did not want to be seen as an associate of the perpetrator of this grave offence.

But in the end I was delivered safely and deposited in a country that we had apparently conquered but which, on first sighting, seemed to be doing a lot better than we were. The people were clean, plump and ruddy faced and their clothes, stylish and new in appearance, gave them a look of affluence. I wondered if it would have been more prudent to have lost the war.

Horst Fascher met us at Hamburg airport and transported us to our hotel a short walk from the Club. The Hotel Germania in Detlev-Bremer Strasse was a large dwelling that had at one time been a family house but which now traded as a bed and breakfast establishment. Again here there was no sign of the relative poverty I had just left. We were all six of us installed into one room. But it was a very large room, we were uncramped and the bed linen was clean and far superior to anything I had known at home. We slept under duvets, at that time unknown in Britain. Warm and comforting marshmallow bed coverings that enveloped and cradled you with the softness of a mother's love.

The Star Club was a ten minute walk away, situated in a narrow unimposing street at one end of the notorious Reeperbahn. The Reeperbahn itself was a wide thoroughfare which ribbonned from the seedy dockland district of St Pauli towards the centre of Hamburg. There the stores stocked with goods for the affluent in the light of a new rising post war prosperity and towering offices of burgeoning multi-national corporations seemed a world away from the sexually charged and decadent streets of St Pauli and Altona.

St Pauli, despite its international reputation as a dark and dangerous place existing on and supported by vice was in fact a dichotomy. On one side of the carriageway round the clock porn would be screened in tiny shop sized makeshift cinemas while on the opposite sidewalk stood the impressive St Pauli Theatre presented productions whose content could never be impugned on grounds of dubious respectability. On Saturday nights the elegant Café Keese, just a few doors along from the Top Ten Club, played host to bejewelled ladies enjoying a weinbrandt and coffee before setting out to sample the excitement of a naughtier and more dangerous environment than they were used to. Slumming it in St Pauli was chic. In perhaps a slightly patronising way the meritocracy of Hamburg found such proletarian attractions very amusing indeed

Grosse Freiheit can be translated to mean Great Freedom but in fact the great freedom originally referred to was not, as you might imagine, the liberty to indulge in a limitless variation of licentious sexual activity, but rather to the religious and commercial independence enjoyed by Altona in the days when it had once existed as a virtually separate state from Hamburg proper. But in the early sixties the appellation seemed both fortuitous and appropriate. This narrow roadway, with barely enough room for one car to pass another, was inhabited by cabarets and clubs offering sex, sex and more sex. And if you got bored with that well, just along the road there was perhaps someone offering a different kind of sex.

Establishments such as the Tabu and the Regina presented live shows of stripping and copulation that would never have been allowed in other more prudish countries and you paid for such exclusivity in the high price of your alcoholic intake. And if you objected to the high price and attempted to avoid the reckoning you might well pay with your life although apart from a few unfortunate incidents the most you could expect was a good beating. And the waiters and bouncers certainly knew how to beat very well indeed.

Oddly enough the night life of the Grosse Freiheit came to an abrupt halt after only a few hundred yards from which point it reverted into the more ordinary guise of a simple street with not much happening apart from a traditional western style bar called the Blockhutte on the right and, at the furthest end on the left, the Indra, once a somewhat tawdry rock & roll club which secured its place in history by having both presented and housed the early Beatles but which was now a club waiting to die.

Immediately adjacent to the new Star Club nestled the Monica Bar, a transvestite establishment whose appeal lay in the presence of exotic figures in glamourous gowns, killer hair dos and with makeup of a thickness necessary to cover up the ever present manly stubble. Any one of them could have been the prototype of Ray Davies' legendary *Lola.*

On my first visit to Hamburg the American helicopter carrier the USS Thetis Bay was in port and if the dark brown voice succeeded in fooling any stray sailor who had wandered in with the intention of taking mister sausage to tuna-town then the game was most definitely up when at the end of his journey he discovered that what was waiting was yet another sausage and quite possibly one bigger than his own.

Call me cynical if you like but I have a feeling that not many of them were actually fooled in the least. I suspect that the frocks merely provided an excuse, albeit a flimsy one, when all along they knew all too well what forbidden and unique experiences lay ahead.

We were impressed with the club itself and after our first performance we found that the club was impressed with us. Horst Fascher loved the band. How could he not? We were given a prime mid-evening slot for our debut. And because we were flavour of the month we were required to perform only three hour-long sets for the most part as opposed to the four or more that other less celebrated outfits had to labour through.

On the celebrity front the venue was treated to a visit by Johnny Kidd and the Pirates who went through their swashbuckling dramatic stage act with great panache. They were a top ballroom back in the UK and the Germans too loved the camp but effective routine of matelot-clad gents in thigh high leather boots and striped tee shirts kerranging their way through a power packed set while their leader, complete with black eye patch covering a perfectly good working optical organ, plunged a sabre into the stage. It was a terrific piece of theatre when the sword stuck which on many occasions it did not.

The Pirates at that time comprised Frank Farley on drums, Johnny Spence on bass and a brilliant guitarist destined for near legendary status, Mick Green, on guitar. In absolute terms they were not in fact the original bunch that played on hit records like *Shakin' All Over*, and the classic Kidd recording *Please Don't Touch*. But this was the combination that most people would remember as the classic Pirates line-up.

In fact those very early original long gone Pirates, whom I remembered so well from their appearances at Staines Town Hall and the Southall Community Centre, had featured legendary session man Clem Cattini on drums, Brian Gregg on bass and Alan Caddy on guitar. And the iconic guitar solo was in fact played neither by Mick Green nor Alan Caddy. It was actually the work of Scottish session player Joe Moretti. Such details do tend to get lost or distorted in the mists of time. But in the end who cares? It would forever be Green, Spence and Farley who would forever be remembered as The Pirates.

Another rocker booked for a short season that turned out to be shorter than anyone expected was Vince Taylor. Taylor was a dark haired handsome guy from Hounslow who affected an accent from Los Angeles and styled himself in the leather suited fashion that had been pioneered by Gene Vincent on Jack Good's television show *Oh Boy*. He liked people to believe that he was an American and in fact it does appear that he had spent a short time in the States as a teenager but certainly not long enough to appropriate an American identity with any real justification.

He had cultivated a wild and brooding Presleyesque image to some degree of success but his somewhat bland and tuneless voice never quite matched up to his appearance. Despite that however he had managed to produce what arguably only two others - Johnny Kidd (*Shakin' All Over*) and Cliff Richard (*Move It*) - had done. *Brand New Cadillac* qualified as that rarest of beasts, a genuinely original and authentic sounding British rock & roll record.

Any vocal inadequacies were fortunately compensated by a dynamic stage show that was non stop action from start to finish. If he wasn't racing back and forth across the podium like a whirling Dervish he was as likely to be found writhing around on his back atop the grand piano. And if his career in Britain had stalled almost as soon as it began the French took to his leather and chains persona like frogs legs to a dinner plate. Along with home grown star Johnny Halliday, the most famous Gallic rocker of them all, he became one of the biggest sensations on the stages of La Belle France.

His opening show was received ecstatically by the Star Club regulars. His final show was received with exactly the same amount of enthusiasm. After all they were one and the same. Vince was, to put it succinctly, one stop short of East Ham which, if you check your London Underground map is Barking.

He was currently in the throes of a romantic involvement with a girl in Paris and it was obviously affecting him to the point where pragmatism and responsibility were definitely 'out la fenetre'. The very next morning he had departed Germany and was on his way back to his troublesome mademoiselle waiting on the Rive Gauche. If Taylor had only jumped in the river we could have stated without fear of contradiction that he really was in Seine.

As a teetotal rule-keeping novice I always felt that my lack of sophistication and awkwardness in the company in the company of these brash and adventurous young musicians was written all over me but much later in life I learned the valuable truth that you should not compare yourself to others. They are usually more screwed up than you are.

Unfortunately he had neglected to tell his musicians or to make any arrangements for their repatriation. Nor had he paid them which caused a minor crisis for drummer Bobby Woodman who was stranded in St Pauli without a sous, or indeed a pfennig. Or any other kind of currency whatsoever. Which is where I came in.

His only way out was to sell what possessions he could in order to pay for his train fare back. I was offered a rather expensive silver grey silk suit at the bargain price of one hundred Marks. I capitulated and passed over the necessary cash for this exotic garment. It was elegant and it had a certain vulgar style. It had been made to measure for Mr Woodman. Alas it had not been made for me. There were acres of shiny silk still flapping around me when I put it on but somehow I never noticed. At eighteen years old I was still very naïve to say the least. My senses of proportion and observation were not yet fully developed. I was experiencing déjà vu. The name Brian St George comes to mind. What was it about me and silver grey suits? Would I ever learn?

Among the other bands appearing at the club, the common-or-garden groups with no special pedigree or fame attached to them, were a group from Nottingham called the Jaybirds. They featured an impressively fast figured lead guitarist called Alvin Dean who, on a Chuck Berry number, could out-Chuck Chuck. The band would eventually arrive at world-wide fame as Ten Years After when the renamed Alvin Lee would take on the mantle of heavy metal guitar hero.

It was their bass player Leo Lyons with whom I got on well. A friendly, unassuming guy, he was deadly serious about his instrument and spent all his spare hours practising. I remember calling for him at the flats opposite the club where Weissleder billeted the bulk of his artistes to find Leo fast asleep across his bunk, his Fender Precision Bass still strapped to him in the playing position. This kind of dedication was to pay off handsomely when Ten Years After blew away the crowd at Woodstock and went off to international fame.

There were attractions from the South. Groups like the Checkmates, Emile Ford's old backing band. London estuary based Bern Elliot and the Fenmen and the Flintstones from our patch, Middlesex.

Sharing the spotlight with Roy Young, Colin Milander, Ricky Barnes and John Watson in the Star Club Combo who were the resident house band was Tony Sheridan, the rocker whose career in England never really travelled beyond the confines of the 2Is coffee bar. Sheridan was wild and unpredictable. His dextrous guitar technique was an odd but fascinating and impressive amalgam of rock, blues and jazz and he took his music very seriously indeed. On a good day he was a handsome charismatic rock god with a tremulous and unique voice that could rip the soul out of a tune better than anyone. On a bad day he was slightly more off the wall than Humpty Dumpty.

When Cliff Richard's first manager John Foster was forming a backing group for his young star's debut tour Sheridan was top of the list on his target guitarists. On the night Foster went to the 2Is he wasn't there but Hank Marvin, along with his chum Bruce Welch, was. Marvin got the gig and Sheridan was consigned to a future of relative obscurity if you discount the tenuous reflected glory afforded by his association with the Beatles. Had things been different the troublesome Sheridan might have become a Shadow and the ever-youthful Peter Pan of pop might have prematurely aged overnight having been saddled with this eccentric and troublesome, if talented, musician.

I couldn't help but notice that a disproportionate amount of groups with odd names like The Strangers, The Big Three and The Undertakers and Mark Peters and the Silhouettes hailed from a part of England that up till now had merely been a spot on the map somewhere north of Watford. How far north I had no idea then. After all, I was from London, the centre of the universe. Why would I know or even care about a dreary seaport two hundred miles away on the western coast called Liverpool?

6

The Banks Of The Mersey

In the bleak post-war years of the mid fifties Liverpool was still pitted and pock-marked with the damage that had been wrought by the Luftwaffe in its vain attempt to cripple Britain's financial viability by annihilating its merchant shipping industry. As it transpired all the might of Hitler's air power could neither destroy the city's commercial infrastructure nor the indomitable spirit of its inhabitants. Liverpool's population may have been but a fraction of London's but it would be a fool indeed who would confuse a great city with merely a populous one.

This bustling north-western seaport straddling the banks of the River Mersey is a tough place that breeds tough people, their hardy nature tempered by a corporate sense of humour which, depending on your point of view, is either a learned behavioural pattern or an inviolate genetic quirk of nature. Scousers, so named after the inexpensive but tasty stew made from leftovers that once formed a major part of the region's working class diet, are funny. And if they are not funny then they still think they are.

Life was not only hard in a country more or less bankrupted by the Second World War it was also extremely simple compared to the high-tech gadget-filled consumer society of today. Radio was still the most important piece of leisure equipment in the average household although television, with sets prohibitively expensive for most families to buy and the medium still in its infancy, was making its presence felt. Most fun was home made.

In and around the city centre small clubs, often with barely room to accommodate more than a couple of hundred people or so, sometimes a lot less, had sprung up providing not only a platform for live music aimed at the kids and not the parents for once but also a space for effecting introductions to members of the opposite sex. These were innocent times when courtship was a long and drawn out process with very little guarantee of any physical interaction at the end to show for your efforts. If you met it was usually through dancing. At least this way you touched. Dancing cheek to cheek was a primitive but often effective form of 'floor play'. But that was about as far as it went.

Virginity was still a very much prized and protected possession. At least for women who, under threat of becoming social outcasts, tried to keep it at all costs. Males on the other hand were desperately trying to lose it but had a great deal of trouble finding a willing partner to accept their precious offering. 'Do you fancy a shag?' would have been for the most part a pointless question in the fearsome fifties. Pregnancy was a condition rewarded by either shame or marriage, often a high degree of one followed quickly by the other. The price of passion was high. With an irate father to deal with and the distinct possibility of a shotgun wedding hanging over your head, a misadventure with a member of the opposite sex could well be a case of wife or death.

Jazz had for a number of years been the youth music of the day and the strains of trombones, clarinets, trumpets and banjos could be heard escaping from smoky rooms and dark, sweat-filled cellars in and around the city centre. Bearded beatniks skip jived in corduroy pants and floppy oversized sweaters, their women decked out in what could only be described as carefully contrived peasant dress. The general aim was to look as intellectual as you could and to pontificate seriously on any subject under the sun whether or not you possessed the necessary qualifications to do so. It was an earthy and downmarket look but they took much pride in their stance of 'anti-glamour'. Flamboyantly smoking a Gauloise helped enormously.

But the sounds of rock & roll were about to take over. By 1958 the writing was on the wall. If Bill Haley didn't get you then Elvis Presley would. Or maybe it was the frantic uninhibited rhythms knocked out by the black artistes like Little Richard, Chuck Berry or the Coasters. Eventually Great Britain was to produce its very own rock & roll stars like Cliff Richard, Marty Wilde and Liverpool's own home-grown sensation Billy Fury, a sultry-eyed ex-docker who had ditched his birth name of Ronald Wycherley for something a bit more enigmatic and moody.

And with the sounds of rock came the chance to change the face of fashion in a cool but cheap way. Blue jeans and white tee shirts for the lads. Tight sweaters and flaring skirts for the girls, many home made and kept in shape by layers of thick petticoats beneath. Yet another barrier to thwart the attentions of wandering hands. But what the hell, you weren't going to get anywhere anyway so just keep dancing was the general rule of thumb. Most young men had to settle for a piece of pre-slumber self-induced satisfaction played out to the accompaniment and encouragement of the evening's memories. Memories of what might have been in a perfect world but which rarely occurred in your own.

For lads with a bit of extra cash and a penchant for real rebellion a teddy boy suit in a fetching shade of powder blue with a black velvet collar could be made to measure at Burtons or John Collier. These menacing dandies, according to headline hungry newspapers, were threats to society and carried weapons of war in the shape of flick knives or knuckle-dusters, constantly on the lookout for someone to fight. It was considered prudent to give them a wide berth or maybe even cross to the other side of the street if you saw them coming.

To get a genuine pair of American jeans the place to go was Chetwyns situated up by the Mersey Tunnel and if a rare pair of imported Levis was beyond your budget then their own house brand was a good substitute.

Teenagers were fast becoming an important new socio-economic group. They had their own music, their own styles and their own money. More than any generation before them. But they also required their own environment where they could indulge their passions for pop music, which could only be infrequently heard over the radio. Places where a lad could meet a girl and vice versa.

The Liverpool club scene began to take off towards the latter end of the fifties with coffee bars and dingy function rooms being made over on special evenings for the enjoyment of, in the main, old style jazz. Ken Colyer, Terry Lightfoot and Chris Barber were the kings of the dance floors. The radical new sound coming from the States called Rock & Roll was taboo in these diehard strongholds of traditional music.

Because of the worldwide fame and celebrity that was eventually to be achieved by the city's favourite sons the Beatles, the beat venue that eventually attained the greatest degree of fame was without doubt the Cavern, a dank basement in Mathew Street right in the heart of Liverpool. It was originally a dingy set of cellars beneath a group of seven storey warehouses used to store wine. Ironically the club, which was opened in 1957 by a local doctor named Alan Sytner, served neither wine nor any other alcoholic beverage. It was soft drinks only for the youngsters who descended the eighteen stone steps to an interior that was most definitely luxury denied.

Now transformed into a place of entertainment it remained the same dingy set of cellars and little was done to alter its appearance other than the installation of a number of uncomfortable wooden benches facing a simple low stage framed by three arches. The stark simplicity of the place only added to its atmosphere, which Sytner had intended to replicate the bohemian gathering places he had encountered on trips to Paris. There was only one entrance and, more significantly, only one exit. If a fire had occurred there would have been a massacre. In the fifties health and safety was for wimps.

By '59 Sytner had got married and moved to London but managed to find an enthusiastic purchaser for the premises in Ray McFall, who had not only acted as his accountant but who had also gained experience by advising the nearby Temple Club in matters financial. Although still subscribing to Sytner's view that jazz was good, skiffle was just about acceptable and rock & roll was the spawn of the devil and therefore banned, McFall was a more pragmatic man and when he realised that the writing was not only on the wall but that the wall was about to collapse if he didn't give in, the ban was lifted. Things were never the same again. The introductory lunchtime rock sessions were popular beyond all expectations and soon after jazz musicians found their positions being usurped by spotty faced, guitar twanging rebels. Rock & roll was king.

The Cavern was by no means the only place where these new groups could test their skills in public. Just south east of Mathew Street, Alan Williams had opened the Jacaranda in Seel Street. Williams, later to become known worldwide as 'the man who sold the Beatles', also ran the Blue Angel, a late night drinking establishment frequented by the artistes, musicians and 'in crowd' of Merseyside.

The Casbah, further out in the wilds of West Derby was a makeshift coffee bar opened by Mona Best as somewhere her drummer son Pete, who was to become the Best with the worst luck in the world, could gain experience playing in public with his group the Beatles within her sight and theoretically out of trouble. Everything here was very much a family affair with anyone available lending a hand on the decoration which included murals by John Lennon. Coffee and fizzy drinks could be purchased but nothing stronger.

The Mardi Gras in Mount Pleasant was yet another rendezvous for youth. It was managed by Joe Flannery, the elder brother of local singing celebrity Lee Curtis whom he also managed, a good looking and talented vocalist with a strong local female following. Regrettably, none of the artistes whose careers he guided ever made it to national fame and Joe was gently teased in the press with a cruel but clever witticism that advised 'Flannery will get you nowhere'.

The list of musical venues was not endless but it was certainly extensive. The Zodiac, the Black Cat and the Odd Spot in the centre. The Lathom Hall down by the docks in Litherland. And if you wanted a grander stage and a sense of spectacle then you could catch one of the package shows that were regularly presented at the Tower Ballroom in New Brighton and which mixed and matched cheap but popular local talent with genuine headline acts of the day both home grown and from across the Atlantic Ocean.

Billy Kinsley of the Merseybeats, still recalls the band supporting the great Little Richard at the Tower Ballroom back in 1962.

'We were only young kids and we didn't really think too much about what we should or shouldn't do in our set. We were just starting out. Tony Crane and I were mad keen Everly Brothers fans and we went into their version of *Lucille*. Pretty soon we noticed Little Richard in the wings shaking his fist and calling us every name under the sun. We'd forgotten it was one of his big hits. It just hadn't occurred to us at the time. When we came off he was yelling, "You bastards, you're stealing my song, you bastards." We were so embarrassed. We couldn't think of what to say so I just said, "Sorry about that Little".'

With such a plethora of venues able and willing to accommodate them and their equipment, beat groups of varying degrees of quality swarmed from one to the other like locusts for a few pounds per session, often performing at more than one place in an evening.

Back in the centre of the city Temple Street, a narrow roadway joining Dale Street and Victoria Street, was home to two favourite haunts. The Temple, where Ray McFall had supervised monetary affairs, was a pub which presented jazz. Further along was the location for another converted cellar named the Iron Door.

The Cavern may have grabbed the major portion of fame but the Iron Door was by no means the poor relation. It had its own crowd, its own atmosphere and more room in which to accommodate them when needed. And the Iron Door precociously wrong-footed its illustrious neighbour by introducing exclusively rock & roll sessions first. It was a smart and a necessary move in those changing times. The Cavern held onto its diehard traditionalist principles for as long as it could but once rock rhythms had unleashed themselves on the teenage patrons they were unstoppable.

It was called The Iron Door by its owners Geoffrey Hogarth and Harry Ormersher in 1958 for obvious reasons but went through some name changes in its early incarnation, including periods as the Pyramid, the Liverpool Jazz Society and the Storeyville Jazz Club. It was still officially the Liverpool Jazz Society when Sam Leach started to promote his rock & roll sessions but hardly anyone referred to it as anything other than the Iron Door. Sam's first all-nighter presenting beat rather than jazz music was on March 11th 1961 and they managed to pack in two thousand people during the mammoth twelve hour, twelve band event. With a paltry fifty paying customers on that same evening it took the Cavern just ten days to see the error of their ways and declare itself at last to be a rock & roll friendly venue.

While the Cavern jealously guarded its association with the Beatles as the top-drawer attraction in their list of local attractions the other establishments too had their special favourites. The Bluegenes, who eventually dropped their trad jazz image and banjo to espouse the good time sounds of rockabilly music, at the same time adopting a new title as the Swinging Blue Jeans, had a seemingly unassailable position as one of the top bands on Merseyside and were the darlings of the Mardi Gras. And the Iron Door became the adopted home of a band whose sharp, professional image and skills in country and pop were gaining more fans for them week by week and who were digging their heels in to stake their legitimate claim as the number two contenders to John Lennon, Paul McCartney, George Harrison and, for the time being, Pete Best. They were The Searchers.

7

The Classic Line-Up

The beginnings of The Searchers had their roots in an unnamed skiffle group formed in the late fifties by John McNally and a constantly changing bunch of boyhood friends. John was born in the Kirkdale district of Liverpool on August 30th 1941 where he lived with his typically large Catholic family. He was one of five brothers and a sister who, tragically, was not to live beyond the age of nineteen.

It was a tough life for everyone back then. The war had brought down much of the city and most of the houses had cracks in the walls and other peripheral damage. A young John, he must have been about three or four at the time, remembers a fighter plane crashing near his house in St John's Road. As it came down it knocked the steeple off St Alexander's Church.

Like every other young lad in the fifties most free time away from school was taken up with knockabout games of football on the local 'rec' or in the street where a pile of coats marked out the goals and sides were arbitrarily picked as to who would go 'pudding' or 'beef'. In a city obsessed by the sport that someone once called 'the working man's ballet' you formed your allegiances early on in life. You were either a Blue or a Red. It was either Everton or Liverpool. The rest of John's family were Evertonians through and through and, showing an early sign of rebellion and a stubbornness that was to remain an essential part of his character, the young John McNally decided that Anfield was the place for him. Liverpool FC would have his undying support.

When rock & roll hit the airwaves football was quickly resigned to a subordinate position in his order of priorities. The sound and image of the guitar captured his imagination and he very soon taught himself to strum a few basic chords on an arch top Broadway instrument that his brother, a merchant seaman, had brought back from the States for him. Along with his best pal Brian Dolan who also played guitar and had a good voice, he would hold impromptu skiffle sessions on the corner of the street, their instrumentation augmented by any of the other half dozen guitar strumming friends who deigned to show up.

John harboured ambitions to follow in his sibling's footsteps and spent the immediate post-school years in preparation for a life on the ocean waves. His initial position in the offices of Alfred Holt organising the despatching of parts for the Blue Funnel line led to a period of training at sea school in Barmouth where he learned all the required maritime skills to cement his future. Alas when the time came for the final examination that would allow him to pursue a deep sea career he was failed because of a lazy eye. But his fixation on beat music helped to soften the blow.

He also worked for a time at the Vactite company in Bootle who manufactured cabling, where friends remember him wearing a blue boiler suit three sizes too big. The cables tended to cut into the flesh of his hands so he wore gloves, which resulted in a fair amount of mickey-taking from his mates who handled the goods with their bare flesh. But John was not about to risk damaging his fingers when he had every intention of putting them to good use making music.

There were skiffle groups on many street corners in those days, and further along St John's Road where it crossed into Bootle, a young Mike Prendergast was also making music with his bunch of friends. Their paths often crossed and they discovered a like-mindedness in both their tastes in music and in their attitudes and ambitions. As their proficiency increased so the line-up regularised itself. And as the funds allowed they upgraded their instruments and acquired the necessary amplification to allow them to play the rock repertoire they aspired to. Mike was soon recruited into the ranks of John's outfit.

Born on March 3rd 1941, Michael John Prendergast received his primary education at St Winifred's in Bootle near where he lived in the St John's Road. A fellow pupil at the time was a certain Christopher Crummey who was to figure in the story a few years down the line. Mike's youthful interests were music and football, not necessarily in that order, and in fact he was good enough at soccer to play for Everton Boys for a while. But it was pop music that eventually won the day and his fortuitous meeting with John McNally provided the nucleus of what was eventually to become one of the most famous groups in the world.

Education at Major Street School had ended for young McNally. The failed attempt at life as a sailor was followed by the job as a trainee fitter at Vactite and he was now earning a wage that was not good but allowed him to trade up from the Broadway to a Futurama solid bodied electric model that almost looked like the instrument played by Buddy Holly.

Mike had actually seen Buddy Holly perform with The Crickets at the Philharmonic in Liverpool on March 20th 1958 when he toured Britain for the first and only time. It was the UK's first sighting of a real live Fender Stratocaster, the solid bodied Holy Grail of guitars that Holly played and which any budding rocker in Britain would happily have committed murder to own. It was the coolest instrument on the planet bar none.

John had missed out on that concert but had seen another American rock & roll star Charlie Gracie at the Empire singing his hits *Butterfly*, *Fabulous* and *Wandering Eyes*. Charlie, a more traditional guy in his approach and tastes, opted for a splendidly over the top Guild X350, a three pickup arch top model that boasted an impressive row of six push-button tone switches and whose large dimensions appeared to dwarf the diminutive but very sharp looking Philadelphian. Holly and Gracie were rare in rock & roll terms. They were two rock stars who could actually play their instruments.

Another pal by the name of Tony West, known to everyone as Joe and older by a couple of years, was fresh out of the Army which had demanded a three-year term of national service and where he too had a skiffle group. They were called the Sixty Six Slicks having been formed from friends of the Sixty Six regiment with whom he had completed his period of conscription. He willingly dumped his guitar and bought an electric bass, still a somewhat rare instrument at the time, in order to join John's bunch. After all guitarists were quickly becoming ten a penny.

Even more importantly he could drive and owned a dark blue 1955 Humber Hawk, registration UKA 456 which ferried the group from gig to gig. With Joe's Tuxedo bass guitar in the instrumentation there was no more having to put up with a shoddy and amateurish tea chest with a broom handle and a length of string to thump out the low notes. And no more washboard providing a rhythm once they had recruited a real live drummer in the shape of Joe Kennedy.

As their proficiency increased so did the ultra-keen McNally's desire for a better guitar. The Czechoslovakian made Futurama had weak electronics and, whilst looking the dog's bollocks with its aerodynamic Fender-esque styling, tremolo arm and bank of three rocker switches to control the triple pickup layout, it just did not have the power and the punch he was looking for. A Gibson Les Paul was what he wanted. But Les Paul's were not just thin on the ground in England, they weren't on the ground at all. Even if he could have raised the cash, which he could not, American instruments were still subject to an import ban in Britain.

Hofners, made in Germany, were the top of the range that was currently available and he had seen a Club 60 model in a shop in Preston. It was blond and beautiful with twin pickups and elaborate 'mother of toilet seat' inlays along the neck and on the headstock. John and Joe West made the trip in the Humber and eventually the deal was agreed. Unfortunately John's age, he was eighteen at the time, meant that he could not legally take out a hire purchase agreement without the guarantee of a parent. Back to Liverpool went the pair and with the papers duly signed by John's father they raced back to Preston. With the precious purchase finally on board they sped off to that night's gig making the venue with barely an hour to spare before they were due on stage.

For a period some of the lead vocal honours were taken by Ron Woodbridge, a tall and zany rocker who curiously hailed from the namby-pamby and highly disapproved of South, a land of wimps and 'Flash Harrys' in the eyes of the average Scouser. A nomadic character, he was temporarily domiciled in Tancred Road in the Anfield district just a couple of streets away from the ground of Liverpool FC and would eventually fetch up in the eighties in Scotland. John had gone along with Mike and bassist Joe West to see him perform at the Glass House, a large pub in Old Swan.

They were impressed at his ability to perform energetically in front of a crowd and to get the girls excited but at their first gig, the Lathom Hall in Seaforth, he was perhaps a bit too energetic and the girls a bit too excited for comfort. Ron was pleased to attract so much female attention as they gathered at the front of the stage to point and giggle at him. What he didn't realise was that he had forgotten to zip up his flies. The group needed exposure but perhaps not quite so much and certainly in an altogether different area. While the girls were amused the guys were not quite as thrilled, seeing this as an insult to their women and a threat to their own position. A fight broke out and the group had to make a very hasty exit out the back way.

Always referred to as 'Big Ron', his little-known but significant claim to fame is that he was the very person who gave the group its legendary name, coming up with the suggestion while they waited at a bus stop in the rain one early evening, which is a pretty good claim to fame by any standards.

The Searchers was of course the title of an immensely popular western film from 1956 starring John Wayne. There was no other significance to the choice other than it sounded cool and the others happily went along with Big Ron's suggestion. The film in fact has contributed more than once to the history of pop music. Unable to get a much repeated phrase of Wayne's out of his mind a rising star from Lubbock, Texas, named Buddy Holly finally built a song around it and *That'll Be The Day* took him and his group The Crickets into the charts for the first time.

When it was time for Big Ron to continue his meanderings they didn't have to look too far for a replacement. Mrs McNally worked alongside a Mrs Beck at a bakery and she passed on her suggestion to her lad John that they consider her son Billy who was, in her opinion, a wonderful singer. A mother's praise is not always the most sensible yardstick to go by but she proved to be a wise and unbiased judge.

His rich and powerfully deep voice was tuneful and perfectly suited to the country feel their communal tastes veered towards. In the mid fifties the lines between rock and country were still blurred. It was all music with a beat sung in American accents to the rhythm of electric guitars. Country artistes such as Johnny Cash (*I Walk The Line, Bal-*

lad Of A Teenage Queen, *How High's The Water Mama?*), Guy Mitchell (*Singing The Blues*, *Knee Deep In The Blues*, *Rockabilly Rock*) and Sonny James (*Young Love*) were happily accepted into the fraternity of performers approved of by teenage music fans, who were also getting into the sounds of Elvis Presley, Gene Vincent and the Everly Brothers. Indeed the Everly Brothers were really a country act who had taken their good looks and sweet harmonies just a few precious steps nearer to the rhythms of rock & roll.

The inclusion of Billy Beck into their ranks, performing under the slicker adopted name of Johnny Sandon, did nothing but advance the reputation of his new cohorts the Searchers in Liverpool. He could more than approximate the vocals of Eddie Arnold, a western star one of whose most notable record successes was a song called *The Tennessee Stud.* Jack Scott's hit *What In The World's Come Over You?* also received a favourable treatment by Beck/Sandon. And if they felt like veering away from the realms of this happy hoedown music the songs of Brook Benton, renowned for his beautifully emotive and honey-coated bass notes, could easily appease the sensitivities of the aficionados of the more tempered and melodic forms of black soul.

Billy Beck, whose new stage name derived from a pub called The Sandon not far from the Liverpool FC's ground at Anfield, was no oil painting. He was tall and geeky looking with a long face and spectacles which fortunately for him had been stripped of their previous taboo status with the arrival of Buddy Holly. But the band looked a sharp unit with their black pants, matching red sweaters, white shirts and ties and twin Hofner Club 60 guitars (Mike had also acquired one) powered by a triangular fronted Watkins Dominator amplifier. And they were starting to sound very good indeed. Johnny Sandon's deep throated tones could not fail to impress.

Realising that his new venture in the second hand car trade needed his full time effort if it was to provide him with the secure and financially stable future that music was highly unlikely to, Joe West decided that playtime was over and real life at last had to kick in. His departure left them depleted in the bass department for a while but Mike and John soon had his replacement in mind. They had seen a guy at the Cross Keys, a large pub, more often than not referred to as The Stadium because of its proximity to the city's boxing arena, where they themselves performed fairly regularly. It was situated at 13 Earle Street in the Liverpool 3 district just a few streets inland from the Princes Dock near the Old Hall/Queensway junction.

Tony Jackson was a thick set, aggressive looking character with a mass of dark hair and sharp facial features exaggerated by a distinctive Roman nose. And if he looked hard he in fact was hard. The tough district he was raised in required that you sometimes had to fight for your survival and Tony was no slouch in that department. Because of his extremely short fuse and tendency to use fists rather than words to emphasise his side of an argument he acquired the nickname Black Jake. It suited him well.

Although for public consumption after the onset of fame he gave his year of birth as 1941 Jackson was actually born on July 16th 1938 in the working class Edge Lane district of Liverpool near Sefton Park, where he attended St Bernard's Roman Catholic School. Although offered a scholarship at St Francis Xavier Grammar School he opted instead for Walton Technical College. Part of the curriculum there was a day release to Liverpool Art School where from time to time he would bump into a young John Lennon. Tony remembered Lennon as 'the nutter of the school'.

While serving his electrical apprenticeship, developing skills that would come to serve him well in the world of pop music and its necessary accompanying electronic paraphernalia, he began to spend his limited free time in forming a skiffle group. Didn't everyone? In the music-mad fifties it seemed at times that there were more teenagers in skiffle groups than not. Their particular ensemble was called the Martinis and boasted the standard line-up of guitars, washboard and tea chest bass, the numbers and instrumentation always dependent on who was in or out of the group at any given time in the course of their ever-changing personnel.

By the time of the Cross Keys days, where Jackson's band was an occasional feature and played for 'thirty bob and as much beer as we could drink', skiffle had more or less run its course and rock & roll, along with guitars that were electric and loud, was in. Tony was a rhythm guitarist and singer with a voice well suited to the new style of music that was pulling in the paying, or rather drinking, customers.

When he met his future partners in fame Tony was already married to Margaret Parry, the first of his three wives. Mike and John went along one Saturday night when they knew he would be playing to check out that their hunch was right. As good as Sandon's voice was, it would be an advantage to spread their appeal as wide as possible. Both John and Mike helped out with the vocal duties during an evening's set but Jackson's cutting tones, well suited to the raunchier material some of their audience favoured, would given them an even greater range with which to work. They got chatting and mutually agreed to give the suggested new alliance a try.

Bass guitarists were a scarce commodity on Merseyside and Tony had found the switch from rhythm to bass a not too difficult one. It was an instrument that would provide more opportunities for employment in bands who were crying out for bass players. Not only that but his equipment came via his own fair hands. The electrical apprenticeship had paid off in spades. He constructed his own amplifier which worked well enough even when compared to the shop bought stuff available.

And it didn't matter if a costly Fender was not within his grasp. A precocious artistic talent, unexpected from a guy who had the external appearance of a street-wise hard man to whom the little niceties of life were simply not on his agenda, was displayed when he produced an instrument that could fool the eyes of most into believing that he was the owner of a genuine Precision Bass from the prestigious American manufacturer.

It was a time of flux in the band and a replacement was needed for a departing Joe Kennedy. Again drummers were not as plentiful as guitarists and in constant demand but Norman McGarry, who had also played with Tony at the Cross Keys occasionally along with a bass guitarist called Jimmy Moran, was brought in as a replacement. But McGarry like many people locally worked at the bakery and a switch to a permanent night shift made his continuation with the group difficult. It was another headache that Johnny Sandon & the Searchers could have done without but life in a rock & roll band back then was a constant struggle to find enough players to keep it all going. Girlfriends, jobs or parental opposition - there were plenty of reasons for someone to drop out at a minute's notice.

Luckily Mike Prendergast had known a fellow pupil at St Winifred's, where he received his primary education, who had taken up drums. Christopher Crummey was not a native Liverpudlian. He was born in Oldham on August 26th 1941 but the family relocated to Merseyside when he was four years old. He was always an oddball child with an extrovert nature, growing his hair long when he was fourteen, an age when anyone daring to be different was taking a big chance. And long hair was pretty big on the difference scale back then.

But Chris was blessed with an unshakeable faith in his own ability and where he was going. In his mind anyone who aimed beneath the stars aimed too low. His demeanour and attitude to life and people in general was mature for his age and his style of dress was urbane and elegant. In the Crummey household he was treated like a minor deity and if his demands weren't met he would throw a tantrum until he got his own way. But any tantrum thrown by Chris were usually followed by deep remorse and his sensitive and basically caring nature required him to make reparation by way of a gift or maybe just some kind words accompanied by a huge grin.

His musical ambitions had actually begun, like so many others, on a guitar together with a smattering of self taught piano and a short fruitless spell on the violin, but he soon discovered that he would never reach the levels of skill he would need to make it big and the process of banging drums seemed a much more sensible solution. His sense of rhythm and timing was good. Frank Hessy's, the foremost music shop in the centre of Liverpool, had a bright shiny blue Ajax kit for sale and his dad signed the hire purchase papers for them. To Chris the fact that they were blue and shiny probably counted more than the actual make or their sound. They appealed to his innate sense of style.

It was while making one of the regular monthly payments that he happened to run into Mike Prendergast, his old pal from those far-off schooldays. Chris was by now working in a furniture store called Swifts, situated in the Stanley Road near the family home at 30 Florida Street, Bootle. Along with furniture, Swifts sold prams and bikes and the like. The Florida Street house is no longer there, having long since made way for a Marks and Spencer store, and Swifts was demolished to make way for the New Strand Shopping Centre.

Crummey accompanied Mike along to a casual rehearsal at John's house and it was soon pretty evident that he would undoubtedly be an asset to the group. He was in and, with little ceremony or preparation, started his career as a Searcher more or less immediately. Chris, in an interview with Spencer Leigh in 1998, recalls his first evening with them at the Wilson Hall in Garston but tells the tale as going straight into a show without reference to the introduction to the others at the rehearsal at John's house. This may or may not be right but John most definitely remembers the rehearsal as their first meeting and believes that the Wilson Hall date is probably correct although he can't be sure.

Chris's memory in his later years is not to be relied on too heavily. In the same interview he clearly states that he joined the band before Johnny Sandon but an existing photograph of the 'red sweater' line-up, the band being clad in dark slacks and scarlet pullovers, white shirts and black ties, with Joe Kennedy on drums and Sandon on vocals along with McNally, Prendergast and West wielding guitars prove this not to be the case. Chris's recollections proved to be both selective and a tad defective.

As a singing drummer with a keen sense of harmony he brought an added dimension to the band. Five musicians, five voices each one distinct from the others. Johnny Sandon & the Searchers had featured in the top five Merseyside groups in the 1961 poll of Merseybeat, the local music newspaper started and operated by an enthusiastic young journalist called Bill Harry. Mike had switched from the Hofner to a quirky looking British made Burns Vibra Artiste guitar, a flashy looking piece of kit with three pickups and a striking cherry red finish.

The guys looked and sounded good, the naff though admittedly smart and parent-friendly red sweaters having been replaced by dramatic black polo necks and black jeans. They quickly established a solid reputation on the Merseyside group scene and joined the legion of rival outfits doing the circuit of the city's beat clubs. On April 18th Johnny Sandon & the Searchers debuted at the Cavern Club in Mathew Street. A few months later on July 14th they returned to the cellar club. The headliners on that Friday night were ostensibly the White Eagles Jazz Band but the evening was to be remembered in musical history for the appearance of another bunch of wannabee rock stars.

Less than two weeks later on the 26th July the Beatles, Gerry & the Pacemakers and Johnny Sandon & the Searchers constituted the line-up with not a jazz band in sight.

The Beatles, who had up to this point been known, and barely known at that, as the Silver Beetles had returned from their second visit to Hamburg. And they had returned in triumph with a new look, a new sound and with new skills. John McNally remembers the night well and was mightily impressed by the foursome who had up to that point been dismissed by most of Liverpool's musical fraternity as a nothing group going nowhere fast.

As for the Searchers they were well satisfied with their swift upward progression within the beat group community. Nothing could stop them now, or so it seemed. But in February of 1962 Johnny Sandon was poached away from them, not by any old rag tag outfit but by the Remo Four, one of the most respected and admired bands on Merseyside which featured the superb skills of guitarist Colin Manley. While others were struggling to find the right chords or trying to make their fingers work fast enough to provide an acceptable solo Manley could faithfully reproduce the skilful and dazzling runs of Gene Vincent's axeman, Cliff Gallup.

Their excellent drummer Roy Dyke was to find fame some time later as one third of Ashton, Gardener and Dyke who scored in the charts with *The Resurrection Shuffle*. It was a difficult offer to turn down and one which Sandon did not. Part of the enticement was the offer of a tour of US air bases in Germany. Johnny Sandon & the Searchers was no more. There now existed a four-piece group simply called the Searchers.

With the indomitable spirit of youth when faced with a crisis the remaining quartet quickly set about retrenching and assembling a repertoire that would enable them to continue along their chosen path. There was little doubt that until they re-established their reputation in the area they would be looked on as a slightly diminished product in many people's eyes. After all they had been deserted for something seemingly more desirable by a home-grown talent who was highly thought of. But somehow the new economical format had a better image. Darker and more cutting edge. This was now much more a rock & roll group than a pseudo country and western ensemble.

John's sense of drama and style caused him to have his blond Club 60 refinished in black by John Griffin (or Griffiths perhaps, they can't quite remember) the person who was currently ferrying them to and from gigs. He was in the business of vehicle repairs and saw no difference in changing the colour of a guitar rather than a car. Along with John Lennon's Rickenbacker, which coincidentally had also undergone a change from blond to black, it became one of the most iconic and recognisable guitars of the period.

There was a lot of competition around and at the top of the list were now the Beatles who had gone to Germany as raw and inconsequential unknowns only to return as seasoned veterans, having honed their skills in front of a foreign crowd that held no preconceptions but cheered them on with each tiny step of their progress. By the time John, Paul, George and Pete trod the stage of a new venue in Hamburg called the Star Club in the summer of '62 they were exciting to watch and to listen to and clearly going places. The Silver Beetles returned from the fatherland as the Beatles and showed them all how it was done.

When Horst Fascher arrived in town to search out new talent for the Star Club where he was the manager he included in his list of suitable bands the Searchers. Germany was calling and holding out fistfuls of Deutschmarks to tempt them. Lead us most definitely into temptation was their swift reply.

8

Time For A Change

By the end of 1962, along with the rest of the country, Cliff Bennett & the Rebel Rousers were feeling the first embryonic stirrings of what was eventually to be known as Merseybeat, spearheaded by a group of whom we learned during our June visit to the Star Club and who appeared under the odd sounding name of the Beatles. It had become quite apparent from the murmurings amongst the bar girls of the Star Club that there was something special about them and we were intrigued. We wanted to know what all the fuss was about. We were once more heading back to the Reeperbahn and about to find out for ourselves.

A lot had happened in the past six months both for us and for them. After a seemingly fruitless trudge around the major - and minor - record labels of the capital their manager Brian Epstein had managed to secure them a deal with Parlophone records, coincidentally the very same label that we were signed to. It was very much a last ditch effort. He had been turned down by everyone including EMI's main competitor Decca who had signed up Brian Poole & the Tremeloes and saw no reason to add another guitar, drums and vocal ensemble to their roster.

Hitherto merely an heir to the family's Liverpool-based electrical goods operation, this was the theatrically-oriented Brian's first venture into to the foreign fields of showbusiness management. He was dispirited and desperate At this point he would have even considered the tacky Embassy label which specialised in cheap, badly produced and performed covers of current chart hits and who only sold their un-cool product in Woolworths. George Martin's willingness to give it a go came like manna from heaven.

In truth Martin would not have been the producer of choice for Epstein or the Beatles. He had no track record to speak of in the field of pop music, having specialised mainly in novelty discs and was perhaps best known for his anarchic and near insane efforts with The Goons and Peter Sellers. They were taking a chance and so was he. The difference was that Martin had a choice.

By the time their first disc came to the market the Beatles had acquired a new drummer. All of the photos I had seen on the walls of the Star Club had incorporated the mean, moody and handsome face of Pete Best but he had been unceremoniously dumped and replaced by a gentleman with the exotic and highly unlikely name of Ringo Starr.

This surprised me. While strolling along the Grosse Freiheit during my previous Hamburg sojourn back in June I had been told by a very excited Ted 'Kingsize' Taylor, whose group The Dominoes were practically resident there, that Starr, despite being energetically courted by the Beatles, had just written informing him that he was willing to join his outfit. It seems that almost before the ink was dry on the paper the former Richard Starkey had second thoughts. Goodbye Kingsize, hello Beatles.

At their first demo session for EMI at the studios in Abbey Road it seems that George Martin had not been impressed by Best's drum technique He considered it too amateur and inconsistent for professional purposes although he made no demands with regard to who they employed for their live appearances. It was of no concern to him. But the seeds had been sown in that restless and impatient cabal of ruthless ambition and their minds were set.

Pete, who was considered by many to be a powerful and effective driving force in the group, not to mention being a teenage heartthrob and the object of fluttering hearts and lustful sighs among the young ladies of Liverpool, was devastated. But the dirty deed was done and Best was on his way to becoming the most pitied person in the history of pop music.

Ringo settled into the band immediately but appeasing the miffed maidens of Merseyside was an altogether different proposition. Best, with his dark, brooding film star looks, had been their idol. Ringo was curiously cute and cuddly with a personality that would not only carry him through but which would provide him with an appeal that was infectious and carried its own kind of charisma. But in the looks department you wouldn't exactly crawl over James Dean to get to him.

The girls rebelled. They camped out in Best's garden and picketed Beatles shows at the Cavern to demonstrate their solidarity. All to no avail. Their cry might have been 'Pete forever, Ringo never' but it was a fait accomplit. The facts were incontrovertible. Ringo forever, Pete, on yer bike.

Love Me Do, their first offering for Parlophone, was released on October 5th 1962. It was a simple and catchy yet surprisingly unadventurous piece of pop music, heavily influenced by the Everly Brothers in the harmony department and by Bruce Chanel's harp player Delbert McClinton in their use of the previously un-hip harmonica. Ironically, in view of Best being replaced in the band, George Martin was not convinced of Ringo's suitability for sessions and drafted in veteran studio drummer Andy White. It is assumed that it is his drumming which is heard on the single but as tracks were apparently laid down by both Starr and White no one is willing to commit themselves absolutely. It is natural that George Martin might err on the side of diplomacy rather than state for the record that Ringo did not perform on *Love Me Do*. Or perhaps he genuinely is uncertain.

Their decision to write only one verse for the song which is simply broken up twice by a very basic middle section was both surprising and radical. Considering that their whole future in the music industry was hanging on this debut disc you would be forgiven for wondering whether it was sheer naivety or an astonishing youthful arrogance that made them think they could get away without the need to write a second verse.

In fact without Epstein's power and influence it might never have worked at all. His NEMS Stores in Liverpool was an important purchaser of EMI product and the fact that they could be guaranteed a bulk order out of all proportion to what could normally be expected for the debut record of a virtually unknown act was a serious consideration when the initial meeting between Epstein and Martin had taken place. *Love Me Do*, propped up by NEMS money, made it to a modest but respectable number seventeen in the charts before dropping out of sight again.

Unknown to me I had already played alongside the Beatles earlier that year. On Saturday March 31st 1962 we had apparently been half of a bill at the Subscription Rooms in Stroud which advertised a night with 'top vocal & instrumental group – stars of Polydor Records – the sensational Beatles', plus the Rebel Rousers. To gain entrance would have cost you five shillings unless you were either a teddy boy or were wearing stiletto heels, in which case you were considered a menace and would be refused entrance. Teddy boys wearing stilettos would have no doubt been shot before reaching the door.

I have absolutely no knowledge of the evening or of them. I don't recall watching them or if I did of any lasting impression created by what would eventually prove to be the most important beat combo in the world. It was only brought home to me by the discovery decades later of a metal reproduction of that evening's poster. I have little doubt that I would have been extremely miffed at the top billing of a group that I had never heard of from a place I had never heard of. We were a respected act from the capital of the country and recording artistes of long standing. Almost a year in fact. My god, that was virtually a lifetime in rock & roll terms. If only I had known. Ah well...

If the tides were shifting for the Beatles we had traversed a few choppy waters ourselves. The tenuous and uncomfortable situation with the terrible twosome, Hopkins and Watson, could not continue. The whole band had become very unsettled and it was left to Cliff once again to inform them that their musical input, brilliant though it was, would be more appreciated elsewhere. Go directly to jail. Do not pass Go. Do not collect two hundred pounds. Fuck off.

It was fortuitous that our departed sax player Sid Phillips had been finding civvy street, with its long days filled with nothing but mending typewriters, more than a little dull and, with the blessing of his wife Mavis, was ready to rouse with the rebels once again. And this time Sid brought a baritone sax in addition to his tenor model thus providing us with a bottom end that really rocked like nothing we had heard outside of Little Richard and Fats Domino records.

Furthermore Dave Wendells, with a generosity of spirit and forgiveness that surely few others would have managed to rustle up after the shoddy way we had treated him, accepted a renewed offer to be our lead guitarist. As the year headed to a close our new line-up looked forward to presenting a new Rebel Rousers to the audience of the Star Club.

We nearly didn't make it. On December 30th 1962 Britain was at the beginning of a big freeze that saw the whole of the country in a very pretty but crippling whiteout. Heathrow Airport had been shut down on the very day that we were due to board our plane leaving us with no idea of when or if we would depart. We were told it would not reopen that day and that we should simply stay at home and check regularly for news.

I couldn't bear to sit in the house just twiddling my thumbs. A sense of proportion is without doubt one of the last senses to develop, and with the restlessness of youth that dictates that every long minute is of mind-blowing importance, I decided to join some friends at the Oldfield Hotel in Greenford where an up-and-coming local outfit called the Detours were fast becoming one of the most popular of the regular bands.

Led by Pete Townshend, their personnel was still in a state of flux. For a while they hovered between names, yo-yo-ing between the High Numbers and The Who before settling on the latter and the classic formation that would become a cornerstone of British rock across the globe. But as yet in these pre-Moon the Loon days they still had a guy called Doug Sandom on drums and Roger Daltrey was content to handle the lead guitar while the vocals were delivered by Colin Dawson. They were very good and getting better all the time.

Getting to the Oldfield wasn't as easy as it sounds. I was in fact car-less at the time. With my new-found wealth courtesy of Herr Weissleder and the good people of Germany I had recently purchased my first set of wheels, a second hand Ford Anglia, registration number YXR 757. After three attempts I finally passed my test in Cliff's tiny grey mini van, the economy transport forced on him by the repossession of his beautiful Sunbeam Rapier. I was now a fully-fledged driver and my vocabulary started to change for the worse. Let's face it, you never really learn to swear until you start driving.

I was proud of my wheels. It was a pale blue model, the one with the distinctive and stylish swept-back window, albeit the standard model and not the deluxe which boasted additional chrome trim and padded dashboard. It had cost me three hundred and seventy five pounds cash and I was so proud when I drove it away from the garage. I continued to drive proudly right up to the point where I skidded on ice and embedded myself in a bollard a few days after Christmas.

So there I was in Greenford having managed to find enough buses still running to get me to where my chums had gathered. In the middle of the evening I decided it would be prudent to get an update on our travel plans. When I rang our sax player Moss's house, to my horror I was told that the airport had reopened and our plane was due to leave at ten. I rushed from the hotel and with the luck of the gods, which I clearly did not deserve, managed to find one of the very few cabs that must have been plying their trade on that most inhospitable of nights.

We stopped at my parents' house and I grabbed the bag that I had packed the day before, said the quickest and most discourteous of goodbyes to my parents who were still traumatised from my recent accident and disappeared into the chilly black and white night. I made it in time. The others were in the café area and the flight had not yet been called. I breathed a sigh of relief. Throughout my life good fortune has always been on my side when I have least deserved it.

Hamburg, when we landed, was in pretty much the same state as the UK. A vast area of thick snow with houses, traffic and people camouflaged somewhere beneath the brilliant white frosting. Apart from the forbidding weather we also had to deal with a small drama regarding our accommodation. The Germania had been fine on our initial visit but this time round we were driven to the block of flats in the Grosse Freiheit opposite the club. 'Flats' was too grand a title to bestow on them. They were a set of interconnecting rooms installed with basics bunks beds laid out barrack room style, musicians – for the use of.

As far as Mr Bennett was concerned they were shabby dormitories, had no style or comfort of any kind and were certainly not going to be for the use of these musicians. We were not used to luxury but we were certainly used to better than this. Having been treated with a certain amount of reverence last time it seemed that familiarity was perhaps breeding contempt. We decided that they had become a little too familiar and we were about to show our contempt. After a short kerfuffle, during which time it was quite apparent that Cliff was going to stand his ground, we were transported about a quarter of a mile to the wide street known as Neuerpferdmarkt (the new horsemarket) and the modern, if basic, Hotel Pacific.

The Pacific at least was a purpose built establishment and for us, who were used to bed and breakfast establishments, was approaching luxury. A contrast to the gabled and fussy stuccoed exteriors of the more typical German architecture, it was constructed in a pale yellow tinged brick, all clean lines and metal window frames with curtains in rich vibrant colours in view of the street making it look rather more attractive than it actually was.

In fact the rooms were boxes with beds, nothing more, but this time round it was also home to Bill Haley & his Comets and what was good enough for the founder of rock & roll was good enough for us. We checked into the hotel quickly and trundled off down to the Grosse Freiheit to check out the action at the club and more importantly those precocious new young pretenders the Beatles. We expected to be disappointed. To be truthful I think we hoped we would be disappointed. But alas we were not.

They were raw and vibrant in their personalities and in their playing but way beyond the excitement of the music there was a maturity about them that shone through. They had 'attitude' before attitude had been invented.

There was nothing particularly precise or clever about what they played or the way they played it. It wasn't complicated and it wasn't new but it swung like a sack of doo doo. Mostly, like the rest of Britain's beat groups, ourselves included, they offered a bunch of reworked American classics from the back catalogues of Chuck Berry, Little Richard, Larry Williams and the like. As we had come to expect from a Liverpool band they eschewed the soft rock clean-cut options of Cliff Richard and the other socially acceptable parent-friendly pop stars to make a musical statement which declared that old black is the new black.

It was very much to our taste and even though there wasn't a sax or a piano in sight the sound was gutsy. The guitars were attacked rather than strummed and their vocals cut through and grabbed an audience that was without doubt excited by lyrics that they barely understood. And the bass drum, un-mic'd in those primitive times, was solid and loud and kept the tempo rock solid. Ass was most definitely being kicked here. They had passion. Cliff Bennett, a guy not too ready with a compliment where British music in particular was concerned, was impressed and so were we all.

The next night it was our turn. The new sound and altered line-up worked well. Over the past weeks our new arrangements had bedded in beautifully and the extra depth provided by the gut-stirring baritone sax more than made up for the missing keyboards. And we even had a new set of cheap shirts in which to launch this latest incarnation of the Rebel Rousers - dark blue Fred Perry style tennis shirts that, like their predecessors, owed their inclusion more to cost than fashion.

If the Beatles played with passion then so did we. Without exception we cared about our music. Bobby Parker's *Watch Your Step*. Larry Williams' *Slow Down*. And the old Chuck Berry stalwart *Talkin' About You*. Our set was tough and unpredictable and, in a coincidental parallel to our Merseyside compatriots, drawn largely from the vaults of black American rhythm and blues.

A little later on in the evening I was heading into the dressing room area when I encountered John Lennon heading out into the club. I decided to introduce myself. 'Hi John.' I began. 'I thought your show was really great. I hope you have a lot of luck with the new record when you get back home.' He did not smile. He looked at me in much the same way a cat looks at a mouse before pouncing to tear the guts out of it. His stare was filled with a curious mix of interest and malevolence and I prayed that it was more the former than the latter.

'Oh yeah, it's Frank isn't it?' Well at least he knew my name. 'I thought you lot were great too. I've been talking to people in the club and it seems that next to Cliff you're the most popular member in the band.' There was a perfectly timed pause before he delivered the *coup de grace*. 'I can't think why. Your harmonies are fucking ridiculous.'

I stood frozen to the spot not quite knowing what had occurred or how to deal with it. I thought I'd been insulted but I wasn't sure. My level of sophistication was not yet at the point where I could be a competent judge of such things. It must be some kind of Scouse humour that I'm not familiar with, I thought. Or hoped. It is said that no-one can make you feel inferior without your consent but at that moment I was giving this prickly northerner *carte blanche* to verbally abuse me. I felt very inferior indeed. I somehow found a voice.

'Well anyway I want to wish you all the best with the new one' I repeated. I had decided to err on the side of quiet dignity. On reflection it was the wisest move I could have made. I could never have competed with the lethal tongue of the still angry young Lennon of the sixties. We were light years away from his 'peace and love in our time' period. 'Yeah, all the best to you too. See you later.' He left. It had not been my finest hour but at least my first meeting with one of the greatest icons in popular music had been a significant one. I did not attempt to meet or talk to or communicate with any other Beatles that night. I was still shell shocked and for all I knew he might have been the nice guy in the group.

The next day the Beatles had gone but of course I had no way of knowing just what they had gone to. Good as I knew they were, I figured they were just another group with maybe a hit or two ahead of them or maybe not. I wish I could say that I knew from the start they were going to be the biggest thing since Fats Domino's Y-fronts but I can't.

I walked into the club that afternoon to find a bunch of the guys listening to some tapes over the PA system. On a shelf in the wings, stage right of the curtains, was a tape recorder, a simple though excellent domestic model used for checking the sound qualities of the in-house equipment and the acoustics of the room.

Adrian Barber, who had deserted the Big Three to become the resident sound engineer, had recorded one of the Beatles' sets the previous evening and he was playing back the fruits of his labour to Ted 'Kingsize' Taylor. The sound coming from the speakers was energetic but primitive and yet in years to come these imprecise and unremarkable reels were to acquire a value out of all proportion to their actual quality.

Nobody at that time could have realised that in time to come even the sound of the Beatles farting would have been a saleable item although Kingsize's shrewd mind told him that the recordings of the Beatles' last ever appearance at the club would be worth acquiring. He eventually did a deal for them and The Hamburg Tapes travelled back to Liverpool with him when he returned home. They were destined to become a genuine, if controversial, historical document in sound. And the controversy was one in which I would eventually figure albeit in a minor way.

I listened for a few minutes and thought nothing of it. When everyone got bored with the tapes Horst Fascher played us an acetate of the Beatles' forthcoming release. An acetate is the shellac-coated metallic demo disc pressed individually to allow a new recording to be played to the musicians, executives, distributors and the like.

It was a vibrant uptempo tune by Lennon and McCartney called *Please Please Me* and it sounded glorious. The first nibblings at success achieved by *Love Me Do*, good as their debut disc was, counted for little against this amazing piece of vinyl. My ears told me that with this one they had propelled themselves into a different league entirely.

The identification mark of the harmonica had been cleverly retained and was more effective this time round if anything. The tune was direct and addictive and the lyrics so simple and effective that they lingered on in my brain long after the disc had stopped spinning. It was pretty obvious that with product like this they were going places. But along with everyone else, with perhaps the exception of Brian Epstein whose belief in his protégés was unshakeable from day one, I just had no idea how far they were going to go.

9

Meet The Searchers

As exciting and stimulating as Hamburg was to most young English musicians I was constantly bored and desperately homesick. One day was no longer than another but they seemed like an eternity especially when it rained, which it did. A lot. For a musician I rose quite early. Usually around ten. The wild ones among our fraternity were unlikely to have been back in their own beds for more than a couple of hours by that time. Many of them would not be in their own beds at all. Goodness knows there were enough beds to sleep in and enough willing bodies to keep you warm and to serve you a hearty breakfast in the morning after an energetic night of copulation.

Compared to some of the other musical ensembles of simmering testosterone more than ready to join the twenty four hour no-holds-barred party that was Hamburg the Rebel Rousers were a tame bunch, more attracted by the possibilities offered by the over consumption of alcohol than any of the many other temptations on tap. With the exception of me, that is, who was still stubbornly resisting the lure of intoxicating liquids. I think it was Brendan Behan who said 'Never trust a man who doesn't drink,' and I'm not sure I entirely disagree with him. God knows I bored for England in those days.

German girls possessed a worldliness far beyond anything experienced in the youthfully immature relationships the lads had left behind in the UK. They fussed over you and took care of your every need. They bought their own drinks and they bought yours as well. There was a liberation in the Fatherland that would have amazed folk back home. And in the area of the bedroom they were the teachers not the pupils. In the England of the early sixties the vast majority of girls simply did not do bedroom stuff and to have it laid out before you like an offering to a god was nirvana. To be a musician around the Grosse Freiheit was for many to live the life of a gigolo. There were oodles of testosterone to be released and so what if there was someone waiting at home and relying on your commitment and your fidelity? Sometimes a young man needs a mistress just to break the monogamy.

I even managed to acquire my own bleach blonde bouffant-haired girlfriend in the form of Monika. She was a dancer and despite her scant knowledge of my language was savvy enough to see the humour in her family name of Pricken. 'I think it sounds a little bit rude in English,' she suggested. When she went on tour with a dance troupe called The Leslie Dancers she would send me postcards of the exciting places she visited. But while she was a nice girl and it was a pleasant diversion I found it a bit claustrophobic. I always liked and needed my own space and didn't want to be anyone's exclusive property.

While many of the musos set up cosy little secret 'homes from homes' with German frauleins who had insinuated themselves into their company with the promise of good sex and, often more importantly, a terrific meal, our lot simply enjoyed the revelry and banter of the post-club gatherings in bars like der Holle which could be found downstairs in the courtyard next door. Here, when the club had closed, you could drink your way into oblivion with your pals without the threat of another show for which you needed to remain sober. Der Holle stayed open until you left or fell over comatose.

If you fell due to the effects of drink it was wise to wait until work had ended. Moss Groves, one of our sax players, misjudged the whole drinking thing on our first trip out and his falling occurred off the front of the stage during one late night session. Not a wise thing to do when your firm is under the control of a strict disciplinarian like Cliff Bennett. The next day, with a king-sized hangover, he was definitely suffering the wrath of grapes and feeling sorry for himself. Not too many words were said but the look of disapproval on Cliff's face said it all. It never happened again.

There was of course the odd bit of straying into even more forbidden territory. One of our members was unfortunate enough to have the pitfalls of indiscreet liaisons brought sharply into focus by a rather disconcerting eruption in the toilet area of his person which, after its refusal to disperse and his need to seek the advice of others, he decided to share with his fellow performers.

The viewing took place in the dressing rooms to the left of the stage early one evening. A group of intrigued pals gathered excitedly in a circle as his trousers were unzipped and lowered for inspection. The deterioration of the condition had obviously gathered pace since he had last dared to peek and when the patient caught sight of the now pulsating mound of multicoloured flesh, slightly reminiscent of a pile of rotting fruit the centrepiece of which was a very unripe and unappetising banana, he fainted.

Horst was called and very soon a car sped off to the krankenhaus where he was incarcerated for the night. With the efficiency of experts very used to treating every hideous sexually transmitted malady that the Reeperbahn could and would throw up, he was back ready for work the next day with his meat and two veg heading slowly but surely towards normal proportions and colour. It was a tough way to learn the lesson 'if you stray you must pay' but indeed his straying days in Hamburg ended once and for all that night. I have no wish to put at risk someone's happy domestic situation simply to satisfy the prurient curiosity of my readers and therefore he shall remain nameless.

Of course if you couldn't find a girlfriend and were desperate for sexual relief there were plenty of efficient and friendly prostitutes plying their honourable trade. But this direction was one trodden mostly by the transient seamen and ne'er-do-wells who passed through the city in search of booze and women before their ship set sail again. The musicians, endowed with a perceived glamour by the simple virtue of their profession, had no need of their services. But for those who did, the easiest way to choose your 'date' was to nip along to the notorious Herbertstrasse.

What would have otherwise been merely an unprepossessing network of cobbled streets that would not normally merit a second glance grabbed one's attention by the solid green metal barriers that hid the buildings from plain sight. They weren't gates. They were heavy iron panels emblazoned with warnings in German that youngsters were forbidden from entering. You simply walked either side of the wide centre panel and into the narrow opening formed by the two smaller side panels to find, hidden behind, a pretty row of picture windowed houses. And what pictures they framed.

Big women. Bigger women. Quite tiny women. More big women. Average-sized women. And positively huge women the size of Panzer tanks. There definitely seemed to be more flesh on these inhabitants than you would have expected to encounter, their Amazonian appearance grotesquely exaggerated by the costumes (you couldn't reasonably call them clothes) of basques and bras and knickers and thigh high boots in a variety of materials from satin and nylon to leather and pvc. Chains, whips and studs were optional. Standards in the flesh trade are odd to say the least because there were grotesque creatures managing to charge considerable amounts of money for their company when in civilian life you'd have a hard time getting the tide to take them out.

To purchase goods from this sexual supermarket you simply made your choice during a leisurely stroll and established a price at the designated aperture and, if agreed by both parties, entered by the adjacent door after which the curtains would be drawn and the fun would begin. Simple, efficient and honest I thought. No objection whatsoever, although I never actually gave them my custom. Too mean? Or too scared? You decide.

The usual routine for me on waking most days was a leisurely stroll over the Reeperbahn and down towards the River Elbe where the British-run Seamen's Mission offered a welcome sanctuary to those of us far from dear old Blighty. There you could get a cheap meal and maybe a discarded newspaper to make you even more homesick than ever. It also served as a money exchange, offering a slightly better rate than you could get from the local bank.

Put off by the distance you could always breakfast on cornflakes at the Mambo Schenke, just a street away from the Grosse Freiheit, where Rosie, the German wife of the Star Club Combo's guitarist Tony Sheridan, worked as a waitress. Or just a few doors along from the club Alphonse und Gretel's small family café could sell you a cheap and spicy frikadelle, a fried hamburger guaranteed to live on in your memory for some time to come as your heart burnt itself to a cinder ramming home the awful truth that your arteries were slowly and inexorably being hardened to the point of complete uselessness. The cut of meat, or indeed the indeterminate animal from which it had been constructed, was never made clear and its food value was questionable. On a good day it was a tasty and inexpensive meal. Quality control was absent. On a bad day it could be saltier than Lot's wife's arse.

One afternoon I wandered into the club to see who was hanging about. A group was rehearsing on the stage. You could usually find one band or another routining new material to keep their act fresh. Three and four hours playing per night used up a hell of a lot of music. Often songs were borrowed from bands you had watched over the previous nights. It wasn't stealing. How could you steal something that had already been stolen itself? It had all been done before and now we were just doing it our own way. The close-knit community of the Star Club was a kind of musical currency exchange.

We had arrived in town playing great R&B tunes like *Stupidity*, *Slow Down* and *If You've Got To Make A Fool Of Somebody* which were soon integrated into the repertoires of other bands who spied on us during our evening sessions. We in turn heard the Big Three, one of the most exciting and competent of the Liverpool combos, playing *Some Other Guy* and *Tricky Dicky* and introduced the tunes to a London crowd on returning home. Little did I know it then but two songs from our current set list were later to figure prominently in the careers of the young men I was about to meet.

Alright caught the ear of Cliff when it was performed on Lonnie Donegan's television show by a black American vocal group called the Grandisons. Lonnie was promoting their career and the tune was their current single. Alas all of Donegan's efforts were to no avail. The single and their career flopped but at least we had acquired a great piece of music which perfectly suited our guitars/saxes and blues-shouting vocals.

Round about the same time we had been presented with a disc brought back from the States by Eddie Normand, the promoter of our local gigs in the West London area. He thought it would be great to do on stage. It was a haunting blues-rock song with a guitar riff that insinuated itself into your brain and a breathy angst-ridden vocal sung by a white girl who knew how to sound black.

Needles and Pins, a flop on the US Liberty Label by Jackie DeShannon, was not what you would call a typical Cliff Bennett & the Rebel Rousers tune but it sure went over big with our regular fans. We had injected droning saxes in harmony to stamp it with our own identification and to give it the gravitas we felt it required to fit into our programme. On reflection it wasn't perhaps the most sympathetic treatment that we could have given the song but it worked for our purposes. Little did we know that we were soon to deliver it to the people who knew exactly how to transform this otherwise unremarkable combination of notes and words into one of the most important hits of the decade, while the aforementioned *Alright* was eventually put to good use by them as a well-respected album track.

The foursome on the stage that afternoon were running through an arrangement of *Walk Right In* which had only just entered the charts by a US act called the Rooftop Singers and they were doing it well. It was a harmony-based song and this was an area in which they were obviously very good. It was yet another Scouse group and in the carefully constructed casualness of their appearance they fitted into the general pattern I had come to expect. I recognised them from the pictures in the bar areas. They were The Searchers.

I caught their set later that evening and liked what I saw and what I heard. They looked good. Young and clean-cut but still with that earthy street kid appeal that seemed to be present to a greater extent in groups from the north of the country than in poncey southerners like us.

Mike, his surname shortened to Pender for the purposes of stage work, was without doubt a handsome young guy with the kind of look that would certainly appeal to women. Strong in appearance and slightly serious with what looked like a chip in his front teeth that, on closer inspection, turned out to be a gold filling and which, like Alma Cogan's beauty spot, was something you either liked or you did not.

John McNally, with a baby face and a hair colour that in a girl might be called strawberry blond, looked about fourteen. I learned to my astonishment that he was already actually a remarkably mature twenty year old. Practically superannuated in my terms of reference. He held his tiny black Hofner guitar high on his chest in the manner that had been adopted by many of the Liverpudlian musicians and looked serious when he sang. I figured this was probably an inbuilt reaction to any resentment felt with regard to his boyish appearance, always a bugbear when you're young but one of life's bonuses when age starts to attack with an unpleasant and unremitting vengeance. Isn't it always the way? No one likes to look young when they're young or old when they're old.

John recalls their journey from Merseyside to Hamburg which, unlike ours, was conducted by ferry. 'We took all our equipment, amps, drums, everything, with us because nobody had thought to tell us that the club was fully equipped and with much better stuff than the crap we had. When we got to Hamburg docks the porters unloaded all our stuff onto the quay. Then they waited for us to tip them, which was something we weren't used to and couldn't afford to anyway so we refused. They called us all the names under the sun then loaded the stuff back onto the hoist and lifted it back onto the ship. We had to go back and take it off ourselves down the gangplank.'

Tony Jackson looked like the tough guy of the gang. He was definitely older by a few years and had an aggressive look about him. Like John he hoisted his instrument, a bass guitar as opposed to a standard six-string, up a few notches from the accepted norm. He seemed to do a fair amount of the singing although, being an ensemble which took the harmony side of things more seriously than most others, the vocals were on the whole spread quite evenly. With the exception of John that is, who joined in on some harmonies and an occasional unison line but whose solo vocals were restricted to a couple of featured numbers during the evening. He seemed to be content chugging out one of the most solid and hypnotic guitar rhythms I had heard in a while. He tended to use the strumming technique normally employed on a banjo but on a standard six- string guitar which is used to being stroked in a much more delicate manner. It was both unusual and extremely effective.

The drummer was altogether harder to figure out. Like Mike, Chris had also abandoned his family name for the more media friendly Curtis. He was without doubt the one in charge as far as their stage presence was concerned. A born communicator, he didn't talk to the people so much as he commanded them, grabbing the crowd and mesmerising it with his gestures, his body language and his instructions from the off and refusing to let them go without receiving the response he demanded. And what he demanded he got. After all they had just gone through a war following orders and were not about to stop now. Old habits die hard.

He looked wild, his extraordinarily long hair falling down thickly way below the collar of the black leather coat he was wearing which, like the others, conformed to the general all black colour scheme of their outfits. And the eyes were nothing less than manic, the insinuated menace within exaggerated by a wide-mouthed grin that indicated either malevolence or exhilaration. It was difficult to tell which. It is little wonder that George Harrison used to refer to him as 'Mad Henry'.

His party piece was the old Ray Charles standard *What'd I Say* and if the vocals were not what you might call controlled they certainly had their effect. The answer and response segment resulted in a mass roar that confirmed without a shadow of a doubt that he had them in his sway. How he kept in time I do not know for he played his kit in a standing position, a not impossible technique but difficult without a doubt and certainly different. I had never seen the like before. In truth he was quite frightening.

When I met them all later I discovered that I was both right and wrong. Tony was indeed the wild party animal of the group, keen to spend his free time in the bars with the other young bucks and the girls, having the craziest and best time of his life while it was there to be had. And why not? There were many times in years to come when I wished I had cut loose a bit earlier and fully enjoyed the privileges and perks of being young.

Mike and John, it turned out, were quiet living and missing their girlfriends to whom they sent frequent and very long letters penned in the dim light of the Spartan quarters of the Grosse Freiheit flats. They were both very personable and friendly. I liked them immediately.

Chris was a different kettle of fish entirely. The wide-eyed aggression I had perceived from his on-stage persona was a complete red herring. He was in fact a gregarious and fun-filled figure whose zany, off-the-wall sense of humour was different from anything I had encountered before. His gestures were large and demonstrative. His turn of phrase theatrical and astonishingly sophisticated. He was a renaissance man in the costume of a thug. It was androgyny before most of us knew what the word meant. Chris was a lot of fun.

His rapid wit would dart off into unexpected lateral directions when you least expected it. We all decided to treat ourselves one night at the local Chinese restaurant, a rare extravagance in those penny-pinching times. The place was called the Chug Ooh which Chris inventively translated as 'The House Of The Little Train That Hurt'. That was the way his mind worked. I enjoyed the company of my new friends and the days passed more quickly, but communicating with other musicians was not always so easy.

John Kay, the guitarist with Bill Haley's Comets at the time, certainly remembers the guy he always thought of as 'Crazy Chris'.

'Yes, I remember that he liked to play practical jokes on other bands, like unplugging amplifiers just as a band would go on stage. And there was another time when he and the Searchers threw me in a fountain apparently because they liked me. Chris would point out the female groupies that he said not to have sex with, because they had VD. I really don't know if it was the truth or not. But I stayed away from them just in case. He also told our bass player, Al Rappa, that a transvestite was a woman and he should go after her. I don't believe Al did though.'

John Kay adds 'Chris always was telling jokes and really liked to laugh a lot. I remember liking to watch him perform on stage. He had a lot of energy in his drumming and vocals. I really liked to hear him sing. He had a kind of a primitive yet polished sound to his voice. He told me that the music scene in the US at that time was playing watered-down R&B and rock & roll crap and that all of the 1950s musical energy was gone. England was just "giving us our own music back in a more pure, raw form that was missing in the US." I agreed. And we all know what followed. British rock & roll and R&B became the hottest music Stateside.

'He liked the Comets because we played pure rock & roll and we kept the 50s feeling alive. That made me feel really good. He loved American Blues & Rock artistes. The Searchers made a definite impression on me too. I am not the kind of person who remembers every little detail of the past but I remember "Crazy Chris"'.' Kay's recollections more or less matched my own.

The Undertakers, who I also liked a lot, were a band like no band I had seen before. Like all the other Merseysiders they were garbed in the mandatory black and played a raunchy style of music that was accompanied by an equally raunchy stage presence. Most of their set consisted of frantically paced rhythm and blues numbers that were not surprisingly loud and compelling.

But the most unusual aspect of the Undertakers' performance was that as they sang they stamped their Cuban heeled boots hard into the wooden stage with a relentless pounding and a most impressive synchronisation that made the front line look like the Tiller Girls on acid. It was truly an awesome sight and one I had never witnessed before. As I watched from the side of the auditorium with Moss Groves we both found ourselves laughing at this spectacle which was, to put it mildly, different. Our amusement was by no means malicious. We both found it quite impressive and anything that grabbed one's attentions I felt was definitely an asset in rock & roll terms.

When it came to the Rebel Rousers' time to take the stage I trundled to the amplifier set behind the closed curtains where Jackie Lomax, the Undertakers' wiry framed bass man, was unplugging his lead. He fixed me with the kind of look you see on a rottweiller just before it is about to clamp its teeth into your leg.

'If I see you taking the piss out of us again I'm going to smash your fuckin' face in.'

There is something about a threat in a Scouse accent that imbues it with an extra dimension of malevolence and makes you take it just that little bit more seriously. The sudden intake of fear had my arse twitching like a rat's nose in a cheese factory. For a brief second I considered explaining his misreading of the situation but plainly here was a man not open to discussion, not at this moment in time anyway.

Had I been a person used to a life of conflict and fisticuffs I would have called his bluff and invited him outside to sort out our differences in the time-honoured fashion. But being the lily-livered wimp I was, I did the sensible thing and offered a grovelling apology. I always think a good grovel is far more preferential to having your face smashed in. Disfigured features when you're in showbusiness is not a good look.

As time went on wounds healed and Jackie and I got on fine. All of the Undertakers were nice guys and together they were a terrific band. As were almost all of the Liverpudlian groups. Kingsize Taylor & the Dominoes, the Strangers, the Big Three, the Searchers, and of course the Beatles. The city seemed to be overrun with raw but exciting musical talent. Unlike their southern compatriots who had mostly adopted the echo embellished crystal clear guitar sounds pioneered by Hank Marvin and his acolytes, these guys eschewed effects and substituted them with guts and passion.

If I had to pick a favourite it would have to be the Big Three. Initially consisting of Johnny Gustafson on bass, Johnny Hutchison on drums and Adrian Barber on guitar, later to be replaced by Brian Griffiths when Barber decided to make his home in Hamburg, they made a trio sound like there were half a dozen people up there on stage and their choice of material was to our taste exactly. But there were few on the stage of the Star Club who didn't match up to the exacting standards expected.

Mike, John and Chris were like-minded people whose company I enjoyed. I hardly ever saw Tony. He was always missing, presumed having a good time. The rest of us would hang out together substituting the temptations of booze or pills for the delights of good conversation and some innocent laughs. Mike and John had serious girlfriends at home to whom they were committed. Their sojourn in the seedy depths of Hamburg allowed them to enjoy their music and amass the wherewithal to return home and marry in unions that, true to their Catholic religion, would be for life.

Someone once said that anyone who doesn't live life on the edge is taking up too much room. We must have been occupying acres of space in a lifestyle that would have made Mother Theresa look like the all time party girl. I must impress upon you that at this time and in fact for a couple of decades yet to come I was an absolute teetotaller. Alcohol did not pass those virgin lips.

If drink wasn't enough for some people to keep the rush of energy flowing through their veins then there were the tiny pills called Preludin to aid and abet their search for enough stamina to get them through the night. Sold as a dietary aid, they were amphetamines which would kill your appetite and embody you with the power and desire to rave on until your body caved in to the exhaustion built up over hours of partying. The sum total of two Preludin tablets were, and have remained, the entire illicit drug intake throughout my less than wild days as a pop star.

A few evenings into our stay I succumbed to what was known as 'the Hamburg throat', an infection which made it painful to sing, almost impossible to swallow and even harder to sleep at night. I was desperate and I sought out Tony Sheridan as my saviour. Tony was known to be a free flying character who had tried just about anything and everything and who, like most people in the club, had employed the effective pick-u-ups when necessary. I explained my predicament and he handed me two tablets. I took them both and waited. Nothing seemed to happen. I waited and I waited and as I wondered when they were going to kick in I realised that they already had. I felt fine. More than fine. I was soaring. The throat was smooth and open and my spirits were high.

I got through the show with no problems whatsoever and, still on a roll, I spent the rest of the night telling anyone who would listen how wonderful these amazing little pills were. But then I discovered the other side of the coin. When the highs wore off the lows took over. I went into a deep depression that worried the hell out of me. The next day I got to a doctor and had my malady treated in the proper manner with antibiotics. And my illicit drug taking ceased from that moment on. I never took another amphetamine. Coke remained something that I drank out of a bottle not shoved up my nose. And I never experienced the attractions of that most innocent of drugs of choice, pot. It neither makes me proud nor ashamed to state that I am drug free. That's just how it is.

Apart from the fact that we were making an extraordinary amount of money in comparison to what we were used to back home, we were also afforded the immense privilege of being in the company of and working on the same stage as our rock & roll heroes. The very people who had inspired us to jump on this precarious and rickety old bandwagon to which we had hitched ourselves.

Apart from those already mentioned there were others who would eventually grace and enhance our time there. The Everly Brothers, two young guys with the sweetest harmonies this side of anywhere and more good looks than one is legally allowed to possess. Joey Dee & the Starliters who surprised us all, as we were expecting a vapid dose of light pop with a twist of banal choreography and instead got a an act full of white soul with a dynamic and charismatic front man who knew how to wrench every amount of emotion out of songs that previously we thought could only be justly delivered by someone with a darker shade of skin

Bo Diddley was an R&B legend and his insistently repetitive 'shave and a haircut - ten bob' rhythm had secured an important position in the development of rock and blues but for me, who was recruited to sit in on bass for his Star Club performances, bashing out one beat on one chord for half an hour was not the most satisfying experience of my life. Still, it was a powerful sound, he was an originator and a legend and the crowd loved him. If the style was not my cup of tea I still consider it a privilege to have been on stage with him. Bo was a really nice guy with a friendly attitude, a warm smile and a stage outfit made from curtain fabric both for cost effectiveness and effect. Both of which results he achieved.

Gene Vincent, my old rockabilly hero whose amazing recording of *Be Bop A Lula* was the second disc I ever bought (*Heartbreak Hotel* of course was the first) turned out to be as mad as a box of frogs. He might have been a dynamic performer but I've seen more brains in a head of lettuce. He was obsessed with crippling karate grips and always carried guns and knives. He was best avoided at all costs.

I was sorely jealous of my chums the Searchers who had managed to be in residence when two real heavyweights visited - Fats Domino and Ray Charles. They don't come much bigger, better or more important in the annals of popular youth music.

What locals we met were almost without exception friendly and welcoming. The bar girls at the Star Club were our confidantes and friends. Rosie, Goldie, Astrid, Bettina and the rest were there to give us comfort and encouragement and to dispense advice should we need it. Bettina was the matriarch of the bunch, big, blonde and buxom with a body you could hire out as a bouncy castle, a heart as big as Germany and a cleavage like a sumo wrestler's bum. John Lennon would trade banter with her from the stage and dedicate her requests for her favourite songs. 'Ein wunsche fur Betty' Lennon would yell as they launched into *Dizzy Miss Lizzie.*

Musicians working at the Star Club existed under a code of protection. They were greeted warmly in the clubs and bars and their special status prevented them from being ripped off which was considered mandatory treatment of the average drunken punter. Abuse of privilege however was not to be recommended. Even the local gangsters were morally bound to obey the unwritten rules. Freddie Fascher, Horst's younger brother, was beaten up in the wings of the club one evening while we were on stage pounding out our set. His transgression was allegedly an unwise dalliance with the girlfriend of a Hamburg hood while the man was languishing in jail. After his punishment Freddie was unceremoniously marched out of the club in full view of the audience. Justice must not only be done, it must be seen to be done.

The young lady in question, I was told later by Cliff Bennett, was also reprimanded for her part in the tryst and, like Freddie, was forced to leave her place of abode in an extremely undignified manner, via the window. Had the window been a ground floor one it would not have been too bad but alas it was on the third floor. I don't believe she ever transgressed again.

Astrid Kirchherr was a talented young art student and photographer who had become involved with the Beatles from their first trip to Hamburg, and in particular their bass player Stuart Sutcliffe to whom she had quickly become engaged. When the not yet fab four returned home Stuart had stayed on to live with Astrid and carry on with his art studies at a Hamburg college, but sadly a brain haemorrhage was to kill him within months.

Astrid was a beautiful girl who, though almost all the published pictures show her with a close cut gamine style of haircut, at that time wore her blond locks shoulder length in a look reminiscent of the French singer Francoise Hardy. Her striking half-lit photographs of the young Beatles, slavishly copied by someone else for their EMI

1. Jack Jackson, the grandaddy of British deejays (Alan Bailey)

2. Me as Wishee Washee in the William Byrd school panto. Back row, fourth from left

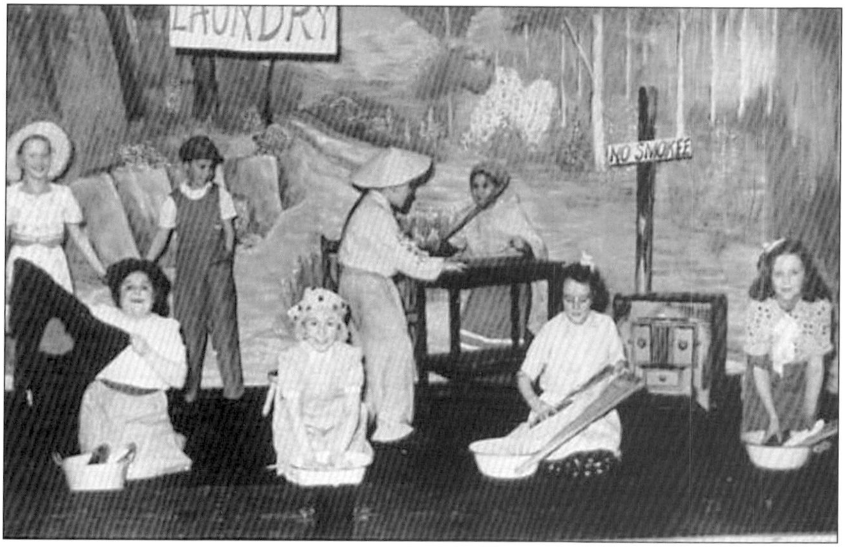

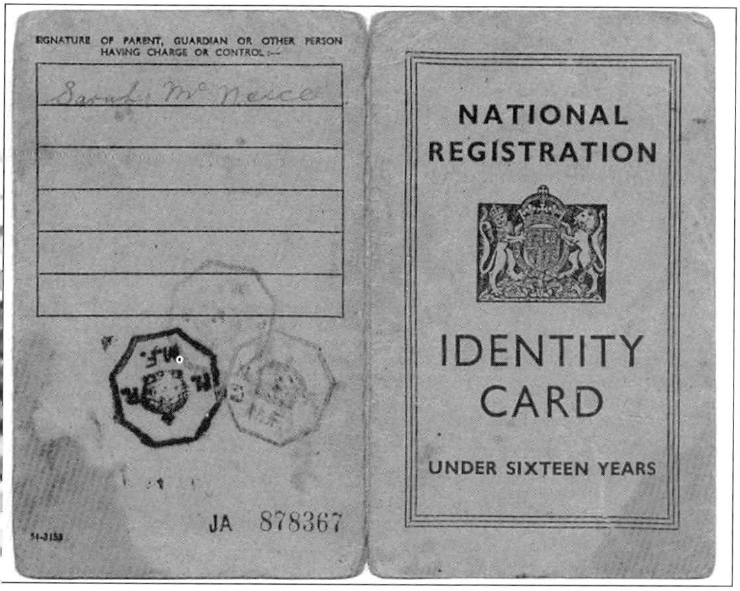

SIGNATURE OF PARENT, GUARDIAN OR OTHER PERSON HAVING CHARGE OR CONTROL:—

JA 878367

NATIONAL REGISTRATION

IDENTITY CARD

UNDER SIXTEEN YEARS

3. My wartime identity card

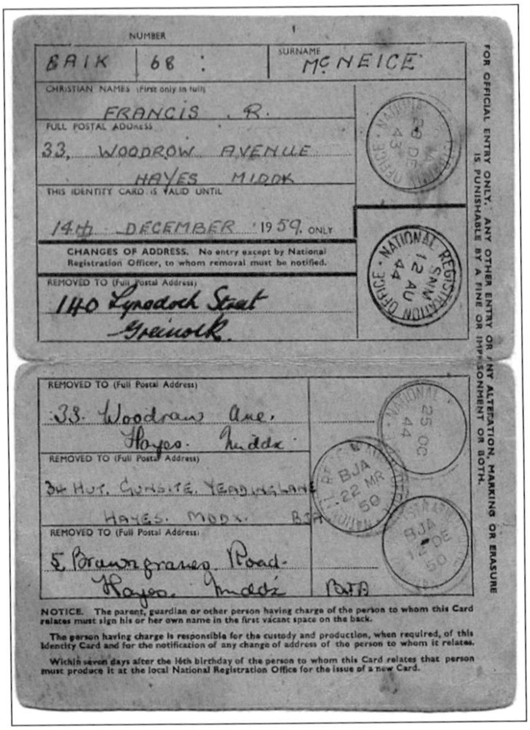

NUMBER | SURNAME

BAIK 68 : | McNEICE

CHRISTIAN NAMES (First only in full)

FRANCIS R.

FULL POSTAL ADDRESS

33, WOODROW AVENUE

HAYES MIDDX

THIS IDENTITY CARD IS VALID UNTIL

14th DECEMBER 1959. ONLY

CHANGES OF ADDRESS. No entry except by National Registration Officer, to whom removal must be notified.

REMOVED TO (Full Postal Address)

140 Lynedoch Street

Greenock

FOR OFFICIAL ENTRY ONLY. ANY OTHER ENTRY OR ANY ALTERATION, MARKING OR ERASURE IS PUNISHABLE BY A FINE OR IMPRISONMENT OR BOTH.

REMOVED TO (Full Postal Address)

33 Woodrow Ave.

Hayes. Middx

REMOVED TO (Full Postal Address)

34 HUT. GUNSITE. YEADING LANE

HAYES. MIDDX. BJA

REMOVED TO (Full Postal Address)

5 Braungraves Road

Hayes. Middx BJA

NOTICE. The parent, guardian or other person having charge of the person to whom this Card relates must sign his or her own name in the first vacant space on the back.

The person having charge is responsible for the custody and production, when required, of this Identity Card and for the notification of any change of address of the person to whom it relates.

Within seven days after the 16th birthday of the person to whom this Card relates that person must produce it at the local National Registration Office for the issue of a new Card.

4. Inside, with the address of our Nissen hut home, Hut 34, the Gunsite, Yeading Lane

5. Mum, Dad and me at the seaside in the 50s

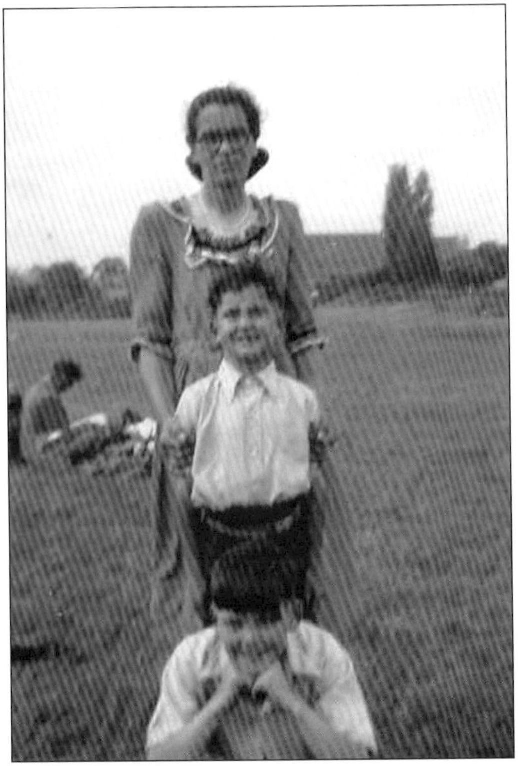

6. Mum, me and brother Jackie

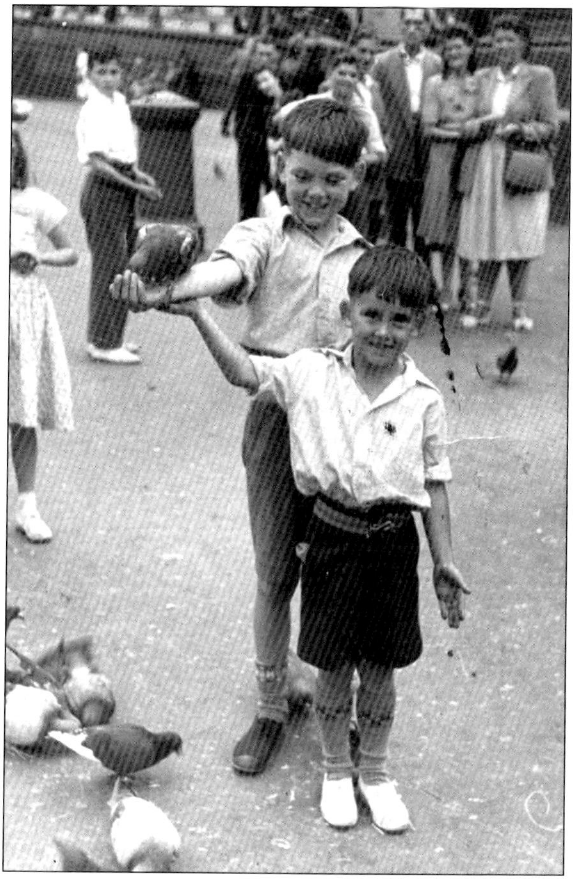

7. Jackie and me feeding the pigeons in Trafalgar Square

8. My GCE certificate for English Language, French and Woodwork – useless!!!

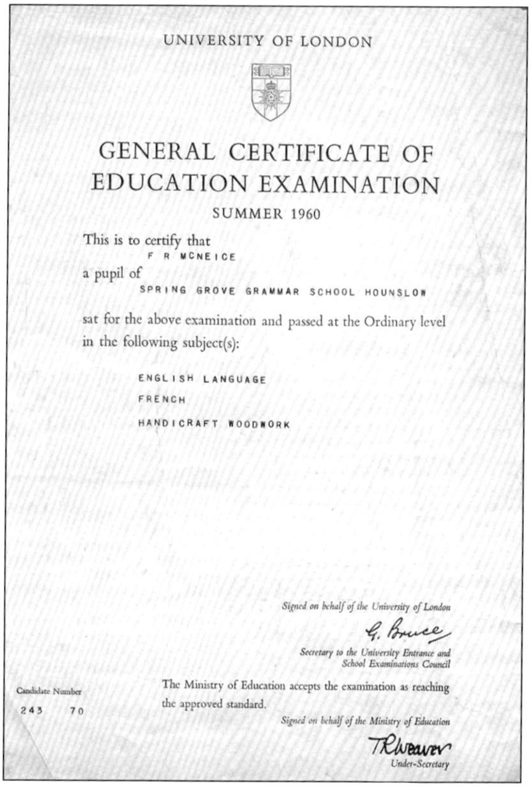

UNIVERSITY OF LONDON

GENERAL CERTIFICATE OF EDUCATION EXAMINATION

SUMMER 1960

This is to certify that

F R MCNEICE

a pupil of

SPRING GROVE GRAMMAR SCHOOL HOUNSLOW

sat for the above examination and passed at the Ordinary level in the following subject(s):

ENGLISH LANGUAGE

FRENCH

HANDICRAFT WOODWORK

Signed on behalf of the University of London

Secretary to the University Entrance and School Examinations Council

Candidate Number

243 70

The Ministry of Education accepts the examination as reaching the approved standard.

Signed on behalf of the Ministry of Education

Under-Secretary

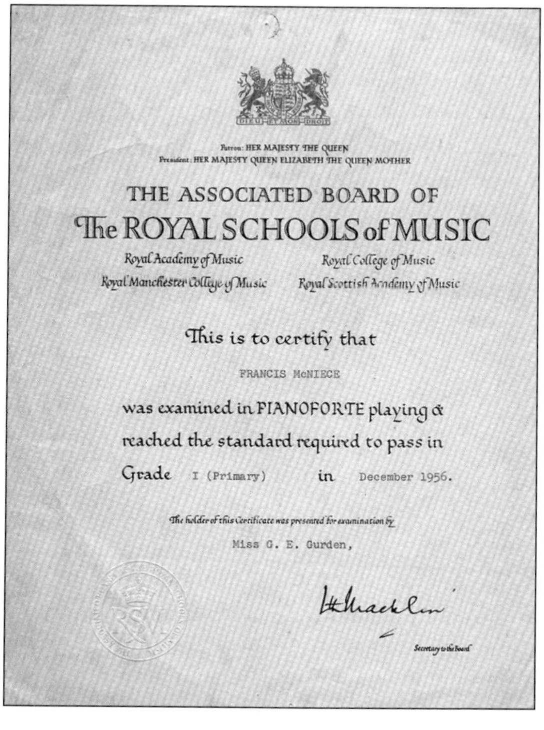

Patron: HER MAJESTY THE QUEEN

President: HER MAJESTY QUEEN ELIZABETH THE QUEEN MOTHER

THE ASSOCIATED BOARD OF

The ROYAL SCHOOLS of MUSIC

Royal Academy of Music — Royal College of Music

Royal Manchester College of Music — Royal Scottish Academy of Music

This is to certify that

FRANCIS McNIECE

was examined in PIANOFORTE playing & reached the standard required to pass in Grade I (Primary) in December 1956.

The holder of this Certificate was presented for examination by

Miss G. E. Gurden,

Secretary to the Board

9. Grade One piano is as far as I got

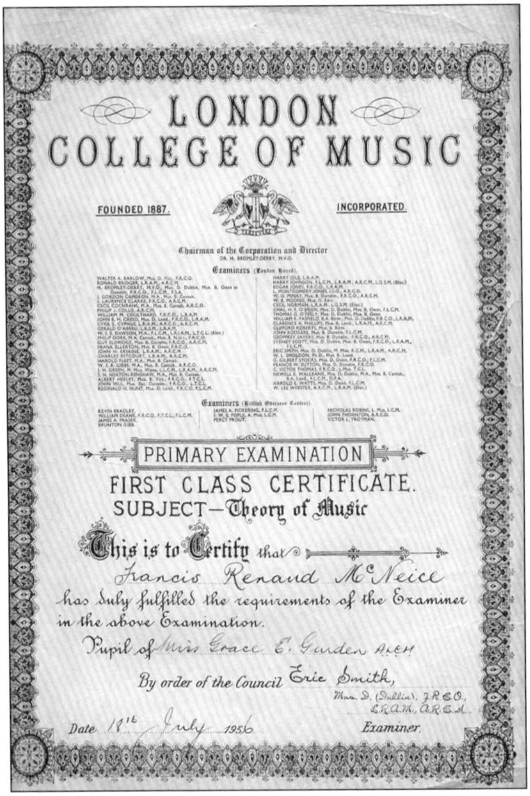

LONDON
COLLEGE OF MUSIC

FOUNDED 1887. INCORPORATED.

Chairman of the Corporation and Director

PRIMARY EXAMINATION

FIRST CLASS CERTIFICATE.

SUBJECT—Theory of Music

This is to Certify that Francis Renaud McNeice has duly fulfilled the requirements of the Examiner in the above Examination.

Pupil of Miss Grace E. Gurden A.R.C.M.

By order of the Council Eric Smith, Mus. D. (Dublin), F.R.C.O., L.R.A.M., A.R.C.M.

Date 18th July 1956 Examiner.

10. The same goes for my music theory

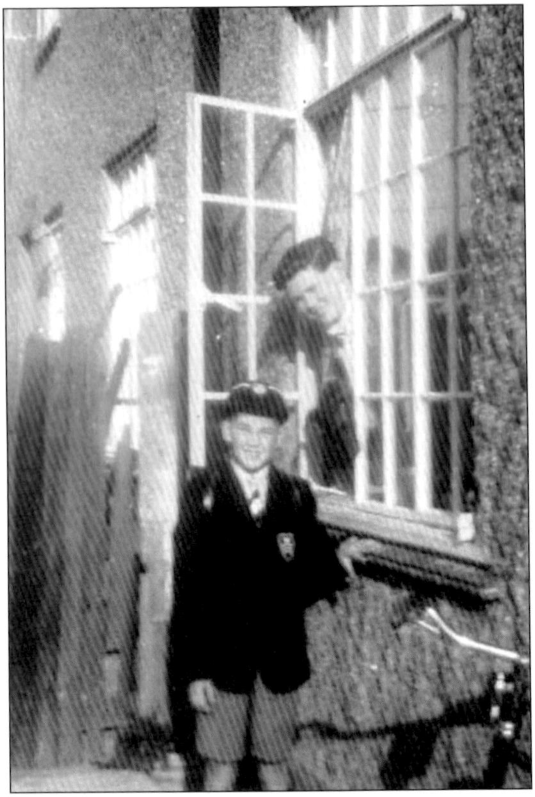

11. Off to my first day at Spring Grove Grammar School with Jackie at the window

12. The Ambassadors skiffle group. Tom Hanlon, Derek (surname forgotten), Jonathan 'Taffy' Evans, John Botterill, me.

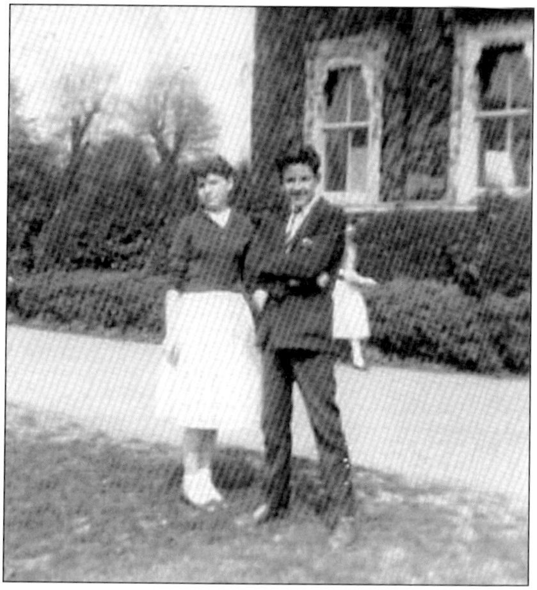

13. In front of Spring Grove Grammar School with Lyn Coleman who shared her sugar caramels with me

14. The Skyways at the Clay Pigeon, Eastcote, Sept 28th 1959. l-r Mick Burt, me, Brian St George, John Marin

15. The Skyways at Wilton Hall Bletchley c.1960 l-r Clive Smith, me, John Carroll, John Marin, Mick Barker

16. Cliff Bennett and the Rebel Rousers, Gaumont State, Kilburn 1961. l-r Sid Phillips, Ben Jordan, Cliff Bennett, Ricky Winter, Mick Borer, me. (Steve Terry)

17. Joe Meek

18. The Rebel Rousers on tour in Scotland 1961.

19. The new Rebel Rousers line-up 1962. l-r me, Moss Groves, (a friend Derek Potter), Cliff Bennett, Nicky Hopkins, Bernie Watson, Mick Burt.

20. Mr 'Hey Baby' Bruce Chanel, Bernie Watson, Delbert McClinton

21. The Searchers 'red sweater line-up'. l-r Joe Kennedy, Tony 'Joe' West, John McNally, Mike Pender, Johnny Sandon.(John McNally collection)

22. Johnny Sandon and the Searchers c.1961 l-r John McNally, Mike Pender, Johnny Sandon, Chris Curtis, Tony Jackson (John McNally collection)

23. The Searchers 1962. back row l-r Mike Pender, Chris Curtis, Tony Jackson. front John McNally (John McNally collection)

24. Iron Door membership card (Margo Newman collection)

25. Iron Door membership - inside (Margo Newman collection)

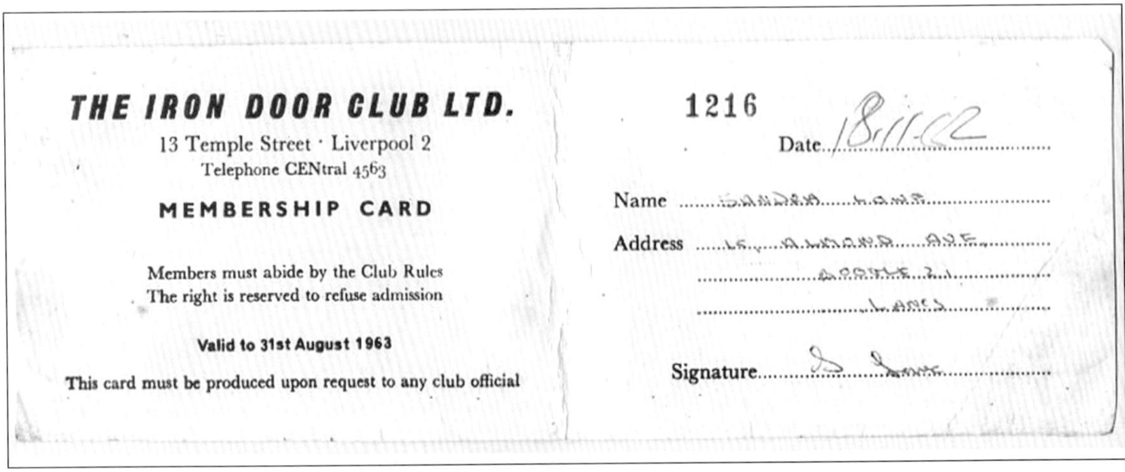

THE IRON DOOR CLUB LTD.

13 Temple Street · Liverpool 2
Telephone CENtral 4563

MEMBERSHIP CARD

Members must abide by the Club Rules
The right is reserved to refuse admission

Valid to 31st August 1963

This card must be produced upon request to any club official

1216

Date ....

Name ....

Address ....

Signature ....

26. A historic Beatles & Rebel Rousers gig at Stroud that no one remembers

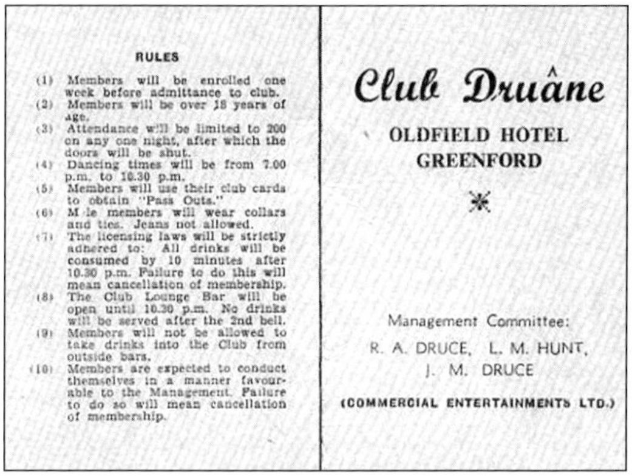

RULES

(1) Members will be enrolled one week before admittance to club.
(2) Members will be over 18 years of age.
(3) Attendance will be limited to 200 on any one night, after which the doors will be shut.
(4) Dancing times will be from 7.00 p.m. to 10.30 p.m.
(5) Members will use their club cards to obtain "Pass Outs."
(6) M le members will wear collars and ties. Jeans not allowed.
(7) The licensing laws will be strictly adhered to: All drinks will be consumed by 10 minutes after 10.30 p.m. Failure to do this will mean cancellation of membership.
(8) The Club Lounge Bar will be open until 10.30 p.m. No drinks will be served after the 2nd bell.
(9) Members will not be allowed to take drinks into the Club from outside bars.
(10) Members are expected to conduct themselves in a manner favourable to the Management. Failure to do so will mean cancellation of membership.

Club Druâne
OLDFIELD HOTEL
GREENFORD

Management Committee:
R. A. DRUCE, L. M. HUNT,
J. M. DRUCE

(COMMERCIAL ENTERTAINMENTS LTD.)

27. The Oldfield Hotel, Greenford membership card where I used to watch the Detours before they became The Who

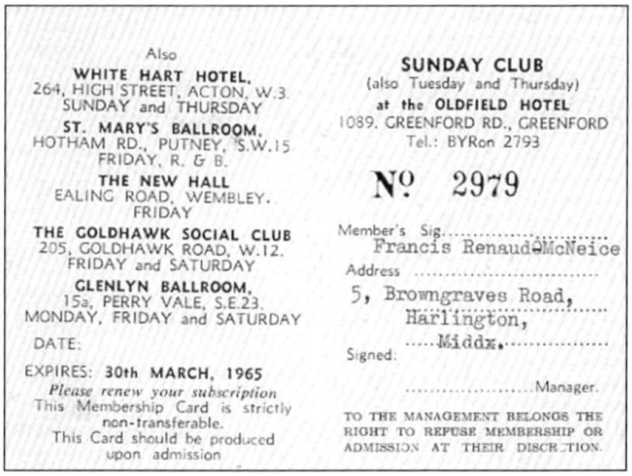

Also
WHITE HART HOTEL,
264, HIGH STREET, ACTON, W.3.
SUNDAY and THURSDAY
ST. MARY'S BALLROOM,
HOTHAM RD., PUTNEY, S.W.15
FRIDAY, R. & B.
THE NEW HALL
EALING ROAD, WEMBLEY.
FRIDAY
THE GOLDHAWK SOCIAL CLUB
205, GOLDHAWK ROAD, W.12.
FRIDAY and SATURDAY
GLENLYN BALLROOM,
15a, PERRY VALE, S.E.23.
MONDAY, FRIDAY and SATURDAY
DATE:
EXPIRES: 30th MARCH, 1965
Please renew your subscription
This Membership Card is strictly non-transferable.
This Card should be produced upon admission

SUNDAY CLUB
(also Tuesday and Thursday)
at the OLDFIELD HOTEL
1089, GREENFORD RD., GREENFORD
Tel.: BYRon 2793

Nº 2979

Member's Sig. Francis Renaud McNeice
Address 5, Browngraves Road,
Harlington,
Middx.
Signed:
.... Manager.

TO THE MANAGEMENT BELONGS THE RIGHT TO REFUSE MEMBERSHIP OR ADMISSION AT THEIR DISCRETION.

28. The Oldfield Hotel membership - inside. Note my real name in full.

29. Cliff Bennett Star Club publicity card (Peter Scotti collection)

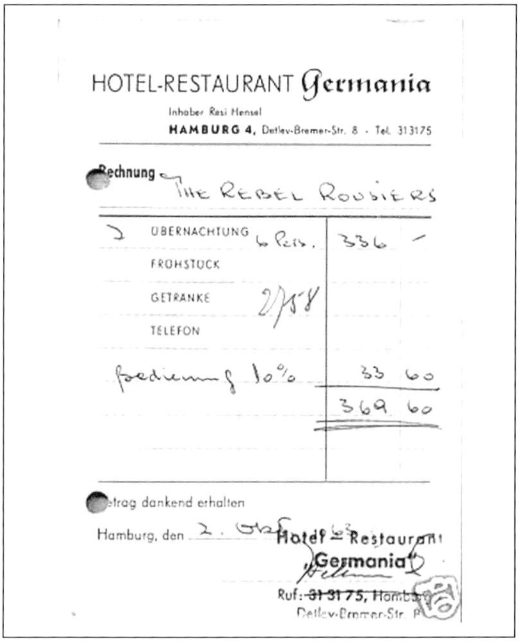

30. Hotel Germania invoice for the Rebel Rousers (Peter Scotti collection)

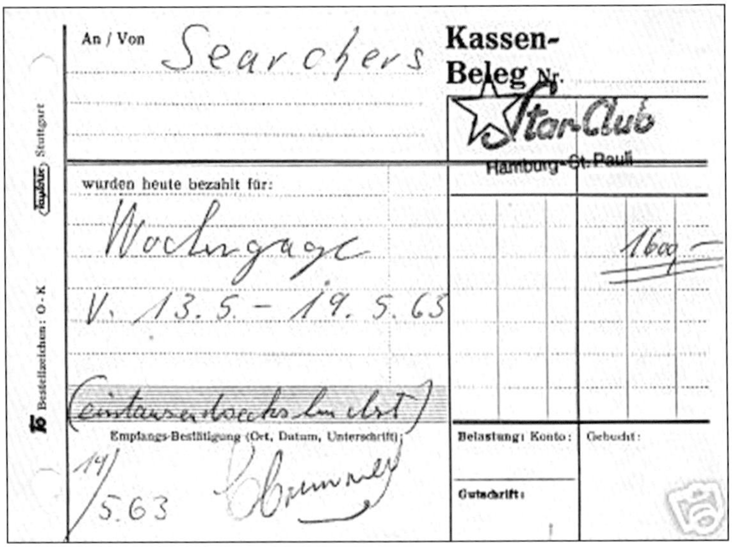

An / Von Searchers

Kassen-Beleg Nr.

Star-Club Hamburg-St. Pauli

wurden heute bezahlt für:

Wochengage	1600.–
v. 13.5. – 19.5.63	

(eintausendsechshundert)

Empfangs-Bestätigung (Ort, Datum, Unterschrift):

14/5.63 Crummey

Belastung: Konto: | Gebucht:

Gutschrift:

Bestellzeichen: O-X | Stuttgart

31. Receipt for Searchers' wages signed for by Chris Crummey (Peter Scotti collection)

Star-Club

Treffpunkt der Weltelite

HAMBURG

Getränkeauswahl

Drinks Grand choix de boissons Stor sortering i drycker

Flasche Bier	0,33 l	1,80	Eierlikör	2 cl	1,50
Glas Wein		1,80	Curacao	2 cl	1,50
Steinhäger	2 cl	1,50	Cherry Brandy	2 cl	1,50
Doornkaat	2 cl	1,50	Pfefferminzlikör	2 cl	1,50
Aquavit	2 cl	1,50	Cacao mit Nuß	2 cl	1,50
Gin	2 cl	1,50	Apricot Brandy	2 cl	1,50
Jamaica-Rumverschnitt	2 cl	1,50	Triple Sec	2 cl	1,50
Reiner Weinbrand	2 cl	1,50	Cassis-Likör	2 cl	1,50
Flensburger Dokator	2 cl	1,50	Cordial-Medoc	2 cl	1,50
Underberg	2 cl	1,50	Mampen-Kaffee	2 cl	1,50
Wodka	2 cl	1,50	Bärenfang	2 cl	1,50
Whisky nach Wahl	2 cl	2,50	Jägermeister	2 cl	1,50
Orig. Franz. Cognac	2 cl	2,50	Mampe Halb und Halb	2 cl	1,50
Orig. Pernod Fils	2 cl	2,50	Cointreau, orig. franz.	2 cl	2,50
			Chartreuse, orig. franz.	2 cl	2,50

dazu Soda DM 0,50

Coca-Cola	1,35	Zitronenlimonade	1,35
Fanta	1,35	Anjola, Ananas-Getränk	1,80

Preise zuzüglich 10 % Personalzuschlag.
Extra charge for staff 10 %.
Supplement pour personnel 10 %.
Till priserna räknas 10 % Personalavgift.

Flaschenware umseitig. For bottled beverages see reverse side.
Tarif des boissons en bouteilles au verso. Drycker i flaskor se omstaende sida.

32. Star Club drinks price list (Peter Scotti collection)

33. With my German fraulein Monika Pricken

34. Johnny Gustafson (the Big Three), Monika Pricken, Brian Johnson (the Strangers) on the Reeperbahn

35. Promo for the Searchers' live recording at the Star Club (Peter Scotti collection)

36. Backing Bo Diddley at the Star Club

37. Cliff Bennett and me on stage at the Star Club

38. Cliff Bennett and me in the famous Abbey Road, Studio 2.

39. Sid Phillips & Moss Groves, the Rebel Rousers' sax section

40. I'd kill to look this good again. Taken by Beatles photographer Astrid Kirchherr (Astrid Kirchherr, K&K, Redferns)

LONDON TO MARGATE AND BACK

BEAT BOAT

SUNDAY, 18th AUGUST Leaves 9.30 a.m. Returns 9.15 p.m.

Aboard m.v. ROYAL SOVEREIGN from Tower Pier with

GERRY AND THE PACEMAKERS

FREDDIE AND THE DREAMERS

BILLY J. KRAMER AND THE DAKOTAS

THE HOLLIES

ORIGINAL CHECKMATES

SOUNDS OF THE ECHOS

SCREAMING LORD SUTCH

CLIFF BENNETT'S REBEL ROUSERS

CYRIL DAVIES RHYTHM & BLUES ALL STARS

BARRY JAMES SHOW ● THE FEDERALS

ROBB STORME & THE WHISPERS

CHRIS FARLOW & THE THUNDERBIRDS

FRANK KELLY & THE HUNTERS

TICKETS £2/10/0 each (You can pay by instalments)

Details from: MODERN MUSICAL EXCURSIONS

22 NEWMAN STREET, LONDON, W.1 (S.A.E. please) (LAN 0184)

ALSO FROM KEITH PROWSE AGENCIES.

41. London-Margate beat boat advert

42. Cliff Bennett and the Rebel Rousers on the London-Margate beat boat 18th August 1963

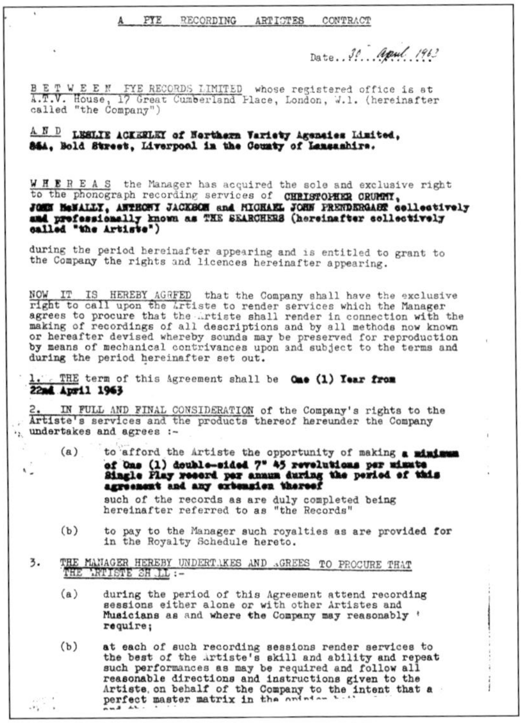

A PYE RECORDING ARTICTES CONTRACT

Date..30 April 1963

BETWEEN PYE RECORDS LIMITED whose registered office is at A.T.V. House, 17 Great Cumberland Place, London, W.1. (hereinafter called "the Company")

AND **LESLIE ACKERLEY of Northern Variety Agencies Limited, 86A, Bold Street, Liverpool in the County of Lancashire.**

WHEREAS the Manager has acquired the sole and exclusive right to the phonograph recording services of **CHRISTOPHER CRUMMY, JOHN McNALLY, ANTHONY JACKSON and MICHAEL JOHN PRENDERGAST collectively and professionally known as THE SEARCHERS (hereinafter collectively called "the Artiste")**

during the period hereinafter appearing and is entitled to grant to the Company the rights and licences hereinafter appearing.

NOW IT IS HEREBY AGREED that the Company shall have the exclusive right to call upon the Artiste to render services which the Manager agrees to procure that the Artiste shall render in connection with the making of recordings of all descriptions and by all methods now known or hereafter devised whereby sounds may be preserved for reproduction by means of mechanical contrivances upon and subject to the terms and during the period hereinafter set out.

1. THE term of this Agreement shall be **One (1) Year from 22nd April 1963**

2. IN FULL AND FINAL CONSIDERATION of the Company's rights to the Artiste's services and the products thereof hereunder the Company undertakes and agrees :-

(a) to afford the Artiste the opportunity of making **a minimum of One (1) double-sided 7" 45 revolutions per minute Single Play record per annum during the period of this agreement and any extension thereof** such of the records as are duly completed being hereinafter referred to as "the Records"

(b) to pay to the Manager such royalties as are provided for in the Royalty Schedule hereto.

3. THE MANAGER HEREBY UNDERTAKES AND AGREES TO PROCURE THAT THE ARTISTE SHALL :-

(a) during the period of this Agreement attend recording sessions either alone or with other Artistes and Musicians as and where the Company may reasonably require;

(b) at each of such recording sessions render services to the best of the Artiste's skill and ability and repeat such performances as may be required and follow all reasonable directions and instructions given to the Artiste, on behalf of the Company to the intent that a perfect master matrix in the opinion ...

43. The Searchers' original Pye contract

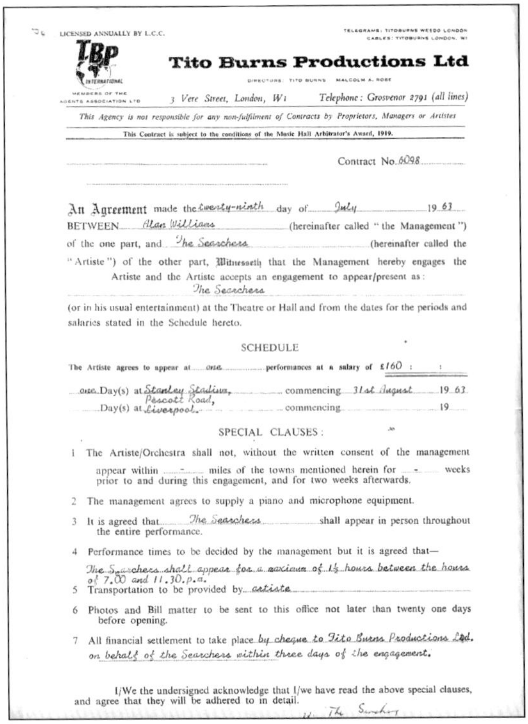

LICENSED ANNUALLY BY L.C.C.

TELEGRAMS: TITOBURNS WESDO LONDON
CABLES: TITOBURNS LONDON, W1

TBP INTERNATIONAL

MEMBERS OF THE AGENTS ASSOCIATION LTD

Tito Burns Productions Ltd

DIRECTORS: TITO BURNS MALCOLM A. ROSE

3 Vere Street, London, W1 Telephone: Grosvenor 2791 (all lines)

This Agency is not responsible for any non-fulfilment of Contracts by Proprietors, Managers or Artistes

This Contract is subject to the conditions of the Music Hall Arbitrator's Award, 1919.

Contract No. 6098

An Agreement made the twenty-ninth day of July 1963 BETWEEN Alan Williams (hereinafter called "the Management") of the one part, and The Searchers (hereinafter called the "Artiste") of the other part, Witnesseth that the Management hereby engages the Artiste and the Artiste accepts an engagement to appear/present as: The Searchers

(or in his usual entertainment) at the Theatre or Hall and from the dates for the periods and salaries stated in the Schedule hereto.

SCHEDULE

The Artiste agrees to appear at one performances at a salary of £160 : :

one Day(s) at Stanley Stadium, Prescott Road, commencing 31st August 1963

Day(s) at Liverpool. commencing 19

SPECIAL CLAUSES:

1 The Artiste/Orchestra shall not, without the written consent of the management appear within - miles of the towns mentioned herein for - weeks prior to and during this engagement, and for two weeks afterwards.

2 The management agrees to supply a piano and microphone equipment.

3 It is agreed that The Searchers shall appear in person throughout the entire performance.

4 Performance times to be decided by the management but it is agreed that— The Searchers shall appear for a maximum of 1½ hours between the hours of 7.00 and 11.30.p.m.

5 Transportation to be provided by artiste

6 Photos and Bill matter to be sent to this office not later than twenty one days before opening.

7 All financial settlement to take place by cheque to Tito Burns Productions Ltd. on behalf of the Searchers within three days of the engagement.

I/We the undersigned acknowledge that I/we have read the above special clauses, and agree that they will be adhered to in detail.

44. Contract for the Searchers at the Stanley Stadium, Liverpool, 31st August 1963

45. Tony Hatch hard at work (Tony Hatch collection)

46. Flyer for the Helen Shapiro/Bobby Vee/Bobby Rydell tour, Stockton 13th Dec 1963

47. Up on the roof at 38 Pont Street, 1963 (Roy Clough collection)

48. Ecstatic in their Knightsbridge apartment (Roy Clough collection)

49. Smiles of success (Roy Clough collection)

50. The Rebel Rousers at the Cavern Dec 10th 1963 l-r me, Cliff Bennett, Sid Phillips, Dave Wendells, (hidden) Roy Young, Mick Burt, Moss Groves

51. John McNally with his iconic Hofner Club 60 (John McNally collection)

album covers, were ground breaking and set the pattern for the image that Britain would soon come to know. She created an iconic image and a style for which she never received the due recognition or rewards she richly deserved.

She introduced herself to us and indicated that she would like to take some studio shots. We were flattered. Her family home at Eimsbutteler Strasse 45a in an affluent middle-class suburb of the city indicated a cultured and privileged upbringing. Her bedroom at the top of the house was lined completely in silver foil, perhaps a tad childish and over dramatic in retrospect but quite shocking and different to young guys from our mundane background where our post war decorative techniques consisted of little more than basic paintwork in brown, cream and green.

The images she captured of us were in the same style and mood as those of the Beatles but with the contrast a little less intense. The faces she seemed most interested in were Cliff's, mine and guitarist Dave Wendells'. When the results were presented to us she raved about the magnificent bone structure of Dave's face. I was slightly miffed, being someone wracked with youthful insecurities and having a need for constant attention and approval. I wanted to be the one with magnificent bone structure. I would have been an analyst's dream back then. In many ways I still am.

My portrait seemed ordinary. I decided that I looked like any other spotty-faced kid to whom classic good looks had patently been denied. When I came across the picture again in the early part of a brand new millennium I was astonished. Looking at it with fresh eyes I realised that I would gladly kill to look that good again.

10

Merseymania

By the time we arrived home from Hamburg in the middle of January 1963 everything had changed and, although we did not know it at the time, nothing would ever be the same again. The Beatles had shot to a number two position with *Please Please Me* and all heaven was about to break loose. It was the beginning of a musical revolution that was desperately needed but which no one could have envisaged.

The last great eruption in the pop world had been Elvis Presley. But an Elvis only came along once in a lifetime if you were lucky. Furthermore Elvis looked like a god and hailed from America. The last place you would look to find a contender for world domination would be a grey northern city in England, and even then a coarse and somewhat down-market bunch of working class scruffs would not be an obvious choice as objects of a quasi-religious adoration.

Please Please Me had been robbed of the top spot by Frank Ifield, the Antipodean import who was still on a roll with *The Wayward Wind* following the spectacular success of *I Remember You.* Oddly enough both artistes still relied heavily on the sound of the harmonica, a sound once looked on as old fashioned and naff but very much in vogue again since Delbert McClinton's effective playing on the Bruce Chanel hit *Hey Baby.* But while Ifield, a performer not a writer, looked to old standards that he could revamp into commercial recordings the Beatles had the Lennon-McCartney partnership to deliver an endless supply of tailor-made material for their group. *Love Me Do* had been an interesting and promising start but *Please Please Me* had lifted their game to a whole new level.

As for myself I was mobile again at last. The powder blue Ford Anglia had been repaired and restored to pristine splendour. Alas there was no establishment that could effectively repair my driving skills which were to remain woefully wanting and when I took to the roads once more the roads quaked with fear and the whole world remained at risk.

Things were looking up for the Rebel Rousers. We even had a new recording deal. Our Managers, Bob and Jean Alexander, had removed us from Joe Meek's control and affected an association with John Burgess, an in-house producer at EMI. Joe Meek might have been a genius but he was the wrong genius for us. We liked Burgess, a slim urbane and well-groomed gentleman with a pleasant and affable nature who had begun his career as the assistant to Norman Newell, an elder statesman of the recording industry, who had written and produced hits for the likes of Shirley Bassey, Johnny Mathis and a host of other major entertainers of the time.

When other commitments prevented Newell from overseeing a session for Adam Faith, an up-and-coming pop star who had achieved a degree of fame as a regularly featured performer on the BBC television programme *Drum Beat*, Burgess had been left in charge and by default found himself the producer of Faith's first hit, *What Do You Want?*. Newell, who had originally intended to be Faith's producer, magnanimously decided it was only right to let Burgess continue supervising Adam's recording future. It was a generous gift that saw the Burgess/Faith alliance deliver an impressive run of more than twenty hits.

Being a West London lad Burgess was obviously a fan of the Rebel Rousers and it was probably his enthusiasm for our band that precipitated the switch from the Holloway Road to Abbey Road. There was hardly a person in Middlesex with an affection for rhythm and blues music who was not a fan to some degree or another. We were looking forward to getting into the hallowed halls of EMI's Abbey Road where their number two studio would be our new recording home. EMI had up-to-date professional equipment, and for overdubs we would no longer have to stand in a stairwell or a bathroom.

But things were changing fast. Whereas London had been the be-all-and-end-all for anything and anyone that mattered in the music industry, the furore created by the Beatles now meant that all roads led to Liverpool. Brian Epstein had begun to assemble a stable of stars to eclipse the prototype created by Larry Parnes in the late fifties. He quickly signed up Gerry & The Pacemakers and under George Martin's auspices the cheeky Scouser and his band produced their first disc, a great arrangement of a Mitch Murray song previously recorded and rejected by the Fab Four called *How Do You Do It?*.

While these precocious northerners were grabbing the charts and the adoration of audiences the length and breadth of Britain, we were continuing with the happy humdrum rounds of the local haunts like the Blue Moon and Burtons. On March 2nd you could find us performing at the California Ballroom in Dunstable alongside Russ Sainty and the Nu Notes for an entrance price of six shillings and six pence. New kid on the nationwide block Gerry Marsden, who no-one away from the banks of the Mersey had heard of a month or two before, was heading for the top of the charts with his very first release. We watched with a jealous awe at the rapid and radical way the scene was changing.

I had been telling my pals about the Beatles. My praise was unstinted and the fervour in the press seemed to bear me out. I encouraged a bunch of them to join me when I knew they were to appear at the Gaumont State Ballroom in Kilburn on April 9th. It was still early days and not a great problem to get tickets.

The State Ballroom was a run-of-the-mill dance-oriented venue on the Kilburn High Road just on the edge of central London and typical of Top Rank entertainment centres up and down the country. The dance floor was adjacent to a low stage where the audience was in touching distance of the performers. Although their star was quickly rising, the Beatles were still just another up-and-coming attraction who nobody really expected to be around for too long and were in no immediate danger from the fans to whom they were still little more than a parochial if currently popular curiosity from some strange place up north.

They were to perform two half-hour sets. Cliff Bennett had also arrived with a couple of the Rebel Rousers, our sax section Sid and Moss. The first set came and went and while the teenage audience, a pretty even mix of boys and girls, screamed their approval my chums remained rather unimpressed. They had been reared on the big band rhythm and blues sound of the Rebel Rousers and these Liverpudlian wannabees sounded tame and ordinary to their ears.

When the interval came I joined Cliff, Sid and Moss and we went backstage to have a chat with John, Paul, George and Ringo. They were affable and welcoming and remarkably unfazed by the fame that had so quickly been thrust upon them. They took it very much in their stride with a sophistication that would have been notably absent from us had we been in the same position. It was all quite academic as any similar sort of position seemed unlikely to be on the cards as far as our careers were concerned.

They spoke about their new single. George mentioned to me that apart from *How Do You Do It?* they had also been offered a song called *I Like It* written by Mitch Murray. He was quite dismissive of Murray's latest offering. 'It's all about I like your hat, I like your boots, I like your bike and stuff like that.' He remarked in that slow and sardonic Harrison drawl. 'It's not for us. It's crap. We wanna write our own. Gerry can have it.' EMI had previously put pressure on them to release their version of *How Do You Do It?* but they had wisely dug their heels in for the ground-breaking *Please Please Me*. In the light of the hysteria that was beginning to build around the group it was hard for EMI to usurp them. We would never have dared to take such a rebellious stand. But we weren't the Beatles

When we eventually left the cramped cupboard that pretended to be a dressing room my friends were getting impatient. They were hungry. They weren't mad about the Beatles, didn't fancy staying for the second set and wanted to go for a Wimpy, the only fast food burger then available in the UK that vainly passed for the more impressive and altogether more authentic and substantial American version. It beggars belief in the light of all that was to come that a bunch of teenagers passed on the chance of stopping to see what was to become the most famous band on the planet for a four-inch patty of cardboard-tasting gunk that purported to be a hamburger.

Two days later, on April 11th, the Beatles' third single, *From Me To You*, was released. Da da da da da dum dum da. A line of gibberish and a stroke of sheer genius. Within hours the whole of Britain was singing it and rushing in their hundreds of thousands to buy it, starting a run of number one hits the like of which had never been witnessed before in the history of popular music.

Just one week later a tiny advertisement in the music press announced the release on the American Liberty label, distributed in the UK by the giant EMI company, of *Needles and Pins* by an American girl singer called Jackie DeShannon, an event studiously ignored and unnoticed by the record buying public in general. Although Cliff and the Rebel Rousers had already cottoned on to the catchy and emotive song and had been including it in the set for some time via an import, its official release on these shores came and went with all the explosive impact of a feather crashing into a sponge.

I had kept in touch with Chris Curtis who would reply in letters crammed with hysterically funny lines that were so idiosyncratic and off the wall that I would show them to my friends who marvelled at his peculiar kind of zany wit. This man was certainly a one-off. In his more serious musings he expressed concern about the future of the Searchers. They seemed to be getting left behind.

Epstein had signed up the good-looking Billy J Kramer and endowed him with the distinct advantage of hand crafted Lennon & McCartney songs to record. Something that was now seen as just about failsafe. And in the coming months he would set about addressing the issue of a male bias by signing up ex-Cavern cloakroom girl Cilla Black, changing her name from the virginal sounding White in order to inject an air of strength and mystery. It was a trick that the great Larry Parnes, the original music Svengali of the fifties, had used many times to great effect when assembling his legendary 'stable of stars'.

Eppy had already passed on signing the Searchers after having gone to view them at the Cavern in the days prior to them reducing to a four piece. He liked them very much, there was no doubt about that. And their reputation in the city was a good one. But on the night in question the setting up of the equipment was followed by the downing of ale in the Grapes across the street from the club. It was the Grapes that separated the men from the boys. Those who could spend their pre-performance hours at the bar yet still manage to descend the steps down to the Cavern and deliver the goods.

When the Searchers eventually took the stage Tony Jackson, a wild living youth and with a longer and more enthusiastic history of alcohol intake than his moderate-minded companions, and singer Johnny Sandon who also enjoyed a pint or six, were visibly the worse for wear. Wires were stepped on and pulled out. Arrangements were delivered with a distinct lack of precision. It was not a good night for them. They had blown their golden chance, it seemed. The Grapes had not only separated the men from the boys, it had on this occasion separated the Searchers from a potentially important management contract.

For their first outing to Hamburg in September '62 they had acquired absence of leave from their various professions but their success at the Star Club had resulted in a return booking set for January '63. They would not be granted leave for a second time. It would need them to forgo the security of their jobs and to endure the wrath of their parents who, whilst happy to encourage them in a harmless hobby, were not keen to see their futures cast aside for a five-minute fling on the flimsy structure of the pop stage.

Chris allowed no place for doubts on his landscape of ambition whatsoever. Music was his future and they would make it without a shadow of a doubt. Tony, always intent on living life to the full, was game for anything and his previous adventures in St Pauli had convinced him he wanted to get back there as quickly as possible and at any cost. John and Mike needed a little persuasion, but not much. Jobs were still plentiful and if it all came to nothing they could pick up more or less where they had left off.

As Spring approached, having returned from Hamburg and with yet another return set for May, they continued their round of regular dates which included the Hollyoaks, the Blair Hall and St John's Hall. But there was still a very pressing problem demanding a solution. The matter of a record contract, or rather the lack of one, had to be addressed. A&R men (Artistes and Repertoire) were arriving in Liverpool by the train-load and signing up just about any guitar-strumming bunch of ne'er-do-wells who could deliver a simple tune and a cheeky smile.

The Big Three, one of the finest and most respected outfits on Merseyside, had already been signed up by Decca who were determined not to miss out on the chance of the next phenomenon from the hometown of the Beatles. But once again their instincts proved wrong and their gutsy debut disc *Some Other Guy*, which they released in April, eventually stalled at a lowly number thirty-seven. Handsome hometown hero Lee Curtis had been also been signed to Decca but 'local boy makes record' does not necessarily mean 'local boy makes charts' and his first offering, *Little Girl*, in March had disappeared without trace.

The nets were being cast even wider afield. Freddie & the Dreamers from neighbouring Manchester had been signed up by John Burgess and their first recording *If You Gotta Make A Fool Of Somebody* was destined for an eventual number three spot. And the Hollies were about to release their first offering on Parlophone, a cover of the Coasters original *Ain't That Just Like Me* at the start of what was to be an impressive run of hits that was to continue long after many others had fallen by the wayside as far as the best selling lists were concerned. But no matter whose door they knocked on, the path that led to the Searchers thus far remained unsullied by the feet of the talent scouts.

With a surprising degree of enterprise and maturity beyond their years they had taken matters into their own hands, producing their own demonstration album that they hoped would grab the interest of the all important record companies down south without whose help they were doomed to failure. Aided by Les Ackerley, who operated the Northern Varieties Agency and was to all intents and purposes their manager in name though, as he was to discover to his regret, not in contract, they arranged a primitive recording setup on the stage of the underground premises of the Iron Door which he had access to as club manager.

A simple domestic tape recorder, which had been hired from a shop near the Adelphi Hotel in town, had to suffice. There were no professional studios in the city that they knew of and if there had been their finances would not have run to that kind of expense. The vocals were handled by the house public address system which, like the similar one at the Cavern and many other venues on Merseyside, had been installed by Brian Kelly. It consisted of a couple of open-backed speaker cabinets powered by a typical 30-50 watt commercial amplifier. The vocals were handled by Reslo ribbon mics which were very much standard for the time and about as good as you were going to get until American Sure microphones arrived in the UK. A couple of microphones from the tape machine judiciously placed captured as good an overall sound as they could manage.

Despite the limitations the inexperienced bunch of enthusiastic hopefuls set about recording the major part of their on-stage material, achieving a surprisingly creditable balance. The vocals were fairly evenly spread with Tony Jackson taking the honours on *Sweets For My Sweet* and *Let's Stomp.*

Mike Pender joined him in unison vocals for *Sho' Know A Lot About Love* and *Ain't That Just Like Me*, the latter being embellished with wild and soulful interjections by Chris. This was the very same tune the Hollies chose for their debut disc. In a smoother vein Mike took the lead and showed a softer and more melodic side for the sentimental *All My Sorrows* before proving that he too could rock it up on the old Hank Williams party song *Jambalaya* and Chuck Berry's evergreen *Sweet Little Sixteen.*

And it was to Chuck that Chris turned for his own solo piece, singing about an old jalopy called *Maybelline* as it raced and eventually beat the much more prestigious and glamourous Cadillac on the highways of the USA. Very few people in Britain had ever seen a Cadillac, or any other American car for that matter, outside of movies and magazines but this was rock & roll and rock & roll was Caddies and Chevvies not Austins and Vauxhalls.

John McNally too was given not one but two turns at the lead microphone and chose the old Liverpool pub anthem *Maggie Mae* and a Fats Domino album track called *Rosalie*. Matching the deep vocal tones of the massively rotund Fats Domino with the light framed and boyish looks of McNally would have seemed absurdly incongruous had it not been for the fact that out of that cherubic mouth came a booming bass voice that went on to embellish many a Searchers track.

One other track, a Chris Curtis composition called *Darling Do You Miss Me* was to surface in the following year as the B side of *When You Walk In The Room* and retitled *I'll Be Missing You*. By this time the group had begun to share songwriting credits as a fairer method despite any original authorship.

Their equipment was not the finest American gear available but comprised good quality European makes and in their safe hands it sounded professional and punchy. Chris was using his blue pearl-effect Ajax kit while Mike played his Burns vibra artiste guitar and Tony used the home-made pretend Fender. John's Hofner Club 60, now sprayed black by one of their occasional drivers who also happened to be a car repairer, was hoisted high on his chest in a pose that was soon to be instantly recognisable around the globe.

The Hofner had also been extensively rewired by Adrian Barber of the Big Three while they were in Hamburg and thus acquired a tone slightly different from other Club 60s. Adrian remembers the task in hand.

'I removed the faceplate and figured out how I would have to change the impedances by comparing the windings on the pickups with diagrams of other circuitry I had brought with me from England. In the end it was really a matter of trial and error. I changed the capacitors and resistors, tried them out and did it again and again until it sounded right. I was not really a trained electronics technician so it was very hit and miss but whatever I did it worked in the end'.

Ackerley had a number of acetates pressed and distributed to the main record companies in London but the response had been disappointing. Decca had turned them down. Others had not even afforded the courtesy of a reply. They had the feeling that despite living in one of the country's most important seaports they were about to miss the boat.

Acetates are for demonstration purposes only and the quality deteriorates quickly with multiple plays. It was a venture that cost the not inconsiderable investment of forty pounds and whether or not this investment would pay dividends or not depended upon whose ears they reached. Luckily, the sounds of the Searchers were to be heard by a pair of ears that were to play a vital part in the group's history.

11

Contractually Speaking

Tony Hatch was a West London lad, born in Pinner on June 30th 1939. Showing an early precocious talent at the piano he followed a classical musical education, which included him being made head chorister at All Saints Church, Langham Place, just off Oxford Street.

When schooling finally came to an end he filled any free time from his post-education employment as a tea boy, filing clerk and general dogsbody at a publishing company with running a weekend dance band, playing in pubs and providing the accompaniment for the local dance. In addition to this most necessary supplement to his meagre income he painstakingly taught himself the intricacies of orchestration, the essential skill that he needed to secure his successful future.

In 1960, at the audaciously youthful age of twenty one, he wrote and produced his first hit for the newly formed Top Rank label, *Look For A Star,* featuring a young singer called Garry Mills. The tune was helped in its sales by its inclusion in a tacky and macabre film called *Circus of Horrors*. Tacky it may have been but bearing out the credo that there's no such thing as bad publicity its mass exposure via the giant cinema screen was a stroke of luck for Tony. Popular music, particularly in the fast- changing tastes of the times, was a young man's game and Hatch was the right young man in the right place at the right time.

When his progress was interrupted by a term of compulsory National Service, during which he opted for a three-year extension as a military bandsman with the Coldstream Guards, he moonlighted, albeit with permission, as a freelance musical director for Top Rank, but by the time his spell in the Army had ended the label had folded.

Luck and talent however were on his side and he soon found a position at one of the new kids on the block, a small but enterprising and ambitious label called Pye, managed by Louis Benjamin and based in the Marble Arch area of London, just at the point where the lush green fields of Hyde Park give way to the bustling shops of Oxford Street and the Edgware Road.

Lacking the huge money that sustained the massive EMI, Philips and Decca operations, the big three of the recording industry, the label ran a small but smart basement set-up of two well-equipped studios in Great Cumberland Place and, along with developing their own roster of artistes, distributed the catalogues of American record companies such as the Red Bird label who needed a British outlet to repeat their successes abroad. The studio has long gone and if you check out the site now you will find a sparkling new office block called York House which in its turn replaced the luxurious gambling casino that initially commandeered the old premises. The casino seemed a fitting substitute. So much of the recording scene at the beginning of the sixties was a gamble in itself. The pragmatic but soulless office development that followed perhaps less so.

Some of Tony's productions such as *Warpaint* and *Ain't a Gonna Wash For A Week* by the Brook Brothers stormed the charts while his efforts with the Kestrels vocal group failed to hit the mark. When he wasn't producing his own acts he was used by the company to provide arrangements for its top artistes like Lonnie Donegan and Kenny Ball. Tony was an easy person to get along with and with his boyish charm and sharp and zany sense of humour fitted in well with the increasingly changing atmosphere of these less formal times. The days of the mandatory collar and tie regime for record producers were speedily coming to an end.

When the Merseybeat phenomenon began to cause its first small but significant waves the roads that once only led away from the grimy and grey North to the prosperous South now turned to point in the opposite direction. Suddenly all roads led to Liverpool. Important people who hitherto would not have deigned to venture north of Watford were now boarding trains and driving their limousines up to the city that had spawned the Fab Four. There was gold in them there docks and four nuggets of pure gold called the Searchers were waiting impatiently to be discovered.

But here is where the chronology becomes slightly blurred. As the mists of time inexorably descend and the brain gets fogged the memory can no longer be relied on as a failsafe piece of equipment. There are two faculties that are first to deteriorate in human beings. The memory is one and I've quite forgotten the other.

John McNally does not remember Tony Hatch coming to see them in Liverpool and is under the firm belief that their contract resulted from a demo which landed on his desk. Hatch remembers it differently and a certain credence has to be afforded his version due to the specific way he recalls the events, recollections that are ratified by Margo Newman, his companion on the journey at that time, still singing under the name of Margo Quantrell.

Tony was in the habit of using a trio of girl backing singers who performed under the name of the Breakaways and who had virtually cornered the UK market in tra-la-laahs and shoobey-doobey-waahs. Margo Quantrell, Vicki Haseman and Betty Prescott had split from the sixteen-strong Vernons Girls who had achieved fame with their regular appearances on Jack Good's groundbreaking television shows Oh Boy and Boy Meets Girls. They supplied the vocal decoration to many of Hatch's productions, the most notable perhaps being the Petula Clark hit *Downtown*.

The Vernons Girls had been formed in Liverpool as a part of the social side of the giant football pools organisation from whence they took their name. Margo Quantrell had suggested to Tony that there were many more terrific groups apart from the Beatles performing in the clubs and ballrooms of her home town and that he should get up there and check them out before someone beat him to it.

Together they drove up on a Friday night and stayed at Margo's mothers house, a modest three bedroom terraced house in the working-class district of Bootle, a little over a mile from the city centre and close to where she had worked at the Vernons offices in Linacre Lane. As a young girl she would often see a good-looking young lad called Billy Ashton walk past on his way to work every morning from his home round the corner in Hankey Drive. In those early amblings Billy Ashton was doubtless dreaming of the time when he could dash into a phone booth, spin round a few times and emerge as a shiny silk suited super hero called Billy J Kramer.

In the summer of 1960 Margo was transferred to another Vernons branch at Vermail House in the Old Roan district where she worked as a wages clerk until her boss, without her knowledge, had arranged an audition with the Vernons Girls, an audition that would change her life forever. The path her fortunes took would eventually lead to her meeting with Tony Hatch and playing a significant part in the discovery of the Searchers.

Tony mistakenly remembered the trip to Liverpool with Margo as December 1962 but there were good reasons to doubt that which I will come to later. Margo took him to the Iron Door, one of the many clubs she and her girlfriends frequented in those teenage years before fame dragged her off to London and television fame. That evening they saw two bands on the same bill. One was the Undertakers, the foot-stomping, stage-splintering *enfants terrible* of the Merseyside ballroom circuit whose dramatic entrance included carrying one of their number onstage in a coffin, a style reminiscent of that other purveyor of horror and theatrics, Screaming Lord Sutch.

The other group, surprisingly wild in the light of the clean-cut image yet to come and existentialist in appearance with their all black bohemian outfits and a crazy guy on the drums controlling the obviously devoted crowd, was the Searchers.

Tony insists he was taken with them immediately and one song in particular that they included in their set, *Sweets For My Sweet*, grabbed him at once as a potential top five hit. He expressed his interest to their manager, local businessman Les Ackerley and offered a contract to secure the services of the Searchers but was stunned to be given the ultimatum that he must also offer a contract to the Undertakers. It was an astute and uncommonly bold move by the provincial and unworldly Ackerley who of course managed both bands. And it was at this meeting, not by courtesy of the Royal Mail, that Hatch insists he was given his copy of the famous 'Iron Door recordings' of the Searchers.

Signing the Undertakers was not in Hatch's plans. Good as they were their shock-rock ghoulish style, which he likened to 'grim reapers', might not sit well with a record company that took pride in maintaining a clean-cut family image. But he did not want to lose the Searchers and decided it was worth the gamble. On the more positive side he thought that Jackie Lomax, the Undertakers' dynamic and good-looking singer and bass player, was fantastic.

The following night Margo took him to some other clubs including the Cavern but in his opinion none of the bands performing that evening possessed any of the excitement and potential of either the Searchers or the Undertakers. After listening to the demonstration album when he returned to London, Hatch's instincts remained the same. The groups produced a commercially attractive sound and *Sweets For My Sweet* still impressed him as the standout track. A contract for the Searchers was eventually drawn up and signed on 30th April 1963.

The doubts about the actual date of the visit to Liverpool were eventually cleared up by Margo. Her memories of the event taking place in March 1963 made much more sense. If the trip had taken place in late 1962 then the three months between viewing and signing would seem like an extraordinarily long length of time to wait and a substantial risk to boot. Although it would have been known to all that the group was due to be in Hamburg for most of January and February '63, and therefore out of action as far as recordings were concerned, it would be foolish to risk not having their names on a contract at least in the knowledge that other A&R men, in an attempt to find their very own Beatles, might come in and snatch them from behind his back. There would be no problem with the wait as long as they had been signed up.

Furthermore a trip to Liverpool in a dash to sign up a possible rival to the Beatles in the December of 1962 would have been a very impressive display of foresight indeed, not to mention a foolish and dangerous journey in the appalling weather conditions when Britain was under a blanket of snow for much of the month.

In truth the Beatles were not yet a very big deal at the time. Earlier in the year *Love Me Do* had reached a respectable but hardly stunning number seventeen in the charts but as far as anyone knew then it might be the last place in the charts they ever saw. If the tales were correct it had even been helped to its modest position by the huge buying power of the Epstein family owned NEMS stores who were important customers for EMI. Indeed it was this fact, keeping the Epsteins happy, that had secured the Fab Four their chance in the first place. Most people of note in the recording industry thought that they had enjoyed their short time in the sun and most probably would not be around much longer.

Yes, the Beatles were cute. And yes, they were irreverent and a bit different from the plethora of guitar groups who had gone before. But they were still very small fish in a very large pond. The big transformation in their status and fortunes did not happen until the release of *Please Please Me* in January 1963. Suddenly everything began to change and the first stirrings of what was to be known forever as Beatlemania were felt. And it was at that point and not before that the bigwigs in London decided they had to get off their high horses and into their fast cars and head north *toute de suite*.

The actual scenario is certainly that Tony Hatch, in the light of an obvious musical explosion that was taking place before his eyes two hundred miles away and which now included Gerry & the Pacemakers, Billy J Kramer & the Dakotas and a bunch of others, first saw the Searchers on their return from Hamburg late February or early March 1963, which would make a contract signing a month or so later quite reasonable. On top of which I certainly do not recall any of the Searchers telling me that a contract was in the wind while I, as a Rebel Rouser, was hanging about with them at the Star Club at the beginning of the year and such an important development in their career would have been a major topic of conversation. March 1963 was without doubt the time of Tony Hatch's arrival on the scene.

The contract with Pye records which had indicated a space for Louis Benjamin's signature for the company and which was signed by Les Ackerley on behalf of the Searchers, was a wonderful document which in these more enlightened times would almost be mistaken for indentures into slavery. It consisted of six A4 pages typed on an ordinary office machine rather than professionally printed and although Ackerley's signature was witnessed by one Joyce Platt of Sandwick Street, Liverpool 8 who we might assume was his secretary, Louis Benjamin's was missing. Whether this was deliberate or merely an oversight must remain a mystery.

The contract stated an initial term of one year, which for whatever reason ran from April 22nd, one week earlier than the actual signing date, required them to record a minimum of one double-sided seven-inch 45 rpm single play record during that first year. It also provided for four yearly options on the company's part to extend the arrangement. The initial period entitled them to a royalty in the United Kingdom of two percent on eighty five percent of their sales.

Why eighty five percent? This was one of the record industry's most enduring and most iniquitous scams. The fifteen per cent deduction was for promotion and breakages, an allowance determined at a time when 78 rpm discs were made of a highly fragile material and many of which did indeed shatter before reaching their destination. Of course when seven-inch 45 rpm records were introduced in the mid fifties they were constructed of a much more pliable plastic and damage in transit was virtually eliminated. But somehow what was not eliminated was the breakages clause and for whatever reasons for years nobody sought to remove it, at least not successfully.

The royalty rate outside the British Isles was halved due to the need for a sub-leasing arrangement with foreign companies who quite naturally had to make their own profit and for any extra expenses incurred in such an arrangement. For the option terms, should they be taken up, slight increments were allowed for. In a second year of contract Pye Records would magnanimously give them half a per cent increase.

Should all the options be exercised the Searchers would eventually reach the massive rate of four percent on domestic sales and two per cent in foreign territories. In the light of recording deals in the twenty-first century where figures are likely to begin at twenty per cent, the unfairness of the record companies in the sixties and their stranglehold on poorly advised artistes comes sharply into focus. But these were standard rates for everyone and even the mighty Beatles fared little better in those early years. The astute Dave Clark was perhaps the only artiste of that era to recognise the power and financial advantage that producing and owning one's own master tapes could give you. Clark was virtually a lone example of business acumen in a world of commercial pygmies naively prostrating themselves before the hordes of voracious corporate giants.

Now the contractual arrangements, pathetic as they were, had been agreed and ratified, it was necessary to get the group into the studio as speedily as possible. The Liverpool phenomenon was beginning to grip the imagination of not just the teenage record-buying public but the nation as a whole. Gerry & the Pacemakers had reached the very top with their first effort *How Do You Do It?* and Billy J Kramer with the Dakotas had also made number two with *Do You Want To Know A Secret?* Nobody knew how long this new craze would last. If this new phenomenon was a 'milch cow' then someone had better 'milch' it pretty quick.

As the Searchers were due to head out once more to Hamburg at the end of May it seemed sensible to fix a session for the night before, following which they could head on down to Harwich to catch the ferry. A cheap hotel, the Aaland in the nearby Sussex Gardens area, was booked and paid for by the group itself. It was basic, nothing more than a B&B, but at less than a pound it was at a price they could afford. After all the record company had not offered to underwrite their expenses. And it was just a short distance from there to Great Cumberland Place where Tony Hatch waited in Pye's Number 1 studio with his engineer Ray Prickett.

Prickett, who handled the desk for all of Tony's sessions was a pleasant, if slightly dour, fellow with a dry sense of humour and, in Tony's opinion, the patience of a saint. To take his mind off the business of pop music he devoted his spare time to being an auxiliary fireman, or 'fire bobby' as the Searchers would have it.

The studio was set up with the drums in a corner surrounded by screens and the amplifiers facing the wall away from the vocal microphones in order to avoid overspill. Both instruments and voices were recorded together in the manner of a live performance, the same way an audition would have been handled at Pye or any other studio at the time. And because the songs were so well rehearsed, the standard no-frills three-hour afternoon session, which included a B-side, finished ahead of time.

With yet another example of his foresight, Chris Curtis had come prepared with a self-penned song for the flip. *It's All Been A Dream* (actually credited to C Crummy on the label) was another of his simple yet effective beat ballads and not dissimilar in style to his song *Darling Do You Miss Me?* (later to be retitled *I'll Be Missing You*) which featured on the Iron Door recordings. Nothing clever or complicated about its construction and though not in the running for A-side status, it showed a promise that could only bode well for the future. After all the writing was on the wall and the old style Tin Pan Alley songsmiths no longer had it all their own way.

Tony Hatch remembers the group being quite subdued at that first recording session although they all had some opinion to offer on hearing their first efforts committed to tape under truly professional conditions. Chris was uncharacteristically serious and from the off appeared to be the main spokesperson while Mike and John were fairly relaxed, even managing some light banter. He found Tony Jackson to be the most tense and humourless on the day and he put it down to having to shoulder the responsibility of the lead vocal. He recalls that everyone worked hard but even way back then he sensed that this was a three-plus-one group and was not over surprised when the cracks between Tony and the others finally reached breaking point one year later.

Whatever the character traits of the individual members, together they had without doubt produced a fine piece of work which, apart from a few technical refinements afforded by the multi-mic facilities offered by equipment which included the latest US-made Ampex machines and an EMT echo plate but little else, was otherwise undecorated. There were very few other outboard effects available at the time when such things were very much in an embryonic stage of development. It received its final mix in mono later that evening, stereo not yet being readily available in Britain, although a compatible stereo mix was later prepared for the States.

The Searchers had achieved a seemingly impossible task. They had taken a previously released record by one of the most talented and respected soul groups in the world, the Drifters, and improved on it. The tempo was brighter and the backing less cluttered. The performance had more exuberance and the lead vocal cut through like a bright shiny new pin. So who cared if they mistakenly sang *'your first sweet kiss'* instead of *'your tasty kiss'*, which was the actual lyric on the original. They had transformed a merely competent and pleasing sound into a potential smash hit.

12

The 'Sweets' Smell of Success

As *Sweets For My Sweet* was hitting the shops for the first time, Cliff Bennett & the Rebel Rousers were heading back to Hamburg having completed our first recording under our new direct contract with EMI. In a curious parallel to our chums the Searchers, we were also experiencing the joys of a fully professional environment with state-of-the-art facilities. Our souped-up version of an old Doris Day hit *Everybody Loves A Lover*, due for release just prior to our return from Germany, was committed to tape in the Abbey Road studios, on the same equipment which was now used by the Beatles. We were hoping that EMI's legendary number two studio with its cavernous interior and steep stairway leading up the side of one wall to the control room would allow us also to benefit from the magic that was changing the face of pop music across the globe.

Alas, like all our other efforts, the fairy dust was missing and our latest assault at the pop charts was to prove about as effective as a chocolate army in a Spanish heat wave. But at least it was an improvement on previous efforts and in John Burgess we had found someone who would give a free reign to the undoubted vocal talents that Cliff Bennett had.

For whatever strange reason the B-side consisted of a left-over from our Joe Meek days which one can only assume had come under the ownership of EMI and was deemed in the interest of economy not to be wasted. *My Old Standby* was a trite little higgety-hoppity hoedown tune thrust into the hands of someone who did not want it and who did not deserve it.

Cliff Bennett recalls telling Joe Meek that it was a piece of crap which he did not want to sing, words which sadly fell on the deaf ears of a wayward genius who stamped his foot, cried a little and eventually got his own way. The only positive thing that can be said about it is that it is the last example of the inappropriate though highly talented Nicky Hopkins/Bernie Watson coupling as members of the Rebel Rousers.

The record's chances were not helped by a rival version of the A-side released by none other than our old friends the Undertakers. Hatch had been pressured by the Searchers' manager Les Ackerley to take them under his control. Who copied whom? I'm pretty sure that we both latched onto the arrangement after hearing Joey Dee & the Starliters singing it at the Star Club and consequently discovering that the particular arrangement they used had already been laid down by the Shirelles in the first place, so neither group had cause for complaint. It was fair game for anyone. Whether either version would have made the leap into the best-selling lists had the competition been removed is hypothetical but my instinct tells me it was unlikely. It was a good record but on reflection not a hit record.

For this season in Hamburg we Rebel Rousers were no longer sporting cheap polo shirts. Inspired by the new collarless style jackets that had been popularised by the Beatles we had created our own version in a brilliant blue with black piping down the front. With black pants and white shirts to finish off the ensemble we looked sharp and we were playing better than ever.

We had worn them proudly at the Botwell Festival in Hayes, Middlesex a week before on June 3rd when we shared a bill with US star Del Shannon and many of the up-and-coming young northern stars such as Gerry & the Pacemakers, Billy J Kramer and Freddie & the Dreamers. The southern contingent at the glorified summer fete, which was instituted to raise money for the Catholic church in whose grounds it was staged, was comprised of Kenny Lynch, Screaming Lord Sutch, Jackie Lynton and Eden Kane. And from anywhere between Hounslow and Los Angeles, depending on whether or not you believed his story, there was pseudo Yank, Vince Taylor.

Other attractions that day who, despite their talent, time proved to be rather forgettable were Robb Storme & the Whispers, Jimmy Crawford & the Messengers and Johnny, Mike & the Shades. A young man just back from living in South Africa, Mickie Most, had previously been one half of the Most Brothers and had gone there to resurrect a fast failing career but had decided to give the UK another go. I was recruited to play bass for him that afternoon for the princely sum of nothing.

Mickie of course went on to become one of the most successful producers of all time and a millionaire many times over, after guiding the careers of the Animals, Herman's Hermits, Donovan and Suzi Quatro among others. The Rebel Rousers may have created an impression with our outfits that day but we didn't seem to be able to create a hit record if our lives depended on it.

If the schedules had been stuck to we were due to meet up with the Searchers in Hamburg once more, but the enthusiasm for *Sweets For My Sweet* was running high and after only a matter of weeks pressure was brought to bear on them to return home to promote the release. Chris handled the negotiations in Hamburg with Horst Fascher and Manfred Weissleder and they paid a sum of money in order to be released from the remainder of their contract. And home came the conquering heroes with Tony now clutching a brand new Hofner violin bass, the same model as Paul McCartney's, which as much as anything had become a symbol of the sixties.

Despite their at last being on hand to assist with the promotion, things were going too slowly for comfort until they received the unexpected boost of an endorsement from none other than John Lennon, who declared it to be currently the best record to come out of Liverpool, and when Lennon spoke the youth of Britain listened. But there was help from other areas too.

In 1963 Martin Wyatt was a young man of twenty, working in the promotions department of Pye's prestigious new offices and studios in Great Cumberland Place. The company had come up in the world since being taken over by the television conglomerate ATV, who had been mightily impressed by the encouraging financial returns of the small label's high volume budget outlet Golden Guinea and its acquisition of rights to American catalogues such as Chess, Cameo Parkway and Reprise.

Wyatt had been at Pye for about two years and was there working under Ian Ralfini, having come from Essex Music, a music publishing company run by David Platt. Essex was a fast-growing business that published much of the material issued by the old Pye-Nixa label which included hits by Lonnie Donegan, Acker Bilk and Chris Barber. Martin remembers it all very well.

'Although I worked on a variety of Pye releases, I was always very much connected with Tony Hatch's projects and really shared Tony's enthusiasm for the debut disc by his new Liverpool signing. It was a terrific disc. I believed in it so much so that I looked on it almost as a mission to break the record. But my extra efforts in this direction occasionally caused problems with Louis Benjamin, who would frequently remind me that there were six or seven other releases that also required my attention.'

Benjamin's office at ATV House had three doors. Ahead of him was the corridor, on the right was his secretary's room and through to the left was the promotions department. He would spend the day constantly poking his head through the door and yelling 'What's happening?' in an effort to spur his staff into greater efforts for the company.

For the first three weeks action on *Sweets For My Sweet* was disappointingly slow to the point of virtual stagnation. But then Wyatt got a call from BBC producer Bernie Andrews who gave him the good news that for one week only he was taking over from Jimmy Grant as producer of the important Light Programme pop vehicle Saturday Club and that he would be playing the new record by the Searchers.

Fortune continued to smile when another 'Beeb' producer, Dennis Jones, rang to inform him that he too was about to spin the disc in Pick Of The Pops. And at the eleventh hour Easy Beat also decided to include it in that weekend's show. Things were finally beginning to happen and fast. Of course the sudden and unexpected burst of enthusiasm from those in power at the BBC might well have been spurred by the Lennon endorsement. After all there were currently no more important people in the pop firmament market than the Beatles and none more in touch with the tastes of the nation's youth. But whatever the cause, or combination of causes, the record was at last on the move.

The icing on the cake and probably the most important plug of all was an inclusion in an all-Merseyside edition of *Thank Your Lucky* Stars broadcast on June 29th. The show also included the Beatles, Cilla Black, Billy J Kramer & the Dakotas, Gerry & the Pacemakers, the Vernons Girls, the Big Three and Lee Curtis. Scouse actor Kenneth Cope was brought in for the Juke Box Jury inspired Spin-A-Disc.

By the Monday the pressing factory could barely cope with demand for the disc. On July 5th it entered the New Musical Express (NME) chart at number twenty-four and at a single stroke the world of the Searchers was turned upside down.

With offers for their services pouring in from all sides it was quite apparent that they now needed serious representation to handle their bookings. Certainly Ackerley had been instrumental in securing their recording contract, but when it came to marketing an up-and-coming sensation whose future had outgrown Liverpool and was about to include the world in its plans, more clout and expertise was required. Louis Benjamin had steered them in the direction of Tito Burns, an old-style band leader who had spurned the vagaries of the relentless and unreliable ballroom circuit in which one was always held to the ransom of fickle popular taste for the highly lucrative world of the theatrical agent.

Tito was a smooth operator who knew his business well and his business was making money for Tito from his top floor offices at number 3 Vere Street, just off Oxford Street in the West End. Pop artistes were the tools by which he could achieve this and he had indeed handled some of the most important acts of the day. Cliff Richard had been one of his stars for a time until Cliff's father had decided a change of management was in order for his son.

His current number one act was the glamourous Dusty Springfield who had left the popular Springfields and was at the start of a long run as a major star whose success was to cross over the big pond to the States, the very same musical Valhalla from where her beloved soul sounds emanated. The group, which included Dusty's brother Tom Springfield and Tim Field who was soon to be replaced by Mike Hurst, purveyed a repertoire of popped-up western-oriented folk songs that found favour in the charts.

But the group was merely a stepping stone for Dusty whose personal preference in music was rooted in the radically different sounds of black soul coming from the industrial cities of the USA and in particular the Detroit studios of Berry Gordy's

Motown label. Dusty's incredible voice and glamourous persona combined with her notoriously difficult and neurotic character traits was to provide a blueprint for divas of the future at a time when the word was not in common usage

Eden Kane was another important client of the Vere Street set-up although by now at the tail end of his time as a golden boy of British pop. *Well I Ask You*, *Get Lost*, *Forget Me Not* and *I Don't Know Why* had scored heavily for the smouldering Anglo-Indian heartthrob but the time of the silk-suited American styled solo star was nearing its demise as quick-witted Scouse scallywags bulldozed everything in their path.

Tito also had a roster of minor acts on his books to fulfil the more modestly paying and workaday dance hall and club requirements, coupled with the outside chance that they too might strike it rich if the fates decreed thus. The rumour was that he would sign groups willy-nilly to contracts which were carefully filed away in the vague hope that luck would eventually fall upon them, whereupon long forgotten proof of their commitment to Tito would be produced. The stories might have been apocryphal but he had learnt his craft of smoke and mirrors well, as was demonstrated to great effect in *Don't Look Back*, the late sixties documentary on Bob Dylan in which he is seen to be gleefully pulling a fast one on a television company.

And now he had the Searchers who were clearly going places and had every chance of becoming serious rivals to the Beatles. In their favour Tito was certainly a man who had all the contacts and who had the ability to organise complicated prestigious tours and necessary promotional opportunities not only in the UK but also on the world stage. He was someone they needed very much at this important time in their rise in the food chain.

We arrived home from Hamburg on July 11th just in time for our jealous eyes to watch the Searchers racing up the charts. Things were moving fast for them and, still in touch with Chris by mail, by good fortune and coincidence I now found myself a friend of the stars. The general public knew Mike and Chris by their adopted stage names and, although some biographical material still used his family name of Prendergast, the Mike in the Searchers was Pender, while Chris had long since dumped his Crummey surname in favour of the alliterative and slicker sounding Curtis.

Tony Jackson has stated in an interview that it was he who had actually given Chris his new handle, quickly purloining it from Lee Curtis's name which he spotted on a club wall while being interviewed by the press and asked for the names of the group's personnel. But this may or may not be true. And as neither Chris nor Tony are any longer around we will never know for sure.

While the Searchers were riding high on a gigantic wave of success we were still thrashing aimlessly about in the paddling pool of popularity. On July 12th they were nestling at number five in the charts with no sign of stopping while we were appearing once more at the California Ballroom, Dunstable, alongside Roy Star & the Cherokees, whoever they were. Entrance to this extravaganza would have cost you four shillings (20p). Great value. No doubt about it. We were good and we were cheap.

As *Sweets For My Sweet* moved up one more place to number four the following week their old cohort Johnny Sandon, with the Remo Four, was making his own foray at the pop charts with a Colin Manley song called *Lies*. But Sandon without the Searchers was a very different product from the Searchers without Sandon and *Lies* rose without trace in the murky waters of that most infamous sea of indifference. Things were not going well for the depressive natured Billy Beck who was beginning to understand a little of how Pete Best must be feeling.

While Sandon must have hoped his Searchers connection would be a springboard to success the Philips company too realised that they had something valuable in their possession and a bunch of almost forgotten Star Club recordings were announced in the press as a forthcoming release in album format. No indication of the amateur nature of their execution accompanied the adverts. The Searchers featured on three tracks of a compilation from the Hamburg sessions. Their past was about to come back and haunt them.

Efforts were made to litigate against this release of what the band considered to be inferior recordings that were never seriously intended to be on general distribution and for which they had received no payment. But it was to no avail and they were forced to accept the situation and hope that it would not interfere too much with their legitimate and approved releases.

Everyone it seemed was getting in on the act. The tiny Oriole label, its greatest successes being the Chas McDevitt Skiffle Group's recording of *Freight Train* in the fifties and a top three record *Like I Do* by Maureen Evans in the sixties, was considered a label to whom you only went if you had exhausted all other options, put out two albums of Merseyside 'also-rans' entitled *This Is Merseybeat* and for the princely sum of twenty nine shillings and tuppence you got tracks from the likes of Earl Preston & the TTs, Faron's Flamingos, Ian & the Zodiacs, Rory Storm & the Hurricanes, Sonny Webb & the Cascades, Derry Wilkie & the Pressmen, the Del Renas and curiously, in the light of their later substantial success, the Merseybeats.

After another one place rise to three the Searchers finally hit the top spot in the NME charts of August 2nd 1963, knocking Frank Ifield and his *I'm Confessin'* off his perch. Ifield had prevented the seemingly unstoppable Beatles from grabbing a chart topper back in February but he couldn't stop the Searchers. They were, needless to say, elated. In the same edition the paper's columnist Allen Evans reviewed their debut album, a speedily put together collection of what basically constituted their stage show at the time. With the almost impossible demands on their time it is a wonder they managed to get an album together at all.

Evans's review of *Meet The Searchers* was a favourable one and he praised the 'torrid instrumental backing throughout - must be a hit'. He gave it four stars. For such a haphazardly assembled bunch of tracks it contained some real gems. *Sweets For My Sweet* was there of course in all its glory and magnificence but so were numbers that were eventually to be regarded as classics of their time. Songs like *Farmer John*, *Ain't Gonna Kiss Ya* and a tune that some months on was to come out of left field to give them their biggest US hit, *Love Potion No. 9.*

It was straightforward playing with no frills or overdubbing but performed with conviction, heart and energy. Soon, with the onset of ever-expanding multi-tracking facilities and impossibly sophisticated sound enhancements, and along with all this the obligation to make use of such advancements, they would never be allowed to record with that kind of basic simplicity again. Recording is like a garage which you promise yourself you are not going to clog up with junk. Pretty soon it is crammed to overflowing. If your desk avails you of sixty-four tracks you will use sixty-four tracks. It is the nature of the beast.

I discovered from Chris that they were due to play a university in Southampton and so I decided to pay them a visit. My old chums suddenly becoming superstars was very exciting indeed. I steered the powder blue Ford Anglia down the A31 and arrived in Southampton a couple of hours later and with an aching back. The basic upholstery of this most modest of Dagenham's handiwork was okay for running around Hayes but the far from ergonomic design of its seats left a lot to be desired. It had been a cute little car but I figured that maybe it was time to upgrade my transport.

Catching up with the Searchers again after all this time and in the light of everything that had gone by was good. And they all appeared pleased to see me. We headed out to a nearby pub, The Cowherd, to while away the spare time before the evening's show. Tony was recounting to me that although things were going incredibly well they were still fulfilling their commitments to old contracts that had them working for ninety pounds a show. Ninety pounds sounded like a fortune to me. It was three times as much as we earned in a night. The idea of being able to dismiss such a sum as paltry was nothing but sheer fantasy in my tiny little impecunious world. I was jealous but I was also very thrilled for them.

The hall was packed to the rafters and the crowd yelled and demonstrated its devotion as they ran through what was more or less the contents of their new album, which of course in its turn had been their current repertoire. The day of the concept album was still in the far distance. The group before me now had a smarter more streamlined look. In the manner of the Beatles they had 'Epsteined' themselves, shedding the bohemian black polo necks and replacing them with high-cut three-button suits in a dark blue shade of tonic mohair and finished off with crisp white shirts and black ties.

Chris still had long hair but it was now carefully trimmed into a stylish adult version of what had gone before.

The equipment too had moved up a notch. Having been impressed by those at the Star Club they had purchased their own set of expensive Fender amplifiers which stood resplendent in their beige livery as a statement that here was a group who had made it. The old 'make do and mend' predecessors had simply been abandoned in a London bed and breakfast hotel after a recording session.

Chris as always controlled the proceedings, cutting a quite manic figure as he stood erect at the drums, wide-eyed and with a huge rectangular grin that that stretched from one side of his face to the other to resemble a letter box, booming out his orders to the obedient mob. Quite naturally *Sweets For My Sweet* was greeted with the roar that one would expect of a number one hit record but the wildest response was reserved for the uninhibited delivery by Chris of the sure-fire Ray Charles classic *What'd I Say*. It was their showstopper. The call and response style of this rhythm and blues belter never failed them.

I reached home at the end of the evening still buzzing with the excitement of it all and in need of hospitalisation due to my chronically aching back which felt like it had been repossessed from John Merrick, the Elephant Man. The next week I went out and bought a beautiful Sunbeam Rapier, white with a contrasting brown side stripe, roof and upholstery in a matching shade of chocolate.

Tito was quick to get his meal ticket onto the rewarding live circuit and August was packed with a series of one-nighters that had no real sense of logic built into their route. On the 3rd they appeared in Morecambe before driving down to Dunstable for a concert the next day. After a welcome two days free the journeys continued with consecutive shows in Bristol, Margate, East Grinstead and Lincoln. To make life a little easier, along with the fame came a financial power that allowed them the luxury of a full-time road manager in the form of Billy Booker, a pal from Liverpool who they had up to then used on a casual basis.

As well as appearing on stage in Lincoln on August 10th they also featured that night in a pre-recorded Thank Your Lucky Stars along with Alma Cogan, the Shadows, and Cliff Richard who was presented with gold discs for *The Next Time* and *Bachelor Boy*.

The following night saw them at Torquay sharing a bill with Alma Cogan and then it was on to Bath and then Wallington in South London. The schedule was a shattering one but Tito's advice was to always take it while you can for who knew if it would still be there tomorrow? Of course this advice which kept them driving up and down every road in the country while Tito sat in a certain degree of comfort behind his London desk might have had as much to do with his desire to keep his commissions rolling in as anything. Altruism and Tito Burns are not words I would readily juxtapose and his meal ticket could now easily provide him with lobster and caviar.

Sweets For My Sweet spent a third week at number one in the August 13th NME chart with Frank Ifield at number two with *I'm Confessin'* which they had earlier impolitely pushed out of the way to claim the top spot. Over in the Rebel Rousers' camp we found ourselves meeting up with many of our old Merseyside friends as they continued their assault on the nation. On August 18th we joined the MV Sovereign on a musical voyage from Tower Hill to Margate and back, sharing the honours with Gerry & the Pacemakers, Freddie & the Dreamers, the Hollies, Billy J Kramer & the Dakotas, Screaming Lord Sutch and Chris Farlowe. At two pounds ten shillings it represented extremely good value for money.

On a higher plane entirely the Searchers, after more shows in Llandudno, Altrincham and Stourbridge, returned to Liverpool in triumph for a show there on August 22nd. Their hometown gave them a rapturous reception but there was little time to savour the moment as the schedule took them way down south again the very next day. By the time they reached the London suburb of Wimbledon after a two hundred mile trip *Sweets For My Sweet* had dropped to number two. One week on and its descent, understandable after a very respectable tenure in the charts, took them down to five with Billy J Kramer enjoying his second hit with *Bad To Me* at number one.

In that same week the plaudits were being handed out to us as well, as Pender and Curtis along with Billy J's backing group the Dakotas pronounced Cliff Bennett & the Rebel Rousers to be their favourite band. Laden with compliments but bereft of hit records we flew back to Germany for yet another season at the Star Club.

Meanwhile the Searchers kicked off their first important package tour sharing the stage with Roy Orbison, Brian Poole & the Tremeloes and Freddie & the Dreamers. Lower on the bill were Cherry Roland, the Sons Of The Piltdown Men and Gary & Lee, acts that quickly rose to obscurity. The tour would also serve as an important plug for their latest offering on vinyl. *Sweets For My Sweet* might have lived out its term in the charts but the album *Meet The Searchers* was selling faster than the contents of a docker's swag-bag and now launched an extended-play disc of four tracks onto the market. *Ain't Gonna Kiss Ya*, *Love Potion No. 9*, *Farmer John* and *Alright* was a slick combination of tracks which within three weeks would find itself nestling in the singles charts at a very respectable number twelve. No doubt about it, the Searchers were one of the hottest acts around and it looked very much like they were here to stay.

13

Unstoppable

The tour with the verbally laconic but vocally stunning Roy Orbison ended in Blackburn on October 4th with the *Ain't Gonna Kiss Ya* EP in the singles charts at a still more than respectable number sixteen. They could do no wrong it seemed. Even the sub-standard and unauthorised Philips release of the *Sweet Nothin's/What'd I Say* single was to reach forty-eight.

It was now time for the release of the group's second single. The story behind *Sugar And Spice*, a tailor-made clone of the first, is an amusing one which could be looked on as either sharp practise or a perfect display of diplomacy depending on your point of view. Personally I adhere to the latter and admire Tony Hatch's integrity in the matter.

The choice of a follow up is one of the most important decisions an artiste can make. With a first offering they have nothing to lose. With the second they could very easily lose everything. Hatch had ostensibly entered the exclusive world of the record producer as a springboard for his other talents, those of arranging and composing, the latter being his major goal. Closeness to his charges and the control he exercised over them was a distinct advantage when it came to placing songs but this privilege came with a grave responsibility. He could not be seen to be forcing unsuitable self-penned material on them which might not be in their own interests. It might not be illegal but to Tony, saddling them with sub-standard product in the way that Joe Meek did when dealing with Cliff Bennett, would have been morally reprehensible. The method he chose had both subtlety and a sense of fair play.

With a straight face he recounted to them the story of a guy in a pub who had played him a song which he thought might be perfect for the Searchers. The person in question was apparently called Fred Nightingale. On hearing this rather unlikely name they could have been forgiven had they broken out into guffaws of laughter at its Goon-like nuances. Whether the group truly believed this barely credible story or whether in deference to their mentor they merely decided to go along with it, not wishing to upset the boss, is not clear. I am sure they would have had their suspicions. But what certainly was clear is that *Sugar And Spice* sounded like a follow-up if ever there was one.

It had the same tempo as *Sweets For My Sweet.* The same chunky rhythm. And the same repetition of chorus-verse-chorus, with words and tune so ludicrously simple that it could be sung by anyone after a single listening, which indeed it was. Included too were the identifying oohs of its predecessor and the same full sounding harmonies behind a lead vocal which was handled once again to great effect by Tony. In the world of hand-crafted clothing it might not have been a Gieves and Hawkes but it was bespoke tailoring by any standards and fitted like a glove. The old jazz standard *When The Saints Go Marching In*, retitled as *Saints and Searchers*, was put on the B-side.

The true identity of the songwriter, Hatch himself, was revealed only after the song had justified their faith in it and had begun its rapid rise to the top regions of the charts. Over the years it has been somewhat vilified but it has always retained a wonderfully naïve charm and considering the extremely vulnerable position the Searchers were in at the time it is still my opinion that Tony Hatch served them very well indeed.

The group's London accommodation, in the light of their new found wealth and status, had received an upgrade from the cheap hostelries of the downmarket Paddington district to the comparative luxury of the mid-priced but infinitely more comfortable Hotel President just a stone's throw from Euston Station, where the express would deposit them after each long journey down from Lime Street. But the demands on their time to be available in London where the power base lay soon resulted in them taking out a year's lease on a three-bedroom apartment at 38 Pont Street, Knightsbridge, situated on the top floor of a distinguished old terrace of red brick houses which stretched from Sloane Street to Beauchamp Place. It was a prestigious address for a bunch of lads from the lower echelons of Liverpool.

The sixty pounds a week rent for the spacious though necessarily bland rental property which had walls of cream and grey carpeting throughout was a king's ransom in 1963. But it was considered a sensible and convenient economic proposition in the light of the mounting hotel bills they were incurring. Their occupancy was not altogether approved of by the other tenants who found their peace constantly disturbed by scruffy groups of barely teenage girls who began to gather on the steps up to the main entrance in the hope of a glimpse of the pop stars. When the elegant polished wood door was defaced with scratched-in graffiti the Searchers were called upon to pay for the repair and they could hardly refuse.

Back again from Germany and once more with pockets bulging with Deutschmarks we Rebel Rousers were soon followed by Roy Young, the Star Club's pianist/ vocalist-in-residence. When his career as a pop star appeared to have stalled in England at the beginning of the decade he was glad to find an enthusiastic audience and a substantial pay packet waiting for him in Hamburg. But he was shrewd enough to know that this was no help to a wider acceptance, which he still believed would be his. And in the same manner as me a couple of years before, he had seen Cliff Bennett's band and decided that it was the perfect vehicle for him.

And Cliff, never one to let finance get in the way of the music, was keen to have the extra voice and the immensely desirable presence of a piano in the line-up once more. Being true to my canny Scottish parentage, I was a little more concerned that Roy's recruitment would naturally result in less take-home pay for me, but in the end it was Cliff's decision and it was the right one. We were becoming a very powerful outfit indeed. The only other serious contenders in bands of that size were Sounds Incorporated and as a purely instrumental group they had established themselves as a backing outfit to imported American stars rather than an attraction in their own right. They did not have a Cliff Bennett.

Throughout November the Searchers were kept busy as always with a series of concerts alongside Dusty Springfield, Brian Poole & the Tremeloes, Freddie & the Dreamers and Dave Berry, the shows being compered by the dangerously irreverent comedian Tony Marsh, who was requested by artistes as much for his fun on the coach as his competence between the acts. Marsh was eventually to be banned from the touring circuit after his 'mooning' at a performer was so injudiciously positioned as to be seen by a rather sensitive member of the audience. This outraged person had complained vehemently about the horrific sight of a middle aged man's portly arse peering back at her over the footlights. Orbison was so addicted to Marsh's entertainment value on the coach journeys that in future he hired the wayward wag to keep everyone amused on tours in which he was otherwise allowed to play no part whatsoever.

Mid-way through the month *Sugar And Spice* reached its high point of number two or number three in the best selling lists depending on which pop paper you preferred to believe. It even reached the coveted number one in one publication. Remarkably, they were to be denied the chance to equal Gerry & the Pacemakers' feat of achieving consecutive chart toppers with his first three releases. Yet another hastily recorded album was already there to cash in on the sales of the single after which it was named. By November 20th *Sugar And Spice* had slipped to number five but any disappointment was quickly eclipsed by an event two days later which rocked the world, against which nothing else including the fortunes of a trite pop song mattered much.

The Searchers were in Perth, Scotland, staying at the Salutation Hotel on the evening of November 22nd and preparing for a show that night. Several hundred miles south I was driving my newly purchased and very elegant second hand Sunbeam Rapier along the M1 heading once more to the California Ballroom, Dunstable, where we were sharing the honours with Ray Dell & the Rocking Deacons and the Valiants in an evening described as a Hitch Hike Special, entrance five shillings.

The shock on hearing the news over the radio is hard to describe. President John F Kennedy had been shot during a motorcade in Dallas. It was unclear at that moment whether or not he had survived but it sounded ominous. I felt a shiver go through me and not a little sense of real fear. Would this mean a war? These were delicate times. The cold war was still at its height and the Bay of Pigs drama which JFK had controlled and commanded with nerves of steel had almost brought on a nuclear confrontation the consequences of which would have been too awful to contemplate.

Later that evening the worst was confirmed but despite Kennedy's passing the show went ahead although there was quite naturally a certain tension pervading the atmosphere throughout the night. It was very strange. Almost surreal. The secure world of the new Camelot had been blown asunder. And the image of a distraught and confused Jacqueline Kennedy cradling the shattered skull of her husband was forever etched in peoples' minds.

To cap it all, my car ground to a halt at the side of the motorway on my return journey. I panicked. I knew nothing about car mechanics, I was not a member of either the AA or the RAC and I had no money on my person. I remembered the advice someone had once given me. Never buy a car you can't push. I phoned from the nearest emergency box and someone organised for a garage to send out a mechanic. But as I had not spotted an emergency phone on my side of the carriageway I had rather stupidly crossed over the central reservation on foot to where I had seen one on the hard shoulder opposite. As crazy as it seems in 1963 traffic on the motorway was light enough to manage such a dumb feat and get away with it. Try that today and you would be just another piece of road kill.

Having given them the reference number of the phone box, I was then forced to wait on the wrong side of the road where my rescuer, now in possession of the incorrect information, would be heading. Eventually he turned up and after turning back at the next exit we pulled up by the car and he looked into my engine. After approximately five seconds he said, 'Okay, start it up.'

'But it won't start,' I argued having tried several times myself to turn the engine over. 'It'll start,' he insisted. I turned the key and the car started. I was astonished until he informed me that the main HT lead had come unscrewed. I could have fixed it myself had I known what an HT lead was and where it should be screwed. Instead it was me who was screwed. I had to explain to him that I had no actual cash and of course we were still in times when people did not carry credit cards. But I did have a gold watch which he accepted as surety until I remitted their fee which I did the very next day. Another thing I did that day was to join the AA.

We had released yet another record, the second for John Burgess and the first with Roy Young as a Rebel Rouser. It was a cover of the Miracles original *You Really Got A Hold On Me.* Again it was a pretty good disc and again, on reflection, it had about as much chance in the charts as a one-legged man in an arse kicking contest. For the flip side we chose *Alright*, the song Cliff had heard by the Grandisons on a Lonnie Donegan television show and which had been picked up by the Searchers who had included it on their album.

The Searchers on the other hand released a second EP from the *Meet The Searchers* album, the songs being *Sweets For My Sweet, Money, Since You Broke My Heart* and *It's All Been A Dream* and they continued their travels on a seemingly endless round of ballroom dates. In the space of six months they had released two singles, two albums and two extended-play records, all of which had seen chart success. The philosophy of 'grab it while you can' was being adhered to rigidly and possibly to the point where it could eventually prove to be detrimental to their longevity.

And Mike had even contrived to find time to marry his fiancée May Doyle on December 2nd although it was not till after the event that either the group or the press found out. With an impressive degree of secrecy they had somehow managed to make the necessary arrangements for the small private ceremony without the rest of the world finding out. When it hit the television news the next day thousands of young female fans had broken hearts they felt would never mend.

On December 10th we Rebel Rousers had a rather exciting date of our own to keep. We had been booked to play at the Cavern and in truth were quite excited about it. The lowly cellar had been elevated to the position of a virtual shrine in the light of all the kudos brought to it by the city's favourite sons. This was a small room that was a big deal.

We set off on the long journey north and eventually approached the city by way of the A580, whereupon Roy decided that we should stop and ask some kids directions to the Cavern. They looked baffled. 'You know, where the Beatles play,' he explained lamely. It wasn't getting us anywhere so we trundled on. It eventually turned out that the city centre where Mathew Street was situated was miles from where we had enquired. It would be like stopping in Ealing and asking a twelve-year-old for directions to the Palladium.

The show that night at the claustrophobic and sweaty Cavern was a sad disappointment. It was packed and the audience seated on the hard benches in front of the low stage was dotted with musician chums of ours from the Undertakers, the Dominoes, the Strangers and others. Guys we had hung around with in Hamburg. But although we played as well as we knew how, a seated room was alien to our general mode of performance and we gave an inhibited presentation on top of which the change of temperature from the cold dressing room to the hot stage kept putting the brass uncomfortably out of tune. And, great as Cliff was as a vocalist, keeping an audience interested and entertained while the problem was regularly rectified throughout our time on stage was not his forte. We came off feeling deflated.

Jackie Lomax and Brian Jones of the Undertakers tried to make us feel better by saying the peasants there didn't appreciate anything good but in truth we just had not handled the occasion well. We put it down to experience. What was done was done. Onwards and upwards.

Meanwhile the demands on the Searchers were so heavy that they barely had time to eat, sleep or breathe let alone see their families. They had recorded the title track to a cinema feature film, *The System*, which featured Oliver Reed and Julia Foster and which was re-titled *The Girl Getters* for the American market. There was talk of them appearing in the movie but nothing came of it, but another film in which they would both sing and act was announced. Furthermore with *Sugar And Spice* in its descent plans were already in place for them to record their third single. December 16th and 17th were set aside for the sessions and although they did not realise it at the time it was to be the catalyst for a radical change in both their personal and professional lives.

Despite the fact that *Sugar And Spice* had run its course in the charts the group took the chance to boost their profile by performing the tune on a second special all-Liverpool Christmas edition of Thank Your Lucky Stars broadcast on December 21st. Once again it was an impressive line-up and a major high point for pop television in the light of the furore that the brand new Mersey Sound was creating across the country.

The Beatles quite naturally were top dogs and were awarded an unprecedented four-song spot, *All My Loving*, *Twist And Shout*, *She Loves You* and *I Wanna Hold Your Hand*, while their supporting cast had to make do with a single number each. Gerry & the Pacemakers delivered their third consecutive number one hit *You'll Never Walk Alone*, the first act ever to achieve the feat, and Billy J Kramer & the Dakotas sang *I'll Keep You Satisfied* while Cilla Black, the Breakaways and Tommy Quickly respectively gave the massive viewing audience *Love Of The Loved*, *That Boy Of Mine* and *Kiss Me Now*.

Although Cilla's somewhat modest start to record success (*Love Of The Loved* reached a high of thirty five) was to change dramatically in a short space of time, no amount of effort and push from the seemingly infallible Brian Epstein could get *Quickly* higher than a thirty three placing with a subsequent release, *You Might As Well Forget Him* in '64. Alas, the Breakaways were never to grace the charts with their presence.

In a quirky coincidence Johnny Sandon eventually went on to record the Burt Bacharach/Hal David song *Magic Potion*, a significant EP track for the Searchers, as lead singer with the Remo Four, the outfit he was to regret quitting his old cohorts for. And when Sandon eventually departed their ranks the void was filled by *Quickly*. Liverpool had always been a very incestuous environment, musically speaking.

Meanwhile, in Searcher-land Tony Jackson, who had provided the excellent and solid vocals on both hits so far, was in a state of blissful ignorance and still revelling in his position as the focal point of one of the biggest youth attractions in Great Britain. But all that was about to change.

14

A New Direction

The two-day session set aside for recording the new single saw a departure in style that was to change the positions of power in the band forever. Tony's voice had proved to be extremely effective on their hits thus far, and the album tracks on which he took the main part were immensely popular with the fans. *Ain't Gonna Kiss Ya*, *Alright*, *Farmer John* and *Love Potion No. 9* were revered almost as much as the singles that had been released and it was more or less taken for granted that he was their undisputed lead singer.

But when he came to attempt the vocal on a tune that Chris felt would herald a breakthrough for them and grab the interest of their public by virtue of the radical change in their approach and sound, it was quite obvious to all that it was not going to work. *Needles And Pins*, the song that they had first heard the Rebel Rousers performing at the Star Club, was a different 'pot au poissons' altogether. It was softer and more subtle and as such required a radically different approach to what was going to result in a display of the hitherto under-developed romantic side of the group. *Sweets For My Sweet* was a dynamic single and a worthy hit. *Sugar And Spice* was also a good pop song but being hand crafted as a follow up it was by necessity derivative, a musical anagram of its predecessor. *Needles And Pins* would prove to the world that they were not just a one-trick pony.

From the get-go when Mike Pender and Chris Curtis paired their voices on the track, with Mike's melody line richly embellished by Chris's beautiful falsetto harmonies, the contest was over. The result with its intriguing tune, laid back hypnotic rhythm and lyrics which eschewed the trivial and got right down to the meat and potatoes of a fractured relationship, was sheer magic. The combination of the two perfectly matched voices had meshed into a golden partnership which the group - or at least three quarters of the group - was convinced would be a winner.

The finished record was a wonderful example of what I considered to be the Searchers' most valuable talent, that of musical asset stripping. They were not content simply to copy a previous example. Instead they listened carefully to decide which were the bits to be savoured and retained and which parts were to be discarded: to separate the wheat from the chaff and reassemble the remainder into a sharply focussed entity which could sail into a bright future with no unwanted baggage on board to slow them down.

Jackie DeShannon's original version of the Jack Nitzche/Sonny Bono composition was an excellent piece of soulful art but the rambling and difficult-to-remember words towards the end would surely have proved an obstacle to its commercial success. Understanding the advantage of repetition they simply removed the problem section and turned once more to the opening verse which, sung over the immediately identifiable and catchy guitar riff, insinuated itself into the brain immediately and forever.

The guitar sound was to be remembered erroneously by many as one of the earliest examples of the electric twelve-string guitar on a pop single. There was, in fact, no twelve-string used on the session. Instead it was a curious overtone in the mix from the treble tones that created a similar effect between John McNally's little black Hofner and Mike's brand new Gibson ES345 guitar. Whatever the cause it was an accidental jingle-jangle of instruments which was to set off a sympathetic jingle-jangle of cash registers around the country as fans flocked to buy the new release.

The manner in which they recorded this new offering was to change once and for all the routine hitherto employed in the studio. With the exception of *Sugar And Spice*, a new song that they had to learn from scratch on the premises, their debut single and albums had been tried and tested on stage. All that was needed was to commit them to tape in a quick un-fussy session which required little by way of rehearsals other than the mandatory checks for balance among the instruments.

With the constant demands on what little free time they had, either from live shows, television, press calls or quite naturally their families, there was no opportunity to set aside any space for rehearsal. Tony Hatch remembers it as a bone of contention with him.

'This was an intensely long session and lasted from two in the afternoon until well into the early hours of the following day. Chris had the original Jackie DeShannon record of *Needles And Pins* but although the rest knew the song well nobody had actually played it. Hence this expensive recording studio was used for the first part as a rehearsal room.

'This highlighted a big problem. The Searchers, not being songwriters, needed time to search for songs and have adequate time to learn them and try them out. I begged Tito to allow proper time in their schedule for this but it was like talking to a wall. Nobody gets paid for rehearsing and the group was so busy with radio, TV, concerts and clubs that any time off was spent asleep on the bus or at home.

'We never specifically recorded an album and more importantly we never booked a week away from London in a residential studio where we could just live together and make music, never even booked a rehearsal room or a few consecutive days at Pye. The first album was cobbled together from hit singles plus B-sides and spare titles left over and it went that way for the entire time the Searchers were at Pye.'

While the group would doubtless agree with Hatch with regards to the *Meet The Searchers* and *Sugar And Spice* albums it would be truer to say that the ones that followed did indeed have certain specific times set aside for the purpose. And that although there was no cohesive 'theme' behind the recordings (this was some time before the idea of a concept album had been introduced) they did enter the studio with the object of a complete album of chosen songs in mind, and rather than simply committing to tape their current on-stage set they sifted through a wealth of hitherto unfamiliar material in an attempt to lift their game, and prove their worthiness in the hierarchy of pop as it was at that point.

It is just as well that they were sure of the results of their endeavours to present *Needles And Pins* as their new single, because pressure was initially brought to bear for a different track altogether to be issued. *I Count The Tears* was yet another tune that had, like *Sweets For My Sweet*, been previously recorded by the Drifters and Pye Records saw that as the natural follow up to *Sugar And Spice*. It was a good song. It had a bright uplifting tempo and a catchy chorus that easily had the hallmarks of a hit but the band itself felt that *Needles And Pins* would enhance their reputation in a way that *I Count The Tears* would not. It would see them at the cutting edge of pop and put them ahead of the game. They were correct in their assumptions. It was a brave act to stand up against the might of the record company bosses but with two huge hits under their belt they not only had guts, they also had power.

As the end of the year approached they could see exciting times ahead. Their second album, predictably and unadventurously named *Sugar And Spice*, had been almost as successful as the first and already dates for a new package tour were announced for the coming year when February and March would see them criss-crossing the country in the company of Big Dee Irwin (*Swingin' On A Star*), Bobby Vee (*The Night Has A Thousand Eyes, Take Good Care Of My Baby*, *Run To Him*) and Dusty Springfield (*I Only Want To Be With You*). They were seen in a colour feature by Pathe Pictorial in cinemas across the land which was meant to extol the virtues of the pure wool garments they were wearing. The National Wool Council of Britain were pleased. The Searchers were not. The glum faces on the resultant footage gives a clue that they absolutely hated the clothes and frankly did not want to wear them.

The Iron Door held a celebration fan club party on December 29th for their special favourites who had been voted second only to the Beatles in the New Musical

Express poll category of Best British Vocal Group. They were also deemed to be seventh in the world's best vocal groups and *Sweets For My Sweet* was judged to be the sixth best British disc of the year. The Shadows had topped that particular category with the Beatles at number two. Christmas certainly was a time for celebration this time round. 1963 had been an amazing year for the Searchers but 1964 was going to be even better.

When deejay Barry Aldis reviewed *Needles And Pins* for the NME on January 3rd he hedged his bets a little. 'Not quite what we expect from the chart-topping group' he opined, a statement which could be construed as a positive or a negative and he continued with 'rather repetitive melody line adds to the appeal.' 'Not quite' and 'rather repetitive' balanced out 'chart-topping' and 'adds to the appeal' and gave him an out should the disc prove to be a flop. Spin was certainly not confined to the world of politics.

Another favourable review in the Record Mirror was more positive. 'Britain's second most popular group get their teeth into a Jackie DeShannon beater...plaintive guitar line running throughout…great tune very well performed...could well be number one.'

The Record Mirror also reported that there were plans in the pipeline for the Searchers to appear in a major film and not just a token appearance. Opening with the group already in the throes of stardom it would go on from there, and promised there would be acting roles for each of them with stacks of dialogue and at least three musical numbers.

Their one-time lead singer Johnny Sandon, now minus the Remo Four, meanwhile made a bold attempt at putting a brave face on things by declaring that he was happier solo and singing his beloved country and western material and announced his forthcoming release, an updated version of the old Tennessee Ernie Ford tune *Sixteen Tons*. Despite his public optimism he must have been dying inside as he watched his old chums conquer the world without him.

Needles And Pins entered the charts on January 17th at number eighteen and from there its rise was meteoric. By the 24th it had shot up to number four and the following week it had displaced the Dave Clark Five's *Glad All Over* at number one. The whole group was happy with their choice having been vindicated, although Tony Jackson's joy was tinged with more than a little bitterness at losing his prime position in the vocal department. The impact of *Needles And Pins* had been so great that he knew it would be hard, if not impossible, to recapture lost ground, particularly in the face of the opposition of Chris Curtis who had in truth never liked Tony much in the first place.

He was in a no-win situation. The rest of the group were firmly on the side of

Chris whose knowledge of pop music was encyclopaedic and whose ideas at the time seemed to be completely in touch with where they should be going. In both his personality and social habits Tony was out of kilter with the rest of the group. Additionally, Pye Records and the Tito Burns Organisation considered Curtis to be the group's absolute leader. If Chris didn't want it then it just wasn't going to happen. Relations between Tony and his fellow band members had begun to get very strained.

His new financial situation which enabled him to replace the iconic but inexpensive Hofner violin bass with a shiny new Epiphone Rivoli instrument made him feel a little better. But not much. He would gladly have traded a new bass guitar for a new lead vocal. He revelled in the life of a pop star and the kudos it brought him and the heady social whirl of the capital suited him well. He declared to journalist Norman Jopling 'I don't want to go back and live in Liverpool. I can't stand it. It's much better down here.'

Needles And Pins remained on top for two weeks before being replaced by Cilla Black's wonderfully emotive *Anyone Who Had A Heart* who in turn had prevented her Liverpudlian mate Gerry Marsden from completing what would have been an unprecedented quartet of consecutive chart toppers with *I'm The One* which stalled in second place.

There were several shows across Europe to undertake before the tour at the end of the month. Berlin with Trini Lopez at the Deutchlandhalle, a performance and a television show in Hamburg and a trip to Sweden. Everyone it seemed wanted the Searchers. They appeared on the BBC's *Hi There* and a series of recordings for Radio Luxembourg was announced. Summer shows in Scarborough and Great Yarmouth were set for July and August and negotiations were underway for tours of South Africa and Israel. Their gruelling schedule, which showed no signs of easing up as their popularity grew, took its toll and even caused John McNally to miss some shows due to a septic throat.

Amongst all this excitement two records slipped out and promptly disappeared with barely a trace. Johnny Sandon tried for a second time with his previously announced recording of *Sixteen Tons*. The rich bass voice that this song required was a piece of cake for Sandon. Unfortunately, the public decided that it was not the cake of their choice. They were apparently on a diet.

Elsewhere on Cameo-Parkway, a Philadelphian label which had scored heavily in the past with teen stars like Charlie Gracie, Bobby Rydell, and twist king Chubby Checker, issued a single by a black group called the Orlons whose only UK record of note up to that point, despite having achieved five top twenty records in the USA up to October '63, had been a minor hit called *Don't Hang Up*. On hearing their new disc, intriguingly called *Bon Doo Wah*, the public hung up immediately saying 'don't call us, we'll call you' and the Orlons were confined to the remainders bin of history. But nestling on the rear of this unremarkable offering was a song that was very soon to become a major part of the Searchers' career.

As usual whenever the group were in London and commitments permitted I caught up with them and reaped some of the rewards that were dished out to them in the way of pleasant social events. Just prior to the commencement of the Bobby Vee/Big Dee Irwin/Dusty Springfield tour Tito Burns held a party at his house in Finchley and I was invited to tag along. The Burns household occupied a decent sized, if unremarkable, detached house in a fairly typical middle-class suburban district but the gathering that night constituted a guest list that to my rather star-less existence was anything but unremarkable.

I found myself rubbing shoulders with the likes of Alma Cogan, Gene Pitney, a pre-Bond Roger Moore and of course the stars of the forthcoming tour. I also disgraced myself by wandering round with a sheet of paper and asking for their autographs, although no one seemed to mind. And I did redeem myself somewhat by giving a lift home to Gene and Alma. I got the feeling that Pitney, who was crushed in the back seat of my Sunbeam Rapier with the glamourous singing star, was hoping that Miss Cogan would invite him in when we arrived at her apartment above the Christian Science Reading Rooms in Kensington High Street where she shared the space with her mother Faye, but alas she simply got out, said goodnight, and we continued our journey, dropping a disappointed Gene at the Stafford Hotel just off Oxford Street.

A small piece of compensation for Tony Jackson was their inclusion in the full-length feature film *Saturday Night Out.* The promised dramatic roles alas never materialised but there were two songs included on which he was the main voice. Although passed over as actors their one scene had them performing two numbers in a pub, the songs in question being the title song to the movie plus *Saints And Searchers*, the latter being nothing more than their version of *When The Saints Go Marching In*, beneath which they were copyrighted as authors, the number being deemed a traditional folk song and therefore in the public domain. It was a shrewd trick which many a canny performer employed, especially when it came to flip-sides which sold exactly the same number of copies as the reverse. It was Andrew Oldham, the mastermind behind the early Rolling Stones, who was later to emphasise this principle with some irony when he recorded an instrumental with the marvellous title of *Oh I Do Love To See Me On The B-side.*

To their eternal chagrin the Searchers had been talked out of putting a self-penned recording on the reverse of *Needles And Pins* in favour of the movie's title track with the reasoning that the publicity gained from its appearance in the film would give the disc a valuable boost. It did not. The film, respectable as it was as a piece of cinema, came and went with no discernable advantage coming their way. On the other hand they had lost tens of thousands of pounds in royalties that would otherwise have accrued as songwriters of the tune which would have accompanied their greatest and most remembered hit.

What remained unknown to the group for over four decades was the fact that *Saturday Night Out* had actually been co-penned by Tony Hatch in partnership with Robert F. V. Richards, a movie music arranger who was to work on a number of mildly titillating movies with such exotic titles as *The Black Torment* (1964), *School For Unclaimed Girls* (1969) and *Incense For The Damned* (1971). He was also the arranger for the eminently forgettable flick *Gonks Go Beat* (1965) while at the more cerebral end of proceedings Richards was the orchestrator for the blockbuster epic *The Lion In Winter* (1968) which starred Katherine Hepburn and Peter O'Toole.

While the Searchers had quickly become aware of the Fred Nightingale appendage the truth behind this other Hatch persona, Marc Anthony, lay undiscovered for decades. Which was probably just as well. The lads might not have been best pleased to discover that the highly lucrative recording which had been wrestled from their grasp had in fact been delivered to their recording manager with the publishing profits again pouring into the coffers of Tito Burns.

While my famous chums were riding high I was merely stumbling along as the Rebel Rousers trudged around the eternal club and ballroom circuit eking out a respectable living but failing to get anywhere in the all-important charts. Towards the end of March we generously offered the public our version of the old Muddy Waters rhythm and blues favourite *Got My Mojo Working*. The public thanked us for the offer but reluctantly declined. It was a good disc performed at a raging tempo with baritone and tenor saxes in harmony adding colour to Cliff Bennett's terrific vocals.

Derek Johnson of the NME wrote that it was a 'frenzied up-tempo beat, honking saxes, slap-happy hoe-down sound'. He also added that it was a fiery disc that made your spine tingle and more dynamic than a rival version by a group called the Sheffields coincidentally produced by Tony Hatch. The Record Mirror praised its 'big fat sound', called us 'one of the best of Britain's beat groups' and predicted that it should show in the lower regions of the charts. Unfortunately it failed to reach any regions of the charts, lower or otherwise.

For the other side we had once again reworked an old standard in much the same way that we had done with *Everybody Loves A Lover*. This time it was the Stephen Foster song *Beautiful Dreamer* that got the treatment. Whether Foster would have thought it beautiful or not I can only guess but we liked it. Readers will note we had not cottoned on to the age old B-side trick.

If we were getting nowhere fast the Searchers were pouring out hits by the bucket load and not surprisingly in the wake of their massive sales the option on their contract had been taken up by Pye Records. Dated March 2nd 1964, the new period was to run from April 22nd for one year, which would seem to leave three further options open for future years. But they had rather trickily inserted an astonishing five further options into the new document which meant that, should they all be applied, the group would be indentured to the company for an astonishing six more years. They were in the peculiar position of having completed one year, yet ending up with more terms ahead of them than when they started out. I would think even Spartacus managed a better deal than that.

As a reward for their future loyalty their rates would increase by one half of a per cent with each new period except for the fourth option, which for whatever reason increased by a whole percentage point. Their generosity knew no bounds it seems. But one has to remember this was very much par for the time. And at least the record labels clearly laid out their terms, good, bad or awful, in the clauses of the contract, unlike unscrupulous managements who often bought and sold their own artistes while the musicians themselves remained in the dark about these iniquitous double dealings.

By this time Les Ackerley had been gently eased out of the picture. He had been a reasonable-sized fish in a modest northern pond but the rise in the fortunes of the Searchers had dragged him into an ocean in which he was about to drown. There was no more that he could do for them now that the big boys had entered the picture. Tito Burns had the office, the contacts and the expertise to advance their career on not just a national but an international stage.

It was given to Tito to conduct the 'Thank you for all you've done but we'll take it from here' talk. Ackerley was no match for Burns who could be either silver-tongued or ruthless depending on the needs of the moment and he knew the ins and outs of the legal position which for Ackerley was weak. The deed was done, any compensatory arrangements that had to be made were completed and it was back to Liverpool for Les with little more than the satisfaction of knowing he had played his essential role in the rise to glory of the Searchers. Ackerley recalls his time guiding the Searchers with a resigned equanimity.

'In 1960 I owned two clubs in Liverpool, in addition to a public accountancy practice. One was a country and western club taking two hundred members, the other was the Iron Door Club. This was four hundred yards from the Cavern on Temple Street. They took up to six hundred and fifty to seven hundred members – on duckboards – while we took two and a half thousand members.

'It was two six-storey warehouses knocked together. We used the bottom four floors. Three stages for groups, one on each floor, plus cloakrooms. We had up to twenty groups a night. Friday, Saturday and Sunday were all-night sessions. There was also a two hour session at lunch times. Busy days! We even allowed Cilla Black to sing at lunch hours.

'The Searchers had promise but no organisation. I slung them off stage three or four times and had serious chats about improvements. We made progress and built up an act. From there I took out a management and booking contract – 10% on each. Later I arranged a recording contract. I have a letter from Decca telling me they were not up to standard.

'I wanted to get them on the Empire Theatre and other shows controlled by Tito Burns in London. As bait I offered him the booking contract. The increased fees would compensate for the loss of that. Of course Tito worked hard to get the management contract, by hook or by crook. Eventually he did so, but that's a long story.

'Over the whole period I probably lost money on the Searchers, but the clubs were making it – so what?'

It seems the Beatles were not the only Scouse band to be turned down by Decca. The Searchers were in good company.

The new contract was signed by the group members themselves. It was contained in the wording that Chris, who signed under his real name of Crummey, was known professionally as Chris Curtis, while oddly no such affirmation was made with regard to Mike's stage name of Pender. He naturally signed as Michael John Prendergast. Chris's surname was erroneously spelt as Crummy without the 'e' on both this and the previous document.

During the first week of April the group flew to Paris to star in a major radio show called Musicorama which featured them miming to their hits in French. Alternative lyrics in both German and French had been commissioned for a small number of their hits in an attempt to break into foreign charts with more ease and force. The words were written down phonetically and delivered with as much of an authentic accent as they could manage. Although the French were reasonably happy to hear songs in their native tongue, considering France to be the centre of the universe, the Germans had always been content to hear hard rock & roll and pop delivered in English, whether it be with an American accent or not, and so these recordings could be considered to have been more of a hindrance than a help by splitting the sales.

I was pleased to receive a postcard from John while in the French capital saying how much he liked the city. But, he added in typical McNally style, it was very expensive.

The pace dictated by Pye was frantic. No sooner had *Needles And Pins* exhausted its run of success than a follow-up was on the market. *Don't Throw Your Love Away* was issued during the first week of April and was the very same song that had been tucked away out of sight on the other side of the Orlons' ill-fated *Bon Doo Wah.*

The tune had been brought to the attention of Chris Curtis by Pat Pretty, a publicist on the payroll of Pye Records and who was married to Jack Bentley, a columnist for the Daily Mirror. Still with his finger very firmly on the teenage public consciousness Chris immediately saw the potential in this hitherto undervalued composition.

It was arranged in very much the same way as *Needles And Pins*, the public having latched onto the new Searchers sound and given it a most definite thumbs-up of approval. Once more Mike was given the lead with Chris on his distinctive and appealing falsetto while the others added more harmonies when required. Instead of the 'pseudo twelve-string' this time round they chose to use a tremolo effect on the guitar, a sound that had been around for some time but which had not featured on anything significant since the days of Duane Eddy. Having achieved 250,000 orders in advance of release it was a guaranteed success.

Derek Johnson's revue on April 7th was predictably positive. 'slightly less forceful than Needles...absolutely captivating melody...intriguing tang of nostalgia...a perfect vehicle for the boys...fascinating harmonies...dancers will love the irresistible beat...whether it reaches number 1 will depend on how long the Beatles' *Can't Buy Me Love* stays at the top.' Sticking to the pattern of self-penned B-sides the Chris Curtis composition *I Pretend I'm With You* completed the coupling.

With two number ones so far, another only missing out by the narrowest of margins and no less expected from their latest offering, they were on the crest of a wave and being feted and pursued from all sides. A million sales of *Needles And Pins* had earned them a gold disc which was presented to the band at a special Variety Club Gold Disc lunch where they were the guests of honour And they headed a star-studded line-up also staged by the Variety Club of Great Britain at the Empire Pool in Wembley. In addition, they had been booked to appear on the prestigious *Ed Sullivan Show* in New York which, having seen the light after the sensation caused by the Beatles, signed up a bunch of British acts including Dusty Springfield, Freddie & the Dreamers, Gerry & the Pacemakers and Brian Poole & the Tremeloes.

The Sullivan television show was without doubt the most influential variety entertainment across the States and the all-important catalyst for them with the USA just waiting to be conquered. The Beatles had barnstormed their way into the hearts of American youth in a fashion that could have never been predicted. For a British disc to achieve success there was big news. For a British outfit to monopolise the best-selling lists, to the point where the Fab Four had all of the top five singles in the Billboard chart of April 4th, was nothing short of phenomenal.

The songs chosen to perform on the *Ed Sullivan Show* on April 5th 1964 were the new single *Needles And Pins* and *Ain't That Just Like Me* which was about to be coupled with *Ain't Gonna Kiss Ya* for a separate US release. The rest of the bill that night was a mish-mash typical of a Sullivan presentation which was designed to grab the attention of a wide age-ranging demographic.

Dan Rowan and Dick Martin of Rowan and Martin Laugh In fame supplied the bulk of the comedic content but Nipsy Russell was also on hand to further amuse the audience. To balance out the Searchers there was a contribution from an Italian tenor called Franco Corelli which offered a touch of Neapolitana. And there was even ventriloquism, if that was your bag, in the shape of Señor Wences. The internationally popular puppet Topo Gigio and a dance duo with the intriguing names of Mata and Hari spread the appeal even wider in a show that was completed by the Little Singers of Tokyo. An Ed Sullivan bill was nothing if not catholic. All that was missing was a troupe of singing dogs and a horse that could tap out his age on a drum.

But despite the extensive content there was little doubt, especially in the light of Brit-mania initiated by the world-conquering Beatles, that the Searchers were the big attraction in this particular week. Despite one guitar amp refusing to work throughout the totally live performance they acquitted themselves very well and received a better review than the Beatles had on their Sullivan debut.

'Most professional group to appear on the show...initial impression more favourable than the Beatles or the Dave Clark Five...melodic flow and a reasonably good harmonic blend, their sense of rhythm rather stiff but no stiffer than other British groups...sustained exuberant mood punctuated by several unison jumps in the air...even in the R&B number *Ain't That Just Like Me* they showed a more subtle command of dynamics than the two groups that preceded them.' It was a good push for their first US tour set for the end of May.

15

Enter The New Boy

Some time towards the end of April 1964 I met up with Chris Curtis in London. We dined at a favourite eaterie of his called Antonio's, a Spanish restaurant in Cranbourn Street just at the point where it is about to meet the main thoroughfare of Charing Cross Road, slap bang in the middle of the busy theatre district of the West End. On the corner diagonally opposite stood the Talk Of The Town, a major cabaret showcase for visiting international stars. These days the old Talk Of The Town has reverted to its original name of the Hippodrome and is currently an impressively luxurious high tech disco.

Antonio's purveyed predictable but excellent anglicised Spanish cuisine and was renowned for its presentations of Flamenco dancing performed on the tiny floor adjacent to the diners. As many will have realised while enjoying sun-soaked holidays on the Costa del Sol, spectacular and colourful as it may be, not to mention highly skilled, a little Flamenco goes a very long way. Castanets and Castilian heels in full stomping mode make a very invasive sound indeed. It is very easy to overdose. But still, evenings at Antonio's were very enjoyable and Chris was always a highly entertaining dinner companion.

Chris, by now a major pop star and a recognisable face wherever he went, was a valued customer and we were welcomed warmly and shown to the best table - or the worst table, depending on how you felt about the noise of those bloody Castilian heels deafening you, and acres of polka dot skirt swirling dangerously near your gazpacho. Conversation began in a pretty typical way as we talked of the latest changes, all upwards, in their fortunes. Their new release *Don't Throw Your Love Away* had been climbing the charts and was heading for a top position, which it finally achieved in May, although the rise was not quick enough to displace the Beatles. It was left to Peter and Gordon to do that with *A World Without Love.*

But then Chris began to tell of discontent in the group. It seemed all was not well in paradise. There had been a rumour in the press that Mike Pender was about to quit.

The rumour was emphatically denied by Tito Burns. Perhaps the press had simply assumed that his unexpected marriage in December was a sign that domestic bliss would lessen the appeal of a hectic life on the road. If they had learned of dissention in the ranks they were quite correct. But they were homing in on the wrong person.

It was with Tony Jackson that the other three were not getting on at all well and it had come to an impasse. They were arguing all the time. He wasn't performing well. He was getting drunk before shows and not tuning up properly, they claimed. Tony claimed (erroneously) in a '90s interview with Spencer Leigh that he was being given the wrong times and dates on purpose. And there was a clash of personalities, not just with Chris with whom he had never bonded but with John and Mike too. It had even come to fisticuffs.

Prior to a show at the Sophia Gardens in Cardiff he had spent too long at the pub and the others, anxiously waiting and wondering if he would turn up at all, had tuned his bass for him to which he strongly objected. The argument continued right up to show time. As the announcement faded and the curtains opened the two figures of Pender and Jackson were seen to be grappling against the amplifiers and about to beat the shit out of one another. Hostilities thankfully ceased speedily enough to allow the show to continue.

Tony was not happy about the Pender/Curtis coupling on the record front despite its obvious runaway success. He had always considered himself to be the rightful lead singer and found the perceived demotion hard to take. *Don't Throw Your Love Away* was already in the top three on its way to number one, their fourth hit and third chart-topper in less than a year. He was not in a strong position to object.

Jackson's weakened position was sealed by the fact that the new direction and vocal style the band had taken was continued with the new album that was now finished and ready for release. *It's The Searchers* was in fact the title of its second issue. On the initial cover design the words had been prefixed with the in-vogue but excruciatingly embarrassing *It's Fab, It's Gear*, fab and gear being cute, if toe-curlingly mawkish, slang promoted in conversation by none other than those custodians of hip, the Beatles. But not even an endorsement from John, Paul, George and Ringo could convince them that this could do anything but rob them of their credibility. They demanded that Pye should withdraw the record and reissue it with the offending words removed. Such was their power that their demands were met although there could be little doubt that in the end the cost of such an operation would be deducted from royalties. A few stray *'Fab, Gear'* copies did find their way onto the market.

The choice of songs and their arrangements on the LP showed a maturity that had advanced significantly since the first two releases and Chris Curtis's stamp was firmly on many of them. *This Empty Place* in particular, a Bacharach-David composition, was not on the face of it an obvious choice for a mere pop combo whose repertoire up to then never ventured too far from the three or four chords tricks of the simple r&b formula it had mostly adhered to. The breathy Chris Curtis vocals and intriguing octave jumps of the melody line with its quirky but always interesting timing threatened to put them streets ahead of their rivals who were still sticking to the most simplistic and direct forms of pop.

I Can't Help Forgiving You, penned by one of their favourite writers Jackie DeShannon, was another haunting tune with a subtle and complimentary guitar figure running in the background. They may not have used a twelve-string guitar on *Needles And Pins* but the real deal was featured on this track, albeit an acoustic instrument and not the jangly electric model they would become associated with. And *Where Have You Been?* was an appealing beat ballad given its emotional boost by the intimate Curtis vocal style. All in all, with the inclusion of the last two smash hit singles, it was a strong product.

But it was noticeable that Tony Jackson, whose voice had featured in a lead role on no less than ten out of the twelve tracks that comprised their debut album *Meet The Searchers*, and seven out of the twelve tracks on the follow up LP *Sugar And Spice* (totalling 62% of the album output thus far), had no solo singles at all on their third release one year on, with the exception of a joint contribution tucked away in the mix of *Sure Know A Lot About Love.*

Just when they should have been overjoyed at all that had come their way in such a short time and reaping the benefits, it was becoming impossible for them to work together. Enough it seemed was enough and changes would have to be made. Tony had to go. Instinctively I knew what was coming and without actually asking the obvious question Chris said, 'But I suppose you're happy with Cliff Bennett?'

I was happy with Cliff although I would have been a great deal happier with the kind of mind-blowing success that the Searchers had seen over the previous twelve months. I explained that, following recommendations from almost every artiste in his stable from the Beatles down, we had just been signed by Brian Epstein. I was scared of rocking the boat now that we could finally be on the verge of making it. Chris opined that he understood, and knowing Eppy he could envisage my quitting possibly might make a difference. We changed the subject and spoke no more of it that night.

I told no-one about this save a couple of close friends until a few weeks later when, on a short and unsuccessful tour of Ireland (we only got paid for half of it), I was walking with our sax player Moss Groves down the main street of a small village the name of which is lost to my memory. For whatever reason I decided to tell him of my conversation with Curtis. Moss looked at me with total incredulity. In his strong, dour Brummie accent he said 'You've turned down a job with one of the biggest groups in the country? Don't be so fucking stupid. Get on the phone, tell them you want the job and ask them if they want a sax player as well.'

He had a point. It was the catalyst I needed. I tossed it over in my mind for a while and finally made the fateful decision. There was a problem though. I had neglected to bring Chris's telephone number away with me and he was ex-directory. I don't know how I managed it but I eventually sweet-talked the operator into getting through to the Crummey household and asking if they would accept my call. Luck was with me. Chris was at home and seemed pleased at my decision. From there it was no going back although I decided not to break the news to Cliff until Chris had discussed it with Mike and John. It would be foolish to burn my bridges only to find that I had to get back to the side from whence I had come.

There was also the small matter of bringing things out into the open with Tony when the time was deemed appropriate. For the time being the erroneous rumours that someone was about to quit the band still centred on the newly-married Mike Pender. Mike had, in fact, been married for four months by this time.

It wasn't long before I came into contact with the whole group again as we had been booked for a series of Sunday night concerts Brian Epstein was to present at the Prince of Wales Theatre just off Leicester Square in the heart of London. The opening headliners for May 3rd by coincidence were the Searchers. Subsequent attractions advertised were Billy J Kramer & the Dakotas plus Brian Poole & the Tremeloes on the 10th, Roy Orbison and Eden Kane on the 17th, Freddie & the Dreamers and the Applejacks on the 24th, the Beatles and Kenny Lynch on the 31st, Gerry & the Pacemakers and the Mojos on June 7th and finally Dusty Springfield topping the bill of the final concert on June 14th.

The cast of support acts in residence throughout the run, apart from Cliff Bennett & the Rebel Rousers, included the Lorne Gibson Trio, the Chants, the Harlems and the Vernons Girls, now reduced to a trio and who were unfortunately to be backed by us. Great as it was, our band was never any good as accompanying musicians and the poor Vernons suffered weekly at our incompetent hands. We were performers in our own right and could not easily fill the role of a group like Sounds Incorporated who were experienced in providing brilliant backing to numerous and demanding American artistes. Sounds Incorporated, although not advertised, were drafted in for the opening concert due to the non appearance for whatever reason by the unpredictable and increasingly unreliable ex-Shadows drummer Tony Meehan.

During the evening Chris introduced me to Tito, explaining that I was the person who would be joining them. Tito's greeting was curt to say the least and certainly non-committal. I got the impression that he was not overjoyed at the prospect of any disruption that might affect his star turn. Perhaps he thought it was something that would blow over. He definitely did not want anyone killing the golden goose before she had laid sufficient golden eggs.

The concerts, at least as far as the initial one was concerned, were under-rehearsed and the opening night stuttered through a roster of acts that varied greatly in their ability to present quality entertainment to a finish that was saved by the Searchers' bravura performance. Columnist Chris Hutchins under the headline 'Searchers OK in Chaotic Concert' wrote 'After a chaotic first half the Searchers were great...exciting act...went off to a tremendous reception from an audience that sounded capacity even though it wasn't.' He also dished out some praise to Cliff Bennett & the Rebel Rousers and to Sounds Incorporated which was nice. The Vernons I imagine might have gathered some plaudits too if they had not had us behind them ruining their act.

The shows got better as we all settled in and naturally the night the Beatles appeared was an absolute sensation. Beatlemania had gripped the land firmly, and once again I watched from the wings in awe but still somehow not realising that from this point on these four lads from Liverpool had become the new reference point for all guitar-based pop music in the future.

By this time press attention had switched to John McNally whose engagement to Mary Hollywood had leaked out. He stubbornly refused to disclose the date and venue of their forthcoming wedding saying 'I don't want my fiancée to be bothered.'

Later in the month while I was patiently biding my time in readiness for the big move and hoping that all would not go 'tits up' we appeared again with the Searchers on Whit Monday when they formed part of the bill at the now annual Botwell Festival in my home town of Hayes. It was a stellar line-up that day with the Animals, Georgie Fame, Eden Kane, the Migil Five, Julie Grant and Screaming Lord Sutch among the featured acts. I did think however that the Searchers were taking their proletarian image a little too far when they all bundled out of their green Ford Thames van minibus.

But green minibus for transport or not, their career was most definitely riding on the crest of a wave as the new album received a four-star review from Allan Evans. On May 24th they topped the bill on television's most popular variety show Sunday Night At The London Palladium and a few days later jetted off to begin their first tour of the United States. Sharing the stage with them as they bussed from city to city starting at the World's Fair in New York were the Dovells (*Bristol Stomp*) and Dick & Dee Dee (*The Mountain's High, Turn Around*).

Although neither of these acts achieved any significance in the UK Len Barry, the lead singer of the Dovells, had a major British chart success in 1965 with *1 - 2 - 3*, at the same time managing to alienate a large proportion of the record buying public by boasting that he would be bigger than the Beatles.

John and Mike had taken along May, Mike's new wife, and John's fiancée Mary

Hollywood, whose wedding to John was now set for June 27th. With Chris a lone gun and hardly a fitting companion for Tony, it further exacerbated Jackson's isolation from the others. He had not yet been told of what was in the wind but the atmosphere was going from bad to worse. The upside was that in a package tour of this kind there are enough distractions on the social side with other performers to interact with, not to mention people one may meet on the road, that unpleasant matters are easily pushed into the background temporarily at least.

Even in America 'Black Jake' was as controversial as ever and managed to make his mark in a quite spectacular way. Overhearing a policeman in a backstage area utter a remark that he perceived to indicate that he might not be 'as other men are' (I understand the word was 'faggot') he decided that even American cops should not be immune to the penalties deserved over such a slur to his manhood. He promptly landed one on the poor unsuspecting law enforcement officer. Fortunately what could have been a disastrous situation was defused by someone with sufficient tact and authority and the band lived to play on. But it was one more nail in the coffin of Tony's demise as a Searcher.

Dee Dee Sperling, one half of the duo Dick & Dee Dee, looks back on the tour fondly. 'I remember how shocked the Searchers were to see us eat French toast and syrup for breakfast. They thought that it was the most disgusting thing they'd ever observed. The tour was done by bus and I remember standing in a fairground after a performance one night and a frantic fan raced up to me waving an autograph book in my face and screamed, 'Are you somebody?' That question has haunted me over the years.

'We all went to Niagara Falls one day. I guess we must have done a show near there. We had our pictures taken at the edge of the falls. And I remember Mike Pender's wife May borrowed my sun tanning lamp and burned her eyes badly. We had to take her to the emergency hospital in New York. We drove through the Bronx on the way there and I was shocked to see people passed out in the gutters, something I'd never seen before.

'The places we played were medium-size venues, not huge arenas or small night clubs, and as far as I can remember we weren't joined by other performers in different towns. It was just the three acts on the tour. The Searchers starred on the bill with the Dovells and Dick & Dee Dee as opening acts. The American kids went wild for the Searchers. It was at the height of the British Invasion and you could get mobbed for just talking with a British accent.'

By mid-June the Searchers were back in the UK and ready to record their new single, *Someday We're Gonna Love Again*, which was achieved by chartering a plane from Blackpool to London, completing the session and promptly flying back to Blackpool for a show at the Ice Rink that same evening. Once again the old B-side plundering trick had been used, this time from an American songstress called Barbara Lewis.

When it hit the stores on July 7th Derek Johnson's review in the NME was muted, stating that it was not as strong as *Don't Throw Your Love Away* but predicting, not surprisingly in the light of their undiminished popularity, that it would be a hit nonetheless. Disc described the tune as 'Easier to hold than a piece of tacky toffee' while the Record Mirror praised the brilliant guitar work and suggested that it would in all probability go to the top in a very short time. On the reverse *No One Else Could Love Me*, a self-penned song as was the general rule, completed the single.

In the Record Mirror popularity polls, which were curiously held in mid-year unlike the more normal end of the year polls that most publications favoured, the Searchers figured strongly. In both British and World vocal group categories they were placed at number three with only the Beatles and the Rolling Stones above them. In the World section the Beatles took the top spot over the Stones while in the British list the one and two positions were reversed. *Needles And Pins* was voted the ninth most popular disc of a year that ran from June 1963 to June 1964.

Somehow in the tiny gap between the recording and the release John and Mary McNally had managed to fit in their wedding which, in contrast to the Prendergasts' clandestine nuptials, was conducted in the full glare of the public, the couple having caved in to pressure from both the press and the Tito Burns office.

On June 27th at St Alexander's Church in Kirkdale over two thousand people gathered to watch the childhood sweethearts wed. There were none of the pop stars many might have expected to see. Liverpool was a long, long way from London and John rarely mixed with celebrities, but Tito Burns drove up in a Rolls Royce which caused a stir. And John's sister with her blonde bouffant hair was mistaken for Dusty Springfield. A policewoman was jostled in the chaotic melée and her tights were torn. Mary's mother sent her a new pair and a box of chocolates to make up for it.

As happy as he was with his new bride John was equally unhappy with the new platter, which he thought was disappointing and un-commercial. He made a wager with Tito Burns that it would not reach the top ten. He was unfortunately proved right when by the latter part of the month it stalled at number eleven, a relatively poor showing for such consistently high placing hit makers.

There was still the matter of a confrontation with Tony to deal with. Although his relationship with the others was at an all time low, he could not have foreseen just how far things had sunk. Again it was left to Tito to broach the subject and offer what might be considered an acceptable solution. He explained how the others felt and that the best way out for all was for Tony to be set up with a backing group of his own and be promoted from within the Tito Burns Organisation as a solo star. The words solo and star hit the right chord. Although it would not have been his first choice to exit such a successful outfit, he could see the advantages of a career in which he would be not just the centre but the sole object of attention.

His departure would be headline news and he had his own share of their substantial fan base to provide him with a ready-made public which would support him if his product was good enough. After all he was a popular member and there was little chance of him simply being deserted and hung out to dry. Instead of the Searchers on the billboards it would be Tony Jackson in letters as high as his ego required them to be. But he was furious and unforgiving of what he saw as a betrayal by the others and Chris Curtis in particular was to receive his anger.

There was a particularly vitriolic confrontation during which Tony threatened to reveal some unpleasant facts about Chris to the newspapers. I discovered later that Tony intended to announce to anyone who would listen that Chris wanted him out so that he could get 'his boyfriend' in. When I eventually found out the gist of his venomous attack I was vaguely amused although I could see where he was coming from. He was, however, very wrong.

Certainly I was a friend of Chris Curtis and more so his friend than of Mike or John at the time although I liked them all very much. Also at twenty years old I might just have got away with being called a boy. But the actual truth of the matter was that Chris was a friend purely because he was an incredibly interesting and funny guy to hang around with. He was never anything less than great company and I admired him a lot. Never ever dull and possessing a sense of style which I was not able to emulate. And the fact that we had become friends before the onset of celebrity disproved any notion that I might simply be a hanger-on to a well-known person basking in reflected glory.

Throughout the entire time I knew him Chris and I never had a conversation that revolved around sex. Those were different and more innocent times and it was not that kind of a group. They were not people who played around and any debauched rock & roll lifestyle one might wish to imagine was conspicuous by its absence. I never once asked Chris about his sexuality and neither did he ask me. I may have opinions on what his lifestyle might or might not have involved but even today I have no proof whatsoever of where his proclivities lay. If you were to ask me if Chris was straight, gay or even prone to shagging the odd sheep I would have to tell you that I could not answer with certainty.

I most certainly did not have any romantic notions towards Chris Curtis and if he held any such notions towards me then he never displayed them. Tony always believed the rumour though. And so did Cliff Bennett as I discovered at a time when someone interviewed him for a proposed biography of the Searchers some years ago. I certainly don't blame either of them. In their place I would no doubt have formed the same conclusion. And in any case there is nothing to blame. I don't have a problem with it. What people do with their own bodies in the comfort of their own homes and in the comfort of their own minds is perfectly fine. But they were mistaken in their belief of this myth because a myth is all it is and was.

Now that everything was finally out in the open, although still being kept from the press, it was agreed for me to start with the group at the end of August following a series of weeks in variety with Dusty Springfield and Eden Kane. It was also time to tell Cliff and the others. Coincidentally, I was in conversation yet again with Moss Groves who told me that during a gathering at which I was not present I had come in for a certain amount of verbal abuse from some of the band. Moss had defended me saying that though they may be 'slagging Frank off' as it were, he had showed astonishing loyalty to them by turning down an offer from the Searchers. At that point I had to tell poor deluded Moss that he would now have to eat his words because I had taken his advice and their offer.

Cliff took the news stoically and set about retrenching. They decided to approach Bobby Thompson, the Liverpudlian bassist with Kingsize Taylor with whom they had all got on with extremely well. He was a like-minded person both socially and musically and would fit in well. The problem was that he had only recently decided to quit Kingsize and had sold his bass guitar. As I wouldn't be needing mine I agreed to loan him my instrument until I needed it in about a month and a half's time. Meanwhile I would enjoy a rest and listen to the Searchers recordings so that I would be well prepared when the time came.

Chris and I had yet another meal at Antonio's during which I thought I'd better make some enquiries as to what my earnings would be. So far the mention of filthy lucre, always an embarrassing subject at the best of times, had been avoided. Chris's answer was that he didn't actually know what they earned because they drew money weekly and the rest was banked for the purposes of tax and expenses plus whatever surplus would accrue for when they would wish to draw on it.

His reply amazed me. What I was asking in fact was what wage they would pay me and here I was being told that I would share equally in the spoils. I asked him if that was the intention and he said that he hadn't envisaged it any other way and neither, as far he was concerned, had Mike or John. I thought they must be mad. After all I had contributed nothing to the enormous success of the band and as far as I could see could not possibly expect that kind of recompense for simply filling in a gap in the instrumentation. But if it was being handed to me on a plate I was not about to turn it down. I still thought they were crazy though.

As it turned out they were not quite as daft as Chris imagined them to be. In an embarrassed phone call a short while later he explained that the other two would not hear of an equal share and that I would be on a wage, the amount of which was still to be decided. I replied that it was fine with me and that he shouldn't bother himself about it. Not willing to leave it there, having been forced to renege, he promised me that he would make sure it would happen before long. It seemed he was far more concerned about it than me, who could see that Mike and John were simply being business-like.

After all, despite the fact that the public somehow sees a musical combination as some kind of Utopian democracy, we all have to remember that entertainment is essentially a business and subject to the same kind of philosophies and necessarily hard-nosed decisions. And far from being a democracy you will find that once the power base has settled in a band the survival of the fittest usually results in a form of dictatorship, hopefully a benevolent one but more often than not a rod of iron rules the obedient roost. Furthermore it is usually the dictatorship that tends to continue in a greater state of efficiency. A hired hand I was and a hired hand I was content to be.

Just as I was relaxing into my very welcome and enjoyable hiatus matters took a different turn. Word had leaked to the press and denials were issued both by Tito's office and by Tony Jackson himself. He had been forced to deny that he was leaving the Searchers saying that they had probably confused him with Ray Jones, the bass player of the Dakotas who was quitting their ranks allegedly due to personality clashes.

In the Record Mirror of July 25th Chris Curtis also insisted that Tony was not leaving. However, the Daily Mirror, only days later, printed a piece by Patrick Doncaster that stated 'Tony Jackson was definitely leaving, whatever his professional associates might say to the contrary.' The game, it seemed, was up.

The information they now possessed, which included my name, was too precise and a glib denial was no longer effective. Tony Jackson in an interview with Barry May of the Record Mirror gave his side of the story. It was not, he explained, an argument between him and the band so much as differences between him and Chris Curtis. 'We both know what sound we want and they are two different views. I don't want to be the star. I just want to be a quarter of the group which I am not now. I couldn't do a vocal on *Needles And Pins* because of laryngitis. After that Chris said that he didn't want me to do the vocals anymore. The decision to leave was a 50/50 one. We decided there was a clash of styles and a break would be best.'

Tony was skirting around the truth. The chasm between him and Curtis was bound to bring things to a head sooner or later. They were both volatile people of strong and determined character, each convinced of his own merit and when one egotist meets another it's an I for an I.

Tony's final day as a Searcher was set for 2nd August when they would play a Sunday night concert at the Aquarium, Great Yarmouth. My debut, Tito explained, would be brought forward to 3rd August, the first date on the variety tour whose opening week was to be at the Coventry Theatre in the Midlands. In one week's time I would take my place on stage with them.

There was also an announcement in the music press that week that Cliff Bennett & the Rebel Rousers had been signed by Brian Epstein's NEMS company and that Bobby Thompson, formerly of Kingsize Taylor & the Dominoes, would join them in place of Frank Allen who was replacing Tony Jackson in the Searchers.

In the Mersey Beat music paper of 6th August a full length page was devoted to the split under the heading 'A New Look For The Searchers'. Chris, John and Mike said nice things about me joining and Tony was quoted as saying he wanted to break away from the Searchers' image and market. He indicated he was auditioning for new members to join his new group.

'I don't know if I will have anyone from Liverpool in the group. In fact I've only received one application from a Liverpool musician.' He did not name anyone but indicated it was a drummer. One can safely assume it was not Chris Curtis.

There were however the small matters of acquiring a bass guitar until I could retrieve mine from Bobby Thompson and of a rehearsal. Luckily I managed to borrow a similar model to mine from the very obliging folk at Sound City on Shaftesbury Avenue, London's major musical store which had been opened by the Searchers themselves back in March. As for rehearsals, so far I had not played a note with them but I knew the chords and lyrics of their major hits and album tracks and so it would not be a great problem. In those simpler times a top of the bill show consisted of little more than half a dozen tunes strung together and there was no production attached to the presentation of a mere pop group's headlining act. We reasoned that an afternoon's run-through at the theatre on the day would suffice. There was no need at this point for me to learn more songs than were required to fill their segment of the show.

On Monday 3rd August I caught the 10.30 a.m train from Euston which arrived dead on schedule at 12.46 and I made my way to the Coventry Theatre. It was a hive of activity with other performers checking out equipment and testing the mics for balance under the guidance and control of tour manager Fred Perry. It would have been foolish for anyone to mistake Fred's theatrically camp nature for weakness. He ruled with an iron evening glove. Fred's main *raison d'etre* in the company was his absolute devotion to Dusty Springfield, whose lighting cues by his fair hands were far and away more elaborate and effective than anyone else's. Madame was a star. Everyone else was just pop.

Most of the cast just required a perfunctory few minutes on stage. They had all done it before. Dusty's regular backing band, the Echoes, did what they had to and gave way to Eden Kane's Downbeats. British-based American import Peppi Borza, a dancer turned singer and a close friend of Miss Springfield, was performing his fashionable twist routine on the show and a rotund, middle-aged impressionist called George Meaton, whose speciality was delivering quite realistic reproductions of noises that could be heard at Crewe Station, was there to balance things against the heavily weighted musical content.

Two o'clock came and went as did three o'clock and four o'clock with no sign of the Searchers. As the first of the two shows was due to go up at six o'clock this was more than a little disconcerting to me. Cliff Bennett would have been spitting tacks by now. Finally at four thirty they piled out of the plebeian green Transit with seemingly not a care in the world. Instead of a run-through with electric instruments on stage we settled with a quick routining of the set we were going to play in the dressing room. Luckily there were no surprises in it for me and I could foresee no problems in my duties that lay ahead.

It might have been my first day but there was still the matter of finance to be settled. Things had moved swiftly without the space for such discussions. As a solution they had ordered their accountant Bob Glatter of Blick, Rothenberg and Noble to present himself in their dressing room where he would conduct the formalities. It was an expensive way to tell me what my weekly wage would be. As a senior partner Glatter's hourly rate would have been in the region of £250 in today's terms. A day away from the office plus all the incidental expenses incurred must have resulted in a tidy sum, but the Searchers were high earning pop stars. They were earning it and they could spend it as they saw fit.

The amount they finally decided to dispose of in my direction was £70 per week with the band taking care of the tax, plus the basic expense on the road which would include hotels, train fares and a certain food allowance. That might sound like a paltry sum to anyone used to today's values but the approximate £100 total when tax was taken into account has to be multiplied by somewhere between ten and fifteen times to make one realise that I would be getting an equivalent of between £1,000 and £1,500 per week. It was a fortune and I was very grateful.

The time finally came when all the supporting acts had done their bits and received due applause. It was top of the bill time and the screams of teenage girls from beyond the tabs were deafening and getting louder. The announcement was made and we ran on stage. At last I was a Searcher.

16

Off To See The World

If you were to believe the columnist from the NME on August 7th, the issue following my debut as a Searcher, you would no doubt have envisaged scenes of chaos and disappointment in the Coventry Theatre that night of August 3rd 1964. George Tremlett wrote 'Searchers shock – fans shout for Tony Jackson' and went on to underline its general theme that all the yelling from the teenage crowd was for the Searcher who wasn't there.

He continued 'As Chris introduced *Memphis Tennessee* his voiced was drowned by shouts of "Where's Tony?" and fans chanting "We want Tony". Clearly rattled, Chris shouted "Shut up" over and over again into the mic only to have the same trouble when they had finished the number.' It made good reading. After all who is going to be grabbed by a headline that tells you everything went quite well on the whole, thank you?

To balance things out the reviewer in the Disc issued one day later gave a truer and more objective account of the evening's happenings. Entitled "Searcher swings in" he wrote that 'the audience at the Coventry Theatre gave bass guitarist Frank Allen an encouraging welcome on Monday when he made his first appearance with the Searchers.

'Frank gives the Searchers a new look even if the sound is much the same. Whereas Tony Jackson held his guitar up chest high, Frank prefers to play his red bass guitar on a long strap'. This was cutting-edge stuff. No sign of controversy so far. He continued 'The number in which he comes into his own is Buddy Holly's *Listen To Me*. It's a lilting number and his voice is obviously well suited to this type of material.' If it was well suited it was purely coincidental. Before our miniscule pre-show run-through in the dressing room I had never actually sung this song on stage before.

In fact, the reality of the event was somewhere in between the two reports. I stood there alongside my new workmates overawed and amazed at my situation, spruced up in my high-buttoned black suit of lightweight mohair which, with white shirt and black tie had become the defining uniform of the smart lads of pop. Mine was not the real thing but was a remnant of my days as a Rebel Rouser, as they had also adopted this mode of dress. The genuine article was still under construction by Tony Bone of Hitchin in Hertfordshire as well as an alternative suit in a pale grey and black dog-tooth pattern.

There were some voices calling out for the missing Tony when the curtains drew apart and I would have been surprised if there had not been. After all, merely a week before he had been an important member of the line-up and his departure was premature due to the leak in the press of the changes that were in the wind. Many years later I learned that the leak had come from an acquaintance from my locality in West London who was rewarded with the not inconsiderable sum of ten pounds for the information. When you consider that the average wage in 1964 was roughly twenty pounds a week it was not bad remuneration for a quick phone call. Ten out of ten for initiative.

But the cries of anguish from the Jackson supporters were really quite limited and diminished quickly after an irate Chris Curtis admonished the culprits from the stage where he commanded the proceedings in his inimitable way. Chris was excellent in the on-stage verbal department. He had a black belt in 'tongue fu'. I just stood there and grinned sheepishly trusting that an innocent and cherubic look would gradually bring them over to my side.

In fact it all went smoothly, there were no noticeable boobs in the music or arrangements and I came off quite elated. The congratulations from tour manager Fred Perry and Dusty Springfield were most welcome and boosted my confidence considerably. 'Just carry on doing exactly what you're doing' were Fred's words of wisdom. From Dusty I got a kiss. I'm not sure if Fred wanted to kiss me as well but I was pleased he didn't make a move as refusal often offends.

With the chance at last for some time at home the rest of the group were commuting from Liverpool each night, a journey which took a couple of hours each way, while I was billeted in the luxurious Leofric Hotel in the city centre for the week's run. But on the third day Mike informed me that I was to travel back with them and that I could stay at May's mother's house with him and May for the rest of the week. It was an extremely kind gesture made because they thought that it was a bit unfair for me to be on my own, particularly at that delicate time.

The newly-wed Mike and May were living with Mrs Doyle at her small terraced house in Lambeth Road, Bootle, just off the St John's Road until they decided what they were going to do about a first real home of their own. Mrs Doyle was a lovely lady, small and smiling and devout in her strong Catholic beliefs, as were my fellow Searchers and their families (though John did manage to lapse considerably as the years passed) and who bore nothing but goodwill to everyone.

I had sometime since abandoned religion as an unlikely and unreliable, not to mention dangerous set of suppositions at best. After all, the Bible was written by the same people who said the earth was flat. There are however three truths I'll go along with. Jews do not recognise Jesus as the Messiah. Protestants do not recognise the Pope as the leader of the Christian faith. And Baptists do not recognise each other in a liquor store or a strip joint.

Each night we would arrive home around one in the morning - still in the dreaded green Thames van - and Mrs Doyle would have a supper ready before we went to bed. We would find a delicious crab salad or maybe an omelette on the table within minutes of being dropped off by our road manager Billy Booker. The only downside of this for me was that I had actually been enjoying my unaccustomed taste of luxury in the very well appointed four-star Leofric and, having no great sentimental attachment to Liverpool, I would have been happier without the long drive at the end of the night. I was never a person who was afraid of being on his own. But I could never have tossed their kindness back in their faces by letting them know that.

After a couple of days into the Coventry run Dusty brought her brother Tom Springfield up from London to provide a bit of fun, company and the welcome addition of conga drums to her backing, which greatly enhanced her closing number, the Latin tune *La Bamba*. Tom had just begun to get his post-Springfields career under way and would before long achieve great success, and a considerable fortune, by writing and producing a string of hits for the Seekers, Ken Dodd, Jose Feliciano and others. It was a nice touch for Dusty to bring Tom in on some vocals to give her act an added dimension, and it was the start of a lifelong friendship for Tom and me.

The social side of my life too had taken an upswing the like of which I could never have foreseen. On August 12th we were the guests of Brian Epstein at his penthouse apartment at the top of Whaddon House in Williams Mews, Belgravia, where he was holding a soiree for anyone who was anyone in the entertainment world. Brian, with his innate sense of sophistication and style, had effortlessly transposed himself from the unprepossessing setting of the banks of the Mersey to the elegant salons of London, where he brushed shoulders and more than held his own with the upper echelons of the cream of society.

We arrived after the sumptuous meal had been consumed, as we were continuing our short tour of variety dates having moved on from Coventry to Southend. But as it was only a hop skip and a jump to central London we arrived in plenty of time to enjoy a major portion of the party. Our names were checked against the guest list and we ascended to the penthouse apartment following Cilla Black who also must have been performing somewhere that evening. Dusty who was on the bill with us and never one to miss out on a shindig had only just arrived before us.

The reason for the party was to celebrate the forthcoming debut concert tour of the Beatles across America. As I sat with John and Mary at a table talking to Paul McCartney and his then girlfriend the actress Jane Asher, trying to keep fairly quiet rather than risk what reputation I didn't have by uttering something banal, I gazed in open-mouthed awe at the star-studded throng.

Comic genius Tommy Cooper, as big and awkward as Judy Garland was small and frail, vied to rub shoulders with the likes of the Beatles, Cilla Black, Peter and Gordon, Dusty Springfield, Mick Jagger, Keith Richards, Tommy Steele and Lionel Bart. I was impressed and it must have showed. I was not a good enough actor to be anything else.

Judy Garland, her tiny sparrow-like frame as fragile as her grasp on life, had caused some confusion when she arrived only to be refused entry due to the fact that neither her name nor that of her escort Mark Herron were on the guest list. It seems that after bumping into her by accident the previous night at the fashionable Caprice restaurant in Belgravia, Brian had issued a verbal invitation but had neglected to add her to the official list. After a tense wait while a message reached a mortified Epstein she was eventually allowed entry.

Fresh from one of her many suicide attempts, cut wrists on the most recent occasion, she caused a mild panic when she disappeared into the toilet for an inordinate length of time only to finally emerge looking rather over-refreshed. Rock musicians in the sixties might have considered themselves as pioneers of the drug generation but Garland, having been raised on barbiturates throughout her years as a childhood star in Hollywood where she downed uppers and downers like bags of candy, was a past master of the art of stimulated recreation. All these Johnny-come-latelys were absolute beginners to her.

A grand star of yesteryear she may have been but she was now looked upon as a slightly wacky and faded celebrity who was past her sell-by date and had precious little attention paid to her by the Fab Four. John Lennon spent most of the evening flitting between Jagger and Richards and Alma Cogan. And although Paul spent a few moments discussing the current Broadway scene with Garland, he and Jane seemed more than content to sit talking with John and Mary McNally and myself.

I looked on the scene with envy, jealous of Lennon's self assurance and ability to intimidate with simply a look and in sheer admiration at Alma's talent to amuse and her capacity to light up any room the moment she entered it. Little did they both know then just how little time they had left. Alma was to die of Leukaemia just two years later while John was shot dead at the hands of Mark Chapman outside the Dakota Building in New York on December 8th 1980, still sixteen years on but far too young to die at forty years of age. Judy Garland never made it past the summer of '69 when she died of an overdose in the toilet of a London apartment.

There was almost a fracas when Tommy Cooper perceived that John Lennon, always the caustic wit and never one to consider someone's feelings before throwing a sarcastic line their way, had been offensive to his wife. The comedian rose and confronted the rock star. Cooper was an awesome size, a tall bulky man with the face of a seasoned boxer and the kind of looks that suggested that in a fight he was unlikely to emerge the loser. Luckily for Lennon, who was known to have played the hard man usually when he knew he was dealing with a weaker opponent, an aide quickly intervened to salve the situation.

The Beatle was relieved to have someone save face on his behalf. John was the guy who put mild mannered Cavern deejay Bob Wooller in hospital for daring to suggest that he might have indulged in a sexual liaison with Brian Epstein, but would never have dared to front up to a real Liverpool hard case like Big Three drummer Johnny Hutchinson

From Southend we moved on to Bournemouth. Meanwhile Tony Jackson had started to get his new career into gear by undergoing cosmetic surgery on his somewhat prominent and ungainly nose to give him a more streamlined appearance as befitted a solo star. The results were impressive and he came out looking a whole lot better than when he went in. Whereas before you might have described him as rugged he could now legitimately be called handsome.

He was also, under the guidance of Rolling Stones' manager Andrew Oldham, about to audition musicians for his new backing band and was reported to be considering Chris Curtis's predecessor in the Searchers, Norman McGarry, but that came to nothing and he eventually recruited his Vibrations, the name given to the new outfit, from elsewhere. In came Ian Buisel on guitar, Martin Raymond on organ and Paul Francis on drums. Francis amusingly enough had once played drums for Rolf Harris and the Kangaroos. Once his new ensemble had been put together Jackson found himself in the same position as ourselves, that of having to find a new hit single with which to re-establish our ranking in the public eye.

Having decided that the Knightsbridge apartment was an unnecessary luxury rather than a sensible economic proposition, the band decided not to renew the lease when it came up for renewal in September, reverting instead to hotels when needed. For most of the year it had lain vacant and was mostly used as a London crash pad for Tony whilst clubbing. Their days off were so few and so precious that as soon as a space without commitments appeared in the diary they would rush back to Liverpool on the express from Euston for some precious quality time with wives and families.

Someday We're Gonna Love Again meanwhile was bearing out John's premonitions when it stalled at a disappointing number eleven in the charts and was now on a downward spiral. It was important to get into the studio and come out with a strong new track to eradicate the memory of the last one and to firmly establish the new line-up in the consciousness of the public. Furthermore Tony had raced into Pye to make his debut disc in a deal arranged between Tito Burns and London Records. It would not look good for Tony to come out with a better and, heaven forbid, more successful product than us. And thus the date of August 31st was set for my entrée into, hopefully, the world of the pop charts.

The song we chose between us was *When You Walk In The Room*, a powerful Jackie DeShannon piece chock full of ingredients that were the hallmarks of a Searchers hit. The simple but effective melody, embellished by the expected harmonies and one of the most memorable of all guitar riffs, could have been tailor-made for us, although it was not. As with *Needles And Pins,* Jackie had tried previously with this one herself and failed. But if we learned of her displeasure at having chart honours snatched from under her nose on that first occasion, we were not to receive any such complaints this time round. As the writer she would reap considerable royalties via a group who could generate many more sales, and therefore revenue, than she herself could, and it is astonishing how monetary rewards can assuage one's disappointment at times like these.

Tony Hatch was kind and welcoming and I was made to feel at home. And as far as I could tell the engineer Ray Prickett saw no problem other than the need to adjust my bass playing style of slapping the strings in between notes as I was used to doing on stage. Once I had altered my technique to rid us of the extraneous and unwanted noise all was fine. There was work to be done on all our parts and we were all happy that a difficult situation had been resolved and that we could now get on with it.

Not only was I playing on my first single as a Searcher but I also found myself becoming a lead singer, not a natural position for me as someone having a voice that was adequate but without any great merits to speak of. It was at Chris's initial suggestion and with everyone else's agreement that we decided to try doubling the vocals. It was normal for most artistes to double-track, which is the process of having the singer repeat his performance on a separate take in order to give it a texture and body that would be lacking in one voice on its own. The difference this time was that Mike and I sang the lead line together and then proceeded to double both vocals thus giving it twice the power in theory.

Because we were using this technique the sound was a tad different from the recordings that had gone before. Mike's voice matched my own very well and in fact throughout much of the record mine tended to cut through more. So much so that when a cover version was recorded in 1981 by a studio ensemble called Tight Fit, in a medley entitled *Back To The Sixties* during a vogue for nostalgic party medleys, the lead vocal replicated my voice exactly. I don't know who they brought in to sing on that session but every time it comes on the radio I can clearly hear my own tones. It is uncanny.

If the melody line and the great lyrics, which managed to rhyme *me you want* with *nonchalant* - a word seldom if ever heard in other pop songs - were incredibly strong, no less importance could be placed on the guitar figure without which the finished item would have been a very different, and lesser product. We had gained an erroneous reputation for using a twelve-string guitar on *Needles And Pins*. This time we decided to emphasise the riff by bringing one in for the recording.

Twelve-string guitars were not thick on the ground but luthier Jim Burns, who was a pioneering figure in British built instruments, had included one in his new range and we had one sent round. It worked well and on that session the archetypal sound of a Searchers record was established. The first model of a Burns twelve-string was finished in white and we acquired at the same time the matching six-string and bass guitars. They in turn were followed by instruments in a translucent green finish. Unfortunately they were very soon followed by an invoice finished in black ink. We had been under the impression that they were being supplied in an endorsement arrangement (can you imagine David Beckham paying for his trainers or track suits?) but we were wrong. We paid the bill - reluctantly.

My Burns Bison bass was a monster of an instrument. A huge slab of wood finished in white and surmounted by some very flashy scratch plates in blue 'mother-of-toilet-seat'. The neck, which ended in an elaborate scroll, looked as though it stretched for a mile and the pick-ups gradually worked themselves loose along with various screws and metal fittings. After a short time everything seemed to rattle. The design of the solid body incorporated a pair of massive cow horns forming the cut-away of the body. If it was a cow to look at it was a pig to play. But it was probably the most recognisable and iconic instrument I ever owned, in the mind of the general public.

Although we were in possession of the Burns guitars, John actually played a Fender Telecaster on the session. His little black Hofner had gone to Sound City for re-fretting and they had loaned him the 'Tele' while the work was carried out. When the Hofner eventually came back he considered the re-fret a disaster and kept the Fender as compensation, eventually changing the finish from sunburst to white.

Beating the release of *When You Walk In The Room* by one week was a new single from Cliff Bennett & the Rebel Rousers. Like *Sweets For My Sweet, One Way Love* was also an old Drifters song that we had been playing on stage during my tenure with the band. It was punchy and had a strong hook in the staccato unison sax lines which ran counter to the melody throughout. In fact during that limbo period between leaving them and joining the Searchers I had called in on a rehearsal one day at the Ivy Leaf Club in West Drayton, one of our old regular venues and the scene of our weekly

Thursday rehearsals which were to be missed on pain of death. John Burgess was vetting their repertoire for a possible new single. Bobby Thompson, my replacement, drafted in at short notice from Kingsize Taylor's Dominoes, was not yet familiar with the song so I stepped in and played the tune with them that afternoon. When it eventually came on the market Derek Johnson of the NME wrote 'great sound on mid tempo...broken beat rocker...punchy brass and beat backing...this could give Cliff Bennett & the Rebel Rousers their long overdue chart debut'. He was quickly proved right.

No sooner had we recorded *Room* than we were obliged to head off for a trip around the globe. It was an exciting prospect for me, whose foreign travel had never extended beyond Germany, but not perhaps the wisest plan of action for a band who badly needed to affirm and re-establish their position in the hierarchy of pop. But we left the shores of Britain safe in the knowledge at least that our new single was on an upward journey albeit a slow and steady one.

Our trip to America which began on September 7th 1964 was a big event for me. The others had already experienced a short visit for television promotion and the two-week long tour with the Dovells and Dick & Dee Dee. I may have missed out on those but on our immediate horizon was something far more exciting. I made a return journey to Great Yarmouth for a Sunday concert the day before and caught a cab on the Monday to Heathrow Airport to meet up with the others. Pop stars we may have been but there was no First Class comfort for us as we slummed it in the rear of the plane. But I cared not a jot. I had no experience of First Class travel anyway and what you don't have you don't miss. However one looked at it this was my first trans-Atlantic flight and I was bound for the home of the brave and the land of the free. Or rather the home of Rock & Roll.

The Murray the K holiday show at the Fox Theatre in Brooklyn boasted a bill that I could never have envisaged being a part of. Marvin Gaye, the Ronettes, the Supremes, Martha & the Vandellas, Smokey Robinson & the Miracles, the Temptations, the Contours, Little Anthony & the Imperials, the Shangri-Las, the Dovells, the Newbeats and Jay & the Americans. As Louis B Mayer had once said about his great studio, there were more stars than there are in heaven. At least it seemed that way to me. As if that were not enough, accompanying us from the shores of the UK were Dusty Springfield and Millie. Millie, who had scored big on both sides of the Atlantic with the reggae style song *My Boy Lollipop* was promoted with her full name of Millie Small in the States.

Forget First Class. We travelled bog standard economy in the back of the plane with the rest of the chicken and geese, the aero equivalent of the green Thames van. In-flight movies had just been introduced but you had to buy your headphones if you wanted to while away an hour or two watching *Major Dundee*, the full-length feature on our particular excursion. In-flight entertainment equipment was in its infancy and the headphone set resembled a plastic stethoscope rescued from a kids' doctors and nurses set. It probed and prodded the inside of your ears to the point where skin was in danger of being removed and hearing permanently damaged. The person who once advised most sensibly that one should never insert anything into your ear smaller than an elbow would have winced at the perils we were introducing to our aural receptors.

But I didn't care. To fly across the Big Pond was reward enough. When we reached New York we rode to Manhattan in a limousine and listened to Martha & the Vandellas on the radio with their unbelievably great new hit single *Dancing In The Streets*. It sounded so powerful and infectious that it seemed to set the tone for the days ahead. We checked into the impressive Americana Hotel on Broadway and no sooner had I turned on the television set in my room than I found myself watching Eddie Cochran in his unforgettable scene from the movie *The Girl Can't Help It*. It was surely a sign. I was in rock & roll heaven.

That night John McNally and I went out on the town and halted at the Peppermint Lounge where The Twist as demonstrated by Joey Dee & the Starliters had first hit the public with all the force of an atom bomb. When we tried to enter we were challenged at the door for ID to prove we were old enough to enter an establishment that sold alcohol. I was amazed. Back home no-one really cared as long as you looked post-pubescent.

We explained that I was twenty, two years above the legal drinking age in Britain, and that John was two years older than me. We had not known that in most US states you needed to be twenty-one to drink. Here in New York the age was eighteen so we were both fine and luckily the guy believed us and didn't insist on us running back to fetch our passports. Moreover, being musicians (we had managed to slip in the fact that we were pop stars) we were not required to pay the cover charge.

Joey Dee, who we both knew and loved from his sensational appearances at the Star Club, was no longer one of the club's attractions. He now had his own establishment in the city. That night there was nobody of any consequence on stage and all in all it was really quite dull. But what the hell, we were actually in New York sitting in the Peppermint Lounge. It felt surreal and I wasn't going to let anything spoil that. There are times when you should not let daylight in on the magic.

Murray the K was the alter ego of Murray Kauffman, a middle-aged Jewish deejay who had quickly realised the potential of the Beatles before his rivals could work out that they were not just another five-minute wonder and had latched firmly onto their coat-tails as the self-proclaimed fifth Beatle (how many fifth Beatles were there for goodness sake?). For a man who had identified himself with the current kings of all that was cool his own cool quotient was notably lacking with his preppy college cardigans and Sinatra-esque hats that might have suited Old Blue Eyes but were in truth at odds with the radical styles that were being imported from the new centre of the musical universe, Britain. Whatever look he was going for, he missed.

But he had the Beatles playing ball, he had the ears of a vast youthful radio audience and he had the power to bring together packages of stars who were willing to perform for less pay than a Taiwanese sweat-shop worker for the chance to promote themselves to the American public as part of a prestige production. And the analogy is not altogether inappropriate, for his presentations required six shows a day beginning at an unearthly ten o'clock in the morning and ending at ten at night. A shop it might not have been. Sweat we most certainly did.

The Fox was an ancient cinema cramped in the backstage area and devoid of any form of comfort. When we arrived we found the US acts were in the process of ordering, at their own expense, air-cooling units to fit to the windows of their cell-sized dressing rooms. Seeing excessive heat as a previously denied luxury, not to mention the cost of hiring one an unwanted expense, we declined. The Yanks thought we were mad. If a moth entered our room it was allowed to live on the principle that it was the air conditioning.

Because of the layout, which comprised tiny rooms on several floors, there was not a lot of opportunity to meet and mix with the other artistes and no green room where we could assemble. Space was at a premium. But still we managed to get to know in a small way some of these legends many of whom we were still very much in awe.

The Supremes had just enjoyed their first serious hit with *Where Did Our Love Go* and were still at the time a little way behind Martha & the Vandellas in status although that was about to change very dramatically, partially due to Berry Gordy's obsession with making Diana Ross a star. I met her briefly and she was rather charming to me. No hint of the difficult diva at that time.

Mary Wilson stated in her autobiography *Dream Girl* that Ross, who was christened as simply Diane and who was still referred to by all the Motown people in that manner, suddenly announced as they approached the opening of their debut season at the Copacabana in New York in June 1965 that there had been an error on her birth certificate and that from now on she would be called Diana. I checked my copy of the Motown Revue album that I got her to sign and she most definitely inscribed herself as Diana that day back in September '64.

Smokey Robinson was a soft spoken and charming gentleman who had nothing but positive things to say about us and about the British scene in general. He had a very generous spirit. Their show was action packed and as they gyrated through a terrific routine on *Mickey's Monkey* they made clever use of strobe lights which produced the effect of a jerky Mack Sennett movie.

Most of the performers were allowed just one song in a fast-moving revue which opened on an airport scene complete with US and British flags and banners in which the acts were welcomed one by one before the music really got into gear. We were of course self-contained but the other acts were backed by the Earl Warren Orchestra who replicated the Motown sound to perfection.

The fabulous Ronettes who were favourites of mine sang *Be My Baby* and as a bonus I enjoyed an innocent bit of puppy love with Nedra Talley, cousin to Ronnie and Estelle Bennett, as we kissed and flirted by the side of the stage. One day in their dressing room we listened excitedly to an acetate of their new record, *Baby I Love You*, which Phil Spector had delivered to the theatre. I was hoping that the great man would put in an appearance but he never showed up. Having since been made aware of his fondness for firearms and his dramatically aggressive nature, I think I was perhaps fortunate.

Without exception they were all great acts on the show and I watched with amazement and felt very privileged. As a British group we could do no wrong. Despite all that immense talent on display it was the guys who looked like the Beatles and spoke in a British brogue that the kids screamed for. Throughout the day our part of the show was the highlight for the young US audience. It was only as night descended that things changed somewhat. As the young guys and girls went home to bed in their safe, white neighbourhoods the colour of the audience changed and soul came into its own. At night there was no doubt that this show belonged to Marvin Gaye.

Many nights I watched him from the side of the stage with admiration at the sheer coolness with which he imbued his performance. Long and lean in his short-waisted white suit, the smooth silky sound of his voice sounded ethereal. Almost angelic. There was none of the wild and raucous entreaties to get up or get down or go wherever from the super smooth Mister Gaye. The words and the melodies flowed towards an audience that was mesmerised.

I spoke to him one night as he came off and he told me how much he loved our music and the whole British sound altogether. He was grateful that groups like the Beatles and ourselves had raved about Motown and given such a boost to their careers. In the US they had been taken so much for granted. But if the Beatles liked them then so did the kids.

There was something aloof about Marvin. Not in a negative or arrogant way. It was just that he had such confidence and self-assurance. Like almost everyone I met he seemed so much more mature than me. It didn't matter that the Supremes were Berry's darlings. Or that the Temptations were enjoying a string of hit records. Marvin knew that he was the king of Motown. He said something very significant to me. I was praising the whole concept of the Motown sound, the organisation and its godfather, Berry

Gordy. Marvin pointedly replied 'In this business you have to watch everyone.' How prophetic those words turned out to be when he was eventually shot dead in the bath by his cross-dressing father.

A couple of times we managed to sneak out of the theatre during the daytime when there weren't too many screaming teenage girls to block our path but most of the time we just hung about in our little cell and bided our time. If we needed food there was a young black kid around who was our 'gofer' and who would go for hamburgers or sandwiches and coffee or whatever we needed. I suppose he existed on tips but he would never have got rich off us. As council house lads who had come through the strictures of post-war austerity we knew the value of money. We were not big tippers.

There was precious little time for rest between the end of the last show till the early start the next day but some of us did venture out one night to Joey Dee's Starliter Club. John and I didn't get to see him at the Peppermint Lounge but after the show on Friday 11th September Mike and I went with a couple of the Ronettes and Larry Kurzon from the William Morris Agency to pay our respects at his new place in Manhattan.

Joey was thrilled to see us again especially as the visit was a complete surprise. We were given the best table at the front of the small, low stage and watched a girl group called the Rag Dolls do their act. Nedra introduced me to a young black guy who stopped by our table to say hello. He was tall, slim and nervous looking. I didn't recognise the face although I should have, but I sure knew the name when it was announced. He was Frankie Lymon, the teenage wonder of the fifties who was the prototype for Michael Jackson and so many other black stars and who took the Teenagers into the charts again and again with songs like *Why Do Fools Fall In Love, I'm Not A Juvenile Delinquent* and *Baby Baby.*

He was one of my first rock & roll heroes whose records on the green and silver Columbia label I played again and again until the scratches made them unplayable. He was friendly but distracted, I felt, as if there were more pressing things on his mind. I would never get the chance to meet him again, for within a short number of years he was dead from a heroin overdose.

Dusty had found her spiritual home among the purveyors of the music she loved and always strived to emulate, and they in turn recognised a stupendous talent and the possessor of one of the great voices in soul no matter that her white skin and Irish heritage should by all rights have barred her from entry to such an exclusive fraternity. But although accompanied by her Australian manager Vic Billings she felt homesick and alone. To relieve her anxiety she would resort to her weird habit of purchasing stacks of cheap crockery with the sole purpose of smashing it up in an attempt to smash her frustrations away at the same time.

Martha Reeves was deputed to extend the hand of friendship and take this British oddball under her wing. They became lifelong friends. The downside for Martha was that she was forced to suffer the innuendos that went with being a female friend of Dusty's. Although she never 'came out' officially during her lifetime there is no doubt that Dusty was in essence lesbian in an age when sexual equality and acceptance was just a pipe dream, although her great friend Peppi Borza did tell me at one time that he knew of men with whom she had enjoyed intimate relations. It's just a shame that anyone actually cared who Dusty, or anyone for that matter, chose to share her bed with. It was her bed and her body to do with as she wished.

Naturally when she and Martha began fraternising the Motown star was suspected of being more than just a friend. The rumours were wrong. Martha was a totally 'straight' woman and she must surely have resented such untrue and unwarranted aspersions but Martha was her own person. A strong lady who had been brought up in the tough projects of Detroit and secure enough in her own sexuality to ride through it with her head held high and proud of her friendship with the eccentric Irish star.

17

The Other Side Of The World

When the Murray the K show finally ended we packed our bags and set off to tour the rest of the country, joined by Eden Kane. The first stop was Tulsa, Oklahoma, on September 14th. Tulsa was also the last stop for Miss Springfield who had revelled in her time in New York with all her new Motown chums, but saw little appeal in trekking from anonymous town to anonymous town performing in unsuitable halls along with all the bad sound and lighting that came with the territory.

While strolling in the warm Tulsa air with Vic Billings he informed me that 'Madam' was not feeling well. She had a sore throat and had retired to her bed. He doubted very much if 'Madam' would be contributing to the show the following night and nor indeed was he expecting things to improve. Vic said this with a sardonic twinkle in his eye and a resignation to the whims and foibles of his supremely talented yet extremely unpredictable client. Dusty had had her fun. She now wanted to go home.

Although bad for the package it was probably a wise move for her. She would not have enjoyed the primitive make-do-and-mend conditions that were part and parcel of such a tour. Lights were what was available, if available at all. Public address systems in those bygone days were basic and the sounds they produced were often abysmal. But amidst the incessant screaming for us it was almost irrelevant. On the plus side we were carrying our own backline with us so that we could at least feel comfortable and familiar with the sound our instruments were producing.

As all of the journeys were by plane on this tour the weight of the amplifiers incurred a very hefty bill in excess baggage charges but we were unperturbed by this. Having dumped the Fenders for a sponsored set of British-made Vox amps, the company had agreed to pay to cart them across the USA reasoning that the resulting publicity would be more than worth the cost. In a schedule such as ours there was no possibility of sending them by the cheaper, but longer, freight method, and somehow any of our personal excess baggage seemed to get lumped onto the Vox bill.

The Tulsa show began very strangely. We managed to open with *Don't Throw Your Love Away* in two different keys at the same time which is pretty weird for a song that we knew back to front. But we quickly pulled into line again and the little *faux pas* was soon forgotten. Amidst the screams of teenage girls and the natural reverb of the cavernous interior it was doubtful anyone would have been aware of the mistake anyway. The scheduled concert for the 15th was cancelled and so we remained in Tulsa for an extra day before continuing on our travels to Madison (16th) and then on to Los Angeles (17th) where we had been booked to appear on the important Steve Allen Show, followed by more shows in Sacramento (18th), Portland and Oregon (19th) after which we returned to Los Angeles (20th). There we were able to rest up a little, the only exertion being a lip-synched appearance on the Lloyd Thaxton television show.

Los Angeles was the mythical land of our youthful dreams. We had time on our hands and we managed to find rich people to party with in Beverly Hills.

The Gromans had the monopoly on Jewish funerals in LA with their logo to be found on the backs of the benches that were positioned by bus stops throughout the city, and daughter Charlene Groman threw a pool party for us. I was impressed by anyone who lived in a house with a pool and even more impressed that the pool had its own jukebox. Back home jukeboxes stood against the walls in cafes and required the insertion of money before they made a sound. This one pumped out music all night long for free. I even managed a rare romantic and most intimate dalliance with Charlene's friend Elaine Corlett. On the other hand Eden Kane, being much more mature and adventurous than me, returned a few years later to marry Charlene.

We were staying in a hotel on Sunset Strip called the Thunderbird Inn. It was a mid-price establishment with pleasantly spacious rooms and a small pool on the first floor terrace, adequate for our needs without being overly extravagant and eating into our budget too much. Years later it closed down and reopened as a retirement home. How fitting. At the end of the nineties the building was taken over and developed into a prestigious and fashionable minimalist hotel called the Standard, just the kind of place we could not afford to stay in.

Our American sojourn finally came to an end on September 22nd and from Los Angeles we flew on to Honolulu to join up with Del Shannon and Peter and Gordon who were to make up the rest of the bill for the Australasian portion of the tour. A delay in departure from Hawaii meant that we missed our connection at Fiji and we stayed over for the night to allow those who needed to rehearse with local backing bands in New Zealand to take the spare seats available on the next flight.

It turned into a very pleasant break for us as we were treated to a Fijian poolside cabaret and barbecue under the soft relaxing moonlight. The next day we had time to kill before catching our flight so we got a driver to take us to the beach. When we got there it resembled Britain only in that there was sand. Other than that all similarities were notably absent. This was Bounty Bar country. Acres of golden beach and not a deck chair or fish and chip stall in sight. Absolutely nothing. There were palm trees with coconuts dangling from them and a brilliant blue sea waiting for us to splash about in and we had it all to ourselves.

When we did venture into the waves the effect was most disconcerting. Instead of the terra firma one was used to in Blackpool or Bournemouth the mud beneath our feet here was soft and gooey. It was as if we had strolled onto a bed of baby poo. Not very nice at all. When rain clouds began to roll our way we became quite worried. We had asked the driver to return three hours later and here we were about to get caught in a tropical downpour from which there was no escape. Fortunately, the man was endowed with a degree of good sense and came back early to rescue us from our predicament.

After all the excitement and hustle of America, New Zealand was so slow as to be almost comatose. Every day seemed like Sunday and Sunday seemed like the rush hour on Mars. With hormones racing and the feckless impatience of restless youth to deal with, I never gave it a fair chance. It would be years before maturity would allow me to appreciate the absolute beauty and understated vibrancy of a land that achieved a perfect balance between the tranquillity of times long gone and the unstoppable march of progress. And in doing so it had managed somehow to filter out the vulgarity that normally comes with the territory. In 1964 New Zealand would just have to bide its time until I grew up.

We caught up with the rest of the tour after a hairy dash that involved connections in Wellington and Christchurch before reaching our destination. We finally made the theatre in Dunedin at 9.30 p.m. and were on stage at 10 p.m. Everyone breathed a sigh of relief. None more so than Harry M. Miller who was the promoter of the tour. From there we performed in Wellington and Auckland (where we received the news that *When You Walk In The Room* was at number nineteen in the UK charts) before continuing on to Melbourne for two days of concerts in a venue that was more used to staging boxing matches.

Finally, we arrived in Sydney, which in our parochial and untravelled minds was what represented Australia to us. This city was a little less suburban than those we had so far experienced but it was still a long way behind the UK both musically and socially at the time. Television had not long been introduced there and the music scene in Australia was still merely second-hand versions of what emanated from Britain or America. Little did we imagine then how this great land was a sleeping giant and that Aussie bands would one day show the world just how it was done.

The Opera House down at the harbour was still under construction and controversy raged around its dubious design and the spiralling costs. The final bill was many multiples of the original budget but whatever ungodly sum they eventually paid it was cheap. The sight of the white-tiled roof in the shape of an elegant ship's sails, which one wag described as being like a bunch of nuns in a rugby scrum, set beside the old 'coathanger' bridge is, and will remain, one of the most awe-inspiring vistas of the modern world.

We were staying at the Town House, a good example of the new and fashionable boutique type of hotel situated at the beginning of Elizabeth Bay Road, just around the corner from the Anzac fountain, the dandelion-shaped water feature that commemorated the sacrifice made by the Australian troops in the Second World War. It was in the King's Cross district, the red light area of Sydney. Strippers, hookers and assorted ne'er-do-wells hustled their trade from the Williams Street junction where Darlinghurst Road stretches its short, seedy way along to the crossroads and the fountain which still spouts its unceasing spray of devotion and gratitude to its long dead heroes and from where McCleay Street winds its way down past the naval base to the harbour.

Today the Cross is much more open and blatant but even in 1964 it was hard to walk the short stretch without being propositioned for sex by the long-legged whores or tapped up for a few pence by the down-and-outs who lived on the sidewalks and in the doorways.

The Town House, whose rooms were comprised of mini-suites that were not over large or imposingly grand but which provided a more personal and individual environment for an international coterie of VIPs bored with the bland and uninspiring boxes hitherto provided by the big hotel chains, was soon brought under the umbrella of the giant Sebel group and became a second home for rock stars and showbusiness personalities who landed up in Sydney, until it eventually closed its doors at the end of the millennium to be replaced by a prestigious block of luxury apartments called Encore.

We got word from home that Top Of The Pops had nothing with which to represent *When You Walk In The Room*, which had been released while we were away and was fast ascending the best selling lists. The disc had received favourable notices. The NME wrote 'Mike Pender and Frank Allen duetting on melody lines....infectious mid tempo rhythm...attractive blend of voices...the boys have made an excellent job of it.' Record Mirror's thoughts concurred. 'Similar to Jackie DeShannon's...jerky, effective group vocal work...first rate guitar work...should be a sizeable hit at least.'

In its first week *Room* had debuted at twenty-nine and in the press that week Tony Jackson's first effort *Bye Bye Baby* was praised by Ian Dove. 'Could have a hit with this one...up tempo pounding beat...a lot more raw and beaty than the Searchers although he retains occasional touches from his former group.' In a newspaper interview Tony expressed his frustration with ballads, stating a preference for a more up-tempo kind of song. He was sporting his newly refined nose, which cost him a reputed £200.

It was all becoming very incestuous with the Searchers, the Rebel Rousers and

Tony Jackson, having played musical chairs in a fairly spectacular way, were now in competition with each other for the charts. Sadly for Tony, he was to be the relative loser with a final chart placing of number thirty.

A Sydney-based film company was deputed to make a promo of us miming to the track, what nowadays would be a video and very much an essential part of the promotional campaign, which in the sixties was the exception rather than the rule. We were shipped out to Fort Denison, a tiny island in the harbour and filmed with the Opera House and the bridge in the background. As a bonus the cameraman managed to include a shot of a sailing ship as it glided by. It was a beautiful image that should have been preserved for posterity. The BBC in its wisdom decided years later to discard such inconsequential nonsense and recorded over the footage in the interests of economy.

The Australian 'Queen Of Bluebeat' Dinah Lee was our home-grown support for the tour and we were joined by local outfits along the way as we performed in all the major cities. On occasions the musicianship of those elected to back the solo acts left a little to be desired and on a couple of the shows Gordon Waller and myself supplied a rhythm guitar and bass from off stage. But in the main it was fine. The old Sydney Stadium, a huge tin construction and just about on its last legs, offered a revolving stage and revolting acoustics, and the Festival Hall in Melbourne was not much better. But the atmosphere was electric and the crowds wonderful and in those prehistoric times of tiny amplifiers and inadequate and effect-less PAs it was perhaps just as well that the screams covered our failings.

I found Peter Asher a great guy to get on with and made a good friend of him during that tour. Born of a wealthy London family, his father was a doctor and his mother a music teacher, he had been raised in some degree of splendour in a grand town-house in Wimpole Street and was as intelligent and sophisticated as I was gauche and naïve. His bespectacled nerdy look and quiet unassuming persona I felt hid a different and more raunchy Peter Asher who lurked beneath. I suspected that he and Dinah Lee had an affair during that tour but I could not state that for certain. I never asked them. One day I will.

Del Shannon, a genuinely nice guy who started out in life as plain Charles Westover and who hid a darker history of depression behind a cheerful visage, coped with his downgrading in the hierarchy of the pop world with equanimity. Two years before he would have been an unchallenged top-of-the-bill, singing his great hits such as *Runaway, Hats Off To Larry, Little Town Flirt* and *Swiss Maid* but changing fashions dictated that he now closed the first half. He was a big favourite with the audiences and they loved him no matter where he happened to appear in the running order. He in turn loved the luxuriant bathrobes supplied by the Town House. So much so that he appropriated one on checkout. The bill followed rapidly and he was forced to bear the cost of the expensive garment.

We covered the other major cities of Brisbane, Newcastle and Adelaide and finished in Perth. Australian pop music was still in its infancy and a long way from being the major force that it was to become.

Five long weeks after we had set out we began the long trek home. In those days aeroplanes required more fuelling stops and we touched down half a dozen times and were fed after each take-off until we finally arrived exhausted and fat at Heathrow.

Fortunately our absence had not prevented *When You Walk In The Room* from rising up the charts. From a first entry at twenty-nine as we left the UK it moved slowly but steadily. On September 25th it had moved up seven places and the following week was at fifteen. By coincidence Cliff Bennett's *One Way Love* had also entered the charts that week and at twenty-nine, exactly the same starting position as *Room*. And the coincidences did not stop there. Tony Jackson & the Vibrations, according to the NME, were just one place below.

One week on and we were at number nine in the NME with Cliff at twenty and Tony at twenty-five. Johnny Stewart, the producer of Top Of The Pops, said to me as we were about to mount the podium for our spot, 'There's only one record heading for number one and its yours.' Unfortunately he was wrong. The front page of the Record Mirror proclaimed the 'Sensational Searchers – well up in the charts with their latest disc'.

Although the NME had our disc peaking at number six it fared much better in most other trade papers and eventually reached its zenith on October 16th at what was to be its generally accepted high spot of number three. Although the New Musical Express had always been my music paper of choice and it was their charts I usually deferred to, in this case I quite naturally decided to take as gospel the highest position anyone was willing to afford it. As far as I was concerned number three it was.

Perhaps if we had been on hand to help with the promotion the extra boost would have given us another well-deserved number one. If that had happened it would surely have signified a new benchmark in our careers because without a doubt the years have proved *Room* by its reception in our stage performances to be the strongest and most enduring of our hits. My old cohorts the Rebel Rousers meanwhile were at seventeen and rising while Tony Jackson's *Bye Bye Baby* had already waved bye bye to the charts.

Despite the chart positions as stated by the NME, by the time an average had been taken for the accepted standard of the Guinness Book Of Hit Singles and other chart reference books the variation could be quite significant. Tony Jackson's debut single, despite its generous placing in the NME, is officially on record as having reached a high of thirty eight and was to be his only chart entry.

With a big hit on our hands it was a good time to start our new UK tour, which opened on October 17th at Sheffield City Hall to a poor audience and a good sound, followed by an excellent night at the Liverpool Empire where Mike, John and Chris were on home ground. I had flown to Speke Airport in Liverpool and rested up in a hotel the night before the start of the run, taking in the cinema before hitting the sack. *Tom Jones* was showing. The movie, not the Welsh warbler, that is.

The bill was strong. We were all fans of Dionne Warwick, Chris Curtis in particular, and he had arranged for us both to pop up to where she was staying at the Mayfair hotel in London a few days previously. She was warm and friendly and we had a lot of fun playing records on a portable that Chris had brought along. The management did ring up to the room to complain about the noise at one point but we turned the volume down a little and carried on. I did get to see a slightly tetchier side to La Warwick when, on my mentioning that I loved Eartha Kitt, she offered the opinion, 'Well she can't sing, that's for sure.' I got the impression that Dionne would be a little happier if compliments to female singers were aimed in her direction only. But despite the sensitive ego she was good company and appreciated the welcome.

The Isley Brothers were the other US act brought over for the tour. They were legends among musicians being not only a dynamic soul act but also the ones who had introduced *Twist And Shout* to us. We had been told by Vic Sutcliffe, one of Tito's henchmen at the Vere Street office, that they were so good on stage that no-one could follow them and therefore they would close the first half, thus preventing them from detracting the attention from us.

It was true that they were an exciting and seasoned act. And it was true that their all-action stage show was dynamic. It was not true however that no one could follow them. The young Brits in the stalls had alas not been trained in the art of being a soul audience and managed very easily indeed not to bring themselves to a frenzy if the manner of a crowd such as they would command at the Apollo in Harlem. The Isleys went over well but were not any kind of a problem at all.

Ronnie and Rudolph appeared to be the subservient siblings while O'Kelly was the alpha male and dominant member of the trio. I was very amused by the fact that, having been used to the American system of paying for the price of a room rather than the number of occupants, they were not thrilled when they found they were not allowed to cram the three of them into a room that was priced for two persons only. They were not getting paid a king's ransom for this tour and the extra outlay dented their budget badly. Their shaving routine was also a wonder to me and I watched them smear a grey gooey depilatory mixture on their cheeks to be scraped off a couple of minutes later taking the stubble with it. It seemed to work well enough for them but when I tried it the effect was negligible.

They were not good on punctuality and even worse in the geography of the United Kingdom. When they missed the coach rendezvous at Alsop Place just around the corner from the Planetarium, arriving minutes after the very strict Fred Perry had ordered its departure, they panicked and hailed a black cab ordering the driver to take them to Birmingham. The cabbie, having figured Christmas had come early, did their bidding but was brought down to earth with a mighty bang at the end of the trip when Fred negotiated a distinctly smaller fare than he had originally demanded.

Elsewhere on the show were our cohorts from the Burns office the Zombies who had put *She's Not There* into the charts and a comedy duo called Syd and Eddie, later to find fame as Little & Large. Backing for the Isleys and Dionne was provided by jazz band-turned-soul band Alan Elsdon & the Voodoos.

Apart from the unusual opener, an upbeat arrangement of *Red Sails In The Sunset*, our set was pretty predictable and included *Needles And Pins*, *Someday We're Gonna Love Again*, *When You Walk In The Room*, *What'd I Say* and a plaintive folk ballad we had just found called *What Have They Done To The Rain* for which Chris would come to the front and move onto a set of bongos. It was visually attractive and a nice musical contrast to the usual up-beat theme of our set. We had heard the song, not a traditional folk song, but one which had been penned by a lady called Malvina Reynolds who was also the composer of *Morningtown Ride*, on a record by Joan Baez.

Miss Warwick chose a superb selection of *Any Old Time, Don't Make Me Over* (her first ever hit in the US), *Anyone Who Had A Heart*, *Walk On By*, *You'll Never Get To Heaven* and, most peculiarly in the knowledge that we as top of the bill were also performing the song, *What'd I Say*. But we didn't care and we didn't complain and the audience didn't appear to mind either way.

Among others the Isleys included *Nobody But Me*, *Talk To Me* and of course *Twist and Shout*, while the Zombies sang *She's Not There* and a bunch of blues standards such as *Road Runner* and *Sticks and Stones*.

We were only a week into the tour when *When You Walk In The Room* began its fall. Disconcertingly Cliff Bennett's *One Way Love* continued to rise and for a while it seemed like an embarrassing situation would arise, but it halted at twelve and faces were saved. My old band had at last achieved a well-deserved hit while our number three effort left enough places between us for a happy ending for all.

Strong as the roster of stellar names was, the business varied wildly and for no explicable reason Stoke on October 24th boasted a very thin crowd while the following night in Woolwich was packed. The next day our car broke down at Basingstoke on the way to Taunton but we made it with time to spare. Taunton seemed jinxed. One of the backing US musicians managed to set fire to his room and the hotel was evacuated while the fire brigade doused the flames. Chris Curtis, assuming it was the usual false alarm, remained in his room until it became clear that there was indeed a conflagration of significant proportions. So significant in fact that he had to be rescued from his chamber by a fireman who hoisted him down a ladder on his back.

If its rise had been leisurely, the descent of *When You Walk In The Room* was a very satisfyingly slow one, moving down to seven, eight, ten, fifteen and twenty-four before finally disappearing from the best selling list of November 17th, by which time Dionne had disappeared from the tour.

During a walkabout on the afternoon of the Glasgow concert on November 9th she had inadvertently looked the wrong way while crossing the road and had collided with a tram. Having seen the edgy side of Dionne I would not have been surprised if the tram had come off worst, but it was the chanteuse who sustained injuries to her arm. She appeared at the theatre later on with the damaged limb in bandages and then vanished from our lives forever. Whether it was actually severe enough to warrant such action was irrelevant. In truth this was not the kind of tour she wanted to be on and she had a point. She was destined for more sophisticated venues where the subtlety of her undoubted talent could be better appreciated. Inevitably her career continued on an upward path that made her one of the great divas of our age and she deserved it.

In the audience that evening was a young and very disappointed Scottish footballer by the name of Alex Ferguson. He had not come to see the Searchers or the Zombies or even the Isley Brothers. The future knight of the realm and manager of Manchester United had come to see his favourite singer Dionne Warwick. In the end he had to put up with us. Oh well, whoever said that life was perfect? Dionne's vacant place in the show was quickly filled by a number of available substitutes including Dave Berry and Eden Kane.

The plaintive little folk song that we had introduced to audiences on the tour received great applause every night and we decided to record the song with a view to changing our style for the next single. We took time from the schedule to get into Pye's Great Cumberland Place studios and commit it to tape. Its soft sound and slow, lilting pace was a contrast to our previous efforts and Tony Hatch added a string section from the third verse onwards, the first time we had used strings on a single. We were pleased with the result. As a projected single the change of pace represented a significant risk but one we were prepared to take.

Having an accomplished arranger like Hatch around was a definite advantage. At a moment's notice we could have charts for orchestral embellishments or a piano for added weight to a track. Somehow we got it into our heads that it was also obviously cheaper than employing outside people. What we didn't realise was that Tony, quite rightly, put in an invoice to Pye for any session work or arrangements undertaken on our behalf.

If we suddenly decided informally that a cute piano figure would help our sound, Tony was recruited to provide it in an instant. It might only take a short time to achieve but Tony would receive a standard session fee to augment his salary. And if Tony's arrangement with Pye was anything like George Martin's less-than-satisfactory deal at EMI, it would be money he needed and deserved. Producers, like the artistes they produced, were held on a tight monetary reign by the record labels.

So important was it seen to be that one single followed hot on the heels of another, *What Have They Done To The Rain* was reviewed by Derek Johnson of the NME during the first week that *When You Walk In The Room* failed to chart. There was hardly time to breathe between releases. 'I found it altogether compelling...a contrast from previous discs...appealing to all tastes...one of the boys' best yet.' The words were glowing and encouraged us despite the fact that Tito declared that it was a funeral dirge. We plugged the song on the Billy Cotton Band Show, a piece of television variety entertainment whose content was not very rock & roll at all but which had large viewing figures.

While *What Have They Done To The Rain* was being promoted, another of our discs was already charting. An extended-play record called *The Searchers Play The System* featured the title track to a movie currently on release – *The System* - and for which the group had been recruited to record some music. Despite previous hints that the Searchers would be debuting as thespians in a forthcoming movie, they were required to neither appear nor act.

If *Room* had made slow progress initially, *Rain* raced up the charts like a dog with no legs and on December 4th we set off on a short run of dates in Scandinavia hoping upon hopes for a miracle. Such was the innocence and ease of international air travel in those blissful and never to return terror-free days that, despite the fact that I managed to forget my passport, I undertook the entire ten-day tour without any problems at customs either here or abroad.

The disc failed to show up in the charts the first week and over the next two weeks limped up rather pathetically from twenty-one to nineteen and then eighteen. We arrived back from Sweden on December 14th, my twenty-first birthday. Never big on birthdays in the McNeice household, nothing had been planned and I simply grabbed a few friends together and we went for a meal at the Lotus House, London's most fashionable Chinese eaterie on the Edgware Road just around the corner from Pye studios, where on any given evening I could, and did, find myself sitting next to luminaries such as Bobby Darin, Roger Moore or Steve McQueen.

By Christmas *Rain* had moved one pathetic place to a very poorly eighteen. We hoped our appearance on the Christmas Day transmission of Ready, Steady, Go, where we shared the honours with Herman's Hermits, Wayne Fontana, the Nashville Teens and the Four Pennies, would boost the sales.

While I was jetting my way around the world and seeing countries that up until then had only been points on the world map, my simple Scottish parents, who had never even left the shores of Britain, looked on with a great deal of wonder and a small amount of fear. I have little doubt that their imagination was running riot as they envisaged the kind of trouble I could be getting into. I'm sure they were confused. I'm sure they were scared too. But I am just as sure they were proud.

My Christmas gift to them that year was a refrigerator. That might seem like very small beer in today's terms when fabulously wealthy rock stars buy their folks mansions with barely a second thought, but in our family money had always been scarce and presents were of necessity basic and inexpensive. I was not a rock star. Not really. I was a very lucky boy but still a paid employee with an excellent but limited wage. In 1964 fridges were still an expensive luxury and there were many houses without them. In the summer months milk bottles stood in pans of water in a cool hallway and still managed to go sour, while fresh food was bought daily from the local shop. Supermarkets had not yet been introduced in Britain. My mum was totally overwhelmed at the sight of the pristine white box which I had kept secreted at Cliff Bennett's house until Christmas Day and which now stood gleaming in the kitchen. It was barely three feet high but it caused the tears to flow and I was happy for her.

It had been an amazing year. At the beginning of it I was no-one. Now I was in the music papers most weeks and even had a pop star girlfriend in Julie Grant, a stablemate with whom I enjoyed a relationship that was mostly, but not entirely, platonic. Julie was a lovely girl, dark haired, bubbly and fun. Her limited success in the charts - a trio of minor hits which included a number thirty-three with her version of *Up On The Roof*, a cover which had to compete with both the original Drifters' version and a high placing recording by Kenny Lynch - belied her very evident talent although she was frequently on television and toured constantly with such great stars as Bo Diddley, the Everly Brothers and the Rolling Stones.

Her family were not entirely thrilled with our association. A nice Jewish boy would have been welcomed warmly but if I picked her up at her North London home I would knock at the door but never went in. I never blamed them. They were simply trying to protect their daughter and preserve their family traditions. And when my mother was shown an item in the music press that asked 'Is it wedding bells for the Searchers' Frank Allen and Julie Grant?' she wondered if her baby boy was perhaps getting in a little too deep. They needn't have worried. We were only kids having fun.

On 29th December I got my chance to meet royalty for the first time when we were asked to perform in front of Princess Margaret and Lord Snowdon at the Savoy Hotel in aid of the Docklands Settlement Ball. At the end of our set, which was extended from two numbers to nine due to the Princess's enthusiasm for pop music, we were presented to the royal couple along with other luminaries such as multi-millionaire John Paul Getty.

Poor Julie Rogers, the hit maker of *The Wedding* who was also due to appear, had good reason not to be pleased that night as her performance was cut due to our overrunning and the fact that the seated audience had been encouraged by us to get up and dance which was not at all suited to her performance. It was extremely bad form for us to behave in this way to a fellow artiste but in our defence we were more or less acting under royal orders. But there was compensation of sorts for the lovely Julie. When she explained, after being asked by Lord Snowdon as to why she had not appeared, he and the Princess invited her to perform for them personally at a small gathering upstairs that was to follow the main event. All's well that ends well.

In the long term *What Have They Done To The Rain*, despite its relatively poor performance as a hit single, proved to be one of the most endurable of our hits maintaining its place in our set when higher climbers had long since fallen by the wayside. As 1964 ended and we performed on the Ready, Steady, Go New Year's Eve edition along with the Kinks, the Animals, Sandie Shaw, Billy J Kramer, Susan Maughan, Manfred Mann, Dusty Springfield, the Dave Clark Five and Kenny Lynch, we had only managed to reach the fourteen spot. Oh well, Happy New Year everyone.

18

Hanging In There

With *What Have They Done To The Rain* still stuck at number fourteen in the first week of 1965 and clearly about to begin its descent it was clear that we would have to choose very carefully with our next offering on vinyl. By the end of the month it was out of the charts altogether but we were still a huge name and the world of television was still very much begging for us.

We were to appear in a tribute to the great American composer Burt Bacharach along with Dionne Warwick, Dusty Springfield, Cilla Black, Sandie Shaw, Adam Faith, the Merseybeats and Chuck Jackson to be pre-recorded at Granada Television's Chelsea studios. Burt was without a shadow of a doubt the one that everyone looked up to. He had reinvented pop by having the courage to introduce odd changes of time signature in his clever arrangement. Burt avoided the obvious and took the genre to a higher plane altogether.

Our contribution would be *Magic Potion* which we had recorded on our new album *Sounds Like Searchers*. These were still times when acts were more or less left to their own devices as far as presentation, or the lack of it, was concerned. Our three minutes of lip-synching with minimal movement or expression will not go down in the annals of history as a high point in musical entertainment. The director even managed to capture John McNally at a point when he could not quite remember the words and anyone watching might be forgiven for thinking he was miming to the Spanish version. All in all the whole show, being studio based and without an audience to give it some life, was without any great merit considering the heavyweight stature of the subject it was meant to be honouring.

Somehow we had managed to squeeze in enough studio time despite the never-ending round of touring and media work to complete the new album and had, I think, come up with a very creditable product. The Record Mirror called it 'a vibrant, exciting album...the great thing about the Searchers is that they can take an old number, record it in their own individual style and it still sounds good...stand-out tracks are *Bumble Bee*, *Let The Good Times Roll*, *A Tear Fell* and *Something You've Got Babe*.'

And there was praise too from Derek Johnson in the NME. "One of the most satisfying and stimulating group LPs I've heard in many months. Unsurpassed flair for blending melody and rhythm." I can't help but think that the progress of *Goodbye My Love* helped him to be a bit more on the positive side this time round.

There was still no particular cohesion or plan to the songs on our LPs. It would take the likes of *Sergeant Pepper* and *Pet Sounds* to change people's thinking on this front. But our choices were catholic and had a wide-ranging appeal. We could be proud of the material we were cutting.

We may have suffered a slipped disc on home ground but *Love Potion No. 9*had been selected for a US release and had shot up to the number three spot over on the other side of the pond. Meanwhile the newly-departed Tony Jackson had, on the advice of Tito Burns, issued his own version. In a slightly contrived piece of PR we placed an advert in the music press congratulating him on a fine record. Tony replied in kind saying 'Thanks for ending the feud. Thanks for the generous space in the advertisement you bought last week in the NME to say so…thanks for your good wishes for the success of our new disc. So put it there fellers...and shake.' I don't recall us ever shaking hands at that point but neither was there any great animosity hanging around. We were too busy to fight. Our first priority was to snatch a new hit from the results of a recent session.

Wherever the demos of great songs were they didn't seem to flood our way. We patiently listened to the acetates that had been sent in to Tony Hatch and discarded them as either awful or not bad but missing that special ingredient that separates a hit from the rest. In the wheat and chaff departments we seemed to be getting more than our fair share of chaff while the wheat was being sent in other directions. There was a song that we had in mind but we didn't have it in our hands.

Goodbye My Love was a haunting tune that had been recorded by an American called Jimmy Hughes although his preferred title had been *Goodbye My Lover Goodbye* for the US market, the same title that had been used in a previous recording by one of the song's trio of composers Robert Mosley. It had first been played to the band by Big Dee Irwin while in tour in 1964 but we didn't have the Hughes disc and we didn't know who the publisher was. But luck was with us. Gene Pitney just happened to be in town and, hearing that we were at Pye, dropped in to say hello. We were talking about the Hughes record which it turned out Gene knew very well indeed. We had booked the Great Cumberland Place set-up for two days and the next day Pitney had obtained a demo and had it sent round to us. We got on with it straight away.

It was an exciting session. We had to make an impact with this one so we went for a big sound and for the first time double-tracked the drums, something that might have been second nature to Phil Spector but which was seldom tried by producers in Britain. John McNally devised a captivating 'swishing' sound on his rhythm guitar which gave an intriguing focal point to the track. We took our time to obtain as near a perfect result as we could and it was night time before we got round to overdubbing the vocals.

As was the norm we double-tracked the voices to get a bigger and more impressive sound, which would be souped up even more in the final mix by an ethereal echo, and in the pursuit of a faultless result it was necessary to stop and 'drop in' from time to time. For anyone who does not understand the jargon of the studio world this refers to an imperfect portion of the performance that would spoil an otherwise good take. A button is pushed at the point of repair and the defective part sung again, at the end of which the button is pressed once more to halt the record mode. Technology has advanced to such unimaginable degrees since then that such repairs are devoid of any dangers. Even an out-of-tune voice can now be made perfect with the aid of a pitch shifter. In 1964 it was a much more primitive world.

The session had gone on longer than we would have wished but we were excited by the results. It was now gone midnight and a passage immediately preceding the middle eight - or the bridge - had to be done again. Mike and Chris sang the harmonies and stopped, happy that they had been in time and in tune. There was a stunned silence in the control room and Tony Hatch glanced over to the tape operator, a nice young guy called Malcolm Eade. He was still learning the ropes but was nonetheless an efficient assistant and learning fast. We all knew what had happened but hoped otherwise. It had been a long and tiring day for all of us and minds were understandably wandering. Malcolm had neglected to punch us out of record at the end of the insert.

Two bars of the backing track which had taken all day to achieve had been erased. There was the strong possibility that the entire recording would have to be begun again from scratch. We were horrified. Tony, with an absence of any noticeable panic and the most magnificent display of diplomacy and tact quietly motioned for Malcolm to come outside. After his gentle admonishment, which was done out of our earshot, the two returned.

Tony listened to the recording and figured that the phrase was repeated once more over the space of the next four bars. He sent us to rest for ten minutes while he and Ray Prickett sorted out the problem. In modern recordings of the twenty-first century edits are carried out by simply moving a cursor on the monitor screen. But this was the sixties and razors and adhesive tape had to be implemented. The section of the recording was copied and, after the useless erased taped had been snipped out, slotted into the gap. Tony played it back. Happily, the result was good enough to use. If you listen to the record of *Goodbye My Love* very closely it is just possible to hear a slight 'swoosh' at the point of entry. It sounds almost like a sigh. It was a sigh of relief for us.

In the NME of February 26th Derek Johnson wrote 'Twelve notes in one word...very impressed by intriguing harmony blend...appealing styling with infectious slow beat and unusual backing...should climb reasonably high.' It sounded as though, in the light of our sticky position, he was hedging his bets. Johnson, it seemed, was a reviewer for all seasons. His technique would have made Pontius Pilate proud.

On the flip-side was a song that has proved to be our most enduring and loved composition - *Till I Met You.* I have seen it credited to Curtis and Pender and I have also seen it marked down as a combined effort from the entire group. In fact this beautiful song with its simple and moving words was written by John McNally alone for his wife Mary.

In the early days Chris gathered the bulk of the B-sides, realising that there was more kudos and longevity not to mention monetary reward in being a songwriter. But eventually as we cottoned on to the fact that the actual merit of the reverse of a single was usually a subjective thing and difficult to argue in favour of as good, bad or indifferent, it was going to accrue the same income as the all-important hit, we agreed to combine the credits no matter who was the originator of the piece. It seemed fairer on the whole.

At the same time it was announced that we were to tour at the end of March and our co-stars would be Dusty, Bobby Vee, Heinz, the Zombies and, most bizarrely, Tony Jackson. Making his usual train noises would be our old variety stalwart George Meaton. There was little doubt that with this nepotistic bill, Vee excepted, there would be a great deal of commission heading towards the coffers of Tito Burns.

Apart from touring with stars I was also meeting people I had only gazed at from a distance before. I was invited by record producer Norman Newell to attend a recording session by Eartha Kitt at the Abbey Road studios. I was thrilled, having been a long-time fan of the purring sex kitten who had been dubbed by Orson Welles 'the most exciting woman in the world'. Dressed very casually in pants and sweater with a band tied across her hair she could not have been more charming and chatted like an old friend as we posed for photos. But I was being lulled into a false sense of security. I was later to see an entirely different side to her character.

Meanwhile our profile in the US was being maintained by an appearance on the latest hit teenage-oriented television show Hullabaloo. Each show featured a star guest who would host the programme and perform a selection of the latest chart songs in a super-medley. Sammy Davis hosted on February 23rd on a show that included amongst others Bobby Goldsboro, the Beau Brummels, Joey Heatherton and the Drifters. We were performing two numbers, *What Have They Done To The Rain*? and our recent Stateside smash *Love Potion No. 9.*

But we never saw any of the other acts or met Sammy because the British section was pre-recorded at Shepperton Studios near Staines in West London. The UK segment was introduced by Brian Epstein in a somewhat stilted and detached manner which would have amused the Americans and in the eyes and ears of their more casual and egalitarian society must surely have appeared to reek of class.

The Moody Blues were also present on the day although filming their segment for a different transmission date. We discovered that their new single was to be a cover of a Drifters tune *I Don't Want To Go On Without You*, a song which we had coincidentally just included on our new album *Sounds Like Searchers*. In a mischievous mood we played our version loudly in the adjoining dressing room just to wind them up a little. Whether it worked and made them a little concerned that there might be a rival version vying for chart honours I have no idea but it amused us at the time. Gosh, we Searchers certainly knew how to live the rock & roll lifestyle.

By way of a footnote, the lead dancer on Hullabaloo was an up and coming dancer and choreographer by the name of Michael Bennett. He was soon to become a Tony-winning Broadway legend creating the style for *A Chorus Line*, *Follies* and *Dreamgirls* and a host of other hit shows until his untimely death from AIDS in 1987.

Goodbye My Love charted in its first week at twenty-four on March 5th which was encouraging and we flew to Paris for a major television show and ate horsemeat for the first (and last) time in the studio canteen. It was the only time I can remember the band flying First Class, although First Class on such a short flight is a waste of both luxury and money. No doubt the French paid, for we never would have. It took from morning till night to record our tiny segment of the show and by the end of it we were so exhausted that we gave up the idea of seeing Paris. We got the cab driver to pass by the Eiffel Tower, stepped out for about half a minute simply to be able to say that we had actually been there and went straight to bed.

The new single leapt up to number ten the following week. Brian Epstein had already made a bet that it would top the charts after being played an acetate of the finished product by Chris Curtis before its release. By the middle of the month it was up another three places and it seemed that Eppy might be right. Perhaps we could dislodge the Rolling Stones' *The Last Time* from number one. We performed the tune of the Eamonn Andrews Show, a favourite late-night chat and music show, which gave it a push and joined a host of stellar names at a special ball in aid of the SOS, the Stars Organisation For Spastics, held at the Empire Pool, Wembley.

It was an impressive list with P J Proby, Adam Faith, Dave Berry, Lulu, Billy J Kramer, the Zombies, the Fourmost, the Merseybeats and the Pretty Things. Top deejays of the day Alan Freeman, David Jacobs and Don Moss compered the event. Tom Jones was also included which produced a tricky and potentially explosive situation.

P. J Proby, who had been born James Marcus Smith in Houston, Texas on November 6th 1938, had been a major attraction with hits like *Somewhere* and *Maria*, arguably the greatest currently popular male performer in Britain, until he had been either unwise or unlucky enough to split his tight velvet trousers during a concert on January 29th 1965 at Croydon's Fairfield Hall during his headlining concert tour. Whether it was deliberate or not only Proby himself knows. Two days later the renting of the sacred velvet was repeated and more flesh revealed to a pubescent audience.

In retrospect such a slight baring of flesh around the knee would not even rate a mention in today's prurient times but the so called decadent sixties were in fact still only a few steps removed from the puritanical morals of the Victorian era. A few years on and the reaction would more likely to be somewhere between stifled yawns and yells to get it all off.

One day he was king of all he surveyed and on stage creating scenes of mass hysteria amidst a writhing audience of hormone riddled teenage girls. The next he was off the tour and replaced by the up and coming Tom Jones, a ruggedly handsome Welshman with a voice to equal the American's, who promptly donned the crown and never returned it. With the publicity and the prestige provided by those unexpected weeks on a prestigious sold-out theatre circuit *It's Not Unusual* had shot to number one. There was no stopping the boyo now.

Someone from the SOS organisation contrived to introduce them to each other and the scene was reminiscent of two wildcats cagily assessing each other, pawing the ground like panthers while figuring who was going to make the first move. The arrogant and rangy Texan was not happy at having his status usurped by this young pretender and could see it all slipping away, while the macho man from the Welsh valleys, well aware of his immense talent and the possibilities that now lay in his grasp, was not about to concede any of the ground he had gained. It was quite fascinating to watch from the safety of the sidelines. Eventually they managed to extend their hands at more or less the same moment and with good grace entered into some friendly small talk. The feeling of relief in the room was palpable.

The first night of our new tour, which opened at the Stockton-on-Tees Odeon on March 25th, left us with an odd feeling. It was the first time we had really had any contact with Tony Jackson since the acrimonious split eight months before. Our brief conversations before the show were friendly enough although quite naturally Tony seemed a little self-conscious. Natural curiosity made us go to the side and watch as he took the stage with his new outfit, the Vibrations.

They sounded good and were well turned out. But Tony, probably in an attempt to quell his nerves, had been drinking prior to the show and it was not helping him. He was altogether trying too hard and the excessive intake of alcohol was clouding his judgement and robbing him of his sense of proportion. In an attempt to whip up the crowd he ventured to the front of the stage and put his hand out to grasp hold of the arms extended to him. Somehow he ended prostrate on the floor, the upper regions of his body teetering over the edge, and continued nearer and nearer the abyss at the end of the podium.

Eventually the edge of the stage came and went and Tony lay on the floor in front of the first row of seats where he had fallen. In his state of inebriation, made even harder by his ardent female admirers who were doing their damnedest to keep him amongst them, he found the climb back extremely difficult and it seemed like an eternity before he managed to scale the heights and regain his position in the middle of his band, swaying precariously and stumbling towards an uncomfortable close. It was a sad sight and we all felt sorry for him. Despite our differences this was something we never wanted to see. It only happened once and for the remainder of the tour Tony was sober and competent enough to perform nightly without any further unfortunate incidents.

It was a strong bill with the magnificent Dusty in yet another supporting role to ourselves. In truth, with good management and promotion, Dusty should have been headlining her own sell-out concerts by this time. Instead she was forced to compete against the hysterical screams of teenage girls there to worship at the feet of the latest idols although she always managed to more than hold her own. Everyone loved Dusty. How could you not?

Bobby Vee was always a guaranteed winner with a roster of hits which, while temporarily out of fashion when compared to the latest groups from Great Britain, would outlast any of the current fads and see him through to the end of the century and beyond. Not only were his songs addictive, his boy-next-door personality and beaming grin were guaranteed to win over any crowd. He was always one of my favourites and a great guy to be on tour with. Bobby was the perfect complement to our similarly clean-cut but slightly more raucous and energetic style.

Capitalising on the success of their debut disc *She's Not There* the Zombies scored strongly with the kids despite a more sophisticated musical style that often crossed over from pop into jazz territory. Colin Blunstone's smooth and smoky voice was different from anything else around at the time when hard-edged vocals were the thing and Rod Argent's expertise on keyboards was a distinctive fusion of classics and rock.

Low man on the totem pole in the vocal department was the blond, bouffant-haired ex-Tornado Heinz. He had been launched on record because his pretty boy looks made record producer Joe Meek's heart beat a little faster. Despite a lack of talent that was obvious to everyone except Meek, who was deeply in love with his protégée, and Heinz himself, Joe had actually achieved the near miraculous feat of providing him with a sizeable hit record, *Just Like Eddie*.

Having been told by Meek that he was immensely talented and a true star he compensated for his tunelessness by hurling himself around the stage like a whirling dervish, jumping on top of the piano and scaling any available heights in order to grab the attention of the audience which was not always known to harbour kind thoughts towards him. Never a favourite of the lads who considered him to be nothing more than a 'dyed haired poof' he had actually come to bodily harm at their hands on more than one occasion. While girls held their hands out to touch him as he performed at the front of the stage the male members of the audience reached forward simply to try and punch him in the face.

One of his favourite tricks was to disappear off the side of the stage and to reappear minutes later down the centre aisle having run around the outside of the theatre and in through the main doors. For most of the time this worked well but there were a few disasters when managements locked the doors after the show started. On these occasions his band had to soldier on manfully with seemingly endless guitar solos until the frantic rocker, dishevelled, sweating and out of breath, finally stepped back into the spotlight from the very point from whence he had left an eternity before.

Although really quite harmless and a reasonably pleasant guy his very existence seemed to engender rage in the ranks of the serious musicians who comprised Dusty's backing band. Their contempt for him reached its apotheosis when on one particular occasion, having realised that the front entrance would be firmly locked, they proceeded to bar the stage door as well. The solos were a little longer that night.

The tour followed the usual pattern which in effect was no pattern at all although this time round the journeys weren't too arduous. From Stockton we headed on to Doncaster, Newcastle, Liverpool, Worcester, Bradford, Bristol, Colchester, Salisbury and Taunton before finishing in Cardiff on April 10th.

After one of the shows Dusty gave me a ride back to town in her brand new Buick Riviera, a monstrously huge and glamourous left hand drive coupé with silver grey paintwork and red leather upholstery. The car was beautiful and so was Dusty. It was a wonder we made the journey intact as Dusty was as blind as a bat and would not wear her glasses. Driving with her was always a life-threatening experience but we survived.

We turned into the cul-de-sac where my parents lived in their simple pebble-dashed council house around one a.m. As I got out and thanked her I badly wished the whole street would wake up and look out their windows. I wanted to shout 'For Christ's sake, look at me you buggers. Dusty Springfield is giving me a lift home.' But no-one looked and I walked to the door in the dark as the Riviera glided silently and anonymously away.

By the first week of April *Goodbye My Love* had gone as far as it was going to go. Brian Epstein had lost his bet but a number four hit was a vindication of our position on the group scene. For the time being we were still very hot stuff.

Mike Pender and John McNally had more to fit into our insane schedule than me, having decided it was time for them to enter the property market. John had acquired a plot near the sea-front in the affluent Liverpool suburb of Blundellsands and designed his own detached dwelling which was still under construction, the kind of residence that well suited a local boy made good. He had originally intended it as a single storey build but when it became obvious that the neighbouring houses would tower over him and make his place look slightly odd the plans were altered to include another storey.

Mike had gone in on a more modest level purchasing a sizeable semi-detached house over the water in Wallasey. It was away from the hustle and bustle of Liverpool giving him and May a more tranquil life, but hell for road manager Billy Booker who had to make a vast detour to drop him off each time on their return from a show. Chris Curtis was still happy to live with his family who had shifted from Bootle to a new home in the Old Roan district neat Aintree.

My own pretensions to being a house owner were for the time being on hold. I was still very much in residence at my parents' council house in Browngraves Road, Harlington, where the only concession to my elevation to pop star status was the installation of a telephone in a bright shade of red. I was doing okay but not to the point where I was at liberty to indulge my whims without serious consideration and certainly not where bricks and mortar were concerned. The thought of perhaps buying somewhere of my own was vaguely in my future plans but the idea of a mortgage in such an unpredictable and precarious profession was too scary for now.

On stage we were still very much in the top bracket and once more shared the stage with the biggest names of the day which included the Beatles, the Rolling Stones, Freddie & the Dreamers, Georgie Fame, Twinkle, the Seekers, Herman's Hermits, the Ivy League, the Bachelors, Wayne Fontana, Cilla Black, the Rocking Berries, Donovan, Dusty Springfield, Tom Jones, Dave Davies and the Animals when it came time for the NME's annual Poll Concert on April 11th.

Pop journalist Keith Altham threw compliments our way, declaring that we looked distinguished as we came on stage in immaculate dark suits and neatly combed hair which he wrote was quite a contrast to the devil-may-care look of some other artistes. Rebels we were not but we had an image and we knew how to use it.

Altham commented on our usual first rate and polished performances but also pointed out that the crowd was disappointed that we didn't play *Goodbye My Love.* Instead we sang *Let The Good Times Roll* and *Bumble Bee.* It was in truth an odd omission and one which recurred decades later when time and time again we somehow could not find room for this top three hit in our set.

Our bias towards *Bumble Bee* however was justified when the extended-play record of which it was the lead track entered the EP charts and stayed in the top spot for two weeks. We might not be the current kings of the castle but we were still very much in residence.

Naturally the Beatles once again were the main event of the concert and just about scooped the board as far as awards went. If they'd entered Crufts no doubt they would have won that too. The legendary singer Tony Bennett was on hand to present them with their trophies. As they prepared to take their place on the stage I stood at the side gazing on in awe at this phenomenon which, like a runaway locomotive, seemed to be absolutely unstoppable. They were clad in black slacks and polo neck tops over which they wore high cut Nehru jackets in a shade of beige. They managed to look at the same time both smart and casual and impossibly cool. How could any of us hope to compete with them? The naked truth was that we could not. We simply had to try to keep in step and play catch-up as best we could.

The four of them were joined by minions and admirers in a tightly packed throng at the foot of the small flight of stairs. In the mid-sixties the smartest place to be was next to a Beatle. George Harrison looked over and yelled 'Hi Frank.' I was taken aback. Sure I'd met them many times but I was very aware of my place in the scheme of things and never attempted to promote myself to a position of intimacy. Despite the relaxed charm of Paul McCartney, whose PR skills put one at ease from the outset, my dealings with John Lennon had made me very aware indeed of the dangers of over-estimating the goodwill on offer. I smiled back and returned his greeting.

George extracted himself from the pack with some difficulty and came over to me. We lounged side by side against the wall for what seemed an eternity while my scrambled and inadequate brain tried in vain to formulate any sentence that might vaguely interest, or at least not offend, a Beatle. The more I tried the more my intellectual capacities locked firmly. Nothing would come. I could hardly enquire as to how things were going. Inside I panicked. Outside I must have appeared remote and uncommunicative. In my defence George didn't seem able to instigate a subject either.

He stood silently cradling his Rickenbacker twelve-string on which he would soon be picking out the riff to *Ticket To Ride*, their new single, as we both stared awkwardly into the middle distance. Maybe this image I had of them being all-powerful and worldly beings endowed with supreme confidence and sophistication was just a myth. The silence between us was deafening and I was dying inside. Eventually George uttered 'Well, I've gotta go,' and he trundled off to join the other three gods who were poised to head up to where the screams awaited. I was mortified. My puny level of self-confidence, low at the best of times, had just sunk a few fathoms deeper.

19

Slip Sliding Away

With the benefit of hindsight I firmly hold to the opinion that the slide for us began with the release of *He's Got No Love* in the first week of July 1965. It might sound odd to suggest that a disc that reached a more than respectable high of a number ten placing in the NME can be classed a failure but it has become noticeable through the passing decades that the tune, catchy and as well made as it was, has only ever been requested a handful of times. I have known records that barely entered the top thirty which have made a significantly greater impression on people's memory banks. Glen Campbell's *By The Time I Get To Phoenix* does not show in the Guinness Book of Hit Singles but is considered an unforgettable classic.

It suggests to me that most of the success *He's Got No Love* attained had been on the strength of the one that had gone before, *Goodbye My Love*, and the momentum that our still-healthy career carried all things along with it. After all there are hits of more modest proportions that we could not dream of ignoring for too long lest certain sections of the audience suffer from withdrawal symptoms. The proof of the pudding is in the eating and after giving it the taste test first time around the customers declined second helpings.

Don't get me wrong, it was a good record but on reflection it lacked the strength of the kind of material that we should have been searching out and waiting for. We needed to come out with another *When You Walk In The Room* or even something with the punch and the drive of *Sweets For My Sweet*. But it's easy to be wise after the event and I certainly didn't have wisdom on my side at the time. I went along with the general thought that it was a good recording and well worth a try. It was simple and bouncy with a very lively backing of juxtaposed figures on jangly guitars. And it was our first self-penned A-side.

The song came by accident with John and Mike messing about with a loose approximation of the backing on the Rolling Stones' record *The Last Time*. By this time

Mike had ditched the Gibson ES345 and purchased a Rickenbacker twelve-string semi-acoustic in order that we could successfully reproduce the distinctive sound that we had now become known for. For the anorak obsessed with detail, it was the Rose Morris model 1993 in a red sunburst finish known as fireglo, a limited edition made for export to the UK only via the Rose Morris Music Company in London. On top of Mike's arpeggios John's Telecaster overlaid a six-string figure enhanced by putting it through a tremolo effect and taking the chord down a tone and up again in a constantly repeating and almost hypnotic pattern.

Mike and Chris combined to come up with a tune and lyrics to fit the sound and with nothing else of any noticeable strength on tape at the time, and a record company itching for another Searchers release, we adhered to Chris's suggestion that we should run with it. After all, we still considered Chris the man at the helm when it came to the bulk of ideas in the studio. He had been right more often than not and was becoming more and more involved in production, having written an upcoming single for Alma Cogan called *Snakes And Snails* (*And Puppy Dog's Tails*). P.J. Proby had also taken Chris's advice and planned a Ben E King song *Let The Water Run Down* as his next offering at Curtis's instigation. Not a great chart success for the crazy Texan, it was, Proby insists, the disc that gave him at least a foothold in his native America. In fact Jim's memory might just be a tad out of kilter there as *Niki Hokey* was his only US top 40 hit.

In truth some record reviewers were carried away just as much as we were. Derek Johnson of the NME, which featured the group on its front page that week, called *He's Got No Love* a 'unique, startling sound...almost like a steel guitar on echo.' Norman Jopling of the Record Mirror was somewhat more hesitant. 'Not exactly the best thing they have done...quite a complicated song with more vocal harmony than of late.' On reflection Jopling was more astute than Johnson.

It entered at an optimistic number forty-eight in its first week, only two positions lower than its predecessor *Goodbye My Love* and one place higher than *What Have They Done To The Rain* had. We were booked to appear on Thank Your Lucky Stars, an important and necessary plug which unfortunately coincided with a short break I had planned to visit friends in Freeport in the Bahamas. John McNally was adamant that I should cancel the holiday and appear on the show. Chris was on my side and figured a way round the problem. To resolve the situation the bass player with the folk group the Settlers deputised for me, standing way back in the line-up, in shadow and with no close-ups. It did not however go unnoticed and rumours flew that I had left the band.

A holiday in the Bahamas might sound like the privileged peccadillo of a *nouveau-riche* pop star but in fact I was flying courtesy of my father's concessionary rights as an employee of the British Overseas Airways Corporation and the entire trip was eating into my meagre bank account to the exotic tune of eighteen pounds return air fare.

I got back home from the Bahamas by the skin of my teeth. It never for a moment occurred to me that, as I was travelling on a standby basis, there might not be a seat for me. In fact the plane was well under capacity on the way out. But when I tried to check in at Nassau for the trip home, having said goodbye to my chums and taken the early morning connecting flight from the island of Grand Bahama to New Providence, the check-in clerk dourly stated that the plane was full and without another word disappeared to the airport equivalent of 'backstage'. I panicked. This was something I had not made provision for. I had brought just enough cash for my holiday and, like most other travellers in those primitive times was not in possession of a credit card. Very few people at that time used such things.

I was suddenly in danger of being stuck in the Caribbean with barely a penny to my name, and being the low season BOAC only operated two flights a week to the UK. If I didn't think quickly I was in danger of missing our next run of shows back home and the thought of facing the wrath of the others, particularly when I should have been at home plugging our latest hit rather than swanning about in the sun, was something I did not relish. I vaulted the desk and trespassed into the staff recreation room where I found the check-in clerk playing poker with his chums. 'I've got to get on that plane' I insisted. He looked up obviously annoyed. 'I can put you on as far as Bermuda.' I accepted. God knows what I was going to do there but being poor in Bermuda would surely be no worse than being poor in the Bahamas. And it would give me time to think.

Once on the aircraft I grabbed an air steward (not, I might add, in the biblical sense) and explained my predicament, with an emphasis on my staff connection. I figured the workers-of-the-world-unite angle might be my best chance of success. When we landed in Bermuda there was a member of the ground staff waiting at the foot of the steps to lead me to a check-in desk and an onward ticket. My relief was so evident and delicious it was almost edible. It never occurred to me though that while I would be moving onwards my luggage would not. I had neglected to collect it and re-check it in. I never saw it again.

I was back in the UK and back in the old routine again. The record was still at the beginning of its climb as we departed our home shores for another tour of the States accompanied by our chums and stable mates the Zombies. For economy's sake this one was undertaken by a combination of bus and plane as we covered mile after mile hitting towns that may have seemed mundane to Americans but whose names sounded mighty glamourous to us.

We started off on July 16th with three days in Chicago, having been voted the world's tenth best vocal group and sixth best British vocal group by readers of the Record Mirror, below groups like the Beatles, Stones, Animals, Hollies and Manfred Mann. We had slipped a little but we were still contenders and a force to be reckoned with.

At McCormack Place we were supported by the Kingsmen of *Louie Louie* fame and Chad Stuart, newly split from his singing partner Jeremy Clyde. This duo who had only managed moderate success in Britain had become big in the States with *A Summer Song*, *Yesterday's Gone* and *Willow Weep For Me.*

When we checked into the Palmer House Hotel the desk clerk asked if we were students. Sensing a special rate on offer we answered in the affirmative and obtained a discount. When the hotel was besieged by hordes of screaming fans over the next two days the mistake was quickly rectified and our bill increased appropriately. Well, it was worth a try.

From Chicago we carried on to Nashville and joined up with the Beach Boys. While we were lounging around the pool at the Holiday Inn we heard the Beatles' new record *Help!* for the first time and realised how far ahead of the game they were compared to anyone else. It was dynamic and we couldn't help but reflect that perhaps our own choice had been a trifle hasty with competition of this standard.

On we travelled to Louisville (20th), Terre Haute (21st), Montgomery (23rd) and Jacksonville (24th) where we re-joined the Beach Boys. Added to that show were Sam the Sham & the Pharaohs, the Shangri-Las and Lesley Gore. We stayed in Florida for the next five days performing in Winter Haven, Orlando, Pensacola, Panama City and Tampa. From there we headed to Columbus, Georgia, after which we received three days off for good behaviour. Or maybe lack of interest, I'm not sure which and cared even less. It was all becoming a haze.

Back in the UK *He's Got No Love* had reached its zenith of number ten in the NME on July 30th (or, if you prefer, twelve once the listings had been averaged out for the official records) and was stuck there for one more week before moving on down and out. On the whole we were quite pleased with its progress. A top ten disc was a respectable achievement especially with one of our own compositions, but we would have to choose carefully from now on. The top five was the only territory we should be inhabiting if we were to remain frontrunners in the current market.

Part of our problem, I felt, was planning. We always seemed to be abroad at a time when we should have been maintaining a high visibility in our home market to give the latest disc a much-needed boost. And usually on a long tour on far distant shores. Our office appeared not to have the capability or foresight to liaise with Pye so that we would be at hand for the necessary television and radio promotion. Furthermore we were individuals who, apart from the gregarious Chris Curtis, were not pushy personalities or controversial enough to insinuate our names and our faces with sufficient force into the minds of the public.

On August 3rd I got a telegram from Pam Jenkins, our fan club secretary from Coventry in England, congratulating me on my first anniversary as a Searcher. Had it really been a year? It had flown by. The significance of the day had escaped me completely. I didn't even know what town I was in by then. We ticked off the exotic names from our itinerary. Chattanooga (4th), Charlotte (6th) and Richmond (7th) where we joined up with Dick Clark's Caravan Of Stars. Why they needed the Searchers and the Zombies added to a list of names that already included Tom Jones, Brian Hyland, Peter and Gordon and a whole bunch of others I didn't know but it was fun having some new pals to mix and to talk with.

The Searchers and the Zombies left the Clark team after New Haven on the 9th and continued our own trek through Burlington (10th), Biddeford (11th), Pittsfield (12th) and stopping for three days in Oklahoma City. On the way from the airport I managed to connect with a dark-haired girl in a blue Chevvy Sting Ray. I got off the bus into the 'glamour-mobile' and she looked after me during my stay. The dangers of such hastily made liaisons was brought home to me on my return when my parents received a call from the girl's poor distraught husband asking me to break it off. I was horrified. In fact there was precious little to break off but it worried me for a moment that there might be unpleasant repercussions.

In Oklahoma City I discovered our old friend Bobby Vee was performing at a nearby state fair so we met up and spent a pleasant evening together after his show. He arrived wearing Bermuda shorts, not a common sight back home and not, might I suggest, a good look for Bobby. Bobby was a nice guy and I liked him a lot.

Our final stop was in Los Angeles where we taped and appearance on *Shindig* for transmission on 8th September. Tito Burns joined us for that portion of the trip with the glamour of Hollywood, Beverly Hills, the exclusive stores of Rodeo Drive and a bunch of his family residing in the area as an incentive. Typical. Agents rarely turn up in some Godforsaken backwater devoid of glamour, shops or, dare I suggest, relatives.

We performed *He's Got No Love*, *Bumble Bee*, which had been released as a single there and reached a very creditable twenty-one in the charts, and of course *Love Potion No. 9* which was to forever remain our most important hit that side of the Atlantic. Our co-performers on that show were mostly unknown in the UK. Bruce Scott, the Collins Kids and the Guilloteens meant nothing in Britain while Gene Chandler's past hits and generally low profile in England left him a virtually forgotten man.

Coincidentally Barbara Lewis, who had made the original record of *Someday We're Gonna Love Again* was also included singing her latest disc *He's A Real Gone Guy*. During a break I sat beside her and made what I thought was pleasant small talk, mentioning that we had covered her song, a fact of which she surely must have been aware. I thought she would be pleased and therefore friendly. Her reply was curt and almost monosyllabic. It seemed to me that our appropriation of her work was possibly a point that rankled. While we were there we also put *Needles And Pins* in the can for inclusion in a show to be aired on December 2nd before heading on home to Britain.

There were some one-nighters to take care of and a two-day trip to Holland in order to film our own television special but as usual the pressure was immediately back on to provide Pye with some product and we began to put down tracks that would hopefully provide us with a new album and with any luck a new hit single.

Once more Chris was very much in charge and flexing his muscles with that usual single-mindedness which underlined his character. Having produced the single with Alma Cogan on which he used Doris Troy and Madeleine Bell on backing vocals, he had also taken charge of an Eden Kane session and was beginning to see his future as much a producer as a musician. He told the Record Mirror that he had formed a production company with Tito Burns which he looked on as a creative challenge and an enthralling assignment. Adding that it would not interfere with the Searchers, Chris explained that production gave a musician a deeper understanding of the problems and the techniques used to overcome them. 'I now know a good deal more about what the man in the box behind the glass panel has to do.'

He was not one to believe he could be mistaken. Such blinkered self-confidence is an admirable trait indeed - as long as you are proved not to be wrong. Knob twiddling was no doubt an essential part of the producer's skill but he had perhaps overlooked the fact that above and beyond everything else the most important ingredient was the song, without which the game was up. He was convinced that a tune he had picked up in the States, an obscure Bobby Darin A-side, was the answer to all our problems. It had a tempo similar to *Needles And Pins* with melodic harmony vocals and a guitar riff that would have continued the style with which we had become identified. It was called *When I Get Home*. And it was a disaster.

52. Live on stage soon after their first success (John McNally collection)

53. A postcard to me from John McNally in Paris

54. Complaining about the cost, of course

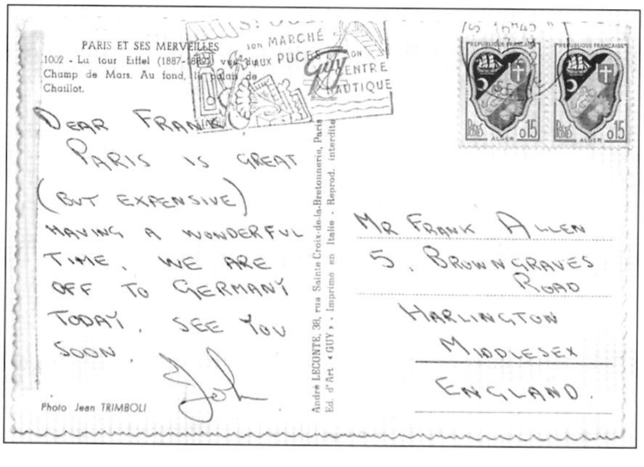
PARIS ET SES MERVEILLES
1002 - La tour Eiffel (1887-1889) vue du Champ de Mars. Au fond, le palais de Chaillot.

DEAR FRANK
PARIS IS GREAT
(BUT EXPENSIVE)
HAVING A WONDERFUL
TIME. WE ARE
OFF TO GERMANY
TODAY. SEE YOU
SOON.
John

Photo Jean TRIMBOLI

André LECONTE, 38, rue Sainte Croix-de-la-Bretonnerie, Paris
Ed. d'Art « GUY ». - Imprimé en Italie - Reprod. interdite

MR FRANK ALLEN
5, BROWNGRAVES
ROAD
HARLINGTON
MIDDLESEX
ENGLAND.

55. In New York for the Ed Sullivan Show 1964 (Roy Clough collection)

56. Me kissing the Blarney Stone. Excellent training for a front man.

57. The Rebel Rousers backing the Vernons (badly) at the Prince of Wales Theatre, London 1964

58. The Botwell House Festival programme, June 3rd 1963

59. On stage on their 1964 Summer tour of the U.S.A (Roy Clough collection)

60. John McNally hits the heights. Top of the Empire State Building, Summer 1964 (Roy Clough collection)

61. Tony Jackson at Niagara Falls, 1964 U.S tour (Roy Clough collection)

62. Mike and May Pender and Tony Jackson at Niagara (Roy Clough collection)

63. Seaton Carew Big Beat Night pre-show July 1964 (Ian Wright)

64. Seaton Carew Big Beat Night - on stage (Ian Wright)

65. The Searchers with the new boy, Knightsbridge, August 1964

66. Tony Jackson & the Vibrations (Roy Clough collection)

67. With Ronettes Nedra Talley and Estelle Bennett at the Fox Theatre, Brooklyn 1964. l-r John, me, Nedra, Chris, Estelle, Mike

68. Me with Jackie DeShannon

THE OFFICIAL

Searchers Fan Club

(Victorian Branch)

87 1948

President: R. E. HALL
51 Mitcham Road,
Mitcham
87 1948

69. Melbourne fan club membership card (Rob Hall collection)

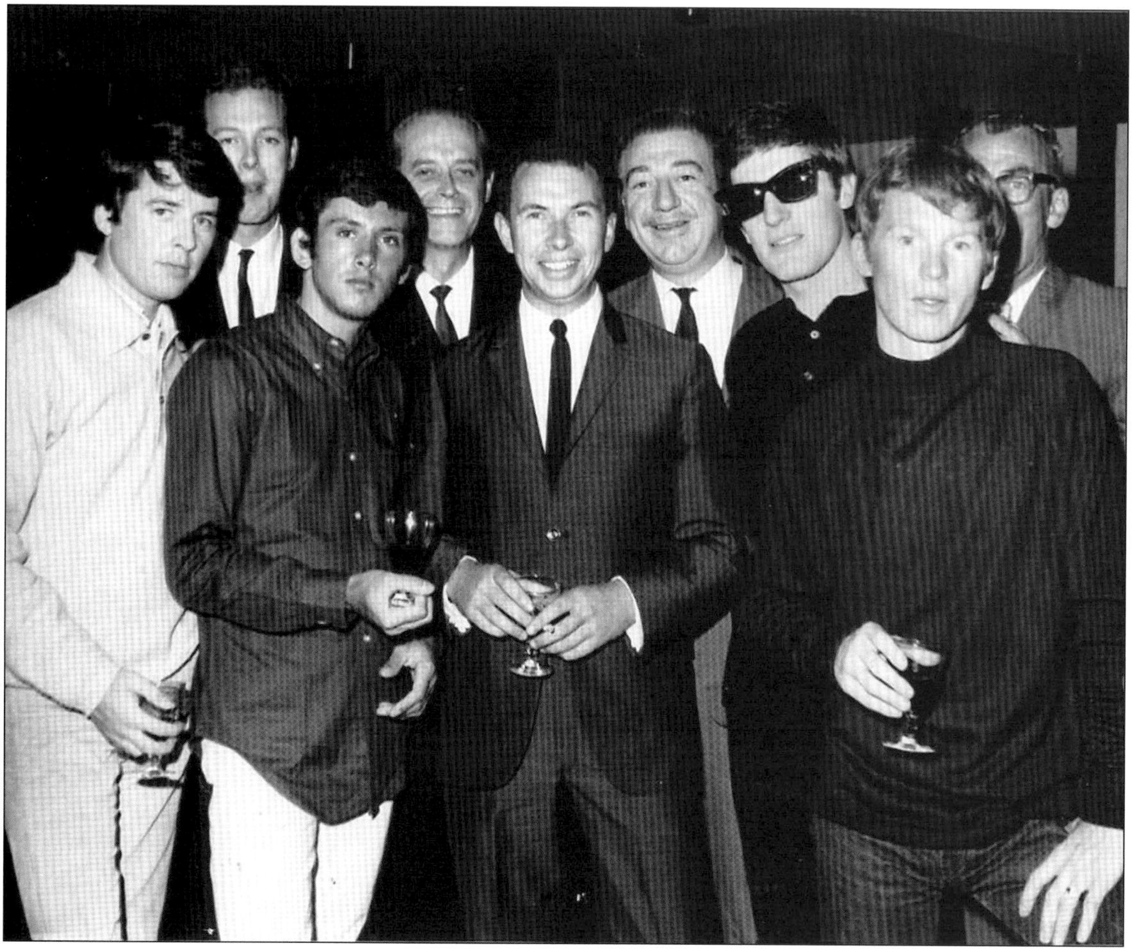

70. With record executives in Australia, September 1964

71. Sensational Searchers - Record Mirror cover

72. Rehearsing for What Have They Done To The Rain on Ready Steady Go (Roy Clough collection)

73. With my pop star girl friend Julie Grant

74. Being presented to Princess Margaret at the Docklands Settlement Ball with (left) Julie Rogers (Doug McKenzie)

75. NME Pollwinners Concert 1965

76. Another flight. '65 U.S tour

77. Oklahoma 1965 with Bobby Vee in Bermuda shorts. Not a good look.

78. The girl in the Sting Ray

79. The Araneta Colosseum, Quezon City, Manila, March 1966

80. With Filipino film stars March 1966

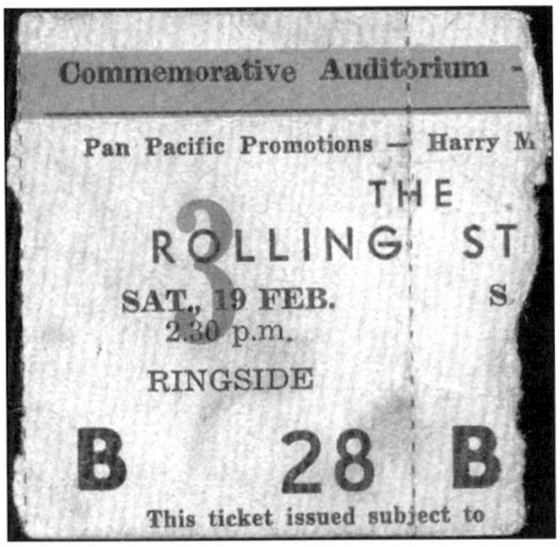

81. 1966 ticket stub, our tour with the Rolling Stones

82. Mike Rispoli (tour manager for the Stones for the Oz 1966 tour), me, Searchers roadie Barry Delaney, at Lennons Hotel Brisbane

83. John on stage at Brisbane City Hall 21st Feb 1966

84. Charlie Watts and me, Melbourne 1966 (Colin Beard)

85. The Searchers' new line-up with John Blunt 1966

86. In the Ford Thames outside the Fiesta, Stockton, August 7th 1967, l-r John Blunt, me, Mike Pender, John McNally (Ian Wright)

87. Fans approving our new drummer John Blunt

88. Germany, in my very silly shirt so much admired by Graham Nash. Late 60s (Erhard Preuss collection)

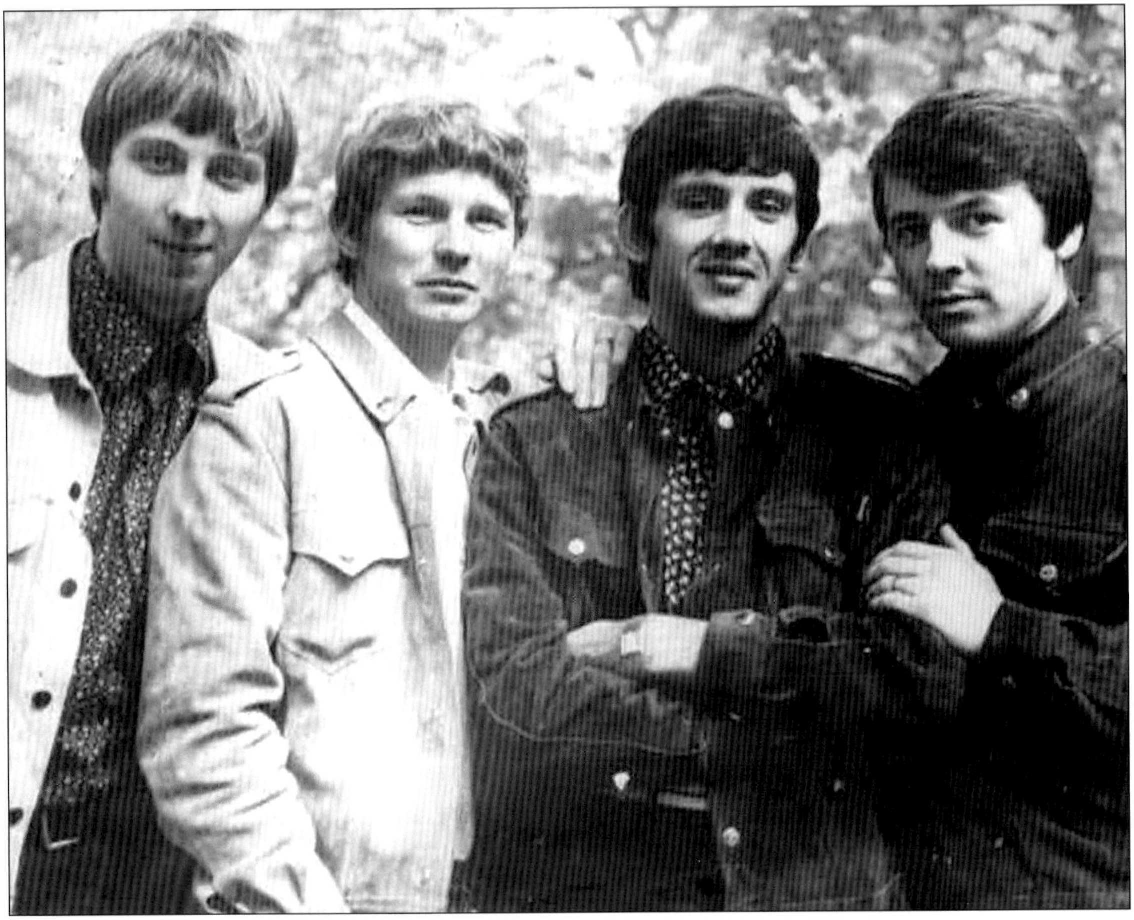

89. 1966 to 1969 line-up. John Blunt, John McNally, me, Mike Pender

20

Deeper And Down

It was actually quite a good record. Even now when I look back and analyse *When I Get Home* the ingredients appeared to be in place. It was medium paced, tuneful and emotive and the lyrics were well crafted. The guitar figure, played on a twelve-string once more, had the hallmark of a Searchers single. And the harmonies were full and precise.

We devised a trick at the beginning to make it interesting. After playing the opening guitar figures we dropped the key one semitone and stayed there until the last verse when, to give it a lift, we raised the pitch once more to the original key. Finally on reaching the end we reverted to the lower key for the final lingering and mournful chord. Raising a key to increase the level of excitement is an old ploy and one that works well. Lowering a key is, on reflection, possibly not such a wise move. If a move upwards lifts the spirits it follows that a drop will tend to depress things a tad. But one can argue the pros and cons until the cows come home. A record will usually be sold in the first minute and anything that occurs at its conclusion will have had little effect on its sales. In the end it remains a fact that it was just not a hit song. Certainly not by us and possibly not by anyone.

If you had read Derek Johnson's review you might well have been encouraged to shell out your hard-earned cash for a new Searchers hit with a certain degree of optimism. 'Written by Bobby Darin...an exhilarating and stimulating disc...moves along at a fast moving pace....distinctive and ear-catching guitar sounds in which the band specialises...I expect it to do a little better than the last release.' Oh that he had been right but he could not have got it more wrong. More on the mark was Norman Jopling in the Record Mirror. 'Not exactly the best thing they have done....quite a complicated song with more vocal harmony than of late.' Jopling, not convinced about *He's Got No Love*, was once again on the ball.

We made ourselves available for all the usual radio and television promotional spots, on top of which we were booked to appear on the very first show of the new season of the prestigious and important Sunday Night At The London Palladium. Plugs did not come higher than this. It was a British tradition for whole families to gather round the set to watch the nation's premier variety show which had consistently maintained record viewing figures since the fifties.

Our slot on the bill was something of a demotion from two years earlier when we would have rightly expected to occupy the star spot at the end of the hour. Instead we were just one of a bunch of musical items banded together in the middle of the proceedings, a new segment which would present musical artistes performing just one number each in quick succession from their position on the famous Palladium roundabout, the moving circular portion of the stage from which the acts traditionally waved their goodbyes at the end of the show.

The folk trio Peter, Paul and Mary had been brought in from America as second top, which pleased me as I was a big fan and was able to get my albums signed by them before they went on. When I entered their dressing room they looked a little daunted at the size of the pile requiring signatures but applied their names without complaint. It was also without humour or any kind of expression whatsoever but at least I got what I wanted.

Closing the show that night were Peter Cook and Dudley Moore and the audience loved them. I watched their spot and found I liked them as well although I had never actually heard of them which just goes to show how little television I watched at that time and how out of touch I was with popular entertainment. I told Dudley Moore at the end of the night how much I enjoyed them and he accepted the compliment graciously.

We could not afford to waste this exposure by singing anything other than our latest disc, although the audience sitting there amongst the plush red velvet seats and gilded carvings would have preferred *Needles And Pins* or *When You Walk In The Room.* These were the days before video recorders and because the show went out live we would never have the chance of ascertaining just how well we had performed that night. Not a bad thing perhaps as I can't imagine we would have had any great reason to be overjoyed. New songs take time to bed in and we had never actually played this one live in public.

Just as we took our positions on the revolve I discovered my guitar lead was not working. Panic ran through my whole body as I sent our road manager Barry Delaney to fetch a spare from our dressing room. Disaster loomed. We were about to deliver an unfamiliar and difficult song to around ten million people through microphones that were devoid of any desired studio effects such as echo or reverb and probably without a working bass guitar. He returned just as the stage started to move and I breathed a sigh of relief as my instrument boomed into life.

We came, we sang, we left. It was okay. Neither a complete fiasco nor an unparalleled success. We got through our three minutes without any glaring mistakes and received generous applause at the end. The audience had now heard our latest release and, having listened, made an instant corporate decision not to buy it. In fact unknown to us the show had been recorded and our segment turned up in 2008, forty-three years later, on YouTube. And surprisingly it didn't sound all that bad.

Throughout September and October we were booked for other programmes essential for getting the tune over to the public. They included Granada Television's Scene At Six Thirty (29th), Top Of The Pops (30th), Ready Steady Go (Oct 1st and 22nd) and Thank Your Lucky Stars (9th) as well as important Light Programme radio spots like Easy Beat and Saturday Club. Alas it was all to no avail. It was becoming quite obvious that nothing could save this record. It made its debut at number forty-four which, as it happens was very much par for our releases of late. So far so good, we thought. The following week however it hobbled wearily up to thirty-five, decided it was all too much effort and started to flop down again with an exasperated sigh. It was the first legitimate single of ours that had failed to enter the top thirty.

And that was where the indomitable spirit of Chris Curtis came into its own. When asked by the press how he felt about us having our first flop he replied, as only Chris could, that we had planned it that way. He stated with a completely straight face, as we gazed on in open-mouthed incredulity, that we had been a little too successful of late and it would be beneficial to keep things low for a while and then come back with a bang. You have to admire such chutzpah. To his credit the journalist in question did not break down and writhe on the floor in hysterics as he would have been fully entitled to do. The man was obviously much too polite.

Dear Chris, who was always so kind and so crazy and full of fun and ideas and boundless enthusiasm, was never the same after that. We all panicked but maybe he felt it most of all. Having tasted success at the highest level his ego was ill prepared to be anything other in life than top dog and the fact that the runt of our litter had just been offered and turned down in no uncertain terms had a disastrous effect on his always-delicate state of mind. He became increasingly remote from the rest of us and his amusing off-the-wall strain of conversation which we had once found such a joy was now very often a jumble of incomprehensible riddles.

We were still busy and popular and after recording an appearance on the children's show Crackerjack we flew to Germany and then to Lisbon before heading for Scotland where we played at the Raith Ballroom in Kirkcaldy (Nov 5th), the Market Hall, Carlisle (6th) and the Lennox Hotel in Ballock (7th).

Towards the end of November the new album, called *Take Me For What I'm Worth* after what we decided was to be the lead track, was put out and at almost the same time that the eponymous single was thrown into the market place. On reflection the speed at which this was achieved was both remarkable and insane. It was less than two months since our last release and we were at a very dangerous point in our career. We would have benefited by taking our time to study our options more carefully before making hasty decisions about further product.

The P. F. Sloan song was a good one with deep thought-provoking lyrics at a time when Bob Dylan and his ilk were making this style all the rage. Sloan had just scored a number one for Barry McGuire with *Eve Of Destruction* and we hoped his magic would rub off on us. It had a soft verse and a contrasting chorus which lifted things a lot and encouraged hands to clap along. It did not have a middle eight section but then neither did *Sweets For My Sweet*, *Someday We're Gonna Love Again* or *Sugar And Spice*.

Reviewers praised its folk beat style and Dylan-like quality, considering it to be different from anything we had done before. The section where the rhythm went into double time was described as particularly stimulating and really vibrant. It did better than the last one - just - peaking at number twenty.

As our chart career began to go into freefall there was little to celebrate that Christmas though the New Year held some interesting prospects in the shape of foreign travel. A projected trip to the US and Hawaii failed to materialise but firmly in place was a tour that would take us to Hong Kong and on to Manila in the Philippines before joining up with the Rolling Stones for a series of concerts across New Zealand and Australia, once again promoted by Aussie entrepreneur Harry Miller.

Despite our poor sales and diminishing status our star had not dropped out of the sky completely. As we entered 1966 we stood in the UK section of the NME points polls at thirty-two which, in consideration of all the other charts acts vying for honours, was not a total disgrace. And in the States we were only two points below at a respectable thirty-four.

On a personal level I had the satisfaction of seeing myself named in the Record Mirror's Fave Raves "Best Lookers" along with Alan Buck of the Four Pennies, Denny Laine of the Moody Blues and Graham Nash and Tony Hicks of the Hollies. I was pleased. It's always reassuring, particularly if like me you have a self-esteem that tends to plummet alarmingly from time to time, to be told you're not exactly a dog's dinner.

As we set off for the Far East on January 24th John McNally managed to miss his plane from Liverpool to London and thus his connection for Hong Kong. Such an event did not cause any shock waves whatsoever. Usually either Mike or John would fail to be on the express down to Euston and we were using air travel these days in very much the same way as we would use a bus or a train. A seat was found for him on the next flight out and he was there in plenty of time for our concerts at the City Hall where the Chinese kids went absolutely doo-lally, racing down the aisles and hurling themselves at the stage to get at us.

The press was full of it the next day. Hong Kong apparently was not used to such unruly behaviour. They interviewed Mike Love and Bruce Johnston of the Beach Boys who were in the audience that night. Johnston had recently taken the place of Brian Wilson who had opted out of live shows in favour of masterminding the group's recording career at their studios back in Los Angeles.

When asked what they thought of the show Love and Johnston, who had been quite sociable and friendly during the Nashville and Florida concerts the year before, suggested that we were no better than any average American group. I can't argue that they were doubtless being truthful and that they were not mightily impressed. It was a legitimate opinion and they were perfectly entitled to it. But as a piece of PR it lacked a certain degree of diplomacy and did not endear them to us.

John was particularly incensed as he had found their on-stage harmonies, so rich, full and precise on their records after hours of Brian Wilson's genius having been lavished on their construction, very thin and imprecise in a live situation. I don't think they would liked to have read that in the press any more than we enjoyed their criticism of us. But hey, they made incredible records and have stood the test of time and when I ran into them again in the late sixties they were absolutely charming. It's just so many surfing waves under the bridge.

China, albeit the Westernised part as opposed to the communist controlled mainland, was fascinating with different sights and smells to stimulate our still very parochial senses. Small people in odd garments eating strange food. Britain was fast becoming used to Chinese restaurants but it was a truncated and carefully contrived version to suit the European palate. Here in Hong Kong there was none of the usual sweet and sour pork or lemon chicken. Much of the authentic cuisine seemed to be messy and steeped in liquid and the natives pushed their faces close to the bowl and scooped furiously with chopsticks with a skill that was most impressive.

The art was not one that we had yet mastered. It was peculiar to have liquid based foods that were to be tackled by cutlery that resembled knitting needles. In England a mother would use a small spoon to feed her baby. What, I wondered, was their Chinese equivalent? Toothpicks? I am reminded of that famous Chinese proverb, a man with only one chopstick goes hungry.

The Philippines was something else. In the difference factor it was off the scale. Guns and glamour. Poverty and paranoia. Diamonds and dust. It was a microcosm of life at both ends of the spectrum but with very little in between. It seemed you either lived a life of unimaginable riches or spent your days struggling for survival. I'm sure that's not how it was at all but that's how it appeared to us.

We were collected at the airport, where hordes of fans hung from the terraces screaming hysterically at us, by the promoter Mr Ramos's right hand man Bobby Grimald and driven in a motorcade that consisted of 1950s American automobiles. Buick Electras and Chevrolet Impalas, DeSoto Fireflytes and the like. It was not a PR gimmick. We soon discovered that most of the transport in the Philippines comprised of leftovers from departing members of the large US troop contingent still stationed there.

Public conveyance was by Jeepneys, old military utility vehicles tarted up with lashings of bright shiny chrome and elaborate multi-coloured paint decorations slightly reminiscent of something you might find on a vintage gipsy caravan in the UK. Fares were cheap and it was a hop-on-hop-off arrangement wherever you decided to begin or end your journey. In a traffic situation in which the survival of the fittest seemed to be the only rule anyone paid lip service to, if you arrived alive it was a bonus. Health and Safety would have had a field day here.

We were there to perform a series of concerts at the huge fourteen-thousand-seat Araneta Colosseum in a suburb of Manila called Quezon City, supported by Julie Rogers who appeared not to hold any grudges about our outrageous upstaging of her at the Savoy the previous year. Or perhaps she was simply too much of a lady to publicly vent any annoyance that might still be festering. At the press conference in one of the arena's lobbies she conducted herself with the decorum expected of her.

As for us, on the whole we were quite chirpy and affable but a certain tension entered the proceedings when Chris Curtis, on being asked of any unfulfilled ambitions, replied that he wanted to play Jesus Christ in a movie. The gasps in the room were not actually audible but it was a close call. In a strongly Catholic country like the Philippines any reference to the Saviour should be most carefully considered and jam packed with reverence. Somehow it was glossed over and we moved on. I can only thank Heaven that we were not in a Muslim country.

Neither was the first show without controversy. When a young Filipino girl ran down to the front with a garland Chris came forward from his drum stool and bent down to accept the gift. Had he stopped there all would have been fine. But he dropped to his knees and began to embrace her in a manner that was perhaps a bit too personal and too enthusiastic for the sensibilities of the rather prim and prudish audience who were horrified at this open display of what they saw as licentious behaviour. There were quite audible boos from sections of the crowd and we all knew immediately that something was wrong. Although the noise only emanated from small pockets of people a throng of fourteen thousand in a state of mild displeasure can be quit unnerving.

Chris, whose job it was to control the crowd tried to smile his way out of it and lighten the atmosphere by tossing the garland back into the audience, which in his mind was a demonstration of affection and generosity but in their view was like having a gift tossed back in one's face. In the end their natural politeness came to the fore and the incident was soon forgotten. We ran off to a huge wave of applause, much relieved and having learned some valuable lessons that would serve us well over the coming days.

For the entire stay in the Philippines, Chris managed to exist separately from the rest of us. Whether it was his conscious decision or whether we had unconsciously banded together and closed ranks from someone who was not quite in sync with the majority I cannot recall. But it was very soon an 'us and him' situation. When we went to the cinema to see the latest Bond film *You Only Live Twice* Chris stayed behind at the Colosseum. And it was just the three of us who went to view a nearby restaurant that had been named in our honour. In truth he did not miss much. It was actually little more than a sandwich bar but it was flattering and the owner was friendly. When we used the pool set in the private garden of our living quarters in the huge building Chris was not to be seen, either in, out of or near it.

Five minutes before showtime on the last night our drummer, who by now seemed to be meandering to the beat of a different drum entirely, was conspicuously absent. Bobby Grimald was sent to his room but returned drummer-less. Mild panic began to set in. Our road manager Barry Delaney was deputed to continue the search. He was more successful. He had apparently found Chris sitting on a chair inside his wardrobe writing songs. It was all a little bit worrying. One of Chris's most admirable qualities was not being afraid of that space between dreams and reality. He believed that if you can dream it then you can make it so. But now the line between them was becoming blurred to the point where reality was just something he occasionally dreamed of. And these days any similarity between his reality and ours was purely coincidental.

The original plan had been to play a couple of dates in Japan once we had completed our duties in the Philippines but that had come to nothing, and rather than waste the time some extra shows had been tacked on at a couple of US air bases. The concert at Clark Air Base just outside Manila was going quite well until Chris found fault with his microphone which admittedly was intermittently cutting out. Lacking the rational train of thought that would simply require him to point out the problem and smile benevolently until one of the crew brought out a replacement, he decided to demonstrate his displeasure by hurling the offending item into the audience. I suppose it's not really surprising that the burly black American airman was far from thrilled at being hit in the head by a flying metal object and at the hands of someone who was actually expecting applause for his outrageous behaviour.

The mood got ugly to the point where we were forced to bring our part of the evening's entertainment to an early close and hightail it out of there. To remain would have been highly dangerous to our health and I doubt that pointing at Curtis and saying 'It was him, mister' would have saved the rest of us from injury. We were all being tarred with the same brush and would doubtless have been smashed by the same fist. He who fights and runs away is thinking along the same lines as me.

We left the Philippines for New Zealand with a lot of memories, some good and some positively terrifying. Had we known then the kind of dangers the Beatles were going to put themselves in during their visit later that year we would have been a lot more scared that we actually were. We were now about to begin a tour across Australasia that coupled us with the Rolling Stones, a combination almost as bizarre as putting Pearl Carr and Teddy Johnson on the road with Megadeth. It was the good, the bad and the downright unlikely.

The Stones' career was quite rightly heading towards the stratosphere. They had expanded on the Beatles' irreverent treatment of the media and single-handedly created punk rock before punk had been invented. All the ingredients were in place for the image that took them to the forefront of British rock, leaving us and most of our well-dressed and polite chums way behind.

Mick Jagger was the master showman who, like Paul McCartney, possessed the natural public relations talent of one who knew just when to shock and when to charm. And he could do both with immense skill. Keith Richards was the eternal anti-hero unwilling to compromise on any level. He would do it his way or not at all. Brian Jones was the posh totty of the group, a pretty and blond haired middle class Lothario from Cheltenham who was more than willing to take advantage of all the sexual favours on offer from female fans, which he enjoyed all the more with the benefit of having little or no conscience. They were there to be enjoyed and discarded.

Bill Wyman and Charlie Watts were the stalwarts, the bedrock of normality in the minds of the general public although Bill by his own admission spent those rock & roll years bedding as many women as he could lay his hands, or various other parts of his body, on. If I communicated with the Stones it was usually with Charlie, Bill or Charlie's wife Shirley, a lovely, intelligent lady who was, like her husband, friendly, welcoming and down to earth. I felt awkward for her when the others would swap stories on the bus of the various activities entered into with groupies.

On one instance, they were on a bus discussing a conquest from the previous night who apparently had tattoos in the most unusual places, particularly shocking in those relatively innocent years when tattoos on a female at all were pretty decadent let alone indelicately positioned ones. But in their defence they were young men, free and single for the most part and this was their territory and their workplace. Any intruder must naturally play by their rules or stay the hell away.

Charlie was an absolute gentleman with a truly English demeanour and an elegance that you would never expect to find in a musician playing in a rock band. Being a Rolling Stone was what he did for a living. Jazz was his passion. His style came naturally. Charlie Watts displayed on a daily basis the kind of perfectly-fitted garments on which Savile Row based its international reputation.

Bill was overtly friendly and easy-going. There was no side to him and a distinct lack of pomposity. When he decided to visit some old friends who had settled in New Zealand he hired a car and invited me along with him and we spent a very pleasant and normal evening in very good company. He wrote in his book Stone Alone of the surprise in the Rolling Stones' camp at hearing that on the first Sunday the Searchers had all gone to church. Very un-rock & roll. They had indeed gone to a service with the exception of me who had chucked any belief in religion a long time ago. Despite my diet of regular indoctrination by way of Sunday school each week my inquisitive and questioning mind had by my teens more or less dismissed the 'good book' as a collection of myths and fables that I found hard to take seriously.

The Stones had cleverly begun to assemble an anti-social image that would prove to be everlasting having realised very early on that it was controversy not convention that had the staying power. To pretend to be one of the unwashed poor was a good way to end up as one of the very washed and, although a trifle scruffy, rich. Even more shrewd was Jagger's ability to maintain a persona of rebellious menace whilst at the same time elevating his social position to where his friends were rich, aristocratic and culled from the very cream of society. He may have been just a lad from Dartford but he does like crap games with barons and earls. He is no doubt happy to flounce into Harlem in ermine and pearls. And while I'm not quite sure whether he dishes the dirt with the rest of the girls it is a fact that Sir Michael Jagger is no tramp.

I spoke to Mick, Keith and Brian only occasionally. I would have loved to have got to know Mick better. There was a twinkle in his eye that just made his face light up when he grinned. He looked like he could be a good friend and a lot of fun. But like John Lennon, he scared me and for the most part I stayed away, although on the few occasions we spoke together he could not have been nicer. And Keith was even scarier still. I can barely recall a conversation with him if indeed we had one at all. Over the years I have regretted not making more effort. I'm sure that if you didn't give him any bullshit Keith would have been brilliant company.

Brian was remote. I can't think of another word for him. It may have been that the balance of power in the group had already begun to shift irrevocably and he knew it. The band he had put together was by a natural osmosis being taken away from him and there was no way he could stop it. But I only realised this much later with the benefit of hindsight. We were too busy taking care of our own internal problems to notice those of others.

When we moved on to Sydney the Rolling Stones were staying in luxurious splendour at the Chevron Hilton while we were booked in at the Sheraton across the road at number 40 MacCleay Street in Pott's Point. The hotel has long since disappeared and the space is now taken up by the Azure apartments, a soulless and unlovable structure that we can only hope in time will again be disassembled by someone with at least a degree of imagination and an edifice of greater worth erected in its place. The Chevron Hilton too has gone, replaced by an ultra-modern block of apartments and offices which include the Ikon building.

Unfortunately our reservations had not been handled at all well and we ended up all staying in one large room. The problem could not be remedied as the place was full so we just had to put up with it. In the light of the dramas that were unfolding within our ranks the last thing we needed was to be was on top of each other twenty-four hours a day but there was nothing we could do.

The shows, this time the venue was the Festival Hall rather than the creaky old Sydney Stadium, went well and although there was no doubt that the Stones were the kings of the castle and we were there merely in a supporting role we came off to a very satisfactory amount of screams and applause. In the second show Chris seemed to stumble a lot and at one point toppled from the podium injuring himself slightly but we made it through to the finish. It was clearly that something was rotten, if not in the state of Denmark then certainly in Camp Searchers.

There was the usual round of radio and television promotion to take care of. We assembled backstage at a Sydney TV studio ready to lip-synch to one of our hits and the girl in charge of us began to eye Chris nervously over her clipboard. 'Is he alright?' she asked. Curtis was indeed looking fragile. His eyes had glazed over and he was moving oddly. 'Oh, don't take any notice. He's just being affected' replied Barry Delaney contemptuously who, like the rest of us, was used to his extravagant gestures and increasingly theatrical behaviour. He had hardly completed the sentence when Chris crashed to floor and remained there motionless.

After someone called the medics who arranged for him to be whisked off to hospital we continued with the show which, because of the playback situation, allowed us to perform as a three piece unhindered by any lack of musical quality. On returning to the Sheraton we rummaged through the big black leather doctor's bag Chris always travelled with and unearthed a bag of pills that resembled a month's worth of product from the M&M factory. The only thing we could think of doing was to tip the lot down the loo and flush our problem out of sight, at least for the moment.

Chris of course refuted the insinuation that he was using the pills as stimulants or that they had affected him adversely, saying that he couldn't do that sort of thing and perform properly. Yet in a 1999 interview with Radio Merseyside's Spencer Leigh he admits that he was not quite himself.

'I hated Australia. I thought it was a country of dreadful people and I was off me cake. I fell off the stage and I still have the scar on my leg. I went out with an Australian girl who said "You need some sleep, darling, come home with me." She had this marvellous flat, more like half an apartment building, with a wonderful view over the harbour. During the night I was drinking coffee and thought I would leave before she woke up. The windows were open and it was a heavy door. I opened it but it came back and smashed on this finger. Nearly took it off, but I went back to them with my bad leg and my bad finger. I went to my doctor's bag to find something for the pain in my finger, and I found that they had emptied the entire contents, all my tranquillisers, down the lavatory. They thought they were doing me a favour, and I told them that was it, I couldn't take anymore, but they made me finish the tour. On the way back home, I wrote a Searchers' song on a sick bag but it wasn't used as I left the group. When I got back to Bootle, they tore the nail out at the hospital.'

In his telling of the tale his timing is slightly out. The night of the great pill-tipping he actually spent in the hospital but I can certainly verify the facts with regard to the girl, having also spent a night with her at her flat down by the harbour. Her name was Julie Adams and it was indeed a splendid apartment. I also shared the bed and her company a little later on. She loved the band and in particular was very taken with John's song *Till I Met You*. Personally I found it sad that Chris failed to appreciate the attributes of a country that I have grown to love more and more as the years go by.

The next day our black sheep was back in the fold and by the day after he had found a local doctor willing to replenish his supply of medicinal nibbles. We were at a loss as to how we should handle the situation and in the end decided to call for help at a higher level. Promoter Harry Miller was summoned and we explained the dilemma and asked if he could take over. Harry was a man used to taking charge and gathered us all together, giving Chris a verbal dressing down in which he made it very plain that if anything of this sort should occur again he would have no hesitation in blowing the whistle and bringing in the police. This was quite bizarre. The Rolling Stones to whom controversy was life's blood were happily rambling through a tour while the Searchers, meek-mannered choirboys in comparison, were threatened with scandal and possible incarceration.

After that nothing much more happened. Unless you count Chris getting arrested, that is. Still in Sydney the rest of us were sitting around in our large room that was pretending to be a suite at the Sheraton in the company of Vic Sutcliffe and Mike Rispoli, both of who worked for the Tito Burns organisation. Vic was looking after us on the tour while Mike Rispoli, being in a slightly senior position, was put in charge of Messrs Jagger and Co. The phone rang and Sutcliffe took the call. It was from the local naval base just down the hill in Pott's Point. The naval police it seemed had apprehended a person in a restricted area and were looking for confirmation that he was who he said he was, one of the pop group called the Searchers.

When Vic returned it was with a very quiet and reticent Chris who made a point of staying very much out of our way. There was not a lot of communication on offer to say the least. As for us, we were not about to press the point. With things at such a delicate state of play we were anxious to avoid any further confrontations. Vic explained that Chris had apparently wandered into the dockyard with a view to asking a sailor to sell him a bag he was carrying and which he liked very much. It was a bizarre tale to say the least and nobody managed to satisfactorily explain how he got past the security guards in the first place. Chris Curtis, with his long hair, formal clothing despite the heat of the Australian summer sun and the ever-present dark glasses, would have the greatest of difficulties in passing himself off as your average matelot.

Chris mixed with the Stones a little more than we did and listened with them as they played a pressing of their new album *Aftermath*. One song he took note of was a track called *Take It Or Leave It* which he reckoned would be a good song for the Searchers. What they thought about Chris I have no idea but Chris was never a person to let such doubts enter his head. His supreme self-confidence imbued him with the unshakable belief that when he spoke those on the receiving end would hang on to his every word. It was a very endearing trait.

Whether they appreciated his company and opinions or simply tolerated his presence is anyone's guess. He must have seemed more than a little weird even in their crazy and exaggerated rock & roll world. I certainly recall the baffled looks on their faces as we all sat in an airport lounge one morning waiting for a connection.

Chris, wearing a dark jacket, trousers and tie despite the soaring temperature, was gazing out from behind his shades at an aeroplane on the tarmac. Not a small craft that could possibly pass as a private pilot's simple twin engine hobby machine but a sizeable piece of transport that would happily accommodate a substantial number of paying passengers. This was a vessel that might be used for the short hop budget runs of a legitimate airline. 'I like that plane. I might buy one when I get home.' The statement was outrageous. We were not poor people but to even suggest that we had the kind of money that could purchase such an item was to enter the realms of the ridiculous where few feet had dared to tread. Nobody said anything but we all looked at each other. The Stones exchanged glances between themselves but what they were thinking God only knows.

As it came time for the long trip home, made even longer by the state of insecurity in which we were all existing, our worries about how we could bring our relationship back into line and get our career back on track had been pre-empted by Chris's unexpected and ominous announcement that as from now he was no longer a Searcher.

For now, bad as it was, there was nothing we could do. Tito would have to use his powers of persuasion once we reached the UK. Meanwhile during the tiring twenty-four hour flight Chris passed sets of lyrics written on sick bags to where we sat a comfortable number of rows away. The hastily scrawled rhymes meant nothing to us. He insisted they were the words to hits he would write for us but without the benefit of a tune they were merely the ramblings of an extremely screwed up mind.

Back on home soil we arranged a lunch with the four of us and Tito to hopefully bring the group back to a working unit that, although there were immense problems, still had a chance of staying together and making hit records once more. It was a nice idea but unfortunately it was not going to happen. Chris remained steadfast in his resolve to quit the band and launch himself headlong into record production where he felt his talents, which he had absolutely no doubt were considerable, would be better appreciated. And now we were three.

21

The Wilderness Years

The period between the latter end of the mid-sixties and the close of the seventies has been rather unkindly referred to as the chicken-in-a-basket years. And not without good reason. It was a period when Britain was pockmarked with cabaret clubs where, for a modest entrance fee, you could enjoy an evening in very pleasant surroundings, the like of which had never before been available to the working-class patron - certainly not on one's own suburban doorstep - and, having devoured your simple but tasty supper of chicken and chips, be entertained by a celebrity of a reasonable calibre. In the early days before the gambling laws were revamped to save people from their foolish selves you could even risk the housekeeping money for a moment of chance on the roulette wheel or the blackjack table.

The biggest of our home-grown names and a good portion of American stars trod the boards at these converted cinemas, supermarkets and, very occasionally, purpose-built establishments. Shirley Bassey. Cliff Richard. Dusty Springfield. The Beach Boys. Louis Armstrong. And of course the Searchers. We all accepted the king's shilling and served our time pitting what skill and charm we possessed against the constant clinking of the cutlery and the incessant chatter of the patrons.

I prefer to look back on it as my university years, a time of further education when we boys would at last learn to become men if we were to survive the transition from show business ingénues to seasoned veterans able to hold our own on a stage once the screaming stopped. Now that we were no longer the flavour of the month in the eyes, ears and lustful thoughts of teenage girls, it was not enough to simply stand there and expect to be lauded and applauded with little or no effort on our part other than to perform a selection of our record successes. There was a craft to be learned. It was time to get out of the playground and join the grown-ups. But first there were a few minor problems still to be ironed out.

We were without a drummer and needed to acquire one very quickly indeed if we were to honour the engagements that were already in the diary. There was no real thought of quitting. This was just one more hurdle in our lives. It was not the first and it would not be the last by any means. A solution, for the time being at least, was supplied by office manager Mike Rispoli who knew of a kid, a friend of his son, who played in a semi-pro band around South London.

John Blunt was a mod, whose back-combed hair and pop art sweaters marked him out as an unlikely candidate to join the now mature and conservatively turned out Searchers. Born on March 28th 1947 in Selsdon, a suburb of Croydon a few miles to the south of the capital, he had been employed for a short time as a glass blower but the impish youth with a Pinocchio face was only interested in playing in a band where he could live out his dreams and emulate his hero, The Who's drummer Keith Moon. His group had been called the Trees named after the Tree pub in Fairfield where he made his first public appearance.

At Rispoli's instigation we had a run through with him and figured that we could work with him in a manner satisfactory enough to get through the immediate worksheet, and in truth there was precious little time to spare. We had a major tour only days away. Thrilled at the chance to join a top outfit like the Searchers, though he would doubtless have preferred a more frantic ensemble in which to expend his excessive supply of youthful energy, John Blunt saw this as a permanent position, while to us it was merely a temporary stop-gap until we could find the right man for the job.

Our working arena was about to change in favour of the supper circuit but we still had a final burst of glory as the co-stars of a tour which was to feature the disgraced P. J. Proby. It was his first since the disastrous 'split pants' episode and his final shows before his current British work permit was due to expire on April 1st, following which he would have to return to America and bide his time until his new applications had been processed and approved.

Both Proby and ourselves had peaked in terms of popularity and the bill was not excessively strong although we were still names to be reckoned with. The other supports consisted of acts vainly treading water until the fickle hand of fate pushed their heads under the surface when they finally expired. Shirley and Johnny, Thane Russal & Three, the Action (replaced by the Sorrows at Newcastle) and a four-piece outfit called Shelley.

In the eyes of the music press the Action were the band 'most likely to' but this guitar/drums outfit failed to fulfil the potential predicted by pop pontiffs. Their style was not dissimilar to The Who, but in the end the public simply asked "who?" and thought little more about them. The compere once more was the dangerously irreverent Tony Marsh. His lewd antics on our shows at least were kept away from the public, but some time later he was finally expelled from the prestigious touring circuit after baring his backside from the wings in full view of the first three rows.

Jim Proby, as if not disadvantaged enough by his ban from the important Rank circuit, was exacerbating his deteriorating reputation by conducting what he himself later on referred to as a lengthy affair with Jack Daniels. Fuelled by the fiery liquid in his dressing room through the long spare hours before his appearance in the show he would finally hit the boards in a state of hazy confusion. Most of the time he knew not where he was, what he was singing or indeed the lyrics to the songs. The audience sat before him in a state of confusion and discomfort as one of the great voices and talents in popular music committed professional suicide before their eyes.

Following the opening night at Birmingham Town Hall on March 12th 1966 Norrie Drummond wrote in the NME 'Proby, dressed in maroon velvet suit, pink shirt and black buckled shoes, admitted he didn't know some of the words of some of the new songs and read them from a piece of paper.

'The Searchers were their usual immaculate selves despite the fact that Chris Curtis is out of the tour because of nervous exhaustion. They opened with *Sweets For My Sweet* as well as singing *Needles And Pins*, *Bumble Bee*, *Goodbye My Love* and *Love Potion No. 9.* Although they played all of their hits (some more than a year old) and sang well I thought they should have played some newer material.'

How different the requirements of the press were then while in the years to come they would come to demand almost total commitment to the back catalogue and to deny a group's right to explore interesting new avenues and sounds.

The Record Mirror too covered the first night and wrote 'The Searchers went through their numbers with perfect professionalism proving that they are one of the top groups who can produce their record sounds on the stage. Halfway through P. J's set the drummer collapsed from over exhaustion. A substitute was quickly found and Proby finished the song as though nothing had happened.'

In his anaesthetised state it is quite likely that P. J. was not even aware the drummer had stopped. What was indeed remarkable was that a replacement was found before the end of the song.

Jim had his words placed on a wooden lectern to the side of his microphone for most of the time and in between songs he would launch into long, rambling diatribes against Tito Burns and the lack of advertising the tour had received. I have no doubt his accusations had some merit, the audience figures were not particularly good, but a grumpy old expatriate American with a bad memory and a drink problem was not what they had paid between five shillings and twelve and sixpence to come to see and hear.

Our office for whatever reason was still refusing to admit that Curtis had quit the band and the nervous exhaustion excuse was being traded as fact. But we knew there was no going back because there was certainly to be no coming back. Chris was gone, gone, gone.

We were still determined to find a new permanent drummer more suited to the image and temperament of the band and held a day of open auditions at the Grafton Rooms in Liverpool. A plethora of Liverpudlian cow spankers turned up accompanied by varying degrees of talent, Scouse cheek and waffle. We plodded wearily through the long afternoon listening to thump after thump after thump with no one offering anything more than we already had in the shape of John Blunt. We even had local hero "Joey" Spruce (a.k.a Earl Preston of Earl Preston & the TTs) joining in the melée in an attempt to prove that he was as skilled on the drums as he was in the vocal department, and for a while he was under serious consideration but we finally decided against it. We left as we came. Empty handed.

Back in London I suggested a drummer called Terry Noone who I knew from a group who had appeared with us during my Rebel Rousing days. He was a nice guy, well scrubbed and clean-cut as befitted our image. We decided to take him on and he set about arranging his passport and handing in his notice with the music publishing company he worked for. No sooner had we set the process in motion than Mike and John suddenly changed tack and decided he was wrong for the job after all.

It was left to Mike Rispoli to be the bad guy and deliver the unfortunate news. I felt really embarrassed and so sorry for Terry who had seemingly burned his bridges. I only hoped he would manage to put the fire out and salvage what he could from the ashes. I believe that not too far down the line he achieved enormous success in the publishing field with the copyrights of a bunch of hit songs from the surfing era. I am pleased. He deserved such poetic justice and he earned more than he would have with us I am sure. Que sera sera.

After the show at the De Montfort Hall in Leicester on March 21st we flew to Frankfurt for an engagement and returned in time for the final date of the tour at the Liverpool Empire on the 27th. The concerts with P. J. had failed to save his career or to revive ours to any degree and we concentrated on the task of getting a new single onto the market.

We had decided to carry on with the plans to record *Take It Or Leave It*, the Jagger/Richards composition we had heard in Australia. The haunting quality of the song and the connection with two of the most hip people in rock & roll might be enough to grab some attention and airplay, we figured. With the exuberant John Blunt in the studio on drums for the first time we treated the piece in the only way we could by keeping a steady hypnotic rhythm throughout, embellished by bell-like guitar figures lilting in the background and by our usual tight harmonies at the end of the lines and through the lah-lahs of the chorus.

It was an appealing song and we were pleased with the result, although on reflection our futures would have benefited by our taking a little more time over the selection and coming out with something much stronger and with more impact. But it was ever the case that we were expected to produce a hit single every three months whether we had anything suitable or not. We were under pressure to come up with the goods and Tony Hatch was under pressure to make sure that we did.

Having completed the task in hand we set off to the far North East to undertake our first ever engagement in cabaret on April 2nd. Fortunately we could not have had a better venue at which to begin this perilous venture. The Fiesta Club in Stockton-on-Tees, a medium sized town about forty miles south of Newcastle, was a run down cinema about a mile from the centre and had been the brainwave of the Lipthorpe brothers Jim and Keith, two ex jazz musicians who had seen the possibilities of bringing a more sophisticated environment in which to present quality entertainment to the masses who had more spending money than any previous generation.

The conversion had been undertaken with taste and the final result showed the marks of people who cared. The tiered seating was plush and the low stage with its expensive electrically operated drapes was the perfect framework for top flight artistes to perform within. The facilities backstage had been decorated with the comfort of both the entertainers and the house band in mind, a far cry from the dank, dark, cramped boxes we suffered on the theatre circuit. There were expensive sofas and soft armchairs in which to rest and a television to alleviate the inevitable boredom that was the bane and the real hard work of the performer's life.

We were made to feel welcome and wanted by the management and staff who became lifelong friends. And thankfully we did not let them down. Realising that we were going to need a bit more than just a few hit tunes to impress on this kind of stage we had rehearsed. From now on the show was planned and paced with up-tempo songs being contrasted with soft, sentimental ballads.

Being big fans of Peter, Paul and Mary and cognisant of the importance of the folk boom which had well and truly made its mark on the youth market, we included a version of Bob Dylan's *Blowing In The Wind.* It was in vogue and suited our harmony style perfectly and we brought a visual element to it by the three of us (Mike, John and myself) gathering tightly round the centre microphone to sing it. Furthermore in a display of unashamed pretentiousness I blatantly lifted the introduction of the aforementioned folk group's live recording with which to lead into the song. I remember it clearly. It went 'This song asks nine questions. When we sing the song we ask ourselves the questions and we ask you please to do the same.' Pretentious, moi? Too bloody right. I have no idea how I managed to say it with a straight face but the audience was too polite to laugh me out of existence and it worked very well. The inclusion of *Blowing In The Wind* was a very good move.

The task of linking the show between songs had fallen to me in a very natural way.

Our first gig without the showmanship of Chris Curtis to carry the whole thing through had been at the Savoy Ballroom in Southsea, just prior to the Proby tour. It was one of our regular ballroom venues where the Benny Freedman Orchestra was the band in residence. We had decided that we would take the introductions in turn but Mike found it a problem constructing fluent and cohesive sentences and looked uncomfortable, while John with his slightly thicker Liverpudlian accent tended to talk so fast that it could have been a foreign language for all the audience knew. My own efforts must have been pretty appalling but they were the least appalling of the three and it was certainly going to be less confusing if the matter was dealt with by just one person, leaving the others to get on with their own important functions within the outfit.

Another song that proved to be a winner in our cabaret set was the Roy Orbison classic *Running Scared.* The drama and range of the steadily climbing verses suited Mike's voice perfectly and as the crescendo of the last line was reached and the pin spot closed on his face to a dramatic blackout we would be guaranteed an ovation. It was a show-stopper which must have been a very satisfying feeling for him. He was less than satisfied one night however when one of the Fiesta Fawns, Sandra White, acting under our instigation pushed a cream pie into his face during the last dying notes. The audience thought it was hysterical. We thought it was hysterical. Mike, understandably I suppose, did not.

As our first foray into club land drew to a successful close *Take It Or Leave It* was thrown into the unforgiving bear pit that was the record buying market. And if you had read the reviews you would have thought the signs were good. Derek Johnson's opinion was that it was a 'Great sound...a Jagger/Richards composition...all credit to the Searchers for adapting it to their own style instead of trying to emulate the Stones...rather unusual number, fractionally under mid-tempo...attractively harmonised by Mike Pender and Frank Allen...not particularly strong melody-wise but the group's interpretation is highly colourful and they have got some great sounds going.'

And Norman Joplin in the Record Mirror was equally enthusiastic. Headlined 'Excellent Searchers' he went on to say the disc 'should make it for the Searchers...Similar style to the Stones but with broad-edged vocal sound...needs a couple of plays to establish itself...a smooth, very smooth, production.'

By sheer coincidence another group, the Riot Squad, had simultaneously recorded a single with the same title and for release at more or less the same time although a different song completely. In the face of our higher profile they sensibly altered the title of their release to *I Take It We're Through.* In 1967 a young man called David Bowie was to join them for a while. I understand that eventually he did rather well for himself. It is believed that some recordings with Bowie were made but as yet remain unreleased.

Full of hope we looked forward excitedly to our April tour of the States which was to include a Murray the K television spectacular. The press announcement included the information that Chris Curtis was unlikely to rejoin the Searchers and that John Blunt would travel with the group. But it seemed that nothing was going right for us. At the last minute the trip was called off and we shuffled our feet at home wondering what else could go wrong.

We had been told by Tito that the work permits had not for whatever reason been granted. Some way down the line Tito told us that the real reason had been that the expected bookings had simply not materialised. Hard to believe. After all we were still a group that had several decent-sized US hits and had almost topped the US charts there only two years previously with *Love Potion No. 9*. And I was never one to put any great store in words that came from Mr Burns's mouth.

On April 23rd, the day that we flew to Germany for a television show, *Take It Or Leave It* entered the charts at forty-seven. The mid forties seemed to be the standard entry level for Searchers records these days. Anything could happen.

On the 28th we flew to Rome for a major television show, Studio Uno, and in between rehearsals managed to see a bit of the city including St Peter's to which the very unworldly John Blunt referred quite seriously as 'that big synagogue.' The show was an important piece of exposure for us on the European stage with vast viewing figures. We shared the bill with, among others, a popular singer called Herbert Paganni who performed a wonderful translation of a Jacques Brel song called *Lombardia*. Herbert very much admired the pink and white shirt I was wearing so I took it off and gave it to him. In return he gave me a copy of the record.

The very likeable but eternally chaotic Blunt managed to lose his plane ticket by the time we reached the airport for the return journey home and we had to buy him a new one. Dealing with Blunt's self-induced state of disorder was to become something we quickly learned to get used to. If we arranged to meet him at a predetermined corner he would be waiting at an entirely different intersection. When he failed to appear at Charing Cross underground station for his first ever BBC session we were at a loss as to what to do until someone remembered there was also a main line station. Sure enough there was Blunty, confused and sweating profusely from his nose. His nose always sweated when he was in a panic.

When we arrived home from Rome our record had jumped to twenty-nine in the NME, a very respectable leap, though the chart placing in the Record Mirror at thirty-eight was significantly lower. We preferred to believe the NME. My pal Dusty Springfield was at number one with *You Don't Have To Say You Love Me*.

A week later it climbed further to twenty-five (NME) after which it began its inevitable descent although oddly enough the disc was still moving up in the Record

Mirror before halting at thirty-one on May 7th. But considering our shaky situation it was still a creditable showing but far short of what was required for us to be considered a major force on the pop scene once more. Dusty had by this time been edged out of the top spot by Manfred Mann's *Pretty Flamingo.* A curious postscript to the *Take It Or Leave It* saga is that, at a high of number five, it turned out to be one of our greatest chart successes in the Netherlands.

Big changes were happening at our management company too. It was announced in the press that the Tito Burns Organisation had been taken over by the Harold Davison Agency. Davison was a mighty force in the entertainment industry and the UK representative of Frank Sinatra among others. The Vere Street offices were closed and our representation moved to a larger and more prestigious building on Regent Street.

While we were coping with our stuttering career our errant ex-drummer Chris Curtis released his own assault on the charts in the form of a Joe South song called *Aggravation.* The reviews were encouraging with the NME noting that it 'moves along at a storming pace....contagious, danceable and good humoured.' The Record Mirror suggested that it 'should do well and not only from curiosity sales....big sounds, big beat with girlie group, heavy drums, big brass, just about everything chucked in.....not brilliant singing but commercial stuff.' Apparently not commercial enough it failed to gain any chart placing which was a bit of a relief for us. It would not have done to see our deserter having more success than us and thus confirming his opinion that he was the sole creative force behind anything we had achieved.

With the exception of a track called *You Don't Have To Tell Me,* a cover of a Walker Brothers song which surfaced on a 2007 compilation album entitled *Unearthed Merseybeat,* it was to be Curtis's swansong in recording terms.

When the annual chart points table was published on July 1st we had slipped to seventy-one, a drop of thirty-nine places from the previous year. But it came as no surprise as our chart positions had been steadily falling and looked as though they would continue to do so unless we pulled something spectacular out of the bag, something that would be hard to do in our state of confusion and uncertainty. Still we were considered good enough to replace The Who in Great Yarmouth as they were thought by promoter Robert Stigwood to be unsuitable for family audiences, something that could never be said about the Searchers.

Our perilous predicament was a bit of a worry for me for two reasons. Firstly I had become a property owner. Deciding that acquiring bricks and mortar would be a wise move I checked my balance in our royalty account and discovered that there was just sufficient to buy the most basic of dwellings. Being a complete dingbat in matters financial I had absolutely no idea how to get a mortgage and doubted very much whether a building society would consider me a sufficiently safe risk to advance a loan to me anyway. In the late sixties credit was still far from being freely available. With a career in freefall I doubted I would be looked on kindly so I simply paid in cash. At least I would be relieved of the worry that someone would come along and whisk it all from under my feet.

With my usual inefficiency I avoided the normal and sensible route of viewing various properties to find the most suitable one in my price range. Cliff Bennett's mother-in-law had remarried and wanted to offload her small house in Hayes. Problem solved. She had a house for sale. I wanted a house. Bingo! It was £4,300 and the price reflected the size. It was semi-detached with two average sized bedrooms and a tiny kitchen just big enough to cook an omelette if you didn't use more than two eggs. Cats would avoid entering for fear of having their skulls fractured while being swung in those strict confines. But it was cute with its Dutch barn roof and dolls house character. I liked it. And being the first in my family to own a house I was very pleased.

I treated it as a hobby for the first six months, not wanting to leave the security and comfort of my parents' home where I was waited on hand and foot. Most days I would drive round just to look at it and to oversee some alterations and decoration. I would make a cup of tea and walk through the rooms (a journey of ten seconds tops) proud to be lord of all I surveyed.

I even experimented with cooking and followed a recipe which required the ingredients to be cooked on a low heat for fifty minutes. After ten minutes I got thoroughly bored and went out to visit friends. When I returned the contents of the pan were little more than blackened charcoal and stuck unappetisingly to the metal. It would not be an exaggeration to say that I was not the sharpest knife in the cutlery drawer. It was only by the greatest of good fortune that the house was not engulfed in flames.

But another shadow had unexpectedly loomed over my head. Shortly before the Harold Davison takeover I had been called into the Vere Street office for a meeting with Tito. In the lobby I ran into Chris Curtis who was there on business of his own now that Tito was handling his new career as a record producer, a move that he was later to regret, recounting in an interview with Spencer Leigh years later that 'Tito turned out to be a really horrible man.' He seemed pleased to see me and asked me why I was there but I couldn't enlighten him, although I think he had a good idea.

When I was finally ushered in Burns, suave and sophisticated with the shine from his nail polish glistening ostentatiously from his perfectly manicured fingers, explained to me that with things as they were money was not what it used to be with the group. Their fees had dropped alarmingly and finances were very tight indeed. I knew at once what was coming. I was asked to take a drop in wages. The actual amount was not mentioned but it was immaterial as I somehow immediately dragged up the courage to say that I understood their position and while I would be happy to take a risk with our combined futures, be they good or bad, I was not prepared to take a cut.

How I managed to keep my resolve I'll never know. Goodness knows I had nothing else waiting for me should they decide to call my bluff. Fortunately, Tito did not try to press his argument but accepted my decision and simply said that he would pass the message on. For the moment the matter was dormant and when I finally met up with the group nobody mentioned it at all.

It had worried me but I could attach no blame to Mike and John and truly understood their position. They were paying me very good money and although I had performed on a number of hits by this time their rise to fame was certainly not down to me. They had worked hard to get where they were and wanted to protect their investment. I would have done the same. But it brought home to me that perhaps my life as a pop star was going to be a good deal shorter than I would have liked.

22

Life Is A Cabaret Old Chum

During his probationary period, and because of his contrasting wild and youthful 'mod' appearance set against our long-established immaculate image, we had kept John Blunt in casual attire. But once we realised this situation was going to be a little less temporary than we at first figured we decided that perhaps it would be wise to dress him in a smart three-button suit like ourselves. It satisfied the expectations of both the public and the managements of the cabarets that were now providing us with the major portion of our income.

Along with the dip in our finances and status came an accompanying reduction in the quality of our accommodation. We discovered the world of the bed and breakfast establishment and the delights of the theatrical digs. It came about by accident. We had been booked for a week at the Cabaret Club in Rosegrove, Burnley, one of the independent venues in a circuit that was to the greater extent monopolised at the time by the large and important Bailey Organisation.

Having no knowledge of the hotel situation in that part of the world we contacted the club ahead of time for their advice. They booked the southern contingent of our party into what we understood what was the Piccadilly Hotel situated in Piccadilly Road, Burnley. John and Mike would be travelling the short drive home each night. When we arrived in the town we found our way to Piccadilly Road and scanned the buildings from one end to the other in vain for a hotel. Time was getting tight and we finally opted for heading straight to the club for more information.

On arrival we discovered that in fact there was no Piccadilly Hotel. We had rooms reserved at number fourteen Piccadilly Road, an ordinary terraced house in which visiting entertainers were regularly billeted in what could be described as a state of homely comfort. We were in shock. Up to now we had been a top pop group who would not have been seen dead in anything less than a three star hotel, which in itself was a demotion from the five star treatment we had been used to, but it was late and we decided that for the first night at least we would have to give it a go.

Number fourteen was owned and run by Fred and Doris Hewitt, a London couple who had relocated to the North West, and enjoyed the company of the eccentric theatricals they played hosts to and who brought in a necessary amount of money to augment Fred's daytime job, whatever that was. My memory has let me down on that score. They were a jovial and easy-going couple and we liked them from the off. The place was clean and tidy and whilst the anonymity and freedom of a formal hotel was missing there was a happy family atmosphere which compensated nicely.

The other guests that week were typical of the varied diet of entertainment at a venue such as the Cabaret Club in Rosegrove. Zena Relph was a lady fire eater-cum-magician who was still mourning the long-gone days of variety theatre and who was now suffering by necessity the alternative, although lesser in her eyes, trail of the chicken-in-a-basket rooms as she criss-crossed the country in her Morris Minor accompanied by her dachshund Fred.

She was friendly and full of fun and told colourful tales of the old days when there were real entertainers around and not just beat groups who did nothing but thump, thump, thump. Despite being one of the thump, thump, thumpers I liked her a lot and we stayed in touch long after we left our Piccadilly digs behind.

Also in residence was Jean Jacques Jourdain, a French balladeer brim full of Gallic charm and the unshakeable belief that a Maurice Chevalier accent and a good chat-up line was all one needed to lure a lady into bed after the show. And he was right. Most nights after his performance he would sneak up the stairs, while Fred and Doris pretended not to notice, with a young lady in tow. His conquests were of varying age, quality and morals. He was hardly a matinee idol and what they saw in him escaped me completely, except that he certainly was a friendly and affable guy. Perhaps that was the secret. That and the pantomime Parisian accent.

He was at a time in his life when he was crossing, or had already crossed, the fine line beyond which middle age gleefully and inexorably beckoned and on his head was the most obvious toupee in Christendom. Allied Carpets would be proud to have laid that one. When he took to the stage no one but Ray Charles or Stevie Wonder could possibly have been unaware that this man was most definitely appearing under an assumed mane. The big question in their heads was how on earth he managed to train that cat to sit on his head all through his performance.

We enjoyed our first taste of theatrical digs with its unique atmosphere and continual cabaret in the form of the other inmates, who ranged from the relatively sane to the completely off their trolleys and our future, as far as board and lodgings were concerned, was set. The clincher of course was the price. A three star could not be had for less than thirty shillings per night. Fred and Doris charged twelve and sixpence and for that there was a supper of freshly-cut sandwiches waiting when we got in at night. It was hard to beat.

We were to discover in time that the authoritarian rule of the theatrical landlady ranged from a rod of iron to a blind eye, or sometimes by virtue of a barely believable naiveté. There was the proprietress from Leeds in the fifties who was telling her friends that she had recently accommodated the up-and-coming not to say extremely camp young comic Frankie Howerd and what a nice chap he was. In fact she remarked on how extraordinarily fortunate it was that he should by sheer accident run into his handsome young cousin currently serving in the Bolivian navy and who also stayed for several days. She also believed in the Tooth Fairy and the Easter Bunny.

In between jaunts around Britain there remained the ever-present need for product. It had been four months since *Take It Or Leave It* hit the stores and we had to come up with something new. The song we chose came along in the oddest of circumstances.

Chris Curtis, now a full-time record producer with his own apartment in Knightsbridge, had already announced to the media that under his new Pye contract he could record who and what he liked and that he might also be associated with future Searchers recordings. This was news to us. But approach us he did with a song penned by three of the Hollies under their communal pseudonym of L Ransford. *Have You Ever Loved Somebody* was a good tune and sounded punchy and commercial. The only catch was that if we wanted to record it we would have to use Chris as producer, something we were extremely loathe to do. A split was a split as far as we were concerned and Chris's mercurial personality was too difficult for us to contemplate putting up with at this point, if ever again.

It suddenly occurred to us that whether or not we could record the song only under his supervision was not his decision to make. These things were in the public domain and music publishers were always desperate to get as many artistes as possible to record their product. We simply rang them and asked for a demo and they duly, and speedily, obliged.

Chris was not best pleased to put it mildly but angered by what he saw as our duplicity he did not back off. Instead he went into the studios to cut a rival version with Paul and Barry Ryan with whom he had already produced one quite successful single, *I Love How You Love Me*, which came complete with a Spector-esque backing and a set of bagpipes. Who was it described a gentleman as someone who possessed a set of bagpipes but refused to play them? There may have been a kitchen sink in there somewhere too. It was hard to tell but in the end it charted at a fairly respectable twenty-one.

The good-looking twin brothers were the sons of Harold Davison's wife, ex-band singer Marion Ryan, and to please her Harold was delivering every ounce of assistance in the promotion of her offsprings' careers. They had already made some inroads with their debut disc *Don't Bring Me Your Heartaches* which reached its zenith just outside the top ten at thirteen but were still searching for the elusive 'biggie'. Subscribing to the myth that Curtis was the sole inspiration and talent behind the Searchers' record success, and encouraged by the promise shown by their previous collaboration the Ryans looked to him to provide it.

It was clear there was going to be a fight and we were in a rather strange position. With the Tito Burns office having been swallowed up by the Harold Davison Organisation we were in effect being pitted against our own representatives and there was no doubt that Harold was pulling out all the stops for his wife's baby boys. His power was mighty indeed and television producers were crumbling under considerable pressure to offer the prime plugs to these new kids on the block. When it was pointed out to Davison that they had managed to get on everything bar The Epilogue his retort was that next time he'd make sure they got that as well. And he certainly was a man who could.

Our roster of plugs was much less impressive but we grabbed as much as we could under the circumstances. One portion of luck was on our side when a handy bit of nepotism came into play and provided us with a spot on Southern Television's pop quiz programme Countdown. Its producer, a flamboyant, talented and ambitious young producer called Mike Mansfield, who cut quite a dash with his chiselled features and striking mane of prematurely silver hair, was one of the crowd I hung around with in London, and his loyalty to a friend was strong enough to give him the courage to deny Davison's entreaties to favour the Ryan Twins over us. Cleo Laine was also on the show along with American folk singer Carolyn Hester.

Although Mike was eventually to become one of the country's most important producers of pop television programmes (Supersonic and Cue The Music) and a groundbreaking video director, it would in those embryonic days have been reasonable to expect him to court the influence of someone as important as Davison. Taking our side was a brave move. An additional piece of valuable exposure was thrown our way too when Mike asked me to be a guest on the panel for the quiz section of the programme, along with top deejay Pete Murray and Peter Noone of Herman's Hermits.

The reviews for both discs were very enthusiastic but pretty much non-committal as far as preferences went and, predictably perched on a fence, Derek Johnson of the NME said that he was sure one of the two versions would happen.

There was an air of tension in the music press with regard to the chart battle under way, which was very understandable considering the mix of contestants. The Ryans, produced by Chris Curtis, versus his old band the Searchers versus Harold Davison, who ostensibly represented the Searchers but who was fighting tooth and nail for the Ryans against Tito Burns, who still handled the Searchers but in reality worked for Harold Davison. Oh what a tangled web was being woven.

When interviewed the Ryans stated that the song had been written especially for them which was complete twaddle. The Hollies themselves had cut a version first although it was not released until 1967 when it featured on their album *Evolution,* before handing it to the Everly Brothers. They included it on their album *Two Yanks In London* which was released before either of the Ryans' or Searchers' versions saw the light of day.

Controversy however was considered something to be avoided at all costs in those oh-so-polite times and Chris Curtis declared that Davison had chosen the song, not him, and that furthermore there was no question of him starting a battle with the Searchers. In his private life he was becoming more erratic. It seemed that his ingestion of substances, a habit which was in harmony with the preferences of his frequent pal around town Brian Epstein, had not diminished, and journalist David Wigg remembers a party at his Knightsbridge apartment that almost ended in tragedy.

An occasional smoker of marijuana, Chris had taken a break from the festivities in the other rooms and had retired to his bedroom to enjoy the soothing effects of a joint. Unfortunately he had been soothed a little too much and had fallen asleep with the lighted toke still in his hand. The bedding caught alight and gradually began to flame up. Fortunately Wigg, one of the bright young stars of the Fleet Street showbusiness machine and a friend to most of the current crop of young pop stars, wandered by to find out why Chris was not joining in the fun. Seeing the conflagration, which was in its early stages, he pulled the anaesthetised Curtis from the bed and smothered the flames. There was no real damage either to the bed or its occupant but it could easily have been a much different story.

As well as his record producing ventures Chris was being enterprising on other fronts. He had decided to form a 'supergroup' which would feature handpicked musicians while he would take care of the lead vocals. He had singled out keyboardist Jon Lord and guitarist Ritchie Blackmore as the mainstays of the backing. Both were superb musicians whose reputations were still very much on the rise.

The initial name of the band was to be Embryo but he quickly decided upon Roundabout as a better title, the principle being that people could get on and off at will or whenever Chris decided it was appropriate. An astute Jon Lord wisely spotted that he could well be one of those asked to depart the jolly little merry-go-round at Chris's slightest eccentric whim, and with Chris obviously not being the most stable of characters it was a very precarious position to be in. Eventually Lord and Blackmore left Chris to his own devices and appropriated the band themselves. Their eventual chosen name was Deep Purple, taken from Blackmore's grandma's favourite song. The rest, as they say, is history.

When not plugging the new disc we spent November of nineteen sixty-six touring the ballrooms of Scotland. Braving the cold winds and snow, often playing two towns a night, we entertained the folks at the Raith Ballroom, Kirkcaldy, and Whitburne Community Centre (4th), the Market Halls in both Carlisle and Dumfries (5th), the Dundee Palais (6th), the Kinema, Dunfermline (7th), the Irish Club in Glasgow (8th), Montrose Locarno (9th), Dundee Students Union (10th), Margo's in Edinburgh and the Walker Hall, Kilbride (11th) followed by Perth City Hall, before heading south for Streatham Locarno (17th), Sheffield Mojo (19th) and Manchester Bellvue (20th). It was a hellish pace but we were young and desperate.

The next day we appeared on the BBC Light Programme as guests on a show called Monday Monday which was followed quickly by more ballroom dates in the Bournemouth Winter Gardens (23rd), Pontypridd Municipal Hall (25th) and Huddersfield Plaza (27th). We might have been out of favour but thanks to our glorious past and our reduced fees we were busier than ever.

In the end there were no winners. Paul and Barry Ryan came to a halt at forty-nine while we just managed to save face by resting one place above them at forty-eight. We were never to bother the UK charts with our presence again. In the face of the immense powers we were pitted against and the all-important television promotion denied us, we had acquitted ourselves very well and with a clear run we might well have had something to be really pleased about.

It is still a record that we are fond of and although Chris described John Blunt's drumming as 'like a rat running over the snare drum' there is a power and energy in the grooves that I find very satisfying and which I thought was missing from the opposition's effort. Under a different set of circumstances who knows what the outcome might have been?

Over in the Rebel Rousers' camp Cliff Bennett was on a high achieving a massive hit with a Paul McCartney written and produced *Got To Get You Into My Life*. It was truly a magnificent comeback, beating the odds and making the number six spot after a two-year absence from the top twenty. It was a trifle disconcerting being upstaged by the person I had once deserted and he could justifiably have looked on this excellent piece of work as the musical equivalent of sticking two fingers up to me, but for Cliff it was a one-off and there were no more hits for him and his merry band of men.

In the NME end of year poll we had disappeared from sight for the first time, but on the plus side the record had actually charted in the States, albeit a lowly seventy-four in Cash Box top hundred, our first US hit for some months. We were also the number three most popular group in Germany and I had been voted Europe's top bass player in a poll conducted by European Pop. Wonders will never cease.

We began 1967 with yet another futile stab at the charts. *Popcorn Double Feature* was an interesting departure for us, almost a foray into the realms of psychedelia with lyrics full of allegory and innuendo as opposed to the more direct and non threatening happy-clappy words that constituted the major part of our normal repertoire. We straightened the song considerably from the original demo that had been sent to us and gave it, or so we thought, a more commercial feel. The end result we decided was catchy (it was), an intriguing new route for us to travel down (it was) and a possible return to chart favour for the Searchers (it was not).

Once more the reviews were reasonably optimistic. 'A lack of immediate distinctiveness but it's a good strong song and the presentation is commercial' (Peter Jones, Record Mirror). 'Zounds! Can this mean a comeback for the Searchers? A breathless urgency pervades this sad/happy romp rather in the famous Herman/Noone groove. It depends on how strong the group's image is whether they can drag themselves back into the chart-light' (Melody Maker).

The predictions were naturally vague and allowed for both failure and success. The great sages of the music press were for the most part no wiser than us when it came to hit records and after sitting firmly on the fence would simply stand around picking splinters out of their arses while they waited for the public's decision, the only one that actually counted, following which they would calmly declare themselves to have been correct. *Popcorn Double Feature*, though far from being a disc that we were ashamed of, achieved the distinction of being our first release not to have entered the charts.

I celebrated this perilous situation by purchasing an MGB GT in dark blue, my first-ever new car. Perhaps this was not the wisest way to manage my very limited reserves in view of the fact that my future appeared about as bright as a twenty-watt light bulb. And for Mike Pender and John McNally there were more problems to deal with.

The ever astute Tito Burns had, it seems, decided that he was acting as more than an agent and felt it only right that he should receive a management percentage in addition to fees they were paying. In other words our money had dropped, resulting in less income for Mister Burns and his solution was to extract more at a time when the band could least afford it and for which they would be afforded no discernible advantage. In their current insecure state Mike and John felt unable to combat the pressure put on them and they succumbed.

Along with the changes in my personal circumstances, small parts of my past were disintegrating around me too. On February 3rd Joe Meek, by whom I had first been committed to record back in 1961, had been found dead at his Holloway Road studio having first shot to death his landlady before turning the weapon on himself. Always an unstable person and an obvious candidate for tragedy, his early death was not a gigantic shock although the method and the violence involved was of a particularly horrific nature. Rock & roll was full of casualties and poor Joe was just one more.

Although the cabaret scene, with week leading into week leading into yet another week, was taking up an inordinate portion of our workload there was respite from this every now and again. In March we jetted off to Scandinavia for concerts in Copenhagen, Stockholm, Oslo and Helsinki. They were cold climates but gave us a warm welcome.

And we still had our ardent supporters. A Michael Parker of Claygate in Surrey wrote to the Record Mirror complaining of 'Searchers sound-alike groups like The Who and the Byrds' (he gave examples as The Who's *So Sad About Us* and the Byrds' *Feel A Whole Lot Better*). He urged the Searchers to come back and make a new LP themselves.

Back on the record front we kept on trying although both we and our producer Tony Hatch were becoming increasingly frustrated at this impossible impasse. On reflection I have a feeling that Tony, seeing the writing on the wall as far as the Searchers were concerned, would have been happier honourably extracting himself from the situation and spending his valuable time on more worthwhile projects such as Petula Clark who was hot and getting hotter under Hatch's direction and with Tony Hatch/Jackie Trent songs such as *Downtown* and *Don't Sleep In The Subway*.

We discussed available material and settled on a cover of a song soon to be released by a US group called the Five Americans entitled *Western Union*. If *Popcorn Double Feature* was to remain a song that we had a certain amount of good feeling about, *Western Union* was a dog when we made it and did not improve with age or benefit when viewed through the rose-tinted blinkers of nostalgia.

For the B-side we had penned a number called *I'll Cry Tomorrow* and for whatever deranged reason, because goodness knows we were not using any hallucinogenic drugs, or any other kind for that matter, we embellished the fade-out by recording the sound of us smashing Coca Cola bottles in a bin. Maybe we were just having a laugh. At this point in time anything was worth trying.

On April 7th and 9th 1967 we found ourselves respectively at the ABCs in Aldershot and Romford deputising for our 'arch enemies' Paul and Barry Ryan who, due to prior commitments in Europe, had to take two days away from a tour that comprised Roy Orbison, the Small Faces, Sonny Child & the TNT and P. P. Arnold who was herself replacing Jeff Beck.

It had become fairly routine in our act for the demonic John Blunt to kick his kit across the stage at the end of the performance in the style of his hero, Who drummer Keith Moon. It was a very un-Searchers-like piece of wanton vandalism but it attracted attention. Members of the cast ran frantically to the wings as the word spread that the Searchers' deranged drummer was in the process of destroying his drums on the stage. One of the rubberneckers was the drummer for Sonny Child's band the TNT, a curly mop-headed Scot called Billy Adamson and neither he nor we knew then that he was to figure in both of our futures very soon.

A review in the local paper picked us out as one of the highlights of the show and included a special mention of *Blowing In The Wind*, which managed to silence an otherwise noisy audience.

Once more reviews in the record papers for the new disc were far from bad. 'Very distinctive...trying for different sounds and performed at top flight. Pay up and take your choice. I fancy the British treatment this time' (Record Mirror). It was released on April 22nd and forgotten by most the next day.

While we were struggling the Beatles were still the undisputed kings of the musical world. In July they asserted their dominance with even greater force by appearing on a world-wide telecast called *Our World* performing their new single *All You Need Is Love* in a studio packed with fellow idols, fans and hangers-on as well as a full size symphony orchestra. One day later I was hanging out with Terry Doran at a cottage in Esher, Surrey, which he rented from John Lennon. Doran, a long time friend of the Beatles and now an executive at Apple Records, was reputedly the 'man from the motor trade' in Paul McCartney's song *She's Leaving Home* (for a short time he was a co-owner with Brian Epstein of a garage in Hounslow called Brydor) although this has been disputed.

Along with Graham Nash of the Hollies and a few others we sat chatting about anything and everything when a hand knocking at the door turned out to be attached to the body of John Lennon. He had just received the final mix of the single and wanted Terry to hear it. I felt very privileged to be among that group of people hearing that historic record before it was released to the general public. But having suffered the slings and arrows of outrageous Scousers in the past I did not enter into any conversation but just stayed silent on the sidelines and listened.

John didn't hang around long. After a bit of excited banter about the new disc and the genuine congratulations of the assembled group he was off out the door again and soon speeding into the dark night in his Ferrari. Not a momentous action-packed encounter but still I felt extremely thrilled at merely finding myself in the presence of a Beatle.

It was the time of flower power and that night I was garbed somewhat ostentatiously in a bespoke shirt made for me by a lovely hippie girl from Parson's Green called Barbara Richter. She had translated my ideas perfectly and constructed a loose fitting tunic in purple slub silk. Over my head was dropped a yoke of gold rimmed squares which had been joined together brickwork style and the result was something akin to what a Roman senator might possibly wear on dress-up day at the forum. On the other hand you might also suggest I resembled Frankie Howerd in *Up Pompeii*. Youth in the mid to late sixties appeared to know no embarrassment in the areas of high fashion.

Graham Nash was full of compliments on my design. A couple of weeks later I watched him and the Hollies on Top Of The Pops performing their latest hit *King*

Midas In Reverse and he was wearing a near replica of my Romanesque shirt. I was far from being annoyed. Instead I was flattered that such a talented and important person, not to mention a genuinely nice guy, should feel that little old me had something worth copying.

As autumn went and we felt the first chill of winter, things were not looking good and there was only one thing for me to do. Spend some money. I went out and bought an E type Jaguar in a bright shade of red and with a detachable hard top in black. With my usual lack of objectivity I bought it in haste and once I had set out on a Monday morning to view a couple of examples I had seen advertised I knew I would come home with one that evening no matter what.

The first one, a white roadster for sale in far off Deptford, was too dodgy even for me to consider. The swan-necked rally light on the passenger side set alarm bells ringing that this vehicle, rather than being driven carefully by one lady owner, had seen some rough days and tough treatment in its action packed past. I graciously declined and drove on to Kingston by which time it was well into the afternoon and the light was fading. It took some time for the garage to have the car, which was garaged elsewhere, cleaned and spruced up ready for viewing.

When it was eventually driven up to the showroom the sky was dark but the Jaguar gleamed in the showroom lights. I made a pretence of examining it but in fact this was a *fait accompli*. The deal was done in about ten minutes flat and I became the new owner of a beautiful 4.2 litre red E type roadster registration number KJJ 220D. It was certainly not the best example I could have got for my money but neither was it the worst and I drove it home as proud as punch. My career was possibly in tatters but I felt like a star. I could arrive at my favourite 'in' club, the Cromwellian on London's Cromwell Road opposite the Natural History Museum, in true style and impress my peers, or at least look them in the face. Two days later in another fit of dubious extravagance I bought from the same place a matching mini, figuring that a second cheap runaround would save on fuel and wear and tear on the Jag. I was young and only today was important. I would deal with any impending problems later.

Despite the writings on the wall of War And Peace proportions it seemed that there was still more to come. Mike and John came to me with the news that their rapidly diminishing income could no longer support my substantial wages and, knowing that I was not willing to accept a reduction in wages, they were inviting me to join them as a full partner. In some way that was good news. I had already stated that I was happy to share the ups and the downs with them. The other side of the coin was that we would all have to reduce our weekly take-home pay to a paltry forty pounds for the foreseeable future. We had never really lived the extravagant lives of true pop stars but with this kind of financial constriction we were entering the territory of mere civilians.

As pathetic as it sounds particularly in the light of today's standards with costs and earnings seemingly floating somewhere in the stratosphere by comparison, forty pounds was still round about twice the average working wage and one could get by quite comfortably on it if a little restraint and common sense was shown. More importantly they had also wisely budgeted for a reserve in the group's bank account to take care of general running costs and the all important tax liabilities that had traditionally been the downfall of so many ostrich-minded entertainers. But it was still a sharp reminder of just how difficult and dangerous things had become.

I began to wonder quite seriously if my tenure as a pop star was about to be curtailed ahead of time. Or maybe I had already been given more time than I rightly deserved and my time in the sun was at an end. I nervously considered at that point whether or not I should dig out my GCE certificate and work out in just what areas my O levels in English, French and Woodwork might benefit me in the way of gainful employment should desperate measures call for it. With those credentials I was fit to be nothing more than a cabinet maker in Quebec. I freely admit I was more than a little scared.

23

A Last Slice Of Pye

August 1967 was the summer of the flower children. Along with thousands of other exotically dressed creatures I travelled to Woburn Abbey clad in silk and beads on the Saturday afternoon of the three-day event. I was flower free and my strands of beads were plastic but at least I had made an effort. The Small Faces, the Move, the Bee Gees and Eric Burdon were among the performers over the three days and in a rare display of generosity the unreliable sun shone benevolently on Britain that afternoon. But elsewhere an event was unfolding that for a while would dim the blooms on display.

The next day on the 28th, the Sunday of the August Bank Holiday, the Searchers played a supporting role to Engelbert Humperdinck on a Sunday evening concert at the ABC Theatre in Blackpool. A phone call came through from a newspaper reporter in London wanting to know how we felt about the news concerning Brian Epstein. We had heard nothing. He explained. Brian had been found dead in the bedroom of his home in London's Belgravia, seemingly from a drug overdose either accidental or otherwise.

He had been hosting a house party at Kingsly Hill his recently acquired country home in Sussex but appeared unsettled and distracted. He left the gathering and returned to London alone. In the morning his manservant discovered the body. With his increasing dependence on recreational drugs creating in him a state of paranoia and his fears that the Beatles' contract, which was soon to expire, might not be renewed preying on his mind it was understandable that many thought his death was an act of self destruction, but he was a man with plans for the future and nothing could be taken for granted.

We were shocked to say the least and delivered the appropriate responses of regret and condolence. All the flowers on earth and all the artificial laughter born of a temporary force-fed American fad could not disguise the fact that the world could still be a nasty place. The seeds of malcontent that sparked the end of the Beatles had already been sown but in my mind it was this one specific event that sealed their fate.

But we had our own problems to deal with. We were still ranked sixteenth favourite UK male group in the NME polls and although it was only one place down from 1966 there was little doubt that the descent would accelerate if we didn't do something about it. We still had a contract with Pye Records and we still had to make an attempt at re-establishing ourselves as a chart act.

Secondhand Dealer was a novelty song that told the tale of the owner of a junk shop who, like his establishment, had seen better days. It had been inspired by a young Swedish pop group called the Second Hand Dealers which had been one of our supports on a club tour of Scandinavia a couple of months earlier. We had been intrigued by their name and made jokes about it with them in the dressing room. A few days later Mike Pender came to me with a tune and I had strung together a set of lyrics resulting in a completed song that we all thought, or maybe just hoped, was quite good.

When the disc hit the stores on November 25th Peter Jones called it 'Rather typical Searchers which means a compact sound and useful material. The voices are good, in fact it's a nice record all round. Might do well.' He awarded it a generous four stars. But it did not do well. At the end of the song the store-keeper dies. He was a stiff and so was our record. But at least the store-keeper had enjoyed a reasonable number of years on this earth. Our disc was stillborn. However, it has become our rarest single of the Pye era. Issued with a blue label rather than the normal pink one, it has commanded as much as £110 on e-bay.

Meanwhile we were learning to deal with the odd dichotomy of an abundance of work accompanied by a paucity of financial reward. We were being sold on a bulk-buy basis that meant the pro-rata fee for the Searchers was a truly puny amount, on top of which clubs would frequently combine to share the cost by having us play on more than one stage per night and more often than not in more than one town, which was by no means an unusual state of affairs. It seemed that every town in Britain boasted at least one thriving cabaret club and some cities were positively over endowed in this respect.

In Southend the place to be was the Talk Of The South. Stockton-on-Tees had the Fiesta, our particular favourite, while next door neighbour Middlesborough had Tito's, the Showboat and the Excel Bowl. Also in the vicinity were the La Bamba (Darlington), the Latino (South Shields), Wetheralls (Sunderland) and La Dolce Vita (Newcastle). There was another La Dolce Vita in Birmingham too along with a Big Night Out.

Batley in West Yorkshire was home to the famous Batley Variety Club which had led the way by bringing over high-priced American acts to tempt the British public through its doors, and only a few miles away the Wakefield Theatre Club provided some healthy competition. In Leeds Peter Stringfellow opened the Millionaire which turned into Cinderella-Rockerfellas and on a lesser scale there was the Ace Of Clubs. Blackburn offered the Starlight and the Cavendish. Barnsley meant the Ba Ba and Doncaster had the Ki Ki.

Manchester could provide a seemingly endless round of venues for acts to trudge through during their working year. There was really no need to leave town. Fagins, the Talk Of The North, the Princess, the Domino, the Georgian, the Warren, the Northern Sporting Club, Bernard Manning's Embassy Club and Bredbury Hall. 'Doubles' were fairly routine. The Princess, Domino and Georgian was a well known mind-numbing 'triple' with the equipment having to be packed up and reassembled at each place in order to fulfil our commitments. We tried not to let these crippling and almost impossible logistics affect the quality of our performance but it surely must have.

It was a tiring, educational and sometimes amusing life. At the Ninety-Nine Club in Barrow-in-Furness, where our good friend Liverpool and England footballer Emlyn Hughes would regularly turn up to see us, one of our supporting acts, a comedian, had been warned by the management to eliminate the 'blue' element of his act. When he went on the following evening he began by explaining to the audience 'I've had a few complaints from the committee about being too rude and I'm sorry about that folks. Anyway, there were these three nuns pissing in a tin can...'

The theatrical digs which had now become our homes from home could be quite idiosyncratic mainly because of the proprietors who were a breed apart. When we were in Leeds we were domiciled in a large detached house opposite Roundhay Park run by Helen Bradley, a tiny, gruff Jewish lady with a visage that was lined and lumpy like a map of the Golan Heights. Atop her wizened head perched a horrendous wig that resembled a nest that had long since been abandoned by its occupants and left to rot with the passing years' exposure to the harshness of the elements. Despite her gruffness I became very fond of Helen.

In bed and breakfast terms it was a rather plush place at which Tom Jones and Engelbert Humperdinck continued to stay for a considerable time after they had achieved national fame. Engelbert bought Helen a black spaniel which she named after her famous guest. Freddie Starr always used the apartment above the garage outside the main house. Helen considered him too problematic to cope with at close range and it gave him his freedom to come and go at will.

The main story in circulation was that Helen Bradley's bed and breakfast operation was simply a front for the real business of the house which was one of 'ill repute'. Apparently dear old pensioner Helen had been convicted of keeping a disorderly house several times in the past and despite such setbacks it was still business as usual. I have to say that if the stories were true then arrangements were made in the most discreet manner for I never saw or heard anything more than a few curt phone calls all answered by Helen - no-one else was allowed to answer the phone - and whose replies consisted of a simple 'yes' or 'no'.

Helen, not known for her friendly manner, for whatever reason took a shine to me and in the afternoon would often ask in a basso profundo voice reminiscent of Max from Charlie's Angels 'Would you like a cup of tea Frank?' If I said yes, and I invariably did, the tea would arrive usually accompanied by her excellent chopped liver and motzahs. If I had declined the offer no-one would have got any. Helen definitely had her favourites. She has long since departed this life to manage those pro digs in the sky where she is probably still dispensing chopped liver and motzahs to the favoured few.

In Middlesborough we stayed at a house on the Linthorpe Road belonging to Baxter Jacobs who ran a very stylish and colourful place full of home-produced modern art and who put more effort than most into providing interesting and attractive food. I remember another rock group lodging there at the same time. They were a bit wilder and much more rock & roll than us which I must add was not a difficult thing to achieve. One night when they came home still hungry after a gig only to find that the wise Baxter had sensibly locked the hatch to the kitchen they simply prised it open and proceeded to raid the larder. The group was called Free and Paul Rogers, Andy Fraser, Simon Kirke and Paul Kossoff appeared to be living up to their name.

A few miles up the road in Stockton the Pendelphin was the place to hang your hat and feel at home. It was only a handful of doors along from the Fiesta and run by a couple called Dave and Barrie Ritchie. This was not some 'out and proud' gay partnership. Barrie Ritchie was truly a lady and became the mother hen to many an act. She achieved a muted form of immortality as the Mrs Ritchie in the title of an unsuccessful single by Harmony Grass, a group which developed from Tony Rivers and the Castaways. She took a keen interest in the fortunes of her guests and was a backbone of encouragement or consolation as they planned their futures or mourned their failures in her parlour. When we entered our 'new wave' phase in the early eighties she even spent a number of laborious hours knitting a silver tie for me to wear on television.

There is for me one proprietress who stands head and shoulders above everyone else and who amazed me with her sheer vivacity and lust for life, not to mention her simple humanity, and my admiration for her has remained undiminished over the years.

Philomena Lynott, a statuesque raven-haired Irish woman with a regal bearing and a constant air of serenity and wisdom, owned a large house in the Whalley Range district of Manchester. It catered to strippers and groups and 'civilians' were not encouraged to book in. The white lettering on a rather decrepit awning over one of the downstairs windows declared 'The Showbiz'. The building had enjoyed better times and luxury was not an attribute of the Showbiz. A loving welcome from the non-judgemental lady who fussed over things was. Fussed is the wrong word. Phyllis (her preferred name, the one we all used) never fussed. She simply coped with whatever life threw at her with her ever-present calmness.

Together with her partner Dennis she presided over a household of characters who might have caused concern to a lesser person. Roy and Percy, two black Canadians who were in a rock band, were in permanent residence. Strippers came and went as their fortunes dictated although some like Maxine a 'fuller figured' ecdysiast from Glasgow was pretty much a full time resident.

The bedrooms were very basic and the cheap divans were supported on piles of bricks, their legs long since having parted company with the bases. Having a bath was a major problem. The gas boiler which heated the water as it passed through the pipes and which only operated when a great number of coins were inserted in a slot was a model of inefficiency and a tortoise could have completed its hibernation in less time than it took to draw enough inches in which to bathe. It follows then that baths were only taken in an emergency.

Meal-times in the communal kitchen were very often in two sittings with up to fourteen diners at each and the quality and quantity of the food was very hit and miss as Phyllis was running things on a slim margin of profit and loss. If lamb chops were on the menu you got two of the tiniest examples known to man. They were that small, the miniscule creatures from which they were extracted could well have been the results of premature births. A dessert could well be a peculiar mix of grapefruit and evaporated milk if that's what was in the larder.

But we loved it warts and all and we loved Phyllis. We were not there for the creature comforts of the flesh but rather for the nourishment of our souls while in the company of this wonderful woman. The large basement room remained unused for many years until she decided to apply for a drinks licence. She got it of course. She was adored by both the Manchester constabulary and the judiciary. Normal rules did not apply when it came to Phyllis.

She eventually got the bar up and running and instituted its very odd opening hours. Drinking commenced at two in the morning to coincide with the bars in town closing. Friends approved of by Phyllis then made their way to Whalley Range and after being vetted by a glance from Dennis propped up in an upstairs window were let in to drink till dawn.

The star regular was George Best, the young footballing genius from Belfast who was the uncrowned king of Manchester. Most nights, including those on the eve of a match, his dark blue E type could be found parked against the kerb outside. The first time George was to visit the hotel there was a good deal of excitement about the place.

Maxine in particular was buzzing with anticipation and stripped with an extra burst of speed that night. She entered the room, her suitcase still in hand and an exaggerated walk which she determined would pass for extreme sexually charged sophistication, and sashayed past George sure in the knowledge he had seen her. She reached the counter and Phyllis, smiling ever so sweetly and with a look on her face that could almost have passed for innocence on anyone else, whispered in her ear 'Maxine dear, your knickers are hanging out of your suitcase. Georgie has seen your drawers.' And indeed they were and he had.

There was even more excitement, this time from Phyllis herself, when the news came that her young teenage son was coming over from Ireland where he had been raised by his grandparents. She had not seen her boy for a long time. Too long. Phillip, the result of an out-of-wedlock relationship with a black seaman at a time when it was all she could do to survive away from her native Dublin and the very light of her life, was arriving with his heavy metal rock group of which he was the bass player and singer. They were called Thin Lizzy and though they had a thriving career and an envious reputation on home ground, over the water they were determined to make it on a bigger stage.

The group's name, by the way, came from the Irish pronunciation of the word Thin in which the 'h' is ignored resulting in a comparison with Henry Ford's old boneshaker (Tin Lizzy) rather than a lofty and malnourished female. And while we're busting myths, the family surname is most definitely pronounced Lie-not.

It was a long tough struggle and Phyllis was there to prop them up. She housed and fed them. She gave them money when they had none. And when their equipment was stolen she bought them new gear. Eventually their persistence and their talent paid off and Thin Lizzy, and Phil Lynott in particular, became huge international stars. When Phillip bought her an impressive detached house called White Horses on the Strand at Howth, an affluent Dublin suburb, she and Dennis sold up the Showbiz and moved back to Ireland along with Graham, a friend and helper who had become a permanent member of their extended family.

But all the love in the world could not save Phil Lynott from himself and the perils of a hedonistic rock & roll life style. He, like so many, fell into the trap of believing that personal power, fame and influence was naturally accompanied by power over personal abuse in the form of hard drugs and when he died on January 4th 1986 from pneumonia precipitated by his use of heroin her world collapsed. Of course Phyllis, being the strong, indomitable person that she was, picked herself up and carried on but she had lost something of herself that could never be recaptured. In later years we visited Phillip's grave together and I could see the pain still etched in that beautiful face.

As 1967 ended and we turned the corner into 1968 the situation at Pye was becoming critical. We were groping blindly with no real idea of the style we should be concentrating on or how to raise our profile in the public eye. With no real guidance from our so-called management it would be impossible to achieve the second without some kind of success in the first. We needed a hit. Any kind of hit. Even a modest one would have been welcome at this time.

Tony Hatch decided to take things in hand and instead of merely trusting to our instincts and exercising his guiding opinions when required and translating our choices into suitably attractive sounds on tape, he decided that we should come at the problem from a completely different angle.

Pop music had been undergoing radical changes and it was no longer the domain of simple tunes and banal lyrics. Burt Bacharach was at the forefront in this new world of intelligent pop and had intrigued everyone with his well-constructed melodies with complicated and ever changing time signatures where a one-off three/four or two/four bar might be suddenly inserted into an otherwise regular four/four rhythm. His style was much admired by Tony Hatch who was a writer and arranger much more than a producer. Producing hits, at which he was extremely successful, was merely a conduit for his true vocation. Indeed in time he was to be thought of by some as the British Bacharach.

He came to us with an idea that instead of starting out with a rough guide demo we should simply construct a single from the germ of an idea he had. Far from being a complete song it was at this point just a title and one line of melody that was in his head. He had been following a London double-decker bus which announced its destination as Camberwell Green. The place name had lodged in his brain and he could not get it out of his head. There was a tune to the title line and little more although by the time we began rehearsals it had progressed in his mind at least. Getting it into our minds was a different matter entirely.

The tune, though very satisfying to the psyche of a serious musical scholar, was a bit of a mystery to us and the patterns changed alarmingly from one time signature to another. John Blunt found these changes an almost impossible task as he staggered like a hurdler with a hamstring injury from one bar to another. I have to say the rest of us weren't much better at grasping the subtleties of the piece which in any case was as far from the true Searchers style, if there was one, as you could get.

Things quickly deteriorated with us getting disillusioned, Tony getting frustrated and John Blunt just about rupturing himself behind the drum kit. I'm sure Tony's song in other hands would have resulted in a well crafted piece of pop, after all he was a very talented man who was having enormous success with his own compositions which had lyrics provided by his new wife Jackie Trent, but none of us could envisage anything worthwhile on the horizon. We were not captivated by the tune, or what we had of it so far, and by the end of the first day there was no-one in the studio who was happy at our progress or lack of it.

Tony called John, Mike and myself aside and said that he was not happy with Blunt's drumming and would prefer to use a session musician (shades of Pete Best?). We discussed the matter away from Hatch and felt that perhaps the problem was not so much with Blunt's competence - after all he had already provided perfectly acceptable and energetic drums on three singles already - but perhaps with Tony's lack of understanding as to where we should be going as a group. We hated *Camberwell Green*, or what we knew of it so far, with a vengeance. Perhaps it was time for change.

Without returning to the ill-fated project we parted from Tony without any further contact or formal discussion with him. It was not the best way to end an association with a man who not only guided our recording career through a truly golden period but who had also become a good friend. In his defence I can only imagine that Tony felt a weight removed from his shoulders as the matter was taken out of his hands. He was not a man to quit from a commitment but his talents and time would be best employed elsewhere and in areas where he would acquire personal satisfaction and pleasure as well as mere success.

Talks were held between Tito Burns and Louis Benjamin, who was the big chief at Pye. It was decided that we should be placed in the charge of the company's new wonder boy Tony Macauley, who was having a seemingly unstoppable run of chart successes with the Foundations (*Baby Now That I've Found You*), the Paper Dolls (*Something Here In My Heart*) and Long John Baldry (*Let The Heartaches Begin*). He and his writing partner John Macleod had tapped into the zeitgeist of late sixties pop and their Motown-influenced compositions with their infectious tunes and bouncy rhythms had the youth of Britain buying them in their hundreds of thousands.

We were very pleased to say the least and felt that in the hands of someone with fresh ears and ideas we might somehow resurrect our plummeting fortunes. I had a meeting with Macauley and Macleod who were seemingly as excited as us at the prospect of working together. To them we were legends and they considered it an honour and a challenge to bring us back to glory. They had songs in their catalogue that would suit us and which they felt could be hits. They were hot and I had no reason to doubt them and I returned to impart the good news to my partners. However no sooner had the project been agreed than it was off again. Tito explained that Pye had decreed that if we were to have the services of their brightest new talent they would have to be compensated by a reduction in our royalty rate. If it was true, it was outrageous. Our rate was four per cent at the time. If anything significant was taken from that we might as well be paying them.

Tito added that he thought that was unacceptable and therefore he was removing us from Pye. As he put it, the Searchers had been good for him and it was time that he repay us by investing his own money in the group's future. He would take over the contract and pay for sessions himself. This sudden burst of philanthropy from Mr Burns was not fooling anyone. I think there was little doubt that Tito had discovered the huge rewards that being the owner of master recordings and releasing them at high rates could bring. We were in no position to argue and accepted the plan. Whatever the reasoning behind it a milestone had been reached. The Pye years were at an end.

24

Liberty, Of A Kind

Even though Bill Landis was to have a huge success with Barry Ryan's solo record *Eloise* he was not really a full time record producer. One half of a minor vocal duo called Bill and Brett Landis he had come to work in the Burns office as a general factotum assisting with whatever required his help and advising artistically on the careers of Tito's acts.

He was someone we had known for some time and got on well with and he was placed in charge of our first post-Hatch session. Bill had chosen a song called *The Great Train Robbery* as our first effort. The subject of the song was not the one perpetrated by Messrs Biggs and Co but rather an earlier nineteenth century railway heist in America. It was a plodding piece of tosh, as far removed from a Searchers hit as you could get, and on reflection stood about as much chance in the charts as the Venus de Milo in a darts match. I'm not sure it was ever completely finished and maybe somewhere in the vaults there is a tape with the evidence. Perhaps one day it will be found and foisted on the public by someone with a malicious mind. But heaven must have intervened to save us from such an embarrassment because Tito Burns suddenly announced that he was placing us with Liberty Records, the small American company who had recently launched their new label in the UK. Contracts were completed and the deal was done, or at least what we saw of it. It was all handled by Tito and in our vulnerable state we were too cowed to question or dispute how he was handling things. These were scary times.

All was not doom and gloom though. Salvation came in a swift and unexpected way. The newly franchised London Weekend Television company offered Tito the opportunity to be in charge of its light entertainment department, an offer which he could not and did not refuse. But having management contracts would have constituted an unacceptable conflict of interest and he was obliged to free himself from any such attachments. Our management contract with Mr Burns was suddenly terminated. As well as being released from Tito we were also released from the extra management fee that was crippling our delicate finances. As an atheist-cum-agnostic I was almost prepared at that point to believe there really was a God after all.

Bob Reisdorf who was in charge of the Liberty Records setup put us under the direction of a young American songwriter/producer called Kenny Young who, along with his writing partner Art Resnick had achieved such success with *Sand In My Shoes* and *Under The Boardwalk* for the Drifters, and was a top talent for the April Music publishing company.

He wasted no time in getting us into the studios with one of his own compositions, a hypnotic and surreal tune called *Umbrella Man*. It certainly was a departure following more the style of *Popcorn Double Feature* than *Needles And Pins* and showed promise, but for me the potential of what was in essence a good song was destroyed by a rather irritating drum pattern that caused an instrumental section during a break to stagger and stutter rather than retain the hypnotic and insistent feel that was one of its main assets along with its curious and dream-like words. I sympathised with John Blunt who understandably had a great deal of trouble executing the part and only a drunk with a wooden leg could have danced to it without embarrassment.

On the B-side we placed one of my own compositions, a song called *Over The Weekend*, a tune that had started out as a possible entry to the Eurovision Song Contest. Bill Landis had suggested I might try to write something for the competition and this was the result. Personally I felt it had the bouncy, sing-able and easy-to-remember qualities that fitted the requirements. Having completed it my submission was declined but John Blunt was such a great admirer of the song that he battered the others into considering it as a future single. This resulted in a demo made by the group at the Marquee Studios with the intention of turning *Umbrella Man* into an A-side during our tenure under the Tito contract, and at a meeting with us he was indeed happy to consider the idea until I mentioned that I was forming my own publishing company. Upon hearing that he was not to share in any spoils that might be forthcoming Mr Burns immediately suggested that it would possibly not be considered for a single after all.

Following Burns's departure from the Harold Davison Organisation the recording was now a leftover spare. Kenny had intended to place another of his own tunes on the flip-side but we had long since decided that we were more than entitled to this potentially lucrative perk if nothing else and remained insistent. The *Saturday Night Out* saga had at least taught us that much. On the final product the demo was used as a master recording which was launched on the public with barely a whimper in the November of that year. In the accompanying advertisements we were garbed in casual flowery attire as was dictated by the fashions of the time and beneath exotic umbrellas as was dictated by the title of the A-side. Alas our efforts once again were all to no avail. Chart-wise it did nothing and we exited 1968 as hitless as we had entered.

Meanwhile John Blunt was becoming somewhat of a liability. We felt that his playing was becoming increasingly erratic, possibly aided by his regular enjoyment of cannabis, a substance hitherto unheard of in the Searchers' environs. I'm not sure even Chris Curtis smoked dope until after his departure although his intake of pills had caused us problems. What on earth was it about Searchers' drummers?

Nice as he was, Blunt's tempos were becoming uneven and difficult to put up with and his position with the band was brought into sharp focus when he was arrested for possession while out driving in his blue Jaguar saloon one night. These days one might expect a stern word and nothing more for having one pathetic joint on one's person but as we headed towards the end of what was considered to be an almost decadently liberal and tolerant decade, an indulgence with the weed was almost akin to being in league with the Devil.

He was found guilty of possession and remanded in prison for two weeks for reports before being released into the world once more. How ridiculous. They could have asked me and saved themselves an awful lot of wasted money. He was a young man doing what young men did. He drank, went with loose women and used mild drugs. While he was holed up in Brixton I decided a few words of sympathy were in order and sent him a jokey letter saying that while I realised he had ambitions to leave his parents' home for a flat of his own I thought the method he had used was perhaps a little over the top. I'm happy to say that it caused him a few chuckles while slopping out.

Mike and John felt that we should dispense with his services as it reflected badly on the image of a hitherto unimpeachable reputation, but although I was in doubt as to whether or not he should remain a Searcher it was for reasons of competence rather than lifestyle and I was not happy about kicking someone when they were down. Apart from which there was the sneaking feeling that the incident, heaven forbid, might just have made us a little bit interesting. I talked them out of sacking him - for a while at least.

The relationship between Mike Pender and John McNally, who by now were travelling to shows together, was undergoing the inevitable transformation of young men who had once sought each other's company because of music and friendship, but who were now kept together by reasons of business and finance. When there was once the four travelling together *en masse* the communal atmosphere of camaraderie relieved anyone of the pressure that comes with too much close exposure to any particular fellow human being.

They had both started young families and it was an ever-more-difficult juggling act to keep money matters in check. John Blunt, myself and our road manager were now all London based and as the only two Searchers still living on Merseyside there was no one else to bounce off and to inject a mollifying degree of humour on the long tedious journeys from town to town. Their conversations by necessity concentrated on the problems of keeping the band afloat and when they disagreed on points of action or principle there was no corner in the small four-wheeled vehicle where they could run to hide.

Their outlooks were different. John became constantly frustrated at Mike's wish to take out more money than he considered sensible from the group's bank account in order to pay bills. He had recently moved from his small house to a substantial dwelling at Aughton in the countryside outside Liverpool. It was a large, rambling old house with three floors and seven bedrooms. It was certainly an impressive piece of property but it was of an age that dictated constant repairs and modernisation and it ate up cash quicker than it takes a swarm of locusts to strip a field of grain. It also badly needed a central heating system for which Mike did not have the ready cash, money that he saw was on deposit in the group's account. But John was emphatic that this reserve was laid by for the purpose of tax liabilities and was not to be touched. Many a performer has used up tax reserves to their peril in the past, and will in the future. It is a dangerous road to tread because as sure as eggs are eggs the taxman cometh.

There were other niggles between them that would continue and increase over the years. When John called to collect Mike at the appointed time he would invariably not be ready. They were using their own vehicles as transport on alternating days and John was furious when Mike arrived, not in his Cortina Mk 6, but in a rather clapped out Triumph Herald which had seen better days and which needed topping up with water every few miles. He had sold the other car to pay for the aforementioned central heating.

Perhaps one of the most serious disputes arose when John arrived at Mike's house one day for a journey to Nottingham where the group was to perform at a private party. When Mike came to the door he was evidently not ready and looked very surprised to say the least. It appeared that he had no knowledge of the gig whatsoever. Moreover, he was hosting a party at home and was waiting for dozens of guests to arrive. There was a heated exchange during which Mike said he never got a letter from the office to inform him. This was not at all surprising because it was not standard practice to send out itineraries which would have been obsolete almost immediately as dates were constantly changing. We simply kept in touch with our office and inserted dates in our diaries as they came in. This had been routine for some time for all of us.

Eventually Mike said he would follow on later by himself. As we waited in Nottingham it became apparent that he was not likely to turn up and a phone call to his house confirmed this. After a discussion with the person whose celebration it was, who was clearly very unhappy with things, we gave him the option of cancelling us or accepting a truncated and somewhat limited performance, both in quality and personnel, by only three Searchers, at a lesser fee of course. He accepted the latter and we completed some kind of show. I often wondered if he regretted the decision because it was a pretty awful presentation to say the least.

Our next attempt at salvation by the hands of Kenny Young was a dual strategy. A bouncy brass accentuated curiosity called *Kinky Kathy Abernathy* also failed to excite the record buying public in the July of 1969. On the face of it the song appeared to be very catchy, though in the end it failed to catch a significant number of purchasers to create any waves in the pop world.

For us this was a session with a difference. Kenny explained he would find it easier and more efficient if we used session musicians to provide the backing track. We were not too sure about the ethics of such a move but we were even less sure about our position in the power structure at the time, and so we conceded. At least it would free us up for earning money from gigs which was our sole source of income, inadequate as it was, at that time. By this point we were willing to try almost anything, and in the end we lost out all round. How could we be proud of something that could barely even be called a Searchers product?

At the same session we also put down five other tracks, or at least a bunch of session players who included renowned session bassist Herbie Flowers and ex-John Barry guitarist Vic Flick did. We simply added our vocals to, as they say in the best television programmes, something that had been prepared earlier. John McNally's haunting ballad *Suzanna* was designated the B-side of *Kinky Kathy* while two of the remaining songs were destined for a far more intriguing future.

Under the reasoning that our name and our image might possibly be working against us we decided to release a single under another name in the hope that the discerning record buying public of Britain would realise quality when listening without prejudice. Kenny Young had been inspired to write a song by an article he had spotted in a newspaper. WHO SHOT THE LOLLIPOP MAN? the headline enquired. Creating a fictitious scenario of his own and expanding on an African tune he had heard he presented us with possibly the most valuable record we ever released.

Somebody Shot The Lollipop Man featured a different sound, a different vocal and a different name. The sound was western-cum-pseudo African, the vocal was by me and the name we adopted was that of Kenny Young's dog, an Afghan hound called Pasha. The song I suppose could be called attractive in some ways with its unintelligible and completely made-up native chants in the background. The vocal was dire in the extreme and I look back in horror wondering why on earth someone didn't have the heart to tell me how awful it was. After all it is not like John McNally to be over-sensitive in matters of business and practicality.

The B-side, *Pussy Willow Dream* (erroneously credited as *Pussy Willow Dragon* on the release), was yet another Kenny Young composition and once again the obscure lyrics were incomprehensible to one as unsophisticated as me. It began 'Pussy willow on your pillow, up the hill oh me oh my. Hitch your wagon to a dragon, let me take you beddy bye' and proceeded to get weirder.

Alas the great British record buying public, after having duly listened without prejudice, decided they had no more interest in Pasha than it had in the Searchers. *Somebody Shot The Lollipop* Man failed to make any impression when it hit the stores in July and its sales could have been counted in dozens rather than thousands. The disc-jockey/producer/writer Jonathan King remarked in his column for Disc and Music Echo that this record apparently was by a well-known group going under the assumed name of Kenny Young's dog and the dog could have made a better job of it. A very astute summing up I thought. Harsh but fair. The twelve-string-denied and brass-embellished un-Searcher sounding *Kinky Kathy Abernathy* followed one month later and sank without trace.

There is nothing so mad as the world of pop music and its more fanatical acolytes, and because of its dire sales figures resulting in a rarity value that seems to be in inverse proportion to its actual musical qualities, *Somebody Shot The Lollipop Man* remains our most sought-after and expensive disc to buy, if you can find one at all, which with any luck you won't.

Another master remaining from that session was intended to be our next A-side. It was a cover of an Andy Kim song called *Shoot 'Em Up Baby*. It wasn't bad and in its bubblegum style could well have scored for someone else. The release date and details were still to be sorted out with the Liberty hierarchy once we got Christmas over with and we could begin afresh with the New Year.

On more workaday terms the John Blunt situation was reaching crisis point and we decided that a change was probably long overdue. Our road manager at the time was a big bluff Londoner called Mickey O'Halloran. He was affable and reasonably efficient at his job, which in those simple times consisted of little more than driving the minibus and humping equipment, though we did learn early on in his employment that one of his failings was that he was not too hot at reading. We only discovered this when we found ourselves travelling from London to Bournemouth via Southampton city centre because he couldn't read the road signs.

Mickey knew of a drummer who was available, a Scot living in London by the name of Billy Adamson. We set up an audition at my house in Harlington and ran through a few numbers with the bespectacled, afro-coiffeured drummer in the small living room of 46 Shepiston Lane. After a bit of humming and haahing we decided to offer him the job and poor, lovable but unfortunate John Blunt, far from finding an extra unwanted present from Santa's sack that December, was presented with the sack itself.

25

Dusty Days

The world was changing inexorably. On July 20th 1969 man first stepped onto the surface of the moon. I spent that auspicious evening at the bijou Hampstead home of songwriters Ken Howard and Alan Blakeley, the talented duo responsible for penning the hits behind Dave Dee, Dozy, Beaky, Mick and Tich. *The Legend Of Xanadu*, *Bend It*, *Hold Tight*, *Zabadak* and many others came from the pens of these two enterprising and talented young songwriters.

Exciting and marvellous things were happening in the world and as we stood on the roof of their smart West London house and gazed far up into the skies in bewilderment and admiration, we wondered where it would all end. High in the heavens, a quarter of a million miles away, human feet were setting foot on another planet while my career, while not crashing to Earth with an almighty bang, certainly seemed destined to touch terra firma with a gentle yet ominous plop. There did not seem to be any great heights to which we would be rising in the near future.

The year 1969 slipped almost imperceptibly into the new decade like the gentle fade of a pop record whilst I seemed to be negotiating a tightrope strung between two parallel worlds. My career was not in the rudest of health and while the malaise was unlikely to be terminal there was no sign on the immediate horizon of a miracle cure. But my social life was thriving and as I sped through the streets of the great metropolis of London in my red 4.2 Jaguar E-type roadster I could still manage to give the impression that I was a wealthy young pop star with money to burn. Showbusiness for the main part is built on illusion, and I was the living proof of that clever deception.

Oddly enough in my impecunious state I had also taken the bold step of moving from my small rabbit hutch of a house to a detached property at 1 Carlyon Road in Yeading a few miles away. Mock Tudor with oak beams, leaded lights and a high wall surrounding it, the place looked impressive enough, though in reality it was smaller than it appeared, but there was enough room for me and I was pleased with the purchase. It cost me the paltry sum of seven thousand two hundred and sixty pounds, which I again paid in cash. I was still too scared to take out a mortgage even if I had known how to get one.

I was neither wealthy nor a pop star in the true sense of the words. I was not short of a bob or two but I had precious little to spare for serious luxuries and while pop is short for popular and we still had plenty of admirers, our coin had been devalued to the point where we could no longer be called bona fide members of the current show-biz upper strata. Though I had no great monetary reserves with which to exhibit any rash extravagances in order to consolidate my tenuous position, London was still a relatively inexpensive town in which to party.

Chelsea was still a bohemian village where the bright young things strolled up and down the pavement like puffed-up peacocks in the summer sun daring society to disapprove of their vulgar and showy lifestyle. Carnaby Street, just across the road from the London Palladium, was the hub of the youth-oriented fashion industry and for the first time shops like Donis or John Stephen would sell you a pair of trousers that actually fitted and flared magnificently without the need to have your mother insert a wedge of material into the seam at the bottom. The corporate stores with their unlimited financial resources were still years away from monopolising the high streets and eliminating the owner-operated shops which in those days gave each thoroughfare a deliciously different identity.

London from the mid sixties through to the early seventies was a paparazzi-free swinging city and deserved every bit of its reputation. On any day you could catch one of the Rolling Stones or the Beatles passing you by unmolested as they shopped for garish apparel in the trendy boutiques. By night they would frequent the clubs which were increasing in number almost weekly. You could usually find a Beatle rubbing shoulders with Rudolph Nureyev in the Ad Lib just off Leicester Square or in the Scotch of St James a hundred yards or so to the south of Piccadilly. Georgie Fame could be found delivering his appetising offerings of jazz and blues at the Flamingo in Wardour Street. The Bag of Nails, Samantha's and the Valbonne were also open for your business.

The Speakeasy on Margaret Street was a huge success right from its opening and a guaranteed hangout for most members of the musical glitterati. I recall walking in there one night to find a party in full swing. And not just any party. The Monkees and the Beatles, plus a number of lesser but still great names, were in a back-slapping mutual congratulatory mood doubtless aided by alcohol and whatever was around.

And if you didn't manage to pass your favourite on the street you could go and see them in concert, perhaps at the Odeon in Hammersmith or the Astoria (later to become the Rainbow) in Finsbury Park. In the years before his untimely death in 1967 I had done so for nothing as a guest of Brian Epstein who had acquired the Saville

Theatre on Shaftesbury Avenue. It proved to be an unsuccessful venture for the Beatles' manager, a crippling burden which haemorrhaged money from Brian's NEMS Enterprises, and with his usual immaculate taste he presented some legendary names. But hindsight proved that it was perhaps equally important to keep an eye on the supporting cast.

Fats Domino was a legend whose performance was as perfect as you would ever get from a fifties rock & roll star. His arrangements and tempos were unusually true to the original records and his set was faultless. He was a worthy headliner. But further down the bill almost unnoticed at the opening of the show was a five-piece group who had just come over from Australia where they had already achieved considerable success and were trying to break into the international big time. They were called the Bee Gees and I didn't pay too much attention. Pretty soon though the whole world would notice them.

On another occasion I went to the Saville to see one of my favourite soul singers Garnett Mimms who, with his group the Enchanters, had recorded a magnificent song called *Cry Baby* which I adored. As brilliant as he was he meant less than nothing to the majority of the audience most of who had actually come to check out a newer sensation who was making waves everywhere. The understated and now slightly old fashioned Mimms had no chance against the wild antics of guitar hero Jimi Hendrix whose exclamation mark to a display of unbelievable virtuosity, the likes of which had never been seen before in Britain, was to set his guitar on fire. Try following that.

I had in fact seen Hendrix briefly in my favourite haunt the Cromwellian soon after his arrival in the UK. Someone had pointed out a rather weird looking black guy who had come down the stairs. 'That's Chas Chandler's new discovery. He's just brought him over from the States,' my friend said. Chandler was the Animals' bassist and had spotted the future star at the Café Wha? in Greenwich Village, New York. Jimi's haircut was still quite short I remember and while his clothes were unconventional even for a rock musician it was a long way from the gaudy flamboyance that was to become his trademark.

The Cromwellian was a wonderful place where the Steam Packet, featuring Rod Stewart, Long John Baldry and Julie Driscoll, with Mickey Waller on drums and Brian Auger on keyboards played so often they were almost looked on as the house band. The club was situated on a corner of the Cromwell Road and Exhibition Road and in those freedom-filled days you could actually park your car on the main road outside without the fear of being clamped or towed away. Downstairs, once they had passed Norah on the door its patrons could eat, drink and bop the night away to live music or a disco while the ground floor bar was the domain of ultra camp barman Harry 'the Heart'. Harry dispensed drinks and mildly barbed witticisms to his customers, every one of whom he referred to as 'darling heart', while sipping elegantly at his giant bowl of Campari and soda. I had a lot of fun at the 'Crom'.

Occasionally I would venture further out for my entertainment. I spotted that Eartha Kitt was due to appear at Caesar's Palace, a prestigious night-club in Luton, about fifty miles north of London. With fond memories of our pleasant and amiable evening with this nice lady at EMI a few years before and clutching my photographs of that meeting I set off with a friend up the M1 motorway. The valet parked the gleaming Jaguar and I was given a seat right at the front. Evidently, I still had clout in the wilds of Bedfordshire. Any nearer and I would have been part of the performance.

Eartha's show was slick, dramatic and marvellously camp and she purred her way through a collection of musical *double entendres* that had the audience eating out of her hands. The sultry sex kitten persona that had been and still was her trademark for a couple of decades might have been in danger of entering the realms of pastiche but I loved it and applauded wildly along with everyone.

Behind her on the stage wielding the baton was musical director Tony Osborne who I knew well and who had been present at the EMI session. His son Gary Osborne, later to write hit songs for Elton John and Kiki Dee amongst others, was also a friend of mine. That I figured would make things a little easier when I nipped backstage afterwards for a pleasant reunion with the delightful Miss Kitt. At least it was all good in theory.

We were led by a member of staff to a corridor outside the star dressing room and left for what seemed like a period of time almost as long as the show I had just enjoyed. Small countries have been created and overthrown in less time than I stood there waiting. Eventually the door opened and we were invited in to be greeted warmly by Tony Osborne who broke the ice by asking me if I'd seen Gary lately. I replied that I hadn't seen him for a while. Eartha on the other hand was sitting there looking like she's just plopped her stilettos into a pile of elephants dung and with a glare that could have burst a boil at ten paces.

'What do you want of me?' she asked in a menacing tone that indicated a challenge rather than a genuine inquiry. It occurred to me that this was going to be a bumpy ride. It sounded all the more unpleasant for being delivered in that indeterminate vibrato-enhanced accent that had always puzzled me. She had been born in America but somehow managed to affect a dialect that might have sounded more natural in a remote colony on the planet Tharg. I had always been intrigued by it. Now I felt threatened.

I had in fact sent a short explanatory note ahead of me but figured that maybe she had not received or understood it. I reminded her of the EMI recording session and the photos taken of us together. It cut no ice. 'What do you really want of me?' she continued, the tone even more unpleasant and emphasised with the pointed 'really'. It was an odd question and I was not quite sure how best to answer.

'Well, I thought it would be nice to have you sign the pictures for me.' Still in shock I was trying to maintain my composure and foolishly believed that keeping it light might somehow do the trick. God, was I naïve in those days.

'Give me one reason why I should sign your photographs' she demanded. It was most definitely a demand, not a question. How was I supposed to reply to something like that? Remembering my John Lennon incident I began to wonder if I'd ever learn that perhaps it is best to keep your idols tucked a safe distance away in your rose-coloured memory banks and not attempt to enter their idiosyncratic and distorted versions of reality. 'I suppose there's no reason why you should sign them' I replied. I was not about to lower myself by begging this dreadful woman for a favour.

'Then I refuse to sign your photographs,' she declared. Tony Osborne sat by silently, unable to come up with any suitable rescue plan for this rapidly deteriorating situation. My mind was buzzing with possible options with regard to a suitable comeback. I considered telling her to stick her signature up her arse but in the end decided that perhaps a touch of dignity might be more infuriating to the old witch. 'Old witch' had now replaced the previous 'nice lady' in my assessment of Eartha go-fuck-yourself Kitt.

'Well, thank you anyway. I enjoyed the show very much.' She ignored the compliment. I bade farewell to Tony and along with my friend I exited this chamber of doom and gloom feeling sorry for Osborne who did not even have the option of leaving this rude woman to wallow in her own mire.

I have often wondered whether I dealt with Eartha in the right way. I had kept my cool but afterwards felt very frustrated at not having vented my anger and brought this extremely unpleasant and obnoxious person to book. I know that if it had happened again she would certainly have felt the sharp end of my tongue. I managed to catch one of her last shows before she died. It was at the Carlyle Hotel in New York and at the age of 81 she delivered a mesmerising performance and proved that she was a unique artiste of immeasurable talent. Temperamental and spiteful she may have been but all that went before counted for nothing. She was simply magnificent.

As a post script to this sorry incident I do have the satisfaction of discovering that she behaved pretty much the same to the Supremes in the sixties and even more remarkably to Sir Elton John in 2005 so I am in fairly good company. I have been slagged off with the best of them.

Elsewhere in the stellar firmament my dealings with its heavenly bodies were somewhat more pleasant. There are nasty divas and there are nice ones. Dusty Springfield was one of the nice ones and in the years since joining the band until she defected to the States at the end of 1970 in a futile attempt to achieve the kind of success and, more importantly, to lead the kind of lifestyle she felt was denied her in the UK, I saw quite a bit of her.

Along with Dusty came her brother Tom Springfield and their friend Peppi Borza, an American dancer who had settled in Britain to pursue an entertainment career. For a while, he was a fairly successful exponent of the current dance fads with his act Peppi and the New York Twisters.

Tom and Dusty were fun people. Their eccentric Irish parents, Catherine (Kay) and Gerrard (O.B.) O'Brien, had handed down to them a quirky sense of humour that was off the wall and infectious. These days it would be considered Pythonesque. Tom was a paradox. Lacking any affectation or pretence despite his great successes as a songwriter and producer he seemed to glide through life surrounded by a constant aura of calm. Simplicity was his watchword.

For a time he equipped his spacious apartment in the Vale, a chic address situated directly off the King's Road, with nothing but paper plates and plastic cups and cutlery. figuring that life was too short to wash up. And every item of clothing in his wardrobe was in the same style and in the same shade of khaki. For Tom during this particular period of his life there was never any need to decide what to wear on any given day. Odd as it might seem to some there is a definite sense of logic to this particular way of thinking. It almost has a Zen feel about it.

On the other hand he certainly had moments of eccentricity his parents would have been proud of. At birth he was given the exotic name of Dionysius which was predictably shortened to Dion (pronounced Die-on and not, as many mistakenly believe, Dee-on) while Dusty was plain old Mary. When pop stardom beckoned and the Springfields were formed their chosen pseudonyms went in opposite directions on the glamour scale. Mary became the mysterious and intriguing Dusty while the colourful Dionysius was curiously slummed down to the more mundane Tom.

I received a postcard from him one day which stated that Tom Springfield no longer wished to be known as Tom Springfield. He now wished to be known as Dionysius Plonk. My mind spent a few moments boggling and then I dismissed it. I never paid to spend too much time figuring out the O'Briens. Knitting fog would be easier. A month or two later a second card arrived. It seemed that I was to ignore the previous one and that we were back to Tom Springfield again. Thank goodness, I thought. Sanity reigns. Or at least it did for a while.

Another period passed and a third card dropped on my mat. Tom Springfield now wished to be known as Dionysius Dionysius. By now I was numb. I made a mental note to find out more the next time I spoke to Tom - sorry - Dionysius Dionysius. In the end it didn't matter. A fourth missal brought us back to page one again. Tom Springfield was back with us and there, thankfully, things remained. I never did pluck up the courage to ask him why.

In contrast to her on-stage character of a sophisticated lady complete with elaborate hair, eye make-up and bejewelled gowns her quirky idea of fun ran from the legendary bouts of plate smashing, occasionally at the side of the stage while we were performing a particularly soft and poignant number, to mimicking the voice of Bluebottle, a character from the ground breaking and zany fifties radio comedy series the Goon Show.

Tom and Dusty, in the long and tedious confines of studio rehearsals or cramped cabaret dressing rooms, would often rewrite the lyrics to the songs they performed in the Springfields. A line in *Silver Threads And Golden Needles* was altered from *'I drown myself in sorrows'* to *'I drown myself in custard'* while the title of her first solo hit, *I Only Want To Be With You*, became *I Only Ordered One Meat Stew.*

In the sixties and seventies if you wanted cheap and colourful entertainment with a wicked and slightly vulgar edge to it, the pub circuit around the capital provided for your needs in the form of an enormous number of drag artistes who strutted their stuff and shocked their audiences with the kind of vulgarity and camp innuendo that was rarely allowed into our living rooms via the television, with the exception of Danny La Rue who was considered by both the establishment and by royalty to be respectable. These were still rather innocent times, and cocks in frocks were still considered shocking.

Hostelries like the Black Cap, the Cricketers and the Vauxhall Tavern packed their bars with crowds that blurred the lines between gay and straight. East End dockers drank side by side with those of a quite different persuasion although appearances can often be deceptive, and more than a few of those dockers found it very easy to be persuaded to succumb at the end of a boozy evening and often went in search of such illicit adventure.

Our favourite stop was the Union Tavern in Kennington just across the Vauxhall Bridge where Lee Sutton reigned supreme. Clad in the kind of pantomimic over-the-top brocade trouser suit that no real woman would dare to be seen in he would use and abuse his devoted followers nightly unleashing the sharpest of tongues and armed with the quickest of wits. Hecklers would be destroyed in a nano-second and revelled in every masochistic moment of their discomfort. Beautifully crafted standards that had been slaved over lovingly by talented songwriters would have their meanings mangled by Sutton's home-grown lyrics. The big hit song from Fiddler On The Roof now became *If I Was A Rich Bitch* while *If They Could See Me Now* from Sweet Charity kept its title but now contained rhymes like *If she could see me now you'd hear my mother say, I told you so, I knew he'd go the other way.* Nothing and no one was sacred.

Dusty loved Lee Sutton. When our bunch paid a visit at least a couple of us had to get there early to reserve a table and defend the vacant seats against all comers until 'Madame' arrived. You could hardly expect Dusty to stand in the middle of that mighty crush and she never arrived on time. She had turned late-coming into an art form. The reactions were not always pleasant when people were turned away from the apparent free spaces on our table for six but all was forgiven when the great diva arrived. The only person a Union Tavern crowd loved more than Lee Sutton was Dusty Springfield. Well, maybe Bette Davis would have created a bigger stir.

As a devoted tennis groupie she enjoyed hanging around with her chums Rosie Casals and Billie Jean King whenever they were in London for the tournaments at Wimbledon or Queen's and Tom would throw impromptu parties at the Chelsea apartment which was spacious enough for a decent knees-up. Rosie and Billie Jean were fun people and bonded well with their new celebrity pal.

I got a call one morning towards the end of Wimbledon fortnight as I was lying in bed in my newly-purchased detached house in Yeading. Dusty wanted to go to the tennis and could find no-one around who would take her. She had centre court and players enclosure tickets, precious items that some people would kill for. But I had no particular interest in the sport and anyway I had made arrangements to go out to dinner that evening.

My excuses cut no ice and she was a hard person to refuse. She pleaded until I gave in on the understanding that I had to leave at six p.m. We had a great time. The summer sun shone with a vengeance and in the break we scoffed miniscule portions of horrendously expensive strawberries and cream. She had a glass of champagne. I was still teetotal. On returning to our seats an Australian guy in the seat next to me turned and spoke. He was holding a choc-ice in each hand. 'Excuse me mate' he said in an almost exaggerated Antipodean tongue, 'I've just bought these ice creams but my friend doesn't seem to have come back. I wondered if you'd want one?'

I was not at all in the mood for one but I felt it would be churlish to refuse the kind offer so I accepted with thanks and took the ice. 'That'll be one and sixpence please.' I was so stunned all I could do was fish in my pocket for coins and hand over the dosh while Dusty surveyed the scene. 'What did he say?' she asked. I told her and she shrieked and when Dusty shrieked there was no avoiding it. In fact neither of us could stop laughing for the next ten minutes much to the annoyance of the prim and staid tennis fans around us.

There has come to be little doubt about Dusty's sexuality, particularly in the wake of revelations that came to light after her death, but Peppi insisted to me that there were men she had been involved with. He knew them but never supplied me with any names. I think he was just trying to point out that things are rarely as black and white as they seem.

Dusty talked to me with great enthusiasm about the attributes and attractions of footballers. In particular she liked their muscular frames and the thickness of their thighs. The fact that I hung around with Chelsea soccer star Alan Hudson fascinated her and she encouraged me to organise a dinner at my house so that she could meet him. I had known 'Huddy' from his early days at the club when he was a junior in the first team squad and we used to spend most evenings in the pubs of the King's Road or at Alexander's restaurant underneath the Markham pub. His brother John had been a Chelsea player too, along with my good friend Barry Lloyd, but failed to make the grade. Alan was the one with the magic feet in the Hudson family.

On the appointed night I prepared the food and waited for the guests. I had organised a friend of mine called Tony Lynch to round up the diners in his very smart Rolls Royce Silver Cloud and ferry them out to the Yeading house, picking up Dusty and Peppi first and then going on the collect Alan Hudson and his footy playing colleague Tony Frewin. The Hudson home in Chelsea was a prefab, one of those ready-made temporary dwellings that had been erected soon after the war to alleviate the acute housing shortage. Top-flight footballers had plenty of status back then but precious little reward to match their profile or talent.

When the vehicle eventually pulled up outside my house it was two passengers light. Apparently Alan's mother had opened the door and explained that a friend had been involved in an accident and that they had to rush to the hospital. The main purpose of the dinner had suddenly been eliminated but we had a fun night anyway. I was to learn from Alan some time later that they had been at home all the time hiding in a back room and too scared and unsure of themselves to spend an evening with such a star as Dusty Springfield.

Dusty liked to drink but I only saw her really smashed on one occasion. I called by one evening at her smart modern town house just off the Bayswater Road between Holland Park and Notting Hill. She had purchased 38 Aubrey Walk in 1968 but spent some time and a considerable amount of money in bringing it up to her exacting demands before finally taking up residence in '69.

It was not a large house by London standards but it impressed the hell out of me with its clean modern lines, white walls and ultra-fashionable downlights set in the ceiling. The bathroom was pretty special. An enormous burgundy tub with a Greek key design round the rim in gold and recesses at each end for gold cushions on which bathers could sit (you could comfortably fit two in there) was a special order from Bonsack's.

At first Aubrey Walk was shared with her pal the soul singer Madeleine Bell, who had initially attracted attention when the American musical Black Nativity hit London, and who stayed on to become a solo artiste and renowned backing vocalist. But when the friendship cooled Norma Tanega moved in to take care of Miss Springfield and she always needed a great deal of looking after. Norma had achieved a modest degree of fame with her hit *Walking My Cat Named Dog* but for the moment had forsaken the pop world for art and spent much of her time working on her very idiosyncratic modern paintings.

I had driven there in my mini, leaving the more glamourous E-type at home, as we intended to go out clubbing, but in the end Norma opted to stay home and it was just Dusty, Peppi and I who headed for a club called Yours And Mine situated on Kensington High Street in the basement beneath a Spanish restaurant called El Sombrero. The restaurant, run by a Swiss entrepreneur by the name of Harry Laubscher and his young Italian friend Amadeo, had experienced mixed fortunes but turning the virtually unused below ground space into a meeting place for a mixed but mainly gay clientele proved to be a goldmine.

Again the patrons ran the gamut from militantly gay through androgynous to hopelessly heterosexual and the atmosphere was always lively. On this night it was packed and naturally the buzz increased with the arrival of a celebrity and one who was a gay icon. She drank Bacardi and Coke along with Peppi. I bypassed the Bacardi and stuck to plain Coke, the drinking kind of course. Once more the conversation turned to sportsmen and her fascination for footballers. Her object of adoration this time was the Leeds goalkeeper Gary Sprake whose curly blond locks and boyish charm she went on about at length. Gay or not, and I never ever asked her outright about her sexuality and neither did she about mine, she certainly seemed to genuinely have the hots for this golden goalie.

When it came time for us to call it a night Peppi was nowhere to be seen. We learned later that Dusty and I had been so engrossed in conversation that he felt out of it, got bored and grabbed a cab home. We got up to leave and a very unsteady Dusty wavered through the throng as best she could in the light of all the booze she had consumed. As she headed towards the exit a woman came towards her and, throwing her arms around her, planted a smacker of a kiss full on the lips and she responded. I was both amazed and amused. Dusty usually went to great lengths to avoid any such public display that might give cause for even more gossip than she already had to contend with. But on the other hand it was rather sweet to see her so relaxed and open for a change.

The red Austin Mini was parked just a few yards along the street and we got in. I started the engine and was about to move off but she obviously had things on her mind. Holding my hand she started to talk about her body clock ticking away and how she longed to have a child before it was too late and she appeared to be very much in earnest. She suggested that if we had a child together it would be a beautiful baby and that she'd take all the responsibility for looking after it. Fair comment I thought as long as it had her singing voice and not mine.

The thought of fathering a child, when even in my mid-twenties I still felt like a gullible and naïve teenager, was a frightening one. As far as I was concerned if I wanted to hear the patter of tiny feet I would put shoes on my cats. She loosened her grip and to my absolute astonishment placed one of her hands slap bang in my groin to where my small, limp appendage was cowering in absolute terror beneath a worryingly thin piece of clothing. If the hand had remained for much longer there is little doubt that arousal would have occurred but momentous decisions made in the heat of passion are almost always doomed to disaster. A hard-on does not count as personal growth.

It wasn't that I couldn't have managed the dirty deed. I have been required to wield my puny pod of passion on many occasions and over the years I have often wondered, had I called her bluff, what the results and consequences would have been. But it was all too sudden and unexpected. She had caught me completely on the hop. And she was an international star while I was virtually a fallen idol with a huge inferiority complex.

In the event it all began and ended so quickly that the pressure was suddenly off. She realised that perhaps this was not the time and place and she was not in the most rational state of mind for such important matters to be decided upon. We sped off back to Aubrey Walk and to Norma, who was highly amused at the legless Dusty and proceeded to take pictures with my little Kodak instamatic camera.

Soon after her death when my book Travelling Man was published a columnist for the Express newspaper commented that perhaps it was fortunate that Miss Springfield was no longer around to confirm or deny the story. I sympathised with him. The most scurrilous and untrue stories are certainly apt to surface after someone's demise. But in fact mine was confirmed both before and afterwards.

In early 1999 I had written to Dusty, then in the last stages of cancer and being cared for by her devoted fan and backing singer Simon Bell, not to be confused with Simon Napier-Bell the co-lyricist of *You Don't Have To Say You Love Me.* I wanted her to okay what I wanted to put in the book and mentioned the episode. She replied to say that it was fine to publish but to be careful about writing too much. Even then, knowing her time was coming, she was still very protective about her private life.

She admitted she had forgotten the 'willy fiddling' episode and added 'I must have been smashed - or intrigued.' I wrote back this time relating every detail of that night. After her funeral in Henley, Simon Bell, who I had never met until then, sought me out to thank me and to say that he had come to tell me what a hysterical time they had reading the story together. They had both laughed so much over the letter as the memories came flooding back, and it brought a lot of fun to her life at a very low point. I felt very good about that.

Further confirmation came later in a letter from her old tour manager and lighting designer Fred Perry who all these years later was living in Los Angeles and running an art gallery. I still have his letter dated August 17th 2000 in which he says that Dusty used to tell him everything 'and I stress everything' he added. Apparently they were out one day and she asked Fred what he thought of me. He told her he thought I was quite fanciable and asked why. Then she told him about what she referred to as 'the incident'.

I have no idea whether Dusty ever told Norma about her proposed sexual shenanigans. Maybe I'll get to ask her myself one day. Days with the great and unforgettable Dusty were great days indeed.

26

RCA

By 1970 we were once more without a recording contract. That was bad. But, having vacillated for far too long, we had at last grasped the nettle and done something about the extended apathy surrounding the drummer situation. That was good.

Billy Adamson was born on May 27th 1944 and raised in the Bellshill district of Glasgow. His band, the Bellrocks, had featured a talented young singer by the name of Marie McDonald McLaughlin Lawrie who was eventually to become a major star known by the much more catchy name of Lulu. After moving down to London, a transfer which every serious Scottish musician had to at least consider if he wanted to give himself a chance of climbing up the shaky ladder to success in the music industry, he served terms with Jet Harris, Emile Ford and Sonny Child & the TNT, the band that had coincidentally shared the stage with us on our short stay with the Roy Orbison tour in April 1967

The job with the black American soul singer Sonny Child finally came to an end and he had been patiently sitting things out and waiting for offers in a small flat which he shared with his young Scottish schoolteacher wife Pat in Fitzjohn's Avenue in Hampstead, a leafy street running parallel to the busy Finchley Road in North London. In fact the recruitment into our ranks almost never happened at all.

Shades of the Terry Noone situation occurred when, barely a day after my having delivered the good news to Billy, Mike and John phoned down from Liverpool to tell me they'd changed their minds. They did not now feel he was right for the group. Whether it was the look or the playing technique I'm not quite sure but the thought of having to pull the rug from under the poor guy's feet horrified me and I fought his corner with the result that, without Billy realising there had been any such crisis, the move was back on.

A letter to the BBC from John McNally on January 12th informed them that Billy Adamson had replaced John Blunt on drums. We were due to record a session for the

Terry Wogan show two days later for the stratospheric fee of forty-five pounds to be broadcast between the twentieth and the twenty-sixth of that month. Pro-rata that worked out at nine pounds per show, remembering that the fee was for the entire group and not per person. Nobody got rich on BBC recordings. We were also booked for a February recording of the Jimmy Young show to go out in March and despite our letter, Blunt's name remained on the contract. However by April the Beeb had finally realised that our membership had changed and Adamson's name was included in their paperwork.

His look certainly was at odds with everything the oh-so-clean-cut Searchers were presumed to be all about. An Afro haircut that threatened to take over the world and pair of oversize spectacles were not what people expected. But as we were going through one of our sadder sartorial adventures in the form of a series of casual and contrived stage outfits that were so awful they really should have been illegal, his avant-garde image did not look quite as awful as it might otherwise have done. 'Avant' it might have been but in the light of things maybe we would have been wiser to let our 'garde' down and stuck to our 'Searcher-Man' suits.

We were clutching at straws. The world of pop apparel was changing and we felt we were getting left behind. Instead of realising the strengths of our established image, which was such a classic one that it proved in time to transcend all passing fashion fads, we tried in vain to regain our 'cool' quotient by dipping into the nursery dressing-up box and playing at being trendy. Such things have to occur naturally or the odds are that it is never going to work. It did not for us.

Our futile and quite laughable attempts at keeping up with the latest rock & roll fashions, which were themselves soon to look passé and almost tame when compared to the outrageous glam and glitter that hit the scene barely a few years, nearly resulted in disaster during a club tour of Southern Ireland. It was at the beginning of what was to be known as 'the troubles' and a bubbling anti-British sentiment was growing with a slow but menacing certainty.

Presenting our show was no problem. We hit them with the old songs they knew and loved and they responded with the kind of enthusiastic applause we had always received and indeed expected in what we looked on as a country full of warm and friendly folk. We left the stage at the end of our set satisfied that we had another success under our belts. A couple of very angry looking young Irish lads rushed to where we were putting our instruments away in the dressing room.

'Tell your drummer to take that fucking shirt off' one of them yelled in a tone that told us in no uncertain terms this was no laughing matter. We looked over to Billy. Oh, my God. Oblivious to its significance in this particular setting he was wearing his usual short sleeved Union Jack shirt, an item that up to now we had just looked on as a nice, colourful, fun piece of clothing. Wearing such a garment in Dublin in those delicate times when people were getting killed or maimed for their allegiance to the British Crown was akin to sticking up two fingers and shouting 'fuck the Pope' in O'Connell Street. It was removed with great haste. Well, anyone can make a mistake, said the Dalek as he climbed down off the dustbin.

Up to now our dealings in that part of the world had been nothing but pleasant. Steeped in a history of musical appreciation that favoured heavily our kind of middle of the road and country-influenced pop we were welcomed with open arms. And we in turn loved the charming eccentricity of Irish logic.

We found it necessary to ask directions on many occasions and, without wishing to be in the slightest patronising, the replies were often uniquely Irish. 'Ah to be sure, if I was going there I wouldn't start from here.' Simply fabulous. There were others. 'Well, I tell you what. You head straight on to the town and then you just follow the flow of the traffic. But there won't be any traffic at this time of night.'

One night in a little country village while waiting for our turn to appear at midnight in what seemed like a deserted cowshed we set out into the square to find coffee. There it was listed on the side of the burger van and so we ordered. 'Ah, we don't sell coffee.' We pointed to the writing on the side of his stall. He leaned over the counter and looked at it as if he had seen it for the first time. 'Oh, to be sure, that was there when I bought the thing.'

We turned up at a country ballroom one night a little before showtime only to find little or nothing happening. We soon discovered that the owner had sold the place a few weeks before. We never performed that night.

But the maddest eccentricity of all came when we had to rush from one venue to another for the second half of a very tight double. We leapt into our car at the end of the first set and sped off leaving our roadie, Chris Cottrell, to collect our guitars together and follow on. When by showtime he had not appeared we were forced to borrow instruments from the resident show-band in order to play. At the end of the night we found him outside sitting in the minibus. He had arrived in plenty of time but despite explaining to the intransigent man on the door that he was a part of our organisation and was bringing our instruments he was refused entry unless he paid the entrance fee. Where else could that happen? It's a wonderful and unique country indeed.

Our public profile had slipped considerably in just a couple of years and we realised the importance of being in the public eye and ear. An internal letter dated September 29th 1970 from M. Lipscombe to the booking department of the BBC informed them that the Searchers would like to do more live shows for them and that we had particularly expressed an interest in Radio One Club, a big listening programme for the youth market at the time. Apparently we also wished it to be pointed out that we could do covers of hit parade numbers and that *Needles And Pins* need not form part of our repertoire unless particularly asked for. There was an air of mild desperation in our camp. As compensation the fee for a radio session had risen to an extravagant fifty pounds.

By the middle of 1971 we had moved agencies, the Harold Davison organisation having been bought out by Gordon Mills' MAM in New Bond Street. Our bookings were handled from there by Barry Dickins, one of the go-ahead and ambitious young bloods in the industry, and we had been without a recording contract for two years, the longest time since *Sweets For My Sweet* shot to the top in 1963. We were far from being the latest rage any more and were in great danger of joining the ranks of the untouchables. Rescue came in the form of the giant RCA company whose UK operation was enjoying great success with acts like David Bowie and the Sweet. As the penchant for androgyny, cross-dressing and tinsel caught the imagination of the great record-buying public, tykes in tights and guys in glitter were challenging the accepted perceptions of manhood and young women's make-up bags were no longer safe from the prying hands of their fashion-conscious boyfriends and husbands.

Thankfully they were also a company with enough traditional instincts and background to cater for the middle-of-the-road market, and had the Everly Brothers and Neil Sedaka under contract as well as ourselves. The Everlys, like us, were swimming against the tide having enjoyed their time in the sun and could not manage to ease themselves back into the best sellers despite making some excellent albums like *Pass The Chicken And Listen* and *Stories We Could Tell.* It would be a while yet before these temporarily fallen idols would hang on in there long enough to become living legends, at least on the concert circuit if not in the charts. Sedaka on the other hand had managed to once again place his finger on the pulse of popular taste and had come back with a very impressive album for RCA, *Emergence*, and a bunch of songs that would provide new hits for the likes of Kiki Dee and Andy Williams.

Our inclusion on RCA's books was due to the unbridled enthusiasm of Richard Swainson, a young executive in the A&R department and a keen Searchers enthusiast. Whether his overall bosses Olaf Wiper and, lower down on the scale, Mike Everett were quite as keen is uncertain. In our meetings with them they were distant and po-faced. There was no warmth towards us. But Swainson was given a reasonably free hand to organise our future with the company. It was apparent from the start that apart from launching an assault on the charts with brand new singles that would fit with the current tastes in music, he would dearly like us at some point to re-record a selection of our old hits. We made it quite clear that we were very much against such a move. Like most artistes we hated the idea of new versions of songs that were revered as little pieces of the sound track of our lives.

Facilities were now far superior to those available in our Pye days but perfection was not the point. Indeed we had learned to love the little mistakes we had somehow missed in our old speedy and simple four-track recordings. Any beautifully executed lines and multi-layered facsimiles we might be able to construct in a state-of-the-art modern studio would not and could not compensate for the natural feel of an original recording which captured the zeitgeist of the moment. Richard accepted our arguments on that point – for the time being at least – and we were signed up on the principle that we would be tackling new material.

The producer chosen for our first release on the new label was David Paramor, the nephew of the legendary Norrie Paramor the man who, amongst his other achievements, was the guiding light behind Cliff Richard. David existed under the broad shadow of his famous uncle and, having yet to prove himself, was keen to be the one to bring us back into public favour. He was an all round nice guy and we bonded very well.

Together we agreed on a Valerie Avon/Harold Spiro song called *Desdemona*, the demo of which was played and sung by a still up and coming Elton John. It was catchy and up-tempo although not a typical Searchers sound by any means, if indeed there was ever such a thing. In fact the variation in style, tempo and content of our recording repertoire through the years was quite remarkable for a group that had somehow acquired a fairly solid image of sweet melody embellished by rich harmonies.

It hit the stores – those that bothered to order any copies – in August 1971, and received virtually no airplay and promptly stiffed. On the other side of the big pond there was some consolation when it reached number 94 in the Billboard charts, on account of the fact that the wife of a small regional radio station took a shine to it and insisted on a heavy rotation for the track. Local sales took it into the listings for a week or two before it went back into hiding, never to be seen again.

We could perhaps have pretended that people were simply confused with another song of the same name released sometime previously by John's Children in 1967 and one that was banned by the BBC for containing the (for that time) racy lyrics 'lift up your skirt and fly'. I recall one night at a party given by journalist David Wigg in his central London house trying to encourage DJ Alan Freeman to give it a spin but he stated firmly that it was too late for a song that had already failed by someone else and not too long ago at that. I realised at that point that he had never even listened to it. He had simply assumed it was the same song. But sensing his resolute disinterest I gave up trying to press the point. I had long since discovered that when an act was out of favour disc jockeys avoided it as if they had a particularly contagious disease. Scared stiff of their own inevitable ageing process in a youth-oriented business they fear failure by association. We were out of favour and therefore infected.

In truth I think the record managed to die on its own account with no other help or hindrance at all from the cloned Marc Bolan title. It was a good track. Not our best but neither were we ashamed of it. But it was gone and all the excuses in the world would not bring it back. For us it was a case of onwards and downwards.

Having tried his best and failed, Paramor was passed over for the next try and instead Swainson placed us with Phil Swern and Johnny Arthey. Arthey was an established big band leader and arranger whose name was more often heard in connection with variety entertainment and radio shows, while Swern was a pop archivist who had a musical brain that buzzed with the kind of facts and figures that could both fascinate and amaze. His knowledge of popular music was extensive to say the least. As a fan, cognisant of the contribution the Searchers had made to the industry, he looked on it as a labour of love to raise us back to where he felt we belonged.

Love Is Everywhere was written by Hot Chocolate vocalist Errol Brown and the fact that it had not been used as one of their own A-sides should have given us the clue that it was possibly not one of his strongest songs. Hot Chocolate had enjoyed a string of big hits which owed as much to Brown's strong visual image and one of the most idiosyncratic vocal styles on the record scene as it did to the excellent material he rolled out with ease.

As the session ground to a close and the last notes were played and sung there was a tiny moment of tension when, fifteen minutes after Swern and Arthey had begun to mix, they pronounced the task completed. John McNally was horrified. We were all well aware that no matter how long and hard one had toiled in the studio it was often in the laborious yet all-important mixing process, an art form in itself, that hits were made or lost. Fortunately, they were open to reason and recommenced the task with John looking on anxiously until we eventually arrived at a mix we could all accept.

The result was a workmanlike recording that was hypnotic and tuneful but once again lacked that 'difference factor' that was now needed to grab the attention of those who were to buy the product. Stripped of Brown's distinctive styling it was just another good record. It was no longer good enough to deliver a track that people might like to have. We were now at the point where we had to come out with a disc that people could not stop themselves from buying despite their preconceptions and prejudices. And, pleasant as it was, this was not that disc. But at least Swainson and RCA seemed undeterred although that was possibly due more to Richard's enthusiastic support rather than the record company's continuing faith in us. He appeared committed and in particular seemed besotted with Mike Pender. We were soon to find out just how besotted.

There were perks at RCA that we had never enjoyed during our previous contracts. Pye, despite the enormous income that the Searchers must have generated for them, barely put their hands in their pockets at all. The only lavish reception (if one could call a gathering at the Lotus House Chinese restaurant just across from the studios as lavish) I recall while under that banner was as much for Dionne Warwick as it was for their top-selling act and headliners of an important upcoming tour. Maybe more so. They were easily impressed by an American diva. There were no limousines laid on for us and if they had been their costs would have been deducted from any royalties due.

Our time at Liberty Records too had been a passing phase that seemed to go as soon as it had come. There were no frills, no perks, no cars or grand receptions. We came. We recorded. We left. Oh yes, I forgot. And we argued before leaving.

But when we took breaks in our RCA sessions they picked up the tab for the food and drinks. And when our van broke down in Leicester one day we got Mike to ring up Richard at home in London and talk him into coming to our rescue, which he did while barely pausing for breath. After our show Richard was waiting and we were ushered into a huge Daimler limousine and chauffeured back to town in luxury. Furthermore, while our Ford Transit was being repaired he organised a replacement with the bill being sent to RCA, never to be seen by us again.

These little expenses would have been set against our account somewhere along the way but as we weren't generating any income by way of sales such matters were of little or no consequence to us. The way things were going they might be the only profit we would ever see. We might as well enjoy them. The Liberty adventure had resulted in nil royalties so a Daimler limo and a free van hire from RCA had put us quids in already.

As the two whizz kid producers presented so far had provided no successful results we decided to take matters into our own hands and went into the studios with nothing but a few self-penned songs and some vague idea of what we wanted to sound like. Of the tracks put down it was one of John McNally's, an attractive tune written in waltz time, that seemed to have the most appeal. But a waltz did not exactly fit the idea of what the public would go for. The solution? Change the rhythm and the meter to something more commercial while retaining the actual lyrics and melody.

What we ended up with was a quite catchy reggae style song with a mass chorus that with a bit of luck we thought might just insinuate itself into the consciousness of our defecting customers and drag them back into the fold. This was not to be, but for one week *Sing Singer Sing* sat at the number one position of the charts in Bangkok. Okay, it was one week only and in a far-off land but a number one is still a number one in our book.

So at least there was still the tiniest glimmer of hope and RCA were not about to abandon us yet but we felt the need to keep them sweet so we finally capitulated on the point of re-recordings. A week in the studios resulted in *Second Take*, a 'best of' style of album which contained new versions of the best remembered of our singles and album tracks plus *Desdemona* and the B-side of *Sing Singer Sing*. It was neither a labour of love nor a source of pride. We could legitimately rename it *Second Take - The Worst of the Best of the Searchers*. The songs retained for the most part, although not in their entirety, the original arrangements but we were ten years down the line and now played them differently.

On the sleeve we looked more like a seventies wannabee outfit styled somewhere between Crosby Stills & Nash and Creedence Clearwater Revival but without the natural authenticity and certainly without a current roster of hits to brag about. Gone were the smart suits to be replaced by dubious casual attire set off by an abundance of hair that can only now be seen in vintage shopping catalogues. John had acquired a beard while I was displaying an unseemly expanse of flesh underneath a flimsy vest and tresses down to my shoulders. Mike wore a large-collared shirt perhaps more suited to the Drifters but he too was heavy on the hair. Billy's hair had resembled a novelty tea cosy from day one so at least there was no change there.

The main benefit to us was that we were still in with a fighting chance on the singles market. To their advantage RCA now owned a bunch of valuable titles that for very little outlay would sell steadily through the years, although on playing they could do nothing but disappoint any serious sixties enthusiast who might have unwittingly purchased them believing them to be the original recordings.

In August 1972 a maxi-single comprising the tracks *Needles And Pins*, *When You Walk In The Room* and one of our own compositions *Come On Back To Me* was released as a taster to the forthcoming album and though the general public took no notice whatsoever of its appearance it certainly caused an unforeseen flurry of activity in the offices of Pye Records.

Richard Swainson informed us that the rival outfit had issued legal warnings which stated that the group's original contract barred it from producing new recordings of any titles previously taped for Pye, and what's more the bar applied in perpetuity. Pye had also been particularly astute in applying such restrictions to any form of recording as yet unknown, an omission in most other companies' agreements which was to provide an escape route to many artistes when the brand new format of CDs arrived on the market in the not-too-distant future.

An 'in perpetuity' clause was in fact a most unusual inclusion in such agreements and Swainson, having discussed the situation with RCA's own legal department, appeared quite dismissive of their objections. The company's lawyer was of the strong opinion that such a clause constituted a restraint of trade and would not hold up in a court of law. Their man was looking forward gleefully to a battle and Richard was getting quite carried away on the wave of such optimism. We cared not a jot. This album of ersatz hits was no source of pride to us but simply a means by which we could prolong our presence in the record market. If the lawyers were happy to fight it out then so be it. We just wanted to be left in peace to set about planning our next single. But then the shit hit the fan.

Things were changing on the music scene and at the cutting edge of change was David Bowie, another RCA artiste, whose androgynous posing and tantalizingly allegorical and thoughtful lyrics had most definitely got my attention. Not a person to keep up with trends or show much interest in new music, my tastes were firmly embedded in the authentic rock & roll of the fifties and virtually came to a grinding halt once we had passed the middle of the next decade. But I loved Bowie which surprised me as much as anybody else. The dressing up amused me but it was the music that made me want to go and see him at the Rainbow in Finsbury Park that August. *Hunky Dory* had been a brilliant album and *Ziggy Stardust* had even surpassed it. Virtually every track was memorable and its running theme of the problems bands encounter when ego and fame start to corrupt caused it to hit home even harder. I did not know it then but that very theme was soon to threaten my own livelihood.

I was also very interested in the support band that night. I had been told by a friend of mine that a mutual girl friend of ours was going out with a guy who was the singer in a group and that the group never played any gigs. They simply rehearsed and rehearsed and rehearsed. I had never heard of such a thing. From the moment I had been in bands it was considered vital to play anywhere you could, not just to earn money, which was of course a most important factor, but also to gain experience. Not to mention the sheer joy of strutting about in front of an audience and wallowing in its applause.

A short while later outside the Royal Albert Hall, where my idols the Everly Brothers were to appear, that same friend introduced me to a young man who came running up to say hello. 'This is Bryan,' my friend Paul MacBeth said. I shook his hand and said 'So you're the guy with the band that never does any shows. Apparently you just rehearse.' He was amused and appeared to be a really affable person who like me had an immense admiration for the Everlys. And anyone who loves the Evs has to have a lot going for them in my opinion. 'Well I hope you do very well,' I offered and he was off to find his seat. I was soon to find out just how well they would do.

In the end their master plan worked and Roxy Music, fronted by Bryan Ferry, stormed the charts with *Virginia Plain*, a disc with an exciting new sound and enough energy to power the national grid for a year. On the night Roxy Music were just fabulous. Ferry's hypnotic, vibrato-laced vocals were riveting and Brian Eno's weird electronic embellishments set them apart from any other sounds around at the time. This was obviously just the beginning for them. I was captured.

And Bowie too was magnificent. Every bit as good as I expected and wanted him to be and more as he depicted the tale of Ziggy and the Spiders From Mars in a style that was a combination of western pop, Gallic mime and Japanese Kabuki. The only hiccup for Bowie came at the end of his set when he and the band left the stage to await their inevitable and deserved encore without giving enough signals to the crowd as to what exactly was happening. The audience sat there bemused and unsure if this was just another vignette in the drama they had just witnessed.

After Bowie et al had disappeared into the wings the clapping died down and the auditorium became silent and the silence was deafening. Confusion reigned as a fidgeting crowd wondered if they should start clapping once more or if this was indeed the end of the concert. What happened was quite bizarre. Bowie emerged from the side to a smattering of applause and came to the microphone where, in the manner of a rather shy cabaret performer, he thanked everyone for coming and hoped, as he put it, that they enjoyed their little show. He and the band then proceeded into the planned encore and finally departed to the sound of the ovation he fully deserved.

As much as I had loved the evening's entertainment the second half was slightly marred by a feeling of discomfort due to an encounter with Mike Everett during the interval. I was enjoying a 'freebie' ticket as a guest of RCA while he was there in his capacity of an executive of the company. When I spotted him I went up and greeted him warmly but the warmth was far from being returned. In fact he was quite surly as he pointed out the problems we were causing them due to our breach of the Pye contract. He insisted that we would have to arrange a meeting to sort the matter out. This was hardly the place for me to offer explanations and our short and disagreeable encounter ended as unpleasantly as it had begun.

I could see his point that there were problems to be ironed out but he could certainly have handled it better. There are perfectly reasonable ways to mention on what was a social occasion that there was a need to discuss some important matters later. But it seemed quite clear to me that Everett was not a fan of ours and that we were simply an annoyance who were highly unlikely to provide RCA with any significant rewards for their investment.

We were summoned to RCA's plush offices in London's Curzon Street and again reminded of the trouble we had caused. Realising that a full explanation in our defence could possibly cause problems for Richard Swainson, our only ally in the camp, we stayed silent and refrained from mentioning that we had not instigated the trouble, that we only made this piece of dross in order to please them in the first place and so they could hardly heap the blame onto us. RCA, Everett explained, were not prepared to lock horns with Pye on the matter despite the previous display of bravado from their legal team and they instructed us to accept a set of terms drawn up at Great Cumberland Place which required us to forfeit a proportion of any royalties earned from the titles concerned. What the hell!! We were never going to get any royalties anyway. We signed.

It was all very unfair but you learn very quickly in life that when the shit hits the fan it is very rarely evenly distributed. As a post script to this unpleasant saga two years after the release of the *Second Take* album the same compilation was put out on an RCA budget label, given a different cover and called *Needles and Pins.* The intervening gap had not served to make it sound any better.

A couple of months later we were appearing at the Latino in South Shields, a Bailey club and the headquarters of that organisation, when two people entered our dressing room as we were preparing to go on stage. Newton Wills was someone with whom I was just barely acquainted and I was not quite sure just what position he held in the entertainment industry but he was fun and a nice guy.

Accompanying him was the lead singer of Roxy Music whose name at that moment stubbornly refused to enter my head. Introductions were required and I had to think fast. 'This is who I've been telling you about,' I announced to the rest of the band and indicating the sleek-haired pop singer. At that instant, thank the Lord, his name popped into my brain and I was able to add, 'This is Bryan Ferry of Roxy Music.'

We chatted for a while until it was time to take the stage and during the show I introduced Ferry to the crowd, heaping genuine praise on him and his group. They applauded politely but really had no idea who he was. Bryan was a local lad from Washington but it would be some time before they would realise that he would become one of the region's most famous sons. Newton, Bryan and I went out for a drink and a bit of socialising later that night at a club on the seafront and enjoyed possibly one of the last periods when Ferry could mingle unnoticed and unmolested in such an environment.

We were added to an RCA bill presented at the London Palladium which also featured the Everly Brothers, still looking good and dressed in non-matching country garb. It was at a time when their personalities were not matching either and sibling rivalry was beginning to turn brotherly love into brotherly dislike.

Dan Loggins opened while we closed the first half. The three acts were sympathetically juxtaposed with melody and sweet harmonies complimenting each other throughout the night. I enjoyed our set enormously and felt comfortable and powerful in a theatre whose intimate atmosphere belied its size. I recall my opening words declaring that I was thrilled to be standing on the very same stage that had also been graced by Dorothy Squires. It must have been a very camp crowd in that night because the throwaway line received an enormous cheer. I also cheekily announced that it seemed rather odd having the top of the bill on in the first half. It got a goof guffaw in response but in retrospect it was a childishly arrogant thing to say even in jest.

It was easy for those who liked the Evs to appreciate our work and vice versa and although we were to feel no special advantage at having played such a prestigious show it still felt like a feather in our cap. Playing to a packed house at possibly the most famous variety theatre in the world can never fail to be a thrilling experience.

Our next single, again recorded under our own control and without the aid of any imported producer, was a cover of a Loggins and Messina track entitled *Vahevala*, an up-tempo and dynamic sea shanty complete with an atmospheric solo played by a Caribbean steel band. For me it was the closest we had come so far to regaining the vital spark that had been missing from our records for some time. I loved the tune and the way that the verses and choruses changed from normal to double time drawing the listener in and increasing the excitement quotient to the hook lines. The dual harmony guitar lines also exploited our musical ability in a way that had not been done before. The finished product did not, I felt, sit quite as comfortably as the original Loggins and Messina version but all in all we acquitted ourselves very well. It was a stirring disc and one to be proud of and I still love the song today.

We even managed to get some television exposure in the form of a BBC2 programme called They Sold A Million in which the artistes were entitled to perform one of their great classics plus a current release. From our back catalogue we played *Goodbye My Love*, which did not sell a million, or at least if it did we were never paid for a million. We appeared in casual dress and I had borrowed a fringed buckskin jacket from my neighbour, soul singer Arthur Conley.

My domestic situation had recently changed. My love affair with glamourous cars had ended and, not wishing to waste any money on the costly maintenance and repairing of the E-type, I part exchanged it for the cheapest brand new vehicle I could find, a very mundane and un-glamourous Vauxhall Viva. And following a series of break-ins at the house, which always looked as though it might promise more valuable contents than were actually within, I decided that it might be more prudent to live as far from the ground as possible.

I had purchased a smart apartment on the tenth floor of a tower block at Wheatlands, a private estate in Heston, West London. I was at 39 while Arthur, whose hit *Sweet Soul Music* was an R&B classic, rented number 38. Immediately above me in one of the penthouses was actress Hannah Gordon and next to Arthur was motor-cycle ace Mike Hawthorn. Thankfully no burglars put in any appearances while I was in residence.

Good as it was and despite our TV appearance Vahevala proved not to be the breakthrough we were looking for and we immediately got on with the next attempt. The atmosphere at the top in RCA was as chilly as the weather in February 1973 but we just got on with our job. Swainson had played us Neil Sedaka's new album which had been recorded in conjunction with Graham Gouldman, Eric Stewart, Kevin Godley and Lol Creme of the hit team that made up the group 10cc. It was choc full of great commercial songs. Richard expected us to choose one of the brighter tracks to cover but we immediately honed in on the emotive ballad Solitaire. Everything about it screamed 'quality' and quite possibly 'hit'. This was excellent material with a superb tune and meaningful lyrics that tugged at the emotions.

Fi Trench provided us with an excellent string arrangement and even showed me the piano part that, despite my more than limited expertise on the instrument, would allow us to reproduce the track on stage. Mike Pender's vocal was crystal clear and the tone was as good as anything he had done so far. But once again we could not get the level of radio plays or any television exposure at all that we desperately needed to boost sales. It was a record that we were justifiably proud of but it failed to make any headway into the best sellers.

Six months later Andy Williams released his version of the song. Disapproving of the reference to cigarettes in the line 'a little hope goes up in smoke' he ordered a new verse to be written. I was not fond of the new lines. I felt they lacked the grittiness and depth of the original and, as great a star as he was, I honestly felt our version had the edge. Andy Williams shot to number four and our stay at RCA was at an end.

27

Small Acts Of Betrayal

Our recording career was at a standstill but elsewhere our graph had begun a slow but steady upward slope despite the strong signs indicating otherwise. As the seventies dragged on the fashion for cabaret clubs very gradually began to wear thin. The gaming laws in Britain were altered and gambling establishments eventually had to have their own entrance, and under a separate membership. Casual temptation, which had once been placed before those who otherwise might never have considered wagering the housekeeping money on a slot machine, a roulette wheel or a blackjack table, was removed.

Up to then the profits, or in some case losses, resulting from the entertainment in the showrooms had been almost irrelevant. In the manner of the great Las Vegas casinos the star names were there in the main as an enticement to bring the customers into the vicinity of games of chance, which was from where the major share of the revenue was derived.

As the novelty of having a night club on one's doorstep and open seven nights a week waned, and with a high proportion of the gaming revenue taken away, the clubs were walking a very delicate tightrope. Though it had never gone down the gambling route the Batley Variety Club had begun paying vast sums to bring over legendary American entertainers like Louis Armstrong, Roy Orbison and Gene Pitney, and people were willing to shell out the higher entrance fee for the rare opportunity to watch such stellar names on home ground.

The downside of such enterprise was that many of the run-of-the-mill British stars seemed very small beer in comparison to such glamourous international attractions. Having watched Jack Jones or the Beach Boys one week a patron might not get too excited by the prospect of Danny Williams or Vanity Fayre the week after. There were simply not enough top-flight entertainers with the kind of magnetism required to pack the venues night after night. The likes of Cliff Richard and Shirley Bassey and a handful of others could guarantee sold-out notices every time. But with so many clubs and such a small pool of 'A' list attractions to draw from performers soon became too readily available. The audiences predictably became jaded and blasé.

For some 'name' acts it was a testing time indeed. And for many unknown supports who had been enjoying the security of sixteen-week 'bulk buy' contracts from the mighty Bailey Organisation as they trudged from one town to another with barely a day off, it was a death knell that sounded ominously in the distance.

Somehow for us it managed to work the other way. As the clubs began to close their doors we suddenly discovered that once again there was a string of one-nighters out there begging for our services. And we could accumulate the paltry sums we were being paid for a week on the cabaret circuit in as few as three such gigs, with the added bonus that we were at last finding ourselves with time for friends and families. We had been undervalued and undersold for too long and at last it was to be our time, if not in the sun then at least in some fairly clement weather.

Though work was plentiful the future was still very much an unknown quantity and my personal budget had been suitably adjusted. The Vauxhall Viva was cheaper to fuel and maintain than the more glamourous E-type but certainly not a mode of transport one could effectively pose in. The fact was brought home to me one afternoon when I pulled up at a set of traffic lights by a roundabout in Hounslow West. My spatial awareness not being all that one would desire meant that the offside front wing had been, shall we say, 'customised' by the latest of my many collisions. Within the group I had been nicknamed Katy Crunch and in truth I had no real defence to the charge.

The sound of a horn alerted me to a vehicle which had pulled alongside. It was an enormous black Lincoln Continental, an ostentatious and impressive example of Detroit's finest and a model which I had long admired and coveted. We were neck and neck at the lights but the rear of the outrageous Lincoln was parked about three blocks behind me.

The driver smiled and waved. It was Pete Townshend. My, how times had changed. I recalled his envy at my induction into the world of fleeting and fickle pop fame during our brief encounter at the Oldfield Hotel in the summer of 1964. In just a short space of time the balance of power had shifted irrevocably. The Who had reached giddy heights from which they would never have to descend, while I sat there in my glamour-denied transport, its crumpled bodywork resembling a discarded crisp packet. I smiled shyly and acknowledged the iconic guitar hero as the signal changed to green and the Continental sailed smoothly and majestically into the distance like a beautiful ocean going yacht leaving me to paddle along shamefully in its slipstream. It was now my turn to be envious but there was no animosity. Pete was one of the nice guys and I wished him nothing but well.

As a group we were getting along fairly amicably although we never lived in each other's pockets. We shared rooms on tour and economy still dictated that Billy Adamson and I travelled from London in the minibus with the road manager and the equipment, not exactly pop star stuff, but as we were okay in each other's company it was not too big a deal. Mike Pender and John McNally's journeys by car from Liverpool carried a little more tension but on the whole it was quite a civilised existence, if far from ideal. In the light of stories of other bands like the Kinks or The Who fighting like demons in the dressing rooms our relatively civilised co-existence seemed very calm.

There could be periods of sullen silence between us and from time to time some raised voices but it was not all doom and gloom by any means. There were also a lot of laughs when we managed to put our differences behind us, although John was frequently annoyed with Mike at having to wait for him on a pick-up for a gig and of course there were the constant disputes about how much money was considered safe to withdraw from our partnership accounts without putting us in jeopardy with the tax man.

From time to time situations arose that shook the very foundations of our organisation and brought home to us that what we had, little as it was, could all come crumbling around us. We had not long departed from RCA and were on a tour of social clubs in Scotland, when Billy revealed to us that he had discovered from friends that Mike, under the guidance and help of Richard Swainson, had recorded a solo track in secret. Whether Richard supplied the backing or Mike financed the venture himself we never found out.

Such an underhanded manoeuvre was a betrayal in our eyes and it had given us a glimpse of the personal ambition and self-interest that was lurking in the shadows waiting to rip the group apart. We were all horrified, none more so than John whose relationship with his one-time friend was now filled with cracks. When Mike next appeared the atmosphere could have been cut with a machete. We had initially decided to swallow our pride and stay silent on the matter rather than risk letting the problem get dangerously out of hand, but eventually John could not settle for such a wishy-washy attitude of non-confrontation whatever the dangers.

Mike's surprise at his duplicity being discovered was evident. His explanation, that he wanted to try something on his own and that he didn't see that it would affect the group, did not wash. Nor did it appease. It was never going to. We were too upset. He dismissed it glibly saying that nothing had come of it anyway, as if that made everything okay. It was plain to us that if anything had indeed come of it we would have been tossed aside like old rags. Mike, we now felt, was working for Mike and could never be totally trusted again. Having faced him with our displeasure we eventually tried to put the matter behind us as best we could. It was either that or affect a split and the ramifications of that were just too awful to contemplate at the time. We were not in a strong position. A very uneasy truce now existed between us as we tried to make the best of our lives and our career.

The social scene in London was ever present to take my mind off such worries if only for a short while. Dusty Springfield, now living in the States and with new high-powered American management, returned in 1972 for what she hoped would be a triumphant return at the Talk Of The Town.

For whatever reason I had left it too late to arrange a table and on the night before phoned my contacts to see if I could be squeezed in somewhere. It was an event I didn't want to miss out on. In the end I had not one but two places reserved for me. Tom Springfield had come up trumps and found a seat at his table along with Dusty's managers. But I had also been fitted in on a table which included journalist David Wigg, public relations guru Tony King and Elton John.

I opted for the latter and we waited excitedly for Madame's appearance which was behind schedule already. She had throat trouble and we knew there might be problems. Forty minutes after her scheduled appearance time there was still no Dusty and a strong rumour gathered pace that she might not be able to go on stage at all. Elton was getting fidgety and intimated that if there was a problem he would go up there and perform himself, and indeed he would have. Apart from being a Dusty Springfield fan of massive proportions he was an entertainer who loved nothing so much as a stage and an audience.

It was after midnight when a highly medicated Dusty finally appeared. Her voice was barely there and she struggled courageously through her set apologising profusely and explaining, 'You know damn well I can sing better than this.' Of course we did and we ignored the imperfections and willed her to make it through. There was a certain poignancy to the night as we witnessed a performance of heroic effort from a woman who, under normal circumstances would have been, and should have been, tucked up at home in bed. She received an ovation that evening as great as any I saw given to her, and she deserved every handclap a thousand times over. Elton was on his feet and cheering like an excited schoolboy. The whole audience was on its feet.

We went back stage afterwards and gave her our congratulations in person. Naturally she was disappointed in herself but the sincere compliments from her peers after the concert must have compensated to an extent. That first night at the Talk Of The Town was also her last. Later in the week while she was still resting under her doctor's advice the theatre cancelled her contract.

Much of our work throughout these wilderness years was mundane, but despite the long hours of travelling, and for those of us at the southern end of the organisation the interminable hanging about at the end of the night while the gear got dismantled and packed away, it was not exactly coal-face labour. The travelling was the worst part with the clogged-up motorways getting worse year by year. There was the constant need to speed in order to make a show after yet another jam had threatened the schedule and the realisation that such an excess of speed could lead to disaster. The person who drives like hell is bound to get there in the end. But even at its worst it was infinitely better than facing the real world and getting a proper job.

We kicked off 1973 with a tour of Scandinavia leaving on January 18th and arriving home again at the end of the month. It was cold but simply being in a foreign country felt infinitely more interesting than chugging up and down the motorways of England.

From time to time the opportunity would arise for something with a bit more to chew on and we travelled to territories with a bit more glamour than was available on our home ground. The Australian market had opened up for us once more although this time our stages were in clubs and bars rather than the concert halls we had been used to. Although the financial rewards were somewhat wanting at least it took us out of the British market for a month or so and allowed us to enjoy our poverty in the sun for a change.

We flew out from London early April and landed in Perth after touching down in Zurich, Teheran, Bombay and Singapore on the journey. Things have changed a lot and these days it now only requires a single refuelling stop and far fewer hours between departure and arrival.

From our base at the Red Castle Motel in Perth we travelled to towns that most Australians never got to see. Karatha, Kalgoorlie, Newman, Geraldton and Manjimup. The tour also took us to Hobart in Tasmania and to Melbourne before flying home from Sydney a month later. We managed to land with some semblance of a tan although the other guests at our motels and hotels had looked on in astonishment as we desperately lay out in weather that was way past the parameters that encompassed an Australian summer. To them it was freezing. In truth it was far from being warm even to us but come hell or high water we were determined to arrive home with a respectable colour.

That same year we had been asked to form part of a British Invasion package to tour the States. It was the tenth anniversary of the time when the Beatles, The Searchers and a host of other British bands had showed them that there was more to the UK than bowler hats, bicycles and friendly policemen. The time was ripe and on June 25th we boarded Air India flight 101 bound for the Big Apple.

Peter Noone in a long awaited reunion with his old pals in Herman's Hermits, with whom he had not been on good terms with since his split to go solo, was headlining. Along with the Dave Clark Five they had come nearest to rivalling the Beatles in popularity although 'nearest' was still light years away from being 'near'. The Fab Four had always rightly been always in a league of their own.

We still had enough clout on those shores and enough chutzpah to demand a clause in our contract giving us the second most important position, that of closing the first half. Completing the line-up were Gerry & the Pacemakers, Wayne Fontana & the Mindbenders and Billy J Kramer, now a solo performer after having worked with the Dakotas for his hit parade years. In fact Gerry's Pacemakers and Wayne's Mindbenders too were new versions of the long-departed originals.

The years had been very kind to Billy J. He looked every inch the pop star with a lean and toned frame and a healthy and thriving mane of lightened locks. It could not have been easy for him. With a tendency to chubbiness Billy had always fought a weight problem and the peak condition he was in now could only have come from sheer discipline. Peter Noone too was in very good shape, still looking the cute pop star with the goofy grin and mop of blond locks. Gerry as ever was the eternal joker and in very good voice, while Wayne was an affable 'boy next door' type with a terrific vocal ability and a still good head of hair which unfortunately for him was not going to be around for too much longer.

We started the tour at the Saratoga Performing Arts Centre on June 26th and then headed for one of the major prestige dates in New York the next day. We were checked into the Sheraton on Broadway but things had changed since our glory days and we were paying for our accommodation out of our own depleted reserves. An expensive establishment like the Sheraton was champagne taste to our beer bottle pockets and we instantly opted out and checked into a much cheaper place situated in the Empire State Building. The McAlpine was rough at the edges to say the least but it matched much closer the amount we were prepared and able to pay.

Our New York appearance was the prestigious Madison Square Garden on a sweltering July 27th, where the audience was surprised when we included some newer material in our nostalgia-based set list. A somewhat heavy version of Neil Young's *Southern Man* complete with a five minute guitar solo by John McNally was maybe the most radical insertion. John's expertise on his instrument along with his insatiable appetite to devour the best and the latest material had seen a role reversal in the lead guitar department with all but some basic old solos played by Mike on the early discs now taken by him. The *Southern Man* solo might have seemed a bit self-indulgent to some but we saw the trip as a chance to display our right to be in there with other contemporary groups.

Though there may well have been murmurs of disapproval among those members of the public who prefer to have their memories left un-tampered with, our programme found favour with the New York Post's Anthony Mancini. He wrote 'Although the headliners were Herman's Hermits the laurels went to the Searchers. The contemporaries of the Beatles drew foot-stomping reactions from the 13,000 ticketholders with hits like *Needles And Pins, Sugar And Spice* and renditions of Carole King's *You've Got A Friend* and Kris Kristofferson's *Sunday Morning Coming Down.* They showed themselves to be a versatile, mature rock group.' On the other hand another critic stated that we 'confused the audience'.

The mention of those two songs pleased me as I had switched to piano while John took over on bass for their duration. I was both delighted and astonished that I appeared to have fooled the Post's music critic because I am to the piano what Mike Tyson is to neuro-surgery. But at least I can legitimately include on my CV that I have played piano at Madison Square Garden.

The same journalist was rather more perplexed though by Billy J's decision to perform one song in particular which, considering its incongruity in the sweltering heat of a New York summer was either genius or sheer lunacy. In one paragraph of his summation of Billy's act he wrote 'The same performer conducted a sing-along to White Christmas "Dedicated to the great man - Mr Bing Crosby." He didn't explain.'

Whilst in the Big Apple we took the chance to visit 48th Street where the latest US instruments were for sale at highly discounted prices. I could hardly afford to turn down a beautiful black Rickenbacker 4001 bass guitar which Manny's music store had on sale at a fraction of the UK price.

Whilst we were there John put pressure on Mike to buy a new 12-string instrument. His own Rickenbacker had been stolen from the pavement outside the Lafayette Club in Wolverhampton a couple of years previously after having been left unattended by our then roadie Chris Cottrell. Needing a replacement for the next day's show he had bought a Bellzouki model, very cheap and not very good and, as we discovered when bits of it soon started wearing away, made of hardboard. Not the finest material with which to construct a professional instrument. The intonation was suspect and in those primitive times before electronic tuners made life so much easier a well made, well set-up guitar was essential.

He took the strong hints and acquired a small blond Rickenbacker 360 6/12, a solid body guitar with a comb-like attachment which in theory could at a stroke lower six of the twelve strings thus converting it into a standard instrument. At least that was the theory. In practice the converter never worked very well and, apart from being clumsy to operate, tended to put it out of tune. But at least it was bye bye Bellzouki.

From the Big Apple we flew to Toronto for a show at the huge Maple Leaf Gardens where the Canadian audience was once again bemused to find that Christmas had come early. Once again our performance found favour with journalist Robert Martin who wrote:

'The best of the groups, although not the most successful commercially, was the Searchers. While the other bands stuck mostly to their old hits and some specially written soppy song about it being nice to be back, the Searchers actually played some contemporary material and did it well.

'They did their biggies like *Needles And Pins* and *Love Potion No. 9*, but also included a creditable version of Carole King's *You've Got A Friend* and Kris Kristofferson's *Sunday Morning Coming Down*. The lead guitarist even took an extended solo on America's *Sandman* and it held very nicely with a solid, tough feel to it.' John's burgeoning expertise on his instrument and his elevation to lead guitar within the band was paying dividends and again my piano thumping had thankfully managed to fool them.

The tour continued. Springfield, Massachusetts (30th), Providence, Rhode Island (July 1st), Cape Cod (2nd), Binghampton (3rd). In Atlantic City on July 6th we played a date at the Steel Pier where our rival attraction was the famous diving horse. A fully-grown horse was led up a ramp adjacent to the theatre several times a day to be launched (whether it was coerced, compelled or complied willingly I know not) from a platform into a tank of water below. How could we compete with that?

Appearing at the same venue the day after us was the Killer himself, Jerry Lee Lewis, the pumping piano from Ferriday, Louisiana. To children of the fifties like us he was a hero and a bunch of us went along to catch his set. Unfortunately, the cantankerous ivory tinkler was in one of his rebellious periods where he was, to the greater extent, denying his affiliation to the raucous rock & roll which had brought him to fame. He proceeded to deliver to a somewhat bored and jaded crowd a succession of dreary country ballads.

Billy J shouted out for *High School Confidential* only to be instantly rebuffed. 'I'll play what I want, boy,' retorted the Killer with a look that certainly could have killed. We didn't argue.

We criss-crossed the country with varying degrees of success. Columbia, New Jersey (7th), New Haven, Connecticut (9th), Independence, Michigan (11th), Minneapolis (12th), Sioux Falls, Dakota (13th). On July 14th we learned from our tour manager Ray Reneri, that the Everly Brothers were playing a concert at Knotts Berry Farm at Buena Vista, California, not too far from where we were staying, and we might just be able to dash over and catch at least some of their set after our show. Some of us were extremely keen. The Everlys were gods in our eyes. Particularly me and Billy Kinsley, the ex-Merseybeats bass player who for the purposes of this tour was standing in as part of Gerry Marsden's current crop of Pacemakers. They were due to perform three shows at the theme park. But before we set off Ray came to tell us that there was no point in rushing.

Their ongoing sibling feud had apparently surfaced on stage apparently caused by Don's extreme state of drunkenness and after smashing his Gibson Everly jumbo guitar onto the floor, an instrument that today would be worth tens of thousands of pounds, Phil had walked off vowing 'never to appear on stage with that man again.'

Oddly enough considering his inebriated condition, Don completed the remaining two shows as a solo act but, for a whole decade anyway, the Everlys were no more.

The major towns sold well. The middle American cities and towns less so. The shows at the Los Angeles Forum and the Cow Place in San Francisco were cancelled due to poor sales and instead on July 15th the entire tour was the feature of the Midnight Special television show hosted by cult deejay Wolfman Jack.

Maurice Gibb of the Bee Gees came to pay his respects and delighted in showing his exciting new toy, a super slim Polaroid camera that allowed you to hold your pictures in your hand a few seconds after having taken them. I was seriously impressed. The problem with such a thing is that the subject invariably wants the picture thus leaving you empty handed. He took one of me playing my new 'Ricky' and of course I snaffled it from him. After the show we went with Maurice to a house he and his brothers had rented nearby and hung out for a while.

Lyn Paul of the New Seekers was also living in LA at the time and hosted a party for us at her rented apartment. It nearly turned to tragedy when Gerry's drummer Pete Clarke was discovered lying face down on the bottom of the pool. Karl Green of the Hermits dived in and pulled him to the surface just in time. Two days later after an enforced hospital stay Clarke rejoined the tour but it had very nearly been all over for him with no chance of a comeback.

From Los Angeles we continued our long trek visiting Winnipeg (16th), Kansas City (17th), Cuyahoga Falls, Ohio (18th), Milwaukee (19th), Columbia, Ohio (20th), Cedar Rapids, Iowa (21st), St Louis, Missouri (22nd). The tour was scheduled to end at that point but the promoters had seen fit to add on an extra date in the Hamptons, the wealthy Long Island holiday resort not far from New York, a favourite weekend destination for wealthy burghers of Manhattan.

They should have left well alone. Last night japes, a long-established touring tradition, got more than a little bit out of hand and for my part completely spoilt the entertainment on offer, and which had been paid for by patrons rightly expecting a slick and professional show which, up to that point, it had been. But despite the sour note we had to end on, which included a near-fisticuffs dressing room confrontation between Gerry Marsden and his drummer Pete Clarke over financial matters, it had been an enjoyable and mostly successful few weeks.

Back home again in Britain we continued to coast through waters that were sometimes calm and sometimes very choppy. We were again without a recording contract but we put down some demos for CBS who were considering taking us on. They eventually declined.

Along with the resurgence in the one-night-stand circuit we also managed to make inroads into Europe. Germany had been the catalyst for many of our contemporaries.

Along with the Beatles and virtually every other beat group worth its salt at the time we had pounded the stage at the Star Club, increasing our repertoire and expanding our virtuosity as we were aided and influenced by our fellow musicians, as they were in turn by us.

When the glory days ended and we had to think in smaller terms rather than the theatres and concerts our fame had raised us to, we would occasionally undertake a run of German bars, clubs and bier-kellers. The return to Deutschland, along with the camaraderie of these adventures and the booze which was always flowing, was a fun thing to do. We all travelled together in the same Ford Transit for a change and during the periods where old disputes and quarrels could be, if not forgotten, at least laid aside for a while we almost felt like a real group again in the old sense of the word.

Our return to the Grosse Freiheit on one such trip was not to our beloved Star Club, which had since been converted into a sex club called the Salambo, but to the place that was once the legendary Kaiserkeller. The Kaiserkeller, situated immediately opposite Manfred Weissleder's Star Club, was a basement set of rooms where Bruno Koshmeider had once kept his musical slaves the Beatles toiling set after set after set each night until they would have faced collapse from exhaustion had not the always available Preludin tablets kept them stimulated and awake.

By 1974 the Kaiserkeller had become the Easy Rider and was now operated by a young entrepreneur called Rainer Haas, a diehard pop aficionado whose knowledge and record collection would surely have rivalled that of Phil Swern. As a teenager he had been a regular pressing up at the front of the stage in admiration for the British and American bands imported for rock-starved kids like him in the sixties.

He was now a young, handsome and well-heeled club owner with a glittering future ahead of him but his initial venture, the success of which allowed him to purchase the Easy Rider, was not a musical one. He had seen the potential in staging a come-back fight for Albert Westphal, a thirty-nine year old retired German heavyweight boxing champion who had in his career beaten three ex-European champions. The promotion was a huge success, subsequent attempts markedly less so, but Haas now had the capital he needed for his future visions still to be realised.

We liked him from the start. A hell of a lot more than the sleazy promoter who had set up the run of dates we had come out to undertake. And our appearance at the Easy Rider packed the sweaty underground space to bursting point. At the end of our second set we left for the dressing room to a cheering audience and of course returned for the obligatory and traditional encore. The cheering went on and on as they chanted the German equivalent of 'more' and 'Searchers'.

As was usual in the UK we decided to leave them wanting more. In England enough is considered as good as a feast. Unfortunately we could have done with a short lesson in local customs where only a feast is as good as a feast because we were apparently expected to return again and probably again in order to satisfy the baying mob. We held fast in our tiny dressing room not realising that, on sensing they were definitely not about to receive any more music from us, the kids had added another word to their chant. 'Searchers - shit!!' was now the war cry. Thankfully, we were not told until some time later.

One evening Rainer took us to see what had become of our old stomping ground across the road. In fact the interior of the Star Club had not changed all that much but what was happening on stage was something else. The beat bands had been sexy. Now what was occurring on that same stage was real sex in its basic form. When the Beatles brought their set to its climax it was altogether different to the climaxes we were now witnessing.

A series of tableaux were being presented on a revolving platform atop which were various combinations of copulating figures. The running theme which connected these set pieces was a gentleman dressed as Napoleon. A trouser-less Napoleon whose dangling and lifeless member was being teased and tickled by a frustrated but determined Josephine seemingly to no avail. Instead of *Twist And Shout* the music now had a classical tone. *Orpheus In The Underworld* blared from the speakers. It would have been more appropriate to re-title it as *Orpheus Without His Underpants.*

On the final revolve the music had changed. La Marseillaise, now trumpeted out and the Tricoleur flared triumphantly as Napoleon appeared once more with a huge grin and an impressive flagpole of his own to brandish. On reflection, I sincerely think our shows were more entertaining. I also think they had more sex appeal.

Before we left Hamburg and realising that we had encountered not only a very personable young guy but also a clever and enterprising businessman, we suggested to Rainer that he could easily assemble a string of German clubs for us to play in. We were not happy with our current promoter there and he was someone we felt we could trust. Less than six months later Haas rang with the okay and we began an association that was to provide us with a territory that would serve us well for decades. He would become the foremost presenter of 'Oldie Nacht' concerts staged in vast arenas all over that vast country.

As the circuit grew and Rainer increased his expertise and his connections, John McNally supplied him with the names and numbers of other groups including the Swinging Blue Jeans and the Tremeloes and others who could fill the gaps when we were not available or when we needed to be rested. There are numerous bands from our era who owe a great debt to John in delivering to them, with no reward to himself, a market which would constitute for many the greater proportion of their livelihood throughout the eighties and nineties.

In 1977 the country was celebrating. It was the twenty fifth anniversary of Queen Elizabeth II's accession to the throne and television programmes were arranged to take advantage of the heightened interest and the potential viewing figures the festivities would accumulate. Appearances on 'the box' were rare for us these days and it was an unexpected bonus to be included in the day's schedule as part of a programme which was to present a microcosm of her reign. The various changes in music would quite obviously emphasise the salient points of progress over the years and there was no more important period than the Merseybeat phenomenon. They couldn't get the Beatles so they got us. A pretty poor exchange but it made us happy.

Despite this bright spot on the horizon I was not in a happy frame of mind having had to deal with problems of my own. A few days previously, on the third of June my mother collapsed and died of a heart attack. Though she had been frail and unwell for most of her life this was a shock from out of the blue. She was fifty-nine years old. I was devastated.

In a blind panic I had driven the few miles to my parents' home with my mind racing. To my eternal shame I recall that one of the thoughts among the many that threatened to burst from my skull as I gunned the car towards Harlington was who was now going to take care of my washing? It was pathetic and I was both amazed and horrified at my capacity for self pity. I think the mind goes a little crazy at times like this.

The day before the broadcast we drove to a trading estate in Wembley to record the track as we were to mime our segment. It was early and we were all tired. The following morning, Tuesday June 7th, we presented ourselves at the Television Centre in Shepherd's Bush ready to roll. As we stood on the podium for the rehearsal Bob Wellings, the presenter, stood at the end of our line-up and explained that before the music he would interview John McNally. Although John did few interviews, usually preferring to depute either Mike Pender or myself, that was more than fine as far as I was concerned. But it was not, it seemed, all right with Mike who instantly began haranguing Bob to interview him as well.

Wellings quietly explained that it was not possible because of the restrictions of time and that it would only be John that he would be speaking to as arranged. This was not good enough for Mike who insisted that he should interview the two originals. Well that puts me in my place, I thought. It's good to know where you stand. After all I had only been in the group for thirteen years, I was a full partner and I was being cast aside as some Johnny-come-lately. Bob however stuck to his guns maintaining steadfastly that the director's instructions would have to be followed.

We were quite taken aback at the arrogance Mike was demonstrating not to mention the sheer stupidity of causing trouble at the all-important BBC. We had been presented with our first high-profile television spot in ages and he was making giant waves.

We completed the rehearsal in an air of bewilderment and anger. When we trooped morosely back to our dressing room silence was the only sound we could make and Mike only remained briefly within its confines.

When it came time for the broadcast proper we reassembled on the platform, hardly able to disguise the chilly atmosphere that engulfed us. Bob Wellings moved into position and announced that things had apparently changed. He would now be interviewing Mike instead of John. If our previous reaction had been surprise and anger it now hovered somewhere between abject disbelief and barely containable fury.

In reply to Wellings' question as to why he thought Liverpool was the place it took off, Mike's reply was that he really couldn't answer that. Priceless. An answer worth fighting for indeed. When prompted by Bob that maybe Liverpool was full of talented people Mike agreed that perhaps Liverpool people had a certain amount of musical ability. He also added that he thought that the Beatles might have had something to do with it. A shrewd observation. This was not cutting edge repartee by any means.

Somehow we got through *Needles And Pins* and a short medley of our hits and even made some attempts to smile through those songs that had once brought so much hope and joy. Perhaps some psychic intuition had subliminally forewarned us of the gloom ahead because the tape we had made the day before was so slow and plodding that our biggest hit record now sounded like something that would have been considered too miserable even for a funeral cortege.

We stood there and sang in front of the dancing dolly birds, they clad in authentic Carnaby Street fashion items and we in a set of black velvet safari suits with flared trousers that would have done a dray horse proud. And while the false smiles stuck to our teeth our innermost senses dwelt on little but the bitter taste of betrayal. When we confronted Mike he lamely said that he thought they should have interviewed all of us. It was of course rubbish. We pointed out to him that he had not achieved that at all. He had simply demanded that the attention be focused on himself at all costs. What we had witnessed was another demonstration of a monstrous ego and self obsession.

On August 16th of that year the King of Rock & Roll, Elvis Presley, was discovered dead on the floor of the bathroom in his Memphis mansion, Graceland. At the tender age of forty-two he had died of a surfeit of prescription drugs, an impacted colon and goodness knows what else. My childhood was disappearing little by little and if my great musical god could slip away so easily then what were the chances for me? My own mortality was brought very much into sharp focus.

28

Back To The Cool

Seymour Stein was barely into his twenties when he founded Sire Records. A contemporary of ours, the brash young Jewish New Yorker had been weaned on the rock & roll revolution of the fifties and was of a generation that could not fail to be excited and influenced by the British Invasion of 1964, when all that had until then had been deemed the property of the United States was suddenly under threat from the Beatles and their peers. Two years later on he started a record company that was eventually to provide home and shelter to a new wave of American groups and artistes who were assembling their own musical ammunition to limit the damage inflicted by these presumptuous foreign invaders.

In 1976 he almost single-handedly created punk by signing four young guys from the New York borough of Queens whose black leather and denim garb, topped off by dark glasses worn not only on days when the sun was not shining but even indoors, flew in the face of the glamour that was expected in the glitzy world of showbusiness. The Ramones stood moody, unsmiling and motionless on stage while churning out pole driving rhythms that bordered on the musically primitive yet were charged with enough energy to power the whole of Manhattan.

Stein's instinct for what was happening in the world of rock and pop was almost unerring. His roster of signings increased to take on board Talking Heads, Richard Hell & the Void Oids, the Pretenders and the Flamin' Groovies. Spreading his wings he signed the Undertones, Echo & the Bunnymen, the Rezillos and Aztec Camera from the UK. And within a couple of years he was to see the potential in an ambitious girl singer from Bay City, Michigan, with the intriguing and highly controversial name of Madonna, upstaging everyone by providing her with a base from where she could put into effect her master plan for world domination.

Stein's casual garb of jeans and leather bomber jacket was at odds with the 'suits' who in the main still controlled the record industry in New York. But they were savvy enough to realise that he was in touch with and understood the word on the streets.

With crotchets and quavers running through his veins in place of blood he not only knew what was happening in the youth market, he had the knack of knowing what was going to happen.

On a trip to Europe in 1979 a casual discussion about the popular music that made up the soundtrack to his adolescence brought up the subject of the influence of British groups and he was amazed to discover from Paul McNally (no relation to John) who was Sire's UK A&R manager at the time that the Searchers, who he opined held an important position in the seismic explosion that had been the Mersey Boom, were still very much in existence and without a recording contract.

Paul had been involved in booking the group for a graduation ball at Loughborough University a few years before, where we had scored a big hit with the young crowd who were somewhat shocked that a band from a previous generation could still pump out music that was valid in their eyes and ears. The university circuit was an important one for us in that late sixties to mid seventies period when they seemed to be the only source of a half decent fee. Perhaps the fact that it was not their money they were risking had something to do with it.

Few could fail to appreciate the trademark sounds that had been established by this Liverpool based quartet and assimilated by young American musicians who had gone on to greater things. Bruce Springsteen on his somewhat low key first-ever tour of Britain played little other than Searchers tracks at his after-show gatherings according to Henry Marsh, keyboardist with the group Sailor (*Glass Of Champagne*, *Girls, Girls, Girls* and *World Wide Traffic Jam*) and often included the classic *When You Walk In The Room* in his live set. Bootleg recordings of the song are in existence.

Tom Petty took the jangly sound of the Rickenbacker twelve-string to greater heights but he was Brit-baked all over and there was little doubt where the seeds were sown and by whom. Likewise Marshall Crenshaw owed a small debt to the Searchers. And even the bêtes noir of the beat scene, the Ramones, were to cover *Needles And Pins* in a version that varied very little from the Searchers' original.

Perhaps the most obvious and enduring comparison was with the Los Angeles based Byrds who over time acquired the lion's share of credits for pioneering the distinctive harmonies and twelve-string combination. Roger McGuinn rarely if ever confessed to a Searchers influence, preferring to bask in the personal glory of 'king of the jangle' but in a 2005 interview with Liverpool music journalist and historian Spencer Leigh, guitarist Chris Hillman at last graciously owned up for them, albeit in a limited way.

'We knew about them and listened to them, sure, and we certainly owe the Searchers something. They were a harmony group and it was similar to what we were doing but Roger McGuinn took the twelve-string to a giant level of proficiency, way beyond George Harrison and the Searchers. I don't think that *Needles And Pins* influenced *Mister Tambourine Man* but if you listen to Gene Clark's song *I'll Feel A Whole Lot Better* you can hear that we stole something from *When You Walk In The Room.* That opening guitar riff is the same.'

Intrigued by the possibility of having such a historically significant group on his label, where he felt they would sit very comfortably alongside the guitar based simplicity of the 'new wave' bands, Seymour was happily pointed in our direction by Rob Dickins who at that time was the managing director of Warner Brothers Music Publishing. In time his rise in the industry would be meteoric, and in 1983 he became the youngest-ever head of a UK record company at the tender age of thirty-two when he was made Chairman of the Warner Music Group.

Rob's connection with us stretched back some way. His older brother Barry Dickins had been our booker at the giant MAM agency and we were the first big name act for whom he had secured engagements. Barry eventually left MAM to form ITB, an organisation that would set up hugely successful tours for Crosby, Stills & Nash, Z Z Top, Diana Ross, Bob Dylan and a host of others. As if that was not enough to give a cachet to the family name, their father Percy Dickins had introduced the first-ever British chart for record sales in 1953 when he was the advertising manager of the New Musical Express.

In his days at Loughborough University with Paul McNally, Rob had in his capacity of Social Secretary for the Students' Union been the person in charge of booking us to perform there. Later, around 1978 or so, he had supervised a recording session of ours at a small studio in Denmark Street, a short thoroughfare off the Charing Cross Road that has been forever known as Tin Pan Alley. Rob's conviction that we were due for a revival alas came to nothing and the tape of an obscure Bob Dylan song called *Lay Down Your Weary Tune* lies neglected and gathering dust in a Warner's vault somewhere, waiting to be rediscovered for a collection of rarities in a future life.

Initial negotiations were conducted with Paul McNally. Paul was fun and easy to get along with and bore more than a passing resemblance to the English comedian of the forties and fifties Cardew 'The Cad' Robinson. He had also been endowed with a laid-back sense of humour that would not have disgraced the Cad himself. Paul McNally had been in Rob Dickins' employ at the time of the *Lay Down Your Weary Tune* session.

With Mike and John being domiciled two hundred miles north in Liverpool, I was seconded into eventually meeting up with Seymour Stein who was in London organising the UK base of his company. I arrived at the apartment just south of the Euston Road to a scene of mild disarray with furniture and filing cabinets lying around waiting to be set in position. There were boxes still unopened on the floor while Stein and his minions worked to create order out of chaos.

Seymour was a smallish, chunky man and friendly enough though not especially outgoing on this occasion. There was obviously a lot going on and it was not a time to spend a moment more on any matter than it warranted. Our encounter was quick, direct and to the point. He asked how we saw our recording future and I replied to the effect that we felt we were still a valid force or at least could be once more and that we wanted to make contemporary sounds that would still use those identifying features that had been so much a part of our history. We would use songs by the best writers available in order to make the kind of album that would bring back our credibility in the eyes of the record-buying public.

A short time later he and a bunch of his Sire cronies journeyed to the seaside town of Southend, barely an hour's drive from the capital, to watch us in cabaret at the Talk Of The South. Despite the very un-punk setting of a room full of less than cool, middle-aged diners reliving a few teenage memories while feasting on cheap and cheerful mass produced food, Stein saw beyond the jaded present and believed there could also be a promising future. We gathered in the cramped dressing room after the show. His words were laconic and to the point. 'Yeah, let's do it.'

Our next task was to sift through the thick American-style contract produced by Sire's legal team. This cleverly worded document bore little resemblance to the primitive typed pages presented by Pye a decade and a half before. It was extremely thorough and protected Sire's interests efficiently. One clause prevented us from ever suing the company on a contingency basis which is the method we have come to know in more recent times as 'no win – no fee'. And any such case would have to be fought in the United States. In other words if we were to contest them we would have to put our money where our mouths were. Money we did not have and were unlikely to risk in any event.

The royalty rate, in the light of the much more artiste-friendly deals today's acts are used to receiving, was far from generous but at around eight percent it was twice as much as the pathetic slave wages paid to us by Pye, the company for whom we had earned millions. And the line of record companies desperate to obtain our exclusive services was noticeable by its absence. We had the document perused as economically as we could by lawyers we could barely afford and finally, after a couple of alterations, finished up with something we could live with.

Our biggest problem with regard to recording was having to be off the road for long periods with no income to take care of the bills which still needed to be paid. We were a working band. All our earnings in those days came from our constant stream of one-nighters which did not bring in untold millions but which at least allowed us to exist and to support our families. But if we stopped working for a moment there was an immediate cash flow problem. We had not made a penny from any recordings made since we had left Pye. Returns from the old hits had long since reduced to a trickle, mostly being derived from the cheap compilations on the economy Marble Arch label. The amounts received were sometimes so low it would have almost felt more decent for us to pay them.

Eventually Sire agreed to pay us a subsistence for each week of recording which would more or less approximate the fees we would be losing. For them it would simply replace any advance monies they would normally expect to pay. As for us no-one had ever given us any advance before so it was a very welcome treat and overcame the obstacle nicely. At last we were a recording band once more and without selling one disc we had actually made money. This was a truly novel experience.

By the summer of seventy-nine we were ready and heading west to the Rockfield recording studios just outside Monmouth. This was a brand new sensation for us having been used to the busy claustrophobic confines of central London where, at the end of a hopefully productive day we would head homewards, or hotel-wards, for some rest before repeating the whole process the following morning. For the next month Rockfield would be our workplace and our home with little to disturb us but the bleating of a few lambs in the nearby fields.

Never has a studio been given such an appropriate name but far from being the fancy of a publicity-conscious entrepreneur it is the actual name of a place. To find the small village of Rockfield you head along the M4 motorway and cross the River Severn towards Wales. Further along the road if you make a right turn on the A449 and continue on the A40 it will take you on to where the picturesque and tourist-friendly town of Monmouth sits alongside the Forest of Dean. Rockfield is then merely a wiggly manoeuvre on the B roads off to the left.

The studio complex was once a working farm owned and converted by two brothers and semi-professional musicians, Charles and Kingsley Ward. Barns and outbuildings had been turned into what was then a pretty much state-of-the-art recording facility complete with an accommodation block. Once ensconced you need never be more than a short stroll away from a microphone or a mixing desk.

The buildings formed a quadrangle with the studio on one side, two-storey chalets with bedroom upstairs and a lounge below on another and administration offices, store rooms and glass-baffled acoustic echo room taking up the remaining two. The chalet-style guest quarters were basic but comfortable and there were videos and televisions in each. The rustic wood construction gave them the feeling of a ranch. A communal room with a large kitchen was the rendezvous for the evening meal brought in each night by smiling ladies who looked as though they enjoyed their food as much as we did. They were lovely smiling women whose flesh wobbled when they laughed as they dished up good wholesome country cooking that pandered little to style but which filled the belly very nicely.

Our recording was put under the direction of the main in-house producer, Pat Moran, a slightly-built person with the look of an impecunious student. Along with a devotion to his art that bordered on obsession he had acquired a 'studio tan', that curious insipid pallor that inhabits flesh that has only rarely been introduced to natural sunlight. Pat was mild mannered and very easy to get on with. The only fault I could attach to him was the limpest of handshakes that made greeting a slightly unsettling experience. But in the light of his other attributes such a minor oddity was mere bagatelle.

He and John McNally bonded particularly well, both being studio animals. In the initial four weeks ahead they would spend hour upon endless hour in the control room together fussing and fretting over the minutiae of the layering process that constitutes making a satisfactory record in a modern age. Gone were the days of one-take singles and albums made in a matter of hours.

For the first few days we were housed in the Old Mill, a detached property near to the entrance to the farm, where we sifted through the material on offer and routined the titles we decided we would attempt. Unlike our Pye era we were royally supplied with an abundance of good songs. There were no rules. We listened and if it was good we recorded it, whether or not we knew of the writer's track record. In fact we cared not a jot if they had form or not. A good song was a good song as far as we were concerned and were glad to grab them.

The first tune to be taken was *Hearts In Her Eyes*, an up-tempo number very much in the old style we were used to but with more punch. Written by Will Birch and John Wicks of a group called the Records, it had it all as far as we were concerned. Rhythm, a catchy melody line with simple yet interesting lyrics and a guitar riff that could have been tailor-made for us.

It's Too Late was a John David song. David worked part time at Rockfield as an engineer and occasional session musician to supplement his income as a member of the group Airwaves. As with *Hearts* it had all the elements we required. John wrote very much in our style, which was hardly surprising having worked a lot with guitar guru and rock aficionado Dave Edmunds who lived in nearby Monmouth. A false myth has grown up that Rockfield was in fact Edmunds' studio probably due to the proximity of his home but the rumour is a false one. Though he has used its facilities many times the operation was firmly in the hands of the Ward brothers.

Noel Brown's *No Dancing* was our 'chunk of punk' and it surprised us as much as anybody else that we not only recorded such an irreverently frantic tune but that it worked really well. Another off-the-wall inclusion was Mickey Jupp's solidly rhythmic *Switchboard Susan* while the haunting Tom Petty ballad *Lost In Your Eyes* pandered to our romantic leanings. *Love's Gonna Be Strong*, written by Ronnie Thomas who was in a band called the Heavy Metal Kids, owed much to the dampened vamping guitar style of the up-and-coming new wave groups and stood up to the best of them, I felt.

A Bob Dylan out-take from his Street Legal album written with one of his backing singers, Helena Springs, *Coming From The Heart,* was maybe a bit laboured but it served the purpose of contrasting nicely with the more frantic content. The years of planning shows for a cabaret audience had taught us the value of light and shade.

Our own self-penned efforts did not take precedence over other material much as we wanted the chance to show what we could do but did include *This Kind Of Love Affair* (John McNally's) and *Don't Hang On* (mine).

The major burden of work fell to John and Pat who worked in tandem to make sure the end product was as faultless as it could be. Things were a lot easier for Billy Adamson and me. After the initial rhythm tracks were laid down Billy was more or less done, while I simply had to bide my time until they were ready to add my harmonies or the rare lead vocal. A studio environment has never been my favourite habitat. Hours of repeating the same guitar phrase or drum pattern with the anxiety factor rising to the point of maximum frustration is anathema to me. Any sunny work-free days for me were spent soaking up the sun in the spacious courtyard, getting browner by the hour to the point where Pat Moran gave me the nickname of Rajah. Billy, meanwhile spent much of his time re-caning a wickerwork chair.

I am happiest on a live stage where every few minutes I am rewarded by enthusiastic applause from a delighted public. And each evening after enjoying the marvellous country cooking delivered by the ever-smiling village ladies I simply wanted to relax in front of the television. The prudent course would have been to refuse an extra helping of apple pie and custard and thus avoid the resulting lethargy that inevitably accompanies a sated stomach. It was a tough call. Studio or apple pie? Apple pie or studio? No contest. The apple pie won every time. The sight of Mike or John dragging themselves away from the meal table for a long evening's labour in the studio laying down more lead vocals or yet another layer of guitar overdubs created no feeling of envy in me whatsoever.

Fortunately John was never happier than tinkering endlessly with the recordings in that futile search for perfection that is a producer's dream and also his nightmare. He and Pat made a great team. Long after they should have succumbed to a sensible night's sleep they would push each other further into the early hours before sheer fatigue made them quit. It could not have been healthy for either of them but their complete dedication had my undying admiration.

In '64 it would have been Mike inserting the solo parts for the guitar but things had since shifted radically and irreversibly. John's prowess and technique had come so far that duties in that department had undergone a complete turnaround. Once the initial basic rhythm track with all of us playing together was on tape it now fell to John alone to layer all of the subsequent guitar parts. Acoustic rhythm. High strung six-string. The iconic sound of the twelve-string. It was John on John on John ad infinitum. A simple technique and ability might have once sufficed for the magnificent if simple riff to *When You Walk In The Room* but what was needed as we headed into the eighties was the level of skill that could compete with today's guitar wielding young studs and John had raised himself to that level.

With little to distract us work progressed at a good rate but as the four weeks neared an end it was apparent that more time would be beneficial if we were to end up with the kind of product that we were aiming for. An album to be forever proud of. Fortunately Sire seemed to be thrilled and excited at the way things were turning out and we received the okay from their offices in Floral Street in Covent Garden that the budget would be extended to accommodate the necessary extension.

Time for us as a constantly working outfit was at a premium. We had commitments that could not be altered. But there was a period where our gigs were more or less all in the Midlands and we figured that we could record during the daytime and still fulfil our obligations in the evenings. At the end of the week we were shattered and worse still we discovered that our tired ears had deceived us. Almost everything we had put down was substandard and virtually unusable.

From somewhere we found a free week and returned to Rockfield, much to the annoyance of families who were seeing very little of their spouses and parents. Even so it was still a matter of working right up to the very last minute which caused yet another bit of friction between Mike and John. There were still instrumental parts that required finishing touches, and although the plan was to return to Liverpool early evening on the final day of recording Pat and John were still poring over the desk as the night drew in.

Mike, unlike his fellow Scouser, was content to accept a compromise and sacrifice quality for an earlier departure while John was determined to finish the job properly. His anger could barely be contained as Mike positioned the car outside the studio with the engine running and constantly urged him to speed things up. The journey back to Merseyside was another silent one.

29

It's Too Late

'S*earchers'* – for whatever reason we felt that omitting the definite article would somehow give us a more contemporary edge – hit the shops in November 1979 in its original 'airplane' sleeve. The shiny chrome objects soaring over a beach into the sunset which many mistook for alien space craft were in fact hood ornaments from American cars from the fifties. It was a world away from our old 'jolly quartet of smiling faces' formula that dictated every album cover in the Pye days.

On the reverse were four individual pictures snapped at Rockfield, each of us holding one of the car mascots and looking moody. Beneath each photo was a white space which in time came in very handy for applying an autograph but in reality was simply a standard part of the Polaroid pictures from which they were reproduced.

The US release was to use the same basic design but with a lighter colouring and with the definite article reinstated. It was felt that 'Searchers' minus 'The' would be too confusing for the American public. And in the white space below the individual shots on the reverse side our names and the instruments we played were printed. Quality control must have been at lunch that day because they somehow managed to spell my name wrong.

The finished album was something we were more than happy with. The collection of songs was eclectic and interesting. You would be strange if you could not find something to like amongst its tracks and the carefully executed layers of swirling guitars not only retained but also expanded on a distinct sound that was a part of our history and our heritage and not to be discarded lightly.

Mike had sung well, his voice clear, crisp and in tune and devoid of the disconcerting vibrato that was to spoil his undeniable vocal talents somewhat for me in later years. It was the Searchers brought up to date in a style that dragged us into the current frame of pop fashion while being more than able to satisfy those diehard traditionalists who both resent and fear change.

90. The advert for our single Umbrella Man

91. With Eartha Kitt at Abbey Road, the calm before the storm

92. With Dusty Springfield on the night of the famous 'willy fiddling' incident

BANGKOK
(Courtesy: HSA Radio)

This Week

1 SING SINGER SING—Searchers
2 FROM MY HEAD TO MY TOE—Barry Ryan
3 MY GUY—Mary Wells
4 THE HARDER THEY COME—Jimmy Cliff
5 LOVE LIFTED ME—Ray Stevens
6 WALK WITH ME, TALK WITH ME, DARLING—Four Tops
7 SUGAR ME—Lynsey De Paul
8 IT'S FOUR IN THE MORNING—Faron Young
9 RICE-PAPER MOUNTAIN (SCAT IN THE DARK)—Alan Haven
10 COUNTRY FREEDOM—Vicky Leandros
11 YOU'RE A SONG (THAT I CAN'T SING)—Frankie Valli & Four Seasons
12 DON'T GO DOWN TO RENO—Tony Christie
13 KATE—Johnny Cash And The Tennessee Three
14 WHERE IS THE LOVE—Roberta

93. A number one is still a number one wherever it is. Sing Singer Sing tops the Bangkok charts

94. 1970 the new line-up with Billy Adamson (right)

95. With RCA a&r man Richard Swainson and Neil Sedaka

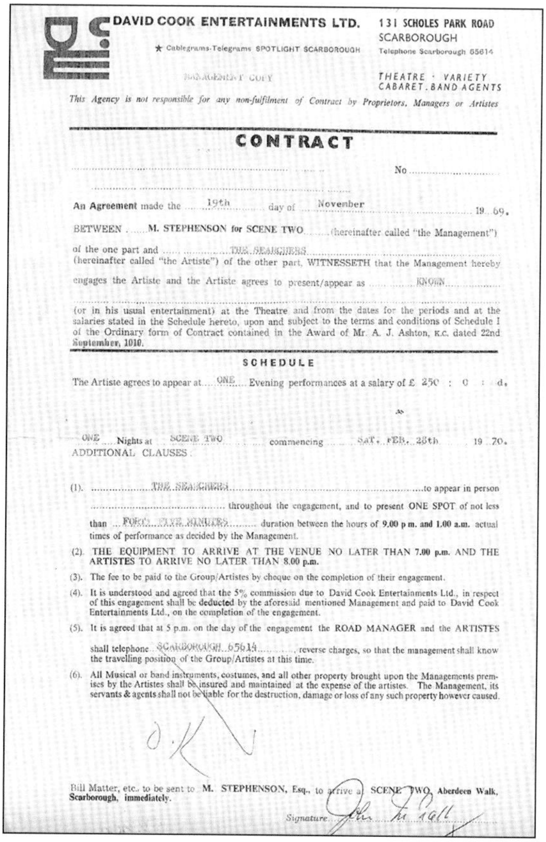

DAVID COOK ENTERTAINMENTS LTD.

★ Cablegrams-Telegrams SPOTLIGHT SCARBOROUGH

131 SCHOLES PARK ROAD
SCARBOROUGH
Telephone Scarborough 65614

MANAGEMENT COPY

THEATRE · VARIETY
CABARET. BAND AGENTS

This Agency is not responsible for any non-fulfilment of Contract by Proprietors, Managers or Artistes

CONTRACT

No ....

An Agreement made the 19th day of November 19 69.

BETWEEN M. STEPHENSON for SCENE TWO (hereinafter called "the Management") of the one part and THE SEARCHERS (hereinafter called "the Artiste") of the other part, WITNESSETH that the Management hereby engages the Artiste and the Artiste agrees to present/appear as KNOWN

(or in his usual entertainment) at the Theatre and from the dates for the periods and at the salaries stated in the Schedule hereto, upon and subject to the terms and conditions of Schedule I of the Ordinary form of Contract contained in the Award of Mr. A. J. Ashton, K.C. dated 22nd September, 1010.

SCHEDULE

The Artiste agrees to appear at ONE Evening performances at a salary of £ 250 : 0 : d.

ONE Nights at SCENE TWO commencing SAT. FEB. 28th 19 70.

ADDITIONAL CLAUSES:

(1). THE SEARCHERS to appear in person throughout the engagement, and to present ONE SPOT of not less than FORTY FIVE MINUTES duration between the hours of **9.00 p m. and 1.00 a.m.** actual times of performance as decided by the Management.

(2). THE EQUIPMENT TO ARRIVE AT THE VENUE NO LATER THAN **7.00 p.m.** AND THE ARTISTES TO ARRIVE NO LATER THAN **8.00 p.m.**

(3). The fee to be paid to the Group/Artistes by cheque on the completion of their engagement.

(4). It is understood and agreed that the 5% commission due to David Cook Entertainments Ltd., in respect of this engagement shall be **deducted** by the aforesaid mentioned Management and paid to David Cook Entertainments Ltd., on the completion of the engagement.

(5). It is agreed that at 5 p.m. on the day of the engagement the ROAD MANAGER and the ARTISTES shall telephone SCARBOROUGH 65614, reverse charges, so that the management shall know the travelling position of the Group/Artistes at this time.

(6). All Musical or band instruments, costumes, and all other property brought upon the Managements premises by the Artistes shall be insured and maintained at the expense of the artistes. The Management, its servants & agents shall not be liable for the destruction, damage or loss of any such property however caused.

O.K.

Bill Matter, etc., to be sent to **M. STEPHENSON, Esq.**, to arrive at **SCENE TWO, Aberdeen Walk, Scarborough, immediately.**

Signature John McNally

96. Contract for the Scene 2, Scarborough, Feb 28th 1970

97. Backstage at the Fiesta Stockton with owner Jim Lipthorpe

99. Jerry Lee Lewis at the Steel Pier, Atlantic City 1973, ignoring Billy J's requests

98. Knocking down pennies in a Stockton pub for charity (Trevor Harland collection)

100. The main attraction. The diving horse, the Steel Pier, Atlantic City

101. With Maurice Gibb after the Midnight Special recording, L.A

102. With Rainer Haas, our German connection

103. John McNally & Paul McNally (no relation) at Rockfield Studios

104. Me, John McNally and Pat Moran at Rockfield

105. Mike and John rehearsing at the Old Mill, Rockfield

106. The Old Mill, Rockfield

107. The Hearts In Her Eyes sleeve

108. With the Police in Baden Baden. l-r Stewart Copeland, Sting, me, Andy Summers

109. The Sire period

110. Ed Stasium and Martin Hughes

111. Martin Hughes, our drummer on Play For Today

112. Being presented to Queen Elizabeth II at the 1981 Royal Variety Show (Doug McKenzie)

113. Peter Collins

114. With Ritchie Blackmore, My Father's Place, Long Island

115. The famous Jack Bender poster

116. Chris Spedding, John Turner (roadie), Joey Costellano (tour manager), David Essex in Heartbreaks, New York

117. Me with a songwriting legend. Jerome 'Doc' Pomus, the Lone Star Café, New York

119. First Class with l-r Spencer James, Eddie Richards, Robin Shaw (Spencer James collection)

118. John McNally and Robert Pratt in happier times

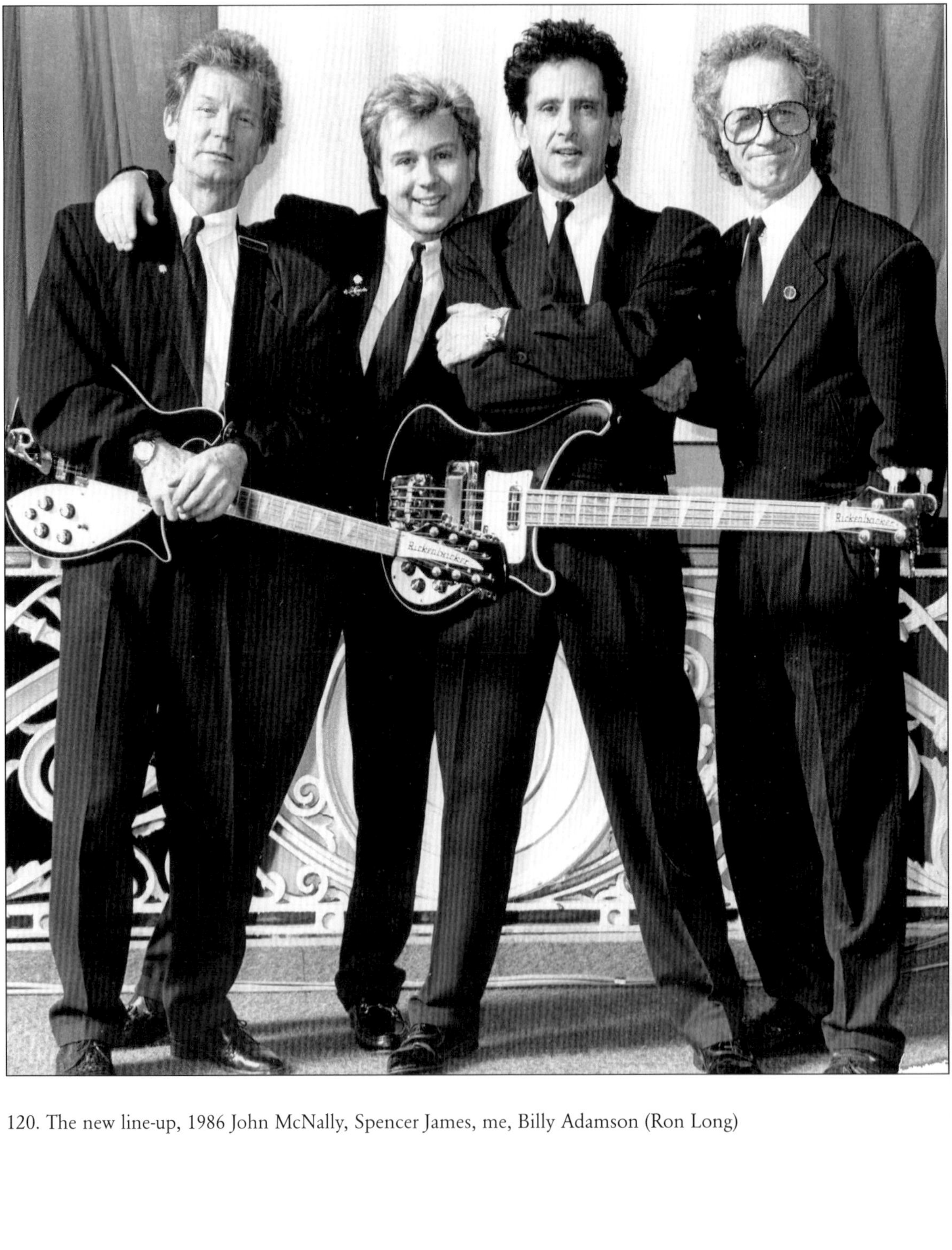

120. The new line-up, 1986 John McNally, Spencer James, me, Billy Adamson (Ron Long)

121. The British Invasion tour. U.S.A 1986

122. The British Invasion artistes. Searchers, Gerry, Chad & Jeremy, Freddie and a Mindbender

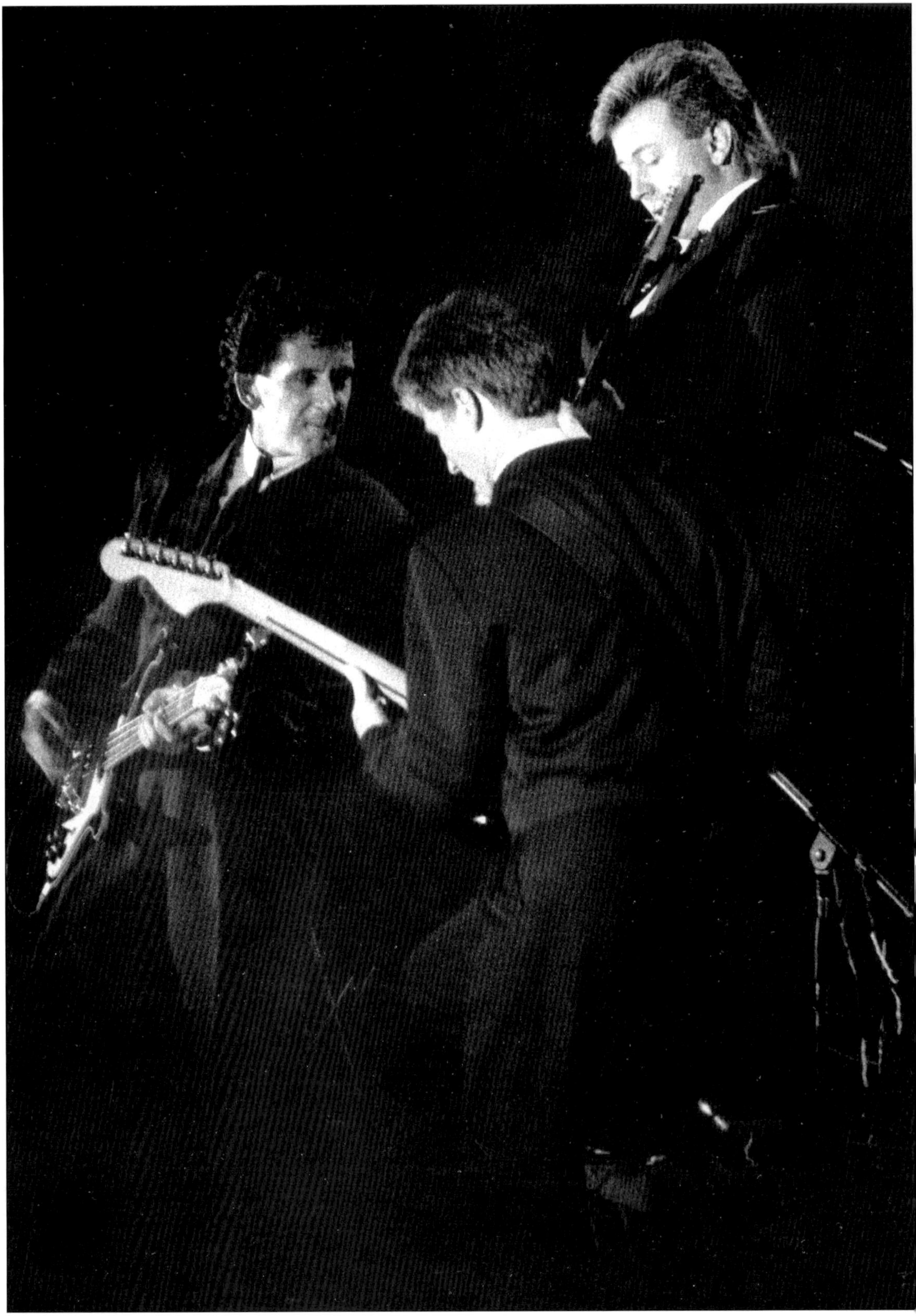

123. The new front line (Ron Long)

124. Kings Lynn or bust

125. The London Palladium, the opening night of the first Solid Silver Sixties tour.

126. Me, John McNally, Paul McCartney, Roy Wood at the Sgt Pepper CD launch

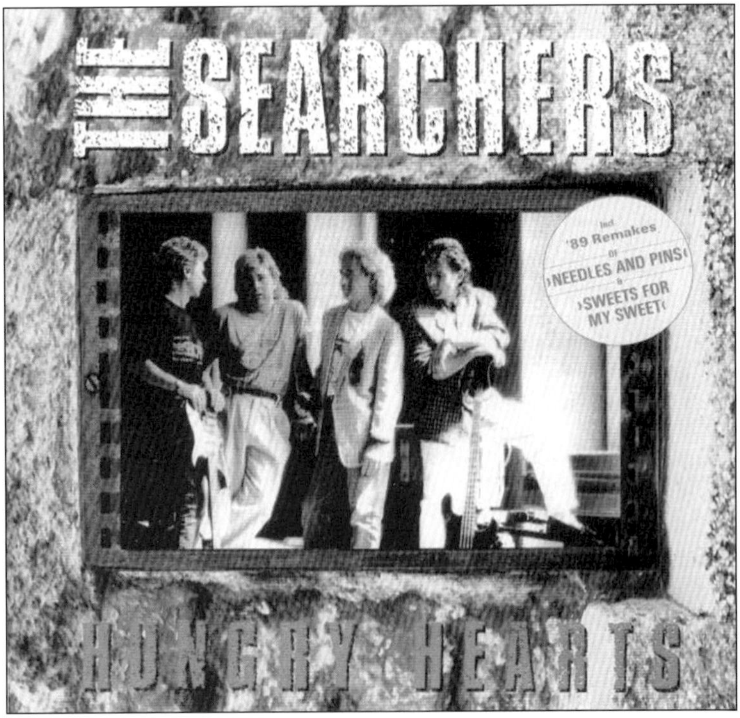

127. The sleeve for Hungry Hearts

The reviews were good to excellent and the label's publicity machine garnered acres of news space for us the like of which we had not enjoyed for years. 'A remarkable comeback by the second best group to come from Liverpool' wrote Charles Catchpole in the Daily Mail. 'Resisting the temptation to dwell in the past they tackle a batch of contemporary material with a verve and freshness that makes you wonder why they ever went away.'

In SHE magazine Bob Kiley declared 'they're back - rocking out with an invigorating chunk of high class pop which shames those who have written them off as tarnished golden oldies. Half of the ten contemporary tracks on the new album have singles potential and with the 60s revival maintaining a presence in the charts it's a delight to see one of the original groups of that era upstaging the imitators. Welcome back, Wack.'

And there was more. Hugh Fielder of Sounds awarded it an impressive four stars while Bob Edmonds for the NME called it 'an immaculate return to prominence by one of the most influential groups ever.' He went on to add 'They've come up with a seamless blend of pop, country and rock & roll that's so effortlessly fine it's enough to make Rockpile (Dave Edmunds' outfit) give up in despair.' All of the signs were good and we could be forgiven for thinking we were heading back into the mainstream with a bang.

As a taster the single *Hearts In Her Eyes* had been released a few weeks earlier in October with my song *Don't Hang On* making up the flip. It was the obvious contender for our first assault at the charts. It harked back easily to our glorious past while matching any current offerings from the so-called 'new wave' groups. The jangle meter was on high to overload and the guitar riff followed on from where *When You Walk In The Room* and *Needles And Pins* ended.

If press coverage had been easy to come by, radio and television were different matters entirely. Disc jockeys who had keenly courted our company when we were riding high were not so enthusiastic about forging associations with a past from which they were forever trying to distance themselves. We needed more airplay to make an impact, particularly on Radio One, and we weren't getting it. Television spots were few and far between and there were hotter acts than us after them but we did manage a number of regional stations and the occasional national spot such as the lunchtime Midlands show Pebble Mill At One and Tim Rice's late night talk and music show Friday Night, Saturday Morning on BBC2.

We travelled abroad to gain exposure when it was offered and flew to Baden Baden in Germany to appear alongside another new British band who, after two hits under their belt already were up and coming but unlike us were not about to stop. The Police were destined for greater things and had 'sensational' stamped all over them. I was amazed and pleased to find that they were incredibly friendly towards us and chatted happily in the concessionary between takes.

Sting I remember was still full of the joys of fatherhood and talked enthusiastically about his young son Joe. I'm afraid I could not help showing my cynical side and ventured my opinions on the wisdom or otherwise of long-term relationships which more and more seemed to come to grief under the pressures and temptations of modern society. 'You're starting to depress me' he commented. Maybe I had hit a little too close to home as it wasn't that long before his marriage to the actress Frances Tomelty collapsed. But he soon cheered up and presented me with a tiny tin Police badge which I affixed to the loose fitting white boiler suit outfit I was wearing for the transmission.

Andy Summers was an extremely nice guy, good fun with a charmingly unaffected nature and he made a point of commenting favourably on my outfit. He was also being extremely helpful in advising me where to go to obtain a sponsored instrument and directed me to the distributors of the Ibanez bass Sting was using with the instruction to tell the guy Sting told me to call. If for any reason that did not work I was to ring him at his home number which he wrote down for me and he would put me onto the Aria people.

When I got home I followed his advice and when Ibanez turned me down I called Andy. True to his word he gave me the relevant names at Aria. They were extremely receptive to my approach and not only was I handed a TRB650 bass completely free of charge but a whole selection of instruments to equip the entire band, including drums plus another bass for me, this time an electric blue fretless model, soon followed.

When I next saw the Police on television plugging their new record I couldn't help but be amused to see that Andy was wearing a white boiler suit exactly like mine. Shades of Graham Nash, I thought.

In the end *Hearts In Her Eyes* failed and we entered 1980 mildly dispirited but ready to try again and in February *It's Too Late* was released with John McNally's song *This Kind Of Love Affair* for the B-side. It too received very favourable notices. Not quite as unstinting as *Hearts In Her Eyes* but its qualities were once more noted by the press and once more pretty much ignored by radio and television. Over in the States it was our debut single from the album and a slowed-down version along with an added piano and handclaps was put out as a tester with *Don't Hang On* used again for the coupling. It fared no better.

The powers at Sire had a rethink about their strategy and concluded that it had been a wrong move to issue the album at Christmas-time when the market was flooded with big names all vying for the massive numbers that a seasonal hit could deliver. They took the unusual decision to halt promotion and withdraw the album in order to re-present it to the public with a fresh assault of promotion and a new look entirely. It seemed they had second thoughts about the wisdom of the 'airplane' cover which many considered too arty and vague.

With three additional titles *Love's Melody* by Andy McMasters, *Silver* by Dave Paul and *Back To The War* by John Hiatt and with Bob Dylan's *Coming From The Heart* removed from the track list it was rescheduled for a March release in the UK. We looked magnificently sullen in the new stark black and white photograph taking up the entirety of the front cover, as befitted our new serious image and the name, now with the definite article back with a vengeance, in luxurious silver lettering. We posed threateningly on the back cover in an empty photographic studio somewhere in Covent Garden. Heaven knows what all this cost but we could not accuse Paul McNally and his minions at Sire of not trying.

Love's Melody, remixed from the album version, was chosen as the single and was, we felt, very worthy of attention. It was pounding and powerful. It had been recorded previously by the writer Andy McMasters' own group Ducks Deluxe but in our minds we had raised the impact a notch or two. Again, we thought we were in with a chance though it had just been proved that nothing was certain.

We dutifully did the rounds of the trendy London gig circuit where the press could get to see us without too much effort, and we enjoyed it immensely. The Electric Ballroom where we supported the B52s was as street cred as a group could get and the Nashville Rooms in Earl's Court was packed out with such luminaries as Hugh Cornwall from the Stranglers and Bette Bright, and from the Banshees Siouxsie Sioux joining the throng.

The Venue in Victoria was another success and the student audience at the Albany in Deptford, a venue that was destined to attain a certain significance in the Searchers' history, loved the intriguing mixture of classic hits and samplings from our current crop. We were supported there by Any Trouble, a band tipped to make big waves mainly due to the very promising talent of their bespectacled singer/songwriter Clive Gregson. After our set the drummer approached Mike in the dressing room and introduced himself. 'Hi, I'm Andy, Any Trouble.' Mike, totally ignorant of who the support was or that a group by such a name even existed, turned for a second, replied 'No mate, no trouble at all. I really enjoyed it' and returned to his conversation leaving the poor guy baffled and dejected.

In the end, despite the British press in the main getting behind us and predicting a comeback, the album and single failed to make a dent and it was back to the drawing board. Fortunately, Sire were still very enthusiastic about working with us and were happy to take another chance. Plans were set in motion for a second album for the following year. Seymour Stein along with his US Director of Artists Development Ken

Kushnik had trekked even further than Southend this time, bringing with them a potential American manager to a holiday camp venue in Devon.

They had even hired a light aircraft to take them there rather than endure the long drive. They sat and watched us in the bizarre Hi De Hi setting and tried to see further than the jolly cabaret banter we by necessity relied on in order to pull in the gigs. They had made the transatlantic crossing in even greater style having shelled out for hideously expensive Concorde tickets. I had already flown on Concorde myself to New York and knew what it cost.

The American manager eventually flew back and left us with a contract to peruse at our leisure and hopefully sign. It was even more frightening than the Sire record contract. At least that wasn't going to cost us anything. As far as we could tell our US management was entitled to First Class air tickets and necessary expenses (unspecified). I, on the other hand, was travelling to engagements in the back of a Ford Transit at a time in my life when a little more comfort would have been more than welcome. A couple of modest trips on our behalf by this flash American could have put us firmly in the bankruptcy court.

And there seemed to be no clause indicating that any fees would be from US earnings only or that any expenses incurred could not be claimed against our UK income. He would certainly have had a struggle getting a Concorde ticket out of us. Maybe a couple of long bus rides but anything more would need serious consideration. Something that we would have probably signed without a second thought at nineteen now represented a terrifying prospect in our late thirties. We eventually declined his gracious offer and remained under our own control. Sometimes it pays to be young and naïve.

There was yet another bombshell to come and one that could not be so readily ignored. After a promotional meeting in London John and Mike grabbed a cab to Euston for their train home and were surprised to find Ken Kushnik and Paul McNally insisting on sharing the journey. During the short trip they voiced their concerns over the drumming and stated that they very much wanted us to replace Billy Adamson. They did not like his style of playing or his look. They felt the drums had let the album down and whatever the case they would not countenance him playing on the next one.

John phoned me the next day with the news. Personally I couldn't see that it was a big deal. He sounded fine to me. At that point if I had agreed Billy would have been ousted from the band without further ado. But, fence sitting as always, I argued against giving in to someone else's control which I figured was an abuse of power and influence. Billy's job was saved. Years later I cannot help feeling that perhaps I was wrong and that in a tough world I too should have been tough and pragmatic and dispensed with sensitivities in favour of the bigger picture.

Telling Billy Adamson was not pleasant but there was little he could do about it. It was a done deal. He was still in place as our drummer for live engagements but would henceforth be substituted for our recording sessions. In truth I don't think he ever really believed that it was Sire's decision. I am sure that he was convinced of our duplicity but what we told him was simply the truth. But it didn't matter one way or the other who was the instigator. The result was the same and the atmosphere between us and our dour Scottish member plummeted even further.

Unhappiness in his personal life did not help matters. His marriage had broken down and to my mind he was bitter towards the world at that point. I specifically recall him saying one time when marital troubles were becoming particularly strained, 'No more mister nice guy.' And that certainly came to be the case, at least as far as we were concerned. I'm sure that within his personal circle of tried and trusted friends with no axe to grind he was still the same affable fellow in whose company I had once spent many good times. Maybe I had changed and Billy had not.

Luckily for us the unfulfilled promise of *The Searchers* did not deter the people at Sire and plans were made for a follow up. The general feeling in the company was that, despite Pat Moran's excellent and dedicated work on the album, there was a need for an extra depth and edge to any new product, and the American producer Ed Stasium was brought in to add the missing elements. Pat appeared not to object to his influenced being dissipated and together they made an effective and happy combination. Ed was a native of New Jersey and had grown up playing in garage bands around New York until he finally realised that his passion lay on the other side of the glass panel that divided studio from control room.

At the Venture Sound Studios in Somerville, New Jersey, where he was a house engineer he worked on and mixed his first gold single, the smash by Gladys Knight & the Pips, *Midnight Train To Georgia*. Following periods at Le Studio in Quebec and the legendary Power Station in New York where he was responsible for much of the studio design and set-up he began a career as an independent, most notably producing a string of albums for the Ramones which included *Rocket To Russia*, *Road To Ruin* and the classic *Rock & Roll High School*.

We considered ourselves fortunate to have Sire's golden boy at our disposal and as a bonus he turned out to be an extremely nice guy to work with, friendly and fun and very much in tune with our own thinking. Any disagreements, and there were very few, were dealt with in an understated and civilised manner. Diplomacy was an invaluable tool always at his disposal. Not for nothing was he known as 'the Henry Kissinger of pop'.

Ed, Pat and John McNally made a formidable and efficient trio and we spent yet another six weeks at Rockfield assembling a bunch of good songs that we felt ideally suited our style, our history and our future. John was working under extreme difficulty having discovered a problem with gallstones that required an operation as soon as possible. The operation was overdue if anything. Deciding that recording commitments were far more important than his personal health he postponed treatment until the album was finished, though the endless hours at his amplifier and in the control booth were stoically endured under a great amount of discomfort.

Ed's input and experience with the punk driven Ramones beefed up the bottom end of our work and gave it an added power. Taking over the drum stool from the ousted Billy Adamson was a young Irish lad called Martin Hughes who had been recommended by Paul McNally. About half our age, his youthful enthusiasm and rock solid bass drum provided the perfect bedrock for the new tracks. He was quiet and unobtrusive and though he seemed a little overawed at being asked to sit in on these sessions with a group who had been part of an era that had become the new reference point for all guitar based bands since, Martin fitted in beautifully and acquitted himself without fuss or fault throughout.

The only speck of trouble during our stay was a barrage of calls from the long departed Chris Curtis who had read of our prestigious signing with Sire and decided that here was a chance for a re-entry into the world of pop. His short, flamboyant career as a producer had ended when his fragile finances gave out and he had been working as a civil servant back in Liverpool. When the first call came to the Rockfield offices they were not unduly concerned and when we chose to avoid contact, knowing that it would be disastrous to avail him of the opportunity to interfere, which he would have, they politely fobbed him off with a suitable explanation.

Though we were still very fond of Chris and recognised that he had a good heart beneath all that bluff and bluster, we knew full well that any involvement would result in him trying to take over without a whiff of conscience. His self-penned songs would not merely be offered to us. We would simply be told that he had songs we were going to record. It would all end in unpleasantness and that was something we desperately wished to avoid.

When further phone calls failed to get him in touch with us he issued threats to the girl on the switchboard that he would come down and set the studio on fire if he was not put through. Panic spread through the organisation and they came to seek out our advice. They were very frightened and wanted to involve the police. We dissuaded them from this course explaining that Chris was nutty but harmless.

In truth, we were not all convinced in ourselves that he was as harmless as we had suggested. Never an entirely stable person, he frequently caused havoc in the office where he worked which included spontaneously lifting a pile of important papers from a desk one day and, to everyone's horror, hurling them out of the window into the street. In the end they wisely decided to bestow early retirement on him and from that point he was entitled to enjoy his little acts of chaos in his own time and at his own risk. Once left to his own devices with no organised labour to occupy his rambling mind he would find other folk to disturb. On one occasion he wandered onto a crowded bus and promptly began to distribute a sizeable portion of his record collection to complete strangers.

On another he went to visit a woman friend who owned a hairdressing salon. It was a 'pensioners special' afternoon and the shop was crowded with dear old ladies happily enjoying the friendly banter with friends while they waited for their hair to turn to elegant shades of blue and purple. Their pleasure at being offered delicious chocolates by this excitable and seemingly funny man soon turned to confusion and fright when he locked the door and refused to let any of them leave. In the end they obtained a merciful release, but for a short while it was not at all pleasant.

Even as we told the Ward brothers that their property was perfectly safe we couldn't help thinking to ourselves that he could just as easily carry out his threats. Eventually he stopped calling, much to everyone's relief.

Once the project was completed we departed for home and the next morning John checked himself into a private hospital in Liverpool for his operation. But the heavy workload he had put himself through had weakened his immune system and the surgery had to be postponed for two days due to exhaustion. He was deemed not fit enough to endure the debilitating abuse to his body which lay ahead.

Meanwhile there were still a number of contracted gigs to be completed and though we had originally intended to bring in a standby guitarist to deputise for the ailing John in the end we fulfilled out obligations as a three-piece unit. There were no great objections and even though we were underpowered we did not encounter any insurmountable problems. We just put our heads down and played the hits.

Two weeks later John, now sporting the beard he had been growing during the Rockfield recordings and clutching the new 'must have' item of the moment, a Sony Walkman which was a get well present from Paul McNally, Ed Stasium and Pat Moran at Sire Records, was back in the fold and, against medical advice, undertook a heavy touring schedule which included a number of club dates in Germany. His damaged stomach muscles required time to repair themselves and he was forced to be seated while on stage. In truth he should never have been on the road at all but this was showbusiness and the show had to go on.

Play For Today was released in the May of 1981. The title was a play on words, having been lifted from the popular BBC drama series and the black cover featured a radio tuner drawn in contrasting green lines. It was a nice use of a phrase that would serve to strike a chord of identification with listeners in Britain. In the US the cute play on words meant nothing and the packaging was completely revamped to show a simply drawn country lane and a signpost topped by a red heart. The title for American consumption was changed to *Love's Melodies* and though it took the eminently sensible route of establishing the name of the preferred track that was to be the first single, it conversely gave a false impression of the content. It was a hard driving rock album and not a collection of soppy love songs.

Most of the songs included were typical bright, up-tempo guitar-based pop that played on the group's strength in this field. Without prior information a potential buyer could easily be misled into believing there was a wealth of soppy slush and romance waiting inside the cover when in fact there was anything but. *Murder In My Heart, Silver, Infatuation, She Made A Fool Of You, Radio Romance, Back To The War, Everything But A Heartache, Almost Saturday Night, September Gurls.* They were all good strong spirited tunes. Our one concession to sentiment was the haunting John David song *New Day*. We were allowed our own input with *Another Night*. Another track, *Ambulance Chaser*, complete with a brass section, was committed to tape but considered unsuitable and was rejected.

Taking an unexpected turn Sire decided to go down a different avenue for the choice of a single and plumped for John McNally's offering, *Another Night*, figuring that it might eliminate any preconceptions about what we were or were not expected to be in musical terms. *Another Night* was slightly surreal and almost psychedelic in its construction and lyrical content. Furthermore its drug-oriented words seemed to refer to the use of cocaine which is not at all what one would expect from the sanitised Searchers.

Coming from the pen of the completely drug free and clean living McNally it was almost as radical as Cliff Richard espousing the joys of illicit group sex. But of course it was perfectly legitimate. After all a novelist does not have to be a confirmed killer to write a murder mystery and a song is nothing more than a mini novel. Though not typical of anything that we had done before it was a good recording with a driving track whose guitar sound lay somewhere between Blue Oyster Cult's *Don't Fear The Reaper* and Martha & the Muffins' *Echo Beach.*

For the purposes of establishing our new image we turned to wearing casual clothes for our concerts, something we had never done before. This was fine for the London rock circuit but after the opening night at the elegant Lakeside Club in Frimley Green in Surrey, now the premier location for important televised darts tournaments, the gruff but lovable owner Bob Potter remarked that 'My waiters are better dressed than you.'

He was dead right. We decided there and then that we had better smarten up for such places and dredged out an old set of safari suits to wear. Unfortunately, they had been constructed at a time when enormous flares - the wider the better - were *de rigeur* and I was most definitely not going to parade myself in such out of date monstrosities in these 'straight legged' times. I spent my one evening off that week laboriously toiling with needle and thread reducing the lower portion of the trousers to a more suitable parallel design.

We had the usual struggle to get plugs on the disc though we did at least manage one national television spot as guests on Moondog Matinee, a Muriel Young production put together as a showcase for her new discoveries, a teenage outfit from Ireland called the Moondogs. They were chums of the Undertones and the connection with our Sire stablemates had helped to cement our inclusion on the show. The Moondogs' boyish charm and good looks were supposed to propel them to international fame and fortune. They did not. Neither did the plug propel our new release into the charts. There was a complete absence of propelling on all sides.

We dutifully played the London rock circuit in an effort to stimulate interest and sales. Mike Gardener gave us a great review in the Record Mirror for the album and also for our Dingwalls show. He wrote 'This Dingwalls set showed that their strengths are even stronger (than last year) especially with the addition of the sparkling material available from their new album *Play For Today* like *Little Bit Of Heaven*, *Murder In My Heart*, *Silver* and the superb single *Another Night.*

'There can be no doubting their energy or commitment and their new found attack and bite is not far from making a great night out, where classics from the past like *Goodbye My Love*, *Needles And Pins* and *When You Walk In The Room* mingle well with latter-day pop standards like *Hearts In Her Eyes*, *Switchboard Susan* and *It's Too Late* in a formidable experience.'

Bob Edmunds in the NME declared that 'If the Searchers had had access to material of this calibre in the 60s their career would never have floundered.' Tony Jasper writing for Music Week called the single a 'full blooded fighting spacey number, well performed.' A reviewer in Time Out declared that if every deejay in the land was doing their job this would be number one. Sadly every deejay in the land ignored his advice.

But in the end it was all to no avail. Neither *Another Night* here in the UK nor the American choice of *Love's Melody*, left over from the previous revamped version of the first album which was unissued over there, managed to chart and sales of the album failed to reach the benchmark that would have guaranteed a third try which was already in the planning stages.

We were disappointed but it had been a good time for us. Again the promise had been unfulfilled in commercial terms but at least we had left a legacy of terrific material to show to future generations that we had not been entirely a waste of space, or that any worthwhile ideas had been used up by the end of '66. It had been a very satisfying and productive experience and there was no-one in the company we did not get along with. For once it almost felt like family.

We had been very hopeful that Sire would remain committed to a third album but they had other young hopefuls to invest their time and money in, and the big changes in the power structure at WEA (Warners, Elektra, Atlantic) who were the giant company who distributed the Sire product, where a new team had been brought in to get their finances back on track, could not have helped. By the middle of 1981 we were again footloose and fancy free.

30

Maybe It's Not Too Late

With our Sire adventure finally at a fruitless end we returned to the more mundane task of taking care of business in the real world once again. In fact things on that front weren't at all bad. The extensive press coverage and the low key but nonetheless distinctive buzz caused by the association with Stein's label had lifted our profile several notches. Along with our cabaret and corporate function dates we were now accommodated on the rock circuit and anything that could widen our market place was more than welcome. Our money had been rising steadily to the point where we could hardly call ourselves rich but at least we were making an acceptable living and managing to pay the bills. There were many who were forced to toil in industries they loathed and which were considerably less rewarding in both financial and psychological terms. We could count ourselves lucky.

If our hopes on the recording side had once again been at least temporarily dashed there was at least an unexpected treat in the offing in a phone call from Tim Rice to Mike Pender. He had long been a fan of the group and we had in the past performed in the garden of his imposing Oxfordshire manor house for the enjoyment of his local cricket club.

It transpired that Tim had been asked to assemble a line-up of entertainers who might be deemed representative of the various phases of British pop music throughout the past quarter of a century for the 1981 Royal Variety Performance. Would we be available? It was an exciting prospect but one which Mike explained we would unfortunately have to decline. The October date fell slap bang in the middle of a Scandinavian tour that was signed, sealed and waiting to be delivered.

Mike's response was exactly the way I would have reacted had I been the one to receive the call. It appeared to be an open and shut case. But John McNally was not one to be put off by such minor difficulties. It was, he quite rightly pointed out, too important for us to miss out on. He insisted that we should ring back and accept the offer and simply adjust the touring itinerary to accommodate the concert. One night of the trip could surely be rescheduled, postponed or cancelled. We could fly home for the day and get back out there in time to resume the rest of the dates.

It was going to be costly. As the Royal Variety Performance was a charity event we didn't even attempt to find out if they would cover our expenses. We simply assumed not and anyway felt it would look cheap to even try. For the thousand pounds or so in flights that we would have to shell out, and of course a considerable sum which constituted the lost fee, it still seemed like very good value for money in publicity terms.

We did have a slight sartorial problem to iron out first. There was no way we could appear in those hideous safari suits. As a temporary solution on our general platform of work they would just about suffice but they were hardly fitting garb in which to strut our stuff in front of, and indeed be received by, royalty.

What are friends there for if not to be used? Mike had a pal in the tailoring business, a man with the iconic name of Tony Curtis, who was happy to make a set of suits in time for the show though there was no opportunity for such luxuries as fittings. We had to trust to his skill and our good luck. Luck as it happened was with us. When they arrived shortly before we set off for Denmark they fitted perfectly. Narrow high buttoned two-piece outfits in shiny black mohair with complimenting black velvet collars and a silk stripe down the side of the pants. The look was perfect and so was the price. One hundred pounds for the lot.

When it came time for us to return to the UK on Monday 23rd November Sweden, Denmark and Finland were cold and covered in a thick frosting of white and it was a treat to take a break, however short, in an environment where the temperature was a couple of degrees warmer. When we arrived at the Theatre Royal, Drury Lane, rehearsals were already in full swing as the glittering array of stars, superstars and jobbing gypsies were running through their routines.

The pop portion of the programme other than ourselves comprised Marty Wilde, Lonnie Donegan, Adam & the Ants, Lulu, Cliff Richard and the Shadows, Donovan, Acker Bilk and Alvin Stardust. It was a pretty fair assessment of how our side of the music business had evolved over the past twenty-five years. At the more cerebral end of the roster was classical violinist Itzhak Perlman while covering the other parts of the spectrum was the usual variety fare.

There was John Inman from Are You Being Served? and Lenny Henry. Perennial stalwarts Jimmy Tarbuck and Dickie Henderson. Anita Harris, the Cambridge Buskers and the cast of the hit West End show One Mo' Time, which included the Clark Brothers, Precious Wilson, Pearly Gates, Patti Boulaye and Kenny Lynch, catered for the more conservative and traditional taste of the royal patron who this year was none other than Her Majesty Queen Elizabeth II. We were not being fobbed off with some 'B' list royal. This was top end of the market stuff.

Both the original and the latest of the Evitas, Elaine Paige and Stephanie Lawrence, were to appear in a segment along with Tim Rice and Andrew Lloyd Webber and Lloyd Webber's cellist sibling Julian.

For whatever reason a French theme had been included with all of the Can Can dancers, sixteen girls and eleven boys, being flown over for the night from the Moulin Rouge in Paris which of necessity had to close for the evening, the first time in its history this had happened. French songstress Mireille Mathieu completed the Gallic content. Charles Aznavour was also originally mooted to be there but for whatever reason was missing from the final cast.

The actor Robert Hardy, who had recently portrayed Churchill on television, compered the evening's proceedings and his uncanny likeness to the man who many considered to be the greatest of great Britons certainly lent an air of authority and a certain gravitas to the event. Unusually for one of these shows there was no big American name on the bill.

There was no need for us to drag our equipment back with us on the plane. We had arranged with the good people at Aria to supply a set of guitars and drums direct to the theatre. It didn't matter that we would not be used to these particular models as our solitary song, *Needles And Pins*, was to be lip-synched to a track we had specially pre-recorded. With the necessarily quick turnover of talent in the pop spot that had room for only one musical offering each, the setting and dismantling of equipment, not to mention the re-balancing of sound, was an impossibility. We were perfectly able to perform the song live, God knows we had done it virtually every night for the past sixteen years, but tonight, along with our other fellow popsters, the movement of our limbs and lips was for visual purposes only.

At the end of the pop section Cliff and the Shadows were due to rise from the bowels of the theatre where their equipment could be kept undisturbed and thus they were able to perform live. Cliff, being only a step or two down in the royalty stakes from the Queen herself was also given time for several of his hits. It was an Orwellian situation. All pop stars might be equal but some pop stars were most definitely more equal than others.

When the time came for our appearance the curtains swept back and I swear there was an audible gasp in the auditorium. The sharp suits with our contrasting white shirts and set off with black ties looked stunning. It was as complete and perfect an image as any Searchers fan could desire. The years had been good to us. Our figures were still trim, there were no bald patches for the lights to bounce off and our faces, at least from that distance, virtually unlined.

The three minutes passed in a flash and we executed a traditional bow to the Royal box. As we strode off to the wings to a warm and gratifying thunderstorm of applause

I felt my guitar cord getting tighter. I had forgotten to pull it out of my bass guitar and began to tug while trying to look as nonchalant as possible and still walking. Just at the point where it began to look like a washing line and was in great danger of wrenching the amplifier head off the speaker cabinet and onto the floor I managed to remove the jack plug from the socket and was mercifully spared the indignity of national, and possibly even international, disgrace.

When the whole thing was over we joined the line of artistes waiting to shake the royal glove and adopt a suitably cap-doffing pose for the benefit of our monarch. Louis Benjamin who had left his position as Managing Director of Pye Records to occupy the equivalent office at Stoll Moss Theatres preceded Her Majesty and introduced each one to her. At least that was the theory.

By the time she had reached our section Louis had lagged behind somewhat and we found ourselves face to face with our sovereign Queen and ne'er a word passing between us. And we were officially not supposed to speak unless spoken to. She eventually spoke to Mike and John and said how nice it was to hear the old songs again. Whether or not that was the truth remains known only to her but it was at least a demonstration of regal diplomacy in action. Having uttered the compliment she seemed unable or unwilling to elaborate any further while Mr Benjamin was still some way back talking to performers who were possibly more in tune with his time and tastes.

She was now in front of me and she stood and looked in impassive silence while I looked back hoping that someone would come to my rescue and perform an introduction. Seconds seemed like hours. It was like a stand-off in a Western movie. Who was going to pull the gun first? At any moment she was about to move on to the next group of people and unless I was introduced the traditional handshake was very unlikely to occur. I decided that this was the only chance I was ever going to get to shake the hand of our Queen and so I simply stuck my hand out, grabbed hers and proceeded to pump up and down. It was like a Marty Feldman sketch I had seen on television. But at least I had my memory and no one could take that away. And for a few seconds she could not take her hand away either, my grip was so tight, but at last she managed to pull herself free from this demented pop person.

The next day we were back in Scandinavia where the weather was still cold but the receptions were warm. We would have to wait till our return to the UK to check out the results of our efforts. The British newspapers dismissed the transmission as too long and disappointing in its content but then I had never known a year when it was any different. I only knew that in the theatre on the day the atmosphere had been electric. Somehow these affairs had trouble in translating successfully to the small screen.

When I finally got the chance to watch it there was no doubt that our tiny fragment looked good and came over well. A downside was the camera work on poor John

McNally who was not given one close-up, at least not on his face. His right hand was zoomed in on occasionally. Both Mike's and my face filled the screen several times and even Billy was covered but all John could look forward to was having the best known strumming hand in the business. His disappointment was hard to hide and rightly so. I felt bad for him and rang to tell him so.

Sire was now history as far as we were concerned, but such was the standing of the name The Searchers that by the latter part of 1982 we were signed to yet another label. Though it was only for a single, with anything further dependent on its success, we found ourselves back at the scene of our greatest triumphs, the old Pye studios in Great Cumberland Place. Of course Pye no longer existed. PRT (Precision Records and Tapes) now owned the facilities and the back catalogue and it was on this label that we would get yet another chance. We seemed to be making more comebacks than Frank Sinatra though his were infinitely more successful.

Matt Haywood was in charge of A&R there and it was his enthusiasm for the group that had instigated the signing. Once more we sifted through a pile of demos and became enthusiastic about a song by a Tyneside composer by the name of Steve Thompson. It was called *I Don't Want To Be The One* and was published by Bruce Welch of the Shadows. A good up-tempo tune with interesting chords and a driving chorus, we felt it had as good a chance as anything.

Matt had called in favours and enlisted the aid of a record producer called Peter Collins who, in tandem with his writing and producing partner Pete Waterman, was enjoying considerable success. They had just reached number one with *Pass The Duchy* by Musical Youth.

After a false start (we turned up at PRT Studios a day early and found it locked - it proved to be our own mistake) the session went well and we were happy with the way things were heading. Peter Collins was a serious guy, small and stocky with a dark, forbidding beard, who was calm and efficient but who did not seem to communicate with us on a personal level, which may have been because he had committed himself to a project that he had little enthusiasm for. I may have been wrong about that but we did not seem to be his kind of people. Or perhaps that was simply his demeanour and common ground was scarce. I don't know. I liked him but did not seem to be on his wavelength.

We used the ex-Roulettes drummer Bob Henrit and finished the task happy that we had given it our best shot which, we felt, had resulted in something that at least had a chance. We waited anxiously to hear the final mix a few days later. John rang me to express his disappointment on hearing the finished disc. He felt it fell short of the powerful track we had left behind at the end of our hard labours but he wanted all of our opinions.

In the end, after playing it through a few times, we all agreed. Peter Collins had removed my bass part, a simple one but one which had been strictly on the beat to push the song as much as possible, and substituted a syncopated line that gave it a more rolling rhythm. I didn't want to sound biased. If removing my part meant we had a better product then so be it despite any blow to my ego. But it really did sound softer to our ears.

Perhaps our jaded ears weren't the ones to use for such an important decision but Pete Waterman was in agreement with us. Collins refused point blank to do any more work on the record. As far as he was concerned he had made the best of it and that was that. But Waterman, taking our part, took us back into the studio, where I replaced the original four to the bar bass line and completed the final mix himself. He was beside himself with excitement exclaiming that it was a sure fire hit. It wasn't. It was duly released by PRT with *Hollywood*, a John McNally song on the flip side and sank without trace. We had even been even afforded the luxury of a basic video to go with the track, a mimed studio performance of the song with some wind blowing through our hair to give it a bit of movement but, apart from a rather nice piece of exposure on Leo Sayer's television series during which he joined us for a medley of our hits, I don't think it ever saw the light of day, let alone the light of a cathode ray tube.

Maybe Collins was right. He was and indeed is a hugely successful producer and knew his stuff. Perhaps we threw a winning formula out of the window. And then again Pete Waterman, who along with Mike Stock and Matt Aitken went on to have one of the most successful careers in production Britain has ever known, became a music legend in his own right. Very soon after our association with him everything he touched turned to gold. Timing is everything.

31

A Change Gonna Come

Having failed under the auspices of Pete Waterman, a man whose touch with everyone except us was such a guarantee of success that he made King Midas look like a pathetic charlatan, we went into PRT for a second effort, this time in September 1983 under the guiding hand of John Verity, who had been the guitar hero-in-residence of the group Argent, replacing Russ Ballard.

His style of playing and taste in music promised to give us a harder edge and with a lot of hope and a bunch of crossed fingers we travelled to Bradford in order to routine the proposed tracks and complete some basic demos in his home studio, before committing them to tape in the more glamourous and professional facilities deep in the dungeons of Great Cumberland Place.

In the end we completed four tracks with Verity, *Innocent Victim*, *A Good Way To Fall*, *In The Heat Of The Night* and *New Heart* before PRT pulled the plug on the project and the proposed releases were shelved. They were not to see the light of day for another nine years when, with the exception of *In The Heat Of The Night* which has not seen a release thus far, they were included on a compilation of hits and rarities put out by Sequel in 1992. Once more that fickle bird of paradise had flown right up our noses and back out again clutching the tattered remnants of our recording career in its beak as it soared off into the distance.

Our time at PRT had not been without some internal tension. One of our regular foreign territories had been Australia, a continent that we had ventured to many times since our first forays to the wonderful land of Oz in the mid sixties. Back then it had been as part of a package and while we were still in the throes of chart success to a greater or lesser degree. Our stages were in theatres and stadiums and our audiences numbered in thousands. Now we were a club act but the smaller crowds and cramped interiors did not dampen our enthusiasm for the place. Well, for most of us anyway.

John McNally and I loved Australia with its seductive climate, fascinating landscape and outgoing, friendly people. Billy Adamson was also keen though he had little choice in any decisions within the group. It was just the three of us who owned and operated the band and Mike Pender was less enthusiastic than either John or myself.

One contributing factor behind his reluctance was that during a previous trip his father had been taken ill and died. He had been unable to get home for the funeral. He was understandably upset at the awful turn of events and was less eager to be that far away from home again. I understood his feelings to a certain extent but considered that a person could not run his life simply on the premise that a similar tragedy might happen again. Life is full of ifs and buts, coincidences and maybe even acts of fate. At some point you simply have to get on with it and take your chances.

We had not worked there for a couple of years but our current absence was due mostly to financial considerations. The money to be earned there was relatively poor compared to our British fees, and we were holding out until we received an offer we could consider realistic. We had talked and between us set an acceptable minimum fee.

A sojourn in Oz was a sensible prospect on several fronts. It would take us off the UK circuit for a while and afford us a certain amount of exclusivity value in a saturated market, pay our bills and give us some pleasant time in the sun, as England suffered its usual depressingly forbidding winter temperatures. Mike was never that mad about lying about in the sun, especially in a sun that was halfway round the world, but our previous trips to Australasia had been regular and without any great problems.

During a break in the *I Don't Want To Be The One* sessions John called us together. An offer at the agreed level had been received a few weeks earlier and the Australian promoters were pressing us for a commitment. Basically, we were merely asking for the okay from Mike. John and I were ready to sign. Without hesitation Mike stated unsmilingly that we could go. But that he would not. With that he left the room.

John and I stood looking at each other, angry and frustrated. We could force a confrontation but that would only precipitate a dangerous situation from which there might be no return. We were certainly not at all sure that we were in a strong enough position to survive a split in our ranks and we wanted to keep our career on track at almost any cost. Reluctantly we decided that there was nothing to do but swallow our pride and get on with things.

Fortunately, there had been a resurgence in interest from America on the back of the Sire association and we found ourselves jetting over there every now and again, usually once a year, for a run of club dates. Again, they paid the bills and kept us out of Britain but US acceptance also gave us a profile a few notches higher that other British bands of our era who had failed to crack the all important and prestigious American market.

We spent some of November 1983 over there, mainly in the New York State area but occasionally venturing further. On the 4th we appeared at a club called My

Father's Place in Rosslyn, Long Island. We were pleased to find Ritchie Blackmore and some of his pals in the audience. Pleased because he was a big deal guitar god and his presence gave the night a certain importance, but also pleased because his group swelled the audience numbers by a significant percentage. It was not a huge crowd.

Even worse was the Marble Bar in Baltimore four days later when just a handful of people rattled about the shabby interior of a building that had seen better days. Parts of Baltimore that we passed through on our way looked depressingly downtrodden and forbidding and the Marble Bar fitted perfectly into the environment. Our dressing room was a dingy space, its graffiti-littered walls with the names of visiting groups scrawled there for posterity. Many of the names were intriguing but none more so than the Wanktones. I would dearly loved to have seen their show. A demonstration of melody and taste without doubt.

Our support for the evening, according to the hastily scrawled handbill put together to publicise the event, were the Re-Searchers. I can only imagine it was meant as a sort of tribute but must have confused some. The aforementioned handbill was a masterwork in itself. Written by hand on A5 paper and reproduced in black and white on a photocopier, it advertised the Searchers (so far so good) from Ziverpool. I'm sure it was meant to be an L but I still have the said item in my possession and it still looks like a Z to me every time I look at it.

Even more wondrous to behold is the additional information that we were the Searchers featuring ex-Moody Blue, Jack Bender. I don't know who should be more insulted, Mike Pinder of the Moody Blues or our very own Mr Pender, or Jumping Jack Bender as we subsequently renamed him.

Having said that, the poor souls who saw fit to book us were absolutely charming and there was no mention of the small fortune they were about to lose. They paid up without a whimper, apologetic that the crowd had not been bigger, and fed us to boot. Lovely people who deserved more. But they really should have researched the project better. During the evening I popped in to watch a bit of the Re-Searchers who were thrashing away loudly in the main room of the dank basement club. I listened briefly to the lyrics and heard the words 'scratch my snatch'. Lovely. Probably a Wanktones song I figured.

We must have managed to instil some excitement into the proceedings because Marc Holan wrote in the magazine Scene that 'Audience and band alike had a blast: this was apparent on everyone's face. In fact I'm sure everyone involved had a much better time than even anticipated. Even the cops tapped their feet as they let the band play up to the very last second.' What on earth were the cops doing there? I asked myself. Maybe they were employed to stop the audience leaving.

On the 10th we were in Ohio at a club in the Flats called Peabody's Down Under.

It was seven and a half bucks to get in at the door (a dollar less if you bought in advance) and this time supported by the Action. Not I must add the British outfit who were less successful contemporaries of ours. The crowd was bigger and again the reviews were excellent.

A week later we performed at a New York club that had really got their act together. They had got their act together years ago and were professionals at presenting cutting-edge quality shows in an intimate setting. The Bitter End on the world famous Bleeker Street down in Greenwich Village had become a bigger legend than many of its performers, having started out as a folk club that was home to all the greats of the sixties. Bob Dylan, Joan Baez, Peter, Paul & Mary and many others. They made the club famous. The club made them famous. It was a mutual admiration society.

Having lost a little bit of ground through the seventies it temporarily changed its name to the Other End in an attempt to revamp its image. It didn't last long and they soon came to realise the value of what they had and what everyone recognised, but it was the alternatively titled venue that hosted our shows on 18th and 19th November 1983.

The long, narrow interior was packed to capacity and throughout our set we could do no wrong. Under the headline 'One Of The Great Shows, Ever' (sic), Bruce Eder of the Aquarian wrote 'The hottest ticket in New York last Saturday wasn't for Yentl or anything happening on Broadway or at the Met - it was for the Other End, where there was a line stretching down the street and around the corner for the Searchers.' His extravagant praise continued with such astonishing hyperbole that you would have thought we were holding a gun to his head. 'No, I didn't see God, but I heard him doing his best Liverpool accent.'

And on it went. There was too much in his paragraphs to reproduce in full so it must suffice that his (almost) final words read 'by the time my head had cooled down after about four hours I could think about a few things: ancillary matters, like seeing if there was a way to arrange for knighthoods and CBEs for the people who brought them to the States and the other people at the Other End for booking them: and important stuff, like the Searchers. They're a fucking unbelievable band.' The appreciation of Mr Eder made up for the disappointing nights we had and still would suffer.

Joey Ramone came to see us that night and we spent some time talking to him in the dressing room after the show. He was very friendly and complimentary and in private far from the threatening image the band portrayed on stage. Joey was to act out the ideal rock & roll dream by dying young but to be truthful the pale and worryingly thin person who hid behind heavy shades that evening could have expired in the next ten minutes and I would not have been at all surprised.

Through the eighties we covered a lot of ground and strutted our stuff on such differing stages as the Chance in Poughkeepsie, where a group called the Police in the very early days of their slog to success had, we were told, drawn less people than we had. And the New Peppermint Lounge in New York, where our loveable but frustrated heavy metal fan roadie John Turner had set out to impress the Americans with his superb drum sounds, thus disastrously eliminating the jangling guitars for which we were renowned and for which people had expected and had paid to hear.

At Christine's in Cape Cod our sound check was delayed by someone moving house. When they move house there they really move house. This one was on top of a truck and inching slowly from one end of the main street to the other. In the end it was a great night and we got on with the club owner so well that despite the loss he suffered he re-booked us for the following year just so he could drink and hang out with us.

We played Jonathan Swift's in Boston and pleased the campus crowd and Brown's Hotel in the Catskills where elderly blue-rinsed matrons watched us in bewilderment and wondered whether it was worth continuing the fight to stay alive before our final noisy encore. In the end we left them happy and determined to stave off the Grim Reaper for a little while longer. The Chestnut Cabaret in Philadelphia was a great venue that would have been wonderful with a decent sized audience. At Heartbreaks in the Big Apple, David Essex and Chris Spedding turned out to watch our show.

On the whole there were no great eruptions within our ranks. We were not that kind of a band and when possible we practised moderation and compromise when it came to dealing with grievances and differing opinions. Eruptions were avoided until they could not be staved off any longer. And while there were sullen and uncommunicative periods in the claustrophobic confines of the dressing room there were also good times when we found a communal root of laughter and almost became friends again.

One focus of Mike's simmering discontent voiced to John when I was not around and which I never learned about till he had departed our ranks, was my position as on-stage front man with the job of communicating with our audience and holding their interest between the musical content of our set. It was from the centre mic that I operated and that was quite unusual. The centre spot has traditionally been the privilege of the lead singer but for whatever reason we decided between us many years before that things would work best this way round. John was stage left and Mike stage right.

But it was not apparently just the position he was objecting to. He seemed to think that he and John should be speaking to the audience as the two originals in the band. I admit that when I eventually discovered this I was furious. He was virtually dismissing my part in the group's existence and my input from *When You Walk In The Room* onwards as of little consequence. Furthermore he was putting himself up for a role for which he was, in my opinion, ill equipped. And in stating this I am not being arrogant.

Talking to an audience always fell easier to me than the others and although my early days must have thrown up some appalling examples of just how not to do it, time and a lot of effort eventually brought me to a point where I felt I could more than hold my own and occasionally excel. Once I got the general hang of it I made it my personal mission to constantly improve. To eliminate clichés and attempt to speak to a whole audience as individual people. There is still room for a hell of a lot of improvement but I am more than happy with the way things have turned out. I even have 'Best Front Man' awards to support my case.

For him to usurp my job would have been akin to me insisting that I should be the lead singer. My voice, while fine on the harmony parts, was not the instrument you would wish to depend on for the main aural focal point. For the occasional main vocal it was acceptable, and indeed Mike and I had sung unison vocals on *When You Walk In The Room*, but if I had been lead I fear our career would have taken a bit of a nosedive.

I have no illusions here whatsoever. Mike's voice was always more than good and when he was really trying it entered the realms of excellence. As a raconteur however he was on shaky ground and I am sure he found out just how hard the task was when he finally took the load on his own shoulders. But at the time I had no idea about this jockeying for power and position.

We were performing at a club called The Gentry in Washington DC and though the room was small the tiny crowd still had plenty of room to rattle around without the danger of bumping into each other. Perhaps thirty or so had paid to see us. As usual the management were treating us like welcome friends rather than a disastrous drain on their shaky finances. The tab for pizzas at the restaurant next door was picked up without complaint and they refrained from voicing any disappointment at our lack of ability to draw a decent sized crowd.

My conscience made me determined to make sure that the occupants of the benches in front of the stage went home happy. They deserved it. In such a situation I make it a principle never to refer to the poor turnout and simply steam on as if it was the best show ever. Sometimes it is not easy but I have always found that if you treat people with respect and humour they will pardon anything. They will happily forgive you for all of your musical trespasses. But make them uncomfortable and you are dead.

This select few were obviously devoted fans who had waited eagerly for our return to their shores and were firmly on our side. There was no problem. At least not in front of me. But on my right hand side while I was attempting to hold their interest between songs, Mike had retreated to his amplifier which had developed an irritating intermittent fault, an annoying crackling which seemed to be caused by a bad connection where the end of his lead plugged into the jack input.

As best I could I tried to keep everyone's mind off it by maintaining a flow of light-hearted chat which was not an easy task. It was one of those technical problems which had no obvious and immediate solution and it looked as though we would simply have to plod on and trust that it wouldn't spoil things too much. But Mike had decided, despite the fact he was curing nothing, to waggle the chord thus prolonging the difficulties, exacerbating the noise and bringing the audience's focus to bear on it. I was having serious problems talking through this unpleasant distraction which could have been more or less ignored if he had only left it alone.

On top of this he had a face like a wet weekend in August. This night was not going to be a commercial triumph. He was not enjoying the experience and it seemed he couldn't wait for it to end. It is an attitude I find almost impossible to understand or to condone. It is so easy to revel in the glory of a packed and excited crowd. Little personal endeavour is required at such times and keeping a happy face comes quite naturally. But you are not automatically entitled to an ovation. It has to be earned. Performances at the dusty end of the spectrum have to be rescued and it takes an extra effort, which I consider one is duty bound to put in. There is almost always a way to do it and the sense of satisfaction at pulling back from impending doom can be immense.

The miserable look on Mike's face was bringing me down and I imagine the audience too. The tension must surely have shown in my eyes and I was struggling to keep the thread of what I was trying to say. I must make one thing clear. I did not hate Mike. There were many times when he was likeable and fun to be with. This was not one of those times and I recall very clearly thinking at that point that if he hated this so much why didn't he just give up? I had no idea of what was to come.

32

Taking Care Of Business

It was the middle of 1985. We did not know it then but the year was to mark a significant turning point in our career. We were in Scotland on a short tour of social clubs, mundane but not unpleasant work that came with the added challenge of having to draw our audience's attention away from its habitual beer-fuelled and noisy conversation. It was par for the course in club land. Not necessarily the ideal situation if one was free to choose an ideal mode of work but still solid employment which we were more than happy to take on.

The weather was deceptively calm and clear and I had no idea of the storm clouds that were about to plunge my life into a dark, depressing gloom. It was near the end of our run and I was driving home from a show, a passenger in the car of our Scottish agent, Robert Pratt.

Robert was a large jovial man with a plump boyish face despite the wiry beard that gave him a more mature and rougher edge. Anxious to discard the outward signs of youth I fancy he felt it lent an air of gravitas to his appearance. I liked him. We all did. It was rare for us to strike up a social relationship with an agent but we had bonded with him and his wife Kathy from the first time he had arranged some gigs for us that side of the border. Quite often after the shows we would go back to their small house in Condorrat, one of the small towns just a few miles outside Glasgow that had been created to offer the inhabitants of the war-torn and run down areas of the city a better environment in which to raise their kids. Kathy would feed us unhealthily generous-sized portions of wonderful home cooked food. The main treat was chocolate caramel shortbread at which she was expert and which was sweet and delicious.

They had two young twin sons Martin and Kevin who were lively as kids usually are and who would jump all over us. We felt like part of their family while we were there and they treated us as such. This time round I was their houseguest while the rest of the group were lodged in a nearby bed and breakfast establishment. I had enjoyed my time with them and looked forward to heading down to London in a couple of days ready to jet off for a week's holiday in sunny Corfu.

Our conversation as we headed back to Cumbernauld was nothing special. The show had been fine that night as indeed they all had been that week. And then it took a rather sinister turn. He asked me if I could keep a secret. Intrigued, I affirmed that I could and he insisted that I couldn't tell anyone. That was fine with me.

Then the bombshell dropped. 'Mike's leaving the band.'

It was like one of those phoney theatrical moments that seemed so surreal that I couldn't quite take it in. I think I asked him if he was serious. He went on to explain that Mike Pender had come to him with the news that he was going to form his own group and that he had asked Robert if he would act for him in arranging his work. He did not know exactly when the parting was to occur but that it wouldn't be for a while.

I thought to myself that this was so unfair. I like to think of myself as a man of my word. Although I cannot guarantee that I have never told a lie or broken a confidence, I have a strong sense of conscience and will usually do whatever it takes to preserve my integrity. I was now obliged to stay silent at a time when I seriously needed to discuss this potentially disastrous situation with John McNally, and I was under a moral obligation not to. I did not get much sleep that night as my brain wrestled involuntarily with the crisis that loomed. Somehow I managed to remain silent and decided to hold off bringing anything out into the open until I returned from the Corfu trip.

It was not easy. The consequences of such an upheaval could at one end of the scale result in my career being prematurely brought to a close. Mike was an important figure in our line-up. Unlike me he was a true original member, something that seemed so important in the minds of the purists. He was also the main voice of the band, having taken over Tony Jackson's parts upon his departure, and though we all took our turns at the microphone neither John and I had the kind of vocal talents that could assume a central role.

If he was setting up in opposition, and that certainly seemed to be the case, would the loyalty of the fans and the confidence of the promoters lie with him or us? And where would we find someone to fill the soon-to-be-vacant position? The thought of listening to endless cassettes filled with the dubious efforts of countless wannabees and the embarrassing confrontations and ultimate rejections that were part and parcel of the audition process was depressing.

I travelled to Gatwick Airport with a very heavy heart and hoped that the hot Grecian sun would lift my spirits a little. I decided to check my answerphone one last time before boarding. There was a message from John asking me to phone him urgently before I set off. I rang his number in Liverpool knowing that his words would hold no surprises for me.

'I've got some bad news' he began. I already knew what the bad news was. 'Mike's leaving.' I decided not to tell him about the conversation with Robert Pratt for the moment. I already felt bad enough about withholding the guilty secret I had been saddled with. He went on to say that he had received the news not from Mike but from club managers who had been told that the Searchers no longer existed. He had informed them that they had got it wrong. We were simply taking a week's break after which it was business as usual. But the guy who had been booking us into the Woodford Halse Social Club near Daventry confirmed that he had been told that from now on he should book The New Searchers with Mike Pender.

Alarm bells had begun to ring in John's head and he said that he had better make some phone calls and get back to him. He rang Mike's number. Mike answered the phone and John immediately asked 'Is this right that you're leaving the group?' Mike answered in the affirmative.

'Don't you think we'd better talk about it?' he asked.

'No.'

'You mean after twenty years together we can't talk about it?'

'We'll talk about it at the next gig' Mike replied. He then hung up without another word.

John asked me what I thought and what I felt we should do. I voiced my fears. It was as big a problem as one could have and there was no telling how we would come out of it, or indeed if we could come out of it at all in any meaningful sense. I stated that if he was willing to give it a go then I was with him. We agreed to discuss things further at the end of the week.

On my return from Greece John and I talked the problem out over the phone and reaffirmed that we were going to at least give it our best shot at surviving this horrifying situation. Neither of us was willing to give up without a hell of a fight. There were avenues to be explored and precious little time to waste. We needed to search out possible replacements and it all had to be done with little or no publicity.

At this point we trusted no-one. We were determined to handle the whole thing ourselves for the time being. We would not tell Mike or Robert yet what our plans were. We would not even tell our own agent Alan Field, other than the fact that there was an impending defection and that we had to deal with it. After all, we figured, everyone would be scrutinising the proceedings in an attempt to suss out where the power base, and therefore the greatest revenue, would eventually lie. It might seem like a wonderfully glamourous world of glittering tinsel and cheesy smiles but in the end showbusiness is often much more about the business than the show.

The atmosphere in the dressing room of the Willows Variety Centre, a large function room that was part of the Rugby Club ground in Salford just by the M602 motorway on the edge of Manchester, was muted to say the least, but our drummer Billy Adamson was blissfully unaware of the machinations afoot. We were dressed and ready to hit the stage and still nothing had been said.

'Isn't there something you have to tell everyone?' John said to Mike.

Mike feigned surprise. John dug in.

'Aren't you going to tell everyone you're leaving the band?' It was out in the open at last. Mike at last had to confirm the fact and the shock on Billy's face was a sight to behold. There was some waffling on Mike's part as he attempted to justify his course of action. He wanted to try and make it on his own before it was too late.

Attempting to usurp the name of the group in one form or another did not quite tally with the phrase 'make it on my own' as far as we were concerned and at forty-four years old surely it was already too late. The words 'spring and chicken' did not readily come to mind in a world of illusion that was largely based on the vagaries of teenage fantasy. Somehow we got through the shows and kept our false grins in place long enough for the audience to go away satisfied and unaware of the Machiavellian processes taking place.

We entrusted the placing of adverts (experienced singer/guitarist required for professional sixties style band etc) in the hands of Tony (Joe) West, our agent pal and original Searchers' bassist in Liverpool, and the tapes came pouring in along with the necessary photographs. There were lots of them. We even had one from a girl but decided that would be a change too far. If anything our music could do with more bollocks rather than less. Some were good. Most were average. Often an excellent voice would be accompanied with a photograph of a troll. Other applicants were either in the wrong area or were of a height that would make John and me look like persons of restricted growth. In the end the solution proved to be much more simple.

On 8th February 1983 we had completed an engagement at the Red Lion, a pub in Brentford, Middlesex, where they presented nights of nostalgia mainly from our particular era. It was a Tuesday evening. Ever interested in what was happening and who was on the scene John had wandered into the main room to check out the band booked to entertain before the main spot. He was impressed by the lead singer, a very good-looking young guy who fronted a group whose repertoire was culled from the sixties and seventies catalogue. They were handled by a friend of ours Tracy Jacobs who had at one time assisted Alan Field before striking out on her own, and John had filed it in his memory banks for the time when we might need a good support band.

He contacted Tracy and invited the young singer, whose name was Spencer James, to submit a tape, if he was interested. He was and he did. Arrangements were made for him to deliver the cassette in person to me at my house, which was only a hop skip and a jump from where he lived. He, like me, was a Hayes lad.

The phone rang as I waited in my main living room with my eye on the front gate. It was John McNally on the other end of the line wanting to know if he had turned up yet. I explained that there was no sign so far at which point a car drew up outside the arch of the ancient twelve-foot high wall that fronted my property. The driver got out.

The person walking down the path was quite short and the baby face sat under a mane of dyed blond hair. He was wearing a white cheesecloth shirt with flared sleeves that only extended three-quarters of the way down the arm. Toulouse Lautrec would have carried off such an item with aplomb I'm sure. The black jeans were sprayed on to a degree where his blood supply had been restricted to danger level and which would have required the sort of implement that one uses to remove riding boots in order to extract oneself from them. The footwear too was a sight to behold. Black suede pixie boots with wide turn downs at mid-calf, a fashion statement which borrowed heavily from one of Anita Harris' old pantomime outfits. I had a deep suspicion that somewhere in the far off Land of Oz one of their Munchkins was missing.

'What does he look like?' John wanted to know.

'Well, he doesn't look like a Searcher right now but I'm trying to imagine him in a suit' I replied in answer to John's question.

He was a very pleasant up-beat person with, it seemed, masses of confidence. He handed over his tape and we briefly discussed the situation. I promised to get back to him as soon as we had listened to his demos. The recordings, which included some compositions of his own, were well executed. The voice on occasion was a trifle nasal and harsh when set against what I had been used to hearing for more than two decades but there was certainly nothing that would strike him out of the equation. I posted it off to John who rang me soon after receiving it.

'What do you think?' he wanted to know. I replied that there was a lot to recommend him although there were some points which possibly needed ironing out.

'Let's do it. If it doesn't work out we can deal with that later.' We were agreed. All systems were go at last. It was a great relief.

Spencer, born just a short distance from me in Hayes, Middlesex, on April 15th 1953, had already achieved a certain degree of success as a member of the hit recording group First Class. The ersatz surfing outfit had originally started out in life as a project of John Carter and Tony Burrows who combined their vocal efforts with Chas Mills at a time when the pop charts were being penetrated by so called groups who were nothing more than a bunch of well experienced session musicians put together to breathe life into the ideas of songwriters and producers with material that required an outlet on disc.

Tony Burrows had gained much notoriety by appearing in no less than three different groups during one edition of Top Of The Pops in 1970. In the space of the half-hour transmission he made quick clothes changes to perform with Brotherhood Of Man (*United We Stand*), Edison Lighthouse (*Love Grows (Where My Rosemary Goes)*) and

White Plains (*My Baby Loves Lovin'*). He was also promptly banned for a period in order to disassociate the BBC with any accusations of fixing.

The studio band for the First Class project included such revered session stalwarts as guitarist Alan Parker, keyboardist Alan Hawkshaw, Les Hurdle on bass and ex-Shadows drummer Brian Bennett. Once the project had attained chart success, with neither Burrows nor Carter keen to tour as they were heavily involved in their highly successful television advertising commitments, it then became necessary to assemble a band which could be the public face behind the name and available to take on the more gruelling task of promoting the discs on the numerous television shows abroad which were keen to have them.

A friend of Carter's, Robin Shaw (guitar and bass), agreed to put a group together which was also to include Spencer James (guitar and vocals) along with Eddie Richards (vocals), Del John (vocals) and Clive Barrett (organ, piano and vocals). At one time all eight members of First Class appeared on Top Of The Pops while the pared down five-piece took on the more tedious but highly essential guise of a travelling unit in order to promote the records on television shows in foreign parts. It was an added bonus that the touring outfit, being a few years younger and more attractive than the seasoned but rather more weathered studio veterans, had a greater visual appeal as a supposed surfing band whose records were being purchased in the main by hormonally bolstered teenage girls.

When the First Class project had run its course Spencer was drafted into a new band which at its initial inception was called Heyday but went on the road as Nightfly. Formed towards the end of 1984 it was to be a musical 'semi-supergroup' whose members included such luminaries as Micky Moody from heavy metal heroes Whitesnake, Boz Burrell from the blues and soul sounds of Bad Company and Zak Starkey, perhaps better known at that time simply for being Ringo Starr's son rather than the well respected and sought-after musician in his own right, that was eventually to be his destiny and indeed his well-earned right.

The signs were good. The management team were the very same people, Colin Johnson and Bob Young, who had so successfully steered the fortunes of denim-dressed rockers Status Quo. And the combined talents were considerable. But despite an extensive winter tour which included appearances on such prestigious stages as London's Marquee Club, the venture simply ran out of steam, and by March 1985 Nightfly flapped its wings for the last time, never to take to the skies again.

Undeterred and barely allowing time to draw breath the indomitable Mister James assembled his own working outfit to which he immodestly attached the name The Spencer James Band and continued to ply his trade on the pub circuit around Middlesex, which was always in need of good quality, dependable and affordable sounds. In a modest way it was a profitable living and was to prove extremely fortuitous for both him and us when the Red Lion in Brentford decided to employ his talents as our support act.

Once the decision had been made to recruit him we went quietly about our business putting the pieces in place. Spencer and I ran through the basic arrangements of the nucleus of our standard set in my living room and I gave him a tape to listen to. The essential plan was to have a complete, if basic, piece of entertainment that we could reasonably present as a show. When that was set in place we could expand and improve at our own pace.

Our initial two rehearsals took place at Hayes Cricket Club about a mile from my house where I had for some years spent my off-duty evenings drinking with my local pals. My old friend Mick Kirby was the steward and made the necessary arrangements for us. The first run-through was okay but not exhilarating. Having been used to certain sounds and phrasing over a period of more than twenty years there were things that seemed alien and grated on our ears. There was no getting over the fact that after that first rehearsal we were having reservations. Minor perhaps but definitely there.

After the second one we were very much more at ease and pretty sure that things would work out just fine. The pieces were slotting into place quite comfortably and we could now think about the eventual parting of the ways with a confidence that had been far from present up to that point. Mike had indicated that his plans were to leave in March 1986 but we quickly decided to take the controlling hand and that any such decisions were going to come from us. Now that we had a settled future Searchers line-up we were keen to get on with our lives and our careers.

We had no intention of being dictated to and informed him and Robert Pratt that we preferred to end our association at the end of the year. It seemed a suitable point in time to make the leap. It was like a marriage. We had agreed to a divorce and now we just wanted to get on with it. They had no problem with the timing, not that what they thought was of any concern to us any more. They were the enemy and the fight was on.

We were due back in Scotland later that year for another week of concerts for Robert with the Nolans as support. They were an excellent act and extremely nice girls and there was no sign that they were particularly aware of the intrigue going on behind the scene. The scene backstage was a fairly civilised environment though naturally the atmosphere between us and the Pender/Pratt camp was a tad frosty. In fact the conditions were arctic.

Robert was very upset by an advert that we had paid for in the Stage newspaper, the so-called bible of the variety world. Once again without informing anyone outside our close-knit circle we had set up a photo session and by way of a half page advertisement let the world know that as from January 1st the Searchers would carry on performing with a brand new member, their first change in twenty-five years.

It had caught Robert unawares and he felt that this should not have been done without his knowledge and especially in advance of his Scottish dates. We could not have cared less. The Stage was a trade paper and the ad was almost exclusively for the benefit of the industry. It was to give bookers plenty of advance warning of the current dramas surrounding the Searchers of which they were already very well aware. Audiences in general would have been oblivious of such things and therefore it mattered not a jot to those attending the shows.

On this run I was in a hotel with the rest of the boys despite the fact that Robert still suggested I stay with him, Kathy and the boys. It was a rather nice attitude, I thought, that despite the obvious tension that he still felt comfortable enough for such an arrangement, but I thought it was wholly inappropriate and opted out. We had closed ranks.

With regard to the revised date for the parting of the ways Robert intimated that Mike Pender had the advantage in that he would have three months to rehearse his band while we would have to get things together in a matter of weeks, grabbing what spare time we had in our heavy datesheet. I was of the opposite opinion entirely, always believing that you can rehearse till the cows come home but things only gel once you are on that stage and the adrenalin is flowing. What's more, Mike had to rehearse three new members and come out the other end with a fluent programme. Not an easy job. Our task was simply to add a new voice to what could be perceived as a ready formed and tested live backing track.

Not only were we sure that our show would be of a suitable standard but we also figured that we would have stolen a very important march on Mike by firmly establishing ourselves on the circuit and a continuing act of quality and worth. We certainly did not feel disadvantaged in any way at all. We were feeling quite perky about the whole episode. After a long term of complacency we had suddenly been given a purpose in life.

Our last gig in Scotland was a club called Smokies in Arbroath. Robert asked if he could record the show as a keepsake. We said no. Call us cynical but our suspicions, rightly or wrongly, were that a cassette of our basic act would be a perfect template for any new band of Mike's to learn the nucleus of a Searchers set at their leisure. After all that was exactly how we did it with Spencer. During the evening our roadie John Turner, a big bruiser of a gentle giant from Barnsley, discovered a cassette recorder in operation on the deejay's console. With a very menacing look that defied anyone to interfere with his actions he removed the offending item. That night we journeyed south intent on assembling all the pieces that would constitute our future in the entertainment business.

On November 22nd we attended a meeting at our accountants' office at York Gate on the Marylebone Road just along from Baker Street, a large, imposing white building, a modest portion of which we felt we had purchased by way of our very heavy fees over the years. Blick, Rothenberg and Noble were not a cheap company by any means but their efficiency and tight reins had kept us up to date with our tax affairs, the traditional banana skin on which many an artiste had slipped with disastrous consequences.

Des Cohen, who was in charge of preparing our yearly returns, was there as of course was Mike. There were a few matters in need of settling. We had already been preparing estimates of the values of our communal assets, amps, PA system, van and cars etcetera. There were no great sums involved here. Second-hand musical equipment does not command high prices and the Iveco truck was a well-worn vehicle which would soon need replacing. A couple of group cars were involved as well as our stage suits and very little else.

We held modest sums of money in our accounts mainly for the purpose of paying our taxes but we were far from being rich people. As fast as money came in it usually went out again. The settlement was agreed upon and a series of instalments laid out until the dissolution agreement for our partnership was signed.

The actual name of course was a major bone of contention which had to be settled between us if we were to avoid expensive litigation. Several alternatives had been bandied about, either reaching our ears by way of clubs who had already been approached, or from Robert who was advising Mike on his future. Mike Pender and the New Searchers was not a consideration in our eyes as it intimated that the old ones might no longer exist. The other main contenders were Mike Pender's Searchers and Mike Pender and His Searchers. The latter was our preferred choice. We felt that it denoted that this was a different animal.

By the end of the meeting Mike had okayed our preference, agreed on the accounts presented by Des Cohen and all seemed more or less settled. We also sensibly insisted that all the letters of his new group's name should be of the same size, style and colouring and that it should all be contained on one line. There were obvious dangers ahead and we wanted to pre-empt any such pitfalls.

Though the estrangement within our ranks provided for a very tense dressing room atmosphere, we tried as far as possible to stick to pragmatics and not let personal grievances add to the stress. John and I had decided that we should remain totally above board if we were going to retain our credibility in the event of any litigation that might be forthcoming. Mike apparently did not see it quite like that.

We had another engagement at the Willows in Salford to complete, the very same place where we forced Mike to reveal his hitherto unannounced defection. Towards the end of our set we were astonished to find him sitting on his amplifier as we launched into *Needles And Pins*. It goes without saying that as the lead voice on our greatest selling single his position should have been in front of his microphone. We were completely baffled and as we went back to our dressing room at the end of our show we tackled him about his odd behaviour.

'I was starved of spotlight' was his explanation. Paranoia, it seemed, had set in. He believed that we had contrived to reduce his profile by manipulating the stage lighting to favour the rest of us. No such thing had either been suggested or carried out. So sure was Mike that he was being plotted against that he berated Maurice the lighting man at the club, who of course denied it, and then came to us to exclaim his amazement and amusement. We in turn complained to Robert Pratt who, to his credit, let Mike know that he was being silly.

In order to be ready for forthcoming shows with our new member we arranged one final rehearsal on the afternoon of our last performance with Mike as well as a full scale dress run-through before the end of the year at Hayes Cricket Club in order to assess what kind of problems we were likely to encounter.

The final show with Mike was to be on December 23rd at the Albany, Deptford, a venue that we had played twice before in its old state, and after an extensive refurbishment. It was a place that was far removed from the cabaret style rooms we often worked in and the audience was largely from the student and rock & roll fraternity. We had first appeared there during our Sire period when we were being launched as a serious rock act again.

John travelled down from Liverpool by train leaving Mike to follow on in the group's Ford Cortina. Most of the work had already been done and the routining of our set was quick and trouble free. Spencer stayed on that evening to enjoy the fun and to see what his soon-to-be predecessor was like. As before we went about our business in a professional manner leaving any unpleasantness carefully tucked out of sight of the paying public.

At the end of the evening there were no sad goodbyes. There was precious little goodwill left between ourselves and Mike to distribute with any enthusiasm or sincerity. At least I could make the short journey home to West London on my own and be finally removed from this hideous, gnawing toothache of a problem. John on the other hand had to travel two hundred miles north to Liverpool in the company of someone he now loathed with a vengeance. In the back seat and not quite comprehending the obvious conflict between these two sullen grown ups was Nathan Prendergast, Mike's young son.

John was driving. He had already foreseen problems before the end of this auspicious night and, tired as he was, did not intend to let Mike get the keys to the vehicle in his grasp. He was correct. When they pulled up in front of Mike's house, Nathan was told to go inside while his dad talked to Uncle John. As he had suspected Mike wanted the keys to the car and a cheque for any balance of monies owed to him by the partnership. How he thought that such important transactions would take place in a Ford Cortina in the early hours of a winter's night it is hard to imagine.

John explained, or rather stated in the most emphatic and unsympathetic terms, that financial matters were to be sorted out in due course by the proper people, our accountants, and that there were two chances of him getting his hands on the car. Slim and none. They did not part on the best of terms. For the Searchers it was the end of one era and the beginning of another. Meanwhile at least there was Christmas for us to look forward to.

33

Legally Blonde

Greeting 1986 was like waking on a bright summer's morning with an unquenchable feeling of optimism bursting in our hearts and at least a glimmer of hope that there could be a bright new future in front of us, when a short time ago it had seemed that there was precious little future at all, bright or otherwise. We had faced our fears and come out of it reasonably unscathed. The worst was over. Nothing could frighten us quite like that again.

We had our new line-up which now included Spencer James and we had rehearsed as much as we felt was necessary. Now we needed to put the product to the test and come out the winner against our rival in our mutual market. This was not differentiating Daz from Omo. It was not the ability to tell Stork from Butter. This was much more important. To us it was the life or death of our future in the entertainment industry.

Our first professional performances with the new line-up in place were to be at the Cabaret Club in Newmarket, ostensibly a converted cinema set at one end of the pretty little Suffolk racing town. It was a venue we had appeared at many times previously and an environment in which we were very comfortable. Fortunately this was a civilised setting for a new beginning, with an audience whose concentration would be on the stage and who, having enjoyed a pleasant meal and a drink or two, would be ready to pay us four nervous artistes enough respect for us to have a fighting chance.

We already knew the set worked. We had run through the whole routine on December 28th once more at Hayes Cricket Club, a small single-storey building set alongside the sports pitch in Wood End Green, Hayes, Middlesex, coincidentally a mere stone's throw from the Beck Theatre which had already played a part in our career and which was to attain an even greater significance in our lives as time went on.

A long-standing ambition of my friend Mick Kirby was to have us perform there but the size of the place had up to this point made the proposition commercially unviable. With a need to bed our new singer in we quoted a price that was not only feasible but in fact could not be beaten. We would play for no fee whatsoever. Mick was delighted and so were the members, most of whom I had known for some time.

We initially intended to treat the evening in a decidedly casual manner, going on in whatever clothes we were wearing on the night and simply playing the songs as best we could, stopping to correct any mistakes or problems as we went along. But at the last moment we decided that if it was to be done at all it should be done properly. The suits were donned and a long-standing tradition was maintained. Despite the non-availability of a phone booth in which to conduct the miraculous transformation, once we put on our shiny black mohair suits, white tab-collared shirts and black ties we each became SEARCHERMAN!!! And our game was lifted to a new level. This instantly became the real deal.

In the event there was no need at all to stop and correct anything. Our worries had been groundless. Whatever mistakes we made were slight and of no real consequence. Our adrenalin was pumping and to a man we concentrated enthusiastically on the task as if we were on stage at the London Palladium. The audience applauded wildly, as well their communal conscience might expect them to considering the bargain price for which they had obtained our services. At the completion of the set, which of course was the sum total of our repertoire, we took our bows and left the floor. We returned for one single pre-planned encore but no more. For the time being we hadn't rehearsed any other songs.

It had been a huge success and an invaluable exercise and we made our separate ways home that night looking forward to the forthcoming New Year celebrations amongst our friends and families. Clutching the bottles of champagne that Mick Kirby had presented to us on behalf of the club we journeyed safe in the knowledge that, barring unforeseen circumstances, we would not disgrace ourselves when it came time to strut our stuff before an audience of genuine paying customers. My journey of course was considerably less than that of the other three, living as I did barely a mile from the club.

The Newmarket engagements on 3rd and 4th January 1986 went seamlessly. As far as Spencer's debut was concerned, a small matter of which the majority of the patrons up to now would have been entirely unaware, we decided to confront the situation head on. We had talked about the best way to deal with it and figured that it would be unwise and more than a little patronising to the assembled bums on seats to pretend that nothing had changed. Indeed a great deal had changed.

After our opening of three segued hits I said the usual hellos and words of welcome and then proceeded to introduce the newcomer to the assembled throng, banking on the assumption that honesty and openness was the best policy. We had not only to present him to them, we had also to commit them to our fledgling member from the outset - to make them feel personally responsible for Spencer's wellbeing, comfort and happiness that evening. It worked perfectly. His boyish good looks and baby-faced grin had them hooked straight away. Once we had achieved our primary aim we could at last relax a little and get on with what we already knew was a winning show.

At the end of our miniscule two-day season we left Newmarket both relieved and sure that we could now get on with our careers in a reasonably trouble-free manner. After all the meeting with our accountants had covered all the salient points of the dissolution and the crinkles had been satisfactorily ironed out. It would now be plain sailing. My goodness, if we really thought that we must have been living in Fairy Dairy Land.

No sooner had the year turned than we discovered a string of misleading advertisements covering appearances set for Mike Pender's new group later in the year. If left unchecked it could have proved dangerous in the extreme for us. A precedent could have been set and one that would have been difficult to turn around if things continued for too long.

Furthermore we were even more perturbed to find that Mike had contacted our bank in Liverpool and managed to freeze the partnership accounts. Cheques we had presented were not being honoured and the situation was serious in the extreme. Without a banking facility in operation we could not trade in any practical terms. The agreements set in place at Blick Rothenberg had been in order to avoid costly and uncertain legal actions. Now it seemed that we had avoided nothing. We badly needed professional advice.

Our accountants pointed us in the direction of Paul Krempel, an ambitious young lawyer in his mid thirties. He kept his office at Chansitor House in Lincolns Inn Fields, the heart of the capital's judicial community, an enclave of beautifully crafted old buildings that boasted the kind of solidity that those engaged in litigation might gain some sort of assurance and comfort from. The kind of artistically elaborate masonry from a bygone age whose magnificence would never be repeated. It was an elegant setting in which to wage ruthless and bloody battles.

We quickly met with Krempel on Friday January 17th and ran through the situation as comprehensively as we could and with as much accuracy and objectivity as we could muster given our naturally biased stance. He was keen to take on the challenge of what he saw was a just cause and we found him very amiable. He was slim and dark haired and had an air about him that was both honest and enthusiastic. We liked him and felt we were in good hands. Rather more disturbing however was his need to know the state of our bank accounts, if John and I owned our own houses, how much they were worth and whether they were mortgaged.

The ramifications of what was at stake slowly began to seep in. Up to that point we were virgins in such dealings, naïve and innocent enough to think that we were right and obviously justice would be swift and simple and hopefully not too expensive. How innocent can you get? We were so dumb we were legally blonde. It now became clear that all our hard-earned savings could very soon be up for grabs and now we had started there was no turning back. It was beginning to feel like some hellish poker game where the doors are locked and you are not allowed to leave until the winning hand has been played.

A letter from Krempel dated January 21st informed us that he had written to our bank demanding the reinstitution of our banking facilities, pointing out that according to section 38 of the Partnership Act of 1890 they had no right to withdraw them in the first place. He furthermore asked them to note that two of the dishonoured cheques were for income tax and VAT and included a warning that they could be held liable for loss or damage resulting from their actions, in which case we would have little alternative but to look to them for compensation. Needless to say we very quickly found our accounts in good working order again.

The letter also contained Paul's opinion that Mike Pender could be prevented from using anything other than Mike Pender And His Searchers as it was a term of the dissolution agreement which we all reached at Des Cohen's office two months previously. His confidence in the facts as he saw them gave us a well needed morale boost.

A reply came from the firm of McManus, Reilly, Campbell who were Robert Pratt's solicitors but who were also acting for Pender. They assured us that Pender would not bill himself as The Searchers but reserved the right to use both Mike Pender's Searchers and Mike Pender And His Searchers, the latter being our preferred choice and the title that Mike had verbally okayed. The words 'cake' and 'eat it' sprang to mind. They also claimed that any agreement had been breached because a sum of £3,000 on account of monies which might be owed as his share of partnership assets had not been paid over to Mike.

Krempel's reply maintained that the monies on account were on condition that the agreement was adhered to and since it had not, the remaining sums would be retained to offset against any damages and losses incurred by The Searchers. He also pointed out the alarm caused by Mike being publicised under a variety of names incorporating the word Searchers contrary to the understandings reached. In particular he was most concerned that Mike, despite it being agreed with Robert Pratt that he would use only the title Mike Pender's Searchers, a name to which we had finally okayed, now also wished to use Mike Pender and His Searchers which we were forcibly against. It was becoming increasingly likely, Krempel stressed, that an injunction was inevitable.

Meanwhile Paul had instructed junior Counsel Richard Miller to prepare a draft agreement containing the terms which had already been settled upon at the Blick Rothenberg meeting. In anticipation of proceedings John and I were required to supply affidavits together with those of our agent, Alan Field, and others to be presented to the Court along with that of Paul Krempel himself. Things were hotting up.

By February 19th we had still not received a decision on the proposals for dissolution from Mike's solicitors and we prepared to go forward with the Court Action. Two days later Pender's solicitors finally sent approval of the terms of an agreement set out in the manner we had demanded, save for the requirement to have all of the name on one line. They maintained that there would be times when this would be impractical and in the end we capitulated on the point.

Via one of our fans we had had acquired studio shots of Mike's new line-up and curiously one set of pictures included Tony Jackson, the original bass player who I had replaced in 1964 and who had sung lead on many of the early recordings. He, it seems, would be appearing on selected dates. Tony had taken on a number of jobs following his unsuccessful venture into a solo career, some of them in the entertainment industry and some in rather more mundane territories. He had at various points sold furniture, been a club rep and deejay in Spain, worked for the railways and even managed a golf club in the Midlands. Having once been a major star he missed the high profile of a name group and wanted to get back in front of an audience again.

It was a shrewd move on Mike's part. Another original face would certainly add strength to the saleability of the attraction. We heard a rumour that Chris Curtis had also been approached to help in some way. But in the end it came to nothing. Tony, not happy with the arrangements and in particular the share of the spoils, eventually declined.

Then suddenly, as we anticipated signing the terms of dissolution as agreed in correspondence between Krempel and McManus Reilly, everything was in disarray once more. It appeared that Mike was now unwilling to enter into the agreement as approved by Pratt's solicitors. Paul Krempel immediately instructed Counsel to settle the proceedings to be brought against Pender and we anticipated an application for an injunction during the coming week. Paul also requested us to submit to him a cheque for £3,500, the sum we had agreed should be passed over on completion of the agreement, as a sign to the Court of good faith in that we were not denying monies owed but that he was holding funds for us which would indicate that we were treating the agreement as binding.

A further complication occurred when Mike suddenly appointed new solicitors in Messrs Brabner, Holden and Company of Liverpool. Mr Brabner, replying to Krempel's warnings of the imminent writ, quite understandably asked for extended time as he had not yet had time to avail himself of all the details of the case and to advise Pender as to whether or not he was bound by the terms referred to in the agreement.

Brabner also stated that Pender had informed him that he had not given McManus, Reilly instructions to act for him at all but that they were merely advising him on behalf of Robert Pratt. The situation was becoming most confusing, not to mention frustrating. Krempel expressed his astonishment at this about turn and informed Brabner, Holden and Co that as far as he was concerned McManus, Reilly were indeed acting for Pender and that he considered that the agreement had been made and that Pender was bound by the terms. Further correspondence passed back and forth between the two law firms but we were getting nowhere fast. There was, in Krempel's opinion, no alternative. The dreaded writ was issued and served on Mike. The application was set to be heard in the High Court on 10th April 1986 in front of Mr Justice Peter Gibson.

The date of the action fell on a working day for us and John and I were trying to figure out the logistics of attending the proceedings and still fulfilling our commitments. In the end Paul Krempel advised us that there was no need for us to be present. He and his team would take care of the matter. In fact the matter did not even enter the court. Mike accepted advice from his solicitors that it would be more sensible and economical to come to an agreement based on the terms previously settled on, and the necessary terms were sanctioned by him outside the courtroom itself.

On 17th April official undertakings were stamped by the Court, preventing Mike from advertising or promoting himself any way other than under the terms set out in the document. The clauses contained in the document demanded that:

HE WILL NOT ANYWHERE IN THE WORLD CALL PROMOTE OR PUBLICISE HIMSELF OR ANY GROUP OF WHICH HE IS PART OF CAUSE HIMSELF TO BE CALLED PROMOTED OR PUBLICISED UNDER OR BY REFERENCE TO ANY NAME INCORPORATING THE EXPRESSION 'THE SEARCHERS' OTHER THAN MIKE PENDER'S SEARCHERS AND (IN THE CASE OF WRITTEN MATERIAL) IN A FORM (SAVE FOR DE MINIMIS DIFFERENCES) EACH WORD IS GIVEN EQUAL PROMINENCE AS TO SIZE COLOUR AND TYPE OF LETTERING.

THAT HE OR HIS MANAGER WILL INCLUDE IN ANY CONTRACT FOR HIS APPEARANCE ANYWHERE IN THE WORLD AS AN ARTISTE OR AS PART OF A GROUP APPEARING UNDER THE NAME 'MIKE PENDER'S SEARCHERS' A PROVISION INSTRUCTING THE OTHER PARTY THERETO TO CALL PROMOTE OR PUBLICISE HIM ONLY UNDER THE NAME 'MIKE PENDER'S SEARCHERS' AND (IN THE CASE OF WRITTEN MATERIAL) EACH WORD IS GIVEN EQUAL PROMINENCE AS TO SIZE COLOUR AND TYPE OF

LETTERING AND THAT HE AND HIS MANAGER WILL FORTHWITH NOTIFY ALL PARTIES TO WHOM HE IS PRESENTLY CONTRACTED THAT HE MAY HENCEFORTH ONLY BE CALLED PROMOTED OR PUBLICISED UNDER THE NAME 'MIKE PENDER'S SEARCHERS' AND (IN THE CASE OF WRITTEN MATERIAL) IN A FORM IN WHICH (SAVE FOR DE MINIMIS DIFFERENCES) EACH WORD IS GIVEN EQUAL PROMINENCE AS TO SIZE COLOUR AND TYPE OF LETTERING

In addition he was given the option that he may elect in writing to substitute the name Mike Pender and His Searchers.

John and I felt elated and more than a little relieved. It was now time to concentrate once more on a datesheet that was looking very full. There were agents and promoters who were still hedging their bets and hanging on to see which way the wind was blowing in the continuing drama of the Searchers.

We had a series of theatre shows throughout the month of April taking in Stevenage, Tunbridge Wells, Eastbourne, Warrington, Folkestone, Cardiff, Northampton, Croydon and Worthing with a second leg set for July. Unwilling or unsure enough yet to take the weight of a whole evening on our shoulders, we were supported by a comedian for the concerts. Though we had future plans for an all-evening show where we could expand the content of our presentations we were still using a support act to take the weight of the first half. It was a little too soon to fly solo but it was to prove an invaluable rehearsal for the kind of act that would become the rule rather than the exception in our touring schedule. Theatres, we figured, were the future. They had class and quality. They would give us the kind of kudos we needed.

Germany too was back on the list of countries for us. We had been absent on that scene for a year or so after a small dispute with our agent there, Rainer Haas. I can't even remember exactly what it had been about but I believe it was something to do with positioning on the bill and our perceived need to retain the status we felt we deserved. Both sides had been intransigent but now practicality took over. We had been flexing our muscle but now there was a lot less muscle to flex.

We made the call and Rainer was openly delighted. For ourselves we had just recaptured a major territory at a time when the whole scene was beginning to boom. Where our circuit there had once constituted modestly-sized clubs it was now concerned almost exclusively with huge sports arenas in which were packed crowds of between fifteen and twenty-five thousand people. We had acted quickly. It would have been disastrous to have allowed Mike to get his foot in first. It was of the utmost importance for us to establish ourselves on every available market or risk losing it to the opposition.

Meanwhile we still had a long list of errant venues to deal with. We sent out a volley of expensive legal warnings to those who had trespassed against us and most took heed and altered or withdrew offending material. In such cases we took no further action although the damage had already been done and they had more or less reaped the benefits without penalty.

Those who refused to toe the line or simply ignored the threats were sued. Any poor fool who thinks that successfully suing someone means that because you are in the right you recover all of your outlay and are not out of pocket as a result of the misdemeanours of others is grossly mistaken. Without going into the whys and wherefores of the British legal system it just doesn't quite work that way. What we were doing cost us a good deal of money but it was necessary. We could not afford to back off or show signs of weakness. It was all quite debilitating but we just had to get on with things as best we could. It seemed that almost every other letter from our legal representative would contain a request for a further fifteen hundred or two thousand pounds to keep up with the work done on our behalf. Signing the cheques began to feel almost surreal.

One piece of news that really stuck in our gullet was the cancellation of some proposed Australian dates due to the fact that Mike Pender and his group were to tour there as part of a sixties package that included Gerry & the Pacemakers and the Manfreds (a slightly re-vamped version of the old Manfred Mann group) among others. Our promoter there did not think the market could support two groups of such similarity at the same time especially as the sixties package would be a high profile and publicly visible item, with nationwide television and radio backing the project, while our venues would consist of clubs and hotels in the main. It particularly hit hard because Australia was a country that we loved. It was also the country that Mike had refused point blank to go to when he was still a part of the Searchers. Such hypocrisy infuriated us but there was little we could do about it.

We complained bitterly to the Musicians Union to whom we had been paying dues for most of our adult lives. They were about as effective as a poodle pissing on a forest fire. And their Aussie equivalent was no better. The only course left would have been to instruct lawyers down under and throw ourselves into an expensive legal action on the other side of the world. Our pockets were by no means bottomless and we reluctantly decided not to start on what could be a ruinously expensive venture. There were quite enough expenses here at home to ruin us thank you very much. We certainly did not feel the urge to go halfway round the world to achieve poverty.

Work took us up and down the country in a variety of settings that ranged from discos and bierkellers in Germany to a birthday party in Chelsea. On a quick trip to Scotland we arrived at a radio station for an interview and discovered that Mike's band, on a similar mission earlier, had signed in as The Searchers. We were incensed.

To think that these Johnny-come-latelys who had no history with the group were attaching themselves to our name was maddening. Technically we could have no complaint if they had inserted Mike Pender's Searchers but this was insulting.

True, there had been changes in our band but such differences were natural progressions that had happened throughout the group's lifetime and no doubt would in the future. Such things are the fate of almost every musical combination but it is an organic and continuous process. The line carries on for better or for worse depending on your outlook, your taste or your position. It bears no relation to a backing band being recruited en masse to replicate an established outfit. They might well in law be Mike Pender's Searchers but they could not and would not be The Searchers. But it was too small an item for us to make capital out of. We set our disgust aside and moved on.

On June 20th we were engaged to play for a 40th birthday party being held at the Duke of York Barracks on the King's Road. An Irish financier called Tony O'Sullivan, who was sharing a joint celebration with fellow City whiz kid Geoffrey Pack, was determined to book his favourite group for the occasion and that group was us.

Tony O'Sullivan had no idea of how to get through to us. But he did remember that we had been handled throughout those bygone glory days by Tito Burns. After a bit of detective work he eventually got through to our old manager, still alive and well and now handling Sacha Distel and Victor Borge. Tito was more than happy to broker the deal. There would be a slice in it for him of course. When Tito in turn contacted our long-standing agent Alan Field, he was informed of the line-up change in case it would make a difference. Tito, as pragmatic and unsentimental as ever and not about to lose a commission, replied that he didn't care who was in the band as long as they sang *Needles And Pins*. Ah, such glorious conscience is so rare these days.

Soon after the deal had been made the date proved impractical for O'Sullivan and a new one, mutually suitable to band and birthday boy, was agreed on. As a by-the-by Burns informed him that there would be an extra charge of one hundred pounds for the altered arrangements. Needless to say none of the supplement ever found its way into our coffers.

For the month of August we were able to get away from the legal traumas temporarily as we jetted off to the USA for a run of club dates. It was still the perceived land of glamour and raised our profile amongst our peers. We had long since realised the wisdom of forgoing the employment of an American tour manager for the simpler and cheaper option of finding our own way about the country. It was a vast continent but with a map and our heads filled with at least a modicum of common sense we rented an Oldsmobile and confidently drove ourselves from state to state without any great mishaps. We started with a rock venue in Grafton, Massachusetts, where we shared the evening with Michigan's favourite sons, Mitch Ryder & the Detroit Wheels.

We quickly became the darlings of the management due to our natural British reserve and good manners. While the Americans brashly demanded their supply of refreshments in the dressing room our polite requests for perhaps some coffee and mineral waters caught the staff by surprise. They were certainly not used to such a pleasant attitude and anything we wanted was ours for the taking. Not being great drinkers or high flyers our wants were few.

At an enormous resort hotel in the Catskills, where a largely ageing Jewish guest contingent came for a short respite from the hustle and bustle of the Big Apple, we eventually won them round after a long struggle. To them we were another raucous rock act while they yearned for the manic humour of Jerry Lewis or the sweet nostalgic ballads of Bobby Vinton. They had no idea who we were. Most of them were so old I doubt they knew who they were. They were content for the most part to sit around and 'kvetch' together and digest enormous amounts of questionable food. It was not the easiest of engagements but it was an interesting experience which I would hate to have missed.

Lulu's in Kitchener, a short drive west from Toronto, boasted the longest bar in America or anywhere come to that. I have no idea whether it was true or not but the large crowd loved us. The large club, formerly a K Mart store and just off the main route to Niagara, was owned and operated by film star Jill Ireland's brother John and quickly became a favourite of ours.

In New York, always a good city for us where the cognoscenti still remembered us and recognised our significant part in the music scene of the mid-sixties, we packed the Lone Star Café and were thrilled to find Jerome 'Doc' Pomus in the audience. The wheelchair-bound songwriter had penned so many incredible hits with his partner Mort Shuman, songs which included *Surrender*, *Viva Las Vegas*, *His Latest Flame* and a whole bunch of others for Elvis Presley, *Teenager In Love* for Dion & the Belmonts and *Can't Get Used To Losing You* for Andy Williams. There are too many singing stars who benefited from his talents to mention. I recalled the time when I was still a schoolboy and he and Mort were brought to Britain by Jack Good to perform their material on the hit television show Boy Meets Girls. To have American songwriters on British television performing the compositions which had become famous by stars of the time was really something to me and the sight of Pomus in his wheelchair was both unusual and memorable.

Their contribution to our rise in the pop firmament was the Searchers' very first hit *Sweets For My Sweet* though it had actually been penned for the Drifters and not us. Still, a hit is a hit and a royalty is a royalty to a tunesmith for whom covers of a song are his pension and Doc was as keen to say hello as we were to meet this legend. He gave me his slightly battered business card and I treasured it like a bar of gold.

We made the trip to Lincoln up in the mountains of New Hampshire for a sold-out date at D. J Wagner's, a rustic holiday camp, all wood condominiums and home-spun artefacts wherever you trod. The cute signposts were in carefully carved wood with gold lettering. It was a modern recreation of Norman Rockwell's American ideal, all shined and polished to a gleam of perfection and with every modern comfort.

Woodstock, the small town outside New York which gave its name to the most famous music festival ever was an intriguing destination on our itinerary. The festival had not been held here at all of course but some forty miles south on Frank Yasgur's Farm in Bethel when they discovered there was no site of a suitable size to be found in Woodstock itself. Three hundred thousand had gathered in the mud and the muck to join in the spiritual experience. For our night in Woodstock we got a mere fifteen. That is not fifteen thousand. It was fifteen people including the bar staff. But no matter. They were terrific to us and we had a ball. A very small ball admittedly but a ball nonetheless. One over-excited lady of indeterminate years even felt compelled to touch me in a most inappropriate place while I was attempting to play. On one hand I felt like explaining that I wasn't that kind of boy while on the other I was flattered to have caused a tiny ripple of excitement and lust in the life of this winter chicken. I'm afraid spring for her had long since gone and the block had most definitely been circuited many times over.

America was a hard nut to crack, or to crack once more to be more correct. It is such a vast area that there was little an act like ourselves could do that would ever cause more than a ripple other than in a local context. But we always enjoyed it and as long as we were making money as opposed to losing it we were content. Once again it removed us from the UK market for a spell and afforded a helping of prestige. There were many of our contemporaries who were extremely jealous of our position. Considering the dramas we had been faced with and the terrible outcome that could so easily have been we were doing quite nicely thank you.

34

Flying High

It seemed we had no sooner touched down again on British soil a couple of days into September 1986 than we were jetting off again to America, and this time it was a much bigger deal altogether. Twenty years ago the Beatles had made the Yanks eat humble pie by bulldozing through the hitherto impenetrable American charts and into the hearts and ears of the teenage fans of that vast continent. And in a piece of clever and meticulous planning even the shiny silver platter on which the pie had first been delivered was being replicated this time round.

Pan Am flight 101 to New York had been a Boeing 707 back in 1966. Now the historically significant number was attached to a giant 747. It was considered an important piece of marketing strategy to reinforce the connection of that first invasion. And while the Fab Four were no longer a going concern as far as live shows were concerned the vessel was packed with a host of names who had once commanded their own fair share of screaming hysterics during those crazy days when the Brits ruled the airwaves.

Along with ourselves the bill consisted of Gerry & the Pacemakers, Freddie & the Dreamers, Chad & Jeremy and the Mindbenders. There had been personnel changes through the intervening years, Freddie's Dreamers and Gerry's Pacemakers these days were simply backing musicians, albeit excellent ones, employed to support and embellish the on-stage presence of their showbiz bosses, and the Mindbenders were an entirely different grouping from the ones who had originally recorded the hits. Their credentials had been obtained by serving time as Wayne Fontana's backing group later in his career. But as far as our own case went we felt justified in that any alterations in personnel had been seamless and natural. A person leaves, a person is replaced. It's a moot point but it is our point.

The principals - ourselves, Gerry Marsden, Freddie Garrity, Chad and Jeremy - flew in the Club section while the backing bands and crew were relegated to cattle class at the back of the bus. Dee Garrity, Freddie's wife, was accompanying the bespectacled comedy songster but the promoters were paying for artistes only and Mr Garrity's finances either could not or would not accommodate such an extravagant outlay. Dee was condemned to slum it with the peasants while her husband made attempts to mollify her by popping down the aisle with a glass of complimentary champagne once in a while. I know many wives who would not have been quite so tolerant. It will come as no shock to discover that the marriage was not to last.

Chad Stuart and Jeremy Clyde, British to the core but much more feted in the States than in their homeland where their success was modest, had rehearsed out there with an American band, but it was thought important enough in image terms to jet them back to Britain solely for the purpose of arriving with the rest of the package in order to present the complete ensemble to the waiting media. The money men it seemed were not skimping on this venture.

We were all put up in a fair degree of luxury at the St Moritz on the Park, a more than comfortable upmarket hostelry straddling the lower western corner of New York's famous oasis of greenery, with the lights of Broadway just around the corner. October 9th, the day we arrived, was by coincidence John Lennon's birthday, he would have been forty-six years old, and John McNally and I crossed Central Park to find a bevy of fans standing solemnly in front of the Dakota Building where he and Yoko Ono had lived together until Mark Chapman had put an early end to their idyll. Throughout the day the crowd continued to grow for a candlelit vigil that evening to mourn the death of the enigmatic Beatle. There was a pervading sadness which I felt myself. True he had been slightly caustic to me on our first meeting a lifetime ago at the end of 1962 but I had very quickly got over that and the offence was not a capital one.

The tour kicked off at Madison Square Garden but unlike the 1973 venture the promoters picked the more sensibly-sized Felt Forum rather than the unrealistic main arena. It was a good start. A big crowd and an enthusiastic reception to kick us into gear. It had nearly turned to disaster for us when Chad and Jeremy's laid back LA-based band took far too much time shifting their equipment while our introduction was being made. As the words came over the main PA an American musician was still fumbling about at John McNally's feet seemingly unaware of the need for haste. A hefty kick from the Scouser's right foot accompanied by an Anglo Saxon threat sped things up a bit. He suddenly realised he was not welcome.

Our odd habit of finishing our short set with a medley reprising five or six of our biggest hits brought fulsome praise from the American promoters. It was something they had never encountered before and they commented enthusiastically on its effectiveness. 'I never realised you guys were so tight' remarked one as we came off. So far so good.

Each act had its own individual appeal and the styles were contrasting yet complimentary. The Mindbenders competently approximated the chart entries of the original group into whose shoes they had stepped and served the purpose of starting the show without one of the main acts having to go on cold.

Gerry, as always, was Gerry. Upbeat, bouncy and effervescent with a roster of hits that had successfully translated to the US market and a Beatle/Epstein connection that was certainly no hindrance. His throaty Mersey-honed voice was still powerful and effective. Oddly his enduring and anthemic *You'll Never Walk Alone*, an ace in the hole which could be guaranteed to bring down any house in his native land, had been a stiff States-wise. Any connection to the song over there was with regard to veteran comedian Jerry Lewis's annual charity telethon and only the dyed-in-the-wool devotees realised its significance in terms of Brit-pop.

Freddie's manic brand of humour was never my cup of Earl Grey but he had cracked it in the US where almost every baby boomer had at some point tried to do 'the Freddie', an insane and manufactured dance which involved the participants leaping up and down with eyes glazed and arms flailing. Not the most elegant piece of terpsichore but remembered by many nonetheless. He was without doubt a weighty name to have on the bill.

Chad and Jeremy's style was altogether much more sophisticated and laid back, possibly influenced by the studied elegance of Mr Clyde in particular whose main occupation nowadays was in the realms of the theatre. He had created a very successful career as a typically effete Englishman in, for the most part, British television dramas. As a distant relation of the Duke of Wellington his innate breeding had certainly been an advantage.

With just one modest hit at home they had found much more favour in America with a run of soft and soothing summer melodies that suited the California climate well. *Yesterday's Gone*, *A Summer Song* and *Willow Weep For Me* had all been big for them and the audience showed just how much they were liked. For me there was much to learn as I watched from the side. When taking their bows there was no frantic rushing on and off the stage but rather a leisurely and confident stroll back and forth, secure in the knowledge that they would be invited back for an encore. While the content of their set was not entirely to my personal taste their manner of connecting with the audience, which consisted of interesting and beautifully enunciated anecdotes, was to be admired.

From the Big Apple we trekked across America in two customised tour buses driven in from Nashville, the major portion of their lives being employed transporting country and western acts from gig to gig. Like many of their current occupants these extravagantly painted vehicles had once seen better days. Soon after the commencement of our travels one of them had to be shipped back in exchange for a replacement that did not pump clouds of diesel fumes into the cabins. But it was a fun way to see the wide-open spaces of that great land.

Gerry and Freddie, along with Freddie's wife and Gerry's personal manager, very quickly opted for hiring a car and travelled separately from the main body of the tour. Freddie, in a display of sheer cheek that was magnificent in its absolute outrageousness, suggested to his already very underpaid backing group that as his departure from the bus had left them more space in which to enjoy the journeys they should make a contribution to his gasoline bill. I believe that 'fuck off' were just two of the many expletives that were included in the reply.

Business was excellent in many places, the major cities in particular, but out in the sticks things occasionally got a bit thin. Tuffy's KC Opry House in Kansas City was not to be remembered for its high position on the success ratio, its two shows containing barely enough people to represent a reasonable attendance for just one. More used to providing a stage for lightly amplified country acts the PA system was not equipped for the amount of mic-ing up we needed to do and while we all wandered off with the boss to be fed at the local fried chicken establishment we left Andy Cairns, Gerry's sound engineer, to effect some modifications. Somehow he managed to cobble the whole thing together after a fashion and the shows finally got under way. He went hungry and we got a sound system.

Unfortunately no-one bothered to check the readiness of the cast before starting the introductory newsreel film which was supposed to lead slickly into the first act. As it came to its conclusion the Mindbenders were still trying to squeeze their expanding frames into a set of over-optimistically tight white trousers and Union Jack shirts on the stairwell. Tuffy's was somewhat under-endowed in the dressing room department. The sparse crowd looked askance at the ensuing chaos as the group was announced followed by a flurry of inactivity. The stage remained embarrassingly bare and stayed that way for a further ten minutes until the pop stars were suitably clad and the show could commence.

But Tuffy's was the only disaster in the logistics department and apart from one of the buses breaking down, resulting in a long wait for a replacement, things ran reasonably smoothly. In Milwaukee Gerry learned that his father-in-law had died and flew home for two days leaving us to close the show and as a sort of tribute, and a bit of fun, we slipped a couple of Gerry's hits into our set which amused the audience and served to satisfy their loss a little.

Massey Hall in Toronto, Canada, turned out to be the highlight of the tour with a capacity crowd padded out with expatriates desperate to hear and cheer their idols from back home. Whatever possessed me I do not know but in the middle of our set I decided to give an anti-drugs speech. In truth I am firmly anti-drugs and I would like to say that it was from a moral standpoint that I made my pronouncements but it would not have been true. I simply realised that a seemingly sincere sermon to the troubled youth on the current times would elicit an enormous reaction of approval and it did. It was an exercise in button pressing that paid off handsomely with a suitable amount of news space devoted to it in the reviews the following day.

Some time later I was told by a bunch of people who were occupying a box that evening that they had listened to my words with a mixture of amusement and embarrassment. They were smoking copious amounts of marijuana and were in fact stoned out of their brains.

There were moments when we could all relax. In Elmira the Holiday Inn was the scene of a tour jam with most of us grabbing the house band's instruments in turn to cut loose and have a bit of fun doing things that were out of our scheduled repertoire.

For an appearance required by the Searchers on Solid Gold, the major nationwide television show hosted by Marylin McCoo and Arsenio Hall, we left the rest of the touring party, rented a car and drove to Burbank. *Love Potion No. 9*, our greatest US success which we lip-synched to, sounded oddly slow. It was the original recording with Tony Jackson singing lead and quite a few beats per minute under the tempo that we had become used to over the years for our live performances. Bobby Vinton and Marie Osmond were also guests on the programme that week and Marie appeared glammed up to the nines and revelling in a big hair day. As a nicely raised Mormon girl I expected her to be an extremely pleasant person and she did not disappoint as we posed for a photograph together.

On a free night in San Diego we stepped up the street to watch Leon Russell and Edgar Winter at a rock club called the Bachannal. Earlier that day we had driven our rental car across the border into Tijuana. The name sounded exotic to us untravelled Brits. The reality was quite different. Quite sleazy and with a great deal of poverty in evidence, it was not a place in which one felt inclined to linger.

Our exit proved the point when a cop approached the vehicle at the border crossing and explained that our hire car was not allowed to be taken into Mexico. He pointed out the clause on our hire document. He was correct. It was there right at the bottom in large black capitals. He knew it the moment he recognised the licence plate as a hire vehicle. It was for suckers like us that he had been looking out and hoping for. For the local cops it was a permanently open season on fleecing errant and unknowing travellers.

He affected a serious expression and explained that we were in big trouble. I got the point immediately and enquired as to whether there was someone not a million miles from here who I could pay to extract us from our predicament. Well surprise, surprise, he was willing himself to help us out. What a nice man. I passed over to him one hundred and eighty dollars. He had declined a lower offer and I had no way of knowing what the going rate was. I just wanted to get us out of there as quickly as possible.

The chutzpah shown by the enterprising policeman I suppose could be reasonably termed Tijuana brass neck. The money duly changed hands and we crossed into America breathing communal sighs of relief and vowing never to return to Tijuana.

The tour ended its run, six weeks after it began, at the Universal Amphitheatre in Los Angeles where a large crowd which included a smattering of minor celebrities such as Stephen Bishop (*On And On*), actor Christopher Cazenove and his actress wife Angharad Rees gave us a magnificent send off. A surprising icon of the sixties appeared in the form of Big Dee Irwin. But the *Swinging On A Star* man, to whom I had first been introduced at a Tito Burns pre-tour house party in 1964, was not there in any kind of celebrity mode. His one-hit fortunes having long since faded he was now employed as the local representative of the Musicians Union. He was surprised and immensely pleased that we remembered him.

A few of us even managed to wander down a nearby grassy slope in the afternoon to visit the old Psycho house which was still on the lot and looking exactly as we remembered it from the creepy old classic black and white film. The Bates Motel was there too but the interiors of both buildings were merely empty, decaying spaces. No bloodied bodies in the shower. No embalmed grandma in a rocking chair. But still we didn't hang around too long.

Whether great profits had been made by the entrepreneurs who had assembled the package I have no idea. We the performers had all enjoyed some of the most fun days we'd had for a long time as we laughed our way across that great country which was the birthplace of the rock & roll we loved so much.

On the plane home John McNally approached Gerry and his manager with the suggestion that such a tour, pared down to an economically viable content, could do well in Britain. Package tours, once a staple diet for us at the peak of our popularity, had become a thing of the past but we saw no reason why it should stay that way. Everyone was in agreement and on our return to British soil the wheels were set in motion. Flying Music, a concert promotions company with a history of nostalgic presentations were more than open to the idea and plans were set in place for a 1987 tryout.

Having enjoyed a fairly trouble-free time away from the legal tussles that were still occurring at home, we now had to get on with sorting out the latest list of misrepresentations. The Belfry Hotel, Sutton Coldfield, the Hatherley Manor in Leicestershire, the Forum, Livingston, and the Meadows Club at Notts County Football Club were only a few of the venues defending our claims of 'passing off' or advertising Mike Pender's outfit as something other than it was legally entitled to be. Mike's new agent, Tony Sherwood, was having a busy time explaining and excusing each breach of the undertakings given, as we saw it.

We had no sooner dealt with one batch than a bunch of others stood in line for our threats of repercussion in the courts. The Percy Main Club, North Shields, the Malvern Winter Gardens, Bianco's - a venue in the North East - and the Crafty Cockney in Burslem all used wrongly-worded advertisements. Mostly they agreed swiftly to correct the errors and in such cases we declined further action. And occasionally we took things to the limit to right the wrongs and defray our quite considerable costs. One leading West London venue was unwise enough to ignore our protestation and neglected to remove misleading posters from its entrance despite having received our very expensive letters. As a result they ended up paying us damages in the region of three thousand pounds, about twice as much as they could have booked us for at the time. But mostly the settlements simply came close to recouping expenses. And several times, to prove we were not money-grabbing opportunists, we handed over any receipts to local charities such as the Butterwick Hospice on Teesside or the George Eliot Trust in Nuneaton.

Meanwhile our big UK adventure finally kicked off at the London Palladium on May 31st 1987 under the banner of the Solid Silver Sixties Show, with two performances completely sold out. But it nearly never happened at all. A couple of weeks before we received an emergency phone call from our road manager Gerry Hope. It seemed that the show in King's Lynn that evening was in fact a show in King's Lynn that afternoon. We were due on stage at four o'clock.

I quickly rounded up Billy Adamson and Spencer James and we set off at the speed of light, or at least the speed of a Ford Sierra 2.3 Ghia which was our group mode of transport at the time. We were making good time and as we left the thirty-mile-an-hour limit of Eye in Cambridgeshire I pressed my foot down in order to make up time at which point a tiny Fiat car in front, crammed with passengers, decided to make a sudden right hand turn. Metal clashed and the Sierra rose gracefully into the air in a beautiful arch that Chitty Chitty Bang Bang could not have executed better. It landed on its side and we found ourselves hanging parallel to the ground below. As I extracted myself from the mangled metal I vowed to drive more carefully in future having been reminded that it is not only cars that can be recalled by their maker. The Sierra and the show were write-offs but thankfully there were no injuries either to ourselves or our opponents in the Fiat other than my wounded pride. The car might not have been able to proceed but, following a short run in Ireland, the Solid Silver Sixties Tour could.

Why it was downgraded to silver rather than gold I have no idea. There had been enough gold in our sales over the years to warrant the grander title but such things were out of our hands. There was a buzz in the air and it felt like the perfect time to lift our game of musical nostalgia to a new level. While Gerry Marsden and ourselves alternated for closing spots the opening act was constant in the form of Peter Sarstedt, the modern minstrel who had created a lifetime pension for himself with his timeless continental-tinged ballad *Where Do You Go To (My Lovely)*.

The swarthy moustachioed singer/songwriter came from a dynasty of talented Anglo-Indian musicians. Brother Richard Sarstedt had found pop fame in the early sixties as Eden Kane with hits like *Well I Ask You*, *Forget Me Not* and *Boys Cry* while their other sibling Clive, under the assumed name of Robin Sarstedt, had charted with a modern version of the old Hoagy Carmichael three-quarter time standard *My Resistance Is Low.*

Whilst we knew of Peter it was the first time we'd met him and we were all pleased to find one of the most congenial people we had ever come across. Here was an erudite and sincere troubadour who took his writing seriously while he took himself with a refreshing pinch of salt. He would prove to be a much-needed calming influence over us all and over the coming months I was to find out that there was so much more to his worth than the one enormous hit, plus a couple of lesser ones, that had entered the charts.

The opening concert went smoothly and the audiences ate out of our hands. The feeling of excitement was palpable and it appeared that the artistes on stage were for once being given a degree of respect that for too long had been withheld. The review that followed by the arts critic of the Guardian was slightly less deferential however. All in all the large amount of newsprint devoted to the article proved the significance of the occasion but each of us suffered a little from a drop of poison in the pen.

Gerry Marsden's somewhat expanded physique was compared to Charlie Drake, the rotund British comedian of yesteryear, while Peter Sarstedt was called an 'incomparably bad lyricist'. I took great exception to that particular comment, knowing how carefully Peter constructed the words to his compositions. *Where Do You Go To (My Lovely)* is to my mind not only impossibly catchy but is a well-observed comment on the superficiality of life among the jet set of Europe. And I still maintain that lyrically *Love Among The Ruins* would be hard to beat.

For ourselves, we drew praise for being slick and still serious about our music but the man could not resist the lure of the barbed comment saying that our outfits were from Man at C&A. Years later, having included wicked comments in a tome of my own merely for their comedic value rather than their objectivity or truth, I can easily understand his motive and find it hard to bear a grudge. After all, everybody has to make a living. More satisfying perhaps to be a Dorothy Parker rather than a Barbara Cartland. And it was indeed a very amusing piece of writing.

Over the four weeks we covered just about every inch of Britain with sold-out notices posted outside virtually every theatre we entered. It was an unqualified success on a scale we had never envisaged and furthermore we had introduced a new sound, or to be more correct, a whole new library of sounds by way of a guitar/synthesiser which Spencer James was now playing. Looking like a standard electric guitar it played in exactly the same way but a specially added pickup which in turn connected to a separate module could convert a note into an amazing range of pre-programmed sounds. With the depression of a foot pedal he could replicate a sweeping string section, a grand piano or even a helicopter though it was unlikely the helicopter would come in for much use. The tour concluded in the Channel Islands at the end of the month on an all-time high and with the promise of more to come. Who said nostalgia ain't what it used to be?

Meanwhile on the legal front, as if things were not complicated enough, Mike had by the end of May changed his solicitors once again to Wright, Webb and Syrett who were a London based firm. He may perhaps have felt that he needed a set-up that was a bit more heavyweight if the fight was showing signs of becoming increasingly aggressive. If the gloves were to come off it would be as well to make sure there was a sturdy set of knuckles underneath with which to inflict sufficient injury.

35

Court In The Act

The lure of the newly introduced Solid Silver package had proved so irresistible that a hastily arranged second leg with the same line-up took over the latter part of January and the entire month of February 1988 with the same 'house full' notices everywhere. Suddenly yesteryear was very big business again. We could not have found a better method of reasserting our position in the current market.

We were now planning our show with much more thought, taking great care to manipulate the emotional sensibilities of our audiences, by contrasting uplifting pop consisting mainly of our hits with dramatic and powerful ballads like *Somebody Told Me You Were Crying,* a little-known song taken from an album by a Christian group called the Allies that we had picked up in the States while on the British Invasion tour. It was a showstopper every night and showed off Spencer James' voice perfectly. The atmospheric bell sounds at the beginning and the sweeping strings that gradually emanated from the newly introduced guitar/synthesiser as the song progressed gave our sound a rich embellishment and identity that few others, if any at the time, possessed.

Our elevation to the theatre platform had in its turn enabled us not only to maintain but to increase our fees on the ballroom and club circuit. It was just as well because as fast as money was coming in it was just as speedily disappearing into the dark abyss wherein dwelt the dreaded and highly voracious litigation monster.

Although it had seemed the first leg had exhausted all the territories in the land, a run of no less than twenty-four hitherto untouched theatres had been assembled to satisfy the needs of audiences who had suddenly discovered the undiluted joys of looking back. It began on January 29th at the Malvern Winter Gardens, which coincidentally was the subject of a possible action with regard to the Mike Pender issue, and ended one month later on February 28th at the Festival Theatre, Paignton.

After a couple of false starts, when it almost seemed that a settlement with Mike Pender could be reached, the time had come to stall no longer. A letter from Paul

Krempel dated February 17th indicated that the delay in reaching a settlement, he felt, was wholly due to Pender and warned us that it might be necessary to reinstate proceedings for a committal. Almost immediately we had found it necessary to serve the papers and one week later we were told that a likely date for the hearing would be some time in May.

There was a matter of the balance of Paul's fees to pay, an amount of £1544.40 was still owing, and the cost of the hearing was estimated at £1500 to £2000 on the basis that it would take two days to clear. That included the cost of Counsel but there would naturally be other amounts incurred. All this of course was on top of the regular payments of £1500 to £2000 we had already been making from the commencement of our troubles. We simply shrugged our shoulders. It was all so surreal that the cheques we signed, once frightening indicators of our financial fragility, had now become a matter of routine. We were fiscally numb. By the end of March it was apparent that because of Counsel's prior commitments no suitable date in May could be found and eventually the day of reckoning was set for June 8th.

We gathered our little team together at Chansitor House on the appointed morning. There was John McNally and myself, suited and booted as befitted the seriousness of the occasion, Paul Krempel and our barrister Richard Miller. Together we walked the short distance through the hallowed lanes to the High Court. It was a bright, cheerful day and everywhere there were black gowns and curly white wigs as the barristers and their clerks hurried to and fro chatting animatedly, often no doubt to those who had a matter of moments before had been opponents pleading and arguing their respective cases. Professional enemies. Private friends. It was quite fascinating.

In the hallway outside the Court itself Pender huddled with his team which included his solicitor, his barrister Mr Bateson, and his agent Tony Sherwood who was to be referred to in the official proceedings by his given name of Anthony Welbourne. The Sherwood part had been adopted during his days as a performer. We barely nodded if at all.

Rather than boasting the dark and musty interiors that we were used to seeing in old black and white films the modern but classic fittings were in a very light wood and the room was airy and quite sanitised. We rose respectfully as Justice Peter Whitford entered and proceedings began.

The arguments back and forth, together with the presentation of evidence in the way of disputed contracts, were dreary in the extreme and if it was so for us then it must have been excruciatingly dull for the judge. I watched him carefully and at one point I could have sworn his eyes were tightly shut. He could have dropped into a power nap but I have little doubt that his razor sharp mind, used to absorbing mass amounts of seemingly complicated facts, was wide awake and taking in every tiny detail. Whenever he glanced through a document handed up to him by a clerk he covered the salient points in a fraction of the time it would take a mere mortal like myself to read through. And, unlike myself, he doubtless understood every syllable.

The name Brian Gannon, one of the many sub-agents used in the entertainment industry, cropped up several times and there was a real Rumpole moment when Justice Whitford lowered his head, looked over the top of his spectacles and in an archaic, rich voice solemnly asked 'Who is Brian Gannon? 'in the manner that an unworldly judge, or perhaps one who wished to appear unworldly for effect, might enquire 'And who, pray tell me, is Elvis Presley? Is he, what I understand to be a 'rock and roller?' Mr Gannon's role in the saga was explained to his satisfaction and proceedings continued.

When the time came for our arguments to be presented our barrister, Richard Miller, pleaded our case with efficiency but not in the kind of beautifully scripted theatrical rhetoric employed in Hollywood movies. This was not Hollywood and he was not Charles Laughton. Real life rarely mirrors drama. Occasionally faltering but still very careful to put the entire facts of our complaints before the court, he stood and faced the judge in a manner that would have been the epitome of elegance were it not for one fact. He was standing on one leg. The other was held at a ninety-degree angle by a free hand. I was transfixed. My future as an entertainer was at stake, along with a considerable amount of the very small fortune I possessed, and I was being represented by someone whose next significant appearance it would seem might well be as Long John Silver in one of the festive season's pantomimes. I was beginning to feel more shaky and unsure with each passing minute.

Our case rested on the agreements set in the previous undertakings given by Mike and in support of this four contracts which either contravened or at least did not entirely fulfil those assurances were produced. One was between Mike and a Royston Jones. The name of the venue escapes me. A second was with the Meadows Club which was situated at the Notts County Football Ground complex. Another was for the Granby Hotel in Leicestershire and the final one for the Lakeside Club at Frimley Green. The contracts, though for Mike Pender's Searchers, failed to include the necessary instructions with regard to size, style and colouring of the wording used.

Two days had been set aside for the proceeding there was nothing so complicated as to warrant more than a day's examination and by early afternoon Justice Whitford began his summing up. It was difficult to tell which way things were going as he mulled over the whys and wherefores of arguments on both sides. There had certainly been breaches, he accepted. He stated that he was extremely unhappy that matters had taken so long to come to court having been instigated by the issuing of a writ on March 25th 1986, and felt it should be disposed of as soon as possible.

The precise technical phrasing he used left us at various points feeling both exhilarated and deflated. Our lack of sophistication in the realms of both the English language and the legal world had us confused as his words took their twists and turns. At one point his deliberations appeared to be going against us. He referred to paragraph 3 of the Notice of Motion in general terms which he apparently had to consider in the light of the relevant provisions of the rules relating to contempt [and the grounds set out in paragraphs 4 and 5 set out breaches in failing to meet the requirements of the undertaking] (sic). What the hell did it all mean? We had no idea but it all sounded so ominous.

The errant contracts were dealt with one by one. Mike had in fact signed the contract for Lakeside himself and, admitting that he should not have, offered the excuse that his habit was to arrive at a club just before a performance and leave as soon as he could and that he did not look sufficiently clearly at the contract when he signed it.

Justice Whitford then summarised the actions taken in dealing with the breaches and seemed to us to be saying that, when pointed out, the mistakes had been rectified. Indeed a writ had been taken out against Lakeside and had been settled. He also agreed with Mike's Counsel, Mr Bateson, that it was a little strange that the motion seeking a penal sanction against the defendant (Contempt of Court carries the threat of imprisonment) was not issued until November, at which time so far as the Granby Hotel was concerned the matter had been rectified and all other incidents were matters of history.

I wanted to yell out that yes, they were behind us but this was all about frightening the bugger into not doing it again which we felt he certainly would if extreme action were not taken. The delays were due to exploring every avenue in order to avoid unwanted litigation which was stressful, fraught with danger and which we could barely afford. It was not sounding good at all. John and I looked at each other and mutually agreed that we had lost.

But almost immediately there was a turnaround and it was clear that he accepted that there had most certainly been transgressions on Pender's part that required reparation in law. Whitford went on to say that he was only concerned with the liability of the defendant in respect of the undertakings he had given and the Plaintiffs had shown that there had been breaches. He added that the Plaintiffs were not seeking to press the matter for committal and sequestration, in other words we were not insisting he be locked up, and he thought it quite right that we were not pressing to such an extreme. We had already decided that it would not look good to be so vindictive. But I have to say it was bloody tempting.

Finally he gave his decision. Imprisonment was wholly inappropriate. (Oh, damn and blast). There was the possibility of a fine being imposed but bearing in mind the circumstances, the time taken to bring the motion, the dilatory way in which the action was proceeding and the full apologies offered, it was enough for the defendant to pay our costs on an indemnity basis. We were not quite sure what he had been saying or what exactly had happened but it appeared that we had emerged victorious. Praise the Lord indeed.

So from now on it would be all plain sailing with our precious name strenuously being protected under the letter of the law. Would it Hell. In fact misuse of our title would be a constant gnawing pain that would continue to plague us throughout our career with varying degrees of effectiveness. But on the whole the situation was at last under some kind of tenuous control.

At least serendipity was on our side. I had taken to exercising my rapidly ageing frame by way of visits to the gym four times a week at the David Lloyd Racquet Club in Heston, not far from Heathrow Airport. To be honest four visits a day would not have achieved the kind of body I would have liked, I was now approaching forty-five years old, and the most I could hope for was some kind of damage limitation.

It was the summer of 1988 and I was relaxing by the coffee counter having completed my work out on the club's Nautilus machines. I was joined by none other than Cliff Richard, Britain's best loved idol and just a plain old mister in those pre-knighted times, who was a David Lloyd regular, albeit on the tennis court rather than the weights. We had occasionally passed the odd sentence or two but were by no means bosom buddies. He knew my name and my history with the band and probably very little more. I knew just about as much of him as any other grovelling unworthy fan, which I most certainly admit to being.

After some small talk he enquired as to what we were doing next June. I had no idea. It was too far ahead. He delivered the news that he was considering taking over the vast 75,000 capacity Wembley Stadium to celebrate his thirty years in the entertainment industry and that 'it would be great to have all our old friends on'. Sorry Cliff, run that by me again. It didn't quite compute, at least as far as the 'all our old friends' portion of the sentence went. Yes, we had spoken and yes, I called him Cliff. Beyond that I was not worthy. But I ventured that whatever the case we would move heaven and earth to accommodate him. I got the feeling that he was nervous about the idea. That perhaps the sheer scale of the project was possibly a bridge too far. Cliff Richard had been a major star for three decades but he had not previously been touted as a stadium attraction. But it was a tantalising prospect and if it were to come to fruition then we would fight tooth and nail to be involved.

When the news was eventually confirmed in the press I immediately rang our agent Alan Field. I strongly suspected that Cliff's offer, made on the spur of the moment over a cup of tea, would be withdrawn accompanied by a suitably phrased excuse. But no. They were delighted to have us on board and much more than that they were going to pay us to be on the show. Little did Cliffie know that we would happily have passed over a reasonable amount of filthy lucre, in a brown paper bag if necessary, to be included in the line-up.

Meanwhile things had suddenly moved in leaps and bounds on the recording front and just when we thought we were dead in the water as far as new recordings were concerned we found ourselves in a recording studio in Germany completing our first album in eight years.

The Coconut studios in a small town called Hennef not far from Cologne was a state of the art facility that had seen a good deal of success in the disco and dance field which was rife and thriving in Germany. It was owned by Tony Hendrik and Karin Van Haaren, an enterprising young couple who were pleased to have what they saw as an enduring legendary name on their youth-oriented label.

Not having the time available to spend an extended period in a studio, which of course would have been without benefit of the essential gig money needed to pay the bills, we resorted to completing the work in a manner we had never tried before. Basic computer-generated drum tracks were laid down ahead of our arrival by our appointed producer, Hans Steingen, along with synthesised string and keyboard pads to provide a bedrock on which we could add our own contribution. Guitars, both six string and twelve string, were layered on top of the prepared tracks followed by lead voices and harmonies which naturally incorporated the trademarks of our long-established sound but which also took advantage of the power and fullness that the new technologies offered.

Many of the songs were Hendrik/Van Haaren compositions but we were allowed enough space on the album for our own works. As was our custom we shared credits although, in the same manner as Lennon and McCartney, we invariably wrote separately. Of course finished songs are embellished and added to by the other musicians during the process of recording. Sharing the rights seemed a fairer method and stopped us arguing about whose songs were best – often a purely subjective argument at best – and who was going to end up with the greater portion of the writing royalties.

Push Push, a slow, bluesy tune was a John McNally composition while the poppier *Every Little Tear* was mine. Spencer James contributed *Fooled Myself Once Again* and I delivered a complete set of lyrics for the Hendrik/Van Haaren melody *Baby I Do*. We also added a complete middle section to *No Other Love* although any composition credits for that one were noticeable by their absence. *Love Lies Bleeding* and *This Boy's In Love* were both entirely John McNally compositions.

It came as no surprise that they requested re-recordings of a couple of our hits for identification purposes and to make the product more saleable. Our natural resistance was tempered by pragmatism. We could see their point and it was important for us to have a disc that would reach the widest possible public. We eventually settled on reworking of *Needles And Pins* and *Sweets For My Sweet* on condition that the new versions would be a radical departure from the originals. A young German arranger, Theo Werdin, was brought on board to translate our ideas into reality.

Indeed it must have come as a great shock to many on hearing the frantic eighties club style of that original Searchers number one hit from 1963. *Needles And Pins* was slightly less jarring to the system perhaps but this time round it opened on a quasi-classical overture built around the distinctive guitar figure. And on the final verse we reverted to the tortured lyrics of Jackie DeShannon's original version.

Probably the stand-out track was one we gifted to the project. *Somebody Told Me You Were Crying,* the beautiful heartfelt ballad that told about the optimism that still remained after death, had been recorded and owned by ourselves and lay on the shelf having failed to secure a commercial release. We remained convinced that in another place and time it could have been one of our biggest hits ever.

We spent several weeks completing the project and the finished album was given the title *Hungry Hearts*, which was on the whole a happy experience. The results might not have satisfied the purists among our fans who possibly expected acoustic drums and more guitars but in truth they were not the market we were aiming for, at least not entirely. If we were to make any inroads into the current markets we had to acquire a whole new army of record buying customers. And over the years the album has found a hardcore of devotees who were quite taken by the immediacy of the songs and who, when it became hard to come by, searched high and low for copies of what in a limited way became a collector's item.

Between October 1988 and April 1989 three tracks were put onto the German market and failed to make any significant impact. *Forever In Love* débuted our Coconut releases followed quickly by the *Needles And Pins* remake and finally *No Other Love.* We remained hitless but were at least content in the knowledge that we had enjoyed the experience and maintained some pride in the fruits of our labours. Twenty-six years after the group's first single we were still a recording band.

36

The Event

The Event, as the Wembley Stadium adventure was finally named, turned out to be one of the major highlights of our career and certainly the largest audience. To be involved in such a gigantic occasion was way beyond our wildest dreams and 1989 promised to be a year of new beginnings and good things to come. Dramas on the legal front had subsided considerably, complicated only by the sudden and tragic death of our young lawyer Paul Krempel.

On February 16th he had been running to catch a bus when he suffered a massive heart attack and died before reaching the hospital. He was thirty-seven years old and had merged his small practice with the larger firm Rochman Landau only two weeks previously. It was a small setback for us but one which paled into insignificance when compared to the tragic and unexpected loss to Paul's family and friends. His duties in handling our case were swiftly assumed by Teresa Cullen, young and enthusiastic and, like Paul, someone we felt a kinship with and in whose hands we felt safe.

Any doubts that Cliff Richard might have had with regard to choosing such an enormous venue as Wembley to celebrate his stellar career soon proved groundless. The clamour for tickets was such that the option of a second day was quickly taken up. Apart from ourselves the final list of names comprised his legendary backing group and stars in their own right the Shadows, reggae band Aswad with whom he had recently recorded, ex-Shadows Jet Harris and Tony Meehan, the Vernons Girls who had provided the glamour quotient of the fifties television show Oh Boy and, as a private joke, the Kalin Twins.

In Cliff's first ever concert tour in those far off days in 1959 when he was a seventeen-year-old teenage idol, he was supporting the American duo who were topping the best sellers with *When*, their one and only success which forever condemned them to the ranks of one hit wonders. Cliff had virtually dragged them out of retirement to provide an expensive punch line to his joke and to allow them one last unexpected moment of glory before retreating once again to pop obscurity.

Naturally they were no longer the fresh faced teen idols of their glory days - none of us were - but they had done themselves little favours by adopting matching goatee beards which made them look even less hip and youthful than they might otherwise have been. And their dated velvet tuxedos added nothing to the glamour quotient. They resembled a pair of well-dressed garden gnomes off to an embassy ball in a tiny emerging third world principality. But Herbie and Hal were nice guys, very respectful and humble and still sounded very much as they did way back *When*.

As a memento and as a display of our gratitude at being invited on board we presented Cliff with an engraved rose bowl around the rim of which we had inscribed *Cliff - 1959 to 1989 - Move It to The Best Of Me - The best from us - The Searchers. The Best Of Me* was his current single at the time.

Our portion of the show, which preceded the Oh Boy presentation, was over in the blink of an eye. Two songs, *Needles And Pins* and *When You Walk In The Room* and that was it. It was just as well. The vastness of it all was overwhelming and the huge gap between us and the first row of faces was greater than the entire length of most venues we were used to. Close to eighty thousand people crammed the stands and the pitch, sweltering and swaying under the blazing summer sun. In Britain nothing weather-wise is guaranteed but with Cliff's connections it came as no surprise to find that we had all been blessed with a surfeit of sunshine pouring forth from the heavens above.

Because of the quick changeover (we formed part of a special sixties section which also included Gerry & the Pacemakers) it was necessary to employ the use of backing tracks. On a live gig such a thing did not settle easily with us. We strongly disapproved of the burgeoning trend towards pre-recorded tracks for supposedly live appearances. We had always been a genuinely live band. But our self-respect was retained by the use of live vocals. Cliff's crowd were there for us from start to finish and we exited elated and pumped up, the roar of the crowd still reverberating around the stadium. Having done our part we could now relax and enjoy the other acts and the hospitality on offer in the beautifully created backstage garden where the food and drinks were set out.

The excellent Aswad were received well but perhaps weren't quite the fare that a Cliff Richard audience was used to. The Shadows on the other hand received a welcome fit for the conquering heroes that they were and delivered a belting set of hit after hit after hit which, though it barely tapped into their seemingly endless catalogue of successes, was sufficient to satisfy the hordes of adoring 'Shads' fans there. And when they were joined on stage by 'the man' the feeling of ecstasy among the crowd was palpable.

Cliff's contribution was in two parts. The Oh Boy segment, presented in the afternoon sun, attempted to recreate his early television shows complete with a packed stage of petticoated, dancing bobby-soxers and augmented by vocal harmonies from the Dallas Boys and the Vernons Girls, his cohorts from the original show.

But the main body of his concert was acted out in the warm evening air when the spectacular lighting rig could come into its own. As sophisticated as the effects were, the greatest crowd reaction was to one of the simplest and most traditional theatrical devices of all. Two giant mirror balls were lowered into sight, sharp pin pointed shards of light twinkling over the arena, and the crowd erupted, giving them a special ovation of their own.

Towards the end of his set Cliff, in a spangled white suit, looked suitably Christ-like as a hydraulic platform raised him high above us all with the entire cast reassembled on the platform for the finale. He was singing the anthemic *From A Distance*. The cameras recording the event moved in for a close up. Cliff was crying.

The second day replicated the first though the emotion could naturally never equal the feelings of the previous twenty-four hours. As for us, a couple of unexpected and unwelcome flies had dive-bombed into our personal pot of ointment skimming away a little of the pleasure in the process. We had already committed ourselves to a show at the Mersey View in Frodsham near Liverpool and, happy as we would have been to forgo the fee, we could not get a release from the contract. It was a regular venue for us and one where we were very popular. The compromise was to dash away after our spot at Wembley and make it in time for the late spot in Frodsham. The logistics were not a problem, there was enough time, but it meant us missing the fun and the camaraderie backstage. It was as if the last delicious lump of ice cream in our cone had dropped out into a puddle. But there was nothing we could do about it.

And to add insult to injury we were left waiting in the wings when Gerry Marsden neglected to call us on for the final chorus of *You'll Never Walk Alone*. We remained at the side frustrated and angry and feeling robbed of our moment of glory as Cathy McGowan and Cliff sang along to the reprise of the song. Gerry swore that it was an oversight. We, rightly or wrongly, decided it was a deliberate act and words ensued. It caused a rift that required a couple of years to heal.

On the touring front we were going from strength to strength and some of the locations were a little more exotic than our normal run-of-the-mill itinerary. In November we were in the resort of Acapulco in Mexico to perform for ABTA, the Association of British Travel Agents, over a five-day period. While we were there we experienced an earthquake which registered 5.6 on the Richter scale. It lasted for a mere three seconds or so but even though no buildings were brought down and there were no casualties that we knew of they were some of the scariest seconds we had lived through.

We spent that Christmas with our families and as 1989 came to a close we took to the skies again and found ourselves in Thailand celebrating the New Year at the luxurious Dusit Thani Hotel in Bangkok, a perfect setting in which to enjoy the festivities and to reflect on twelve months that had, although not without stress, been one of the most momentous of our career so far. In the sultry heat we could at last relax and unwind far away from the court cases and the endless motorway miles that we were required to travel in pursuit of our chosen profession. We toured the splendid temples, lavishly decorated with gold and jade and thrilled through a hair-raising ride as a long-boat powered by an old Chevvy engine whipped us through the narrow jungle river-ways at an alarming speed.

As an extra enticement (up to that point we had always firmly refused Christmas and New Year engagements) we were given a beach holiday at the resort of Pattaya and it was good to be far from the bitter cold of the UK. After all we had been through during the last year we felt we richly deserved it. It was a memorable trip maybe not so much for the actual shows but particularly for the eye-watering sights of the unusually skilled bar girls who could perform the most amazing feats with a part of their anatomy not created for such unexpected antics. It's amazing what a well-rehearsed performer can do with a string of razor blades or a banana.

Balloons were inflated, bananas propelled, razor blades extracted and a live linnet produced from that deep, dark cavern accompanied by a beatific smile of pride and a lack of self-consciousness that to my innocent eyes seemed at odds with the lascivious nature of the display. Where was the shame? I felt sorry that circumstances forced someone to earn a living in this manner but at the same time I was fascinated. I kept watching and joined in with the applause as the tiny bird, in the true tradition of show-business, took its bow. Whoever said that quality entertainment was dead?

With the improvements in the presentation of our show which had been enhanced by some simple yet amazingly effective lighting and pyrotechnics we had invested in, work was increasing and of a better quality and for greater reward than we had previously experienced. The Solid Silver Sixties tours were still packing them in and the mixing and matching by Flying Music meant we were now touring with our old friend Bobby Vee.

We had known Bobby since the early days when, in the wake of the explosion that was generically known as Merseybeat, the Americans were battered into second place. From being a headline act and with a list of more than a dozen monstrous hits to call on (*Run To Him*, *The Night Has A Thousand Eyes*, *Rubber Ball*, *Take Good Care Of My Baby* etc), he had to play second fiddle to the precocious young Brits. But, as is the way of all things, his time had come round again and as a classic hero he was once more headlining while it was our turn to close the first half.

Never ones to take prisoners, we saw the whole thing as a challenge and went in for the kill. Our set was designed to elicit a tumultuous reaction from the crowd, especially in the run up to our finish, and it invariably did. And if the performance and the content was not enough then our simple yet effective lighting set-up, along with some spectacular silver flash pyros culminating in a violent explosion from three front line confetti cannons on the last note, always destroyed whatever opposition we might be facing. This wasn't showbiz. This was war.

On the first night at the Fairfield Halls in Croydon, Bobby was extremely perturbed and felt threatened. He was an immensely talented artiste and proud of his career and his hits. The visual nature of our act left him feeling vulnerable and by the third night he had instructed the promoter to provide him with a similar display (minus cannons) with which to hold his own.

On occasions we would have problems with theatres about the use of our pyrotechnics and the fire marshal would check that the confetti was the proper flame-proof stuff. When asked if it had been treated our roadie, Phil Hayes, replied that we gave it three good meals a day and took it for regular walks so it had nothing to complain about. The fire marshal was not amused.

There were a lot of complaints about the length of our set and in truth we were running over our allotted time by five or ten minutes which is bad form in theatre terms. With so much material that we deemed necessary for the greatest impact, we found it extremely difficult to plan short shows. The major hits had to be in there – even then some big ones were omitted – but there were things that, though they were not part of our recording history, elicited an even greater response from our audience and we felt naked without the armour-plated defence provided by them. On reflection we should have behaved better. In some ways we might have helped Bobby a little. His guitarist, a very amiable chap by the name of Ar Stevens, always confided that when appearing with us he always seemed to move up a gear and never performed better than with the Searchers.

With such terrific hits and a really superb band behind him, which included his three sons, he was under little real threat and always sent them home ecstatic. How could he not? He was one of the great stars of the early sixties and has hung on in there to become a legend of pop music history.

At the Wimbledon Theatre I was thrilled at the appearance backstage of Lonnie Donegan, a particular idol of mine and a man to whom we should all be grateful. As the person who introduced skiffle to Britain he gave us the confidence to believe that, with an acoustic guitar and three chords we could all be performers. Without Lonnie things might have been very different indeed.

The tour was a huge success and ended up at the Dominion, Tottenham Court Road, on April 3rd where once more we very rudely over-ran. My mate Bruce Welch of the legendary Shadows turned up to watch as did a bunch of other celebrities which included Andrew and Julian Lloyd Webber, both avid Bobby Vee fans.

When the tour came to a close we continued at our normal hectic pace. We flew to Belfast to do a television show along with the Tremeloes, Dave Berry and the Swinging Blue Jeans. We were informed that we would be miming to our record in front of a live audience. No problem. That was fairly standard for TV. When we reached the Ulster Hall we discovered that the audience had actually paid for their tickets and had no idea of the lip-synching. As far as they were aware they were going to watch a live concert. As songs faded out rather than having proper live endings the discontent in the theatre grew like a malevolent cancer and the feeling of anger was palpable. Somehow the whole charade came to a finish without fisticuffs or a riot but it was a close call and we all went back to our hotel feeling very uncomfortable. We felt we had been cheated just as much as the audience.

The next morning we flew back to Heathrow and raced to Broadcasting House where we were due to play a number of songs during a special anniversary edition of the Gloria Hunniford Show. It was bizarre. We had just mimed for a live concert in Belfast and played live on a radio show in London. It's a mad, mad world.

For the remainder of the year we kept busy with a short tour of Canada, an Elvis convention in Leicester and our usual round of regular clubs, pubs and conventions. John McNally and I were thrilled and delighted to be asked to appear on Tony Hatch and Jackie Trent's This Is Your Life where we recounted the story of the mysterious Fred Nightingale, the pseudonym under which Tony had written *Sugar And Spice*. It was a fitting tribute to a man who had played such an important part in our lives.

When I got home I was too wired up to sleep and decided to take apart my silver disc for the 250,000 sales of *When You Walk In The Room*. I remembered the wonderful story of the Rolling Stones who, on checking out one of their gold awards, discovered that it was actually a Val Doonican record. I desperately wanted mine to be someone like Vera Lynn or even Mantovani. When I put it on the turntable I was very disappointed to hear *When You Walk In The Room*. What a bummer.

37

Travelling At The Speed Of Light

As we entered the last decade of the twentieth century it felt like someone had packed me and my life into a truck and the driver had died at the wheel with his foot jammed hard down on the throttle. Everything seemed to be going so fast and I longed for the distant days of my childhood when all good things took an eternity to arrive. These days no sooner had Christmas passed than the summer was on us with barely a moment to reflect on what was happening. At this rate it would soon be over and I wasn't just talking about my career.

John McNally and I were discussing the subject one day. He was now at the ripe old age of forty-nine and I was only a couple of years behind. "Do you realise how fast the last twenty years have gone?" I asked. He agreed with me. "Well that's about how long you've got, mate."

Work was still plentiful and things were very satisfactory though at the level we were existing we still had to budget very carefully to make sure there was a reasonable share of the income to provide us with the comforts we felt we deserved at this stage of our lives. We no longer used second-hand Sierras to transport us up and down the interminable miles of motorway. We could now afford brand new Mercedes saloons which we would replace every three years or so when the mileage had reached a hundred and fifty thousand miles or thereabouts.

It was rare for us not to be rebooked and we had therefore established a solid base of regular venues to guarantee the bulk of our work each year. The Mersey View in Frodsham. The Chestnuts, Glentham. The Willows, Salford. Savva's at Usk. The Circus Tavern, Purfleet. The Frontier, Batley. And a whole bunch of others.

We were booked for summer shows in Great Yarmouth, Paignton and Blackpool. There were no rules. Clubs, bars, ballrooms – or what was left of these dinosaurs of the leisure industry – theatres and conventions. It didn't matter. We took on all comers. In June we enjoyed our regular mid-year concert at the Beck Theatre in Hayes, always a sell-out both at summer and Christmas, and then flew straight off for a run of shows for the British troops in Germany. We had hardly touched down in the UK again before we were off to Ireland and then on to Sonderberg in Denmark and then home again, a trip which required six planes in two days.

We played anything and everything and were happy to do so and somehow the other guys, with attention-starved families to placate and take care of, managed to keep their lives and relationships on track. For me it was different. I had no such commitments to uphold. I was a free agent and loved the liberated feeling that doing whatever I wished at any given time provided me. Going home to an empty house was not a penance but a joy and I was more than happy not to be burdened with a responsibility to others. I always subscribed to the 'fish and guests' theory. After three days (with maybe a few exceptions) they all start smelling. And pets do not enter the equation either. They require feeding and looking after and nothing stays in my house that cannot take care of itself. Selfish? Yes. But it's my life and I'll do what I want, as the song goes.

It was unlikely that there would be another Event on the horizon but every once in a while we enjoyed the bonus of something a bit special. On August 25th we headlined at the Chelmsford Spectacular in Hylands Park in front of a twenty five thousand strong crowd and received rave reviews from the Essex press.

That year marked the twenty-fifth anniversary of England's 1966 World Cup victory and on 21st October we provided the suitably nostalgic musical background for a reunion of the team at Wembley Stadium. On this occasion we were inside and performing in the function room, but Wembley is Wembley whichever way you look at it and there were plenty of luminaries to gawp at. Bobby Moore, Nobby Stiles, Geoff Hurst and the rest of the surviving players. Michael Parkinson was there along with Jimmy Tarbuck, the Earl of Harewood and others. Des Lynam compered the occasion. To top it all the great Franz Beckenbauer had flown in from Germany to pay his own tribute. To be honest a group playing, no matter what their pedigree or historical suitability, is very much a secondary consideration in the face of such greatness but we were received enthusiastically and when I dragged Nobby Stiles onto the stage to belt out a chorus of *A Whole Lot Of Shakin' Going On* he put everything he had into his performance.

On another front I was thrilled to received my first solo award, that of Best Front Man In A Sixties Band, presented to me by The Beat Goes On, a fanzine dedicated to the music of our era. It might not have been a gold disc or a Grammy but we are all grateful for a pat on the back from time to time.

Under the auspices of Yorkshire-based entrepreneur and radio executive Tim Jibson our annual Christmas Show that year at the Hull City Hall, another place which had become special and which was guaranteed to sell out every December, was videoed to celebrate thirty years of the Searchers. There were taped messages from the likes of Shadow Bruce Welch and deejay Mike Read and when it was finally released the following year it included filmed footage of Cliff Richard heaping fulsome praise on us. From hero to fan. How good could it get?

Feeling we should be giving something back, both to the people who had followed and supported our shows throughout the recent years and to the world in general we agreed to a suggestion from Tim Viney, who had been operating the Searchers Appreciation Society since 1985, that we hold a convention, something he had been keen on for a while.

On February 9th 1992 at a school in Nuneaton, Warwickshire, we gave our services in aid of the George Eliot Baby Scanner Appeal, a worthy cause that existed to raise much-needed cash for equipment required by the premature baby unit at the local hospital. It was a small affair. We charged a modest entrance fee and auctioned off items of memorabilia. It didn't matter what it was. If it was Searchers-related then it was up for grabs.

There were copies of rare singles and pre-release acetates which included *Vahevala*, *Secondhand Dealer* and *Umbrella Man*. I had saved extra programmes of bygone tours and brochures from the Royal Variety Show and the World Cup Reunion. A leather shirt of mine which had appeared in a seventies handout for the band fetched fifty pounds while a set of hair braids which I had recently removed after suffering a particularly sad attack of male menopause sold for thirty. In all we raised in excess of three thousand pounds. Not a fortune but we felt contented that we had at least done something.

By coincidence we discovered that our ex-bassist, my predecessor Tony Jackson, had been taken into the very same hospital the previous day following a heart attack. He had relocated to the Midlands to serve as a steward for a golf club. John went to visit and they spent a short but happy time reminiscing. There had been much bad blood it's true but time was at last beginning to heal. Black Jake had certainly mellowed over the years.

We had started to do some shows for the British troops stationed in various parts of the world, some exotic and some not, some dangerous and some benign. It quickly became a favourite kind of work for me personally. The experiences were unique and uplifting and we all enjoyed a male camaraderie and sense of bonding that could never be gained in any other environment.

On April 17th we flew via Houston, Texas, to Belize, the Central American country that had previously been known as British Honduras, where the bored and beleaguered jungle-based troops greeted us rapturously. For ten days we camped in the forests and played our songs in the jungle moonlight. In our spare moments we also took the chance to visit the impressive Mayan temples constructed centuries before by the Aztec Indians. The privileges that came with our toils were received and gobbled up with gratitude by us, a bunch of lads who at one time would never have expected to see beyond the British Isles.

Ten days later we were heading off again for a three-day trip to Hong Kong. We were into our fourth decade as a band and no longer in the public eye but there was no sign of things slowing down.

It was around this time that I was pleased to be able to return favours in a small way to my boyhood hero Cliff Richard. We were at Heathrow Airport waiting for a flight to Finland and in a newspaper I spotted a cherished number plate coming up for auction. MOV 1T. It would be sacrilege for it to be snapped up by a removals firm. It was surely meant for Britain's most enduring rock idol and though the E was missing it was the title of his first hit record. I tore out the ad and sent it through to his office in Esher and pretty soon it was adorning his Mercedes sports car. Corny as it might seem I felt proud.

Goodness knows why it had taken so long but three years after the High Court judged in our favour the full settlement was finally signed between ourselves and Mike Pender. The wheels of justice grind exceedingly slowly. But if that was supposed to signify the end of any transgression towards us we would be doomed to disappointment. The mis-advertising, although gradually dissipating, continued to irk us.

A five hundred pounds settlement accepted from another action against the Kirklevington Country Club in Teesside we donated to a local cancer hospice charity called the John Butterwick Trust. We did not want to be seen to be gold diggers in the pursuit of our cause. We could well have done with the cash ourselves. It cost more than that in solicitors fees to take out the action.

Although the years were still good for us, the cabaret side of the entertainment industry was not faring too well and Savva's in Usk, a regular booking for us, closed after a vain struggle to make things pay. George Savva, a big man with a big heart and a veteran of the club world who was loved both by his acts and his clientele, finally had to admit defeat and shut up shop overnight. With his wife Pam he went abroad to lick his wounds and reassess their lives. Deposits were lost and some artistes remained unpaid for work undertaken, ourselves included, but when they returned to these shores some years later with new premises and revitalised, George made sure we were booked. It was his way of keeping the faith and making amends.

The 1993 Solid Silver Sixties tour, a strong bill featuring ourselves, Gerry & the Pacemakers and Billy J. Kramer & the Coustiks, kicked off in the Channel Islands on March 1st and continued its roller-coaster ride right through to its close at the London Palladium on Sunday May 9th. It was pretty much packed out from start to finish and a fun time for us.

As we boarded the plane for a show on the Isle of Man, armed with a brand new set of beautiful black instruments courtesy of the German based ESP company with our names inscribed at the twelfth fret, our sound man, Gerry Hope, was briefly detained when security staff discovered a pair of handcuffs in his hand baggage. They were removed and he was eventually allowed to get on. We never asked him why. It was pointless. He was always off the wall and we just looked on it as par for the course. In the light of the paranoia that surrounds airports these days I fear the repercussions would have been a tad more serious.

The young and lively Coustiks, who were backing Billy J, quickly became the characters of the tour with their infectious humour and zany outlook on life. At one hotel their drummer Chris Cadley got a call from reception reminding him that check-out time was 10.00 a.m. Bleary eyed and still sleepy he asked if perhaps they could be allowed to stay in their rooms until noon. The girl replied that it would be fine except that it was already a quarter to one.

For the one and only time the tour, always a UK only project, flew to Germany to join forces with the Mamas And The Papas, Dave Dee, the Bay City Rollers and others for a gigantic two-day nostalgia spectacular in Stuttgart, presented by Rainer Haas.

The crew bonded beautifully and, at the instigation of Gerry Hope, created theme days on which they would dress or act in the appropriate pre-designated manner. There was a 'shorts day' and a 'bad attitude day' (a complete failure when the mostly female theatre staff turned out to be much too nice to be nasty to) and a hat day.

Hat day occurred while in Cambridge. And Gerry Hope decided that full Muslim garb would be suitable. During the interval, instead of undertaking his usual chores, he came on to the stage, laid out a prayer mat and remained there on his knees, head to the floor in a state of devotion until at the end of the intermission he was lifted bodily from the podium, still in the prone position, by the rest of the crew.

That was small beer compared to the Bradford show which just happened to be 'transvestite day'. The tour's entire crew were in full drag for the night. Schoolgirl uniforms and nurses' garb were donned but again no-one could outdo Mister Hope who carried out his tasks dressed in nothing but a lurex G-string and a see-through nightie. When it came down to loading out at the end of the night it was too hot and so the nightie was discarded. Passers by quite naturally gawped at this strapping moustachioed man with nothing but what looked like a sequinned eye patch hiding his lunchbox.

All of these decadent happenings were captured on film by Pacemakers' bassist Andy Cairns who, at the end of the journey, was to produce a quite remarkable video diary of the adventure, at a time when all that was available to him was a simple hand-held domestic recorder and the unbridled enthusiasm of a passionate amateur. The results were a triumph and to this day I still feel that it was worthy of greater exposure.

On the downside of things, halfway through the tour we managed to fall out once more with Gerry Marsden. To this day I'm not quite sure what sparked it all but by Worthing we were barely on speaking terms. We were alternating the closing spot and on the nights Gerry finished there was a full finale. On the nights where we were last on the finale was minus Gerry who always enjoyed the opportunity to get an early night.

The rota was strictly maintained and the closing night at the London Palladium meant that we took what many still see as 'the top spot'. That sort of thing didn't matter to Gerry who would always have opted for a quick drive back home up the motorway but Flying Music, the promoters, insisted that it would be a finale with the entire cast for such an important venue. The tour had sold every one of the three and a half thousand seats at the BIC in Bournemouth and it was taken as a matter of course that the prestigious London venue would be packed solid for both performances. Among the celebrity guests attending was Cliff Richard, who I had invited. You could feel the buzz of excitement as he entered the theatre. Forty years on and he was still a huge star.

The night was a triumph and a fitting end to a terrific tour. The rift with Gerry took some time to end but end it did eventually. When we were all getting on well he was a fun person to be with, outrageous and outspoken and the life and soul of the party. The feud couldn't remain. It was all too petty on both sides and the alliance too important to be allowed to last. Our two groups on a combined show was a fairly lethal combination.

Despite our undoubted appeal on the circuit and our ability to hold our own with anyone as a closing act, we were rather irked that Flying Music never seemed to pay us the respect we felt we deserved or gave us the support we would have liked. No matter how much effort we put into our performance or how wild the reaction was Gerry would always be given preference and it rankled. We liked Derek Nicol very much but dearly wanted the company to show us that we were valued, and so the next package tour would see a temporary departure from them.

With the tour at an end there were still interesting and exciting things on the horizon. With our usual insanity and inability to resist a logistical challenge we hired a private plane and flew to Germany for an open-air show at the Lorelei near Frankfurt with the Beach Boys, the Hollies and Shakin' Stevens and on the stroke of our final chord dashed back to our shaky little six-seater craft in order to make another booking back home in Stroud, Gloucestershire, that evening. We touched down at the tiny unlit Midlands airfield in the nick of time, the light fading fast. Fifteen minutes later and it would have been deemed unsafe to land, putting the late night gig in jeopardy. This kind of juggling with schedules was nothing new to us and somehow luck was always with us.

The next foreign trip, which began on September 27th, was another for the forces, this time in the far off Falkland Islands and again the military experience was one never to be forgotten. It's a desolate place and the social aspect during a visit by entertainers is as important to the performers as it is for the squaddies.

As we descended into Mount Pleasant airport we were provided with an escort of Tornado F3 fighters. Very impressive and guaranteed to make one feel very important indeed. We played our first show at Stanley Town Hall for the indigenous population before strutting our stuff in front of uniformed audiences at Mount Alice, Mount Byron, Mount Kent and the main base at Mount Pleasant. Most of those in front of us weren't even around at the time we were riding high in the charts, but it made no difference. We sang to them and after our spot we partied with them.

The partying was wildest in the tiny mountain camps where our entire spectators bundled together in the tiny mess hall numbered less than forty and that was a full house. By the time we reached Mount Kent word had gone ahead that we were lots of fun and real party animals. There were banners held aloft as we started up. 'We love you Searchers' the home-made flags declared. They hadn't even seen us yet but they had the recommendations of Alice and Byron to go on. Unfortunately, we were completely partied out and after a couple of post-show drinks I had to admit defeat and head off for some much-needed sleep.

It was without a doubt an adventure of the highest order. Despite being afraid of heights I was talked into ramp riding on one of the Chinook helicopters. Flying at fairly low levels and for short distances they tend to leave the rear loading bay down. Sitting on a flat rectangle of metal with your feet dangling in the air as you zoom over the desolate terrain is a scary trip regardless of the fact that you are held on by a safety rope hooked around your waist. And it is even scarier when the loadmaster waves a retaining hook in front of your face as you perch precariously on what is, to all intents and purposes a flying garage door. The hook is of course from a spare harness but for a brief moment you wonder.

The year ended with the Searchers being voted Favourite Sixties Band and I celebrated my fiftieth birthday with a party. Where had all the years gone? When I was a kid only really ancient people were fifty and I certainly didn't feel ancient by any means. I think the brain stops somewhere around the twenty five mark.

I took over a restaurant in Chelsea and, along with my fellow Searchers, packed it with friends from in and out of the business. There were faces one might recognise and others perhaps more anonymous. My long-term ladyfriend Lee Lowsley was there as was Paper Doll Susie Mathis, just about my oldest and dearest friend in the music industry down the years, who came down from Manchester for the bash. Bruce Welch, who along with John McNally is one of the great rhythm guitarists in Britain. Helen

Worth (Gail Platt from Coronation Street) with her husband actor Michael Angelis. Showbiz journalist David Wigg. The doyen of theatre critics Jack Tinker. Dave Dee. Peter Sarstedt. Martin Lee and Sandra Stevens from Brotherhood of Man. Film producer Norma Heyman and Norman Newell, lyricist of such unforgettable hits as *More, Never Never Never, This Is My Life, Portrait Of My Love* and so many more.

My whole life seemed to have gathered around me to help me cope with the unwelcome but unavoidable ageing process. It was a good way to commemorate a milestone in my life.

38

Just When All Was Calm

The New Year kicked in with an unforgettable trip to Kenya. We flew out of Heathrow on February 13th, spouses and partners included, for an eleven-day trip. It was not a money-making exercise by any means. Ostensibly to play a couple of shows at the Windsor Golf and Country Club in Nairobi, the main purpose as far as we were concerned was to enjoy some rest and recuperation and to take advantage of the safari that came as part of the package. John McNally and I felt that at this stage in life we could afford to cherry-pick to a certain extent and to do things just for the sheer joy of it rather than have to make the books balance at the end.

The Masai Mara game reserve afforded us the opportunity to get close to lions, elephants, giraffes, zebras, hippos and other amazing and exotic wildlife and without the charge that usually accompanied such a privilege. Monkeys swung in the trees outside our lodgings. We stayed under canvas but these were tents in name only. Kingsize beds and hot showers. All the comforts of a hotel combined with all the cuteness of a childhood sleepover in a friend's back garden. Mine, I was led to believe, had previously been occupied by ex-President Jimmy Carter.

Our quiet success continued throughout the year. Another fan club convention provided a further £4000 for the George Eliot Appeal. Our summer show at the Beck Theatre on June 12th was once again sold out and we completed a BBC Radio 2 series entitled Jimmy Tarbuck Salutes The Searchers. Produced by Sonia Beldom and with our old Scouse comedian pal compering, and occasionally joining us in song, we recorded six shows for transmission which included guests such as Georgie Fame, Peter Sarstedt, his pop star brother Eden Kane and the Manfreds, which still included originals Paul Jones, Mike Hugg, Mike Vickers and Tom McGuinness.

There was a change in our crew brought on by personal family considerations which meant Gerry Hope had quit his position at our sound desk. Backline roadie Phil Hayes was at last given his chance to handle the front of house sound and to say goodbye to the many times he was left waving at the airport as we soared off to yet another foreign trip which required and only budgeted for the main man only. A young nineteen year old, John Semark, took over his duties. The young lad had no experience in this kind of work whatsoever apart from a bit of club deejaying around the Northampton area. He had simply seen an ad in the local job centre and thought it was worth investigating.

His try-out was at Barons nightclub in Swansea, a load-in that meant humping our truckload of heavy amplification equipment up four floors for a late night gig in front of a young crowd whose attention to what was happening on stage was minimal to say the least. We explained to him that this was about as bad as it would get. Astonishingly he loved it - the rather young and attractive disco 'totty' might have had something to do with it - and he accepted the job and at the time of writing is still hanging on in there. His next gig with us at Chelmsford was totally at the other end of the spectrum.

On August 29th the Chelmsford Spectacular again packed 25,000 plus into Hylands Park and again we were closing the show. This time round was slightly daunting knowing that two heavyweights, Ruby Turner and the great Edwin Starr, were preceding us. These were serious performers with a gravitas that we perhaps lacked. But no matter. It was a triumph for us and we left the stage feeling like kings. In all we were to play the Chelmsford show five times, more than anyone else I believe.

Still slightly miffed at the lack of respect we felt was coming from Flying Music, 1994's package tour, comprising ourselves, the Swinging Blue Jeans, the Merseybeats, Billy J Kramer and the Coustiks, went out under the banner of the Beat Goes On Tour and was promoted by a North London based promoter Chas Elliott. It ran from October 2nd until November 27th. Forty-one dates in all finishing at the renowned yet decidedly far-from-cosy Hammersmith Apollo. It did good business everywhere and proved our worth as a headline act.

We were also in the charts again in an oblique kind of way. A rap act called C. J. Lewis had combined the catchy chorus of our 1963 hit *Sweets For My Sweet* with an insistent narrative and the combination worked well enough to put it in the best sellers. I was not a rap fan and firmly in sympathy with the story of a club owner (probably apocryphal) whose advice to a comedian arriving at a club was 'Don't talk too fast or they'll start dancing to you round here.' But as rap went this was pretty soft on the ear and surprisingly not too unpleasant on mine.

Our finances were in good shape and our reserves were enough for John and me to exchange our Mercedes 190 models for the new and more luxurious C Class types. As I drove away after having posed for photos in front of H. L. Gorners in Wigan, John commented to the salesman that I'd soon dent mine. I had an unfortunate history of damaging cars. I drove home and put it carefully away in my garage. Unfortunately, I had not reckoned that the C Class was an inch or two higher than my previous Mercedes. As I reversed out the very next morning I watched in horror as my bike, which had been suspended from the ceiling by two metal hooks and which unknown to me had been lifted clear of them by the roof of my new vehicle, slid slowly and inexorably down the window and onto the bonnet scraping the beautiful paintwork on its way.

Before the end of the year we undertook a short visit to Toronto for a company convention and a ballroom date. When we checked in at the Air Canada desk we were taken under the wing of a most helpful and genial concierge with the exotic name of Kelvin Ogunjimi who promptly had us all upgraded from bog standard 'chicken and geese' to the oh-so-comfortable Club Class. I warned our new young roadie who was experiencing his first-ever flight that life would not always be like this.

At the check-in for our return flight we were horrified to find that our sponsored seats had been given away. The only way to get home in time for a show in Manchester was to fly backwards several hours to Edmonton, Alberta, and then to catch a forward connection to Heathrow. It was a horrendous prospect but the only solution to our dilemma and we eventually set off from London, Ontario, on the pointless flight to Edmonton. When I lamented our predicament to one of the airline staff in Edmonton the incredibly nice lady took all of our boarding cards, ripped them up and provided us with new ones for the Club compartment. Young Mister Semark was beginning to think that perhaps life might be like this after all.

After a couple of days off for Christmas which I spent with Eileen 'Red' Bond', ex-wife of Australian beer baron Alan Bond, at Upp Hall, their imposing mansion in Hertfordshire, I rejoined the band for a festive tour of Germany in the company of Chubby Checker, Sailor, Showaddywaddy, Smokie, Harpo and Suzi Quatro which took us to the end of the first week in January. It was great fun and with no driving responsibilities a chance to consume maybe more alcohol than was either usual or wise.

Chubby was a revelation. Delivering a dynamic on-stage set when he twisted like a Dervish despite his considerable size, his off-stage existence gave the impression that he was touring a different planet entirely. A wonderful character, in spite of the fact that communication with him was not the easiest of tasks. Suzi was now officially Mrs Rainer Haas, the two having wed on an impulse in Las Vegas a month before. What a brilliant career move. Marry the boss. Suzi still loves to remind me that in my typically cynical way I gave the union six months tops. At this point in time they are still happily married.

The years continued to flow one into another at a lunatic pace, each with its share of highs and, thankfully, few lows. Our current choice of group material was vindicated when *Somebody Told Me You Were Crying* was voted the favourite of all our recording by the members of the Searchers Appreciation Society.

On April 28th 1995 we joined up with Bobby Vee to boost the bill of his tour on the night it played the Royal Albert Hall, without doubt one of the finest buildings, both interior and exterior, anywhere in the world. We had boobed there (not entirely our fault) some years earlier because of problems with our sound, but this time round it was a joy.

That done we flew over to Belfast for a week of shows for the troops. We had done so many of these CSE shows now that we might as well have joined up, as on August 30th we headed out to war-torn Bosnia for exactly the same purpose. We arrived on the very day that the Allied Forces started bombing the crap out of the country and the first show was cancelled because it was deemed to be too near the action.

In truth I never found the Balkans as scary as Northern Ireland where we were billeted in a hotel in Ballymena. Anyone walking in or out could well have meant us harm. There was no way of knowing. It had been brought home to me when one of our civvy-clad guards poked his head in the minibus as we were about to head out for a show. I asked him what he was looking for. 'I can't find my magazine' he replied. I picked up an old newspaper. 'You can have this if you want it.' He looked at me as if I was retarded and shook his head knowingly. 'Not that kind of magazine' he said as he retrieved his ammunition from behind a rear seat. After shows the wagon would drive a different and ridiculously circuitous route back to our lodgings. But it would have been easy for a militant group to hang about for our exit and silently slip into pursuit.

Although we could hear the noise of battle beyond the horizon, Bosnia was a piece of cake. We were here and they were there. Our lads were British and in uniform and the enemy was not. Apart from that they looked – well – foreign. The most frightening thing while we were there was boarding a helicopter that had waited half a day to be mended. I don't trust helicopters at the best of times. I trust those with mechanical problems infinitely less.

We performed and partied in Zepce before travelling by road through the mountains to Vitez, Gornji Vakuf, Tomislavgrad and Ploce. The signs of constant shelling was everywhere and we were housed in anything available from a bombed-out house with no water or electricity to metal containers lined up side by side in army stations like someone's hellish version of a holiday camp.

We went out for a coffee and a snack in Tomislavgrad and someone pointed out to our drummer Billy Adamson that the town had once been called something else. 'Yes, Shithouse,' was the dour Scot's reply.

The crowning moment without doubt was the final concert in Ploce where around three thousand young squaddies, still wet behind the ears but each one able to beat the shit out of me, sat in dread of what rubbish they were expected to enjoy from these old farts. By the third song we were as one. They reacted in a way we had never before experienced throwing themselves into the spirit of the evening that shocked everyone.

When it came to the guitar solo in *Johnny B Goode* two khaki-clad soldiers leapt on stage and did the Chuck Berry duck walk across the front of the stage with machines guns taking the place of the more usual guitars. At the end of our set they rose as one and gave us the most deafening ovation we had ever enjoyed. Then they stood on their benches and did the Wayne's World bow chanting 'We are not worthy'. It was a truly emotional and unforgettable moment in my career.

There was also a second trip to the Falkland Islands in 1995 and this time there was the added bonus of a stop off in the Ascension Islands to break up the long flight home. If the Falklands were bleak the Ascensions were a hot and sweaty contrast. A paradise in military terms where there seemed to be a lot more socialising than work going on.

Billy Adamson had throughout his time with us gone through a number of self-improvement programmes. I watched him plough his way through The Trial by Franz Kafka. Who knows? He may have been riveted by it. It's a modern classic so I suppose its merits must be great. At one time he took up running and as soon as we got to venues he would change into shorts and set off dashing through the streets like a man possessed. It lasted about a year. Teetotalism did not fare so well.

While in Germany he suddenly announced to the club owner, a stout lady who was insistent we should stay behind and drink with her, that he didn't drink. This was news to us. He had been pissed two nights before. She continued to press and he became slightly irate. She should have been patient for two days later he was knocking it back again like any self-respecting Glaswegian.

By the time of the Falklands tour, encouraged by his current girlfriend, he had become a vegetarian. When the RAF steward came round with the in-flight snack he handed over a carton which contained some orange juice, a bag of crisps, a cheese sandwich, an apple and a sausage roll. With a certain amount of disdain that only ingénue veggies can adopt Billy called out to the guy 'Have you got any vegetarian meals?'

Without missing a beat the razor-sharp steward replied 'Certainly mate,' and reached out to take back the sausage roll. We of course were in hysterics. Billy on the other hand didn't seem to think it was that funny. Unfortunately vegetarianism, laudable a cause as it may be, rarely seems to come in tandem with a self-deprecating sense of humour. As much as I admire the sentiments I would, unless I was forced to kill my own food, find it extremely difficult to become a vegetarian and there is very little I eat that hasn't once looked over a garden gate. Barbaric as it may be to some I do on the whole prefer my food to have had parents.

There was little opportunity in our schedule for time to ourselves but during a short break I managed to get over to Nashville and from there drove to Memphis to see Graceland, something I had wanted to do for years. True, it isn't as big as one might expect but it is still a sizeable pad and if it is a bit gaudy, well we're talking about a down home unsophisticated country boy with all the money he could wish for and dealing with the kind of taste that prevailed in the seventies. I loved it. I'm not one for things spiritual but it was a special feeling to be in the home of the man without who my life might have been very different indeed.

Workwise I was spreading my wings outside the group just a tiny bit. Nothing that would interfere with the main job of being a Searcher. On Only The Lonely, a programme I recorded for Radio 2, I narrated the story of Roy Orbison which was broadcast on September 23rd, and I was pleased with the result. Sonia Beldom, the producer of our previous radio series, had drafted me in for the job.

As 1995 came to an end we spent New Year's Eve in Hannover on a concert which included Suzi Quatro, Dave Dee, Middle Of The Road, the Rubettes, Hot Chocolate and Daniel Boone. Germany, which had been the staple source of work for so many bands of our era, was showing signs of winding down a bit but we were fortunate in having established our solo concerts and most of the time when Rainer Haas would ask about our availability we were already committed. We were in a very fortunate position indeed.

The beginning of '96 did not start too well for me. One day I crossed the road carelessly and had been knocked down by a car resulting in a dislocated shoulder. On hearing the news John McNally's concern was not so much for my welfare as to who was going to play bass at Camberley the next day. Lack of sympathy was a rather endearing trait in the Searchers which I both understand and applaud. Another trait is making the show no matter what and having been discharged in the morning I was dutifully on stage, plucking away with my right arm in a sling, as the traditions of showbusiness demand, although my ladyfriend Lee Lowsley did insist that John should collect me and drive me there.

The year's highlights included a ten-day mini-tour with Billy J Kramer and the Swinging Blue Jeans, a charity show at the Sheffield City Hall supporting Mark Knopfler and the Notting Hillbillies, a cruise around the Mediterranean and once more the gigantic Chelmsford Spectacular.

The cruise, which was to be the first of many such voyages for P&O, was on the Canberra, setting sail from Southampton on July 21st and stopping off in the warmer climes of Naples, Toulon and Palma amongst others. Performing four shows while on board was hardly slave labour and the chance to cut loose from reality for a couple of weeks was the icing on the cake. We scrubbed up pretty well for the black tie dinners and piled on the pounds as a result of the round-the-clock catering available.

Due to previous commitments we had to leave the ship at La Coruna and fly back to the UK, leaving our friends and families to enjoy the remainder of the voyage. Leaving them behind was sad. Leaving Canberra behind was even sadder. Like an old film star she was past her prime but still retained her elegance and grace. We felt thrilled and privileged to be in her company. The following year she was scrapped.

Three days later we found ourselves in yet another magnificent and romantic setting as we sang our hits to a vast crowd gathered in the grounds of Batemans, Rudyard Kipling's former house in Sussex and now a National Trust property preserved in all its splendour for the benefit of the nation. The Marmalade shared the bill with us that day which was to be the first of three visits during the late nineties. One year on minus one day we returned to Batemans, this time supported by the Merseybeats. Our final visit was on August 8th 1999 when we were joined by an Abba tribute band. They amused us greatly when we heard them complaining to the crowd during their set that some former members had set up a rival outfit but that the people should not be fooled. The musicians on stage were the genuine article they proclaimed. It seemed ironic if not ludicrous that they should be proudly boasting that they were the real imitations.

Before 1996 was out we also managed to fit in another fan club convention and another CSE tour of Belfast. I loved it all despite the constant demands on our time. No sooner had we got the festive season over with than we were boarding the aircraft carrier HMS Illustrious sailing from Gibraltar to Marseilles during which we would play a couple of shows. Although we had reached the ship, vital pieces of our equipment - a bag of guitar/synthesiser leads - had been offloaded by BA and had not arrived when the Illustrious departed.

The ship's commander decided that the solution was to send our sound man Phil Hayes back in a helicopter to fetch it. This was thrilling stuff and John McNally and I wanted to go with him. We were denied on account of the medicals one had to go through first. Phil told us later of the James Bond style retrieval of the missing bag with relish. The pilot put the chopper down, Phil ran to the terminal, was handed the item and raced back to his very flash form of transport which soared off down the Med again without further ado. He also told us about the all-important pre-flight medical. Apparently he had been taken to the ship's doctor who asked him if he felt okay. 'Yes' was the answer. 'Okay then, off you go.' Inspection over.

On the whole our lives were happy ones and we found ourselves cruising through the years on a wave of contentment confident that, barring any unforeseen mishaps, this happy state of affairs could and would continue until that time when we would no longer wished it to. But for another of our contemporaries things had turned out very differently indeed.

Back on Merseyside the dark clouds of despair had descended on a desperate and depressed Johnny Sandon, the man who had transformed himself from plain old Billy Beck into a respected entertainer in his home town of Liverpool and whose rich, creamy tones had entranced so many. To have almost made it for Sandon, a man constantly plagued with the private demons of despondency, was worse than never having seen the carrot of opportunity dangling in front of him at all.

The wrong decision at the wrong time had seen him voluntarily part from a bunch of friends who were almost instantaneously whisked off to international stardom while he was left floundering in a band that remained excellent and admired but unfeted and hitless. When his days with the Remo Four ended Sandon reverted to his birth name and tried his hand at being a stand-up comedian playing the clubs around the 'Pool, getting laughs when he could and digging himself deeper into the depths of despair when he could not.

As Britain's revellers enjoyed the bright lights of the holiday season the lights were extinguished in his lonely and desperate world. On Christmas Day his daughter had made a surprise visit to his home in St Paul's Close, Rock Ferry, only to discover her father hanging from a shower cubicle, a dog lead tied around his neck. Johnny Sandon had failed in his ambition as an entertainer and he had failed two previous suicide attempts by overdose. At last he had succeeded in ending his own life, surely the greatest failure of all.

Searchers schedules are often the stuff of legend. We were offered a show in Singapore. The exotic location made it very attractive but the show was on March 20th 1997 and we were due for an already sold-out show at Nantwich Civic Hall on the 22nd. 'We can't do it' I said to John McNally. He was having none of it and suggested checking the flights. We discovered it could just be achieved if none of the return flights delayed us by more than two hours.

'Planes are always delayed,' I said. 'It's too dangerous.'

'Who dares wins' was McNally's answer.

We set off on March 17th for Singapore via Bahrain. Following the show at the Westin Hotel we grabbed two hours of shut-eye before our very early departure for the airport. We caught the 7.30 am flight and changed aircraft at Bahrain, and on landing at Heathrow we dashed to the domestic terminal for the flight to Manchester where we had cabs waiting. We touched down at 7.40 pm. We made the Nantwich show on time and the promoter was delighted. We hadn't actually told him about the Singapore concert. He would only have worried.

My extra-curricular activities continued in the form of an in-flight entertainment programme I had recorded for Britannia Airways, the huge package holiday company. I was delighted. No matter how much I enjoyed being a Searcher there is always something special about something you have achieved on your own merit. To further boost my ego I was once more awarded the "Beat Goes On" Best Front Man award during our summer show at the Beck Theatre, Hayes, on June 15th.

As for the band we were enjoying a bit of unexpected exposure in the release of the 1979/80 Sire sessions on a double CD by an Australian company, Raven. We completed a two week cabaret season at London's prestigious Green Room, light on audience but very enjoyable and so near home for me which was a bonus. And our death-defying tricky manoeuvres continued. In order to play the Chelmsford Spectacular once more on August 25th we had to race down the A10 from Snetterton where we had two afternoon shows. No problem. We were veterans at that sort of thing.

In November I received a curious call from a firm of solicitors with the splendid name of Frere, Cholmeley, Bischoff who had learned that I had been present at the time of the infamous December 1962 Hamburg recordings of the Beatles at the Star Club and committed to tape by Ted 'Kingsize' Taylor. There was to be a case in which the Beatles were plaintiffs and they required my testimony.

On December 1st I presented myself to a Mister Neville Cordell at their offices in John Carpenter Street, EC4, very near to Blackfriars Station. I told my story which was basically that yes, I had been present and yes, I heard them being played over the club PA system the next day and that I knew very little else. He seemed happy with that and I was asked if I would appear as a witness for them. Of course I agreed. These were the Beatles after all. But I couldn't see what help I was going to be. In any case the hearing was not until May of the following year.

Meanwhile everything was going swimmingly and although there were always occasional times of tension within our ranks it had been reasonably drama free since the 1985 departure of Pender. We had even taken tentative steps into the fascinating new world of internet technology by acquiring a web site. It was facilitated by Gary Jackson, a sixties aficionado who convinced us that it would be of great benefit to us as a form of communication and advertising and would require little to no input by us other than supplying titbits of information and an up-to-date list of engagements.

Initially we were simply an inclusion on his My Generation site but pretty soon, being the band from our strata that undertook the greatest number of dates and appeared to have a higher and livelier profile than most, we were afforded a separate entity which soon documented virtually everything about our present, our past and our future.

Invaluable in the running of the site was Wendy Burton, a long-time fan residing in Tonbridge, Kent, and who, with her secretarial and organising expertise gained from her years of working for the National Trust, was able to collate the information provided by me and prepare it for insertion on line by Gary. Together we made a good team and far from having no input I soon found myself working with both of them to provide our devotees with as much material of interest as I could gather. This most definitely was the way of the future. Even a Luddite like me could see that.

Most Saturdays were spent in Germany along with a host of our contemporaries. I always enjoyed those foreign trips. No driving. Nice hotels. The chance to really shut off and enjoy a few drinks after the show. In early February 1998 we undertook a week's tour of the Middle East, playing in the main for the expat community. We found the road signs out there highly amusing. One read: DRIVE SLOWLY OR IT IS A REGRET. Judging by the number of accidents on the roads there many people seemed to have suffered a regret. Another instruction ordered the citizens: DO NOT PUT LITTER IN ANY PLACE EXCEPT FOR A PAPER PLACE ONLY. We obeyed and never put our litter in anything that was not a paper place.

Our dispute with Flying Music had been resolved and the '98 tour went out under their auspices and featured the Searchers, Helen Shapiro and the Swinging Blue Jeans. It ran from February 22nd to May 2nd, packing the crowds in all the way. Helen, who had more or less renounced her pop roots in favour of her beloved jazz and gospel had been tempted onto the circuit and delighted her fans with most of her hit records. She was a highly accomplished performer and a serious draw audience-wise. I felt it was a shame that her career could not straddle both worlds a bit more. Her records were things to be proud of. But every person has a duty to do what makes them happy in a personal sense. The final show was at the Hammersmith Apollo once more.

The previous day I paid my second visit to Frere, Cholmeley, Bischoff and signed my affidavit in readiness for the forthcoming court appearance. A few days later and I made my way to the seat of British justice where the paparazzi had gathered in a state of excitement at the promised appearance of a real live Beatle.

My old boss Cliff Bennett had also been deputed to appear and as we stood outside in the street after the break for lunch George Harrison approached. Cliff and I greeted him and in his slow Scouse drawl he uttered 'Nice to see you Cliff. You're looking well.' There was a pause and he turned to me. 'I don't know about him though.' What was it about me and Beatles that made them feel the need to utter caustic remarks I wondered? Actually, figuring that I had always kept myself in good shape and was extremely well dressed for the time of day in my black pants and hounds tooth high button jacket I was a trifle miffed but said nothing. 'Thanks for doing this for us,' might have been nice.

I delivered my inconsequential knowledge on the witness stand after first having confused the barrister by preferring to 'affirm' rather than swear on the Holy Bible. Affirmation it seems was far from being the norm but having no belief in a deity I saw no reason to be a hypocrite. Certainly not in an environment where every word coming out of my mouth was required to be the truth. I stepped down and took my seat for George's performance. He seemed to have mellowed in the last half hour as he kept turning to me and giving conspiratorial smirks at what he thought were ludicrous question posed to him. The cross questioning barrister was not given an easy time.

George was the Beatle who had drawn the short straw in having to attend the dreary and time-consuming proceedings and he was not happy about it. When it was suggested that they had delivered up their rights the Hamburg recordings for a crate of beer he adopted a contemptuous look and a sarcastic edge to his voice and replied that it was hardly likely. George was a Beatle and about the closest thing you could get to a living god in the eyes of many. Having dealt with the intrusion of an inquisitive media for the best part of his life he was not about to be cowed by a mere lawyer in a black gown and a ludicrous wig. His verbal opponent was visibly uncomfortable.

When it was all over and we trooped out the courtroom there were raised voices at the lift. George was castigating a member of the public who had the temerity to approach him and ask for an autograph. 'You want locking up. You're mad, you.' The diatribe continued until the lifts doors closed and George Harrison finally descended from view. The poor guy turned to me and with a hurt look on his face said in a thick Irish brogue 'Mr Allen, I don't know why he was like that. I don't mean any harm. I'm a fan. I just wanted to say hello'. I felt so sorry for him and in truth could not understand George's reasoning. But then I have never had to suffer being a Beatle. In the light of his tragic and early death it might have been that he knew a lot more than we did at that point in time and was feeling sorry for himself and angry with the world. On May 8th the case was settled in the Beatles' favour.

Twelve days later I had a meeting with a young Welsh publisher called Meuryn Hughes. Having been sent an article of mine by our agent he wanted me to write a book to be published by his small Cardiff-based firm Aureus. It was frightening. I thought I could write quite well. I also felt articles were within my capabilities. A book was a very different matter but I felt I had to accept the challenge and set a deadline of six months. The end result was the publication of Travelling Man.

Apart from a three-day trip to Connecticut where we play two shows at the Mohegan Sun Casino, an engagement arranged by Julie Grant, my old pop singer girlfriend now based in the States, the rest of the year went by without incident until one day in November when once more our calm waters turned somewhat choppy.

It was November 15th. We arrived home after having flown out to Germany the previous day for yet another nostalgia fest. The cabs dropped us at my house where the cars were parked. Suddenly Billy Adamson announced that he wanted to talk to us. There in my kitchen, with barely a space to reply or interrupt his diatribe he told us exactly what he thought of us. We stood there amazed.

True there had for a long time been an atmosphere between him and us, by which I mean myself and John McNally as the owners of the name and the business called The Searchers. It probably began in earnest during the period with Sire Records when the company ordered us to use another drummer. I am sure he always believed that was an excuse. But we never realised just how deep the resentment went.

It was clearly a worker-management thing. After so long with us he felt his position within the set-up should be different. But that was never going to happen as he well knew. At this late stage in our lives and careers, and having survived some upsets which almost destroyed our ability to earn our living, we were not about to decimate our assets or dissipate our power for anyone. After the Pender situation in particular we were never going to give up control of a business that we had struggled to keep afloat through the very lean years. We were not getting any younger.

People do tend to have a rose-tinted view of groups and feel that as they are operating under a single name it is some sort of Utopian democracy, but that is rarely the case. And the more people who have power to influence decisions the harder it is to get things done. Quite often a benevolent dictatorship is more efficient and more beneficial to all. We felt we were fair but I imagine Billy's perception was otherwise. Suffice it to say that after a long rant, which slightly resembled a cartoon of Dennis the Menace in a frantic tizz with steam coming out of his ears, he went out to the car bringing his suit back with him. He threw it on my hall floor and left. It was pretty dramatic.

I don't recall his actual final words but I do remember the last sentence he addressed to me. While pointing a very angry finger he roared 'And I have to play with this shit.' It's a shame when things end like that. I liked Billy.

39

Where's Wally?

We stood silent and bemused in the kitchen of my West London house for a few moments as we digested the scene that had just been acted out in front of us. The Scottish one, no doubt mightily relieved at getting all that pent-up anger off his chest, was speeding towards the M1 to his home in Bedfordshire and a brand new life. Well at least there would be no dilly-dallying about making a decision this time round. There was simply no time. We needed a replacement drummer, either temporary or permanent, and we needed him yesterday. We were due to appear at the London Hilton in five days' time.

Spencer James suggested that Wally had recently given up and had settled down to a steady day job. Wally was Walter Rothe, borne in Buckingham on February 16th 1954, who had until his recent retirement from the world of pop music been the drummer for Les Gray's Mud. The original group known as Mud who had notched up a reasonable list of hits including *Tiger Feet* and *Lonely This Christmas* had long since fractured and their lead singer, as was pretty much standard procedure in the dog-eat-dog world of beat groups, had formed his own version of the outfit which now consisted of itinerant musicians from wherever they could be recruited.

For the last ten years Wally had kept the beat behind the beautifully eccentric, highly amusing and now largely alcoholic Mister Gray but had finally thrown in the towel after deciding that such a career under Les's increasingly erratic leadership was not as rewarding as he would have liked. As he so succinctly put it, 'There were times when my house was making more money than I was.'

Before the Mud saga he had also enjoyed success in his own right when Liquid Gold topped the charts in 1980 with the disco smash *Dance Yourself Dizzy.* Their many television appearances were memorable as much for the outrageous costumes as for the music, the greatest transgressor being Wally, their drummer, whose inhibitions, if indeed he ever possessed such restrictions, had apparently deserted him. Their mimed appearances on Top Of The Pops would have him leaving the drum stool to reveal a pair of shapely legs, a pair of green glitter hotpants and a naked chest on which was painted a set of xylophone keys. He would then pretend to play the solo with his drumsticks on his rib cage with a huge grin on his face and seemingly not an ounce of shame. I have always thanked God we did not have our success in the tack and glitter world of the eighties.

The group, whose lead singer Ellie Hope was coincidentally the sister of our recently departed sound man Gerry Hope, managed a couple of other minor entries including a low pop at the US charts with *My Baby's Baby* before finally calling it a day, their financial well-being only marginally better than when they had started out. Very little changed in the dodgy dealing world of pop and musicians have always been extremely deficient in the area of finance.

Following the Mud years Wally had since retreated to his home in Buckingham, the one asset he had managed to salvage from years of touring the world. When he had purchased the property he managed to complete the move in just one trip with everything he owned crammed into a Morris Traveller proving that a number one hit record is no guarantee of personal wealth. When his musical career gave up on him he took a job at the local Wico factory assembling windscreen wipers.

We knew of him but not too much about him. Spencer said he was a nice guy, easy to get on with and about the same height as us. We had always considered height an important factor as far as our visual image was concerned. We set him off on the mission to contact Wally on his way home to Northampton. At least it might get us out of the immediate predicament even if we decided he was not the man for the job.

Asked if he fancied going to Australia in January (we had at last managed to broker a deal that would open up that wonderful continent to us again after too long away) and, there being no objections from his wife Nicola, he agreed straight away. Rehearsal arrangements were made at a room a few yards from Wally's home for the Tuesday and we gathered to run through sufficient material to present at least the minimum time required in our contracts.

First sighting of the new recruit was a bit of a shock. His hair was down to his shoulders and very much at odds with our neatly trimmed short back and sides. And far from being 'about the same height as us' he towered over our heads. He was Snow White to our Three Dwarfs. There was certainly no chance of him fitting into Billy's old stage suit as Spencer had with Mike's. But seated behind the skins the difference would not be too noticeable, we hoped.

We had one okay, if shaky, rehearsal followed by a better one two days later, before we threw ourselves to the lions. There was one point of contention I had to raise and that was his name. As far as I was concerned we were not about to have a Wally in the band. It was simply not Searchers. Plumbers and brickies were called Wally. He informed us that his middle name was Edgar and I suggested that Eddie would be fine and thankfully he had no objections. In fact I think we did him a bit of a favour there. The final piece of the jigsaw had slotted comfortably into place.

Eddie Rothe's debut was at the Hilton in London's Park Lane. We got through from start to finish without any serious mishap though the tunes were delivered at the speed of a Ferrari but not necessarily with the same quality or precision. Not only were they hard to dance to or to listen to, we were going so fast we had to stretch out a few things towards the end in order to fill our slot. But things somehow fell together and after enjoying his light and ever-cheery personality over the next few days we knew things would settle and it was going to work out just fine.

To be with someone who smiles for twenty four hours a day, after having endured decades of tension with one who clearly was not enjoying either the job or our company, was a blessed relief. He recounted hilarious stories of his Mud days when every journey took an eternity because of Les Gray's need to stop at virtually every pub en route. The quality of their performance always depended on the length of the drive and the number of hostelries along the way.

Life with Les Gray was always interesting. His stage attire was leopard skin brothel creeper shoes and a lurid yellow drape suit with leopard skin collars and cuffs. On one trip abroad he picked up the wrong suitcase from an airport carousel and was surprised to find it contained a very sober and smart business suit. But not as surprised as the businessman who had to attend an important conference in a canary yellow teddy boy outfit.

Fans apparently would regularly approach the band and insist that the ragged apology for a pop star in their midst was not Les Gray, to which they would retort 'Do you really think if we were auditioning for a Les Gray replacement we would have chosen him?'

Our routine on stage had baffled and bothered Ed for some time and in truth he never got completely used to it. Though we sometimes made out a set list we all knew the general plan which was ingrained into our subconscious and we were well aware that, depending on the particular situation and the reaction of that night's audience, we might have to switch in an instant. What changes we would make were largely instinctive. A glance from John was all we needed to prepare our heads for what was coming. Ed's time with Mud had consisted of the same set list in the same order for ten years and it never once varied. 'Searcherland' was foreign territory indeed.

We headed off for our Australia/New Zealand trip in January enjoying the mild euphoria that always comes with encountering and having dealt with a crisis. Mike's obstinacy had stopped us going there before and although his departure had opened up the avenues again it had taken some twelve years before we could get our feet back in the door.

And this time it was not just the pubs and clubs that hosted us. Our market had upped itself to the sports-oriented leagues clubs and RSLs (Returned Services Leagues) which, due to the vast revenue brought in by the pokies, or slot machines, resembled mini Las Vegas casinos and many of them not that mini either. Rooty Hill RSL in a suburb just outside Sydney and Twin Towns RSL at Coolangatta were impressive and superbly equipped clubs with the kind of quality infrastructure you might expect in more prestigious locations and facilities that had rarely been seen back home in the UK since the days of Batley Variety Club and the Sheffield Fiesta. And most of the others were not far behind.

Our last visit had been more than fifteen years ago and in truth the gap had done us more good than harm. The structure and pacing of our shows and our ability to command a stage had improved beyond measure and we felt confident that we could now hold our own in rooms that were used to presenting acts of international stature and renown. Our position was very quickly established and the Antipodean trip became an annual event. One that we would look forward to eagerly. The added bonus was that it allowed us to escape a large part of the cold and dispiriting British winter.

We were particularly glad of Ed's constantly cheerful nature during the first few days of our stay. Placed in the hands of a tour manager who, with his large moustache and buckskin clothing, resembled Wild Bill Hickok, drove barefooted and smoked like a chimney, we set off from our Sydney base for a show in a tiny town called Barooga. We had never heard of it. Unfortunately neither had our driver or indeed any other Australian we came into contact with. The estimated travel time in our itinerary was six and a half hours.

We had already been driving for most of that time when 'Wild Bill', who had already alienated John McNally a mere fifteen minutes into the drive by stopping for a cigarette break having been banned from lighting up inside the vehicle, discovered he had missed the main turn off. The fact that he had started out on the road to a place he was completely unfamiliar with, unaided by anything so basic as a map, was a major contributing factor. After a marathon journey during which it felt as though the globe had seen two world wars and the rise and fall of several small nations we finally limped into Barooga. It had been fourteen hours since we started out yet it felt slightly longer than my entire life so far. But far from being angry and disgruntled we had lapsed into a sort of surreal state of amused insanity spurred on by the ever optimistic and amusing ramblings of the indomitable Eddie Rothe. It had been an adventure to say the very least. Needless to say we were never to use that particular driver again.

The tour of Australia was a success and we continued on to New Zealand. From our last show there, bizarrely on a rugby pitch in the party centre of Queenstown with our audience gathered in the distance like a colony of ants a hundred yards away at the edge of the pitch, we flew on to the Gulf States for concerts in Abu Dhabi, Bahrain, Al Ain and Dubai before heading home. Our new enthusiasm showed on our faces and in our performance. It was a much-needed opportunity to hone our act and get used to each other's company, and we re-entered the UK six weeks later refreshed and ready for the challenges ahead.

On the morning of Tuesday March 2nd I received a call from Tom Springfield to arrange to meet for a meal. Dusty Springfield's brother and I had kept in touch through the years and would catch up with each other a couple of times a year. I couldn't make it that evening but we agreed to get together on the Thursday evening. He warned me however that it might be necessary to cancel if Dusty's situation got worse. She had been suffering from cancer for a number of years and after a period of remission the awful disease had returned with a vengeance. There were reports in the media and much gossip flying about as to how bad things were. One day you would hear she was at death's door and the next the word was that she was fine and still fighting. I never knew which to believe but it was apparent from Tom's concern that the signs were not good.

I hadn't seen Dusty in a while. She had moved back from the States via a short sojourn in Amsterdam and was currently renting a large house by the Thames in Henley where she was being cared for in the main by Simon Bell, a Scottish vocalist who had been a fan first, then a backing singer and finally a trusted and devoted friend.

I never visited her at Henley. It was obvious she was not keen on having visitors. Ever the diva she would not want anyone to see her looking anything other than her best. Some time before this though I had occasion to write to her as I was in the final stages of writing a book, parts of which included mentions of Dusty. There was nothing libellous and nothing untrue so I did not need anyone's permission but I would never have published anything about her that she would not want.

I enclosed transcripts of the appropriate paragraphs and, knowing that she would not be up to writing letters, provided two tick boxes. One requested me to 'delete the offending paragraphs' while the other stated 'publish and be damned'. She ticked the latter although in a shaky scrawl which wound around the edge of the paper she admitted that the incident in my little red mini outside Yours And Mine had completely gone from her memory banks. 'I must have been intrigued, or smashed' she wrote. I kept that scribbled note as a precious keepsake and in order to fill in the blanks in her memory wrote back to her with a very detailed description of the momentous occasion she was referring to.

A few hours after Tom Springfield and I made our arrangements and ended the call he rang again explaining that things had got worse and that perhaps we had better postpone for a while. Dusty died that evening. She was fifty nine.

Her funeral was an affair that would have pleased her. She knew she was dying and she had planned the details herself, expressing the wish that she wanted to stop the traffic in Henley. And indeed she did. The streets were lined with sobbing fans as the glass-walled carriage drawn by four black horses transported her body to the church. A huge display of flowers spelling DUSTY sat atop the coffin as it made its sombre way to the Church of St Mary The Virgin. The singer Lulu and Pet Shop Boy Neil Tennant read eulogies which were both sad and funny at the same time. Her old lighting and tour manager Fred Perry had travelled over from Los Angeles to be there.

At the wake held at Danesfield House in nearby Marlow I was approached by Simon Bell whom I had never actually met. He both surprised and pleased me by saying that he had made a point of seeking me out just to let me know that my letters containing my description of the infamous 'willy fiddling' incident had made Dusty laugh so much that they had done her a power of good at a time when she most needed it. I was very touched by Simon's words and pleased that I had made at least a tiny mark in the life of someone so loved by so many far more important than me.

As for myself I had met my own personal challenge in the form of my first book, Travelling Man - On the Road with The Searchers, which was published that spring. It had originated as a short article which had been taken somewhat more seriously by others than I would have dared to. When I saw the finished work I viewed it with both awe and pride. It was a beautiful object and it gave me a greater thrill than any hit record had done. This was entirely my own effort. From the outset I was not entirely sure I was equipped for the task and therefore with some exceptions restricted the subject matter to just the touring side of my life as a musician, lacing the narrative with as much of my quirky humour as I could muster. It read well, I felt, and it sold well. At the time of my writing this, Travelling Man remains in print and looks like it will remain so for some years to come.

We had long since accepted that the Searchers were a nostalgia act and had started to be proud of our history and our place in the pop firmament. In fact there were greater acts than us still plying their trade more than four decades on from the first stirrings of success who could legitimately fit the description.

The Rolling Stones, with whom we had toured Australia back in 1966, were bigger than they had ever been in their entire career and these days were packing out vast stadiums rather than the city halls and ABC cinemas that had once housed their screaming teenage audiences. The Stones, unlike ourselves, were still very much in the business of releasing new albums with regularity and their star had never dimmed as our own had. They were arguably the biggest touring band in the world. Their immense popularity increased year upon year. There is no other group with their pulling power, and more than forty years on they hold the record for the highest grossing tour. But even they would have to admit that it is their old catalogue of giant and unforgettable hits, embellished by the stunning visual spectacle they provide, that forms the greater part of their attraction. And there is no shame in such a tag.

I went to see them at Wembley in June that year. It was worlds apart from the outfit we had shared the stage with all those years ago. Ever-advancing technology and their vastly improved musicianship, not to mention the unstoppable energy and incomparable stage command of Mick Jagger, made it a magnificent spectacle. Brian Jones had long gone as had Bill Wyman but alongside Jagger and Keith Richards the immaculate and stoic Charlie Watts was still there pounding away on the drums, looking like an elderly retainer in a Hammer film, and keeping everything rock solid at the back. The Stones without Charlie was almost unthinkable.

Ronnie Woods, once the new boy, was now a long-standing fixture and rightly considered an original, at least of this particular Rolling Stones era. There could be no better man for the part than Ronnie. He fitted both the sound and the image of the band like a beautifully tailored leather glove. Who else could compete with Keith Richards in the role of rock & roll rebel? It is reported that Keith once said of Ronnie that if he didn't get his act together he would be dead soon. You can be sure that when Keith Richards worries about your health you are a true member of the rock & roll fraternity.

I ran into Ronnie Woods at the London Palladium a couple of years later. He was in the row behind me for a Flying Music package that featured legendary rockers Bobby Vee, Johnny Tillotson, Freddie Cannon, Little Eva and Brian Hyland. When I turned round to face the extremely noisy and excitable guitarist he pointed straight at me and yelled, 'Fuckin' hell, I used to go and watch him every week at Burtons in Uxbridge.' And indeed he had, in those far-off days when I was a Rebel Rouser and Cliff Bennett's outfit was the 'must see' band in West London. The Art Wood Combo was a local attraction based in West Drayton and Ronnie was Art's little brother.

Later on when he finally managed a nibble at fame with his band the Birds and I was established as a Searcher we both appeared on Thank Your Lucky Stars, a notorious appearance for them in which their drummer, for whatever reason, was lowered onto his kit from the ceiling only to miss the target and end up sprawled over the studio floor. When the show was over they kindly gave me a lift back to London in their battered old van, a vehicle which along with exhaust fumes also suffered from human fumes as they constantly farted their way back to town. I was thrilled that Ronnie, who was now without doubt a legitimate member of rock & roll royalty, remembered me.

Elsewhere in London that year I was reminded once more of bygone times when I caught shows by Marianne Faithfull and Bill Wyman. Marianne's voice, once imbued with a sweetness and innocence, was now harsh and smokey and sounded as though it been trampled on by a troupe of clog dancers from Clitheroe. But there was a truth and reality within that made her performance poignant. She had lived a fascinating life and every husky note she now sang served to remind us.

Bill Wyman had opted out of the Stones in order to discover who he really was and had found a satisfying existence as a restaurateur, a writer and a part-time musician. These days he played for fun and was clearly enjoying being a part of his Rhythm Kings, the excellent big band outfit with a changing line-up of seasoned side men like Albert Lee, Georgie Fame and Martin Taylor, which he had set up so that he could play for enjoyment at last, rather than money. Their brand of pounding forties and fifties rhythm and blues was the kind of material he loved. It was what he chose to play rather than what he was instructed to. Bill was happy at last. One assumes that after a life of drama and near tragedy Marianne too was now comfortable in her own skin. And the Stones were still the kings of everything. Everyone it seemed was to the greater extent happy.

If the hard-living Ronnie and Keith were very much alive and kicking others had not been so fortunate. On June 28th I attended the funeral of Dave 'Screaming Lord' Sutch. My memory strayed back to the old days at the Clay Pigeon in Eastcote where I first heard that this fascinating and 'off the wall' character was about to launch his novelty rock-horror show. In all the years I knew him I never once guessed of the private demons that dwelled within. Like his old recording manager, Joe Meek, he had put an end to his own life. Joe with a gun and Dave with a rope. As we headed towards the final days of the second millennium the facts were being hammered home to me that we were all mortal and that the old maxim was indeed true. The only sure things in life are death and taxes.

That summer I was over at the offices of the Cliff Richard Organisation in Claygate, Surrey, for lunch with his personal assistant Roger Bruce and secretary Gill Snow, a truly lovely woman who, with others, works tirelessly to maintain a semblance of order in the complicated life of Britain's first pop knight. Following the retirement of his manager Peter Gormley, Cliff had taken charge of his own career and headed a substantial set-up, an impressive office building and a large volume of staff. As I went to leave, I was approached by David Bryce, the elegant and diminutive shaven-headed executive who had ostensibly taken over Gormley's role, one for which he was well equipped having organised Cliff's day-to-day activities for many years. David's brother, Dickie Valentine, had been a major heartthrob in the mid fifties.

David wanted to know if we were still free on New Year's Eve. This of course was not just any New Year's Eve. It was the last night of the millennium and celebrations were already being planned all over the globe. For most performers it promised to be the greatest pay-day of their performing lives and we were hearing stories of the unbelievable salaries being commanded by the most ordinary of acts. As yet we had not received any such offer but were confidently expecting something to turn up.

I delicately explained to David that I was very aware that Cliff was donating his fee for what was the final night of a run of dates at the National Indoor Arena in Birmingham to charity but that we were in a different financial league entirely and simply could not afford to be so generous. As well as we were doing, it was always a fine line between making money and losing it and such a night would never happen again. I did however promise that if they wanted us we would keep our fee to a minimum. They did want us and we agreed a figure that was approximately half the amount we could reasonably expect for the last day of the millennium.

It turned out to be a wiser move than we could have imagined. As the time approached many people preferred to forgo the ludicrously expensive commercial entertainment on offer for their own simpler and more cost-effective private celebrations. It had all got out of hand. Many of the planned functions were called off when tickets remained unsold and many an artiste, both household names and otherwise, found themselves the recipients of unexpected cancellation notices. The fantastic fees turned out to be nothing more than fool's gold.

Cliff had been good to us on several occasions and we were thrilled to do the concert for him. And in our own interest it had the advantage of being a high profile engagement which in terms of our profile would do us much good. We were now playing with the big boys. Sharing the bill were legendary Shadows guitarist Hank Marvin and the latest British opera sensation, the young and handsome Russell Watson. An added bonus was that Cliff himself was to join us on stage for *Needles And Pins*. Sadly, this didn't happen as he had a throat infection which almost caused him to abort the concert. Cliff limped bravely through the evening, his voice brilliantly mixed by his expert sound people so that the audience remained unaware of his discomfort, but he had to opt out of our planned duet.

It was a wonderful night for us personally. Cliff Richard's crew treated us with the utmost respect and every setting we had asked for in advance of the show was ready and waiting. Our guys, Phil Hayes and John Semark, could not heap enough praise on them, used as they were to the arrogance of so many backstage staff who lived in the reflected glory of their famous bosses. Praise came the other way too. After a magnificent reception we were told that it was rare for a Cliff crowd to give such support to another act on the bill. I couldn't quite see why we would not be well received. After all we were no threat to a star as big as Cliff and our music was complementary.

The only downside of the night for me was when, in some spare moments during the long evening, I decided to change my bass strings. I opened the boot of my car with the electronic key and fiddled about to find the ones I needed. Having done that

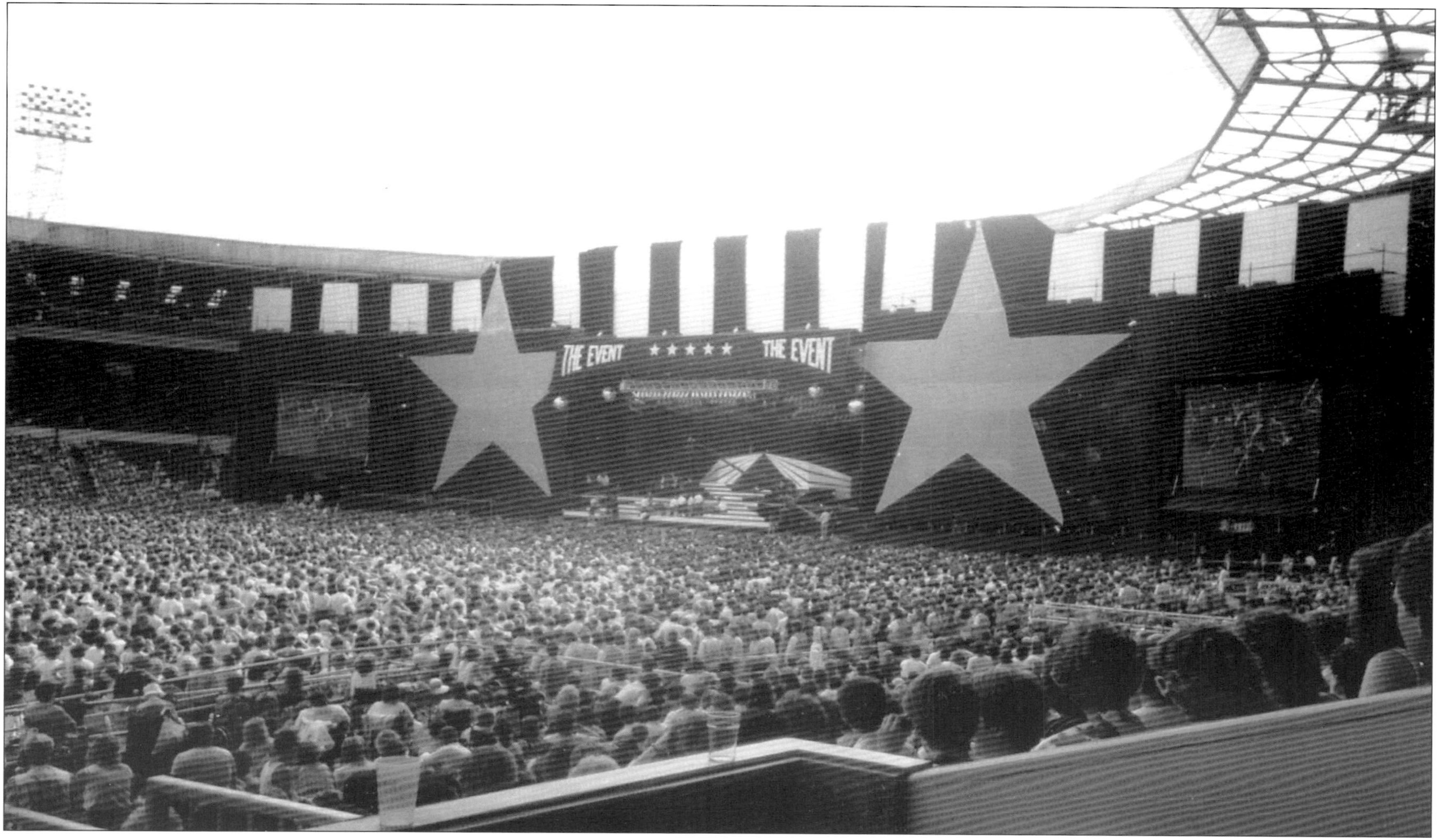

128. The Event

129. Me, Cliff and John

130. The Dynamic Duo, Allen and McNally (Ron Long)

131. John and me with Tony Hatch and Petula Clark at Tony's This Is Your Life

132. The auction at our convention with Searchers Appreciation Society organiser Tim Viney (Ron Long)

133. My first Best Front Man award (Ron Long)

134. With 'the lads' on stage in Bosnia

135. Searchers and crew on HMS Illustrious

136. Ed in his skunk suit with Liquid Gold (Eddie Rothe collection)

137. The new line-up with Eddie Rothe on the right

138. Ed Rothe drumming as a Searcher

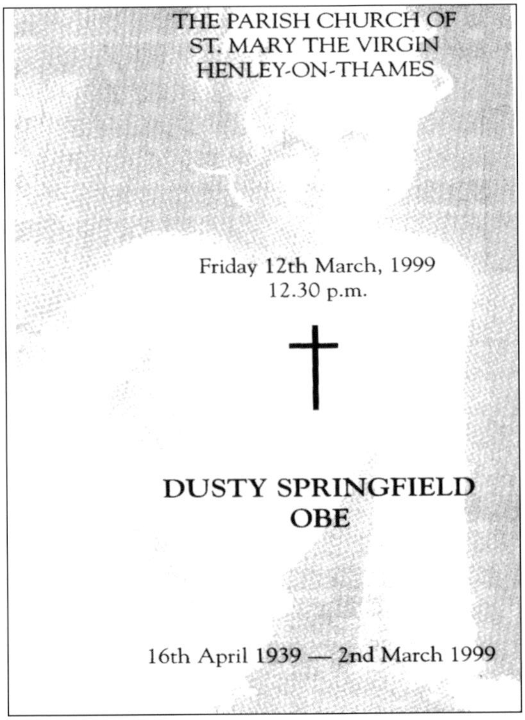
THE PARISH CHURCH OF
ST. MARY THE VIRGIN
HENLEY-ON-THAMES

Friday 12th March, 1999
12.30 p.m.

†

**DUSTY SPRINGFIELD
OBE**

16th April 1939 — 2nd March 1999

139. Dusty's funeral programme

140. With our website team, Wendy Burton and Gary Jackson.

141. P. J. Proby in his dressing room

142. P. J. Proby and me on stage

143. Tony Jackson 1938-2003

144. Tony Hatch with John and me at my 60th

145. The 2007 Solid Silver line-up. Searchers, Gerry & the Pacemakers, Swinging Blue Jeans and Merseybeats (Flying Music)

146. John reunited with his old Hofner Club 60 at the Hard Rock Cafe in Manila

147. On stage with Sir Cliff Richard at Wentworth Golf Club

148. Chris Curtis singing at a Merseycats gathering (Arty Davies collection)

149. Chris Curtis
1941-2005

150. On stage at the Royal Albert Hall

151. John McNally doing what he loves best

152. Sometimes a roadie's life is o.k. Me with our crew John Semark (left) & Phil Hayes (right) on the Arcadia

153. Horst Fascher, the old Star Club manager

154. The Cannery, Las Vegas

155. Backstage at the Cannery with Billy J. Kramer

156. And with Denny Laine

157. John talking 12 strings with one of our V.I.P fans, Steve Van Zandt (John McNally collection)

158. The Searchers' original lead vocalist turns up again in Glasgow 2007. 'Big Ron' Woodbridge

159. With our guest drummer Marky Ramone at the Cutting Room, New York 2006

160. Reunited with Supremes star Mary Wilson in 2008.

161. Plugging the new compilation CD. An acoustic set on the Johnnie Walker show 11th May 2008

162. The Rebel Rousers reunion, 2007. back row - Ben Jordan, Ricky Winter, Sid Phillips, Mick Currell, Cliff Bennett, Mick Borer. front row - Alfie James, me (Sid Phillips)

163. Live on stage in the 'noughties' (Brian Marsh)

164. Still live (Wendy Burton)

165. And happy (Wendy Burton)

166. The promotion worked. Our Silver Discs for The Very Best Of The Searchers

167. The sweater says it all

I slammed the lid shut. Horror of horrors, I immediately realised that the keys remained inside the locked boot which I had released not with the multiple door lock function but with the button that opened the lid to the trunk and nothing else. Like a desperate nincompoop I kept pressing the lock somehow hoping that divine intervention would release the latch. Not a hope. I felt like going to Cliffie and suggesting that as he had appeared to have strong connections with certain powers ethereal he might possibly request a small miracle on my behalf.

Here I was on the last night of 1999 at a major function in a city that had been sealed off by the police until morning. No one was getting in or out until the next day, which of course was a day on which virtually no businesses would be operating across the length and breadth of England. I remained unsettled for the rest of the night and finding sleep was a problem. The major reason for my discomfort was that one day later we were all heading off for our annual trip to Australia. I was only grateful that at least I had a day's grace. Fortunately we were staying next door at the Holiday Inn that night, but somehow I had to retrieve my keys in the morning and get home to London.

It was beginning to look like John McNally was going to have to drive me home to collect the spare key and then straight back to Birmingham to fetch the car. It was a prospect he was not looking forward to. In the morning I managed to contact a Mercedes Benz garage and to my great surprise a mechanic was sent out to help. Unfortunately the locking system on the vehicle was so efficient that we were forced to smash the rear lights in order to get to the bunch of keys. It seemed like an act of sheer vandalism as the glass splintered into my gleaming and beloved Mercedes. This was not going to be a cheap solution but by that time I didn't care about the expense. It had been an unforgettable New Year's Eve but now I just wanted to go home.

40

Into The Millennium

At last the years had reached the magical number two thousand and for the Searchers the pace continued relentlessly, which came as no surprise to anyone. We were used to it. In fact we had never really known anything else. Like zombie hamsters on a wheel of our own creation we ploughed onwards, quite able to effect at least a temporary halt but oddly unwilling to do so.

From Heathrow we flew to Perth in Western Australia, arriving on the morning of January 2nd. Hank Marvin was up the sharp end in First Class luxury on his way home to the city which had been his home for a while now. We were just behind in Club, impostors each and every one of us. We had been upgraded from the deck chair and sandwiches section at the rear by friendly contacts working for the airline. It's not what you know, it's who you know. And how much you are prepared to grovel.

From there we crisscrossed the vast continent playing fifteen concerts and then moving on to New Zealand for the final five before heading back to the UK, touching down in the early hours of February 1st. Two days later, with barely time to draw breath and unpack, we were into the start of the latest Solid Silver Sixties Tour which began its sixty-seven date run most appropriately at the Liverpool Empire. Sharing the bill with us were Gerry & the Pacemakers, the Swinging Blue Jeans and Peter Sarstedt, a combination that had proved its worth over the years and which could still be guaranteed to pack the theatres.

During the tour's run we acquired our very own website domain name *www.the-searchers.co.uk* which was registered on April 17th. At last we were a part of the IT generation whereas previously we had been a mere attachment to Gary Jackson's My Generation site which dealt with the sixties scene in general. Gary, ostensibly the operator of a newsagents and post office in Southampton, along with keen enthusiast Wendy Burton continued to compile and present our pages which were constantly changed, enhanced and updated to hold the interest of those who logged on. As well as Wendy's newsletter I began to deliver one of my own at irregular intervals in order to show that we actually took an interest in the people who supported us. Old articles I had written for our Searchers Appreciation Society magazine were included as were photos, a biography, a discography and the all-important date sheet.

Business-wise it was an essential move. No-one could afford to lag behind. A time to live and a time to die, the song said. Now it was a time to be Googled. Contact details were put on line making it easier for people to employ our services. And along with the normal commercial engagements came bookings from fans who were beginning to reach milestones in their lives and wanted to celebrate in the appropriate manner despite the considerable expense involved. It was very flattering.

The Solid Silver Sixties marathon finally ended on May 28th at the Grand Theatre in Wolverhampton, with the London date again being the Palladium one week before. It was the usual crazy schedule but in typical Searchers style we exacerbated the problems by filling a free day that followed the Nottingham show with not one but two shows of our own. And to complicate things even further they just happened to be in separate countries. By hiring a Piper Cherokee we managed to complete an engagement in Esbjerg, Denmark, and flew back for an evening show at the Grosvenor House in London's Park Lane for a convention of fire-fighters.

As soon as the tour finished we were off to the USA for appearances at the Mohegan Sun Casino in Connecticut and another at the Resorts Casino in Atlantic City. Summer that year was taken up by dates in the holiday spots of Skegness, Scarborough and Great Yarmouth until we finally got to enjoy what we considered to be our real holiday. Our P&O cruise was now a yearly event during which we could switch off entirely and, apart from two show days, wind down to a point where we were almost comatose. Our bodies needed it. This year's trip around the Mediterranean visiting such hotspots as Cadiz, Barcelona, Toulon, Livorno, Cannes and Gibraltar meant that we reluctantly had to turn down another high profile engagement back home. In February our old chum Sir Cliff Richard had asked us to appear with him as part of a charity show to be held at Wentworth Golf Club, the guest of honour being the Prime Minister, Tony Blair. A golden opportunity missed – for the time being.

On November 21st I was catching a plane from JFK Airport back to London after a three-day spot of R&R in the Big Apple. As I turned right into the Business section I encountered Mick Jagger entering the First Class cabin and paused to chat. We were nothing more than acquaintances, our status in the pop hierarchy planets apart, but he was friendly and accommodating. After a while I decided that he might like a copy of Travelling Man, after all there was a picture of us together from the old touring days when I was with the Rebel Rousers. He seemed pleased enough to accept it and I returned to my seat with a smug, self-satisfied smile on my face. At Heathrow I waved goodbye from the opposite end of the baggage carousel but he seemed far from happy.

I could not figure out why. And then I realised that the first thing someone does when receiving a book such as mine is to find one's own name in the index. I remembered to my horror what I had written.

In one paragraph I suggested that Keith Richards' unbelievably rugged constitution meant that with a more moderate life style he might well have ended up looking like Bonnie Langford's love child. In the following sentences however I pointed out that while Jagger still possessed the kind of slim-hipped, tight-bummed figure that would not look out of place on a Spanish bullfighter, these days he seemed to be propping up the face of a Shar Pei.

Oh my god. It was not put there to insult. It was meant to give my book an edge and a touch of wickedly ironic humour, which of course it would apart from when being read by the subject of the offending words. It never occurred to me that Mick would ever see it. I was mortified. I liked Jagger. He always had a wonderful twinkle in his eye that showed there was much humanity within and had never been anything but nice to me. He was an international superstar and a master showman and had masterminded the Stones' career and finances so well that they were richer and more successful than anyone could ever have imagined. I had no right getting a cheap laugh at his expense and if he ever reads this I hope he will take it as my grovelling apology. In my defence there was nobody in the tome I sent up more than myself.

By now our lives pretty much fitted into a pattern. Foreign trips (2001 in Australia and New Zealand with some shows in the Middle East before getting home on March 18th), solo concerts (between April 1st and June 29th we completed another forty one of our 'all evening' shows), German nostalgia fests (on July 7th we were in Hamburg alongside Suzi Quatro, Smokie, Showaddywaddy, Boney M, Harpo, the Tremeloes, Dave Dee, Dozy, Beaky, Mick and Tich, Alvin Stardust, the Sweet, Hot Chocolate, Mickey Finn's T Rex, the Manfreds, Chris Andrews, the Rubettes, Slade, Pussycat and Daniel Boone) and impossible schedules (after our spot on the Hamburg show we flew straight back to the UK for another appearance that evening at the Grosvenor House Hotel, once again for the fire-fighters who seemed to have the hots for us).

Somewhere in that frenzied routine, on April 29th, I managed to attend the unveiling of a plaque in memory of dear Dusty Springfield that had been affixed to her old house at 38 Aubrey Walk, Holland Park, the only property she ever actually owned. The Heritage Foundation organised the tribute and for the first time in three decades I had the chance to peek inside the place that had once been a destination for parties and fun. It did not look so different from the way I remembered it. The kitchen, with its garish seventies tiles that had once been such a modern statement but which now were a touch of kitsch, seemed to have remained unaltered although my memory could not be relied upon.

I never went upstairs. I was too embarrassed to ask the current owners, who were allowing their home to be invaded by complete strangers, if it was permitted. I wondered if the glorious outsize purple coloured Bonsack bath, with its Greek key motif in gold around the top and wonderfully decadent pillows set in recesses at either end, was still there. I doubted it. Such things these days are looked on as vulgar and naff. But as a lad from a council house who had once actually lived in a tin hut I recall thinking it was the most luxurious thing I had ever seen. I was asked to say a few words during the ceremony and I did my best but I know it was gauche and inadequate.

The ghost of Dusty was everywhere and I half expected to see a misty vision of her smiling at me from the stairway just like the spectre of Julie London had appeared to a drunken Tom Ewell in the classic rock & roll movie The Girl Can't Help It. Little by little my past was fading, making me far too aware of my own mortality than was comfortable.

In July I appeared on the television show Through The Keyhole and as the cameras followed the tortured vowelled presenter Loyd Grossman through my West London home I sat behind a screen praying that they would manage to guess my identity to prove my name, or more correctly that of the Searchers, still carried some weight. I had never possessed a particularly high public profile even in those three years of glory before the fame began to fade and I dreaded the ignominy of failure to recognise me. The panel, consisting of broadcaster Alistair Stewart, writer Joan Bakewell and celebrity chef James Martin eventually managed to make the sixties connection but were struggling with the group name let alone mine. Time was about to run out when Alistair Stewart finally yelled 'Is it the Searchers?' David Frost confirmed his triumph. 'Yes, Frank Allen of the Searchers, will you come through the keyhole'. They hadn't exactly named me but honour was saved.

On Monday September 10th we appeared at the Embassy Theatre, Skegness, a favourite venue of ours set along the promenade of the Lincolnshire resort. It had been a good concert and I set off for Great Yarmouth the next day in high spirits. The Vauxhall Holiday Camp was one of our most regular engagements and we were always assured of a wild reception and a wonderful night. The date, September 11th, was a date that would never be forgotten.

I had just passed King's Lynn when breaking news came on the radio that an incident had just happened in New York in which an airplane had crashed into one of the Twin Towers of the World Trade Centre. Details were sketchy. It was thought at first that it was a light plane. Such a thing had happened before. On July 28th 1945 the Empire State Building was struck by a B25 bomber in a tragic accident caused by the fog that shrouded Manhattan on that fateful morning. I assumed this happening would have a similarly innocent explanation. The announcement was quite dramatic but at that moment it did not seem like the kind of earth-shattering news that would change everybody's lives forever.

Moments later while we were digesting the ramifications of the events the newscaster informed us that the other tower had been struck by a second aircraft. Things were taking a bizarre turn. Yet even then it was being suggested that the second crash was due to a spotter plane making an error while investigating the first. It was soon obvious that there was no mistake, that both planes were commercial airliners packed with passengers and that we were witnessing one of the greatest tragedies of our lifetimes. I had in fact been in the basement area of the Twin Towers on the day before my encounter with Mick Jagger on my New York connection the previous year. It was a long gap but it's amazing how close it seemed in the light of what was now happening.

Backstage at the Vauxhall Holiday Camp we were riveted to the television screens as we watched the constant replays of the incredible scenes in New York. As the drama unfolded we learned of the other planes that had also gone down, one crashing into a section of the Pentagon and another that had, we later learned, been destined for the White House but which was forced down into a field after an incredibly brave revolt from a group of passengers who, despite the knowledge that they were surely doomed, decided to do something.

It was hard to play the show as normal that night but we did. There really was no other solution unless of course someone had seen fit to cancel the entertainment. This was show business and as the old maxim states, the show must go on.

With everyone still tender from the memory of 9/11 we tried to get on with our lives as best we could, though the events of that tragic day were never far from our minds. Our package tour for 2001 which ran from October 13th to November 25th went out under the banner of The Beat Goes On and was financed by our friend Chas Elliott rather than the Flying Music Company. The main reason for this was that John McNally and I, always conscious that things were in great danger of becoming too 'samey', had mulled over various combinations and had time and again returned to the idea that we should involve P.J Proby.

At his peak Proby's rich and impressive baritone voice had very few rivals. Tom Jones was one. Scott Walker perhaps another although in a softer vein. Proby's inclusion was an intriguing prospect in our eyes. Unfortunately others saw it differently and no-one was willing to take a chance on the bad boy of pop. They were not convinced that he would turn up for every show or even less that he would make it from one end of the tour to the other. Promoters Mark Howes and Robert Pratt, originally earmarked as the financial backers of the venture, eventually shied away from the project. We were asked to give a guarantee that he would appear. It was something we could not do. In fact we still had strong memories of his erratic behaviour on our tour of 1966. We just thought P.J, when operating on all four cylinders, was still an exciting talent the like of which had never been equalled and we wanted him on our show. Every other combination seemed a little bit predictable and possibly boring. But there could be no guarantees.

Eventually Chas Elliott decided to take the chance. The remainder of the bill was to be Billy J Kramer, always a solid draw with his sixties connection, boyish good looks and impressive roster of hits and the girl singer Billie Davis whose one significant hit was a cover of the Exciters single *Tell Him*. She had been a long time friend of Proby's and we felt that apart from being a name in her own right she might be able to exert a steadying influence on our unpredictable star.

At a pre-tour lunch at the trendy Joe Allen restaurant in Covent Garden Chas was beginning to doubt the wisdom of his involvement. The gathering consisted of John McNally, myself, our agent Alan Field, Chas and P.J who was now several stones heavier than in his prime and sporting a set of mutton-chop sideboards, a far cry from the svelte and handsome, prancing cat-like figure he once was. Proby did not give Elliott an easy ride. It was quite obvious from the outset that 'Jim's' single-mindedness and obstinacy had not deserted him and that he had not mellowed with age. As we exited after a tense round of discussions, during which Jim seemed to eat an inordinate amount of food as one supposes only a Texan can, Chas whispered to John and me 'What the bloody hell have you buggers got me into?'

Neither did his problems end there. We thought the deal with Billy J, now domiciled in the US, was done and dusted but we were to discover this was far from the truth. There was no post Twin Towers fear of flying but he had acquired a new lady manager who was flexing her business muscle. With the publicity material printed and circulated and the newspaper advertisements already in the public domain his increasing demands proved too much for Chas to accommodate and suddenly the tour was one performer less. Things did not bode well and even John and I were now worried. Chas decided not to replace Billy J despite his obvious strength on the bill and we would continue with the remaining three acts. If for any reason Proby threw a wobbly we would be left with just the Searchers and Billie Davis. Not exactly Live Aid. We all crossed our fingers very tightly indeed.

The opening night at the Town Hall in Ballymena on October 13th was as near to a disaster as one would want to come. The venue was old and shabby and the inadequate sound system was not helped by an inadequately populated room that had been constructed before the word *acoustic* had entered the English dictionary. Billie Davis struggled through her spot as best she could. Jim went on and performed his set like a grim-faced automaton who, as was blindingly obvious to the crowd, was not at all happy with conditions. He barracked the lighting man from the stage. His singing that night was not up to par. Up to that point the McNeice genes has blessed me with a paucity of grey hair but I could suddenly feel them pushing through.

We fared better than the others and our reception was excellent although we too suffered from the sound. The next evening in Londonderry's Millennium Forum, a purpose-built and much more suitable theatre, was far superior but there was still an air of doom around the whole set-up. We left Northern Ireland in a state of mild apprehension. There were two days off before the tour recommenced on the mainland at the Rhyl Pavilion.

I sat by the loading bay as Jim's car pulled up. He got out, his arms awkwardly laden with bags, and trudged towards the theatre. I was getting used to the grim look that seemed to be permanently affixed to his face. In an attempt to keep spirits light and cheery I waved and yelled out to greet him. He barely glanced up as he passed me muttering 'This could be my last night on the tour.' My heart stopped. All our fears seemed to be coming true. I have forgotten quite what the gripe was on that particular day but I learned to get used to 'Jim's last day on the tour' speech. It happened with regularity throughout the run but thankfully his threats were never carried out.

Once in mainland Britain his old voice and his old talent seemed to return. It was a well planned act and the off-stage intro, the first stunningly emotive lines of Maria in those incredible tones that I remembered so well, never failed to send shivers down my spine. I made sure I was there every night to wish him well and that I was at the side of the stage at the close of the first half to congratulate him on a great show. I didn't have to lie. I meant it. And I think he did us proud. He knew we had put our necks on the line for him and though there were times when he would have carried out his doom-laden promises I truly feel that his loyalty and gratitude to John McNally and me stopped him.

Proby kept himself very much to himself. There was little socialising with the rest of the entertainers and apart from his entrance and exit from the stage the most I saw of him was when I would pop into his dressing room just to say hello and make sure everything was all right. He came from a service background and all of the objects in his little private domain were laid out with military precision, cowboy boots in a perfect row on the floor, make up and other accoutrements arranged in precise lines and right angles on the dressing table surface. He could not function in a world without order. Any slight deviation either here or within the show itself would upset him. He would sit there sipping his lemon tea, slowly and carefully applying his stage make-up until showtime. It seemed his new regime of sobriety had to a great extent robbed his life of fun but after a lifetime of boozing that proved near fatal he had obviously decided that just being alive was more valuable than such transient frivolities.

The show at Cheltenham Town Hall on Tuesday November 6th was also his sixty-third birthday and to celebrate the occasion I had ordered a cake decorated with what I was informed was a map of Texas. That part of it was, for whatever reason, formed in green icing and resembled an area of anonymous and ill-tended parkland. Anything less like Texas would be hard to imagine but there was no time to have the Lone Star State resculptured. We kept it out of Jim's sight during the hours before he went on.

Before he took his false tabs at the end of his set he attempted to exit stage left. Unfortunately Jim had neglected to do a pre-show 'recce' and was blissfully unaware that the Cheltenham venue had no exit on that side and he came face to face with a brick wall. Silently and with a face like thunder he manoeuvred a full turn like a stately galleon gingerly edging its way out of a particularly difficult harbour. Such things seemed to happen with regularity in Jim's world.

He returned to deliver his final song and as his performance ended our temporary lady tour manager marched on to present him with his birthday surprise. He muttered a few words which everyone took to be some form of muted thanks and left the podium. Immediately afterwards in the confines of his dressing room the young woman felt the lashing of Proby's tongue. He hated the idea of being given a cake on stage. Whether it was because it would remind the audience of his advancing years or he thought such happenings had no place during his show I have no idea but he was not a happy bunny.

Once he discovered that I had been the instigator he seemed to regain his composure and thanked me profusely, adding that the only other person who had ever done that for him was John Lennon. I was more than happy with that. His tiny tantrum did not bother me a jot. Jim was a unique and loveable character. Mystifying and maddening certainly but never ever dull.

As the days went by I became fonder of Jim and felt sorry for a great singer who, by simply being in the wrong time zone had his glittering future stolen from him. Of course he was always a stubborn and difficult man and entitled to share a portion of the blame but he deserved better. On Friday October 26th we played the Fairfield Hall and amused the audience by reminding them with an indelicate phrase that this was the very place where, as Janet Jackson would have put it, a wardrobe malfunction, aided by his long standing affair with Jack Daniels, sent his career 'down the shit chute'. I can only imagine the regrets that must have been running through his mind while on that stage. How many 'if onlys' must there have been in Jim's life.

When the tour, which was a lot of fun and a surprising financial success, came to an end at the Portsmouth Guildhall on November 25th we presented him with a silver plated, bone handled magnifying glass as a keepsake. P.J, as off the wall as ever, bought us musical toilet roll holders.

41

Passing Friends

The year 2002 was as uneventful as life for us would get. Compared to other bands on our circuit it was a very busy year but for us, who were used to going at breakneck speed, the somewhat slower pace was both welcome and alarming at the same time. We all needed the rest. We were not getting any younger. But it took a while to adjust to the kind of leisure time that most folk took for granted.

An Australian tour, something we had come to expect and look forward to, did not happen. The economy on that side of the world was not in its best shape and it appeared that the market could not bear our fees, which I might state were far from excessive. Or it may have been a power play on behalf of our promoters in Oz. Keep 'em lean and keep 'em keen, and maintain or even lower the price might have been the cunning train of thought. Who knows what lurks in the murky minds of agents?

But we still had most of the regular UK venues to rely on and Germany and Denmark as always provided us with refreshing visits to foreign soils. With time to spare we were able to provide the loyal members of the Searchers Appreciation Society with another convention, this time held at the Co-operative Sports and Social Club in Nuneaton on October 13th. These occasions had become increasingly popular with our amazingly devoted regulars and gave us the chance to pay something back.

Apart from the usual auction of memorabilia and a free performance by us the big thrill for the fans was the appearance of Tony Jackson. Our long-departed ex bass player wanted to contribute towards the funds that would be raised for the hospital that had looked after him during his recent heart scare. A lot of water had passed under the bridge and any animosity that had existed between him and us had to the greater extent dissipated.

We did not get him on stage to sing on this occasion. Although perfectly mobile he looked greyer and more fragile than we remembered and he was content to sit and observe the goings-on rather than take part. In fact he had become stooped and his playing days had been curtailed by severe arthritis in his hands many years before but he happily chatted to the thrilled aficionados who came up for autographs and to pay their respects to one of the original Searchers.

It came as a great surprise to us that this burly, hard drinking, rough, tough Scouser whose reputation had earned him the demonistic nickname of Black Jake, was both a cat lover and an accomplished artist. He donated a number of his marvellous pencil portraits for sale in aid of the charity and they were quickly snapped up. John in particular must have wondered how Tony had managed to keep this aesthetic side a secret for so long.

It occurred to us that, in his fragile state, Tony's health was in jeopardy. He certainly did not look well. Year by year our comrades and our idols were being taken from us. Bob Wooller, the iconic and influential Liverpool deejay who had presided over so many Cavern evenings had passed away at the age of seventy, not a great age in modern terms. My boyhood hero Lonnie Donegan finally succumbed to his failing heart while on tour in England. In the company of that other skiffle king, Chas McDevitt I had seen him two years before at the Swan in High Wycombe and he was nothing less than magnificent. His unstoppable energy and his commitment to the music he loved astounded me. Almost fifty years on from his first recordings he was better than ever.

Our annual cruise that year was a short one on the P&O ship Arcadia sailing from Southampton on October 19th and returning just one week later. And the last days of December we were again in Kenya where we saw in the New Year under the African moonlight at a resort in Mombasa. It was hard to differentiate between holiday and work. We were living a privileged life but we needed to recharge our batteries for the 2003 Solid Silver Sixties Tour of Britain which was to take in no less than seventy towns and cities between February 20th and May 18th.

Travel was still a privilege for me but the edge had been taken off the fun in the wake of 9/11 and the necessary security procedures that now made the check-in process a tedious and lengthy nightmare. We had become quite used to the 'missing bags sketch' to the point that arrival in a foreign land without benefit of instruments with which to ply our trade no longer fazed us. We simply accepted the likelihood that they would arrive post-haste and in time for our performance which, fortunately, they invariably did. Our philosophy was that a piece of luggage was like a guitarist with a big amp. Sooner or later it was bound to turn up. But the torture that was now the rule at the outset of a trip was something we could never get used to. Flying was no longer the joy it had once been.

This time on the Solid Silver Tour we were joined by Dave Dee, Dozy, Beaky, Mick and Tich, Barry Ryan, Wayne Fontana and the Dakotas. It was a hoot from beginning to end with everyone bonding well. There was however the constant worry about

Dave Dee's health following his treatment for prostate cancer. When his condition had been diagnosed he had sought advice from all corners including my great friend Bruce Welch of the Shadows. Bruce had developed the same disease some time before and had opted for a straight-forward surgical removal of the prostate. He was fortunate and came out the other end happy and healthy and with every likelihood of a full life ahead of him.

Dave Dee had chosen a relatively new procedure in which radio-active seeds were injected into the area with the hope that they would destroy the cancerous cells. Unfortunately there were complications during and after his operation and Dave's life had since been scarred by immense problems that made his day-to-day life a nightmare. He bore his extremely raw deal with a bravery and strength of character that astounded us all, never once burdening us with his difficulties unless pressed for information. The feat of getting from one end of this arduous tour to the other was nothing short of heroic and he won the admiration of everyone around him.

Our concert at the Theatre Royal in Nottingham fell on the first of May. It was a fine summer's day and we rested in the green room on the first floor between sets chewing the fat and enjoying the light-hearted banter that served as an assurance that this was a happy and contented package. Word came up to us that Tony Jackson, who now resided in the area, had arrived for a visit. We were warned not to look shocked. When he appeared it was hard to hold to the remit. The once solid and stocky bruiser who had taken on allcomers at the mere suspicion of a slight or an insult was now a frail and wizened shell of a man with a haunted look on his lined and prematurely aged face.

He was helped to a chair by John McNally and Larry Williams, the close friend who had brought him. In the mere six months since the convention he had become barely mobile and a sliver of saliva snaked its way down from his mouth as he uttered what sentences he could. His voice was indistinct and though we all tried to make conversation it was of necessity stilted and unnaturally measured. It was particularly hard to take by John who, despite all the rancour and disagreements of the past, only spoke of him in good terms these days. Life was too short for petty recriminations and for some of their most glorious days their lives had been inextricably entwined.

Eventually Tony was taken out to watch the show and when I made mention of his presence during our closing spot the applause was rapturous. I would like to think he was thrilled that people still remembered him and appreciated so much his important part in the career of the Searchers. As for me I had always recognised that I was riding on the coat-tails of a bunch of guys who had already made the big time and I was more than happy to be the 'new boy' to Tony's 'original' tag.

In July John received a phone call from Tony who wanted to convey the news personally that he had been given only a short time to live. Once more that ever-present black Scouse humour surfaced. 'Well, at least that saves me sending you a get well card,' was John's wicked reply. 'You bastard,' said Tony, his tone making it obvious that he understood the pithy ironic sarcasm of his old mate. Their conversation was well timed. On August 18th Tony finally succumbed to the combined effects of angina and diabetes. He was 65 years old.

I received a call from Jennifer Selway at the Express newspaper. They were about to insert an obituary and she wondered if I might be prepared to write it for them. I had already written a couple of pieces for them. One was an article on the origins of the song *Unchained Melody* which I had penned knowing that it was sure to be at number one that weekend by the Pop Idol contestant Gareth Gates. Another was a piece on the history of *Happy Birthday* which I had written to coincide with Prince William's twenty-first celebration.

This latest assignment was different. Was it appropriate? I had not only stolen his job but I was now about to make money out of his death. I accepted and got straight to work as it had to be submitted by four that afternoon. There were things I needed to know about Tony. His real age had been uncertain and I had to phone his friends to check the passport. There was the question of what to keep in and what to leave out from his colourful life. His departure from the group. The fights. His three wives. The eighteen months prison sentence, of which he served nine, for threatening a woman with a replica pistol after a dispute about a phone box. His heavy drinking. And the final mellowing of the Liverpool bad boy turn artist. I put in the facts that I felt told the essential story of Tony Jackson and hoped I got it more or less right. I was on a hiding to nothing so I just had to go with my instinct.

My obituary, which was entitled *Searcher Who Craved A Rock And Roll Lifestyle*, took up the greater part of a page when the newspaper come out the following day. Other publications gave his death similar column inches. We were all astonished at the amount of coverage he received. There were arguably greater celebrities than Tony before and since who had commanded less attention. At least his passing had not been ignominious.

His funeral was held on Wednesday August 27th at the Wilford Hill Crematorium in Nottingham. It was a smaller gathering than I had envisaged and we wondered if perhaps it would have been better had it taken place in his native Liverpool. In the 'Pool it would have been standing room only. Guys from his old group The Vibrations were there but the friends of his boyhood and the bands he shared stages with in those exciting days when the thought of making the big time must have seemed like an impossible dream had not managed to make the journey.

I rendezvoused with John and Mary McNally and Tony West, the group's very first bass player from the pre-Jackson days, at a service area on the M1 and we arrived at the church together. As we drew into the parking area we could see that Mike Pender was already there along with his wife May. John was already insisting that he wanted to keep well away. Mary McNally and I felt that things should be perhaps more civilised and that we had to at least acknowledge them. This was after all a funeral. I walked over and held out my hand to shake his.

'Hello Mike, good to see you,' I said. 'Hello Francis,' he replied in what I perceived to be a somewhat condescending tone. He put out his own hand in return but somehow contrived to avoid moving his body forward with it, or so it seemed to me. It was like joining the receiving line of a minor civic dignitary. Maybe I was being over sensitive. It all felt rather patronising and I was immediately regretting my decision to extend the hand of friendship. I vowed it would not happen again and quickly moved to his wife May before returning to our party.

The service was short and dignified. The arrangements had been taken care of by Larry Williams who had also looked after him during his final days. Mike Pender delivered a eulogy and behind me John McNally, in a voice that I felt was a trifle too audible, was mumbling about hypocrisy. During his oration, Mike talked of not believing the unpleasant things that the newspapers had written and I was in no doubt that this at least in part bore reference to my own piece.

I learned that a number of Tony's friends disapproved of my mentions of his wild days, his fights and his term of incarceration. I felt they had missed the point and misunderstood the difference between a eulogy and an obituary. A eulogy, normally given at a funeral or a memorial service comprises in the main the positive and the humorous aspects of a person's life. Controversy and negativity are usually omitted on an occasion where the object is to celebrate their existence and mourn their passing.

An obituary is a summation of a person's time on earth in which all the significant points, be they good or bad, are remembered. It is a combination of words that truthfully and candidly asserts that person's essential character and affirms the mark that person made on the world. Anything else would lessen the man. To omit the most important aspects of Tony's intriguing and often dramatic life would be as stupid and as condescending as describing Keith Richards, on the day he finally shuffles off his mortal coil, as a clean living, celibate, drug free teetotaller who went to bed every night before ten o'clock with a mug of cocoa. Would Keith be happy with a watered down version of his being that had been diluted to the potency of a fruit cocktail? Not on your life.

Would Tony have preferred to avoid the quite remarkable media coverage and to have been hustled out the back door like some insignificant magnolia-tinted nobody? I don't think so. The only thing I regret about my obituary is that with more time to complete it and with more care in its execution the structure could have been so much better.

Life for Tony was over but business for the Searchers continued unabated with a frenetic run of engagements that took us back to Denmark and Germany as well as our standard routine of criss-crossing Britain. And as we headed towards the latter months I decided to mark my 60th birthday on December 14th by taking over Blushes, a restaurant on the King's Road, Chelsea, opposite the site of the old Duke Of York Barracks a few hundred yards from Sloane Square.

I had initially decided to bypass any such celebrations but, egged on by my good friend the showbusiness writer David Wigg, I changed my mind. The choice of venue, again picked out by David Wigg, could well have been influenced by the fact that it was situated immediately below his London apartment. No need for an expensive cab or any risk of driving under the influence for the very astute Fleet Street scribbler.

Somehow I managed to compile a guest list that did not exclude anyone who might have been mortally offended by their exclusion. The most important people in my life were taken care of first. Susie Mathis, Lee Lowsley, John McNally, Cliff Bennett and of course my brother Jackie McNeice and his wife. Fellow Searchers Spencer James and Eddie Rothe along with our long standing crew, Phil Hayes and John Semark, were there of course along with a reasonable smattering of familiar faces from the entertainment industry. Bruce Welch, Anita Harris, Julie Rogers, Lynsey DePaul, Helen Worth, and a bunch of others.

I was pleased that Tony Hatch managed to attend. Due to pressures of work I had missed his 60th but I was thrilled that he was there at mine. He made a very flattering speech which followed a hysterically funny one from Shadow Bruce Welch. Bruce's old boss Cliff Richard, now a knight of the realm, had to decline because of prior commitments but instead sent a very welcome case of champagne. A surefire way to obtain forgiveness in my eyes.

We still found Australia denied to us for a second year but by way of compensation 2004 was to see us returning to the Philippines for the first time since the fun but troubled tour of 1966. Setting off from the UK on May 25th on a flight by Royal Brunei Airlines we were installed in the very acceptable luxury of the Shangrila Hotel in the heart of Manila. The sights and sounds of that fascinating city brought the memories flooding back for John McNally and me.

There were only two shows planned. The first was at the Hard Rock Café in the Makati district while the second was the massive Araneta Colosseum, the very place where we had caused both boos and screams thirty eight years previously. In nostalgic terms the venue was most appropriate. In practical terms the sheer size and capacity certainly seemed over-ambitious for a band whose pulling powers, though excellent for the circuit on which we now plied our trade, were considerably reduced from those chart-topping glory years.

The Hard Rock was packed and throbbing with atmosphere. An unqualified success. As a bonus we discovered that John McNally's old Hofner Club 60 guitar, surely one of the most recognisable axes of the era, was an artefact on display in the restaurant. It was looking a little shabbier than we remembered and one of the inlays had disappeared from the highly ornate fingerboard but other than that it hung gloriously there before us bringing the kind of smiles of delight that are elicited by a surprise encounter with a dear old friend.

The Araneta Colosseum had not changed all that much from '66 except that almost every inch of the once barren area that had surrounded it was now highly developed with housing and businesses. The little enclosed garden with the pool out back of the enormous circular construction, where we had spent our leisure and meal times, was still there and the crude animal statuary still in place. Even Bobby Grimald, our old minder, now frailer but still recognisable, turned out to greet us. Mr Araneta himself had long since passed away but his son had taken over the mantle.

Unlike our first visit the huge arena was not jammed to capacity this time round but to our surprise the thousands who applauded and cheered with an unbounded enthusiasm far exceeded anything we had expected. It was certainly a more than respectable turnout by anyone's standards.

In the summer of that year we received a second request to perform at the Dreamscope Ball, the charity event that Sir Cliff Richard had wanted us for in 2000. This time the date in our diary had not yet been filled and we said yes. It was for a Saturday night and our acceptance was an expensive move that was to cost us several thousand pounds in lost work to us and fees to our crew, not to mention travel expenses and the other sundries that constitute the crippling cost of touring, but we owed him one. And the charity was a more than worthy cause. It was the least we could do.

This time round on June 26th at the exclusive Wentworth Golf Club Cliff was to be a guest rather than a performer and we were to be the main entertainment of the evening. Ahead of time we received word that the Prime Minister Tony Blair, once again the guest of honour, was quite prepared to don a guitar and get up on stage with the Searchers and we had an amp and a spare Fender Stratocaster ready behind us on the tiny cramped stage. We had no idea what he might want to play.

In the end it was academic. Given the choice of position we had elected to perform towards the end of the evening rather than in the mid-evening cabaret spot and, as they say in our industry, timing is everything. Tony Blair was leaving for the NATO conference in Turkey early the next morning and as soon as his speech, set for the space just before our set, was completed he was escorted to his waiting limousine and off into the night. The Strat remained untested by the PM's virtuosity.

That particular moment of glory, and the resulting attention in the press, might have passed us by but by way of compensation I dragged Cliff up on stage to join us in the middle of our set. Still looking good in an immaculate evening suit accentuated by a red silk scarf draped over his shoulders he willingly stepped onto the podium and agreed to my suggestion that we should perform *Move It*. To object would have done him little good. It was the only Cliff song we had rehearsed in readiness for the evening.

'Original version,' I whispered in his ear. He appeared to assent by giving me a nod and we launched into the iconic guitar riff that session man Ernie Shears (and not Hank Marvin who had not yet been recruited into Cliff's backing group) had ad-libbed on a Hofner Committee back in 1958. We stuck to the record tempo as opposed to the slower pace Cliff and his band were currently adhering to and when we arrived at the line 'Let me tell you baby it's called rock & roll,' in the first verse we stoically stuck to the original and kept the instruments going. Most people, Cliff included these days, either cannot or will not stop themselves from cutting the backing at that point. Sacrilege. One should not tamper with perfection or meddle with one's memories.

So far so good. John McNally executed a pretty true approximation of the solo that was on the disc and we continued into the second time round. And that's where it went wrong for me. In his latter years ex-Drifter Ian 'Sammy' Samwell (pre-Shadows British Drifter, that is) had penned a brand new second verse which Cliff had gratefully grabbed and introduced into his on-stage version. It was his entitlement of course but being a die hard rock & roll fan I much preferred the classic simplicity of the repeat. Into the new verse he went either forgetting or preferring to ignore my pleas at the start and sang about Mississippi mud and goodness knows what. I couldn't tell you what the words to that verse are. My mind always blocked out such heresy. Ah well, it was worth a try.

The crowd were thrilled and we carried on into a rendition of *Johnny B Goode* in which I traded lead vocal lines with Cliff. Why I did that I don't know. On reflection I should have just left him to it. He was the possessor of one of Britain's all-time classic rock and pop voices and I was a vocalist whose equipment dipped its toe into the waters of adequacy and ventured no further. But he was very gracious and seemed unperturbed and content for me to share the glory.

After he left the stage we continued with our regular set and as we approached the end I called him up again to join us on *Needles And Pins*. I also suggested that Cilla Black, who was also a guest that evening and dancing with the knighted popster at that point, might like to come up too. Knowing that as the consummate professional she prefers to avoid such impetuous and unplanned situations I pointed out that we would quite understand if she didn't. I think she would have plumped for that option except that Cliff had her grasped around the wrist and more or less dragged her forward with him. They stayed with us for our greatest hit and the one that followed, *When You Walk In The Room.* I'm not too sure if Cilla, who has recorded her own version of *When You Walk In The Room* enjoyed it but she certainly smiled all the way through and we were more than pleased to have their exulted company that night.

42

More Goodbyes

After the Wentworth show we had a few days to relax before continuing the globetrotting that had become so much a part of our lives with a one-nighter in Holstebro, Denmark. From there it was back home and a few days to repack before heading out to the USA for a brief visit. We were still not at all sure if financially it was worth all the trouble and expense for just two shows but it was fun and we were definitely getting the feeling of a positive build-up of interest in the States again. We decided it was worth hanging in there to see if anything could be made of it.

This time we were to play just one show on our second visit to the Mohegan Sun Casino in Connecticut with a new venue, the Cutting Room on West 24th Street, New York City, the night before, July 9th. The Cutting Room, a real rock club situated just along from the beautiful Flat Iron building in the lower numbers heading down a few blocks from Times Square towards Greenwich Village, was an exciting and challenging prospect.

Co-owned by Sex In The City actor Chris Noth who played the character Mister Big in the hit series, it resembled an old-fashioned gentleman's club. The ante room directly off its unimposing entrance was 'shabby chic' in a style that could be described as Edwardiana and Victoriana meet and kick the shit out of each other. The adjacent showroom was a simple rectangle with an adequate although not huge stage. It was calculatedly tattered and throbbing with atmosphere.

A bunch of our much-valued UK diehard fans, including our Appreciation Society organiser Tim Viney and website co-ordinator Wendy Burton, had made the trip from England. We were impressed by their dedication and the expense they were prepared to go to in order to show their support. American followers, some whose faces we knew and others who, though we recognised their names, were visually strangers. It was a thrilling night.

The audience was euphoric, the management were ecstatic and by the end of the almost two-hour set we knew we had established a firm footing once more in the Big Apple. It was beginning to look as though America was going to be a serious consideration after all.

The Mohegan Sun Casino was familiar territory and we took it in our stride. We were now staying in the on-site hotel that had been erected since our first visit. The gigantic mirrored monolith rose over the landscape, an impressive shard of glass that slashed upwards through the Connecticut sky and drew the eye from miles around. It was the last word in luxury and my accommodation was of a size that required merely one overnight stop on the journey from the panoramic window view to the bathroom. This was a long long way from my Browngraves Road council house.

When it came time for our show it was considered beneath us to trudge through the main gambling rooms in view of the public. Instead we were ordered to assemble in the lobby where we transferred into an outrageous stretch limousine for the five hundred yard journey to the dressing rooms. Once there we were faced with trays of cold cuts and salads, chafing dishes filled with hot snacks and fresh fruits which included strawberries coated in thick, dark chocolate. The refrigerator was stuffed with every kind of drink we might need. At the end of the night most of the food remained where it lay. We had already gorged ourselves earlier in the concessionary.

It was a trifle surreal as we reflected on our early days trudging round the social clubs of Britain in the sixties where not only was the fare likely to be pies and peas, considered by many of the punters to be considerably higher on their list of priorities than us, but that it was usually denied to us lowly performers unless we paid out of our own pockets.

We had played the Wolf Den before and knew just how to handle the open-sided room and to use the constant clink of the slots as an aid to atmosphere rather than look on it as a distraction. We performed two sets to more or less the same audience and threw in just about everything we thought they might want. *Bumble Bee*, merely an EP track in the UK but a chart entry for us Stateside, was dragged out of our song cupboard while *Love Potion No. 9,* which at number three had achieved our highest position there back in '64, was moved further towards the end of the set list for maximum impact. The more than positive reaction confirmed the wisdom of our choices and it was a happy ensemble that flew home to carry on with the general round of dates, the major part of the summer and autumn being taken up with a series of shows at coastal resorts.

My sixty-first birthday that year was never going to be anything as special as the big one I had just passed so I plumped for a night out at my favourite and most regular restaurant, The Ivy, with a couple of pals. The enjoyment was added to when the management presented me with a dinner plate inscribed in chocolate with the words

Happy Birthday Rock God. It was the ironic nickname which had been given to me by my friends and which the maitre d' Kevin Lansdowne and those on the other end of the booking line learned to recognise to the extent that I could jokingly make a reservation without even the need to mention my name. 'Hi, this is a Rock God. Can I have a table for two at 9 tomorrow night?' was all that was required. Silly but fun.

John Reid, Elton John's estranged ex-manager, came in with a party of people that included a true Rock God with no irony needed, Mick Jagger, along with Jerry Hall. They turned right at the reception desk to a booth at the end while I was seated at my regular table along the left hand side of the room. A short while later Reid came over to congratulate me, having been told of the special occasion. I was delighted. We were not by any means close friends, merely good acquaintances. I did not move in the kind of circles that he inhabited but whenever we met he had always been considerate and kind towards me.

At the end of our meal I deliberated about the wisdom of approaching his table to say goodbye but I was hesitant because of Jagger's presence. I was still embarrassed and regretful about the mildly wicked words in my book by which he would most certainly have been wounded. What the hell. I crossed the room and was greeted by nothing but smiles and good wishes from everyone. Mick was charming. He had either forgotten, forgiven or was wearing his very best politician's hat. Thank you Mick.

In 2005, by an odd quirk of fate, we had Australasia back in our clutches. We had been offered the chance to join the QE2 for a leg of a world tour that would take us from Perth to Singapore and to make the trip worthwhile financially we had contacted our Aussie agent Tony Brady about setting up a few dates prior to our setting sail. With arrangements well in hand and Australian dates in the diary Cunard then altered all their entertainment set up and the voyage for us was no more. All of a sudden we were cruise-denied, cast adrift and left to paddle our own canoe. Not good.

This meant that Australia, under our old financial structure, was no longer a viable option and we informed Brady that we would not after all be coming. It then transpired that a mild panic set in. Venues, after our two-year absence, wanted us badly and suddenly money, plus extra dates, were found to the point that this part of the globe would in the future provide a very acceptable addition to our finances not to mention our skin tones and our psychological well-being. The small bunch of shows was now extended into a three-week tour and Australia had become a yearly fixture, going from strength to strength with each visit.

Three days after our return to Britain we were off on yet another Solid Silver Sixties Tour joined by old stalwarts Gerry & the Pacemakers, the Merseybeats and the Swinging Blue Jeans, and the 'sold out' notices were a familiar sight outside of most of the theatres.

John McNally and I had talked about asking Chris Curtis along to one of the shows, perhaps Southport or the Liverpool Empire. We mulled it over and over, wondering about the wisdom of the idea. After all, much as we admired him and as fondly as we remembered him, Chris was an extremely unpredictable person. He could very quickly take you over or go off on an unexpected and unwelcome tangent without any warning. If, in his fragile state of mind, we asked him on stage with us, chaos could and probably would ensue. It would be perhaps wiser simply to ask him along as a guest and announce his presence to the audience.

I gave John the only phone number I had for him, one that had been given to me by Merseyside radio personality and writer Spencer Leigh who had interviewed him for his show. On Monday February 28th John phoned me at home on one of our rare days off from the tour. He had tried the number I had given him and spoken to a lady who had no idea who or where Chris was. The number was obviously very out of date. I had no other to offer him and we left things at that.

The next day John found an old number for Chris and decided to try it. A young woman's voice answered and John asked for Chris. She suggested that perhaps he had better speak to her mother. The young woman's mother turned out to be Chris's sister Rosie, who stunned John with the news that Chris had collapsed with a heart attack and died the previous day, the very day that John had tried to reach him.

The funeral took place on March 9th at the Holy Rosary Church in the Old Roan district of Liverpool where Chris had been living. John and I attended, of course, and it was to be an affair that suited perfectly the flamboyant style that was so indicative of the eccentric and charismatic drummer. The black horse-drawn carriage which carried Chris's coffin on his final journey was handled by sombre and dramatic looking characters in black topcoats and high silk hats. It was the kind of splendid scene that one would expect to see in a Hammer horror film, and Christopher Lee and Peter Cushing would not have looked out of place atop the coach. Chris was certainly not going quietly.

The mourners were many and, being in Liverpool, comprised many of the members of the beat groups that competed for fame and fortune along with the Searchers when Merseymania first shook the world all those years ago. The Undertakers (the pop group, not the funeral directors' staff). The Dominoes. Faron and some of his Flamingos. Some were easy to spot. Others had changed and I found myself in a room full of my contemporaries in various states of bodily decay. A once slim-framed teen idol I remembered from four decades previously was now the size of Warrington and barely recognisable. Time had taken its toll on others and there were those who had aged so much and were in such a shabby state of health that there seemed little point in them going home again.

Faron still looked lithe and fit and pretty much like Faron, and Geoff Nugent - appropriately an Undertaker at a funeral - had not altered to any degree. Many faces were unrecognisable to me. I found myself talking to a gentleman who obviously knew me very well but who was a stranger to my eyes. I nodded in the right places and hoped I wasn't giving the game away. When the conversation ended I asked Mary McNally who the guy was. She answered that it was Billy Booker. I was mortified. Billy Booker had been our road manager at the time I joined the band and we had spent about a year on the road together until he dumped our equipment at Speke Airport and quit on the eve of a Scandinavian tour in 1965. A 'fit of Speke' if you like. I hoped to goodness that he hadn't noticed my lack of recognition. Armed with the necessary information I could now return to Billy and continue our reminiscences with a renewed confidence.

We had already noticed Mike Pender on the steps of the church and tactically kept our distance. Suddenly I saw Mike approaching. Oh well, at least I had stuck to my resolve not to make the first move like last time. 'Good to see you,' was more or less the gist of the conversation from both of us as we shook hands. He turned from me and called out 'John' at the same time making his way to where John McNally was in conversation with a group of people. John looked round unsmiling and uttered 'Sorry Mike,' before turning his back and walking away. There was to be no rapprochement. The wounds were too deep.

On occasions interviewers have enquired as to whether there would come a time when we would perform with Mike again. One even rather aggressively suggested that we should stop the silly arguments and confusing the public and get back together. My reply was that this was perhaps on a par with intimating that an ex-husband should reunite with a divorced spouse after an extremely acrimonious parting in which love had irrevocably turned to hate. In such a scenario I imagine the reply would be on the lines of 'You may quite like her but are you seriously suggesting that I make it up with that evil bitch who nearly ruined my life? When Hell freezes over.' In reality I am not sure that I would ever be that adamant. I don't have that much hate in me for anyone. But there is little doubt that it would take a major miracle for the gap between John McNally and Mike Pender ever to be bridged.

The service and speeches were both sad and amusing and we all continued at the British Legion along the road where food and refreshments had been arranged. The banter and the renewing of acquaintances, all centred around tales of the zany but loveable Chris and the glorious innocent days when Liverpool was the centre of the musical universe, were a joy and I drove back down the motorway happy that I was there to say goodbye to a funny, remarkable, frustrating, kind, maddening, unique, clever and wonderful human being.

The London date for the tour was the Royal Albert Hall on April 22nd, a much grander space than was normal for these packages in the new millennium. Early on I inquired of Flying Music supreme Derek Nicol whether or not they intended to boost the line-up for that show as they had on previous occasions. After all, as successful as these tours were, we were now many years down the line for such productions and they no longer had the novelty value of the first two or three outings. Back then, having been deprived for too long of the opportunity to hear their kind of music in such comfortable surroundings, people grabbed their chance not knowing for how long these performers would be around. By now it was pretty clear that at least a decent selection of them had no intention of going away for a considerable time.

Derek looked surprised and replied that they hadn't considered it. He looked pensive and I figured they might now start thinking about it toute de suite. After all as magnificent as it was the beautiful circular building with its awesome and ornate interior of red and gold embellishment and impressive wall of private boxes might not look so breathtaking when playing host to three nuns and a whippet. As time passed by it became apparent that no additions were to be made and we would stand or fall on our combined appeal. It bothered me. I wondered if there was perhaps a petard nearby on which we would hoist ourselves.

Astonishingly when the night arrived the place was full. A smattering of free seats could perhaps be spotted by the eagle-eyed. And the upper gallery, a place to be avoided anyway especially by the hard of hearing, those suffering from vertigo or anyone susceptible to nose-bleeds, had not been put on sale. But everywhere else was a heartwarming people-packed sight that shouted success. And unlike our previous disaster there the evening was a personal unqualified triumph for us as a group. With me it can be either insurmountable nerves or supreme confidence on such occasions. Fortunately, on this occasions it was the latter, and I was more than a little drunk with the feeling of power during our set. As I stepped down after our set to the roar of the crowd the Swinging Blue Jeans' road manager, Roger Weddup, pronounced 'You came off that stage like a conquering hero,' and I did truly feel like one.

As usual there was precious little time for us to set aside a proper vacation so we compensated ourselves with the yearly P&O cruise, this time on the new Arcadia sailing around the Baltic stopping off at places like Tallin, St Petersburg and Helsinki. The old Arcadia had been sold off to another line and emerged later on as the Ocean Village. Tallin in Estonia was beautiful, like an unreal fairytale concoction daubed in pastel pinks, blues and yellows. No wonder it had been the location for the town centre scenes in the movie Chitty Chitty Bang Bang. St Petersburg was impressive but more impersonal. The grand parts were beautiful, the less spectacular edifices much more representative of our perception of a Soviet city. And Helsinki was far better than I remembered from earlier visits. Maturity now allowed me to appreciate so much more the sights and sounds that we were being treated to. At last I had time to stop and smell the roses.

After our stop off in the resort of Travemunde north of Hamburg the entire town turned out to wave the monstrous vessel goodbye, lining the dock for half a mile like a thick column of ants until there was no more land for them to stand on. Arcadia was the largest vessel ever to visit the tiny port and the sight of what was essentially an enormous floating apartment block drifting majestically out to sea. The dozens of small craft followed alongside honked their sirens and the tiny fire tenders like excited minnows shot sweeping arches of water into the air by way of salute, was an emotional experience. Tears were shed. We held our Union Jacks aloft and raised our glasses of champagne while the hordes on the quayside waved and shouted their good wishes.

While this glorious and unforgettable spectacle was occurring our drummer Ed Rothe was sitting on his balcony on the opposite side of the ship completely oblivious and calmly videoing a lone angler silently perusing the small fish that might be nibbling at his line. We told him all about it later that evening. Sailaway? What sailaway?

Our usual two performance days, encompassing four shows, was not exactly coalface labour and we were glad of the enforced relaxation that is a part of an ocean-going working holiday. Looming up fast were two solid months of all-evening solo concerts that would take us through to the last weeks of the year.

These specialist shows in which we could relate virtually our entire history in music over the space of two hours, with a short interval, now formed the bulk of our touring schedule. Fortunately for us it was the most satisfying form of work and attracted an audience who wanted a little more than a brief display of our greatest hits. And being based around theatre time it meant that we knew exactly when our shows would start and end. No hanging around waiting while a desperate comic, having garnered some laughs at long last clings on to his audience for what seems like an eternity or for chattering diners to finish their pudding and coffee. With no support act we played for longer in these concerts but it seemed oh so much easier and infinitely more satisfying.

We had also talked our Danish promoters into experimenting in the same field over there and the try-out shows in Aarhus and Viejle in November were an unqualified success. Language was no problem. If one spoke clearly and articulately the Scandinavians understood everything. Such would not have been the case if the situation had been reversed. As far as we Brits in our arrogance are concerned the whole world speaks English and that is the way it should be! And that part of the world was no longer restricted to Denmark. A few days after our return we were off to Sweden for concerts in Orebro, Uppsala and Stockholm. And after more endless miles of British motorways, Antwerp in Belgium was graced with our presence before we saw out the last weeks of the year on home ground.

Our enforced two-year absence from the Australian scene from 2002 to 2004 turned out to have been a blessing in disguise. And now New Zealand had re-entered the equation. We were due to play a concert at a Christchurch venue in 2005 but for whatever reason – we were never given the exact details – it had been pulled.

We became a more sought-after commodity and the shows, always well received, were now even better attended. On each previous visit clubs would rebook automatically and new venues, the word of our reputation for delivering the goods having spread, would be added. We left the UK for our 2006 visit on January 18th and returned on February 20th, suntanned, rested and, despite the work, happy.

In March we were reunited with an old friend from the Hamburg days in the shape of Horst Fascher, the old manager of the Star Club. Horst was still getting involved in Beatles and Star Club related events with varying degrees of success and he was co-ordinating an outdoor festival in the smart coastal town of Friedrichshaven not far from Hamburg. He had changed little apart from a heavy growth of grey beard and we spent the limousine journey from the airport reminiscing. That was without doubt a very special time in our lives, but I felt that looking back meant so much more to Horst than to us. The Star Club era and the Beatles association in particular would forever be the focal point of his life. He was drowning in the waves of sentiment while we were much more concerned about making sure we received our fee. Horst, as nice a guy as he was, did not have the most reliable of reputations.

By coincidence I took a call from Gerry Marsden on my mobile while in the limousine. Fascher was ecstatic. We all had been such a big part of his life during those crazy days and none more so than Gerry, except of course the Beatles. They spoke for a few minutes and Horst became quite emotional. It must have brought back many good memories of a time that, no matter how many festivals or nostalgia nights or re-launches of would-be New Star Clubs, would never come again. In the end the concert was a good one and we got paid. We went home happy.

On May 31st that year I was having dinner in the Ivy with our backline and lighting designer John Semark when he brought my attention to a figure standing in front of me waiting for some sort of acknowledgement. It was Bryan Ferry. He had been dining at the far end of the room and had stopped to say hello on the way out. We greeted each other warmly.

I had been a big fan of his since the early Roxy Music days and if anything liked his solo work even more. Bryan was always an acquired taste. People usually either liked or loathed his style. But it was very much my kind of style and for me the urbane and elegantly groomed Ferry hit the right buttons. I always made a point of getting along to as many of his concerts as I could and I was never disappointed.

After a bit of small talk and general enquiries as to how things were going I asked when I was likely to see him again. 'We're doing a concert in London on July 22nd,' was his reply. 'What a pain,' I said. 'We're playing in Las Vegas that night.'

Bryan arched his eyebrows and with a highly amused expression on his face retorted 'Well there's one-upmanship for you.' It was a very comical moment and probably the one and only time I would be able to claim one-upmanship on such a star.

I wasn't lying. We certainly were performing in Vegas albeit at the wrong end of the Strip and a good way on from the main thoroughfare. The US market had been going from strength to strength for us and the one and two day trips of previous years had now translated into a modest but satisfying run of seven dates that took in a variety of venues. The Emelin Theatre, Mamaroneck (July 12th), the Boulton Centre, Bayshore (July 13th), the Mohegan Sun, Connecticut (July 14th), the Cutting Room, New York (July 15th), Bodles Opera House, Chester (July 16th), the Ram's Head Tavern, Annapolis (July 18th), the Power House, Sacramento (July 20th) and finally the Cannery, North Las Vegas (July 22nd).

On our previous visit to the Cutting Room on New York's West 24th Street in 2005 we had anticipated an appearance by Marky Ramone, the drummer with the legendary punk rock outfit who had kept the beat for them since their 1978 album Road To Ruin which had included a cover version of *Needles And Pins*. His manager had asked if the prestigious Searchers fan could possibly sit in on the song. He certainly could. In the end prior commitments had kept him away but on this occasion he had managed to make it along and I spotted him in the bar area looking every inch the menacing New York rock dude with bare arms and flowing locks and a sultry look that could deflower a virgin at twenty paces.

We had never met but I introduced myself. He was absolutely charming, if a little harassed seeing that he had his wallet, along with all his money and credits cards, stolen on the way to the club. Not the best start to a night out. Towards the end of our set I made the introduction, reminiscing about the time I had watched the band in all its glory at Hammersmith Odeon in the early eighties and beckoned him to the stage. Eddie Rothe generously vacated his stool while Marky took over and for the next three minutes we experienced the real power of punk as his bass drum pounded out the bottom end of the rhythm like a steam hammer. A truly remarkable sound. We were extremely flattered to be praised and idolised by one whose band had made an infinitely greater mark in the history of rock than we had ourselves.

I'm not quite sure what Marky made of our friendly, chatty on-stage style and our method of involving the audience in our songs. Punks and rock stars rarely utter more than the title of the song if they are prepared to say anything at all and smiling is definitely not encouraged. It's not considered cool. But we had long since given up trying to be cool. We simply performed in the manner in which we felt comfortable and which in turn pleased our crowd. I hope he enjoyed the night as much as we did. We appreciated seeing and meeting him.

Think Las Vegas and you think vast glittering showrooms set amidst the blinding neon lights that line the hotels of the Strip, the main thoroughfare on which most of the action takes place. It is along the Strip that you find Caesar's Palace, the Luxor, the Venetian, New York-New York, the Aladdin, the Mirage, the Dunes and all the other gilded palaces of sin where you can catch a show, eat your heart out and gamble your life savings away any time day or night.

If you carry on off the end of the main section past the huge tower that is the Stratosphere and continue for around eleven miles you will find the Cannery, placed right next to one of the intersections at East Craig Road. A much more modest construction than the city's major hotels it resembles a large Holiday Inn, but a Holiday Inn in which the foyer is crammed with one armed bandits. It is one of what they call the 'local casinos' and attract an entirely separate clientele to that which sticks to the glamour and the glitter of the main drag.

The show room off to the back next to the open pool is very much more a multi-function concert area rather than a plush cabaret lounge, open to one side so that the moveable seating can be extended into the open air. The atmospheric environment is attractive to the kind of country and rock acts who prefer a bit more street cred around them rather than chandeliers and feather-clad showgirls. It was a perfect place for us and an evening that was advertised as a British Invasion concert. We were closing the show. The opening act was ex-Moody Blue/Wings star Denny Laine, now a resident of Las Vegas himself, and Billy J Kramer, who had by this time been living in the US for a number of years.

Billy J and Denny were excellent but why wouldn't they be? They were both veterans of several decades and knew their business very well indeed. Billy was blessed with a string of unforgettable hits and a Beatles connection that would forever be a valuable currency in the States. His easy-going and informative chat linked the songs to great effect. In the early days Billy had taken a fair amount of stick for having what some considered a less than perfect singing voice but his records were cleverly constructed, in tune and very distinctive. His was a very commercial sound. His hits had deservedly stood the test of time. His enthusiasm was infectious and I liked and admired Billy. We all did.

I did not know Denny personally and had not seen him on stage since his Wings days when he had been a part of Paul McCartney's post-Beatles outfit. He performed a really excellent set and was wise enough to include his hits from both his Moody

Blues and his time with Wings. That might sound obvious but it is remarkable how many otherwise sensible artistes are happy to dispense themselves of their glorious past and alienate an audience whose expectations are doomed to disappointment.

Things could not have gone better for us. The crowd was attentive and responsive. By the end of our hour on stage they were on their feet and rocking. Our set was always designed to climb gradually to a big finish so that we would be able to include the subtlety of the more dramatic and romantic numbers that provided that all-important contrast to the uptempo content. We were never a band to just jump in with a load of 'grunt and bash' unless the occasion demanded it and our set list was always very carefully put together.

Along with our ovation we earned the plaudits of a new agent on that occasion. Selwyn Miller, a Las Vegas based agent had come along especially to check us out with a view to establishing us firmly on the casino circuit, an area where he was very well connected. He was thankfully thrilled with what he saw and promised us greater things to come, a promise which he would soon fulfil.

As we sat in the airport the next day, ready to leave Las Vegas for the connection to Los Angeles and eventually home, I observed and listened to the people around me. On the next bench I overheard a gentleman who was obviously a performer talking to someone on his mobile phone about his Vegas shows which he felt had been an unqualified success. On a second call he announced himself as Sammy Shore and I recognised the name. Sammy Shore was a long-established comedian, a veteran of the Strip. Not impressive in itself perhaps but very significant to me in that for many years he had been the opening act for Elvis Presley. Having never had the chance to meet the King himself, sitting next to a man who had rubbed shoulders with him was at least a small substitute.

I eavesdropped on yet another conversation and heard the man seated next to me, again on his cell phone, leaving a voicemail message for a Mike Hewitson with regard to fixing up tickets for Elton John's Red Piano show at Caesar's Palace. When he had finished I asked him if this was indeed the Mike Hewitson from England, an old friend who had once been Dave Clark's (he of the legendary Dave Clark Five) personal assistant and to whom I hadn't spoken or seen for more than thirty years.

He had remained in my memory as a suave and urbane young man immaculately attired in a perfectly fitting pin striped suit and dealing with Dave's demands in an endearingly idiosyncratic way. I recall one time Dave pretending to be irritated at the fact that 'his roadie' had extravagantly taken a cab into town in order to simply collect his suit from the dry cleaners. The bill for the taxi had vastly outweighed the cost of the cleaning. It suited Dave's sense of style to employ someone whose sense of style matched his own.

My instincts were confirmed and at the man's suggestion I left a message on Mike's voicemail service at the Rio Hotel where he was staying. When I got back to London I found the number of the Rio and asked to be put through to Mike's room.

A voice answered. 'Hello'. It was a little curt.

'Mike Hewitson?' I asked.

'No,' was the monosyllabic reply.

'Is Mike there?'

'Yes, who's speaking?'

'It's Frank Allen of the Searchers,' I explained.

'Frank, it's Elton,' the voice answered in a somewhat more excitable tone. I was gobsmacked. Partly because I was suddenly talking to Elton John, global superstar and also because he actually remembered me and seemed pleased.

'Christ, Elton' I stammered, 'I am so pissed off. We've just done a show at the Cannery and I was walking down the Strip with our backline roadie and we saw your show was on. We would loved to have seen it.' 'Of course you can come to the show,' he immediately offered, upon which I had to explain that we were no longer in America but had returned home to dear old Blighty. Realising we were not going to take up his generous offer his interest seemed to wane and he ended the conversation as quickly as it had begun, said his goodbyes and passed me over to Mike whereupon we verbally renewed our interrupted friendship. As they say, timing is everything.

43

The Big Finish

In truth there is no big finish. At least none that I can see on the far horizon. Our working existence has to the greater extent settled into a rather robust and self-sustaining pattern and, barring any unforeseen mishaps, the pattern appears to be a repeating one. Nothing is set in stone but our workload is pretty firmly embedded on a foundation of regular engagements that guarantee a future work-filled year for as long as we want it, assuming of course that our health stands up and our enthusiasm and enjoyment persists. But maybe I'm being a trifle premature. It could all come falling down around our ears next week. But I doubt it.

2007, a full forty-five years on from the embryonic young Searchers embarking on a professional career back in '62, turned out to be the busiest twelve months in our entire history, with almost two hundred concerts.

Our Australia/New Zealand adventures continued to grow with return visits to practically all of our past venues being added to by a bunch of new ones. After six weeks of touring there we returned to the UK ready, in true Searchers style, to begin our biennial Solid Silver Sixties tour the very next day. In our world days off are for wimps.

We landed back at Heathrow at 5 am on February 20th and barely had time to unload our dirty laundry before heading north next day, jet lagged and tired, for the first night of the tour at the Floral Hall, Southport. Our cohorts this time round were the Merseybeats, the Swinging Blue Jeans and Wayne Fontana, a tried and trusted combination which, far from bringing into play the old maxim that familiarity breeds contempt, once again proved to be a money spinning combination.

From Southport we headed further up to Harrogate and Carlisle and continued upwards for the Scottish run. We may have been away from home for a month and a half but it was still to be another ten days before we were able to sleep in our own beds. Mondays were free days but apart from that the schedule was more or less relentless. When the tour did have a day off on March 23rd we Searchers trotted off to Butlins in Bognor for a performance there. The tour ended its fifty-four date run at the Palladium on April 29th but even then there was little time for rest.

Two days later we jetted off to Canada and the USA for a series of mainly casino engagements - the McPhillips St Station Casino in Winnipeg, The Regina Casino, Frank Sissons' Silver Dollar in Calgary, the Soaring Eagle Casino at Mount Pleasant, Michigan, and the Mohegan Sun in Connecticut - which once again also took in the more street-cred environs of the Cutting Room on New York's West 24th Street. North America was at last turning into a territory that was, after a slow slog of a start, a serious financial consideration.

Our annual cruise, once more on the P&O ship Arcadia, filled up sixteen leisurely days in September allowing us to recharge our batteries, and was fairly similar to the previous one, stopping off at Malaga, Dubrovnik, Venice, Split, Corfu, Malta and Palma. We could hardly argue that the four shows spread over two nights could be called an unreasonable hardship.

Our all-evening solo concerts had become such a success that we were able to assemble them into a full forty-date autumn tour, a significant and important slice of our year's engagements. Utilising the medium-sized theatres around the country we could attract more or less full houses to most shows. A five to six hundred capacity was about par for the course although we often strayed into larger territory and managed to pull in the size of audience that was more typical of a Solid Silver Sixties tour.

On the other hand we occasionally downsized to the three hundred seater halls that if filled could still provide us with a healthy income. That was the advantage of being able to handle an entire evening. The Arts Centre at Pocklington just outside Hull, holding barely more than a couple of hundred, was about as small as it would get but it was intimate, friendly and a lot of fun. Pocklington is a tiny town - three steps in any direction and you're at the city limits. As John McNally was wandering around the town in the afternoon he spotted the headline in the local paper which proclaimed *Donkey Drowns In Pond.* I mentioned it on stage that night adding that I imagined the highlight of the week must be watching the traffic lights change. At that point someone in the audience yelled, 'We haven't got any.' Stadium rock this was not. But that's just fine with us.

During the rest of the year any gaps in these standard work periods were filled by the usual quota of holiday villages, country house hotels, corporate functions and frequent flights abroad to Denmark, Germany, Sweden and other familiar European territories.

We were still trying to break back into the Irish market but it was proving an altogether harder nut to crack. In the old glory days we seemed to be there all the time but in the intervening years following the 'troubles' we had omitted Ireland, both north and south, from our itinerary and we had been largely forgotten.

Our solo concert at the Waterfront complex in Belfast was an unqualified success but the same show in out-of-the-way towns such as Enniskillen, Banbridge and Armagh drew sparser audiences than we were used to. I've had more people round my table for dinner. No matter the size of the crowd the reception was without exception ecstatic, yet spreading the word was difficult. As with the US we simply looked on it as a challenge which we determined in time would be overcome.

We are well aware that we still have the ability to make good albums. The two releases on Sire in the early eighties, *The Searchers* and *Play For Today* and the *Hungry Hearts* album in 1989 on the German Coconut label, have proved that. But of course the recording industry is as much about selling young bodies to other young bodies as it is to music and regretfully we are no longer young, and as well-kept as we may be for our ages it is very much a case of damage limitation in the body department and our share of the market is very limited. As satisfying as the results may have been during the Sire and Coconut periods the financial rewards for both came to absolutely zilch. Nada. Zero. Not a bleedin' sausage.

We are a working band with a constant stream of bills that require paying whether we are actually on the road or not. There is a large diesel-hungry Mercedes truck filled with PA and backline equipment. Everything needs continual repairing or replacing and our two crew, on permanent employ, rather ungraciously demand wages. Our personal vehicles are soon knackered after putting up with a 40,000 miles a year schedule. And we've tried sneaking out the back door of hotels without paying the bill but somehow we never get away with it.

Even if we did feel like setting aside six non-earning weeks in order to settle into a studio somewhere in the wilds of the country our families would somehow feel the need to object having seen little more than mere glimpses of us throughout the touring year. How utterly unreasonable of them. As our twilight years approach with alarming rapidity we find that, much as we love the industry we have chosen and the thrill that goes along with every successful show, we would rather appreciate being suitably paid for it.

As we enter the autumn of our days (my sixty-fourth birthday was in 2007, while John McNally, as already previously stated is two years further on down the line) we find we too would quite like a little more time off. The trouble is we find it very hard to say no, even to the most ridiculous logistical nightmares.

With only three days off for Christmas 2007 we were booked to perform at Nidd Hall, the Warners country house hotel just outside Harrogate in Yorkshire. In theory not an excessive trek for Liverpool-based McNally. A little more of a trek for the rest of us but no matter. Apart from the fact that we then accepted an engagement to perform on a ferry going from Stockholm to an island off Finland, and back on the day before the Harrogate jaunt. This of course involved us, accompanied by our front-of-house sound man Phil Hayes, catching an early flight from Heathrow to Sweden on December 26th in order to connect with the boat. After completing our show we were to sleep on the vessel which would berth on the island before transporting us back to Sweden the next morning, docking at 10 am.

We then had to disembark with our instruments and our baggage from that ferry onto another one which was to depart only a mind boggling fifteen minutes later and take us to a port closer to Arlanda airport from where we had to take the 11.45 plane back to London landing at 1.25 in the afternoon. Immigration having been completed it was then just a matter of a two hundred mile drive to Harrogate where our backline guy John Semark waited with the gear set up and anticipating a scintillating, action-packed performance. The show must go on. Remember. Eyes and teeth, dears. Eyes and teeth. It was madness of the highest degree and an undertaking that no-one else we know would have contemplated. But this, crazy as it seems, is real life in Searcherland.

The 2008 tour of Australasia was another major success to the point where they wanted us to commit for the following year before we had even entered the second week. The early months of the year spent in the southern hemisphere it seemed had become a permanent fixture in our annual schedule. Likewise our fast expanding American itinerary which now consisted almost entirely of casino showrooms, with the exception of the Cutting Room in New York once more, and a cute theatre called the Festival Place in Edmonton, Alberta.

We began the US tour with two days at the Fallsview Casino in Niagara where the 1500 seater showroom was sold out for both nights. Niagara would be a fairly unremarkable town were it not for the rather magnificent water feature which someone had the foresight to install. A stroke of genius if ever there was one.

Edmonton, suffering a complete white-out with the most snow in decades, was next. The show, again a complete sell-out, was most enjoyable with a welcome as warm as the weather was cold. We could not move out of the hotel because of the blizzard. Fortunately we had opted to spend our days off in Vancouver ahead of the two shows we had been booked for there, and took the chance to have a look around a city that we were unfamiliar with which was both picturesque and fascinating.

We were sharing the bill there with Peter & Gordon who had been drafted in to replace the Manfreds when problems not revealed to us had necessitated their withdrawing from their US trip. We hadn't seen the duo since the mid sixties and it was good to catch up and reminisce about the '64 tour across the land of Oz.

From Vancouver we crossed into the States and when our commitment at the Cannery Casino was completed, our second time there, we decamped to Circus Circus on the main strip for a few days R & R. The privilege of a musician's life was once again brought home to me when I was able to grab the chance to see the Grand Canyon from a helicopter, actually landing on the floor of that great natural wonder for a champagne picnic before making the return trip to Las Vegas.

As fearful as I am of heights and as disconcerting as it is hovering thousands of feet in the air from what seems like nothing more than a giant egg whisk, I was overawed by the sheer magnificence of what nature had created and almost as impressed by what man had created as we descended back over the splendid vulgarity and outrageousness that is the gambling capital of the world. Music and a tiny amount of talent had given me opportunities that very few were ever afforded. I was a lucky lad indeed.

The Cutting Room show in New York was to my mind better than our show two years before. It was straighter, edgier and more rock & roll which suited the environment. And the same went for the two days at the Mohegan Sun in Connecticut. We were at home and felt confident and powerful.

Epcot Disney in Orlando, Florida, was a new setting for us. At the World Showcase, an open-air amphitheatre where we were to play three half-hour sets on each of our two days there, the powers-that-be came backstage after the opening show on the second day. It was quite apparent that they were mightily impressed and did not hold back from telling us.

It seems that very few artistes, excellent though they may otherwise be, ever attempted or managed to connect and communicate with the audience, something that had always been an integral part of our stage technique. To Disney we were manna from heaven and they wanted us back. In fact they wanted us back for five days in the Spring for a special theme time there. In the end it proved impossible to organise. We had already managed to move the 2009 Solid Silver Tour back by one week to placate the Australians and they were not going to allow us to chop off another week at the end which is what it would have needed.

We had already blocked off a period in June for a return to North America and they would just have to make do with something during that visit. Much as we hated to disappoint such a powerful organisation there was nothing we could do. And as I've said before, sometimes it's good to say no.

Although some new product on disc is a tantalising idea, we have more or less come to accept that our value still lies with our old catalogue which gets repackaged and reissued with a regularity that is quite remarkable, and the fact that we were able to renegotiate our old pathetic contract to the point where our royalties could almost be considered reasonable was a welcome bonus.

And if there was to be no big finish then at least we were not going quietly. In May 2008 we found ourselves being presented with a delightful surprise that none of us could have foreseen six months before. Almost exactly forty-five years after *Sweets For*

My Sweet gave the Searchers their debut hit we were back in the charts. Not with a single and not with a new recording, but in the charts nonetheless.

The company that owned our original masters, Sanctuary, had been bought out by the giant Universal Music Group and had, under the guidance of its supremo Brian Berg, instituted a strategy of television-advertised back catalogue albums which had proved to be a winning formula. Following on the successful heels of fifties stars Marty Wilde and Billy Fury, *The Very Best Of The Searchers* reached a more than respectable number eleven in the best sellers and remained in the album charts for six weeks.

We were needless to say elated. Frank Sinatra, one place above us, had kept us out of the top ten by a mere two hundred sales. Had we been on a Solid Silver Tour at the time, with three solid months of packed theatres, we could have got it right to the top or as near as damn it.

We did whatever was necessary to plug the release which included an acoustic spot on the very popular Johnnie Walker Radio Show. We performed a medley of our hits on the high-rating This Morning television programme hosted by Philip Schofield and Fern Britton but there was nothing else on offer in TV land. Indeed there was a paucity of spots for any musical performers at all on television in the current climate and what there were to be had were being chased by artistes younger, hotter and prettier than us.

Had television and radio been more willing to accommodate us in order to plug the product I have no doubt we could have pushed the album even higher. But top ten or not the impressive sales earned us a Silver Disc, an astonishing and welcome bonus.

While conducting the endless round of radio interviews the faceless voice on the other end of the phone told me that a week before he had also interviewed Mike Pender who suggested that we could have gathered more publicity if the three of us had got together to promote it. He then asked the eternal question as to whether we would consider doing something with Mike. I replied that at this point in time there was more chance of getting all four original Beatles back together.

Don't get me wrong. I don't hate anyone and I certainly don't hate Mike Pender. There is much to be admired about the man although I considered his ethics as far as the group was concerned questionable. But we had good times along with the bad. There might even come a time in the distant future when we can sit round a table and laugh about the past in an atmosphere of what might pass as friendliness. But the bonds between him and John McNally have, it seems, been inextricably broken. I suppose that is natural. They were boyhood friends many years before I arrived on the scene and there was more history between them. It follows that any hurt would be of a deeper nature. If the hatchet is to be buried John would be more likely to bury it in his head. A little strong perhaps but you get the drift.

In the end *The Very Best Of The Searchers* missed out on a gold disc by a weasel's willy and we had to make do with silver. But on reflection that's pretty good. I used to make an on-stage introduction to our last Guinness Book Of Hit Singles entry *Have You Ever Loved Somebody* which reached the ignominious position of number forty-eight that these days we would gladly kill for a number forty-eight. Well there we were at an amazing number eleven and I didn't even have to commit murder. The gods (who I do not believe exist) were smiling on us once more.

And so this mad and wonderful life goes on. We are always being asked when we are going to call it a day and I honestly cannot give an answer. Two thousand and twelve marks the fiftieth anniversary from that magic moment when Johnny Sandon & the Searchers became simply The Searchers and trudged of to Hamburg and into the history books. Maybe that is the right time. Perhaps when our tired old bodies can no longer dredge up the energy to transport us onto the stage or when there is no audience out there for us to flaunt our limited talents in front of. Or when we have become too crotchety and quavery to play any more crochets and quavers. It is much more likely to be when we find out we are no longer having any fun. I'd just prefer not to think about it right now. This book has to end somewhere and as hard as it may be I must stop here. But as far as The Searchers are concerned right now there is no end in sight.

List of Illustrations

33. With my German fraulein Monika Pricken
34. Johnny Gustafson (the Big Three), Monika Pricken, Brian Johnson (the Strangers) on the Reeperbahn
35. Promo for the Searchers' live recording at the Star Club (Peter Scotti collection)
36. Backing Bo Diddley at the Star Club
37. Cliff Bennett and me on stage at the Star Club
38. Cliff Bennett and me in the famous Abbey Road, Studio 2.
39. Sid Phillips & Moss Groves, the Rebel Rousers' sax section
40. I'd kill to look this good again. Taken by Beatles photographer Astrid Kirchherr (Astrid Kirchherr, K&K, Redferns)
41. London-Margate beat boat advert
42. Cliff Bennett and the Rebel Rousers on the London-Margate beat boat 18th August 1963
43. The Searchers' original Pye contract
44. Contract for the Searchers at the Stanley Stadium, Liverpool, 31st August 1963
45. Tony Hatch hard at work (Tony Hatch collection)
46. Flyer for the Helen Shapiro/Bobby Vee/Bobby Rydell tour, Stockton 13th Dec 1963
47. Up on the roof at 38 Pont Street, 1963 (Roy Clough collection)
48. Ecstatic in their Knightsbridge apartment (Roy Clough collection)
49. Smiles of success (Roy Clough collection)
50. The Rebel Rousers at the Cavern Dec 10th 1963 l-r me, Cliff Bennett, Sid Phillips, Dave Wendells, (hidden) Roy Young, Mick Burt, Moss Groves
51. John McNally with his iconic Hofner Club 60 (John McNally collection)
52. Live on stage soon after their first success (John McNally collection)
53. A postcard to me from John McNally in Paris
54. Complaining about the cost, of course
55. In New York for the Ed Sullivan Show 1964 (Roy Clough collection)
56. Me kissing the Blarney Stone. Excellent training for a front man.
57. The Rebel Rousers backing the Vernons (badly) at the Prince of Wales Theatre, London 1964
58. The Botwell House Festival programme, June 3rd 1963
59. On stage on their 1964 Summer tour of the U.S.A (Roy Clough collection)
60. John McNally hits the heights. Top of the Empire State Building, Summer 1964 (Roy Clough collection)
61. Tony Jackson at Niagara Falls, 1964 U.S tour (Roy Clough collection)
62. Mike and May Pender and Tony Jackson at Niagara (Roy Clough collection)
63. Seaton Carew Big Beat Night pre-show July 1964 (Ian Wright)
64. Seaton Carew Big Beat Night - on stage (Ian Wright)
65. The Searchers with the new boy, Knightsbridge, August 1964
66. Tony Jackson & the Vibrations (Roy Clough collection)
67. With Ronettes Nedra Talley and Estelle Bennett at the Fox Theatre, Brooklyn 1964. l-r John, me, Nedra, Chris, Estelle, Mike
68. Me with Jackie DeShannon
69. Melbourne fan club membership card (Rob Hall collection)
70. With record executives in Australia, September 1964
71. Sensational Searchers - Record Mirror cover
72. Rehearsing for What Have They Done To The Rain on Ready Steady Go (Roy Clough collection)
73. With my pop star girl friend Julie Grant
74. Being presented to Princess Margaret at the Docklands Settlement Ball with (left) Julie Rogers (Doug McKenzie)
75. NME Pollwinners Concert 1965

76. Another flight. '65 U.S tour
77. Oklahoma 1965 with Bobby Vee in Bermuda shorts. Not a good look.
78. The girl in the Sting Ray
79. The Araneta Colosseum, Quezon City, Manila, March 1966
80. With Filipino film stars March 1966
81. 1966 ticket stub, our tour with the Rolling Stones
82. Mike Rispoli (tour manager for the Stones for the Oz 1966 tour), me, Searchers roadie Barry Delaney, at Lennons Hotel Brisbane
83. John on stage at Brisbane City Hall 21st Feb 1966
84. Charlie Watts and me, Melbourne 1966 (Colin Beard)
85. The Searchers' new line-up with John Blunt 1966
86. In the Ford Thames outside the Fiesta, Stockton, August 7th 1967, l-r John Blunt, me, Mike Pender, John McNally (Ian Wright)
87. Fans approving our new drummer John Blunt
88. Germany, in my very silly shirt so much admired by Graham Nash. Late 60s (Erhard Preuss collection)
89. 1966 to 1969 line-up. John Blunt, John McNally, me, Mike Pender
90. The advert for our single Umbrella Man
91. With Eartha Kitt at Abbey Road, the calm before the storm
92. With Dusty Springfield on the night of the famous 'willy fiddling' incident
93. A number one is still a number one wherever it is. Sing Singer Sing tops the Bangkok charts
94. 1970 the new line-up with Billy Adamson (right)
95. With RCA a&r man Richard Swainson and Neil Sedaka
96. Contract for the Scene 2, Scarborough, Feb 28th 1970
97. Backstage at the Fiesta Stockton with owner Jim Lipthorpe
98. Knocking down pennies in a Stockton pub for charity (Trevor Harland collection)
99. Jerry Lee Lewis at the Steel Pier, Atlantic City 1973, ignoring Billy J's requests
100. The main attraction. The diving horse, the Steel Pier, Atlantic City
101. With Maurice Gibb after the Midnight Special recording, L.A
102. With Rainer Haas, our German connection
103. John McNally & Paul McNally (no relation) at Rockfield Studios
104. Me, John McNally and Pat Moran at Rockfield
105. Mike and John rehearsing at the Old Mill, Rockfield
106. The Old Mill, Rockfield
107. The Hearts In Her Eyes sleeve
108. With the Police in Baden Baden. l-r Stewart Copeland, Sting, me, Andy Summers
109. The Sire period
110. Ed Stasium and Martin Hughes
111. Martin Hughes, our drummer on Play For Today
112. Being presented to Queen Elizabeth II at the 1981 Royal Variety Show (Doug McKenzie)
113. Peter Collins
114. With Ritchie Blackmore, My Father's Place, Long Island
115. The famous Jack Bender poster
116. Chris Spedding, John Turner (roadie), Joey Costellano (tour manager), David Essex in Heartbreaks, New York
117. Me with a songwriting legend. Jerome 'Doc' Pomus, the Lone Star Café, New York
118. John McNally and Robert Pratt in happier times
119. First Class with l-r Spencer James, Eddie Richards, Robin Shaw (Spencer James collection)
120. The new line-up, 1986 John McNally, Spencer James, me, Billy Adamson (Ron Long)
121. The British Invasion tour. U.S.A 1986
122. The British Invasion artistes. Searchers, Gerry, Chad & Jeremy, Freddie and a Mindbender

123. The new front line (Ron Long)
124. Kings Lynn or bust
125. The London Palladium, the opening night of the first Solid Silver Sixties tour.
126. Me, John McNally, Paul McCartney, Roy Wood at the Sgt Pepper CD launch
127. The sleeve for Hungry Hearts
128. The Event
129. Me, Cliff and John
130. The Dynamic Duo, Allen and McNally (Ron Long)
131. John and me with Tony Hatch and Petula Clark at Tony's This Is Your Life
132. The auction at our convention with Searchers Appreciation Society organiser Tim Viney (Ron Long)
133. My first Best Front Man award (Ron Long)
134. With 'the lads' on stage in Bosnia
135. Searchers and crew on HMS Illustrious
136. Ed in his skunk suit with Liquid Gold (Eddie Rothe collection)
137. The new line-up with Eddie Rothe on the right
138. Ed Rothe drumming as a Searcher
139. Dusty's funeral programme
140. With our website team, Wendy Burton and Gary Jackson.
141. P. J. Proby in his dressing room
142. P. J. Proby and me on stage
143. Tony Jackson 1938-2003
144. Tony Hatch with John and me at my 60th
145. The 2007 Solid Silver line-up. Searchers, Gerry & the Pacemakers, Swinging Blue Jeans and Merseybeats (Flying Music)
146. John reunited with his old Hofner Club 60 at the Hard Rock Café in Manila
147. On stage with Sir Cliff Richard at Wentworth Golf Club
148. Chris Curtis singing at a Merseycats gathering (Arty Davies collection)
149. Chris Curtis 1941-2005
150. On stage at the Royal Albert Hall
151. John McNally doing what he loves best
152. Sometimes a roadie's life is o.k. Me with our crew John Semark (left) & Phil Hayes (right) on the Arcadia
153. Horst Fascher, the old Star Club manager
154. The Cannery, Las Vegas
155. Backstage at the Cannery with Billy J. Kramer
156. And with Denny Laine
157. John talking 12 strings with one of our V.I.P fans, Steve Van Zandt (John McNally collection)
158. The Searchers' original lead vocalist turns up again in Glasgow 2007. 'Big Ron' Woodbridge
159. With our guest drummer Marky Ramone at the Cutting Room, New York 2006
160. Reunited with Supremes star Mary Wilson in 2008.
161. Plugging the new compilation CD. An acoustic set on the Johnnie Walker show 11th May 2008
162. The Rebel Rousers reunion, 2007. back row - Ben Jordan, Ricky Winter, Sid Phillips, Mick Currell, Cliff Bennett, Mick Borer. front row - Alfie James, me (Sid Phillips)
163. Live on stage in the 'noughties' (Brian Marsh)
164. Still live (Wendy Burton)
165. And happy (Wendy Burton)
166. The promotion worked. Our Silver Discs for The Very Best Of The Searchers
167. The sweater says it all

Essential Discography

Researched and reassembled by Roy Clough

The list is as complete as we have been able to make it but with the wealth of material both official and unofficial that has been on the market over the last five decades it is entirely possible that there may be some omissions.

Any slight variations in placings between this list and the text of the book will be because of the official lists being an amalgamation of the Record Retailer charts (source used by publications such as British Hit Singles published by Guinness, Complete Book of British Charts published by Omnibus Press) and various other periodicals such as NME (New Musical Express), Record Mirror, Disc etc. The main paper consulted for the text of the book was the NME.

- A dash indicates no release. A blank indicates it did not chart.

<u>Vinyl Releases (Unless stated)</u>

Singles - Title	Label UK/US	Year UK	Chart UK	Chart US
Sweets For My Sweet/It's All Been A Dream	Pye/Mercury	Jun 63	1	
Sweet Nothin's/What'd I Say	Philips	Sept 63	48	-
Sugar And Spice/Saints And Searchers	Pye/Liberty	Oct 63	2	
Needles And Pins/Saturday Night Out	Pye/Kapp	Jan 64	1	13
Ain't That Just Like Me/Ain't Gonna Kiss Ya	Kapp	Mar 64	-	61
Ain't That Just Like Me/I Can Tell	Mercury	Apr 64	-	
Don't Throw Your Love Away/ I Pretend I'm With You	Pye/Kapp	Apr 64	1	16
Someday We're Gonna Love Again/ No One Else Could Love You	Pye/Kapp	Jul 64	11	34

When You Walk In The Room/I'll Be Missing You	Pye/Kapp	Sept 64	3	35
What Have They Done To the Rain/ This Feeling Inside	Pye/Kapp	Nov 64	13	29
Love Potion No Nine/Hi Heel Sneakers	Kapp	Dec 64	-	3
Goodbye My Love/Till I Met You	Pye/Kapp	Feb 65	4	52
Bumble Bee/A Tear Fell	Kapp	Mar 65	-	21
He's Got No Love/So Far Away	Pye/Kapp	Jul 65	12	79
When I Get Home/I'm Never Coming Back	Pye	Oct 65	35	-
Don't You Know Why/You Can't Lie To A Liar	Kapp	Oct 65	-	
Take Me For What I'm Worth/Too Many Miles	Pye/Kapp	Nov 65	20	76
Take It Or Leave It/Don't Hide It Away	Pye	Apr 66	31	-
Have You Ever Loved Somebody/It's Just The Way	Pye	Oct 66	48	94
Popcorn Double Feature/Lovers	Pye	Jan 67		
Western Union/I'll Cry Tomorrow	Pye	Apr 67		
Second Hand Dealer/Crazy Dreams	Pye	Nov 67		
Umbrella Man/Over The Weekend	Liberty/World Pacific	Nov 68		
Somebody Shot The Lollipop Man/ Pussy Willow Dragon** (As Pasha)	Liberty	Jun 69		-
Kinky Kathy Abernathy/Suzanna	Liberty	Jul 69		-
Desdemona/The World is Waiting For Tomorrow	RCA	Aug 71		94
Love Is Everywhere/And A Button	RCA	Oct 71		
Sing Singer Sing/Come On Back To Me	RCA	Apr 72		-
Needles And Pins/When You Walk In The Room/ Come On Back To Me	RCA	Aug 72		-
Vahevala/Madman	RCA	Oct 72		-
Solitaire/Spicks And Specks	RCA	Feb 73		-
Hearts In Her Eyes/Don't Hang On	Sire	Oct 79		-
It's Too Late/This Kind Of Love Affair	Sire	Feb 80		-
It's Too Late /Don't Hang On	Sire	Feb 80	-	
Love's Melody/Changing	Sire	Jul 80		-
Another Night/Back To The War	Sire	Mar 81		-
Love's Melody/Little Bit Of Heaven	Sire	May 81	-	
I Don't Want To Be The One/Hollywood	PRT	Nov 82		-
Forever In Love/Every Little Tear	Coconut	Oct 88		-
12" - Forever In Love/Forever in Love (Dream Mix)/ Every Little Tear	Coconut	Oct 88		-
Needles And Pins 89/Fooled Myself Once Again	Coconut	Feb 89		-
12" - Needles and Pins 89/Needles and Pins (Club Mix)/				

Radio Edit	Coconut	Feb 89	-
CD Needles and Pins (Club Mix)/Radio Edit/ Fooled Myself Once Again/Lonely Weekend	Coconut	Feb 89	-
No Other Love/Push Push	Coconut	April 89	-
12"- No Other Love/Push Push/Radio Edit	Coconut	April 89	-
CD No Other Love/Push Push/Radio Edit/ Lonely Weekend (club mix)	Coconut	April 89	-

** The actual song title was Pussy Willow Dream but incorrectly credited on Single as Pussy Willow Dragon.

<u>Vinyl EP Releases UK Only – All EP's contained 4 tracks. (Mini Albums)</u>

EP Title	Label	Year UK	UK EP Chart
Ain't Gonna Kiss Ya **	Pye	Sep 63	1
Sweets For My Sweet	Pye	Dec 63	5
Hungry For Love	Pye	Jan 64	4
The Searchers Play The System	Pye	Jul 64	11
When You Walk In The Room	Pye	Nov 64	12
Bumble Bee	Pye	May 65	1
Searchers 65	Pye	Sept 65	15
Four By Four	Pye	Nov 65	
Take Me For What I'm Worth	Pye	Jan 66	

** This EP sold so well it reached number 12 in the UK Singles chart.

<u>Essential Album Releases</u>

- A dash indicates no release. A blank indicates did not chart.

Album Title	Label	Year UK	Chart UK	Chart US
Meet The Searchers	Pye	Aug 63	2	-
Sugar And Spice	Pye	Nov 63	5	-
Meet The Searchers- Needles and Pins	Kapp	Mar 64	-	22
It's The Searchers	Pye	May 64	4	-

Hear Hear (live at Star Club)	Mercury	Jun 64	-	
Attention (live at Star Club)	Philips	Jun 64		-
This Is Us	Kapp	Oct 64	-	97
Sound Like Searchers	Pye	Mar 65	8	-
Searchers Number 4	Kapp	Oct 65	-	
Take Me For What I'm Worth	Pye/Kapp	Nov 65		
Second Take	RCA	Nov 72		-
Searchers (The Searchers in US)	Sire	Nov 79		
The Searchers (Re-issue of above-extra tracks)	Sire	Mar 80		-
Play For Today	Sire	Apr 81		
Loves Melodies				
(Same as above except slightly different track listing)	Sire	Apr 81	-	
Hungry Hearts	Coconut	Oct 89		-

Notes: All the 5 PYE albums have been released a number of times on CD. One series of releases features all PYE albums on CD with both stereo and mono versions plus bonus tracks

The Second Take album was released on CD, with bonus tracks, plus all the A and B sides of the RCA singles.

In 2008 both USA Sire albums The Searchers and Loves Melodies were released on CD.

Hungry Hearts was released on CD as well as Vinyl. Apart from a very limited vinyl issue of Hungry Hearts to coincide with a Solid Silver Sixties tour the Coconut recordings were really only released in Europe and were difficult to get hold of in the UK.

Compilation Albums

Through the years there have been numerous compilation albums released, far too many to list, on Vinyl, Tape and CD. Those listed below are a good representations of the group's career.

It is also worth noting that some compilations that have been released on budget labels as being by The Searchers and which show photos of the 1960s line up, but which are in fact re-recordings by Mike Pender's Searchers. Indeed some versions have been issued under the correct title but it can be confusing.

If the disc contains the new titles Blue Monday and Red Ferrari you may safely assume that these are by Mike Pender's Searchers. Yet even without these two songs on the track listing you still may be in possession of a Mike Pender's Searchers compilation. These things are hard to police and in the end it is a case of 'buyer beware'.

Album Title	Year of Release	Label
Silver Searchers 25th Anniversary Collection	1988	PRT
EP Collection Vol 1	1989	See For Miles
EP Collection Vol 2	1990	See For Miles
German, French and Rare Recordings	1990	Repertoire
30th Anniversary Collection (3 CD Box Set)	1993	Sequel
Sire Sessions 1979-1980	1998	Raven
Second Take Plus	1999	Taragon
Pye Anthology (2 CD Set)	2000	Sequel
Swedish Radio Sessions 1964 - 1967	2001	Sequel
Iron Door Club Sessions	2002	Sequel
Searchers At The Star Club	2003	Bear
40th Anniversary Collection (2 CD Set)	2003	Sanctuary
BBC Radio Sessions (2 CD set)	2004	Sanctuary
Definitive Pye Collection (3 CD Box Set)	2008	Sanctuary
The Very Best Of The Searchers**	2008	Universal

** Special mention for this release as it was backed by a TV promotion and gave the Searchers their first Album Chart entry in 43 years, reaching number 11 and earning them a Silver Disc.

Live CDs

Over the last few years the Searchers have released a number of limited edition Live CDs comprising a selection of their hits and old album material plus some more recent acquisitions and which are a comprehensive representation of their stage show. These have been available at concerts only.

Videos and DVDs

There have been numerous video compilations featuring various sixties acts and the

Searchers are featured on a number of them. The only commercially released video of an entire Searchers show was "The Searchers – 30 Glorious Years" which was introduced by Cliff Richard and released in 1993 by Pentagon Communications. Likewise there are many DVD multi-act compilations available which include the Searchers. Please note, however, that one DVD showed a photo of the current line up and states that it is The Searchers but in fact features Mike Pender's Searchers performing.

In 2007, after many requests to release their own DVD, a limited number of The Searchers – Live In Concert, again only available for purchase at their shows, was produced by Andy Cairns who for many years was one of Gerry Marsden's Pacemakers and who now is in charge of the media department at Dixons City Academy in Bradford, Yorkshire.

Index

Only surnames have been included in the index. Where forenames alone appear, including those of the Searchers, they have not been indexed.

Only those venues, television, radio programmes etc in which the Searchers or the Rebel Rousers have appeared or which have a particular connection with a specific story or anecdote have been included in the index. Venues which are simply part of a tour list have been omitted.

Likewise song titles recorded or performed by artistes other than current or ex-members of the Searchers and the Rebel Rousers have been omitted. Searchers and Rebel Rousers recordings along with significant songs in their stage repertoire are indexed.